BENCHMARK SERIES

Microsoft® Word

2016
Levels 1 & 2

Nita Rutkosky • Audrey Roggenkamp • Ian Rutkosky

PARADIGM
EDUCATION SOLUTIONS

St. Paul

Senior Vice President	Linda Hein
Editor in Chief	Christine Hurney
Director of Production	Timothy W. Larson
Production Editor	Jen Weaverling
Cover and Text Designer	Valerie King
Copy Editors	Communicáto, Ltd.
Senior Design and Production Specialist	Jack Ross
Design and Production Specialist	PerfecType
Assistant Developmental Editors	Mamie Clark, Katie Werdick
Testers	Janet Blum, Fanshawe College; Traci Post
Instructional Support Writers	Janet Blum, Fanshawe College; Brienna McWade
Indexer	Terry Casey
Vice President Information Technology	Chuck Bratton
Digital Projects Manager	Tom Modl
Vice President Sales and Marketing	Scott Burns
Director of Marketing	Lara Weber McLellan

Cover Photo Credits: © Photomall/Dreamstime.com. **Getting Started Photo Credits:** Page 3: Leungchopan/Shutterstock.com.

ISBN 978-0-76386-921-2 (print)
ISBN 978-0-76386-924-3 (digital)

© 2017 by Paradigm Publishing, Inc.
875 Montreal Way
St. Paul, MN 55102
Email: educate@emcp.com
Website: ParadigmCollege.com

Brief Contents

Contents

Microsoft Word 2016 Level 2

Preface

Benchmark Series: Microsoft® Word 2016 is designed for students who want to learn how to use this powerful word processing program to create professional-looking documents for school, work, and personal communication needs. No prior knowledge of word processing is required. After successfully completing a course using this textbook and digital courseware, students will be able to:

- Create and edit memos, letters, flyers, announcements, and reports of varying complexity
- Apply appropriate formatting elements and styles to a range of document types
- Add graphics and other visual elements to enhance written communication
- Plan, research, write, revise, and publish documents to meet specific information needs
- Given a workplace scenario requiring a written solution, assess the communication purpose and then prepare the materials that achieve the goal efficiently and effectively

Upon completing the text, students can expect to be proficient in using Word to organize, analyze, and present information.

Well-designed textbook pedagogy is important, but students learn technology skills through practice and problem solving. Technology provides opportunities for interactive learning as well as excellent ways to quickly and accurately assess student performance. To this end, this textbook is supported with SNAP 2016, Paradigm's web-based training and assessment learning management system. Details about SNAP as well as additional student courseware and instructor resources can be found on page xiv.

Achieving Proficiency in Word 2016

Since its inception several Office versions ago, the *Benchmark Series* has served as a standard of excellence in software instruction. Elements of the *Benchmark Series* function individually and collectively to create an inviting, comprehensive learning environment that produces successful computer users. The following visual tour highlights the structure and features that comprise the highly popular *Benchmark* model.

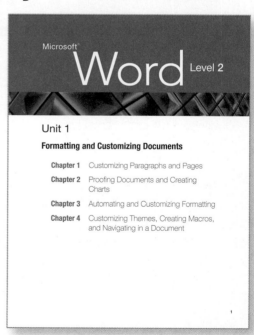

Microsoft

Word Level 2

Unit 1

Formatting and Customizing Documents

Chapter 1 Customizing Paragraphs and Pages

Chapter 2 Proofing Documents and Creating Charts

Chapter 3 Automating and Customizing Formatting

Chapter 4 Customizing Themes, Creating Macros, and Navigating in a Document

Unit Openers display the unit's four chapter titles. Each level contains two units; each unit concludes with a comprehensive unit performance assessment.

Student Textbook and eBook

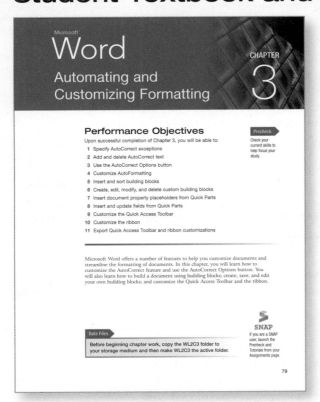

Chapter Openers present the performance objectives and an overview of the skills taught.

Precheck quizzes allow students to check their current skills before starting chapter work.

Data Files are provided for each chapter from the ebook. A prominent note reminds students to copy the appropriate chapter data folder and make it active.

Students with SNAP access are reminded to launch the Precheck quiz and chapter tutorials from their SNAP Assignments page.

Projects Build Skill Mastery within Realistic Context

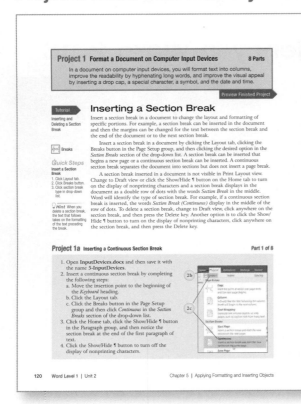

Multipart Projects provide a framework for instruction and practice on software features. A project overview identifies tasks to accomplish and key features to use in completing the work.

Preview Finished Project shows how the file will look after students complete the project.

Tutorials provide interactive, guided training and measured practice.

Quick Steps provide feature summaries for reference and review.

Hint margin notes offer useful tips on how to use features efficiently and effectively.

Typically, a file remains open throughout all parts of the project. Students save their work incrementally. At the end of the project, students save and then close the file.

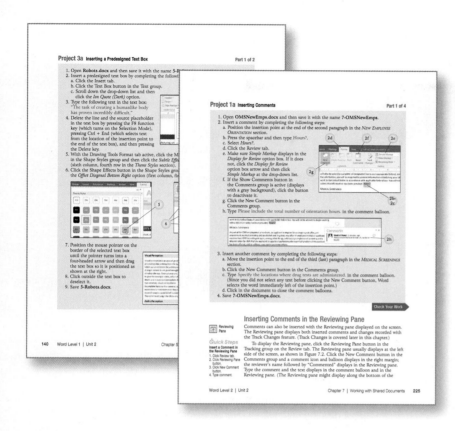

Step-by-Step Instructions guide students to the desired outcome for each project part. Screen captures illustrate what the screen should look like at key points.

Magenta Text identifies material to type.

Check Your Work allows students to confirm they have completed the project activity correctly.

Between project parts, the text presents instruction on the features and skills necessary to accomplish the next section of the project.

Chapter Review Tools Reinforce Learning

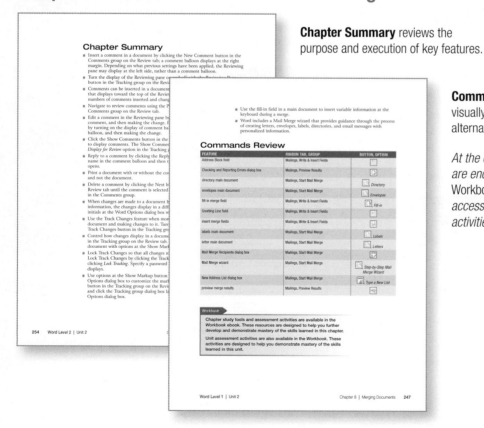

Chapter Summary reviews the purpose and execution of key features.

Commands Review summarizes visually the major features and alternative methods of access.

At the end of each chapter, students are encouraged to go to the Workbook *pages of the ebook to access study tools and assessment activities.*

Workbook eBook Activities Provide a Hierarchy of Learning Assessments

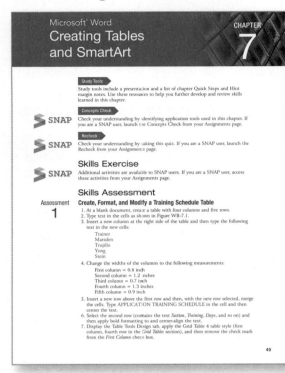

Study Tools are presentations with audio support and a list of chapter Quick Steps and Hint margin notes designed to help students further develop and review skills learned in the chapter.

Concepts Check is an objective completion exercise that allows students to assess their comprehension and recall of application features, terminology, and functions.

Recheck concept quizzes for each chapter enable students to check how their skills have improved after completing chapter work.

Skills Exercises are available to SNAP 2016 users. SNAP will automatically score student work, which is performed live in the application, and provide detailed feedback.

Skills Assessment exercises ask students to develop both standard and customized types of word processing documents without how-to directions.

Visual Benchmark assessments test problem-solving skills and mastery of application features.

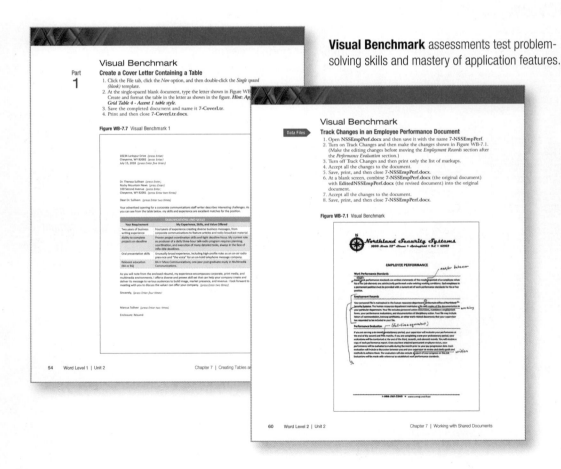

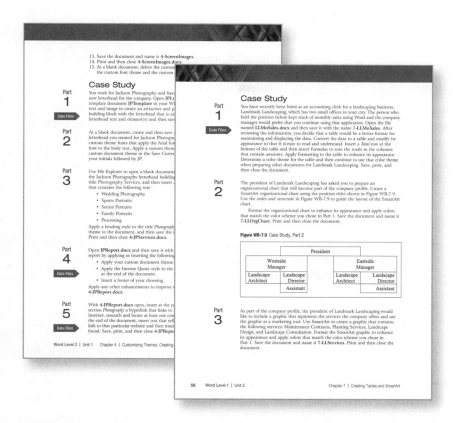

Case Study requires analyzing a workplace scenario and then planning and executing a multipart project.

Students search the web and/or use the program's Help feature to locate additional information required to complete the Case Study.

Unit Performance Assessments Deliver Cross-Disciplinary, Comprehensive Evaluation

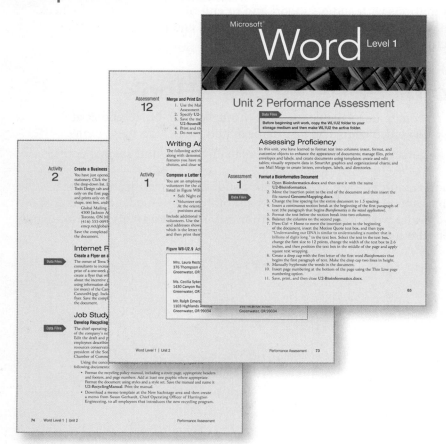

Assessing Proficiency exercises check mastery of features.

Writing Activities involve applying application skills in a communication context.

Internet Research projects reinforce research and information processing skills.

Job Study at the end of each Unit 2 presents a capstone assessment requiring critical thinking and problem solving.

SNAP Training and Assessment

SNAP is a web-based training and assessment program and learning management system (LMS) for learning Microsoft Office 2016. SNAP is comprised of rich content, a sophisticated grade book, and robust scheduling and analytics tools. SNAP courseware supports the *Benchmark Series* content and delivers live-in-the-application assessments for students to demonstrate their skills mastery. Interactive tutorials increase skills-focused moments with guided training and measured practice. SNAP provides automatic scoring and detailed feedback on the many activities, exercises, and quizzes to help identify areas where additional support is needed, evaluating student performance both at an individual and course level. The *Benchmark Series* SNAP course content is also available to export into any LMS system that supports LTI tools.

Paradigm Education Solutions provides technical support for SNAP through 24-7 chat at ParadigmCollege.com. In addition, an online User Guide and other SNAP training tools for using SNAP are available.

Student eBook

The student ebook, available through SNAP or online at Paradigm.bookshelf.emcp.com, provides access to the *Benchmark Series* content from any device (desktop, tablet, and smartphone) anywhere, through a live Internet connection. The versatile ebook platform features dynamic navigation tools including a linked table of contents and the ability to jump to specific pages, search for terms, bookmark, highlight, and take notes. The ebook offers live links to the interactive content and resources that support the print textbook, including the student data files, Precheck and Recheck quizzes, and interactive tutorials. The *Workbook* pages of the ebook also provide access to presentations with audio support and to end-of-chapter Concept Check, Skills Assessment, Visual Benchmark, Case Study, and end-of-unit Performance Assessment activities.

Instructor eResources eBook

All instructor resources are available digitally through a web-based ebook at Paradigm.bookshelf.emcp.com. The instructor materials include these items:

- Planning resources, such as lesson plans, teaching hints, and sample course syllabi
- Presentation resources, such as PowerPoint slide shows with lecture notes
- Assessment resources, including live and annotated PDF model answers for chapter work and workbook activities, rubrics for evaluating student work, and chapter-based exam banks

Microsoft® Office

Getting Started in Office 2016

Several computer applications are combined to make the Microsoft Office 2016 application suite. The applications are known as *software*, and they contain instructions that tell the computer what to do. Some of the applications in the suite include Word, a word processing applicaton; Excel, a spreadsheet applicaton; Access, a database applicaton; and PowerPoint, a presentation applicaton.

Identifying Computer Hardware

The Microsoft Office suite can run on several types of computer equipment, referred to as *hardware*. You will need access to a laptop or a desktop computer system that includes a PC/tower, monitor, keyboard, printer, drives, and mouse. If you are not sure what equipment you will be operating, check with your instructor. The computer systems shown in Figure G.1 consists of six components. Each component is discussed separately in the material that follows.

Figure G.1 Computer System

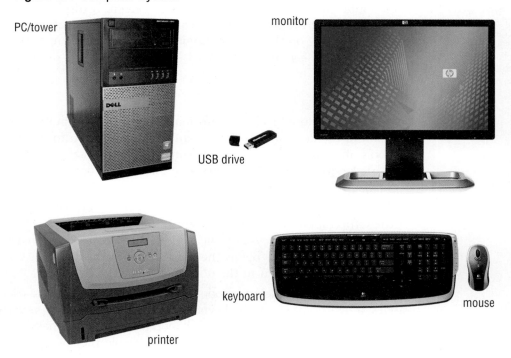

PC/tower

USB drive

monitor

printer

keyboard

mouse

Figure G.2 PC/Tower

PC/Tower

The PC, also known as the *tower*, is the brain of the computer and is where all processing occurs. A PC/tower consists of components such as the Central Processing Unit (CPU), hard drives, and video cards plugged into a motherboard. The motherboard is mounted inside the case, which includes input and output ports for attaching external peripherals (as shown in Figure G.2). When a user provides input through the use of peripherals, the PC/tower computes that input and outputs the results. Similar hardware is included in a laptop, but the design is more compact to allow for mobility.

Monitor

Hint Monitor size is measured diagonally. For example, the distance from the bottom left corner to the top right corner of the monitor.

A computer monitor looks like a television screen. It displays the visual information that the computer is outputting. The quality of display for monitors varies depending on the type of monitor and the level of resolution. Monitors can also vary in size—generally from 13 inches to 26 inches or larger.

Keyboard

The keyboard is used to input information into the computer. The number and location of the keys on a keyboard can vary. In addition to letters, numbers, and symbols, most computer keyboards contain function keys, arrow keys, and a numeric keypad. Figure G.3 shows an enhanced keyboard.

The 12 keys at the top of the keyboard, labeled with the letter F followed by a number, are called *function keys*. Use these keys to perform functions within each of the Office applications. To the right of the regular keys is a group of special or dedicated keys. These keys are labeled with specific functions that will be performed when you press the key. Below the special keys are arrow keys. Use these keys to move the insertion point in the document screen.

Some keyboards include mode indicator lights. When you select certain modes, a light appears on the keyboard. For example, if you press the Caps Lock key, which disables the lowercase alphabet, a light appears next to Caps Lock. Similarly, pressing the Num Lock key will disable the special functions on the numeric keypad, which is located at the right side of the keyboard.

Figure G.3 Keyboard

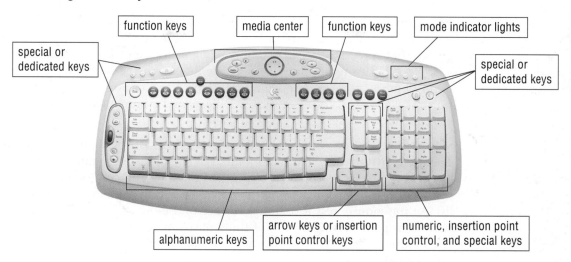

function keys

media center

function keys

mode indicator lights

special or dedicated keys

special or dedicated keys

alphanumeric keys

arrow keys or insertion point control keys

numeric, insertion point control, and special keys

Drives and Ports

A PC includes drives and ports that allow you to input and output data. For example, a hard drive is a disk drive inside of the PC that stores data that may have been inputted or outputted. Other drives may include CD, DVD and BluRay disc drives, although newer computers may not include these drives, because USB flash drives are becoming the preferred technology. Ports are the "plugs" on the PC, and are used to connect devices to the computer, such as the keyboard and mouse, the monitor, speakers, a USB flash drive and so on. Most PCs will have a few USB ports, at least one display port, an audio cable port, and possibly an ethernet port (used to physically connect to the Internet or a network).

Printer

An electronic version of a file is known as a *soft copy*. If you want to create a hard copy of a file, you need to print it. To print documents you will need to access a printer (as shown in Figure G.4), which will probably be either a laser printer or an ink-jet printer. A laser printer uses a laser beam combined with heat and pressure to print documents, while an ink-jet printer prints a document by spraying a fine mist of ink on the page.

Figure G.4 Printer

Mouse

Most functions and commands in the Microsoft Office suite are designed to be performed using a mouse or a similar pointing device. A mouse is an input device that sits on a flat surface next to the computer. You can operate a mouse with your left or right hand. Moving the mouse on the flat surface causes a corresponding pointer to move on the screen, and clicking the left or right mouse buttons allows you to select various objects and commands. Figure G.5 shows an example of a mouse.

Using the Mouse The applications in the Microsoft Office suite can be operated with the keyboard and a mouse. The mouse generally has two buttons on top, which you press to execute specific functions and commands. A mouse may also contain a wheel, which can be used to scroll in a window or as a third button. To use the mouse, rest it on a flat surface or a mouse pad. Put your hand over it with your palm resting on top of the mouse and your index finger resting on the left mouse button. As you move your hand, and thus the mouse, a corresponding pointer moves on the screen.

When using the mouse, you should understand four terms — point, click, double-click, and drag. When operating the mouse, you may need to point to a specific command, button, or icon. To *point* means to position the mouse pointer on the desired item. With the mouse pointer positioned on the item, you may need to click a button on the mouse to select the item. To *click* means to quickly tap a button on the mouse once. To complete two steps at one time, such as choosing and then executing a function, double-click the mouse button. To *double-click* means to tap the left mouse button twice in quick succession. The term *drag* means to click and hold down the left mouse button, move the mouse pointer to a specific location, and then release the button.

💡 *Hint* This textbook will use the verb *click* to refer to the mouse and the verb press to refer to a key on the keyboard.

Using the Mouse Pointer The mouse pointer will look different depending on where you have positioned it and what function you are performing. The following are some of the ways the mouse pointer can appear when you are working in the Office suite:

I

- The mouse pointer appears as an I-beam (called the *I-beam pointer*) when you are inserting text in a file. The I-beam pointer can be used to move the insertion point or to select text.

- The mouse pointer appears as an arrow pointing up and to the left (called the *arrow pointer*) when it is moved to the Title bar, Quick Access Toolbar, ribbon, or an option in a dialog box, among other locations.

- The mouse pointer becomes a double-headed arrow (either pointing left and right, pointing up and down, or pointing diagonally) when you perform certain functions such as changing the size of an object.

Figure G.5 Mouse

- In certain situations, such as when you move an object or image, the mouse pointer displays with a four-headed arrow attached. The four-headed arrow means that you can move the object left, right, up, or down.
- When a request is being processed or when an application is being loaded, the mouse pointer may appear as a moving circle. The moving circle means "please wait." When the process is completed, the circle is replaced with a normal mouse pointer.
- When the mouse pointer displays as a hand with a pointing index finger, it indicates that more information is available about an item. The mouse pointer also displays as a hand with a pointing index finger when you hover the mouse over a hyperlink.

Touchpad

If you are working on a laptop computer, you may use a touchpad instead of a mouse. A *touchpad* allows you to move the mouse pointer by moving your finger across a surface at the base of the keyboard. You click and right-click by using your thumb to press the buttons located at the bottom of the touchpad. Some touchpads have special features such as scrolling or clicking something by tapping the surface of the touchpad instead of pressing a button with a thumb.

TouchScreen

Smartphones, tablets, and touch monitors all use TouchScreen technology (as shown in Figure G.6), which allows users to directly interact with the objects on the screen by touching them with fingers, thumbs, or a stylus. Multiple fingers or both thumbs can be used on most modern touchscreens, giving users the ability to zoom, rotate, and manipulate items on the screen. While a lot of activities in this textbook can be completed using a device with a touchscreen, a mouse or touchpad might be required to complete a few activities.

Figure G.6 Touchscreen

Choosing Commands

Once an application is open, you can use several methods in the application to choose commands. A command is an instruction that tells the application to do something. You can choose a command using the mouse or the keyboard. When an application such as Word or PowerPoint is open, the ribbon contains buttons and options for completing tasks, as well as tabs you can click to display additional buttons and options. To choose a button on the Quick Access Toolbar or on the ribbon, position the tip of the mouse arrow pointer on the button and then click the left mouse button.

The Office suite provides accelerator keys you can press to use a command in an application. Press the Alt key on the keyboard to display KeyTips that identify the accelerator key you can press to execute a command. For example, if you press the Alt key in a Word document with the Home tab active, KeyTips display as shown in Figure G.7. Continue pressing accelerator keys until you execute the desired command. For example, to begin checking the spelling in a document, press the Alt key, press the R key on the keyboard to display the Review tab, and then press the letter S on the keyboard.

Choosing Commands from Drop-Down Lists

To choose a command from a drop-down list with the mouse, position the mouse pointer on the option and then click the left mouse button. To make a selection from a drop-down list with the keyboard, type the underlined letter in the option.

Some options at a drop-down list may appear in gray (dimmed), indicating that the option is currently unavailable. If an option at a drop-down list displays preceded by a check mark, it means the option is currently active. If an option at a drop-down list displays followed by an ellipsis (...), clicking that option will display a dialog box.

Choosing Options from a Dialog Box

A dialog box contains options for applying formatting or otherwise modifying a file or data within a file. Some dialog boxes display with tabs along the top that provide additional options. For example, the Font dialog box shown in Figure G.8 contains two tabs—the Font tab and the Advanced tab. The tab that displays in the front is the active tab. To make a tab active using the mouse, position the arrow pointer on the tab and then click the left mouse button. If you are using the keyboard, press Ctrl + Tab or press Alt + the underlined letter on the tab.

To choose an option from a dialog box with the mouse, position the arrow pointer on the option and then click the left mouse button. If you are using the keyboard, press the Tab key to move the insertion point forward from option to option. Press Shift + Tab to move the insertion point backward from option to option. You can also press and hold down the Alt key and then press the

Figure G.7 Word Home Tab KeyTips

Figure G.8 Word Font Dialog Box

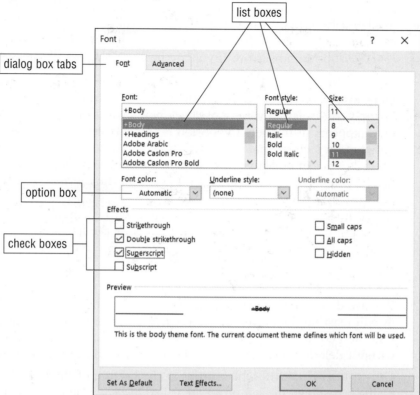

underlined letter of the option. When an option is selected, it displays with a blue background or surrounded by a dashed box called a *marquee*. A dialog box contains one or more of the following elements: list boxes, option boxes, check boxes, text boxes, option buttons, measurement boxes, and command buttons.

List Boxes and Option Boxes The fonts available in the Font dialog box, shown in Figure G.8, are contained in a list box. To make a selection from a list box with the mouse, move the arrow pointer to the option and then click the left mouse button.

Some list boxes may contain a scroll bar. This scroll bar will display at the right side of the list box (a vertical scroll bar) or at the bottom of the list box (a horizontal scroll bar). Use a vertical scroll bar or a horizontal scroll bar to move through the list if the list is longer (or wider) than the box. To move down a list using a vertical scroll bar, position the arrow pointer on the down arrow, and then click and hold down the left mouse button. To scroll up through the list, position the arrow pointer on the up arrow, and then click and hold down the left mouse button. You can also move the arrow pointer above the scroll box and click the left mouse button to scroll up the list or move the arrow pointer below the scroll box and click the left mouse button to move down the list. To navigate in a list with a horizontal scroll bar, click the left arrow to scroll to the left of the list or click the right arrow to scroll to the right of the list.

To use the keyboard to make a selection from a list box, move the insertion point into the box by holding down the Alt key and pressing the underlined letter of the desired option. Press the Up and/or Down Arrow keys on the keyboard to move through the list, and press the Enter key when the desired option is selected.

In some dialog boxes where there is not enough room for a list box, lists of options are contained in a drop-down list box called an *option box*. Option boxes display with a down arrow. For example, in Figure G.8, the font color options are contained in an option box. To display the different color options, click the *Font color* option box arrow. If you are using the keyboard, press Alt + C.

Hint This textbook will refer to the down arrow for an option box as an option box arrow.

Check Boxes Some dialog boxes contain options preceded by a box. A check mark may or may not appear in the box. The Word Font dialog box shown in Figure G.8 displays a variety of check boxes within the *Effects* section. If a check mark appears in the box, the option is active (turned on). If the check box does not contain a check mark, the option is inactive (turned off). Any number of check boxes can be active. For example, in the Word Font dialog box, you can insert a check mark in several of the boxes in the *Effects* section to activate the options.

To make a check box active or inactive with the mouse, position the tip of the arrow pointer in the check box and then click the left mouse button. If you are using the keyboard, press Alt + the underlined letter of the option.

Text Boxes Some options in a dialog box require you to enter text. For example, the boxes below the *Find what* and *Replace with* options at the Excel Find and Replace dialog box shown in Figure G.9 are text boxes. In a text box, type text or edit existing text. Edit text in a text box in the same manner as normal text. Use the Left and Right Arrow keys on the keyboard to move the insertion point without deleting text and use the Delete key or Backspace key to delete text.

Command Buttons The buttons at the bottom of the Excel Find and Replace dialog box shown in Figure G.9 are called *command buttons*. Use a command button to execute or cancel a command. Some command buttons display with an ellipsis (...), which means another dialog box will open if you click that button. To choose a command button with the mouse, position the arrow pointer on the button and then click the left mouse button. To choose a command button with the keyboard, press the Tab key until the command button is surrounded by a marquee and then press the Enter key.

Option Buttons The Word Insert Table dialog box shown in Figure G.10 contains options in the *AutoFit behavior* section preceded by option buttons. Only one option button can be selected at any time. When an option button is selected, a blue or black circle displays in the button. To select an option button with the mouse, position the tip of the arrow pointer inside the option button or on the option and then click the left mouse button. To make a selection with the keyboard, press and hold down the Alt key, press the underlined letter of the option, and then release the Alt key.

Figure G.9 Excel Find and Replace Dialog Box

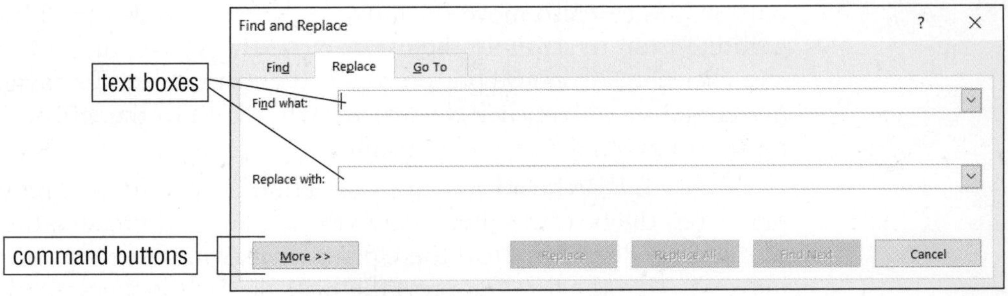

Figure G.10 Word Insert Table Dialog Box

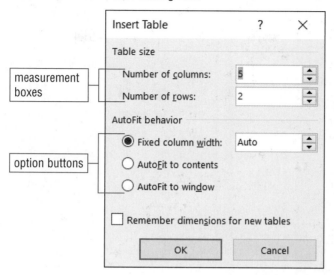

Measurement Boxes Some options in a dialog box contain measurements or amounts you can increase or decrease. These options are generally located in a measurement box. For example, the Word Insert Table dialog box shown in Figure G.10 contains the *Number of columns* and *Number of rows* measurement boxes. To increase a number in a measurement box, position the tip of the arrow pointer on the up arrow at the right of the measurement box and then click the left mouse button. To decrease the number, click the down arrow. If you are using the keyboard, press and hold down the Alt key and then press the underlined letter for the option, press the Up Arrow key to increase the number or the Down Arrow key to decrease the number, and then release the Alt key.

Choosing Commands with Keyboard Shortcuts

Applications in the Office suite offer a variety of keyboard shortcuts you can use to execute specific commands. Keyboard shortcuts generally require two or more keys. For example, the keyboard shortcut to display the Open dialog box in an application is Ctrl + F12. To use this keyboard shortcut, press and hold down the Ctrl key, press the F12 function on the keyboard, and then release the Ctrl key. For a list of keyboard shortcuts, refer to the Help files.

Choosing Commands with Shortcut Menus

The software applications in the Office suite include shortcut menus that contain commands related to different items. To display a shortcut menu, position the mouse pointer over the item for which you want to view more options, and then click the right mouse button or press Shift + F10. The shortcut menu will appear wherever the insertion point is positioned. For example, if the insertion point is positioned in a paragraph of text in a Word document, clicking the right mouse button or pressing Shift + F10 will cause the shortcut menu shown in Figure G.11 to display in the document screen (along with the Mini toolbar).

To select an option from a shortcut menu with the mouse, click the option. If you are using the keyboard, press the Up or Down Arrow key until the option is selected and then press the Enter key. To close a shortcut menu without choosing an option, click outside the shortcut menu or press the Esc key.

Figure G.11 Word Shortcut Menu

Working with Multiple Programs

As you learn the various applications in the Microsoft Office suite, you will notice many similarities between them. For example, the steps to save, close, and print are virtually the same whether you are working in Word, Excel, or PowerPoint. This consistency between applications greatly enhances your ability to transfer knowledge learned in one application to another within the suite. Another benefit to using Microsoft Office is the ability to have more than one application open at the same time and to integrate content from one program with another. For example, you can open Word and create a document, open Excel and create a spreadsheet, and then copy the Excel spreadsheet into Word.

When you open an application, a button containing an icon representing the application displays on the taskbar. If you open another application, a button containing an icon representing that application displays to the right of the first application button on the taskbar. Figure G.12 shows the taskbar with Word, Excel, Access, and PowerPoint open. To move from one program to another, click the taskbar button representing the desired application.

Customizing Settings

Before beginning computer projects in this textbook, you may need to customize your monitor's settings, change the DPI display setting, and turn on the display of file extensions. Projects in the chapters in this textbook assume that the monitor display is set at 1600 × 900 pixels, the DPI set at 125%, and that the display of file extensions is turned on. If you are unable to make changes to the monitor's resolution or the DPI settings, the projects can still be completed successfully. Some references in the text might not perfectly match what you see on your

Figure G.12 Taskbar with Word, Excel, Access, and PowerPoint Open

screen, so some mental adjustments may need to be made for certain steps. For example, an item in a drop-down gallery might appear in a different column or row than what is indicated in the step instructions.

Before you begin learning the applications in the Microsoft Office 2016 suite, take a moment to check the display settings on the computer you are using. Your monitor's display settings are important because the ribbon in the Microsoft Office suite adjusts to the screen resolution setting of your computer monitor. A computer monitor set at a high resolution will have the ability to show more buttons in the ribbon than will a monitor set to a low resolution. The illustrations in this textbook were created with a screen resolution display set at 1600×900 pixels. In Figure G.13, the Word ribbon is shown three ways: at a lower screen resolution (1366×768 pixels), at the screen resolution featured throughout this textbook, and at a higher screen resolution (1920×1080 pixels). Note the variances in the ribbon in all three examples. If possible, set your display to 1600×900 pixels to match the illustrations you will see in this textbook.

Figure G.13 The Home Tab Displayed on a Monitor Set at Different Screen Resolutions

1366 × 768 screen resolution

1600 × 900 screen resolution

1920 × 1080 screen resolution

Project 1 **Setting Monitor Display to 1600 × 900**

Note: The resolution settings may be locked on lab computers. Also, some laptop screens and small monitors may not be able to display in a 1600 × 900 resolution.

1. At the Windows 10 desktop, right-click in a blank area of the screen.
2. At the shortcut menu, click the *Display settings* option.

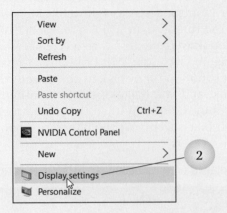

3. At the Settings window with the SYSTEM screen active, scroll down and then click *Advanced display settings*.

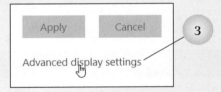

4. Scroll down the Settings window until the *Resolution* option box is visible and take note of the current resolution setting. If the current resolution is already set to 1600 × 900, skip ahead to Step 8.
5. Click in the Resolution option box and then click the 1600 × 900 option at the drop-down list.

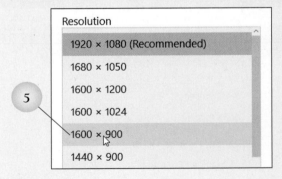

6. Click the Apply button.
7. Click the Keep Changes button.
8. Click the Close button.

Project 2 Changing the DPI Setting

Note: The DPI settings may be locked on lab computers. Also, some laptop screens and small monitors may not allow the DPI settings to be changed.

1. At the Windows 10 desktop, right-click in a blank area of the screen.
2. At the shortcut menu, click the *Display settings* option.
3. At the Settings window, take note of the current DPI percentage next to the text *Change the size of text, apps, and other items*. If the percentage is already set to 125%, skip to Step 5.
4. Click the slider bar below the text *Change the size of text, apps, and other items* and hold down the left mouse button, drag to the right until the DPI percentage is 125%, and then release the mouse button.

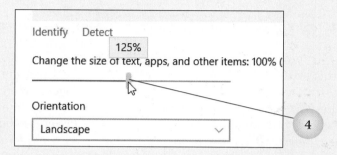

5. Close the computer window.

Project 3 Displaying File Extensions

1. At the Windows 10 desktop, click the File Explorer button on the taskbar.

2. At the File Explorer window, click the View tab.
3. Click the *File name extensions* check box in the Show/hide group to insert a check mark.

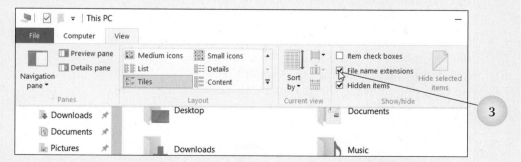

4. Close the computer window.

Completing Computer Projects

Some projects in this textbook require that you open an existing file. Project files are saved on OneDrive in a zip file. Before beginning projects and assessments in this book and the accompanying ebook, copy the necessary folder from the zip file to your storage medium (such as a USB flash drive) using File Explorer. Begin downloading the files for this book by going to the ebook and clicking the Ancillary Links button that displays when the ebook displays this page or any chapter opener page with the Data Files tab on it.

Project 4 Downloading Files to a USB Flash Drive

Note: OneDrive is updated periodically, so the steps to download files may vary from the steps below.
1. Insert your USB flash drive into an available USB port.
2. Navigate to this textbook's ebook. If you are a SNAP user, navigate to the ebook by clicking the textbook ebook link on your Assignments page. If you are not a SNAP user, launch your browser and go to http://paradigm.bookshelf.emcp.com, log in, and then click the textbook ebook thumbnail. *Note: The steps in this activity assume you are using the Microsoft Edge browser. If you are using a different browser, the following steps may vary.*
3. Navigate to the ebook page that corresponds to this textbook page.
4. Click the Ancillary Links button in the menu. The menu that appears may be at the top of the window or along the side of the window, depending on the size of the window.

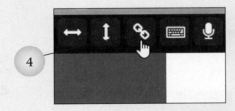

5. At the Ancillary Links dialog box, click the <u>Data Files: All Files</u> hyperlink.

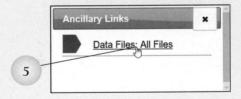

6. Click the Download hyperlink at the top of the window.
7. Click the Open button in the message box when the DataFiles.zip finishes downloading.
8. Right-click the DataFiles folder in the Content pane.
9. Click the *Copy* option in the shortcut menu.

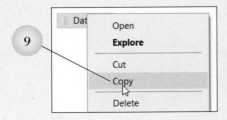

10. Click the USB flash drive that displays in the Navigation pane at the left side of the File Explorer window.
11. Click the Home tab in the File Explorer window.
12. Click the Paste button in the Clipboard group.

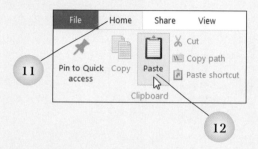

13. Close the File Explorer window by clicking the Close button in the upper right corner of the window.

Project 5 Deleting a File

Note: Check with your instructor before deleting a file.

1. At the Windows 10 desktop, open File Explorer by clicking the File Explorer button on the taskbar.
2. Click the *Downloads* folder in the navigation pane.
3. Right-click *DataFiles.zip*.
4. Click the *Delete* option at the shortcut menu.

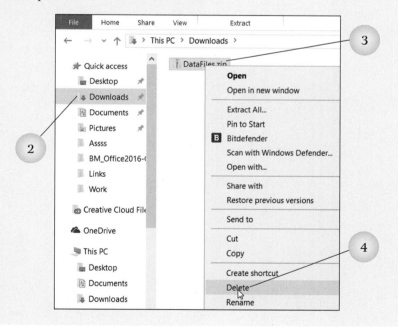

Microsoft® Word Level 1

Unit 1

Editing and Formatting Documents

Microsoft Word

Preparing a Word Document

Performance Objectives

Upon successful completion of Chapter 1, you will be able to:

1 Open Microsoft Word

2 Create, save, name, print, open, and close a Word document

3 Close Word

4 Open a document from and pin/unpin a document at the *Recent* Option list

5 Edit a document

6 Move the insertion point within a document

7 Scroll within a document

8 Select text

9 Use the Undo and Redo buttons

10 Check spelling and grammar

11 Use the Tell Me and Help features

> **Precheck**
>
> Check your current skills to help focus your study.

In this chapter, you will learn to create, save, name, print, open, close, and edit a Word document as well as complete a spelling and grammar check. You will also learn about the Tell Me feature, which provides information and guidance on how to complete a function, and the Help feature, which is an on-screen reference manual that provides information on features and commands for each program in the Microsoft Office suite. Before continuing, make sure you read the *Getting Started* section presented at the beginning of this book. It contains information about computer hardware and software, using the mouse, executing commands, and exploring Help files.

SNAP

If you are a SNAP user, launch the Precheck and Tutorials from your Assignments page.

> **Data Files**
>
> Before beginning chapter work, copy the WL1C1 folder to your storage medium and then make WL1C1 the active folder.

<table>
<tr><td>**Project 1**   **Prepare a Word Document**</td><td>**2 Parts**</td></tr>
</table>

You will create a short document containing information on resumes and then save, print, and close the document.

Preview Finished Project

Opening Microsoft Word

Microsoft Office 2016 contains a word processing program named Word that can be used to create, save, edit, and print documents. The steps to open Word may vary but generally include clicking the Start button on the Windows 10 desktop and then clicking the Word 2016 tile at the Start menu. At the Word 2016 opening screen, click the *Blank document* template.

Creating, Saving, Printing, and Closing a Document

When the Blank document template is clicked, a blank document displays on the screen, as shown in Figure 1.1. The features of the document screen are described in Table 1.1.

At a blank document, type information to create a document. A document is a record containing information such as a letter, report, term paper, table, and so on. Here are some things to consider when typing text:

- **Word wrap:** As text is typed in the document, Word wraps text to the next line, so the Enter key does not need to be pressed at the end of each line. A word is wrapped to the next line if it begins before the right margin and continues past the right margin. The only times the Enter key needs to be pressed are to end a paragraph, create a blank line, and end a short line.

- **AutoCorrect:** Word contains a feature that automatically corrects certain words as they are typed. For example, if *adn* is typed instead of *and*, Word automatically corrects it when the spacebar is pressed after typing the word. AutoCorrect will also superscript the letters that follow an ordinal number (a number indicating a position in a series). For example, type *2nd* and then press the spacebar or Enter key, and Word will convert this ordinal number to 2nd.

- **Automatic spelling checker:** By default, Word automatically inserts a red wavy line below any word that is not contained in the Spelling dictionary or automatically corrected by AutoCorrect. This may include misspelled words, proper names, some terminology, and some foreign words. If a typed word is not recognized by the Spelling dictionary, leave it as written if the word is correct. However, if the word is incorrect, delete the word or position the I-beam pointer on the word, click the *right* mouse button, and then click the correct spelling at the shortcut menu.

- **Automatic grammar checker:** Word includes an automatic grammar checker. If the grammar checker detects a sentence containing a grammatical error, a blue wavy line is inserted below the error. The sentence can be left as written or corrected. To correct the sentence, position the I-beam pointer on the error, click the *right* mouse button, and choose from the shortcut menu of possible corrections.

Figure 1.1 Blank Document

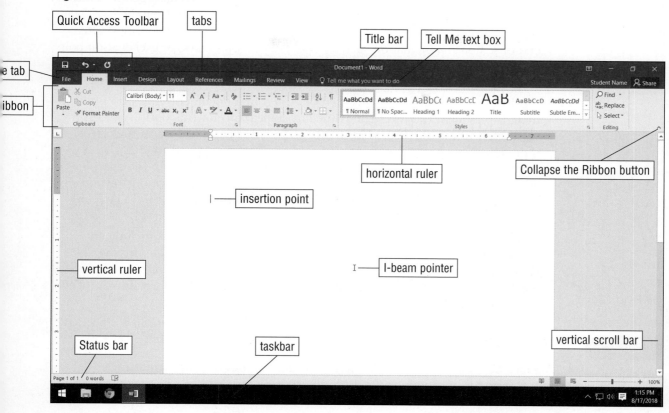

Table 1.1 Microsoft Word Screen Features

Feature	Description
Collapse the Ribbon button	when clicked, removes the ribbon from the screen
File tab	when clicked, displays backstage area, which contains options for working with and managing documents
horizontal ruler	used to set margins, indents, and tabs
I-beam pointer	used to move the insertion point or to select text
insertion point	indicates the location of the next character entered at the keyboard
Quick Access Toolbar	contains buttons for commonly used commands
ribbon	area containing tabs with options and buttons divided into groups
Status bar	displays the numbers of pages and words, plus the view buttons and Zoom slider bar
tabs	contain commands and features organized into groups
taskbar	contains icons for launching programs, buttons for active tasks, and a notification area
Tell Me feature	provides information and guidance on how to complete functions
Title bar	displays the document name followed by the program name
vertical ruler	used to set the top and bottom margins
vertical scroll bar	used to view various parts of the document beyond the screen

- **Spacing punctuation:** Typically, Word uses Calibri as the default typeface, which is a proportional typeface. (You will learn more about typefaces in Chapter 2.) When typing text in a proportional typeface, space once (rather than two times) after end-of-sentence punctuation such as a period, question mark, or exclamation point and after a colon. The characters in a proportional typeface are set closer together, and extra white space at the end of a sentence or after a colon is not needed.

- **Option buttons:** As text is inserted or edited in a document, an option button may display near the text. The name and appearance of this option button varies depending on the action. If a typed word is corrected by AutoCorrect, if an automatic list is created, or if autoformatting is applied to text, the AutoCorrect Options button appears. Click this button to undo the specific automatic action. If text is pasted in a document, the Paste Options button appears near the text. Click this button to display the Paste Options gallery, which has buttons for controlling how the pasted text is formatted.

- **AutoComplete:** Microsoft Word and other Office applications include an AutoComplete feature that inserts an entire item when a few identifying characters are typed. For example, type the letters *Mond* and *Monday* displays in a ScreenTip above the letters. Press the Enter key or press the F3 function key and Word inserts *Monday* in the document.

Tutorial

Entering Text

Using the New Line Command

A Word document is based on a template that applies default formatting. Some basic formatting includes 1.08 line spacing and 8 points of spacing after a paragraph. Each time the Enter key is pressed, a new paragraph begins and 8 points of spacing is inserted after the paragraph. To move the insertion point down to the next line without including the additional 8 points of spacing, use the New Line command, Shift + Enter.

Project 1a Creating a Document

Part 1 of 2

1. Open Word by clicking the Word 2016 tile at the Windows Start menu.
2. At the Word opening screen, click the *Blank document* template. (These steps may vary. Check with your instructor for specific instructions.)
3. At a blank document, type the information shown in Figure 1.2 with the following specifications:
   a. Correct any errors highlighted by the spelling checker or grammar checker as they occur.
   b. Press the spacebar once after end-of-sentence punctuation.
   c. After typing *Created:* press Shift + Enter to move the insertion point to the next line without adding 8 points of additional spacing.
   d. To insert the word *Thursday* at the end of the document, type Thur and then press F3. (This is an example of the AutoComplete feature.)
   e. To insert the word *December*, type Dece and then press the Enter key. (This is another example of the AutoComplete feature.)
   f. Press Shift + Enter after typing *December 6, 2018*.
   g. When typing the last line (the line containing the ordinal numbers), type the ordinal number text and AutoCorrect will automatically convert the letters in the ordinal numbers to a superscript.
4. When you are finished typing the text, press the Enter key. (Keep the document open for the next project.)

Check Your Work

Figure 1.2 Project 1a

The traditional chronological resume lists your work experience in reverse-chronological order (starting with your current or most recent position). The functional style deemphasizes the "where" and "when" of your career and instead groups similar experiences, talents, and qualifications regardless of when they occurred.

Like the chronological resume, the hybrid resume includes specifics about where you worked, when you worked there, and what your job titles were. Like a functional resume, a hybrid resume emphasizes your most relevant qualifications in an expanded summary section, in several "career highlights" bullet points at the top of your resume, or in project summaries.

Created:
Thursday, December 6, 2018
Note: The two paragraphs will become the 2nd and 3rd paragraphs in the 5th section.

Tutorial

Saving with a
New Name

 Save

Saving a Document with a New Name

Save a document if it is going to be used in the future. Save a new document or save an existing document with a new name at the Save As dialog box.

To save a new document, click the Save button on the Quick Access Toolbar, click the File tab, and then click the *Save* option or the *Save As* option, or press the keyboard shortcut Ctrl + S and the Save As backstage area displays, as shown in Figure 1.3. Click the *Browse* option to display the Save As dialog box, as shown in Figure 1.4.

To save an existing document with a new name, click the File tab, click the *Save As* option to display the Save As backstage area, and then click the *Browse* option to display the Save As dialog box. Press the F12 function key to display the Save As dialog box without having to first display the Save As backstage area. At the Save As dialog box, type the name for the document in the *File name* text box and then press the Enter key or click the Save button.

Quick Steps

Save a Document
1. Click File tab.
2. Click *Save As* option.
3. Click *Browse* option.
4. Type document name in *File name* text box.
5. Press Enter.

Hint Save a document approximately every 15 minutes or when interrupted.

Figure 1.3 Save As Backstage Area

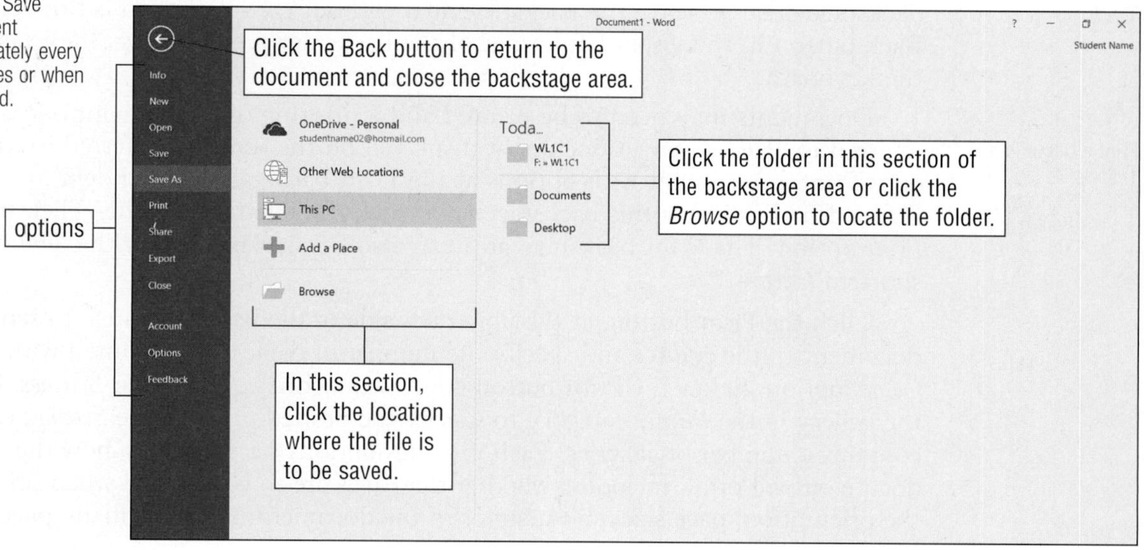

Document1 - Word

Student Name

Click the Back button to return to the document and close the backstage area.

Info
New
Open
Save
Save As
Print
Share
Export
Close
Account
Options
Feedback

options

OneDrive - Personal
studentname02@hotmail.com

Other Web Locations

This PC

Add a Place

Browse

Toda...

WL1C1
F: » WL1C1

Documents

Desktop

Click the folder in this section of the backstage area or click the *Browse* option to locate the folder.

In this section, click the location where the file is to be saved.

Figure 1.4 Save As Dialog Box

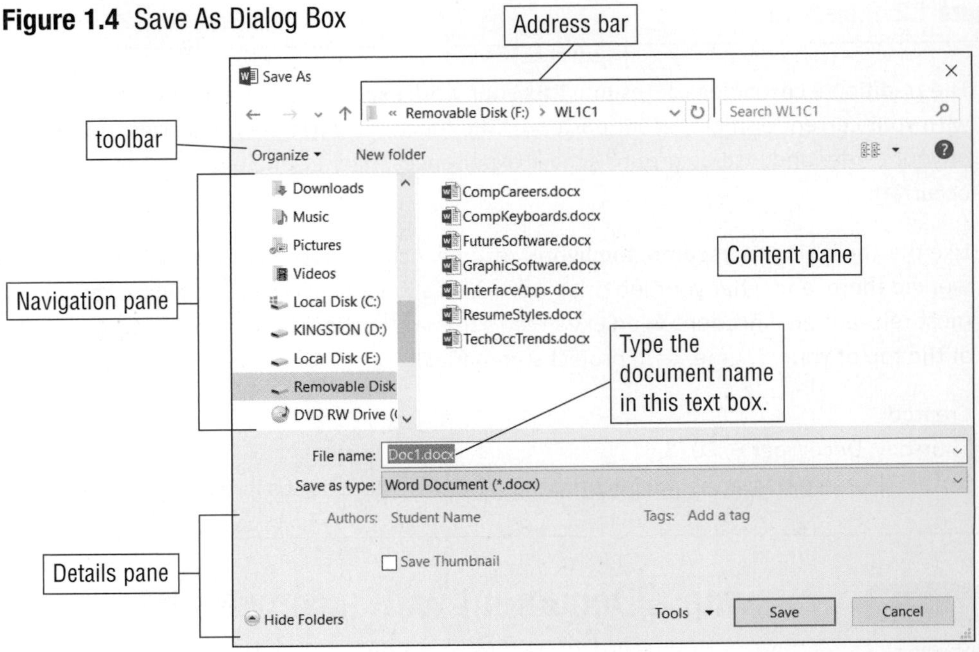

Naming a Document

Hint You cannot give a document the same name first in uppercase and then in lowercase letters.

Document names created in Word and other applications in the Microsoft Office suite can be up to 255 characters in length, including the drive letter and any folder names, and they may include spaces. File names cannot include any of the following characters:

forward slash (/)	less-than symbol (<)	quotation marks (" ")
backslash (\)	asterisk (*)	colon (:)
greater-than symbol (>)	question mark (?)	pipe symbol (|)

Tutorial

Printing a Document

Printing a Document

Click the File tab and the backstage area displays. The buttons and options at the backstage area change depending on the option selected at the left side of the backstage area. To leave the backstage area without completing an action, click the Back button in the upper left corner of the backstage area, or press the Esc key on the keyboard.

Quick Steps

Print a Document

1. Click File tab.
2. Click *Print* option.
3. Click Print button.

Documents may need to be printed and a printing of a document on paper is referred to as *hard copy*. A document displayed on the screen is referred to as *soft copy*. Print a document with options at the Print backstage area, shown in Figure 1.5. To display this backstage area, click the File tab and then click the *Print* option. The Print backstage area can also be displayed using the keyboard shortcut Ctrl + P.

Click the Print button, at the upper left side of the backstage area, to send the document to the printer and specify the number of copies to be printed with the *Copies* option. Below the Print button are two categories: *Printer* and *Settings*. Use the gallery in the *Printer* category to specify the desired printer. The *Settings* category contains a number of galleries. Each provides options for specifying how the document will print, including whether the pages are to be collated when printed; the orientation, page size, and margins of the document; and how many pages of the document are to print on a sheet of paper.

Figure 1.5 Print Backstage Area

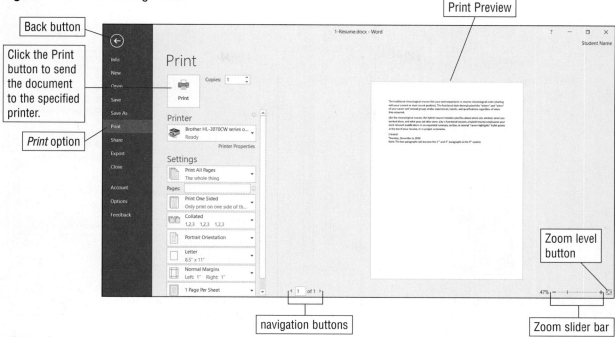

Back button

Click the Print button to send the document to the specified printer.

Print option

Print Preview

Zoom level button

navigation buttons

Zoom slider bar

 Quick Print

Quick Steps

Close a Document
1. Click File tab.
2. Click *Close* option.

Close Word
Click Close button.

Another method for printing a document is to insert the Quick Print button on the Quick Access Toolbar and then click the button. This sends the document directly to the printer without displaying the Print backstage area. To insert the button on the Quick Access Toolbar, click the Customize Quick Access Toolbar button at the right side of the toolbar and then click *Quick Print* at the drop-down list. To remove the Quick Print button from the Quick Access Toolbar, right-click the button and then click the *Remove from Quick Access Toolbar* option at the shortcut menu.

Tutorial

Closing a Document and Closing Word

 Close

Closing a Document and Closing Word

When a document is saved, it is saved to the specified location and also remains on the screen. To remove the document from the screen, click the File tab and then click the *Close* option or use the keyboard shortcut Ctrl + F4. When a document is closed, it is removed and a blank screen displays. At this screen, open a previously saved document, create a new document, or close Word. To close Word, click the Close button in the upper right corner of the screen. The keyboard shortcut Alt + F4 also closes Word.

Project 1b Saving, Printing, and Closing a Document and Closing Word Part 2 of 2

1. Save the document you created for Project 1a and name it **1-Resume** (*1-* for Chapter 1 and *Resume* because the document is about resumes) by completing the following steps:
   a. Click the File tab.
   b. Click the *Save As* option.
   c. At the Save As backstage area, click the *Browse* option.
   d. At the Save As dialog box, if necessary, navigate to the WL1C1 folder on your storage medium.

1a

e. Click in the *File name* text box (this selects any text in the box), type 1-Resume, and then press the Enter key.

2. Print the document by clicking the File tab, clicking the *Print* option, and then clicking the Print button at the Print backstage area.

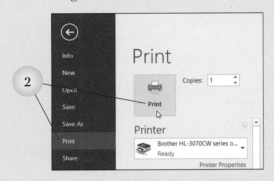

3. Close the document by clicking the File tab and then clicking the *Close* option.

4. Close Word by clicking the Close button in the upper right corner of the screen.

Check Your Work

Project 2   Save a Document with a New Name and the Same Name   2 Parts

You will open a document in the WL1C1 folder on your storage medium, save the document with a new name, add text, and then save the document with the same name. You will also print and then close the document.

Preview Finished Project

Creating a New Document

When a document is closed, a blank screen displays. To create a new document, display a blank document by clicking the File tab, clicking the *New* option, and then clicking the *Blank document* template. A new document can also be opened with the keyboard shortcut Ctrl + N or by inserting a New button on the Quick Access Toolbar. To insert the button, click the Customize Quick Access Toolbar button at the right side of the toolbar and then click *New* at the drop-down list.

The New backstage area also includes the *Single spaced (blank)* template. Click this template and a new document will open that contains single spacing and no spacing after paragraphs.

Tutorial

Opening a Document from a Removable Disk

Opening a Document

After a document is saved and closed, it can be opened at the Open dialog box, shown in Figure 1.6. To display this dialog box, display the Open backstage area and then click the *Browse* option. Display the Open backstage area by clicking the File tab. If a document is open, click the File tab and then click the *Open* option to display the Open backstage area. Other methods for displaying the Open backstage area include using the keyboard shortcut Ctrl + O, inserting an Open button on the Quick Access Toolbar, or clicking the Open Other Documents hyperlink in the lower left corner of the Word 2016 opening screen.

Figure 1.6 Open Dialog Box

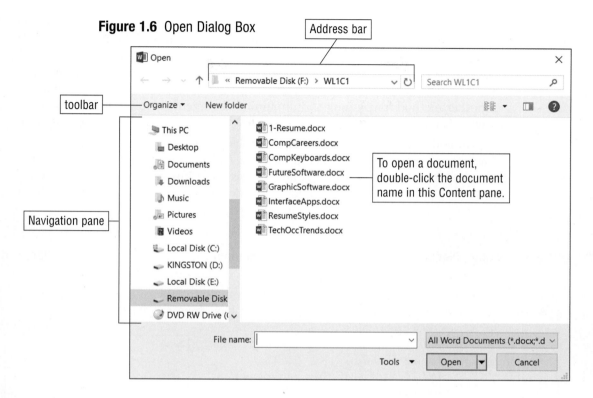

Address bar

toolbar

Navigation pane

To open a document, double-click the document name in this Content pane.

Quick Steps

Open a Document
1. Click File tab.
2. Click *Open* option.
3. Click *Browse* option.
4. Double-click document name.

Tutorial

Opening a Document from the *Recent* Option List

Tutorial

Pinning and Unpinning a Document at the *Recent* Option List

At the Open backstage area, click the *Browse* option and the Open dialog box displays. Go directly to the Open dialog box without displaying the Open backstage area by pressing Ctrl + F12. At the Open dialog box, navigate to the desired location (such as the drive containing your storage medium), open the folder containing the document, and then double-click the document name in the Content pane.

Opening a Document from the *Recent* Option List

At the Open backstage area with the *Recent* option selected, the names of the most recently opened documents display. By default, Word displays the names of 25 of the most recently opened documents and groups them into categories such as *Today*, *Yesterday*, and perhaps another category such as *Last Week*. To open a document from the *Recent* option list, scroll down the list and then click the document name. The Word 2016 opening screen also displays a list of the names of the most recently opened documents. Click a document name in the Recent list at the opening screen to open the document.

Pinning and Unpinning a Document at the *Recent* Option List

If a document is opened on a regular basis, consider pinning it to the *Recent* option list. To pin a document to the *Recent* option list at the Open backstage area, hover the mouse pointer over the document name and then click the small left-pointing push pin that displays to the right of the document name. The left-pointing push pin changes to a down-pointing push pin and the pinned document is inserted into a new category named *Pinned*. The *Pinned* category displays at the top of the *Recent* option list. The next time the Open backstage area displays, the pinned document displays in the *Pinned* category at the top of the *Recent* option list.

A document can also be pinned to the Recent list at the Word 2016 opening screen. When a document is pinned, it displays at the top of the Recent list and the *Recent* option list at the Open backstage area. To "unpin" a document from the Recent or *Recent* option list, click the pin to change it from a down-pointing push pin to a left-pointing push pin. More than one document can be pinned to a list. Another method for pinning and unpinning documents is to use the shortcut menu. Right-click a document name and then click the *Pin to list* or *Unpin from list* option.

In addition to documents, folders can be pinned to a list at the Save As backstage area. The third panel in the Save As backstage area displays a list of the most recently opened folders and groups them into categories such as *Today*, *Yesterday*, and *Last Week*. Pin a folder or folders to the list and a *Pinned* category is created; the folder names display in the category.

Project 2a Opening, Pinning, Unpinning, and Saving a Document   Part 1 of 2

1. Open Word and then open **CompCareers.docx** by completing the following steps:
   a. At the Word opening screen, click the <u>Open Other Documents</u> hyperlink.
   b. At the Open backstage area, click the *Browse* option.
   c. At the Open dialog box, navigate to the external drive containing your storage medium.
   d. Double-click the **WL1C1** folder in the Content pane.
   e. Double-click **CompCareers.docx** in the Content pane.
2. Close **CompCareers.docx**.
3. Press the F12 function key to display the Open dialog box and then double-click **FutureSoftware.docx** in the Content pane to open the document.
4. Close **FutureSoftware.docx**.
5. Pin **CompCareers.docx** to the *Recent* option list by completing the following steps:
   a. Click the File tab.
   b. At the Open backstage area, hover the mouse pointer over **CompCareers.docx** in the *Recent* option list and then click the left-pointing push pin that displays to the right of the document.

   (This creates a new category named *Pinned*, which displays at the top of the list. The **CompCareers.docx** file displays in the *Pinned* category and a down-pointing push pin displays to the right of the document name.)
6. Click **CompCareers.docx** in the *Pinned* category at the top of the *Recent* option list to open the document.
7. Unpin **CompCareers.docx** from the *Recent* option list by completing the following steps:
   a. Click the File tab and then click the *Open* option.
   b. At the Open backstage area, click the down-pointing push pin that displays to the right of **CompCareers.docx** in the *Pinned* category in the *Recent* option list. (This removes the *Pinned* category and changes the pin from a down-pointing push pin to a left-pointing push pin.)
   c. Click the Back button to return to the document.

8. With **CompCareers.docx** open, save the document with a new name by completing the following steps:
   a. Click the File tab and then click the *Save As* option.
   b. At the Save As backstage area, click the *Browse* option.
   c. At the Save As dialog box, if necessary, navigate to the WL1C1 folder on your storage medium.
   d. Press the Home key on your keyboard to move the insertion point to the beginning of the file name and then type 1-. (Pressing the Home key saves you from having to type the entire document name.)
   e. Press the Enter key.

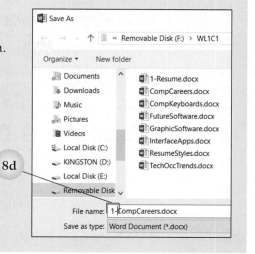

Tutorial

Saving a Document with the Same Name

Saving with the
Same Name

If changes are made to an existing document, save the changes before closing the document. Consider saving changes to a document on a periodic basis to ensure that no changes are lost if the power is interrupted. Save a document with the same name using the Save button on the Quick Access Toolbar or the *Save* option at the backstage area.

Project 2b Saving a Document with the Same Name

Part 2 of 2

1. With **1-CompCareers.docx** open and the insertion point positioned at the beginning of the document, type the text shown in Figure 1.7.
2. Save the changes you just made by clicking the Save button on the Quick Access Toolbar.
3. Print the document by clicking the File tab, clicking the *Print* option, and then clicking the Print button at the Print backstage area. (If your Quick Access Toolbar contains the Quick Print button, you can click the button to send the document directly to the printer.)
4. Close the document by pressing Ctrl + F4.

Check Your Work

Quick Steps

Save a Document with the Same Name
Click Save button on Quick Access Toolbar.
OR
1. Click File tab.
2. Click *Save* option.

Figure 1.7 Project 2b

The majority of new jobs being created in the United States today involve daily work with computers. Computer-related careers include technical support jobs, sales and training, programming and applications development, network and database administration, and computer engineering.

You will open a previously created document, save it with a new name, and then use scrolling and browsing techniques to move the insertion point to specific locations in the document.

Editing a Document

When a document is being edited, text may need to be inserted or deleted. To edit a document, use the mouse, the keyboard, or a combination of the two to move the insertion point to specific locations in the document. To move the insertion point using the mouse, position the I-beam pointer where the insertion point is to be positioned and then click the left mouse button.

Tutorial

Scrolling

Scrolling in a document changes the text display but does not move the insertion point. Use the mouse with the vertical scroll bar, at the right side of the screen, to scroll through text in a document. Click the up scroll arrow at the top of the vertical scroll bar to scroll up through the document and click the down scroll arrow to scroll down through the document.

The scroll bar contains a scroll box that indicates the location of the text in the document screen in relation to the remainder of the document. To scroll up one screen at a time, position the arrow pointer above the scroll box (but below the up scroll arrow) and then click the left mouse button. Position the arrow pointer below the scroll box and click the left button to scroll down a screen. Click and hold down the left mouse button and the action becomes continuous.

Another method for scrolling is to position the arrow pointer on the scroll box, click and hold down the left mouse button, and then drag the scroll box along the scroll bar to reposition text in the document screen. As the scroll box is dragged along the vertical scroll bar in a longer document, page numbers display in a box at the right side of the document screen.

Project 3a Scrolling in a Document   Part 1 of 2

1. Open **InterfaceApps.docx** (from the WL1C1 folder you copied to your storage medium).
2. Save the document with the new name **1-InterfaceApps** to the WL1C1 folder.
3. Position the I-beam pointer at the beginning of the first paragraph and then click the left mouse button.
4. Click the down scroll arrow on the vertical scroll bar several times. (This scrolls down lines of text in the document.) With the mouse pointer on the down scroll arrow, click and hold down the left mouse button and keep it down until the end of the document displays.
5. Position the mouse pointer on the up scroll arrow and click and hold down the left mouse button until the beginning of the document displays.
6. Position the mouse pointer below the scroll box and then click the left mouse button. Continue clicking the mouse button (with the mouse pointer positioned below the scroll box) until the end of the document displays.
7. Position the mouse pointer on the scroll box in the vertical scroll bar. Click and hold down the left mouse button, drag the scroll box to the top of the vertical scroll bar, and then release the mouse button. (Notice that the document page numbers display in a box at the right side of the document screen.)
8. Click in the title at the beginning of the document. (This moves the insertion point to the location of the mouse pointer.)

Moving the Insertion Point to a Specific Line or Page

 Find

Word includes a Go To feature that moves the insertion point to a specific location in a document, such as a line or page. To use the feature, click the Find button arrow in the Editing group on the Home tab, and then click *Go To* at the drop-down list. At the Find and Replace dialog box with the Go To tab selected, move the insertion point to a specific page by typing the page number in the *Enter page number* text box and then pressing the Enter key. Move to a specific line by clicking the *Line* option in the *Go to what* list box, typing the line number in the *Enter line number* text box, and then pressing the Enter key. Click the Close button to close the dialog box.

Moving the Insertion Point with the Keyboard

Tutorial

Moving the Insertion Point and Inserting and Deleting Text

To move the insertion point with the keyboard, use the arrow keys to the right of the regular keyboard or use the arrow keys on the numeric keypad. When using the arrow keys on the numeric keypad, make sure Num Lock is off. Use the arrow keys together with other keys to move the insertion point to various locations in the document, as shown in Table 1.2.

When moving the insertion point, Word considers a word to be any series of characters between spaces. A paragraph is any text that is followed by a single press of the Enter key. A page is text that is separated by a soft or hard page break.

Table 1.2 Insertion Point Movement Commands

To move insertion point	Press
one character left	Left Arrow
one character right	Right Arrow
one line up	Up Arrow
one line down	Down Arrow
one word left	Ctrl + Left Arrow
one word right	Ctrl + Right Arrow
to beginning of line	Home
to end of line	End
to beginning of current paragraph	Ctrl + Up Arrow
to beginning of next paragraph	Ctrl + Down Arrow
up one screen	Page Up
down one screen	Page Down
to top of previous page	Ctrl + Page Up
to top of next page	Ctrl + Page Down
to beginning of document	Ctrl + Home
to end of document	Ctrl + End

Resuming Reading or Editing in a Document

If a previously saved document is opened, pressing Shift + F5 will move the insertion point to the position it was last located when the document was closed.

When opening a multiple-page document, Word remembers the page the insertion point was last positioned. When the document is reopened, Word displays a "Welcome back!" message at the right side of the screen near the vertical scroll bar. The message identifies the page where the insertion point was last located. Click the message and the insertion point is positioned at the top of that page.

Project 3b **Moving the Insertion Point in a Document**   Part 2 of 2

1. With **1-InterfaceApps.docx** open, move the insertion point to line 15 and then to page 3 by completing the following steps:
   a. Click the Find button arrow in the Editing group on the Home tab, and then click *Go To* at the drop-down list.
   b. At the Find and Replace dialog box with the Go To tab selected, click *Line* in the *Go to what* list box.
   c. Click in the *Enter line number* text box, type 15, and then press the Enter key.
   d. Click *Page* in the *Go to what* list box.
   e. Click in the *Enter page number* text box, type 3, and then press the Enter key.
   f. Click the Close button to close the Find and Replace dialog box.

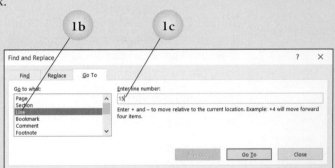

2. Close the document.
3. Open the document by clicking the File tab and then clicking the document name **1-InterfaceApps.docx** in the *Recent* option list in the *Today* category.
4. Move the mouse pointer to the right side of the screen to display the "Welcome back!" message. Hover the mouse pointer over the message and then click the left mouse button. (This positions the insertion point at the top of the third page—the page the insertion point was positioned when you closed the document.)

5. Press Ctrl + Home to move the insertion point to the beginning of the document.
6. Practice using the keyboard commands shown in Table 1.2 to move the insertion point within the document.
7. Close **1-InterfaceApps.docx**.

You will open a previously created document, save it with a new name, and then make editing changes to the document. The editing changes will include selecting, inserting, and deleting text and undoing and redoing edits.

Preview Finished Project

Inserting and Deleting Text

Editing a document may include inserting and/or deleting text. To insert text in a document, position the insertion point at the location text is to be typed and then type the text. Existing characters move to the right as text is typed. A number of options are available for deleting text. Some deletion commands are shown in Table 1.3.

Tutorial

Selecting, Replacing, and Deleting Text

Selecting Text

Use the mouse and/or keyboard to select a specific amount of text. Selected text can be deleted or other Word functions can be performed on it. When text is selected, it displays with a gray background, as shown in Figure 1.8, and the Mini toolbar displays. The Mini toolbar contains buttons for common tasks. (You will learn more about the Mini toolbar in Chapter 2.)

Table 1.3 Deletion Commands

To delete	Press
character right of insertion point	Delete key
character left of insertion point	Backspace key
text from insertion point to beginning of word	Ctrl + Backspace
text from insertion point to end of word	Ctrl + Delete

Figure 1.8 Selected Text and Mini Toolbar

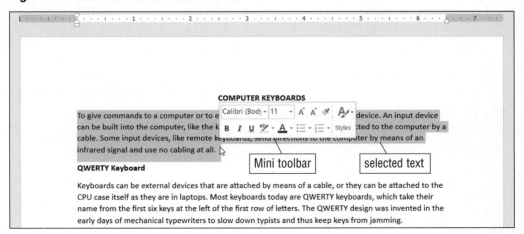

Selecting Text with the Mouse Use the mouse to select a word, line, sentence, paragraph, or entire document. Table 1.4 indicates the steps to follow to select various amounts of text.

To select a specific amount of text, such as a line or paragraph, click in the selection bar. The selection bar is the space at the left side of the document screen between the left edge of the page and the text. When the mouse pointer is positioned in the selection bar, the pointer turns into an arrow pointing up and to the right (instead of to the left).

To select an amount of text other than a word, sentence, or paragraph, position the I-beam pointer on the first character of the text to be selected, click and hold down the left mouse button, drag the I-beam pointer to the last character of the text to be selected, and then release the mouse button. All text between the current insertion point and the I-beam pointer can be selected. To do this, position the insertion point where the selection is to begin, press and hold down the Shift key, click the I-beam pointer at the end of the selection, and then release the Shift key. To cancel a selection using the mouse, click in the document screen.

Select text vertically in a document by holding down the Alt key while dragging with the mouse. This is especially useful when selecting a group of text, such as text set in columns.

Hint If text is selected, any character you type replaces the selected text.

Selecting Text with the Keyboard To select a specific amount of text using the keyboard, turn on the Selection mode by pressing the F8 function key. With the Selection mode activated, use the arrow keys to select the text. To cancel the selection, press the Esc key and then press any arrow key. The Status bar can be customized to indicate that the Selection mode is activated. To do this, right-click on the Status bar and then click *Selection Mode* at the pop-up list. When the F8 function key is pressed to turn on the Selection mode, the words *Extend Selection* display on the Status bar. Text can also be selected with the commands shown in Table 1.5.

Table 1.4 Selecting Text with the Mouse

To select	Complete these steps using the mouse
a word	Double-click the word.
a line of text	Click in the selection bar to the left of the line.
multiple lines of text	Drag in the selection bar to the left of the lines.
a sentence	Press and hold down the Ctrl key and then click in the sentence.
a paragraph	Double-click in the selection bar next to the paragraph, or triple-click in the paragraph.
multiple paragraphs	Drag in the selection bar.
an entire document	Triple-click in the selection bar.

Table 1.5 Selecting Text with the Keyboard

To select	Press
one character to right	Shift + Right Arrow
one character to left	Shift + Left Arrow
to end of word	Ctrl + Shift + Right Arrow
to beginning of word	Ctrl + Shift + Left Arrow
to end of line	Shift + End
to beginning of line	Shift + Home
one line up	Shift + Up Arrow
one line down	Shift + Down Arrow
to beginning of paragraph	Ctrl + Shift + Up Arrow
to end of paragraph	Ctrl + Shift + Down Arrow
one screen up	Shift + Page Up
one screen down	Shift + Page Down
to end of document	Ctrl + Shift + End
to beginning of document	Ctrl + Shift + Home
entire document	Ctrl + A or click Select button in Editing group and then click *Select All*

Project 4a Editing a Document   Part 1 of 2

1. Open **CompKeyboards.docx**. (This document is in the WL1C1 folder you copied to your storage medium.)
2. Save the document with the new name **1-CompKeyboards**.
3. Change the word *give* in the first sentence of the first paragraph to *enter* by double-clicking *give* and then typing enter.
4. Change the second *to* in the first sentence to *into* by double-clicking *to* and then typing into.
5. Delete the words *means of* (including the space after *of*) in the first sentence in the *QWERTY Keyboard* section.
6. Select the words *and use no cabling at all* and the period that follows at the end of the last sentence in the first paragraph and then press the Delete key.
7. Insert a period immediately following the word *signal*.

8. Delete the heading *QWERTY Keyboard* using the Selection mode by completing the following steps:
   a. Position the insertion point immediately left of the *Q* in *QWERTY*.
   b. Press F8 to turn on the Selection mode.
   c. Press the Down Arrow key.
   d. Press the Delete key.
9. Complete steps similar to those in Step 8 to delete the heading *DVORAK Keyboard*.
10. Begin a new paragraph with the sentence that reads *Keyboards have different physical appearances* by completing the following steps:
    a. Position the insertion point immediately left of the *K* in *Keyboards* (the first word of the fifth sentence in the last paragraph).
    b. Press the Enter key.
11. Save **1-CompKeyboards.docx**.

8a-8c

To enter commands into a co
device can be built into the c
computer by a cable. Some ir
means of an infrared signal.

QWERTY Keyboard

Keyboards can be external de
itself as they are in laptops. M
the first six keys at the left of
of mechanical typewriters to

10a-10b

To enter commands into a computer or
device can be built into the computer,
computer by a cable. Some input devic
means of an infrared signal.

Keyboards can be external devices that
itself as they are in laptops. Most keybo
the first six keys at the left of the first r
of mechanical typewriters to slow dow

The DVORAK keyboard is an alternative
commonly used keys are placed close t
install software on a QWERTY keyboard
keyboards is convenient especially whe

Keyboards have different physical appe
that of a calculator, containing number
"broken" into two pieces to reduce stra
change the symbol or character entere

Check Your Work

Using the Undo and Redo Buttons

Tutorial

Using Undo and Redo

 Undo

 Redo

💡 *Hint* You cannot undo a save.

Undo typing, formatting, or another action by clicking the Undo button on the Quick Access Toolbar. For example, type text and then click the Undo button and the text is removed. Or, apply formatting to text and then click the Undo button and the formatting is removed.

Click the Redo button on the Quick Access Toolbar to reverse the original action. For example, apply formatting such as underlining to text and then click the Undo button and the underlining is removed. Click the Redo button and the underlining formatting is reapplied to the text. Many Word actions can be undone or redone. Some actions, however, such as printing and saving, cannot be undone or redone.

Word maintains actions in temporary memory. To undo an action performed earlier, click the Undo button arrow. This causes a drop-down list to display. To make a selection from this drop-down list, click the desired action; the action, along with any actions listed above it in the drop-down list, is undone.

1. With **1-CompKeyboards.docx** open, delete the last sentence in the last paragraph using the mouse by completing the following steps:
   a. Hover the I-beam pointer anywhere over the sentence that begins *All keyboards have modifier keys*.
   b. Press and hold down the Ctrl key, and then click the left mouse button, and then release the Ctrl key.

> install software on a QWERTY keyboard that emulates a DVORAK keyboard. The ability to emulate other keyboards is convenient especially when working with foreign languages.
>
> Keyboards have different physical appearances. Many keyboards have a separate numeric keypad, like that of a calculator, containing numbers and mathematical operators. Some keyboards are sloped and "broken" into two pieces to reduce strain. All keyboards have modifier keys that enable the user to change the symbol or character entered when a given key is pressed.

1a-1b

   c. Press the Delete key.
2. Delete the last paragraph by completing the following steps:
   a. Position the I-beam pointer anywhere in the last paragraph (the paragraph that begins *Keyboards have different physical appearances*).
   b. Triple-click the left mouse button.
   c. Press the Delete key.
3. Undo the deletion by clicking the Undo button on the Quick Access Toolbar.
4. Redo the deletion by clicking the Redo button on the Quick Access Toolbar.
5. Select the first sentence in the second paragraph and then delete it.
6. Select the first paragraph in the document and then delete it.
7. Undo the two deletions by completing the following steps:
   a. Click the Undo button arrow.
   b. Click the second *Clear* listed in the drop-down list. (This will redisplay the first paragraph and the first sentence in the second paragraph. The sentence will be selected.)
8. Click outside the sentence to deselect it.
9. Save, print, and then close **1-CompKeyboards.docx**.

3

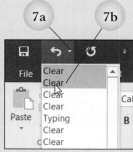

7a   7b

Check Your Work

Project 5 **Complete a Spelling and Grammar Check**   **1 Part**

You will open a previously created document, save it with a new name, and then check the spelling and grammar in the document.

Preview Finished Project

Checking the Spelling and Grammar in a Document

Quick Steps

Check Spelling and Grammar
1. Click Review tab.
2. Click Spelling & Grammar button.
3. Change or ignore errors.
4. Click OK.

Spelling & Grammar

Two tools for creating thoughtful and well-written documents are the spelling checker and the grammar checker. The spelling checker finds misspelled words and offers replacement words. It also finds duplicate words and irregular capitalizations. When spell checking a document, the spelling checker compares the words in the document with the words in its dictionary. If the spelling checker finds a match, it passes over the word. If the spelling checker does not find a match, it stops, selects the word, and offers possible corrections.

The grammar checker searches a document for errors in grammar, punctuation, and word usage. If the grammar checker finds an error, it stops and offers possible corrections. The spelling checker and the grammar checker can help create a well-written document but do not eliminate the need for proofreading.

To complete a spelling and grammar check, click the Review tab and then click the Spelling & Grammar button in the Proofing group or press the F7 function key. If Word detects a possible spelling error, the text containing the error is selected and the Spelling task pane displays. The Spelling task pane contains a list box with one or more possible corrections along with buttons to either change or ignore the spelling error, as described in Table 1.6. A definition of the selected word in the list box may display at the bottom of the Spelling task pane if a dictionary is installed.

Hint Complete a spelling and grammar check on a portion of a document by selecting the text first and then clicking the Spelling & Grammar button.

If Word detects a grammar error, the word(s) or sentence is selected and possible corrections display in the Grammar task pane list box. Depending on the error selected, some or all of the buttons described in Table 1.6 may display in the Grammar task pane and a description of the grammar rule with suggestions may display at the bottom of the task pane. Use the buttons that display to ignore or change the grammar error.

When checking the spelling and grammar in a document, temporarily leave the Spelling task pane or Grammar task pane by clicking in the document. To resume the spelling and grammar check, click the Resume button in the Spelling task pane or Grammar task pane.

Table 1.6 Spelling Task Pane and Grammar Task Pane Buttons

Button	Function
Ignore	during spell checking, skips that occurrence of the word; during grammar checking, leaves currently selected text as written
Ignore All	during spell checking, skips that occurrence of the word and all other occurrences of the word in the document
Add	adds the selected word to the spelling checker dictionary
Delete	deletes the currently selected word(s)
Change	replaces the selected word with the selected word in the task pane list box
Change All	replaces the selected word and all other occurrences of it with the selected word in the task pane list box

1. Open **TechOccTrends.docx**.
2. Save the document with the name **1-TechOccTrends**.
3. Click the Review tab.
4. Click the Spelling & Grammar button in the Proofing group.
5. The spelling checker selects the word *tecnology* and displays the Spelling task pane. The proper spelling is selected in the Spelling task pane list box, so click the Change button (or Change All button).
6. The grammar checker selects the word *too* in the document and displays the Grammar task pane. The correct form of the word is selected in the list box. If definitions of *to* and *too* display at the bottom of the task pane, read the information. Click the Change button.
7. The grammar checker selects the sentence containing the words *downloaded* and *versus*, in which two spaces appear between the words. The Grammar task pane displays in the list box the two words with only one space between them. Read the information about spaces between words that displays at the bottom of the Grammar task pane and then click the Change button.
8. The spelling checker selects the word *sucessful* and offers *successful* in the Spelling task pane list box. Since this word is misspelled in another location in the document, click the Change All button.
9. The spelling checker selects the word *are*, which is used two times in a row. Click the Delete button in the Spelling task pane to delete the second *are*.
10. When the message displays stating that the spelling and grammar check is complete, click OK.
11. Save, print, and then close **1-TechOccTrends.docx**.

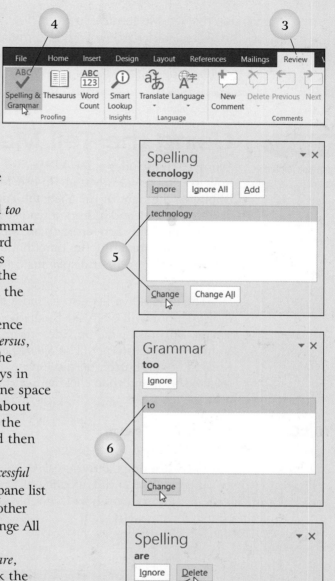

Check Your Work

Project 6 Use the Tell Me and Help Features

2 Parts

You will use the Tell Me feature to learn how to double-space text in a document, display the Word Help window with information on autocorrect, and display the Smart Lookup task pane with information on scrolling. You will also use the Help feature to learn more about printing documents.

Preview Finished Project

Tutorial

Using the Tell Me Feature

Using the Tell Me Feature

Word 2016 includes a Tell Me feature that provides information and guidance on how to complete a function. To use Tell Me, click in the *Tell Me* text box on the ribbon to the right of the View tab and then type the function. Type text in the *Tell Me* text box and a drop-down list displays with options that are refined as the text is typed; this is referred to as "word-wheeling." The drop-down list displays options for completing the function, displaying information on the function from sources on the Web, or displaying information on the function in the Word Help window.

The drop-down list also includes a *Smart Lookup* option. Clicking the *Smart Lookup* option will open the Smart Lookup task pane at the right side of the screen. This task pane provides information on the function from a variety of sources on the Internet. The *Smart Lookup* option can also be accessed with the Smart Lookup button on the Review tab or by selecting text, right-clicking the selected text, and then clicking *Smart Lookup* at the shortcut menu.

Project 6a Using the Tell Me Feature

Part 1 of 2

1. Open **GraphicSoftware.docx** and then save it with the name **1-GraphicSoftware**.
2. Press Ctrl + A to select the entire document.
3. Use the Tell Me feature to learn how to double-space the text in the document by completing the following steps:
   a. Click in the *Tell Me* text box.
   b. Type double space.
   c. Click the *Line and Paragraph Spacing* option.
   d. At the side menu, click the *2.0* option. (This double-spaces the selected text in the document.)
   e. Click in the document to deselect the text.

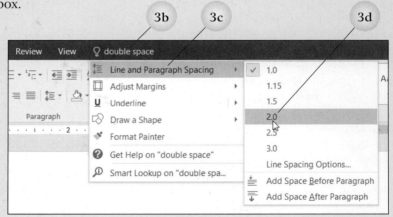

4. Use the Tell Me feature to display the Word Help window with information on AutoCorrect by completing the following steps:
  a. Click in the *Tell Me* text box.
  b. Type autocorrect.
  c. Click the *Get Help on "autocorrect"* option.
  d. At the Word Help window, click a hyperlink to an article that interests you.
  e. After reading the information about autocorrect, close the window by clicking the Close button in the upper right corner of the window.

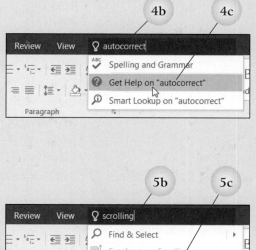

5. Display information on scrolling in the Smart Lookup task pane by completing the following steps:
  a. Click in the *Tell Me* text box.
  b. Type scrolling.
  c. Click the *Smart Lookup on "scrolling"* option. (The first time you use the Smart Lookup feature, the Smart Lookup task pane will display with a message stating that data will be sent to Bing and suggesting that you read the privacy statement for more details. At this message, click the Got it button.)

  d. Look at the information that displays in the Smart Lookup task pane on scrolling.
  e. If two options—*Explore* and *Define*—display at the top of the Smart Lookup task pane, click the *Define* option. This will display a definition of the term *scrolling* in the Smart Lookup task pane.
  f. Close the Smart Lookup task pane by clicking the Close button in the upper right corner of the task pane.
6. Save, print, then close **1-GraphicSoftware.docx**.

Check Your Work

Tutorial

Using the Help Feature

Using the Help Feature

Word's Help feature is an on-screen reference manual containing information about Word features and commands. Word's Help feature is similar to the Help features in Excel, PowerPoint, and Access. Get help by using the Tell Me feature or by pressing the F1 function key to display the Word Help window, shown in Figure 1.9.

Quick Steps

Use the Help Feature
1. Press F1.
2. Type search text in search text box.
3. Press Enter.
4. Click topic.

In this window, type a topic, feature, or question in the search text box and then press the Enter key. Articles related to the search text display in the Word Help window. Click an article to display it in the Word Help window. If the article window contains a <u>Show All</u> hyperlink in the upper right corner, click this hyperlink and the information expands to show all Help information related to the topic. Click the <u>Show All</u> hyperlink and it becomes the <u>Hide All</u> hyperlink.

The Word Help window contains five buttons, which display to the left of the search text box. Use the Back and Forward buttons to navigate within the window. Click the Home button to return to the Word Help window opening screen. To print information on a topic or feature, click the Print button and then click the Print button at the Print dialog box. Click the Use Large Text button in the Word Help window to increase the size of the text in the window.

Figure 1.9 Word Help Window

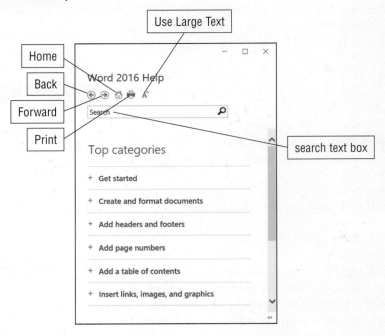

Getting Help from a ScreenTip

Hover the mouse pointer over a certain button such as the Format Painter button or Font Color button and the ScreenTip displays a Help icon and the <u>Tell me more</u> hyperlinked text. Click <u>Tell me more</u> or press the F1 function key and the Word Help window opens with information about the button feature.

Getting Help at the Backstage Area

The backstage area contains a Microsoft Word Help button in the upper right corner of the screen. Display a specific backstage area, click the Microsoft Word Help button, and information on the backstage area displays in the Word Help window.

Getting Help in a Dialog Box

Some dialog boxes contain a Help button. Open a dialog box and then click the Help button and information about the dialog box displays in the Word Help window. After reading and/or printing the information, close the Word Help window and then close the dialog box by clicking the Close button in the upper right corner.

1. Open a new blank document by completing the following steps:
   a. Click the File tab and then click the *New* option.
   b. At the New backstage area, double-click the *Single spaced (blank)* template.

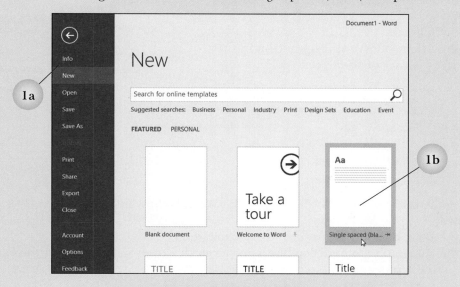

2. Press F1 to display the Microsoft Word Help window.
3. At the Word Help window, click in the search text box, type print preview, and then press the Enter key.
4. When the list of articles displays, click the <u>Print a document in Word</u> hyperlinked article. (You may need to scroll down the Word Help window to display this article.)
5. Scroll down the Word Help window and read the information about printing and previewing documents.
6. Click the Print button in the Word Help window. This displays the Print dialog box. If you want to print information about the topic, click the Print button; otherwise, click the Cancel button to close the dialog box.
7. At the Word Help window, click the Use Large Text button to increase the size of the text in the window.
8. Click the Use Large Text button again to return the text to the normal size.
9. Click the Back button to return to the previous window.
10. Click the Home button to return to the original Word Help window screen.
11. Click the Close button to close the Word Help window.
12. Hover your mouse over the Format Painter button in the Clipboard group on the Home tab.

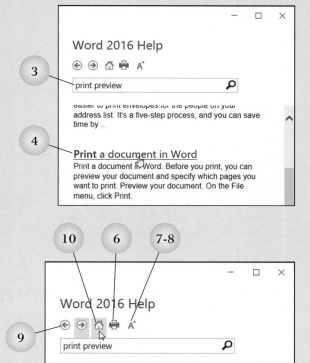

13. Click the <u>Tell me more</u> hyperlinked text at the bottom of the ScreenTip.
14. Read the information in the Word Help window about the Format Painter feature.
15. Click the Close button to close the Word Help window.
16. Click the File tab.
17. Click the Microsoft Word Help button in the upper right corner of the screen.

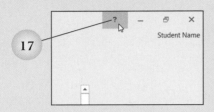

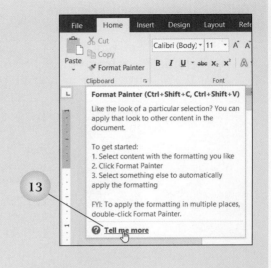

18. Look at the information that displays in the Word Help window and then close the window.
19. Click the Back button to return to the document.
20. Click the Paragraph group dialog box launcher in the lower right corner of the Pararaph group on the Home tab.

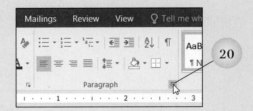

21. Click the Help button in the upper right corner of the Paragraph dialog box.

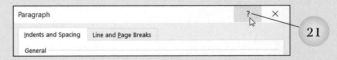

22. Read the information that displays in the Word Help window.
23. Close the Word Help window and then close the Paragraph dialog box.
24. Close the blank document.

Chapter Summary

- Refer to Figure 1.1 and Table 1.1 for an example and a list, respectively, of key Word screen features.
- Click the File tab and the backstage area displays, containing options for working with and managing documents.
- Document names can contain a maximum of 255 characters, including the drive letter and folder names, and may include spaces.
- The Quick Access Toolbar contains buttons for commonly used commands.

- The ribbon contains tabs with options and buttons divided into groups.
- The insertion point displays as a blinking vertical line and indicates the position of the next character to be entered in the document.
- The insertion point can be moved throughout the document without interfering with text by using the mouse, the keyboard, or the mouse combined with the keyboard.
- The scroll box on the vertical scroll bar indicates the location of the text in the document in relation to the remainder of the document.
- The insertion point can be moved by character, word, screen, or page and from the first to the last character in a document. Refer to Table 1.2 for keyboard insertion point movement commands.
- Delete text by character, word, line, several lines, or partial page using specific keys or by selecting text using the mouse or the keyboard. Refer to Table 1.3 for deletion commands.
- A specific amount of text can be selected using the mouse or the keyboard. Refer to Table 1.4 for information on selecting with the mouse, and refer to Table 1.5 for information on selecting with the keyboard.
- Use the Undo button on the Quick Access Toolbar to undo an action such as typing, deleting, or formatting text. Use the Redo button to redo something that has been undone with the Undo button.
- The spelling checker matches the words in a document with the words in its dictionary. If a match is not found, the word is selected and possible corrections are suggested in the Spelling task pane. The grammar checker searches a document for errors in grammar, punctuation, and word usage. When a grammar error is detected, possible corrections display in the Grammar task pane along with information about the grammar rule or error. Refer to Table 1.6 for Spelling task pane and Grammar task pane buttons.
- The Tell Me feature provides information and guidance on how to complete a function. The *Tell Me* text box is on the ribbon to the right of the View tab.
- Word's Help feature is an on-screen reference manual containing information about Word features and commands. Press the F1 function key to display the Word Help window.
- The Word Help window (Figure 1.9) contains five buttons, which are to the left of the search text box: the Back, Forward, Home, Print, and Use Large Text buttons.
- Hover the mouse pointer over a certain button and the ScreenTip displays a Help icon and the <u>Tell me more</u> hyperlinked text. Click this hyperlinked text to display the Word Help window, which contains information about the button feature.
- Some dialog boxes and the backstage area contain a help button that when clicked displays information about the dialog box or backstage area.

Commands Review

FEATURE	RIBBON TAB, GROUP	BUTTON, OPTION	KEYBOARD SHORTCUT
AutoComplete entry			F3
close document	File, *Close*		Ctrl + F4
close Word		✕	Alt + F4
Find and Replace dialog box with Go To tab selected	Home, Editing	🔍, *Go To*	Ctrl + G
Leave backstage area		←	Esc
Move insertion point to previous location when document was closed			Shift + F5
new blank document	File, *New*	*Blank document*	Ctrl + N
New Line command			Shift + Enter
Open backstage area	File, *Open*		Ctrl + O
Open dialog box	File, *Open*		Ctrl + F12
Print backstage area	File, *Print*		Ctrl + P
redo an action		↷	Ctrl + Y
save	File, *Save*	💾	Ctrl + S
Save As backstage area	File, *Save As*		
Save As dialog box	File, *Save As*		F12
Selection mode			F8
spelling and grammar checker	Review, Proofing	ABC✓	F7
Tell Me feature		Tell me what you want to do	Alt + Q
undo an action		↶ ▾	Ctrl + Z
Word Help			F1

Microsoft® Word

Formatting Characters and Paragraphs

Performance Objectives

Upon successful completion of Chapter 2, you will be able to:

1 Change the font, font size, and choose font effects

2 Format selected text with buttons on the Mini toolbar

3 Apply styles from style sets

4 Apply themes

5 Customize style sets and themes.

6 Change the alignment of text in paragraphs

7 Indent text in paragraphs

8 Increase and decrease spacing before and after paragraphs

9 Repeat the last action

10 Automate formatting with Format Painter

11 Change line spacing

12 Reveal and compare formatting

Precheck

Check your current skills to help focus your study.

The appearance of a document in the document screen and when printed is called the *format*. A Word document is based on a template that applies default formatting. Some of the default formats include 11-point Calibri font, line spacing of 1.08, 8 points of spacing after each paragraph, and left-aligned text. In this chapter, you will learn about changing the typeface, type size, and typestyle as well as applying font effects such as bold and italic. The Paragraph group on the Home tab includes buttons for applying formatting to paragraphs of text. In Word, a paragraph is any amount of text followed by a press of the Enter key. In this chapter, you will learn to format paragraphs by changing text alignment, indenting text, applying formatting with Format Painter, and changing line spacing.

Data Files

Before beginning chapter work, copy the WL1C2 folder to your storage medium and then make WL1C2 the active folder.

SNAP

If you are a SNAP user, launch the Precheck and Tutorials from your Assignments page.

Project 1 Apply Character Formatting   4 Parts

You will open a document containing a glossary of terms, add additional text, and then format the document by applying character formatting.

Preview Finished Project

Tutorial

Applying Font
Formatting Using
the Font Group

Applying Font Formatting

The Font group, shown in Figure 2.1, contains a number of options and buttons for applying character formatting to text in a document. The top row contains options for changing the font and font size as well as buttons for increasing and decreasing the size of the font, changing the text case, and clearing formatting. Remove character formatting (as well as paragraph formatting) applied to text by clicking the Clear All Formatting button in the Font group. Remove only character formatting from selected text by pressing the keyboard shortcut Ctrl + spacebar. The bottom row contains buttons for applying typestyles such as bold, italic, and underline and for applying text effects, highlighting, and color.

A Word document is based on a template that formats text in 11-point Calibri. This default may need to be changed to another font for such reasons as altering the mood of the document, enhancing its visual appeal, and increasing its readability. A font consists of three elements: typeface, type size, and typestyle.

A typeface is a set of characters with a common design and shape and can be decorative or plain and either monospaced or proportional. Word refers to a typeface as a *font*. A monospaced typeface allots the same amount of horizontal space for each character, while a proportional typeface allots varying amounts of space for different characters. Typefaces are divided into two main categories: serif and sans serif. A serif is a small line at the end of a character stroke. Consider using a serif typeface for text-intensive documents because the serifs help move the reader's eyes across the page. Use a sans serif typeface for headings, headlines, and advertisements. Some popular typefaces are shown in Table 2.1.

💡 *Hint* Change the default font by selecting the font at the Font dialog box and then clicking the Set As Default button.

💡 *Hint* Use a serif typeface for text-intensive documents.

Figure 2.1 Font Group Option Boxes and Buttons

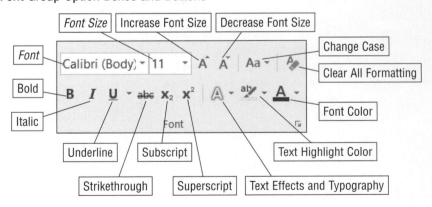

Table 2.1 Categories of Typefaces

Serif Typefaces	Sans Serif Typefaces	Monospaced Typefaces
Cambria	Calibri	Consolas
Constantia	Candara	Courier New
Times New Roman	Corbel	Lucida Console
Bookman Old Style	Arial	MS Gothic

Type is generally set in proportional size. The size of proportional type is measured vertically in units called *points*. A point is approximately $\frac{1}{72}$ of an inch—the higher the point size, the larger the characters. Within a typeface, characters may have varying styles. Type styles are divided into four main categories: regular, bold, italic, and bold italic.

💡 ***Hint*** Press Ctrl +] to increase font size by 1 point and press Ctrl + [to decrease font size by 1 point.

Use the *Font* option box arrow in the Font group to change the font. Select the text and then click the *Font* option box arrow and a drop-down gallery of font options displays. Hover the mouse pointer over a font option and the selected text in the document displays with the font applied. Continue hovering the mouse pointer over different font options to see how the selected text displays in each font.

The *Font* option drop-down gallery is an example of the live preview feature, which displays how the font formatting affects text without having to return to the document. The live preview feature is also available with the drop-down gallery of font sizes that displays when the *Font Size* option box arrow is clicked.

Project 1a   Changing the Font and Font Size   Part 1 of 4

1. Open **CompTerms.docx** and then save it with the name **2-CompTerms**.
2. Change the typeface to Cambria by completing the following steps:
   a. Select the entire document by pressing Ctrl + A. (You can also select all text in the document by clicking the Select button in the Editing group and then clicking *Select All* at the drop-down list.)
   b. Click the *Font* option box arrow, scroll down the drop-down gallery until *Cambria* displays, and then hover the mouse pointer over *Cambria*. This displays a live preview of the text set in Cambria.
   c. Click the *Cambria* option.

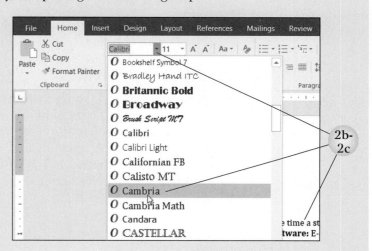

3. Change the type size to 14 points by completing the following steps:
   a. With the text in the document still selected, click the *Font Size* option box arrow.
   b. At the drop-down gallery, hover the mouse pointer over *14* and look at the live preview of the text with 14 points applied.
   c. Click the *14* option.

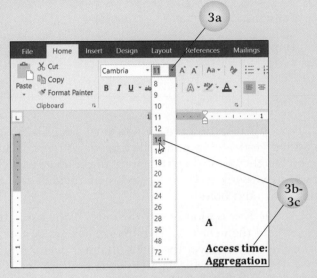

4. Change the type size and typeface by completing the following steps:
   a. Click the Decrease Font Size button in the Font group three times. (This decreases the size to 10 points.)
   b. Click the Increase Font Size button two times. (This increases the size to 12 points.)
   c. Click the *Font* option box arrow, scroll down the drop-down gallery, and then click *Constantia*. (The most recently used fonts display at the beginning of the gallery, followed by a listing of all fonts.)
5. Deselect the text by clicking anywhere in the document.
6. Save **2-CompTerms.docx**.

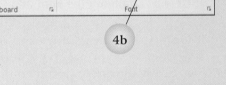

Check Your Work

Choosing a Typestyle

B Bold

I Italic

U ▾ Underline

Apply a particular typestyle to text with the Bold, Italic, or Underline buttons in the bottom row in the Font group. More than one typestyle can be applied to text. Click the Underline button arrow and a drop-down gallery displays with underlining options such as a double line, dashed line, and thicker underline. Click the *Underline Color* option at the Underline button drop-down gallery and a side menu displays with color options.

1. With **2-CompTerms.docx** open, press Ctrl + Home to move the insertion point to the beginning of the document.
2. Type a heading for the document by completing the following steps:
   a. Click the Bold button in the Font group. (This turns on bold formatting.)
   b. Click the Underline button in the Font group. (This turns on underline formatting.)
   c. Type Glossary of Terms.
3. Press Ctrl + End to move the insertion point to the end of the document.
4. Type the text shown in Figure 2.2 with the following specifications:
   a. While typing, make the appropriate text bold, as shown in the figure, by completing the following steps:
      1) Click the Bold button in the Font group. (This turns on bold formatting.)
      2) Type the text.
      3) Click the Bold button in the Font group. (This turns off bold formatting.)
   b. Press the Enter key two times after typing the *C* heading.
   c. While typing, italicize the appropriate text, as shown in the figure, by completing the following steps:
      1) Click the Italic button in the Font group.
      2) Type the text.
      3) Click the Italic button in the Font group.
5. After typing the text, press the Enter key two times and then press Ctrl + Home to move the insertion point to the beginning of the document.
6. Change the underlining below the title by completing the following steps:
   a. Select the title *Glossary of Terms*.
   b. Click the Underline button arrow and then click the third underline option from the top of the drop-down gallery (*Thick underline*).
   c. Click the Underline button arrow, point to the *Underline Color* option, and then click the *Red* color (second color option in the *Standard Colors* section).

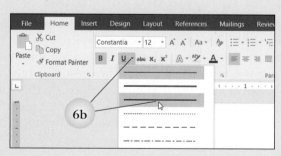
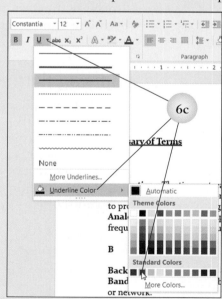

7. With the title still selected, change the font size to 14 points.
8. Save **2-CompTerms.docx**.

Check Your Work ▶

Figure 2.2 Project 1b

C

Chip: A thin wafer of *silicon* containing electronic circuitry that performs various functions, such as mathematical calculations, storage, or controlling computer devices.

Cluster: A group of two or more *sectors* on a disk, which is the smallest unit of storage space used to store data.

Coding: A term used by programmers to refer to the act of writing source code.

Crackers: A term coined by computer hackers for those who intentionally enter (or hack) computer systems to damage them.

 Tutorial

Highlighting Text

 Clear All Formatting

 Change Case

 Strikethrough

Subscript

Superscript

 Text Effects and Typography

 Text Highlight Color

Font Color

Choosing a Font Effect

Apply font effects with some of the buttons in the top and bottom rows in the Font group, or clear all formatting from selected text with the Clear All Formatting button. Change the case of text with the Change Case button drop-down list. Click the Change Case button in the top row in the Font group and a drop-down list displays with the options *Sentence case*, *lowercase*, *UPPERCASE*, *Capitalize Each Word*, and *tOGGLE cASE*. The case of selected text can also be changed with the keyboard shortcut Shift + F3. Each time Shift + F3 is pressed, the selected text displays in the next case option in the list.

The bottom row in the Font group contains buttons for applying font effects. Use the Strikethrough button to draw a line through selected text. This has a practical application in some legal documents in which deleted text must be retained in the document. Use the Subscript button to create text that is lowered slightly below the line, as in the chemical formula H_2O. Use the Superscript button to create text that is raised slightly above the text line, as in the mathematical equation four to the third power (written as 4^3). Click the Text Effects and Typography button in the bottom row and a drop-down gallery displays with effect options. Use the Text Highlight Color button to highlight specific text in a document and use the Font Color button to change the color of text.

Applying Formatting Using Keyboard Shortcuts

Several of the options and buttons in the Font group have keyboard shortcuts. For example, press Ctrl + B to turn bold formatting on or off and press Ctrl + I to turn italic formatting on or off. Position the mouse pointer on an option or button and an enhanced ScreenTip displays with the name of the option or button; the keyboard shortcut, if any; a description of the action performed by the option or button; and sometimes, access to the Word Help window. Table 2.2 identifies the keyboard shortcuts available for options and buttons in the Font group.

Table 2.2 Font Group Option and Button Keyboard Shortcuts

Font Group Option/Button	Keyboard Shortcut
Font	Ctrl + Shift + F
Font Size	Ctrl + Shift + P
Increase Font Size	Ctrl + Shift + > OR Ctrl +]
Decrease Font Size	Ctrl + Shift + < OR Ctrl + [
Bold	Ctrl + B
Italic	Ctrl + I
Underline	Ctrl + U
Subscript	Ctrl + =
Superscript	Ctrl + Shift + +
Change Case	Shift + F3

Tutorial

Applying Font
Formatting Using
the Mini Toolbar

Formatting with the Mini Toolbar

When text is selected, the Mini toolbar displays above the selected text, as shown in Figure 2.3. Click a button on the Mini toolbar to apply formatting to the selected text. When the mouse pointer is moved away from the Mini toolbar, the toolbar disappears.

Figure 2.3 Mini Toolbar

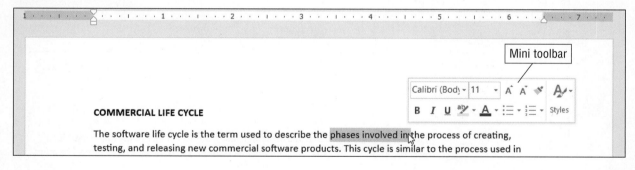

1. With **2-CompTerms.docx** open, move the insertion point to the beginning of the term *Chip*, press the Enter key, and then press the Up Arrow key.
2. Type the text shown in Figure 2.4. Create each superscript number by clicking the Superscript button, typing the number, and then clicking the Superscript button.
3. Remove underlining and change the case of the text in the title by completing the following steps:
   a. Select the title *Glossary of Terms*.
   b. Remove all formatting from the title by clicking the Clear All Formatting button in the Font group.
   c. Click the Change Case button in the Font group and then click *UPPERCASE* at the drop-down list.
   d. Click the Text Effects and Typography button in the Font group and then click the *Gradient Fill - Blue, Accent 1, Reflection* option (second column, second row) at the drop-down gallery.
   e. Change the font size to 14 points.
4. Strike through text by completing the following steps:
   a. Select the words and parentheses *(or hack)* in the *Crackers* definition.
   b. Click the Strikethrough button in the Font group.

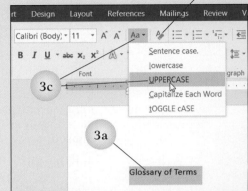

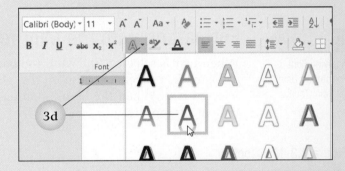

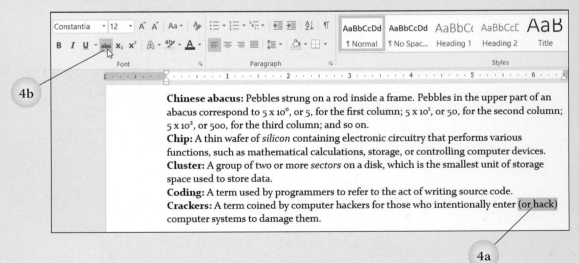

5. Change the font color by completing the following steps:
   a. Press Ctrl + A to select the entire document.
   b. Click the Font Color button arrow.
   c. Click the *Dark Red* color (first color option in the *Standard Colors* section) at the drop-down gallery.
   d. Click in the document to deselect text.
6. Highlight text in the document by completing the following steps:
   a. Click the Text Highlight Color button arrow in the Font group and then click the *Yellow* color (first column, first row) at the drop-down palette. (This causes the mouse pointer to display as an I-beam pointer with a highlighter pen attached.)
   b. Select the term *Beta-testing* and the definition that follows.
   c. Click the Text Highlight Color button arrow and then click the *Turquoise* color (third column, first row).
   d. Select the term *Cluster* and the definition that follows.
   e. Click the Text Highlight Color button arrow and then click the *Yellow* color at the drop-down gallery.
   f. Click the Text Highlight Color button to turn off highlighting.
7. Apply italic formatting using the Mini toolbar by completing the following steps:
   a. Select the text *one-stop shopping* in the definition for the term *Aggregation software*. (When you select the text, the Mini toolbar displays.)
   b. Click the Italic button on the Mini toolbar.
   c. Select the word *bits* in the definition for the term *Bandwidth* and then click the Italic button on the Mini toolbar.
8. Save **2-CompTerms.docx**.

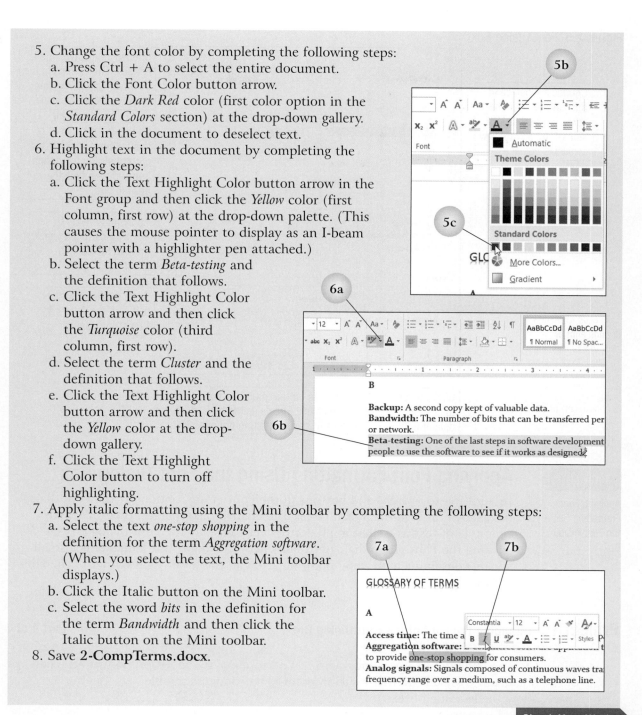

Check Your Work

Figure 2.4 Project 1c

Chinese abacus: Pebbles strung on a rod inside a frame. Pebbles in the upper part of an abacus correspond to 5×10^0, or 5, for the first column; 5×10^1, or 50, for the second column; 5×10^2, or 500, for the third column; and so on.

Figure 2.5 Font Dialog Box

Choose a typeface in this list box. Use the scroll bar at the right side of the box to view available typefaces.

Choose a typestyle in this list box. The options in the box may vary depending on the selected typeface.

Choose a type size in this list box, or select the current size in the option box and then type the desired size.

Apply font effects to text by inserting a check mark in the desired effect check box.

See a preview of the text with the selected formatting applied.

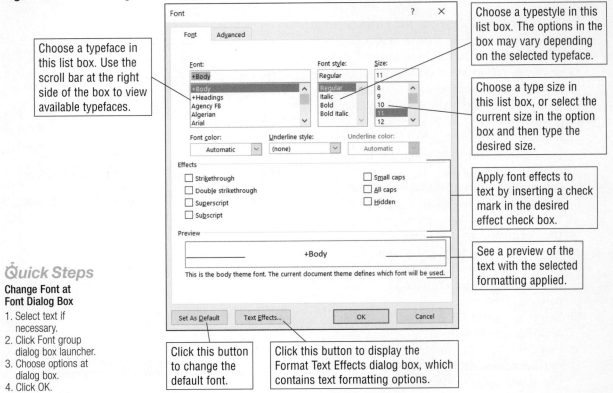

Quick Steps

Change Font at Font Dialog Box
1. Select text if necessary.
2. Click Font group dialog box launcher.
3. Choose options at dialog box.
4. Click OK.

Click this button to change the default font.

Click this button to display the Format Text Effects dialog box, which contains text formatting options.

Tutorial

Applying Font Formatting Using the Font Dialog Box

Applying Font Formatting Using the Font Dialog Box

In addition to options and buttons in the Font group, options at the Font dialog box, shown in Figure 2.5, can be used to change the typeface, type size, and typestyle of text as well as apply font effects. Display the Font dialog box by clicking the Font group dialog box launcher. The dialog box launcher is a small square containing a diagonal-pointing arrow in the lower right corner of the Font group.

Project 1d Changing the Font at the Font Dialog Box

Part 4 of 4

1. With **2-CompTerms.docx** open, press Ctrl + End to move the insertion point to the end of the document. (Make sure the insertion point is positioned a double space below the last line of text.)
2. Type Created by Susan Ashby and then press the Enter key.
3. Type Wednesday, February 21, 2018.
4. Change the font to 13-point Candara and the color to standard dark blue for the entire document by completing the following steps:
   a. Press Ctrl + A to select the entire document.
   b. Click the Font group dialog box launcher.

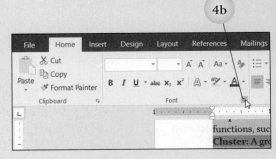

c. At the Font dialog box, type can in the *Font* option box (this displays fonts that begin with *can*) and then click *Candara* in the *Font* list box.

d. Click in the *Size* option box and then type 13.

e. Click the *Font color* option box arrow and then click the *Dark Blue* color option (ninth option in the *Standard Colors* section).

f. Click OK to close the dialog box.

5. Double-underline text by completing the following steps:

a. Select *Wednesday, February 21, 2018*.

b. Click the Font group dialog box launcher.

c. At the Font dialog box, click the *Underline style* option box arrow and then click the double-line option at the drop-down list.

d. Click OK to close the dialog box.

6. Change text to small caps by completing the following steps:

a. Select the text *Created by Susan Ashby* and *Wednesday, February 21, 2018*.

b. Display the Font dialog box.

c. Click the *Small caps* check box in the *Effects* section. (This inserts a check mark in the check box.)

d. Click OK to close the dialog box.

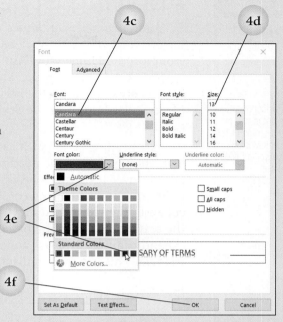

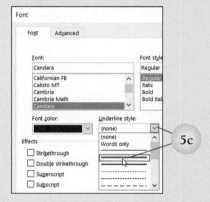

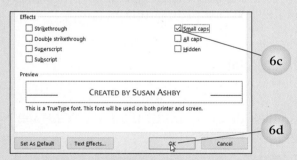

7. Save, print, and then close **2-CompTerms.docx**.

Check Your Work

Project 2 **Apply Styles and Themes** 3 Parts

You will open a document containing information on the life cycle of software, apply styles to text, and then change the style set. You will also apply a theme and then change the theme colors and fonts.

Preview Finished Project

Applying Styles from a Style Set

A Word document contains a number of predesigned formats grouped into style sets. Several styles in the default style set display in the styles gallery in the Styles group on the Home tab. Display additional styles by clicking the More Styles button in the Styles group. This displays a drop-down gallery of style options. To apply a style, position the insertion point in the text or paragraph of text, click the More Styles button in the Styles group, and then click the style at the drop-down gallery.

Quick Steps

Apply a Style
1. Position insertion point in text or paragraph of text.
2. Click More Styles button in Styles group.
3. Click style.

If a heading style (such as Heading 1, Heading 2, and so on) is applied to text, the text below the heading can be collapsed and expanded. Hover the mouse pointer over text with a heading style applied and a collapse triangle (solid, right- and down-pointing triangle) displays to the left of the heading. Click this collapse triangle and any text below the heading is collapsed (hidden). Redisplay the text below a heading by hovering the mouse over the heading text until an expand triangle displays (hollow, right-pointing triangle) and then click the expand triangle. This expands (redisplays) the text below the heading.

Removing Default Formatting

A Word document contains some default formatting, including 8 points of spacing after paragraphs and line spacing of 1.08. (You will learn more about these formatting options later in this chapter.) This default formatting, as well as any character formatting applied to text in the document, can be removed by applying the No Spacing style to the text. This style is in the styles gallery in the Styles group.

Changing the Style Set

Quick Steps

Change Style Set
1. Click Design tab.
2. Click style set.

Word provides a number of style sets containing styles that apply formatting to text in a document. To change the style set, click the Design tab and then click the style set in the style sets gallery in the Document Formatting group.

Project 2a **Applying Styles and Changing the Style Set**   **Part 1 of 3**

1. Open **SoftwareCycle.docx** and then save it with the name **2-SoftwareCycle**.
2. Position the insertion point anywhere in the title *COMMERCIAL LIFE CYCLE* and then click the *Heading 1* style in the Styles group.

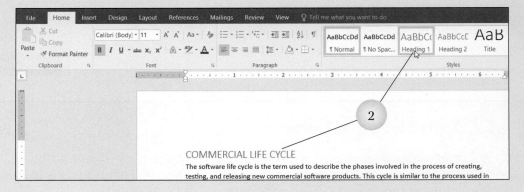

3. Position the insertion point anywhere in the heading *Proposal and Planning* and then click the *Heading 2* style in the styles gallery in the Styles group.

4. Position the insertion point anywhere in the heading *Design* and then click the *Heading 2* style in the styles gallery.

5. Apply the Heading 2 style to the remaining headings (*Implementation*, *Testing*, and *Public Release and Support*).

6. Collapse and expand text below the heading with the Heading 1 style applied by completing the following steps:

   a. Hover the mouse pointer over the heading *COMMERCIAL LIFE CYCLE* until a collapse triangle displays at the left side of the heading and then click the triangle. (This collapses all the text below the heading.)

   b. Click the expand triangle at the left side of the heading *COMMERCIAL LIFE CYCLE*. (This redisplays the text in the document.)

7. Click the Design tab.

8. Click the *Casual* style set in the style sets gallery in the Document Formatting group (the ninth option in the style set). (Notice how the Heading 1 and Heading 2 formatting changes.)

9. Save and then print **2-SoftwareCycle.docx**.

Check Your Work

Tutorial

Applying and Modifying a Theme

 Themes

Quick Steps

Apply a Theme
1. Click Design tab.
2. Click Themes button.
3. Click theme.

Applying a Theme

Word provides a number of themes for formatting text in a document. A theme is a set of formatting choices that includes a color theme (a set of colors), a font theme (a set of heading and body text fonts), and an effects theme (a set of lines and fill effects). To apply a theme, click the Design tab and then click the Themes button in the Document Formatting group. At the drop-down gallery, click the theme. Hover the mouse pointer over a theme and the live preview feature will display the document with the theme formatting applied. Applying a theme is an easy way to give a document a professional look.

1. With **2-SoftwareCycle.docx** open, click the Design tab and then click the Themes button in the Document Formatting group.
2. At the drop-down gallery, hover your mouse pointer over several different themes and notice how the text formatting changes in your document.
3. Click the *Organic* theme.
4. Save and then print **2-SoftwareCycle.docx**.

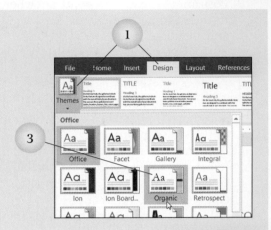

Check Your Work

Modifying a Theme

Modify the color applied by a style or theme with the Colors button in the Document Formatting group. Click the Colors button and a drop-down gallery displays with named color schemes. Modify the fonts applied to text in a document with the Fonts button in the Document Formatting group. Click this button and a drop-down gallery displays with font choices. Each font group in the drop-down gallery contains two choices. The first choice in the group is the font that is applied to headings, and the second choice is the font that is applied to body text in the document. If a document contains graphics with lines and fills, a specific theme effect can be applied with options at the Effects button drop-down gallery.

The buttons in the Document Formatting group display a visual representation of the current theme. If the theme colors are changed, the small color squares in the Themes button and the Colors button reflect the change. Change the theme fonts and the *As* on the Themes button and the uppercase *A* on the Fonts button reflect the change. If the theme effects are changed, the circle in the Effects button reflects the change.

The Paragraph Spacing button in the Document Formatting group on the Design tab contains predesigned paragraph spacing options. To change paragraph spacing, click the Paragraph Spacing button and then click the option at the drop-down gallery. Hover the mouse pointer over an option at the drop-down gallery and after a moment a ScreenTip displays with information about the formatting applied by the option. For example, hover the mouse pointer over the *Compact* option at the side menu and a ScreenTip displays indicating that selecting the *Compact* option will change the spacing before paragraphs to 0 points, the spacing after paragraphs to 4 points, and the line spacing to single line spacing.

1. With **2-SoftwareCycle.docx** open, click the Colors button in the Document Formatting group on the Design tab and then click *Red Orange* at the drop-down gallery. (Notice how the colors in the title and headings change.)
2. Click the Fonts button and then click the *Corbel* option. (Notice how the document text font changes.)
3. Click the Paragraph Spacing button and then, one at a time, hover the mouse pointer over each paragraph spacing option, beginning with *Compact*. For each option, read the ScreenTip that explains the paragraph spacing applied by the option.
4. Click the *Double* option.
5. Scroll through the document and notice the paragraph spacing.
6. Change the paragraph spacing by clicking the Paragraph Spacing button and then clicking *Compact*.
7. Save, print, and then close **2-SoftwareCycle.docx**.

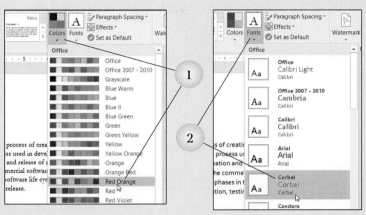

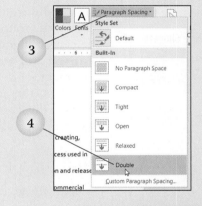

Check Your Work

Project 3 **Apply Paragraph Formatting and Use Format Painter**   **6 Parts**

You will open a report on intellectual property and fair use issues and then format the report by changing the alignment of text in paragraphs, applying spacing before and after paragraphs of text, and repeating the last formatting command.

Preview Finished Project

Tutorial

Changing Paragraph Alignment

Changing Paragraph Alignment

By default, paragraphs in a Word document are aligned at the left margin and are ragged at the right margin. Change this default alignment with buttons in the Paragraph group on the Home tab or with keyboard shortcuts, as shown in Table 2.3. The alignment of text in paragraphs can be changed before text is typed or the alignment of existing text can be changed.

Table 2.3 Paragraph Alignment Buttons and Keyboard Shortcuts

To align text	Paragraph Group Button	Keyboard Shortcut
At the left margin		Ctrl + L
Between margins		Ctrl + E
At the right margin		Ctrl + R
At the left and right margins		Ctrl + J

Changing Paragraph Alignment as Text Is Typed

☰ Center

¶ Show/Hide ¶

☰ Align Right

☰ Align Left

If the alignment is changed before text is typed, the alignment formatting is inserted in the paragraph mark. Type text and press the Enter key and the paragraph formatting is continued. For example, click the Center button in the Paragraph group, type text for the first paragraph, and then press the Enter key; the center alignment formatting is still active and the insertion point displays centered between the left and right margins. To display the paragraph symbols in a document, click the Show/Hide ¶ button in the Paragraph group. With the Show/Hide ¶ button active (displays with a gray background), nonprinting formatting symbols display, such as the paragraph symbol ¶ indicating a press of the Enter key or a dot indicating a press of the spacebar.

Changing Paragraph Alignment of Existing Text

💡 **Hint** Align text to help the reader follow the message of a document and to make the layout look appealing.

To change the alignment of existing text in a paragraph, position the insertion point anywhere within the paragraph. The entire paragraph does not need to be selected. To change the alignment of several adjacent paragraphs in a document, select a portion of the first paragraph through a portion of the last paragraph. All the text in the paragraphs does not need to be selected.

To return paragraph alignment to the default (left-aligned), click the Align Left button in the Paragraph group. All paragraph formatting can also be returned to the default with the keyboard shortcut Ctrl + Q. This keyboard shortcut removes paragraph formatting from selected text. To remove all formatting from selected text, including character and paragraph formatting, click the Clear All Formatting button in the Font group.

Project 3a **Changing Paragraph Alignment**   Part 1 of 6

1. Open **IntelProp.docx**. (Some of the default formatting in this document has been changed.)
2. Save the document with the name **2-IntelProp**.
3. Click the Show/Hide ¶ button in the Paragraph group on the Home tab to turn on the display of nonprinting characters.

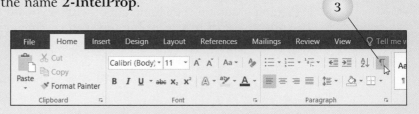

4. Press Ctrl + A to select the entire document and then change the paragraph alignment to justified alignment by clicking the Justify button in the Paragraph group.
5. Press Ctrl + End to move the insertion point to the end of the document.
6. Press the Enter key.
7. Press Ctrl + E to move the insertion point to the middle of the page.
8. Type Prepared by Clarissa Markham.
9. Press Shift + Enter and then type Edited by Joshua Streeter.

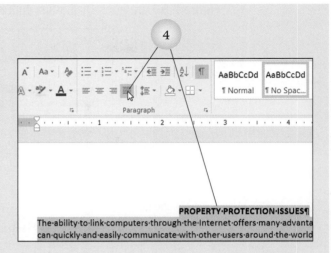

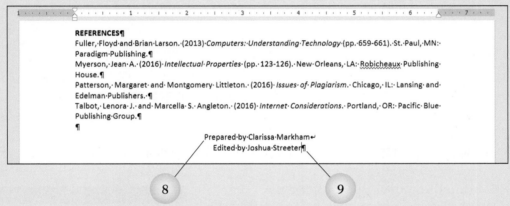

10. Click the Show/Hide ¶ button in the Paragraph group to turn off the display of nonprinting characters.
11. Save **2-IntelProp.docx**.

Check Your Work

Quick Steps

Change Paragraph Alignment

Click alignment button in Paragraph group on Home tab.
OR
1. Click Paragraph group dialog box launcher.
2. Click *Alignment* option box arrow.
3. Click alignment option.
4. Click OK.

Changing Alignment at the Paragraph Dialog Box

Along with buttons in the Paragraph group and keyboard shortcuts, paragraph alignment can be changed with the *Alignment* option box at the Paragraph dialog box, shown in Figure 2.6. Display this dialog box by clicking the Paragraph group dialog box launcher. At the Paragraph dialog box, click the *Alignment* option box arrow. At the drop-down list, click the alignment option and then click OK to close the dialog box.

Figure 2.6 Paragraph Dialog Box with Indents and Spacing Tab Selected

Change paragraph alignment by clicking the *Alignment* option box arrow and then clicking the alignment option at the drop-down list.

Use these options to specify spacing before and after paragraphs.

Project 3b Changing Paragraph Alignment at the Paragraph Dialog Box

1. With **2-IntelProp.docx** open, change the paragraph alignment by completing the following steps:
   a. Select the entire document.
   b. Click the Paragraph group dialog box launcher.
   c. At the Paragraph dialog box with the Indents and Spacing tab selected, click the *Alignment* option box arrow and then click the *Left* option.
   d. Click OK to close the dialog box.
   e. Deselect the text.
2. Change the paragraph alignment by completing the following steps:
   a. Press Ctrl + End to move the insertion point to the end of the document.
   b. Position the insertion point anywhere in the text *Prepared by Clarissa Markham*.
   c. Click the Paragraph group dialog box launcher.
   d. At the Paragraph dialog box with the Indents and Spacing tab selected, click the *Alignment* option box arrow and then click the *Right* option.
   e. Click OK to close the dialog box. (The line of text containing the name *Clarissa Markham* and the line of text containing the name *Joshua Streeter* are both aligned at the right since you used the New Line command, Shift + Enter, to separate the lines of text without creating a new paragraph.)
3. Save and then print **2-IntelProp.docx**.

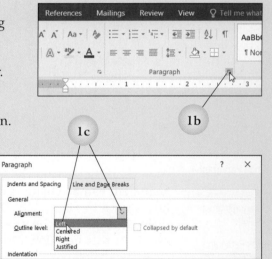

Check Your Work

Indenting Text in Paragraphs

Tutorial

Indenting Text

To indent text from the left margin, the right margin, or both margins, use the indent buttons in the Paragraph group on the Layout tab, keyboard shortcuts, options from the Paragraph dialog box, markers on the horizontal ruler, or the Alignment button above the vertical ruler. Figure 2.7 identifies indent markers on the horizontal ruler and the Alignment button. Refer to Table 2.4 for methods for indenting text in a document. If the horizontal ruler is not visible, display the ruler by clicking the View tab and then clicking the *Ruler* check box in the Show group to insert a check mark.

Quick Steps

Indent Text in Paragraph

Drag indent marker(s) on horizontal ruler.
OR
Press keyboard shortcut keys.
OR
1. Click Paragraph group dialog box launcher.
2. Insert measurement in *Left, Right,* and/or *By* text box.
3. Click OK.

Figure 2.7 Horizontal Ruler and Indent Markers

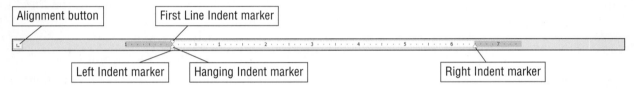

Table 2.4 Methods for Indenting Text

Indent	Methods for Indenting
First line of paragraph	• Press the Tab key.
	• Display the Paragraph dialog box, click the *Special* option box arrow, click *First line,* and then click OK.
	• Drag the First Line Indent marker on the horizontal ruler.
	• Click the Alignment button, until the First Line Indent symbol displays and then click the horizontal ruler at the desired location.
Text from left margin	• Click the Increase Indent button in the Paragraph group on the Home tab to increase the indent or click the Decrease Indent button to decrease the indent.
	• Insert a measurement in the *Indent Left* measurement box in the Paragraph group on the Layout tab.
	• Press Ctrl + M to increase the indent or press Ctrl + Shift + M to decrease the indent.
	• Display the Paragraph dialog box, type the indent measurement in the *Left* measurement box, and then click OK.
	• Drag the Left Indent marker on the horizontal ruler.

continues

Table 2.4 Methods for Indenting Text—*Continued*

Indent	Methods for Indenting
Text from right margin	• Insert a measurement in the *Indent Right* measurement box in the Paragraph group on the Layout tab. • Display the Paragraph dialog box, type the indent measurement in the *Right* measurement box, and then click OK. • Drag the Right Indent marker on the horizontal ruler.
All lines of text except the first (called a *hanging indent*)	• Press Ctrl + T. (Press Ctrl + Shift + T to remove a hanging indent.) • Display the Paragraph dialog box, click the *Special* option box arrow, click *Hanging*, and then click OK. • Click the Alignment button, left of the horizontal ruler and above the vertical ruler until the Hanging Indent symbol displays and then click the horizontal ruler at the desired location. • Drag the Hanging Indent marker on the horizontal ruler.
Text from both left and right margins	• Display the Paragraph dialog box, type the indent measurement in the *Left* measurement box, type the indent measurement in the *Right* measurement box, and then click OK. • Insert a measurements in the *Indent Right* and *Indent Left* measurement boxes in the Paragraph group on the Layout tab. • Drag the Left Indent marker on the horizontal ruler and then drag the Right Indent marker on the horizontal ruler.

Project 3c Indenting Text

Part 3 of 6

1. With **2-IntelProp.docx** open, indent the first line of text in each paragraph by completing the following steps:
   a. Select the first two paragraphs of text in the document (the text after the title *PROPERTY PROTECTION ISSUES* and before the heading *Intellectual Property*).
   b. Make sure the horizontal ruler displays. (If it does not display, click the View tab and then click the *Ruler* check box in the Show group to insert a check mark.)
   c. Position the mouse pointer on the First Line Indent marker on the horizontal ruler, click and hold down the left mouse button, drag the marker to the 0.5-inch mark, and then release the mouse button.
   d. Select the paragraphs of text in the *Intellectual Property* section and then drag the First Line Indent marker on the horizontal ruler to the 0.5-inch mark.

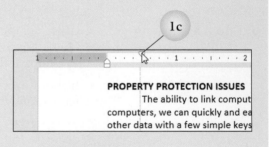

Chapter 2 | Formatting Characters and Paragraphs

e. Select the paragraphs of text in the *Fair Use* section, click the Alignment button until the First Line Indent symbol displays, and then click the horizontal ruler at the 0.5-inch mark.

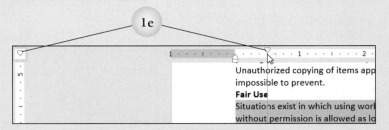

f. Position the insertion point anywhere in the paragraph of text below the heading *Intellectual Property Protection*, make sure the First Line Indent symbol displays on the Alignment button, and then click the 0.5-inch mark on the horizontal ruler.

2. Since the text in the second paragraph in the *Fair Use* section is a quote, indent the text from the left and right margins by completing the following steps:
   a. Position the insertion point anywhere in the second paragraph in the *Fair Use* section (the paragraph that begins *[A] copyrighted work, including such*).
   b. Click the Paragraph group dialog box launcher.
   c. At the Paragraph dialog box with the Indents and Spacing tab selected, select the current measurement in the *Left* measurement box and then type 0.5.
   d. Select the current measurement in the *Right* measurement box and then type 0.5.
   e. Click the *Special* option box arrow and then click *(none)* at the drop-down list.
   f. Click OK or press the Enter key.

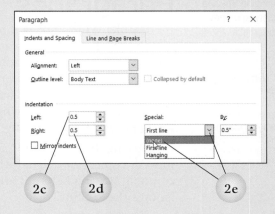

3. Create a hanging indent for the first paragraph in the *REFERENCES* section by positioning the insertion point anywhere in the first paragraph below the heading *REFERENCES* and then pressing Ctrl + T.

4. Create a hanging indent for the second paragraph in the *REFERENCES* section by completing the following steps:
   a. Position the insertion point anywhere in the second paragraph in the *REFERENCES* section.
   b. Click the Alignment button until the Hanging Indent symbol displays.
   c. Click the 0.5-inch mark on the horizontal ruler.

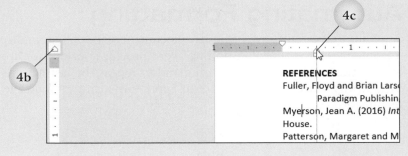

5. Create a hanging indent for the third and fourth paragraphs by completing the following steps:
   a. Select a portion of the third and fourth paragraphs.
   b. Click the Paragraph group dialog box launcher.
   c. At the Paragraph dialog box with the Indents and Spacing tab selected, click the *Special* option box arrow and then click *Hanging* at the drop-down list.
   d. Click OK or press the Enter key.
6. Save **2-IntelProp.docx**.

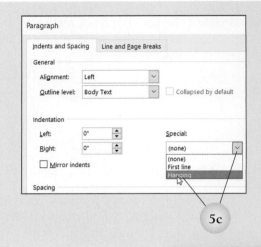

5c

Check Your Work

Tutorial

Changing Spacing Before and After Paragraphs

💡 **Hint** Line spacing determines the amount of vertical space between lines, while paragraph spacing determines the amount of space above or below paragraphs of text.

Spacing Before and After Paragraphs

By default, Word applies 8 points of additional spacing after a paragraph. This spacing can be removed or it can be increased or decreased, and spacing can be inserted above the paragraph. To change spacing before or after a paragraph, use the *Before* and *After* measurement boxes in the Paragraph group on the Layout tab, or the *Before* and *After* options at the Paragraph dialog box with the Indents and Spacing tab selected. Spacing can also be added before and after paragraphs at the Line and Paragraph Spacing button drop-down list.

Spacing before or after a paragraph is part of the paragraph and will be moved, copied, or deleted with the paragraph. If a paragraph, such as a heading, contains spacing before it and the paragraph falls at the top of a page, Word ignores the spacing.

Spacing before or after paragraphs is added in points and 1 vertical inch contains approximately 72 points. To add spacing before or after a paragraph, click the Layout tab, select the current measurement in the *Before* or *After* measurement box, and then type the number of points. The up or down arrows at the *Before* and *After* measurement boxes can also be clicked to increase or decrease the amount of spacing.

Automating Formatting

Applying consistent formatting in a document, especially a multiple-page document, can be time consuming. Word provides options for applying formatting automatically. Use the Repeat command to repeat the last action, such as applying formatting, or the Format Painter to apply formatting to multiple locations in a document.

Repeating the Last Command

Formatting applied to text can be applied to other text in the document using the Repeat command. To use this command, apply the formatting, move the insertion point to the next location the formatting is to be applied, and then press the F4 function key or the keyboard shortcut Ctrl + Y. The Repeat command will repeat only the last command executed.

Project 3d Spacing Before and After Paragraphs and Repeating the Last Command   Part 4 of 6

1. With **2-IntelProp.docx** open, add 6 points of spacing before and after each paragraph in the document by completing the following steps:
   a. Select the entire document.
   b. Click the Layout tab.
   c. Click the *Before* measurement box up arrow. (This inserts *6 pt* in the box.)
   d. Click the *After* measurement box up arrow two times. (This inserts *6 pt* in the box.)
2. Add an additional 6 points of spacing above the headings by completing the following steps:
   a. Position the insertion point anywhere in the heading *Intellectual Property* and then click the *Before* measurement box up arrow. (This changes the measurement to *12 pt*.)
   b. Position the insertion point anywhere in the heading *Fair Use* and then press F4. (F4 is the Repeat command.)
   c. Position the insertion point anywhere in the heading *Intellectual Property Protection* and then press F4.
   d. Position the insertion point anywhere in the heading *REFERENCES* and then press Ctrl + Y. (Ctrl + Y is also the Repeat command.)
3. Save **2-IntelProp.docx**.

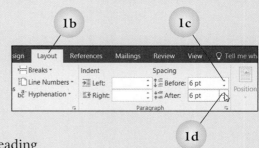

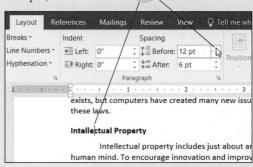

Check Your Work

Formatting with Format Painter

Tutorial

Formatting with
Format Painter

 Format Painter

Quick Steps

Format with Format Painter
1. Format text then position insertion point within formatted text.
2. Double-click Format Painter button.
3. Select text to apply formatting.
4. Click Format Painter button.

The Clipboard group on the Home tab contains a button for copying formatting and displays in the Clipboard group with a paintbrush. To use this button, called Format Painter, position the insertion point anywhere in text containing the desired formatting, click the Format Painter button, and then select the text to which the formatting is to be applied. When the Format Painter button is clicked, the I-beam pointer displays with a paintbrush attached. To apply the formatting a single time, click the Format Painter button. To apply the formatting in more than one location in the document, double-click the Format Painter button and then select the text to which the formatting is to be applied. When finished, click the Format Painter button to turn it off. The Format Painter button can also be turned off by pressing the Esc key.

1. With **2-IntelProp.docx** open, click the Home tab.
2. Select the entire document and then change the font to 12-point Cambria.
3. Select the title *PROPERTY PROTECTION ISSUES*, click the Center button in the Paragraph group, and then change the font to 16-point Candara.
4. Apply 16-point Candara formatting to the heading *REFERENCES* by completing the following steps:
   a. Click anywhere in the title *PROPERTY PROTECTION ISSUES*.
   b. Click the Format Painter button in the Clipboard group.

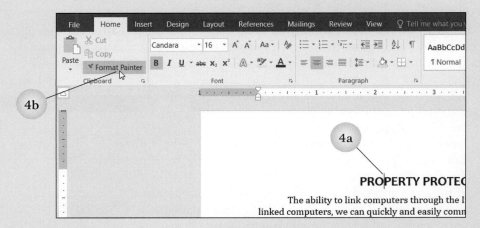

   c. Press Ctrl + End to move the insertion point to the end of the document and then click anywhere in the heading *REFERENCES*. (This applies the 16-point Candara formatting and centers the text.)
5. Select the heading *Intellectual Property* and then change the font to 14-point Candara.
6. Use the Format Painter button and apply 14-point Candara formatting to the other headings by completing the following steps:
   a. Position the insertion point anywhere in the heading *Intellectual Property*.
   b. Double-click the Format Painter button in the Clipboard group.
   c. Using the mouse, select the heading *Fair Use*.
   d. Using the mouse, select the heading *Intellectual Property Protection*.
   e. Click the Format Painter button in the Clipboard group. (This turns off the feature and deactivates the button.)
   f. Deselect the heading.
7. Save **2-IntelProp.docx**.

> **Check Your Work**

Changing Line Spacing

The default line spacing for a document is 1.08. (The line spacing for the IntelProp.docx file, which you opened at the beginning of Project 3, had been changed to single line spacing.) In certain situations, Word automatically adjusts the line spacing. For example, if a large character or object, such as a graphic, is inserted into a line, Word increases the line spacing of that line. The line spacing for a section or an entire document can also be changed.

Quick Steps
Change Line Spacing
1. Click Line and Paragraph Spacing button.
2. Click option.
OR
Press keyboard shortcut command.
OR
1. Click Paragraph group dialog box launcher.
2. Click *Line Spacing* option box arrow.
3. Click line spacing option.
4. Click OK.
OR
1. Click Paragraph group dialog box launcher.
2. Type line measurement in *At* measurement box.
3. Click OK.

Change line spacing using the Line and Paragraph Spacing button in the Paragraph group on the Home tab, keyboard shortcuts, or options from the Paragraph dialog box. Table 2.5 displays the keyboard shortcuts to change line spacing.

Line spacing can also be changed at the Paragraph dialog box with the *Line spacing* option or the *At* measurement box. Click the *Line spacing* option box arrow and a drop-down list displays with a variety of spacing options, such as *Single, 1.5 lines,* and *Double.* A specific line spacing measurement can be entered in the *At* measurement box. For example, to change the line spacing to 1.75 lines, type *1.75* in the *At* measurement box.

Table 2.5 Line Spacing Keyboard Shortcuts

Press	To change line spacing to
Ctrl + 1	single line spacing
Ctrl + 2	double line spacing
Ctrl + 5	1.5 line spacing

Project 3f Changing Line Spacing

Part 6 of 6

1. With **2-IntelProp.docx** open, change the line spacing for all paragraphs to double spacing by completing the following steps:
   a. Select the entire document.
   b. Click the Line and Paragraph Spacing button in the Paragraph group on the Home tab.
   c. Click *2.0* at the drop-down list.
2. With the entire document still selected, press Ctrl + 5. (This changes the line spacing to 1.5 lines.)
3. Change the line spacing to 1.2 lines using the Paragraph dialog box by completing the following steps:
   a. With the entire document still selected, click the Paragraph group dialog box launcher.
   b. At the Paragraph dialog box, make sure the Indents and Spacing tab is selected, click in the *At* measurement box, and then type 1.2. (This measurement box is to the right of the *Line spacing* option box.)
   c. Click OK or press the Enter key.
   d. Deselect the text.
4. Save, print, and then close **2-IntelProp.docx**.

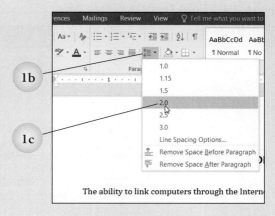

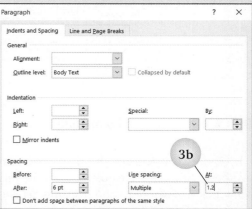

Check Your Work

You will open a document containing two computer-related problems to solve, reveal the formatting, compare the formatting, and make formatting changes.

Preview Finished Project

Revealing and Comparing Formatting

Display formatting applied to specific text in a document at the Reveal Formatting task pane, shown in Figure 2.8. The Reveal Formatting task pane displays font, paragraph, and section formatting applied to text where the insertion point is positioned or to selected text. Display the Reveal Formatting task pane with the keyboard shortcut Shift + F1. Generally, a collapse triangle (a solid right-and-down-pointing triangle) precedes *Font* and *Paragraph* and an expand triangle (a hollow right-pointing triangle) precedes *Section* in the *Formatting of selected text* list box in the Reveal Formatting task pane. Click the collapse triangle to hide any items below a heading and click the expand triangle to reveal items. Some of the items below headings in the *Formatting of selected text* list box are hyperlinks. Click a hyperlink and a dialog box displays with the specific option.

Figure 2.8 Reveal Formatting Task Pane

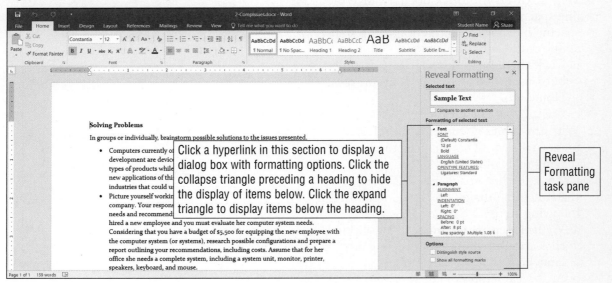

Project 4a Revealing Formatting　　　　　Part 1 of 2

1. Open **CompIssues.docx** and then save it with the name **2-CompIssues**.
2. Press Shift + F1 to display the Reveal Formatting task pane.
3. Click anywhere in the heading *Solving Problems* and then notice the formatting information in the Reveal Formatting task pane.
4. Click in the bulleted paragraph and notice the formatting information in the Reveal Formatting task pane.

Quick Steps

Compare Formatting

1. Press Shift + F1 to display Reveal Formatting task pane.
2. Click or select text.
3. Click *Compare to another selection* check box.
4. Click or select text.

Along with displaying formatting applied to text, the Reveal Formatting task pane can be used to compare formatting of two text selections to determine what is different. To compare formatting, select the first instance of formatting to be compared, click the *Compare to another selection* check box, and then select the second instance of formatting to be compared. Any differences between the two selections display in the *Formatting differences* list box.

Project 4b Comparing Formatting

Part 2 of 2

1. With **2-CompIssues.docx** open, make sure the Reveal Formatting task pane displays. If it does not, turn it on by pressing Shift + F1.
2. Select the first bulleted paragraph (the paragraph that begins *Computers currently offer both*).
3. Click the *Compare to another selection* check box to insert a check mark.
4. Select the second bulleted paragraph (the paragraph that begins *Picture yourself working in the*).
5. Determine the formatting differences by reading the information in the *Formatting differences* list box. (The list box displays *12 pt -> 11 pt* below the FONT hyperlink, indicating that the difference is point size.)
6. Format the second bulleted paragraph so it is set in 12-point size.
7. Click the *Compare to another selection* check box to remove the check mark.
8. Select the word *visual*, which displays in the first sentence in the first bulleted paragraph.
9. Click the *Compare to another selection* check box to insert a check mark.
10. Select the word *audio*, which displays in the first sentence of the first bulleted paragraph.
11. Determine the formatting differences by reading the information in the *Formatting differences* list box.
12. Format the word *audio* so it matches the formatting of the word *visual*.
13. Click the *Compare to another selection* check box to remove the check mark.
14. Close the Reveal Formatting task pane by clicking the Close button in the upper right corner of the task pane.
15. Save, print, and then close **2-CompIssues.docx**.

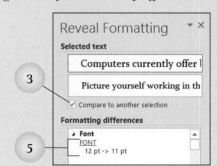

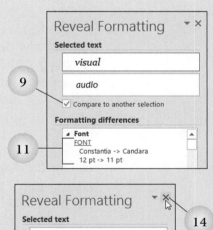

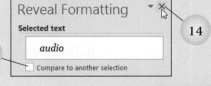

Check Your Work

Chapter Summary

- A font consists of three elements: typeface, type size, and typestyle.

- A typeface (font) is a set of characters with a common design and shape. Typefaces are either monospaced, allotting the same amount of horizontal space for each character, or proportional, allotting varying amounts of space for different characters. Proportional typefaces are divided into two main categories: serif and sans serif.

- Type size is measured in point size; the higher the point size, the larger the characters.

- A typestyle is a variation of style within a certain typeface, such as bold, italic, or underline. Apply typestyle formatting with some of the buttons in the Font group on the Home tab.

- Apply font effects with some of the buttons in the Font group on the Home tab, such as superscript, subscript, and strikethrough.

- The Mini toolbar automatically displays above selected text. Use options and buttons on this toolbar to apply formatting to selected text.

- Use options at the Font dialog box to change the font, font size, and font style and apply specific effects. Display this dialog box by clicking the Font group dialog box launcher.

- A Word document contains a number of predesigned formats grouped into style sets. Change to a different style set by clicking the Design tab and then clicking the style set in the styles set gallery in the Document Formatting group.

- Apply a theme and change theme colors, fonts, and effects with buttons in the Document Formatting group on the Design tab.

- Click the Paragraph Spacing button in the Document Formatting group on the Design tab to apply a predesigned paragraph spacing option to text in a document.

- By default, paragraphs in a Word document are aligned at the left margin and ragged at the right margin. Change this default alignment with buttons in the Paragraph group, at the Paragraph dialog box, or with keyboard shortcuts.

- To turn on or off the display of nonprinting characters, such as paragraph marks, click the Show/Hide ¶ button in the Paragraph group on the Home tab.

- Indent text in paragraphs with indent buttons in the Paragraph group on the Home tab, buttons in the Paragraph group on the Layout tab, keyboard shortcuts, options from the Paragraph dialog box, markers on the horizontal ruler, or the Alignment button above the vertical ruler.

- Increase and/or decrease spacing before and after paragraphs using the *Before* and *After* measurement boxes in the Paragraph group on the Layout tab or using the *Before* and/or *After* options at the Paragraph dialog box.

- Repeat the last command by pressing the F4 function key or the keyboard shortcut Ctrl + Y.

- Use the Format Painter button in the Clipboard group on the Home tab to copy formatting already applied to text to different locations in the document.

- Change line spacing with the Line and Paragraph Spacing button in the Paragraph group on the Home tab, keyboard shortcuts, or options from the Paragraph dialog box.

- Display the Reveal Formatting task pane to display formatting applied to text. Use the *Compare to another selection* option in the task pane to compare formatting of two text selections to determine what is different.

Commands Review

FEATURE	RIBBON TAB, GROUP	BUTTON	KEYBOARD SHORTCUT
bold text	Home, Font	B	Ctrl + B
center-align text	Home, Paragraph		Ctrl + E
change case of text	Home, Font	Aa ˅	Shift + F3
clear all formatting	Home, Font		
clear character formatting			Ctrl + spacebar
clear paragraph formatting			Ctrl + Q
decrease font size	Home, Font	A˅	Ctrl + Shift + < OR Ctrl + [
display or hide nonprinting characters	Home, Paragraph	¶	Ctrl + Shift + *
font	Home, Font		
font color	Home, Font	A ˅	
Font dialog box	Home, Font		Ctrl + Shift + F
font size	Home, Font		
Format Painter	Home, Clipboard		Ctrl + Shift + C
Help			F1
highlight text	Home, Font	aby ˅	
increase font size	Home, Font	A˄	Ctrl + Shift + > OR Ctrl +]
italicize text	Home, Font	I	Ctrl + I
justify text	Home, Paragraph		Ctrl + J
left-align text	Home, Paragraph		Ctrl + L
line spacing	Home, Paragraph		Ctrl + 1 (single) Ctrl + 2 (double) Ctrl + 5 (1.5)
Paragraph dialog box	Home, Paragraph		
paragraph spacing	Design, Document Formatting		
repeat last action			F4 or Ctrl + Y
Reveal Formatting task pane			Shift + F1

FEATURE	RIBBON TAB, GROUP	BUTTON	KEYBOARD SHORTCUT
right-align text	Home, Paragraph		Ctrl + R
spacing after paragraph	Layout, Paragraph		
spacing before paragraph	Layout, Paragraph		
strikethrough text	Home, Font	abc	
subscript text	Home, Font	x_2	Ctrl + =
superscript text	Home, Font	x^2	Ctrl + Shift + +
text effects and typography	Home, Font	A ▾	
theme colors	Design, Document Formatting		
theme effects	Design, Document Formatting		
theme fonts	Design, Document Formatting	A	
themes	Design, Document Formatting	Aa	
underline text	Home, Font	U ▾	Ctrl + U

Workbook

Chapter study tools and assessment activities are available in the *Workbook* ebook. These resources are designed to help you further develop and demonstrate mastery of the skills learned in this chapter.

Microsoft®
Word

Customizing Paragraphs

Performance Objectives

Upon successful completion of Chapter 3, you will be able to:

1   Apply numbering and bulleting formatting to text

2   Apply paragraph borders and shading

3   Sort paragraph text

4   Set, clear, and move tabs on the horizontal ruler and at the Tabs
    dialog box

5   Cut, copy, and paste text in a document

6   Use the Paste Options button to specify how text is pasted in a
    document

7   Use the Clipboard task pane to copy and paste text within and
    between documents

As you learned in Chapter 2, Word contains a variety of options for formatting text
in paragraphs. In this chapter you will learn how to apply numbering and bulleted
formatting to text, how to apply borders and shading to paragraphs of text, how
to sort paragraphs of text, and how to manipulate tabs on the horizontal ruler and
at the Tabs dialog box. Editing some documents might include selecting and then
deleting, moving, or copying text. You can perform this type of editing with buttons
in the Clipboard group on the Home tab or with keyboard shortcuts.

SNAP

Data Files ▶

**Before beginning chapter work, copy the WL1C3 folder to
your storage medium and then make WL1C3 the active folder.**

You will open a document containing information on computer technology, type numbered text in the document, and apply numbering and bulleted formatting to paragraphs in the document.

Preview Finished Project

Applying Numbering and Bullets

Numbering

Bullets

Automatically number paragraphs or insert bullets before paragraphs using buttons in the Paragraph group on the Home tab. Use the Numbering button to insert numbers before specific paragraphs and use the Bullets button to insert bullets.

Tutorial

Creating Numbered Lists

Quick Steps

Type Numbered Paragraphs
1. Type 1.
2. Press spacebar.
3. Type text.
4. Press Enter.

Hint Define a new numbering format by clicking the Numbering button arrow and then clicking *Define New Number Format.*

Creating Numbered Lists

Type *1.* and then press the spacebar and Word indents the number 0.25 inch from the left margin and hang-indents the text in the paragraph 0.5 inch from the left margin. Additionally, when the Enter key is pressed to end the first item, *2.* is inserted 0.25 inch from the left margin at the beginning of the next paragraph. Continue typing items and Word inserts the next number in the list. To turn off numbering, press the Enter key two times or click the Numbering button in the Paragraph group on the Home tab. (Paragraph formatting can be removed from a paragraph, including automatic numbering, with the keyboard shortcut Ctrl + Q. Remove all formatting, including character and paragraph formatting from selected text, by clicking the Clear All Formatting button in the Font group on the Home tab.)

Press the Enter key two times between numbered paragraphs and the automatic numbering is removed. To turn it back on, type the next number in the list (and the period) followed by a space. Word will automatically indent the number and hang-indent the text. To insert a line break without inserting a bullet or number, press Shift + Enter.

When the AutoFormat feature inserts numbering and indents text, the AutoCorrect Options button displays. Click this button and a drop-down list displays with options for undoing and/or stopping the automatic numbering. An AutoCorrect Options button also displays when AutoFormat inserts automatic bulleting in a document.

Project 1a **Creating a Numbered List** **Part 1 of 3**

1. Open **TechInfo.docx** and then save it with the name **3-TechInfo**.
2. Press Ctrl + End to move the insertion point to the end of the document and then type the text shown in Figure 3.1. Apply bold formatting and center the title *Technology Career Questions*. When typing the numbered paragraphs, complete the following steps:
   a. Type 1. and then press the spacebar. (The *1.* is indented 0.25 inch from the left margin and the first paragraph of text is indented 0.5 inch from the left margin. Also, the AutoCorrect Options button displays. Use this button if you want to undo or stop automatic numbering.)
   b. Type the paragraph of text and then press the Enter key. (This moves the insertion point down to the next paragraph and inserts an indented number *2* followed by a period.)

   c. Continue typing the remaining text. (Remember, you do not need to type the paragraph number and period—they are automatically inserted. The last numbered item will wrap differently on your screen than shown in Figure 3.1.)

   d. After typing the last question, press the Enter key two times. (This turns off paragraph numbering.)

3. Save **3-TechInfo.docx**.

Check Your Work

Figure 3.1 Project 1a

Technology Career Questions

1. What is your ideal technical job?
2. Which job suits your personality?
3. Which is your first-choice certificate?
4. How does the technical job market look in your state right now? Is the job market wide open or are the information technology career positions limited?

Automatic numbering is turned on by default. Turn off automatic numbering at the AutoCorrect dialog box with the AutoFormat As You Type tab selected, as shown in Figure 3.2. To display this dialog box, click the File tab and then click *Options*. At the Word Options dialog box, click the *Proofing* option in the left panel and then click the AutoCorrect Options button in the *AutoCorrect options* section of the dialog box. At the AutoCorrect dialog box, click the AutoFormat As You Type tab and then click the *Automatic numbered lists* check box to remove the check mark. Click OK to close the AutoCorrect dialog box and then click OK to close the Word Options dialog box.

Figure 3.2 AutoCorrect Dialog Box with AutoFormat As You Type Tab Selected

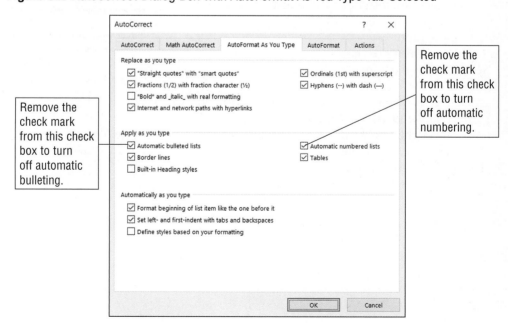

Numbering formatting can be turned on or applied to existing text with the Numbering button in the Paragraph group on the Home tab. Click the Numbering button to turn on numbering, type text, and then click the button again to turn off numbering, or select existing text and then click the Numbering button to apply numbering formatting.

Project 1b Applying Numbering Formatting

Part 2 of 3

1. With **3-TechInfo.docx** open, apply numbers to paragraphs by completing the following steps:
   a. Select the five paragraphs of text in the *Technology Information Questions* section.
   b. Click the Numbering button in the Paragraph group on the Home tab.

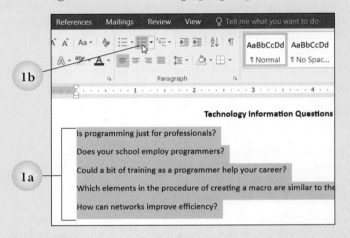

2. Add text between paragraphs 4 and 5 in the *Technology Information Questions* section by completing the following steps:
   a. Position the insertion point immediately right of the question mark at the end of the fourth paragraph.
   b. Press the Enter key.
   c. Type What kinds of networks are used in your local area?
3. Delete the second question (paragraph) in the *Technology Information Questions* section by completing the following steps:
   a. Select the text of the second paragraph. (You will not be able to select the number.)
   b. Press the Delete key.
4. Save **3-TechInfo.docx**.

Check Your Work

Tutorial

Creating Bulleted
Lists

Creating Bulleted Lists

In addition to automatically numbering paragraphs, Word's AutoFormat feature creates bulleted lists. A bulleted list with a hanging indent is automatically created when a paragraph begins with the symbol *, >, or -. Type one of the symbols and then press the spacebar and the AutoFormat feature inserts a bullet 0.25 inch from the left margin and indents the text following the bullet another 0.25 inch. Change the indent of bulleted text by pressing the Tab key to demote text or pressing Shift + Tab to promote text. Word uses different bullets for demoted text.

Bulleted formatting can be turned on or applied to existing text with the Bullets button in the Paragraph group on the Home tab. Click the Bullets button to turn on bulleting, type text, and then click the button again to turn off bulleting. Or, select existing text and then click the Bullets button to apply bulleted formatting. The automatic bulleting feature can be turned off at the AutoCorrect dialog box with the AutoFormat As You Type tab selected.

Quick Steps

Type Bulleted List
1. Type *, >, or -
   symbol.
2. Press spacebar.
3. Type text.
4. Press Enter.

Create Bulleted List
1. Select text.
2. Click Bullets button.

Project 1c   Creating a Bulleted List and Applying Bulleted Formatting   Part 3 of 3

1. With **3-TechInfo.docx** open, press Ctrl + End to move the insertion point to the end of the document and then press the Enter key.
2. Type Technology Timeline: Computer Design bolded and centered, as shown in Figure 3.3, and then press the Enter key.
3. Turn off bold formatting and change to left alignment.
4. Type a greater-than symbol (>), press the spacebar, type the text of the first bulleted paragraph in Figure 3.3, and then press the Enter key.
5. Press the Tab key (which demotes the bullet to a hollow circle) and then type the bulleted text.
6. Press the Enter key (which displays another hollow circle bullet), type the bulleted text, and then press the Enter key.
7. Press Shift + Tab (which promotes the bullet to an arrow), type the bulleted text, and then press the Enter key two times (which turns off bullets).
8. Promote bulleted text by positioning the insertion point at the beginning of the text *1958: Jack Kilby, an engineer* and then pressing Shift + Tab. Promote the other hollow circle bullet to an arrow. (The four paragraphs of text should be preceded by arrow bullets.)
9. Format the paragraphs of text in the *Technology Timeline: Computers in the Workplace* section as a bulleted list by completing the following steps:
   a. Select the paragraphs of text in the *Technology Timeline: Computers in the Workplace* section.
   b. Click the Bullets button in the Paragraph group. (Word will insert the same arrow bullets that you inserted in Step 4. Word keeps the same bullet formatting until you choose a different bullet style.)
10. Save, print, and then close **3-TechInfo.docx**.

Check Your Work

Figure 3.3 Project 1c

> **Technology Timeline: Computer Design**
>
> ➤ 1937: Dr. John Atanasoff and Clifford Berry design and build the first electronic digital computer.
> > o 1958: Jack Kilby, an engineer at Texas Instruments, invents the integrated circuit, thereby laying the foundation for fast computers and large-capacity memory.
> > o 1981: IBM enters the personal computer field by introducing the IBM-PC.
> ➤ 2004: Wireless computer devices, including keyboards, mice, and wireless home networks, become widely accepted among users.

Project 2 Customize a Document on Chapter Questions 3 Parts

You will open a document containing chapter questions and then apply border and shading formatting to text.

Preview Finished Project

Adding Emphasis to Paragraphs

 Borders

To call attention to or to highlight specific text in a paragraph, consider adding emphasis to the text by applying paragraph borders and/or shading. Apply borders with the Borders button on the Home tab and shading with the Shading button. Additional borders and shading options are available at the Borders and Shading dialog box.

Tutorial

Applying Borders

Applying Paragraph Borders

Every paragraph in a Word document contains an invisible frame and a border can be applied to the frame around the paragraph. Apply a border to specific sides of the paragraph frame or to all sides. Add borders to paragraphs using the Borders button in the Paragraph group on the Home tab or using options at the Borders and Shading dialog box.

When a border is added to a paragraph of text, the border expands and contracts as text is inserted or deleted from the paragraph. Insert a border around the active paragraph or around selected paragraphs.

Quick Steps

Apply Borders with Borders Button
1. Select text.
2. Click Borders button arrow.
3. Click border option at drop-down list.

One method for inserting a border is to use options from the Borders button in the Paragraph group. Click the Borders button arrow and a drop-down list displays. At the drop-down list, click the option that will insert the desired border. For example, to insert a border at the bottom of the paragraph, click the *Bottom Border* option. Clicking an option will add the border to the paragraph where the insertion point is located. To add a border to more than one paragraph, select the paragraphs first and then click the option.

1. Open **Questions.docx** and then save it with the name **3-Questions**.
2. Insert an outside border to specific text by completing the following steps:
   a. Select text from the heading *Chapter 1 Questions* through the four bulleted paragraphs.
   b. In the Paragraph group, click the Borders button arrow.
   c. Click the *Outside Borders* option at the drop-down list.
3. Select text from the heading *Chapter 2 Questions* through the five bulleted paragraphs and then click the Borders button in the Paragraph group. (The button will apply the border option that was previously selected.)
4. Save **3-Questions.docx**.

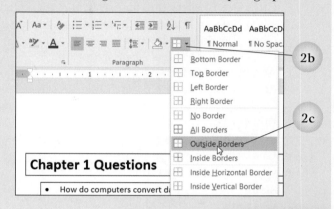

Check Your Work

Quick Steps

Apply Borders at the Borders and Shading Dialog Box
1. Select text.
2. Click Borders button arrow.
3. Click *Borders and Shading* option.
4. Choose options in dialog box.
5. Click OK.

To further customize paragraph borders, use options at the Borders and Shading dialog box shown in Figure 3.4. Display this dialog box by clicking the Borders button arrow and then clicking *Borders and Shading* at the drop-down list. At the Borders and Shading dialog box, specify the border setting, style, color, and width.

Figure 3.4 Borders and Shading Dialog Box with the Borders Tab Selected

Click the *Style* list box arrow to display additional line styles.

Click the *Color* option box arrow to display a drop-down list of color options.

Click the *Width* option box arrow to display a drop-down list of width options.

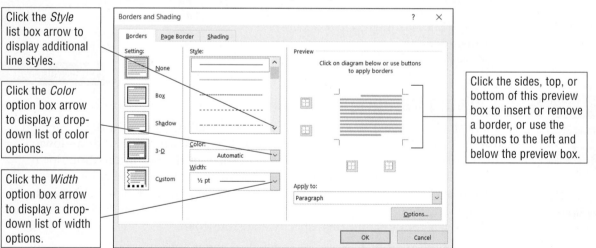

Click the sides, top, or bottom of this preview box to insert or remove a border, or use the buttons to the left and below the preview box.

1. With **3-Questions.docx** open, remove the paragraph borders around the heading *Chapter 1 Questions* by completing the following steps:
   a. Position the insertion point anywhere in the heading *Chapter 1 Questions*.
   b. Click the Borders button arrow and then click *No Border* at the drop-down list.
2. Apply a bottom border to the heading *Chapter 1 Questions* by completing the following steps:
   a. Click the Borders button arrow.
   b. Click the *Borders and Shading* option.
   c. At the Borders and Shading dialog box, click the *Style* list box down arrow two times. (This displays a double-line option.)
   d. Click the double-line option.
   e. Click the *Color* option box arrow.
   f. Click the *Blue* color option (eighth option in the *Standard Colors* section).
   g. Click the *Width* option box arrow.
   h. Click the *3/4 pt* option at the drop-down list.
   i. Click the *None* option in the *Setting* section.
   j. Click the bottom border of the box in the *Preview* section.
   k. Click the OK button to close the dialog box and apply the border.
3. Apply the same border to the other heading by completing the following steps:
   a. With the insertion point positioned in the heading *Chapter 1 Questions*, click the Format Painter button.
   b. Click anywhere in the heading *Chapter 2 Questions*.
4. Save **3-Questions.docx**.

Check Your Work

Applying Paragraph Shading

Apply shading to text in a document with the Shading button in the Paragraph group. Select text and then click the Shading button arrow, and a drop-down gallery displays. Paragraph shading colors display in themes in the drop-down gallery. Use one of the theme colors or click one of the standard colors at the bottom of the gallery. Click the *More Colors* option and the Colors dialog box displays. At the Colors dialog box with the Standard tab selected, click a color or click the Custom tab and then specify a custom color.

Paragraph shading can also be applied to paragraphs in a document using options at the Borders and Shading dialog box with the Shading tab selected. Display this dialog box by clicking the Borders button arrow and then clicking the *Borders and Shading* option. At the Borders and Shading dialog box, click the Shading tab. Use options in the dialog box to specify a fill color, choose a pattern style, and specify a color for the dots that make up the pattern.

1. With **3-Questions.docx** open, apply paragraph shading to the heading *Chapter 1 Questions* by completing the following steps:
   a. Click anywhere in the heading *Chapter 1 Questions*.
   b. Click the Shading button arrow.
   c. Click the *Blue, Accent 5, Lighter 80%* color option (ninth column, second row in the *Theme Colors* section).
2. Apply the same blue shading to the other heading by completing the following steps:
   a. With the insertion point positioned in the heading *Chapter 1 Questions*, click the Format Painter button.
   b. Click anywhere in the heading *Chapter 2 Questions*.
3. Apply shading to text with options at the Borders and Shading dialog box by completing the following steps:
   a. Select the four bulleted paragraphs below the heading *Chapter 1 Questions*.
   b. Click the Borders button arrow.
   c. Click the *Borders and Shading* option.
   d. At the Borders and Shading dialog box, click the Shading tab.
   e. Click the *Fill* option box arrow.
   f. Click the *Gold, Accent 4, Lighter 80%* color option (eighth column, second row).
   g. Click the *Style* option box arrow.
   h. Click the *5%* option.
   i. Click the *Color* option box arrow.
   j. Click the *Blue, Accent 5, Lighter 60%* color option (ninth column, third row in the *Theme Colors* section).
   k. Click OK to close the dialog box.
4. Apply the same shading to the bulleted paragraphs below the heading *Chapter 2 Questions* by completing the following steps:
   a. Click anywhere in the bulleted paragraphs below the heading *Chapter 1 Questions*.
   b. Click the Format Painter button.
   c. Select the five bulleted paragraphs below the heading *Chapter 2 Questions*.
5. Save, print, and then close **3-Questions.docx**.

Check Your Work

You will open a document on online shopping and then sort several different paragraphs of text.

Preview Finished Project

Tutorial

Sorting Text in Paragraphs

Sorting Text in Paragraphs

Text arranged in paragraphs can be sorted alphabetically by the first character of each paragraph. The first character can be a number, symbol (such as $ or #), or letter. Type paragraphs to be sorted at the left margin or indented at a tab. Unless specific paragraphs are selected for sorting, Word sorts the entire document.

To sort text in paragraphs, open the document. If the document contains text that should not be included in the sort, select the specific paragraphs to be sorted. Click the Sort button in the Paragraph group and the Sort Text dialog box displays. At this dialog box, click OK.

 Sort

Quick Steps

Sort Paragraphs of Text
1. Click Sort button.
2. Make changes as needed at Sort Text dialog box.
3. Click OK.

The *Type* option at the Sort Text dialog box will display *Text*, *Number*, or *Date* depending on the text selected. Word attempts to determine the data type and chooses one of the three options. For example, if numbers with mathematical values are selected, Word assigns them the *Number* type. However, if a numbered list is selected, Word assigns them the *Text* type since the numbers do not represent mathematical values.

Project 3 Sorting Paragraphs Alphabetically

Part 1 of 1

1. Open **OnlineShop.docx** and then save it with the name **3-OnlineShop**.
2. Sort the bulleted paragraphs alphabetically by completing the following steps:
   a. Select the four bulleted paragraphs in the section *Advantages of Online Shopping*.
   b. Click the Sort button in the Paragraph group.
   c. At the Sort Text dialog box, make sure that *Paragraphs* displays in the *Sort by* option box and that the *Ascending* option is selected.
   d. Click OK.

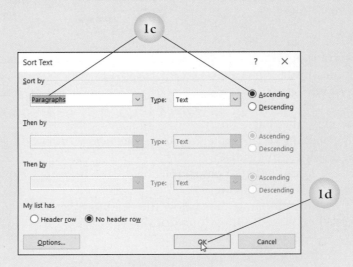

3. Sort the numbered paragraphs by completing the following steps:
   a. Select the six numbered paragraphs in the section *Online Shopping Safety Tips*.
   b. Click the Sort button in the Paragraph group.
   c. Click OK at the Sort Text dialog box.
4. Sort alphabetically the three paragraphs below the title *REFERENCES* by completing the following steps:
   a. Select the paragraphs below the title *REFERENCES*.
   b. Click the Sort button in the Paragraph group.
   c. Click the *Type* option box arrow and then click *Text* at the drop-down list.
   d. Click OK.
5. Save, print, and then close **3-OnlineShop.docx**.

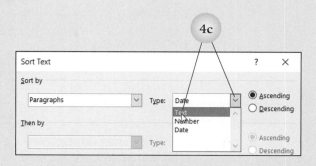

Check Your Work

Project 4   Prepare a Document on Workshops and Training Dates   4 Parts

You will set and move tabs on the horizontal ruler and at the Tabs dialog box and type tabbed text about workshops, training dates, and a table of contents.

Preview Finished Project

Setting and Modifying Tabs

A Word document includes a variety of default settings, such as margins and line spacing. One of these defaults is a left tab set every 0.5 inch. In some situations, these default tabs are appropriate; in others, custom tabs may be needed. Two methods are available for setting tabs: set tabs on the horizontal ruler or at the Tabs dialog box.

Setting and Modifying Tabs on the Horizontal Ruler

Tutorial

Setting and Modifying Tabs on the Horizontal Ruler

Quick Steps

Set Tabs on Horizontal Ruler
1. Click Alignment button above vertical ruler.
2. Click location on horizontal ruler.

Hint When setting tabs on the horizontal ruler, a dotted guideline displays to help align them.

Use the horizontal ruler to set, move, and delete tabs. If the ruler is not visible, click the View tab and then click the *Ruler* check box in the Show group to insert a check mark. By default, tabs are set every 0.5 inch on the horizontal ruler. With a left tab, text aligns at the left edge of the tab. The other types of tabs that can be set on the horizontal ruler are center, right, decimal, and bar. Use the Alignment button above the vertical ruler to specify types of tabs. Each time the Alignment button is clicked, a different tab or paragraph symbol displays. Table 3.1 shows the tab symbols and what type of tab each symbol will set.

To set a left tab on the horizontal ruler, make sure the left tab symbol (see Table 3.1) displays on the Alignment button. Position the arrow pointer on the tick mark (the vertical line on the ruler) where the tab is to be set and then click the left mouse button. When a tab is set on the horizontal ruler, any default tabs to the left are automatically deleted by Word. Set a center, right, decimal, or bar tab on the horizontal ruler in a similar manner.

Table 3.1 Alignment Button Tab Symbols

Alignment Button Symbol	Type of Tab
L	left
⊥	center
⌐	right
⊥	decimal
I	bar

Hint Position the insertion point in any paragraph of text, and tabs for the paragraph appear on the horizontal ruler.

If the tab symbol on the Alignment button is changed, the symbol remains in place until it is changed again or Word is closed. If Word is closed and then reopened, the Alignment button displays with the left tab symbol.

To set a tab at a specific measurement on the horizontal ruler, press and hold down the Alt key, position the arrow pointer at the desired position, and then click and hold down the left mouse button. This displays two measurements in the white portion of the horizontal ruler. The first measurement is the location of the arrow pointer on the ruler in relation to the left margin. The second measurement is the distance from the arrow pointer to the right margin. With the left mouse button held down, position the tab symbol at the desired location and then release the mouse button followed by the Alt key.

Project 4a **Setting Left, Center, and Right Tabs on the Horizontal Ruler**   Part 1 of 4

1. Press Ctrl + N to open a new blank document.
2. Type WORKSHOPS centered and bolded, as shown in Figure 3.5.
3. Press the Enter key. In the new paragraph, change the paragraph alignment back to left and then turn off bold formatting.
4. Set a left tab at the 0.5-inch mark, a center tab at the 3.25-inch mark, and a right tab at the 6-inch mark by completing the following steps:
   a. Click the Show/Hide ¶ button in the Paragraph group on the Home tab to turn on the display of nonprinting characters.
   b. Make sure the horizontal ruler is displayed. (If it is not displayed, click the View tab and then click the *Ruler* check box in the Show group to insert a check mark.)
   c. Make sure the left tab symbol displays in the Alignment button.
   d. Position the arrow pointer on the 0.5-inch mark on the horizontal ruler and then click the left mouse button.

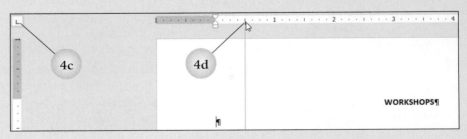

e. Position the arrow pointer on the Alignment button and then click the left mouse button until the center tab symbol displays (see Table 3.1).

f. Position the arrow pointer on the 3.25-inch mark on the horizontal ruler. Press and hold down the Alt key and then click and hold down the left mouse button. Make sure the first measurement on the horizontal ruler displays as *3.25"* and then release both the mouse button and the Alt key.

g. Position the arrow pointer on the Alignment button and then click the left mouse button until the right tab symbol displays (see Table 3.1).

h. Position the arrow pointer below the 6-inch mark on the horizontal ruler. Press and hold down the Alt key and then click and hold down the left mouse button. Make sure the first measurement on the horizontal ruler displays as *6"* and then release both the mouse button and the Alt key.

5. Type the text in columns, as shown in Figure 3.5. Press the Tab key before typing each column entry and press Shift + Enter after typing each entry in the third column. Bold the title and column headings as shown in the figure.

6. After typing the final entry in the last column entry, press the Enter key two times.

7. Press Ctrl + Q to remove paragraph formatting (tab settings) below the columns from the current paragraph.

8. Click the Show/Hide ¶ button to turn off the display of nonprinting characters.

9. Save the document and name it **3-Tabs**.

Check Your Work

Figure 3.5 Project 4a

	WORKSHOPS	
Title	**Price**	**Date**
Quality Management	$240	Friday, February 9
Staff Development	229	Friday, February 23
Streamlining Production	175	Monday, March 5
Managing Records	150	Tuesday, March 20
Customer Service Training	150	Thursday, March 22
Sales Techniques	125	Tuesday, April 17

After a tab has been set on the horizontal ruler, it can be moved to a new location. To move a tab, position the arrow pointer on the tab symbol on the ruler, click and hold down the left mouse button, drag the symbol to the new location on the ruler, and then release the mouse button. To delete a tab from the ruler, position the arrow pointer on the tab symbol to be deleted, click and hold down the left mouse button, drag down into the document, and then release the mouse button.

When typing text in columns, press the Enter key or press Shift + Enter to end each line. If the Enter key is used to end each line, all lines of text in columns will need to be selected to make changes. To make changes to columns of text with line breaks inserted using Shift + Enter, the insertion point needs to be positioned only in one location in the columns of text.

Project 4b Moving Tabs

1. With **3-Tabs.docx** open, position the insertion point anywhere in the first entry in the tabbed text.
2. Position the arrow pointer on the left tab symbol at the 0.5-inch mark on the horizontal ruler, click and hold down the left mouse button, drag the left tab symbol to the 1-inch mark on the ruler, and then release the mouse button. **Hint: Use the Alt key to help you position the tab symbol precisely**.

3. Position the arrow pointer on the right tab symbol at the 6-inch mark on the horizontal ruler, click and hold down the left mouse button, drag the right tab symbol to the 5.5-inch mark on the ruler, and then release the mouse button. **Hint: Use the Alt key to help you position the tab symbol precisely**.
4. Save **3-Tabs.docx**.

Check Your Work

Setting and Modifying Tabs at the Tabs Dialog Box

Tutorial

Setting and Clearing Tabs at the Tabs Dialog Box

Use the Tabs dialog box, shown in Figure 3.6, to set tabs at specific measurements, set tabs with preceding leaders, and clear one tab or all tabs. To display the Tabs dialog box, click the Paragraph group dialog box launcher. At the Paragraph dialog box, click the Tabs button in the lower left corner of the dialog box.

Quick Steps

Set Tabs at Tabs Dialog Box
1. Click Paragraph group dialog box launcher.
2. Click Tabs button.
3. Specify tab positions, alignments, and leader options.
4. Click OK.

To clear an individual tab at the Tabs dialog box, specify the tab position and then click the Clear button. To clear all tabs, click the Clear All button. A left, right, center, decimal, or bar tab can be set at the Tabs dialog box. (For an example of a bar tab, refer to Figure 3.7.) A left, right, center, or decimal tab can be set with preceding leaders.

To change the type of tab at the Tabs dialog box, display the dialog box and then click the desired tab in the *Alignment* section. Type the measurement for the tab in the *Tab stop position* text box and then click the Set button.

Chapter 3 | Customizing Paragraphs

Figure 3.6 Tabs Dialog Box

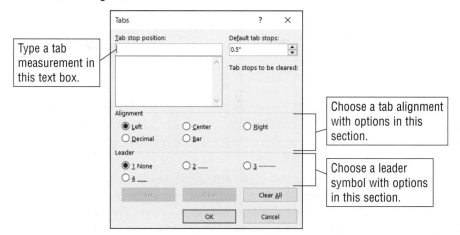

Type a tab measurement in this text box.

Choose a tab alignment with options in this section.

Choose a leader symbol with options in this section.

Project 4c Setting Left Tabs and a Bar Tab at the Tabs Dialog Box   Part 3 of 4

1. With **3-Tabs.docx** open, press Ctrl + End to move the insertion point to the end of the document.
2. Type the title TRAINING DATES bolded and centered (as shown in Figure 3.7), press the Enter key, return the paragraph alignment to left, and then turn off bold formatting.
3. Display the Tabs dialog box and then set left tabs and a bar tab by completing the following steps:
   a. Click the Paragraph group dialog box launcher.
   b. At the Paragraph dialog, click the Tabs button in the lower left corner of the dialog box.
   c. Make sure *Left* is selected in the *Alignment* section of the dialog box.
   d. Type 1.75 in the *Tab stop position* text box.
   e. Click the Set button.
   f. Type 4 in the *Tab stop position* text box and then click the Set button.
   g. Type 3.25 in the *Tab stop position* text box, click *Bar* in the *Alignment* section, and then click the Set button.
   h. Click OK to close the Tabs dialog box.

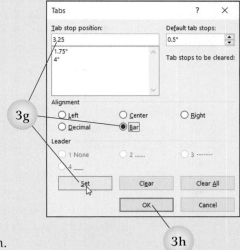

4. Type the text in columns, as shown in Figure 3.7. Press the Tab key before typing each column entry and press Shift + Enter to end each line. After typing *February 26*, press the Enter key.
5. Clear tabs below the columns from the current paragraph by completing the following steps:
   a. Click the Paragraph group dialog box launcher.
   b. At the Paragraph dialog box, click the Tabs button.
   c. At the Tabs dialog box, click the Clear All button.
   d. Click OK.
6. Press the Enter key.
7. Remove the 8 points of spacing after the last entry in the text by completing the following steps:
   a. Position the insertion point anywhere in the *January 24* entry.
   b. Click the Line and Paragraph Spacing button in the Paragraph group on the Home tab.
   c. Click the *Remove Space After Paragraph* option.
8. Save **3-Tabs.docx**.

Check Your Work

Figure 3.7 Project 4c

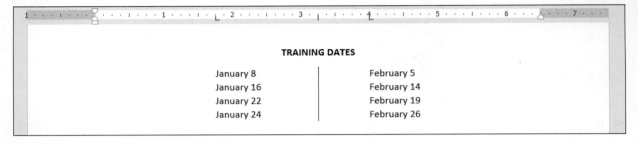

TRAINING DATES

January 8	February 5
January 16	February 14
January 22	February 19
January 24	February 26

Four types of tabs (left, right, center, and decimal) can be set with leaders. Leaders are useful in a table of contents or other material where the reader's eyes should be directed across the page. Figure 3.8 shows an example of leaders. Leaders can be periods (.), hyphens (-), or underlines (_). To add leaders to a tab, click the type of leader in the *Leader* section of the Tabs dialog box.

Project 4d   Setting a Left Tab and a Right Tab with Period Leaders

Part 4 of 4

1. With **3-Tabs.docx** open, press Ctrl + End to move the insertion point to the end of the document.
2. Type the title TABLE OF CONTENTS bolded and centered, as shown in Figure 3.8.
3. Press the Enter key and then return the paragraph alignment to left and turn off bold formatting.
4. Set a left tab and then a right tab with period leaders by completing the following steps:
   a. Click the Paragraph group dialog box launcher.
   b. Click the Tabs button in the lower left corner of the Paragraph dialog box.
   c. At the Tabs dialog box, make sure *Left* is selected in the *Alignment* section of the dialog box.
   d. With the insertion point positioned in the *Tab stop position* text box, type 1 and then click the Set button.
   e. Type 5.5 in the *Tab stop position* text box.
   f. Click *Right* in the *Alignment* section of the dialog box.
   g. Click *2 ......* in the *Leader* section of the dialog box and then click the Set button.
   h. Click OK to close the dialog box.
5. Type the text in columns, as shown in Figure 3.8. Press the Tab key before typing each column entry and press Shift + Enter to end each line.
6. Save, print, and then close **3-Tabs.docx**.

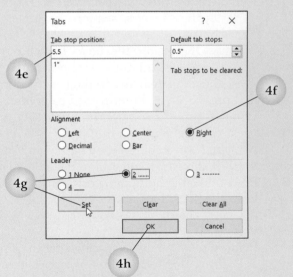

Check Your Work

Figure 3.8 Project 4d

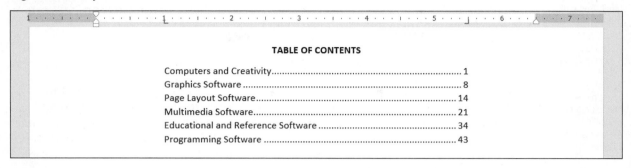

Project 5 | **Move and Copy Text in a Document on Online Shopping Tips** | **2 Parts**

You will open a document containing information on online shopping safety tips and then cut, copy, and paste text in the document.

Preview Finished Project

Cutting, Copying, and Pasting Text

Tutorial

Cutting, Copying, and Pasting Text

When editing a document, specific text may need to be deleted, moved to a different location in the document, or copied to various locations in the document. These activites can be completed using buttons in the Clipboard group on the Home tab.

Deleting Selected Text

Hint The Clipboard content is deleted when the computer is turned off. Text you want to save permanently should be saved as a separate document.

Word offers several different methods for deleting text from a document. To delete a single character, use either the Delete key or the Backspace key. To delete more than a single character, select the text and then press the Delete key on the keyboard or click the Cut button in the Clipboard group. If the Delete key is used to delete selected text, the text is deleted permanently. (Deleted text can be restored with the Undo button on the Quick Access Toolbar.)

Using the Cut button in the Clipboard group will remove the selected text from the document and insert it in the Clipboard, which is a temporary area of memory. The Clipboard holds text while it is being moved or copied to a new location in the document or to a different document.

Cutting and Pasting Text

 Cut

 Paste

Quick Steps

Move Selected Text
1. Select text.
2. Click Cut button.
3. Position insertion point.
4. Click Paste button.

To move text to a different location in the document, select the text, click the Cut button in the Clipboard group, position the insertion point at the location the text is to be inserted, and then click the Paste button in the Clipboard group.

Selected text can also be moved using the shortcut menu. To do this, select the text and then position the insertion point inside the selected text until it turns into an arrow pointer. Click the right mouse button and then click *Cut* at the shortcut menu. Position the insertion point where the text is to be inserted, click the right mouse button, and then click *Paste* at the shortcut menu. Keyboard shortcuts are also available for cutting and pasting text. Use Ctrl + X to cut text and Ctrl + V to paste text.

Quick Steps

Move Text with the Mouse
1. Select text.
2. Position mouse pointer in selected text.
3. Click and hold down left mouse button and drag to new location.
4. Release left mouse button.

OR

1. Select text.
2. Press Ctrl + X.
3. Move to new location.
4. Click Ctrl + V.

When selected text is cut from a document and inserted in the Clipboard, it stays in the Clipboard until other text is inserted there. For this reason, text can be pasted from the Clipboard more than once.

Moving Text by Dragging with the Mouse

The mouse can be used to move text. To do this, select text to be moved and then position the I-beam pointer inside the selected text until it turns into an arrow pointer. Click and hold down the left mouse button, drag the arrow pointer (which displays with a gray box attached) to the location the selected text is to be inserted, and then release the button. If the selected text is inserted in the wrong location, click the Undo button immediately.

Project 5a   Moving and Dragging Selected Text   Part 1 of 2

1. Open **ShoppingTips.docx** and then save it with the name **3-ShoppingTips**.
2. Move a paragraph by completing the following steps:
   a. Select the paragraph that begins with *Only buy at secure sites,* including the blank line below the paragraph.
   b. Click the Cut button in the Clipboard group on the Home tab.
   c. Position the insertion point at the beginning of the paragraph that begins with *Look for sites that follow.*
   d. Click the Paste button in the Clipboard group. (If the first and second paragraphs are not separated by a blank line, press the Enter key.)

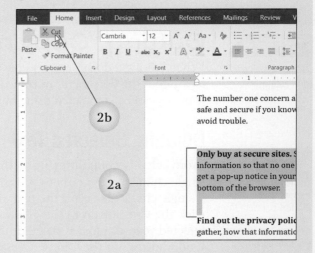

3. Following steps similar to those in Step 2, move the paragraph that begins with *Never provide your social* before the paragraph that begins *Look for sites that follow privacy* and after the paragraph that begins *Only buy at secure.*
4. Use the mouse to select the paragraph that begins with *Keep current with the latest Internet,* including one blank line below the paragraph.
5. Move the I-beam pointer inside the selected text until it displays as an arrow pointer.
6. Click and hold down the left mouse button, drag the arrow pointer (which displays with a small gray box attached) so that the insertion point (which displays as a black vertical bar) is positioned at the beginning of the paragraph that begins with *Never provide your social,* and then release the mouse button.

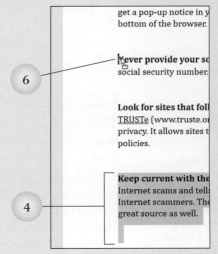

7. Deselect the text.
8. Save **3-ShoppingTips.docx.**

Check Your Work

Using the Paste Options Button

When selected text is pasted, the Paste Options button displays in the lower right corner of the text. Click this button (or press the Ctrl key on the keyboard) and the *Paste Options* gallery displays, as shown in Figure 3.9. Use buttons in this gallery to specify how the text is pasted in the document. Hover the mouse pointer over a button in the gallery and the live preview displays the text in the document as it will appear when pasted.

By default, pasted text retains the formatting of the selected text. This can be changed to match the formatting of the pasted text with the formatting of where the text is pasted or to paste only the text without retaining formatting. To determine the function of any button in the *Paste Options* gallery, hover the mouse pointer over the button and a ScreenTip displays with an explanation of the function as well as the keyboard shortcut. For example, hover the mouse pointer over the first button from the left in the *Paste Options* gallery and the ScreenTip displays with *Keep Source Formatting (K)*. Click this button or press K on the keyboard and the pasted text keeps its original formatting.

Figure 3.9 Paste Options Button Drop-Down List

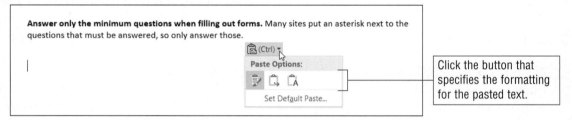

Click the button that specifies the formatting for the pasted text.

Project 5b Using the Paste Options Button

Part 2 of 2

1. With **3-ShoppingTips.docx** open, open **Tip.docx**.
2. Select the paragraph of text in the document, including the blank line below the paragraph, and then click the Copy button in the Clipboard group.
3. Close **Tip.docx**.
4. Press Ctrl + End to move the insertion point to the end of **3-ShoppingTips.docx**.
5. Click the Paste button in the Clipboard group.
6. Click the Paste Options button that displays at the end of the paragraph and then click the second button in the *Paste Options* gallery (Merge Formatting button). (This changes the font so it matches the font of the other paragraphs in the document.)
7. Save, print, and then close **3-ShoppingTips.docx**.

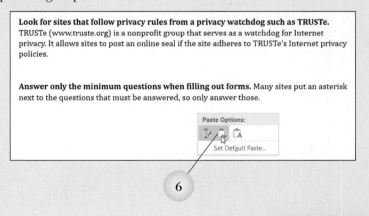

Check Your Work

You will copy and paste text in a document announcing a staff meeting for the Technical Support Team.

Preview Finished Project

Copying and Pasting Text

 Copy

Quick Steps
Copy Selected Text
1. Select text.
2. Click Copy button.
3. Position insertion point.
4. Click Paste button.

Copying selected text can be useful in documents that contain repeated information. Use copy and paste to insert duplicate portions of text in a document instead of retyping them. Copy selected text to a different location using the Copy and Paste buttons in the Clipboard group on the Home tab, the mouse, or the keyboard shortcuts, Ctrl + C and Ctrl + V.

To use the mouse to copy text, select the text and then position the I-beam pointer inside the selected text until it becomes an arrow pointer. Click and hold down the left mouse button and also press and hold down the Ctrl key. Drag the arrow pointer (which displays with a small gray box and a box containing a plus [+] symbol) and a black vertical bar moves with the pointer. Position the black bar in the desired location, release the mouse button, and then release the Ctrl key.

Project 6 Copying Text   Part 1 of 1

1. Open **StaffMtg.docx** and then save it with the name **3-StaffMtg**.
2. Copy the text in the document to the end of the document by completing the following steps:
   a. Select all of the text in the document and include one blank line below the text. ***Hint: Click the Show/Hide ¶ button to turn on the display of nonprinting characters. When you select the text, select one of the paragraph markers below the text***.
   b. Click the Copy button in the Clipboard group.
   c. Move the insertion point to the end of the document.
   d. Click the Paste button in the Clipboard group.
3. Paste the text again at the end of the document. To do this, position the insertion point at the end of the document and then click the Paste button in the Clipboard group. (This inserts a copy of the text from the Clipboard.)
4. Select all the text in the document using the mouse and include one blank line below the text. (Consider turning on the display of nonprinting characters.)
5. Move the I-beam pointer inside the selected text until it becomes an arrow pointer.
6. Click and hold down the Ctrl key and then the left mouse button. Drag the arrow pointer (which displays with a box with a plus symbol inside) so the vertical black bar is positioned at the end of the document, release the mouse button, and then release the Ctrl key.
7. Deselect the text.
8. Make sure all the text fits on one page. If not, consider deleting any extra blank lines.
9. Save, print, and then close **3-StaffMtg.docx**.

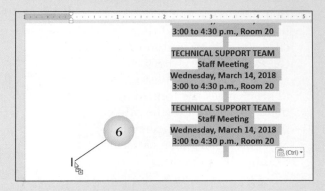

Check Your Work

You will use the Clipboard task pane to copy and paste paragraphs to and from separate documents to create a contract negotiations document.

Preview Finished Project

Tutorial

Using the
Clipboard Task
Pane

Using the Clipboard Task Pane

Use the Clipboard task pane to collect and paste multiple items. Up to 24 different items can be collected and then pasted in various locations. To display the Clipboard task pane, click the Clipboard group task pane launcher in the lower right corner of the Clipboard group. The Clipboard task pane displays at the left side of the screen in a manner similar to what is shown in Figure 3.10.

Select the text or object to be copied and then click the Copy button in the Clipboard group. Continue selecting text or items and clicking the Copy button. To insert an item from the Clipboard task pane into the document, position the insertion point in the desired location and then click the option in the Clipboard task pane representing the item. Click the Paste All button to paste all of the items in the Clipboard task pane into the document. If the copied item is text, the first 50 characters display in the list box on the Clipboard task pane. When all the items are inserted, click the Clear All button to remove any remaining items.

Quick Steps

Use the Clipboard
1. Click Clipboard group task pane launcher.
2. Select and copy text.
3. Position insertion point.
4. Click option in Clipboard task pane.

Hint You can copy items to the Clipboard from various Microsoft Office applications and then paste them into any Office file.

Figure 3.10 Clipboard Task Pane

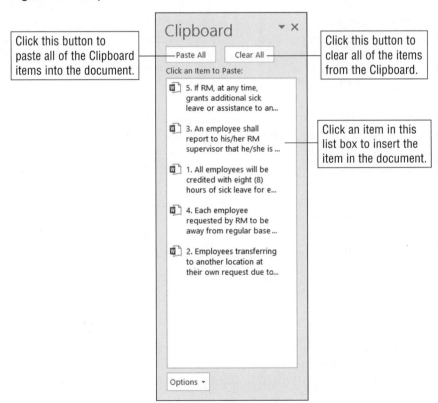

Click this button to paste all of the Clipboard items into the document.

Click this button to clear all of the items from the Clipboard.

Click an item in this list box to insert the item in the document.

1. Open **ContractItems.docx**.
2. Display the Clipboard task pane by clicking the Clipboard group task pane launcher in the bottom right corner of the Clipboard group. (If the Clipboard task pane list box contains any text, click the Clear All button in the upper right corner of the Clipboard task pane.)

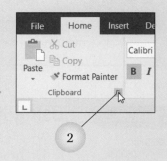

3. Select paragraph 1 in the document (the *1.* is not selected) and then click the Copy button in the Clipboard group.
4. Select paragraph 3 in the document (the *3.* is not selected) and then click the Copy button in the Clipboard group.
5. Close **ContractItems.docx**.
6. Paste the paragraphs by completing the following steps:
   a. Press Ctrl + N to display a new blank document. (If the Clipboard task pane does not display, click the Clipboard group task pane launcher.)
   b. Type CONTRACT NEGOTIATION ITEMS centered and bolded.
   c. Press the Enter key, turn off bold formatting, and return the paragraph alignment to left alignment.
   d. Click the Paste All button in the Clipboard task pane to paste both paragraphs in the document.
   e. Click the Clear All button in the Clipboard task pane.

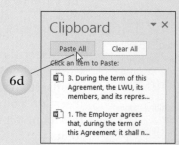

7. Open **UnionContract.docx**.
8. Select and then copy each of the following paragraphs:
   a. Paragraph 2 in the *Transfers and Moving Expenses* section.
   b. Paragraph 4 in the *Transfers and Moving Expenses* section.
   c. Paragraph 1 in the *Sick Leave* section.
   d. Paragraph 3 in the *Sick Leave* section.
   e. Paragraph 5 in the *Sick Leave* section.
9. Close **UnionContract.docx**.
10. Make sure the insertion point is positioned at the end of the document, on a new line, and then paste the paragraphs by completing the following steps:
    a. Click the button in the Clipboard task pane representing paragraph 2. (When the paragraph is inserted in the document, the paragraph number changes to *3.*)
    b. Click the button in the Clipboard task pane representing paragraph 4.
    c. Click the button in the Clipboard task pane representing paragraph 3.
    d. Click the button in the Clipboard task pane representing paragraph 5.

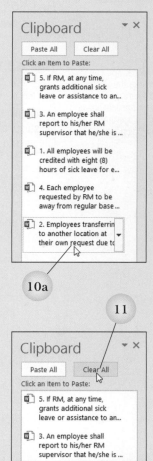

11. Click the Clear All button in the upper right corner of the Clipboard task pane.
12. Close the Clipboard task pane.
13. Save the document and name it **3-NegotiateItems**.
14. Print and then close **3-NegotiateItems.docx**.

Check Your Work

Chapter Summary

- Number paragraphs using the Numbering button in the Paragraph group on the Home tab and insert bullets before paragraphs using the Bullets button.

- Remove all paragraph formatting from a paragraph by pressing the keyboard shortcut Ctrl + Q. Remove all character and paragraph formatting by clicking the Clear All Formatting button in the Font group.

- The AutoCorrect Options button displays when the AutoFormat feature inserts numbers. Click this button to display options for undoing and/or stopping automatic numbering.

- A bulleted list with a hanging indent is automatically created when a paragraph begins with *, >, or -. The type of bullet inserted depends on the type of character entered.

- Automatic numbering and bulleting can be turned off at the AutoCorrect dialog box with the AutoFormat As You Type tab selected.

- A paragraph created in Word contains an invisible frame and a border can be added to this frame. Click the Borders button arrow to display a drop-down list of border options.

- Use options at the Borders and Shading dialog box with the Borders tab selected to add a customized border to a paragraph or selected paragraphs.

- Apply shading to text by clicking the Shading button arrow and then clicking a color at the drop-down gallery. Use options at the Borders and Shading dialog box with the Shading tab selected to add shading or a pattern to a paragraph or selected paragraphs.

- Use the Sort button in the Paragraph group on the Home tab to sort text in paragraphs alphabetically by the first character of each paragraph, which can be a number, symbol, or letter.

- By default, tabs are set every 0.5 inch. Tab settings can be changed on the horizontal ruler or at the Tabs dialog box.

- Use the Alignment button above the vertical ruler to select a left, right, center, decimal, or bar tab. When a tab is set on the horizontal ruler, any default tabs to the left are automatically deleted.

- After a tab has been set on the horizontal ruler, it can be moved or deleted using the mouse pointer.

- At the Tabs dialog box, any of the five types of tabs can be set at a specific measurement. Tabs also can be set with preceding leaders, which can be periods, hyphens, or underlines. Individual tabs or all tabs can be cleared at the Tabs dialog box.

- Cut, copy, and paste text using buttons in the Clipboard group on the Home tab, with options at the shortcut menu, or with keyboard shortcuts.

- When selected text is pasted, the Paste Options button displays in the lower right corner of the text. Click the button and the *Paste Options* gallery displays with buttons for specifying how text is pasted in the document.

- With the Clipboard task pane, up to 24 items can be copied and then pasted in various locations in a document or other document.

- Display the Clipboard task pane by clicking the Clipboard group task pane launcher in the Clipboard group on the Home tab.

Commands Review

FEATURE	RIBBON TAB, GROUP	BUTTON, OPTION	KEYBOARD SHORTCUT
borders	Home, Paragraph		
Borders and Shading dialog box	Home, Paragraph	, *Borders and Shading*	
bullets	Home, Paragraph		
clear all formatting	Home, Font		
clear paragraph formatting			Ctrl + Q
Clipboard task pane	Home, Clipboard		
copy text	Home, Clipboard		Ctrl + C
cut text	Home, Clipboard		Ctrl + X
New Line command			Shift + Enter
numbering	Home, Paragraph		
Paragraph dialog box	Home, Paragraph		
paste text	Home, Clipboard		Ctrl + V
shading	Home, Paragraph		
Sort Text dialog box	Home, Paragraph		
Tabs dialog box	Home, Paragraph	, Tabs	

Workbook

Chapter study tools and assessment activities are available in the *Workbook* ebook. These resources are designed to help you further develop and demonstrate mastery of the skills learned in this chapter.

Microsoft®

Word

Formatting Pages

Performance Objectives

Upon successful completion of Chapter 4, you will be able to:

1 Change document views

2 Navigate in a document with the Navigation pane

3 Change margins, page orientation, and paper size

4 Format pages at the Page Setup dialog box

5 Insert a page break, blank page, and cover page

6 Insert page numbering

7 Insert and edit predesigned headers and footers

8 Insert a watermark, page background color, and page border

9 Find and replace text and formatting

Precheck

Check your current skills to help focus your study.

A document generally displays in Print Layout view. This default view can be changed with buttons in the view area on the Status bar or with options on the View tab. The Navigation pane provides one method for navigating in a document. A Word document, by default, contains 1-inch top, bottom, left, and right margins. Change these default margins with the Margins button in the Page Setup group on the Layout tab or with options at the Page Setup dialog box. A variety of features can be inserted in a Word document, including a page break, blank page, and cover page, as well as page numbers, headers, footers, a watermark, page color, and page border. Use options at the Find and Replace dialog box to search for specific text or formatting and replace it with other text or formatting.

Data Files

Before beginning chapter work, copy the WL1C4 folder to your storage medium and then make WL1C4 the active folder.

SNAP

If you are a SNAP user, launch the Precheck and Tutorials from your Assignments page.

Project 1   **Change Views and Navigate in a Report on Navigating**   2 Parts
and Searching the Web

You will open a document containing information on navigating and searching the web, change document views, hide and show white space at the tops and bottoms of pages, and navigate in the document using the Navigation pane.

Tutorial

Changing
Document Views

Changing Document Views

By default, a Word document displays in Print Layout view. This view displays the document on the screen as it will appear when printed. Other views are available, such as Draft and Read Mode. Change views with buttons in the view area on the Status bar (see Figure 4.1) or with options on the View tab.

Displaying a Document in Draft View

Change to Draft view and the document displays in a format for efficient editing and formatting. At this view, margins and other features, such as headers and footers, do not display on the screen. Change to Draft view by clicking the View tab and then clicking the Draft button in the Views group.

 Draft

Displaying a Document in Read Mode View

 Read Mode

Read Mode

Read Mode view displays a document in a format for easy viewing and reading. Change to Read Mode view by clicking the Read Mode button in the view area on the Status bar or by clicking the View tab and then clicking the Read Mode button in the Views group. Navigate in Read Mode view using the keys on the keyboard, as shown in Table 4.1. Other methods for navigating in Read Mode view include clicking at the right side of the screen or clicking the Next button (right-pointing arrow in a circle) to display the next pages and by clicking at the left side of the screen or clicking the Previous button (left-pointing arrow in a circle) to display the previous pages.

The File, Tools, and View tabs display in the upper left corner of the screen in Read Mode view. Click the File tab to display the backstage area. Click the Tools tab and a drop-down list displays options for finding specific text in the document and searching for information on the Internet using the Smart Lookup feature. Click the View tab and options display for customizing what appears in Read Mode view. Use View tab options to display the Navigation pane to navigate to specific locations in the document, show comments inserted in the document, change column widths or page layout, and change the page colors in Read Mode view.

Figure 4.1 View Buttons and Zoom Slider Bar

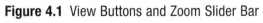
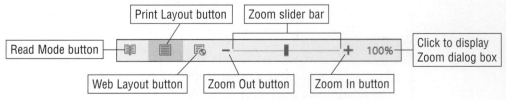

Table 4.1 Keyboard Commands in Read Mode View

Press this key	To complete this action
Page Down key, Right Arrow key, or spacebar	display next two pages
Page Up key, Left Arrow key, or Backspace key	display previous two pages
Home	display first page in document
End	display last page in document
Esc	return to previous view

If a document contains an object such as a table, SmartArt graphic, image, or shape, zoom in on the object in Read Mode view by double-clicking it. The display size of the object increases and a button containing a magnifying glass with a plus symbol inside ( ) displays just outside the upper right corner of the object. Click this button to zoom in even more on the object. Click the button again and the object returns to the original zoom size. Click outside the object to return it to its original display size. To close Read Mode view and return to the previous view, press the Esc key or click the View tab and then click *Edit Document* at the drop-down list.

Tutorial

Changing the Display Percentage

 Zoom

 Zoom Out

 Zoom In

 100%

Hint Click the 100% at the right side of the Zoom slider bar to display the Zoom dialog box.

 Ribbon Display Options

Changing the Display Percentage

By default, a document displays at 100%. This display percentage can be changed with the Zoom slider bar at the right side of the Status bar (see Figure 4.1) and with options in the Zoom group on the View tab. To change the display percentage with the Zoom slider bar, drag the button on the bar to increase or decrease the percentage. Click the Zoom Out button at the left side of the slider bar to decrease the display percentage or click the Zoom In button to increase the display percentage.

Click the Zoom button in the Zoom group on the View tab to display the Zoom dialog box that contains options for changing the display percentage. If the display percentage has been changed, return to the default by clicking the 100% button in the Zoom group on the View tab. Click the One Page button to display the entire page on the screen and click the Multiple Pages button to display multiple pages on the screen. Click the Page Width button and the document expands across the screen.

Changing Ribbon Display Options

Use the Ribbon Display Options button in the upper right corner of the screen to view more of a document. Click the Ribbon Display Options button and a drop-down list displays with three options: *Auto-hide Ribbon*, *Show Tabs*, and *Show Tabs and Commands*. The default is Show Tabs and Commands, which displays the Quick Access Toolbar, ribbon, and Status bar on the screen. Click the first option, *Auto-hide Ribbon*, and the Quick Access Toolbar, ribbon, and Status bar are hidden, allowing more of the document to be visible on the screen. To temporarily redisplay these features, click at the top of the screen. Turn these features back on by clicking the Ribbon Display Options button and then clicking the *Show Tabs and Commands* option. Click the *Show Tabs* option at the drop-down list and the tabs display on the ribbon while the buttons and commands remain hidden.

Hiding and Showing White Space

In Print Layout view, a page displays as it will appear when printed, including the white spaces at the top and the bottom of the page representing the document's margins. To save space on the screen in Print Layout view, the white space can be removed by positioning the mouse pointer at the top edge or bottom edge of a page or between pages until the pointer displays as the Hide White Space icon and then double-clicking the left mouse button. To redisplay the white space, position the mouse pointer on the thin gray line separating pages until the pointer turns into the Show White Space icon and then double-click the left mouse button.

Hiding and Showing White Space

⊢+⊣ Hide White Space

⊢+⊣ Show White Space

Project 1a   Changing Views and Hiding/Showing White Space   Part 1 of 2

1. Open **WebReport.docx** and then save it with the name **4-WebReport**.
2. Click the View tab and then click the Draft button in the Views group.
3. Click the Zoom Out button (to the left of the Zoom slider bar) three times. (This changes the display percentage and *70%* displays at the right side of the Zoom In button.)

4. Using the mouse, drag the Zoom slider bar button to the middle until *100%* displays at the right side of the Zoom In button.
5. Click the Print Layout button in the view area on the Status bar.
6. Click the Zoom button in the Zoom group on the View tab.
7. At the Zoom dialog box, click the *75%* option and then click OK.

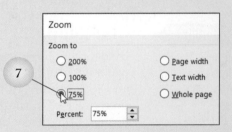

8. Return the display percentage to the default by clicking the 100% button in the Zoom group.
9. Click the Read Mode button in the view area on the Status bar.
10. Increase the display size of the table at the right side of the screen by double-clicking the table. (If the table is not visible, click the Next button at the right side of the screen to view the next page.)
11. Click the button containing a magnifying glass with a plus symbol that displays outside the upper right corner of the table. (This increases the zoom.)

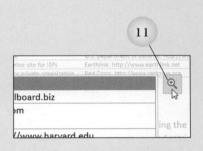

12. Click outside the table to return it to the original display size.
13. Practice navigating in Read Mode view using the actions shown in Table 4.1 (except the last action).
14. Press the Esc key to return to the Print Layout view.
15. Click the Ribbon Display Options button in the upper right corner of the screen and then click *Auto-hide Ribbon* at the drop-down list.

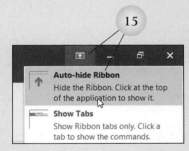

16. Press Ctrl + End to display the last page in the document and then press the Page Up key until the beginning of the document displays.
17. Click at the top of the screen to temporarily redisplay the Quick Access Toolbar, ribbon, and Status bar.
18. Click the Ribbon Display Options button and then click *Show Tabs* at the drop-down list.

19. Click the Ribbon Display Options button and then click *Show Tabs and Commands* at the drop-down list.
20. Press Ctrl + Home to move the insertion point to the beginning of the document.
21. Hide the white spaces at the tops and bottoms of pages by positioning the mouse pointer at the top edge of the page until the pointer turns into the Hide White Space icon and then double-clicking the left mouse button.
22. Scroll through the document and notice the display of pages.
23. Redisplay the white spaces at the tops and bottoms of pages by positioning the mouse pointer on any thin gray line separating pages until the pointer turns into the Show White Space icon and then double-clicking the left mouse button.
24. Save **4-WebReport.docx**.

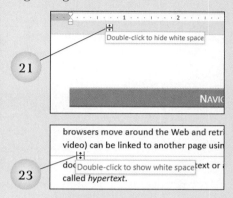

Tutorial

Navigating Using the Navigation Pane

Navigating Using the Navigation Pane

Among the features that Word provides for navigating in a document is the Navigation pane, shown in Figure 4.2. Click the *Navigation Pane* check box in the Show group on the View tab to insert a check mark and the Navigation pane displays at the left side of the screen and includes a search text box and a pane with three tabs. Click the Headings tab to display titles and headings with styles applied. Click a title or heading in the pane to move the insertion point to that title or heading. Click the Pages tab to display a thumbnail of each page. Click a thumbnail to move the insertion point to the specific page. Click the Results tab to browse the current search results in the document. Close the Navigation pane by clicking the *Navigation Pane* check box in the Show group on the View tab to remove the check mark or by clicking the Close button in the upper right corner of the pane.

Q̃uick Steps

Display Navigation Pane
1. Click View tab.
2. Click *Navigation Pane* check box.

Figure 4.2 Navigation Pane

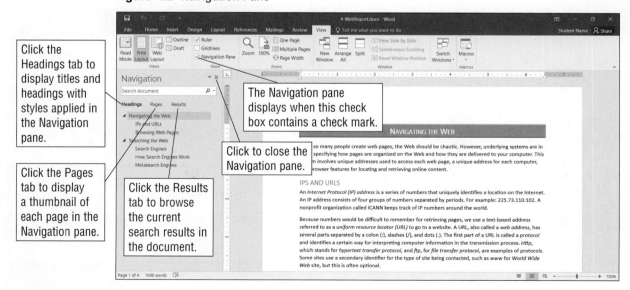

Click the Headings tab to display titles and headings with styles applied in the Navigation pane.

The Navigation pane displays when this check box contains a check mark.

Click to close the Navigation pane.

Click the Pages tab to display a thumbnail of each page in the Navigation pane.

Click the Results tab to browse the current search results in the document.

1. With **4-WebReport.docx** open, make sure the document displays in Print Layout view.
2. Display the Navigation pane by clicking the View tab and then clicking the *Navigation Pane* check box in the Show group to insert a check mark.
3. Click the *Navigating the Web* heading in the Navigation pane.

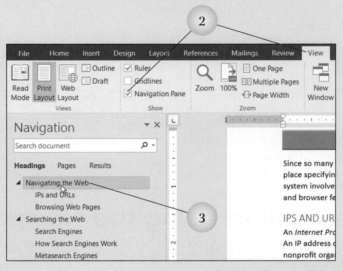

4. Click the *Searching the Web* heading in the Navigation pane.
5. Click the Pages tab in the Navigation pane to display the page thumbnails in the pane.
6. Click the page 4 thumbnail in the Navigation pane.
7. Scroll up the pane and then click the page 1 thumbnail.
8. Close the Navigation pane by clicking the Close button in the upper right corner of the pane.
9. Save and then close **4-WebReport.docx**.

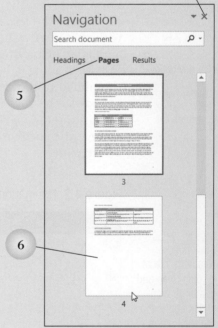

Project 2 **Format a Document on Online Etiquette Guidelines**   **2 Parts**

You will open a document containing information on guidelines for online etiquette and then change the margins, page orientation, and page size.

Preview Finished Project

Changing Page Setup

The Page Setup group on the Layout tab contains a number of options for changing pages in a document. Use options in the Page Setup group to perform such actions as changing margins, orientation, and page size and inserting page breaks. The Pages group on the Insert tab contains three buttons for inserting a cover page, blank page, and page break.

Tutorial

Changing Margins

 Margins

Changing Margins

Change page margins with options at the Margins button drop-down list, as shown in Figure 4.3. To display this list, click the Layout tab and then click the Margins button in the Page Setup group. To change the margins, click one of the preset margins in the drop-down list. Be aware that most printers require a minimum margin (between ¼ and ⅜ inch) because they cannot print to the edge of the page.

Tutorial

Changing Page Orientation

 Orientation

Changing Page Orientation

Click the Orientation button in the Page Setup group on the Layout tab and two options display: *Portrait* and *Landscape*. At the portrait orientation, which is the default, the page is 11 inches tall and 8.5 inches wide. At the landscape orientation, the page is 8.5 inches tall and 11 inches wide. Change the page orientation and the page margins automatically shift—the left and right margin measurements become the top and bottom margin measurements.

Tutorial

Changing Paper Size

 Size

Changing Paper Size

By default, Word uses a paper size of 8.5 inches wide and 11 inches tall. Change this default setting with options at the Size button drop-down list. Display this drop-down list by clicking the Size button in the Page Setup group on the Layout tab.

Quick Steps

Change Margins
1. Click Layout tab.
2. Click Margins button.
3. Click margin option.

Change Page Orientation
1. Click Layout tab.
2. Click Orientation button.
3. Click orientation option.

Change Paper Size
1. Click Layout tab.
2. Click Size button.
3. Click size option.

Figure 4.3 Margins Button Drop-Down List

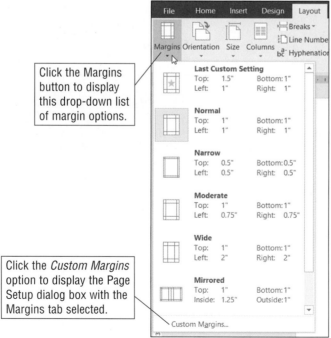

Click the Margins button to display this drop-down list of margin options.

Click the *Custom Margins* option to display the Page Setup dialog box with the Margins tab selected.

1. Open **Netiquette.docx** and then save it with the name **4-Netiquette**.
2. Click the Layout tab.
3. Click the Margins button in the Page Setup group and then click the *Narrow* option.
4. Click the Orientation button in the Page Setup group and then click *Landscape* at the drop-down list.

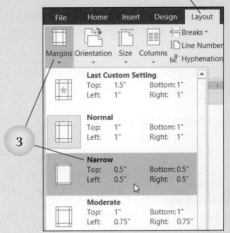

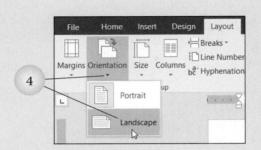

5. Scroll through the document and notice how the text displays on the page in landscape orientation.
6. Click the Orientation button in the Page Setup group and then click *Portrait* at the drop-down list. (This changes the orientation back to the default.)
7. Click the Size button in the Page Setup group and then click the *Executive* option (displays with *7.25″ × 10.5″* below *Executive*). If this option is not available, choose an option with a similar paper size.

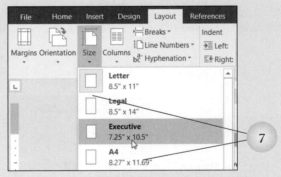

8. Scroll through the document and notice how the text displays on the page.
9. Click the Size button and then click *Legal* (displays with *8.5″ × 14″* below *Legal*).
10. Scroll through the document and notice how the text displays on the page.
11. Click the Size button and then click *Letter* (displays with *8.5″ × 11″* below *Letter*). (This returns the size back to the default.)
12. Save **4-Netiquette.docx**.

Check Your Work

Quick Steps

**Change Margins
at the Page Setup
Dialog Box**
1. Click Layout tab.
2. Click Page Setup
   group dialog box
   launcher.
3. Specify margins.
4. Click OK.

**Change Paper Size
at the Page Setup
Dialog Box**
1. Click Layout tab.
2. Click Size button.
3. Click *More Paper
   Sizes* at drop-down
   list.
4. Specify size.
5. Click OK.

Changing Margins at the Page Setup Dialog Box

The Margins button in the Page Setup group provides a number of preset margins. If these margins do not provide the desired margins, set specific margins at the Page Setup dialog box with the Margins tab selected, as shown in Figure 4.4. Display this dialog box by clicking the Page Setup group dialog box launcher or by clicking the Margins button and then clicking *Custom Margins* at the bottom of the drop-down list.

To change one of the margins, select the current measurement in the *Top*, *Bottom*, *Left*, or *Right* measurement box and then type the new measurement, or click the measurement box up arrow to increase the measurement or the measurement box down arrow to decrease the measurement. As the margin measurements change at the Page Setup dialog box, the sample page in the *Preview* section shows the effects of the changes.

Changing Paper Size at the Page Setup Dialog Box

The Size button drop-down list contains a number of preset paper sizes. If these sizes do not provide the desired paper size, specify a paper size at the Page Setup dialog box with the Paper tab selected. Display this dialog box by clicking the Size button in the Page Setup group and then clicking *More Paper Sizes* at the bottom of the drop-down list.

Figure 4.4 Page Setup Dialog Box with Margins Tab Selected

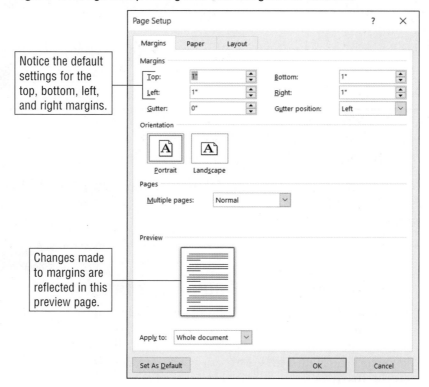

Notice the default settings for the top, bottom, left, and right margins.

Changes made to margins are reflected in this preview page.

1. With **4-Netiquette.docx** open, make sure the Layout tab is selected.
2. Click the Page Setup group dialog box launcher.
3. At the Page Setup dialog box with the
   Margins tab selected, click the *Top*
   measurement box up arrow until *0.7"*
   displays.
4. Click the *Bottom* measurement box up
   arrow until *0.7"* displays.
5. Select the current measurement in the
   Left measurement box and then type
   0.75.
6. Select the current measurement in the
   Right measurement box and then type 0.75.
7. Click OK to close the dialog box.
8. Click the Size button in the Page Setup group and then click
   More Paper Sizes at the drop-down list.
9. At the Page Setup dialog box with the Paper tab selected, click
   the *Paper size* option box arrow and then click *Legal* at the
   drop-down list.
10. Click OK to close the dialog box.
11. Scroll through the document and notice how the text displays
    on the page.
12. Click the Size button in the Page Setup group and then click
    Letter at the drop-down list.
13. Save, print, and then close **4-Netiquette.docx**.

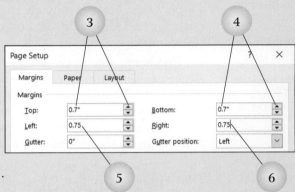

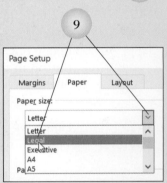

Check Your Work

Project 3 Customize a Report on Computer   3 Parts
Input and Output Devices

You will open a document containing information on computer input and output
devices and then insert page breaks, a blank page, a cover page, and page
numbering.

Preview Finished Project

Tutorial

Inserting and
Removing a Page
Break

 Page Break

Inserting and Removing a Page Break

With the default top and bottom margins set at 1 inch, approximately 9 inches of
text prints on the page. At approximately the 10-inch mark, Word automatically
inserts a page break. Insert a page break manually in a document with the
keyboard shortcut Ctrl + Enter or with the Page Break button in the Pages group
on the Insert tab.

A page break inserted by Word is considered a soft page break and a page
break inserted manually is considered a hard page break. Soft page breaks
automatically adjust if text is added to or deleted from a document. Hard page
breaks do not adjust and are therefore less flexible than soft page breaks.

Quick Steps

Insert a Page Break
1. Click Insert tab.
2. Click Page Break button.
OR
Press Ctrl + Enter.

If text is added to or deleted from a document containing a hard page break, check the break to determine whether it is still in a desirable location. Display a hard page break, along with other nonprinting characters, by clicking the Show/Hide ¶ button in the Paragraph group on the Home tab. A hard page break displays as a row of dots with the words *Page Break* in the center. To delete a hard page break, position the insertion point at the beginning of the page break and then press the Delete key. If the display of nonprinting characters is turned off, delete a hard page break by positioning the insertion point immediately below the page break and then pressing the Backspace key.

Project 3a   Inserting Page Breaks   Parts 1 of 3

1. Open **CompDevices.docx** and then save it with the name **4-CompDevices**.
2. Change the top margin by completing the following steps:
   a. Click the Layout tab.
   b. Click the Page Setup group dialog box launcher.
   c. At the Page Setup dialog box, click the Margins tab and then type 1.5 in the *Top* measurement box.
   d. Click OK to close the dialog box.
3. Insert a page break at the beginning of the heading *Mouse* by completing the following steps:
   a. Position the insertion point at the beginning of the heading *Mouse* (at the bottom of page 1).
   b. Click the Insert tab and then click the Page Break button in the Pages group.
4. Move the insertion point to the beginning of the title *COMPUTER OUTPUT DEVICES* (on the second page) and then insert a page break by pressing Ctrl + Enter.
5. Move the insertion point to the beginning of the heading *Printer* and then press Ctrl + Enter to insert a page break.
6. Delete a page break by completing the following steps:
   a. Click the Home tab.
   b. Click the Show/Hide ¶ button in the Paragraph group.
   c. Scroll up to display the bottom of the third page, position the insertion point at the beginning of the page break (displays with the words *Page Break*), and then press the Delete key.
   d. Press the Delete key again to remove the blank line.
   e. Turn off the display of nonprinting characters by clicking the Show/Hide ¶ button in the Paragraph group on the Home tab.
7. Save **4-CompDevices.docx**.

Check Your Work

Inserting and Removing a Blank Page

Click the Blank Page button in the Pages group on the Insert tab to insert a blank page at the position of the insertion point. This might be useful in a document where a blank page is needed for an illustration, graphic, or figure. When a blank page is inserted, Word inserts a page break and then inserts another page break to create the blank page. To remove a blank page, turn on the display of nonprinting characters and then delete the page breaks.

Inserting and Removing a Blank Page

☐ Blank Page

Inserting and Removing a Cover Page

Consider inserting a cover page to improve the visual appeal of a document or to prepare it for distribution to others. Use the Cover Page button in the Pages group on the Insert tab to insert a predesigned cover page and then type personalized text in the placeholders on the page. Click the Cover Page button and a drop-down list displays with visual representations of the cover pages. Scroll through the list and then click a predesigned cover page option.

A predesigned cover page contains location placeholders, in which specific text is entered. For example, a cover page might contain the *[Document title]* placeholder. Click the placeholder to select it and then type personalized text. Delete a placeholder by clicking the placeholder to select it, clicking the placeholder tab, and then pressing the Delete key. Remove a cover page by clicking the Cover Page button and then clicking *Remove Current Cover Page* at the drop-down list.

Inserting and Removing a Cover Page

▦ Cover Page

Quick Steps

Insert Blank Page
1. Click Insert tab.
2. Click Blank Page button.

Insert Cover Page
1. Click Insert tab.
2. Click Cover Page button.
3. Click cover page at drop-down list.

💡**Hint** Adding a cover page gives a document a polished and professional look.

Project 3b **Inserting a Blank Page and a Cover Page**   Part 2 of 3

1. With **4-CompDevices.docx** open, create a blank page by completing the following steps:
   a. Move the insertion point to the beginning of the heading *Touchpad and Touchscreen* on the second page.
   b. Click the Insert tab.
   c. Click the Blank Page button in the Pages group.
2. Insert a cover page by completing the following steps:
   a. Press Ctrl + Home to move the insertion point to the beginning of the document.
   b. Click the Cover Page button in the Pages group.
   c. Scroll down the drop-down list and then click the *Motion* cover page.

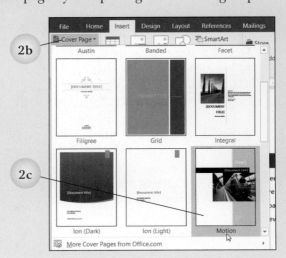

d. Click the *[Document title]* placeholder and then type Computer Devices.

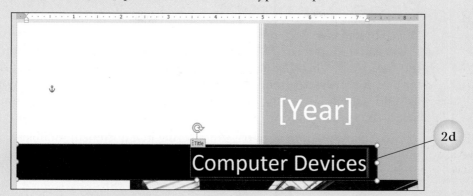

e. Click the *[Year]* placeholder. Click the placeholder down arrow and then click the Today button at the bottom of the drop-down calendar.

f. Click the *[Company name]* placeholder and then type Drake Computing. (If a name displays in the placeholder, select the name and then type Drake Computing.)

g. Select the name above the company name and then type your first and last names. If, instead of a name, the *[Author name]* placeholder displays above the company name, click the placeholder and then type your first and last names.

3. Remove the blank page you inserted in Step 1 by completing the following steps:

a. Move the insertion point immediately right of the period that ends the last sentence in the paragraph of text in the *Trackball* section the bottom of page 3).

b. Press the Delete key on the keyboard approximately six times until the heading *Touchpad and Touchscreen* displays on page 3.

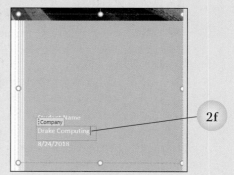

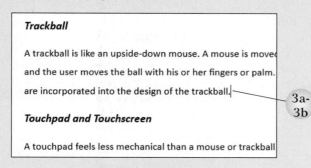

4. Save **4-CompDevices.docx**.

Check Your Work

Tutorial

Inserting and Removing Page Numbers

Inserting and Removing Page Numbers

Page Number

Word, by default, does not print page numbers on pages. To insert page numbers in a document, use the Page Number button in the Header & Footer group on the Insert tab. Click the Page Number button and a drop-down list displays with options for specifying the location of the page number. Point to an option in this list and a drop-down list displays a number of predesigned page number formats. Scroll through the options in the drop-down list and then click an option.

Quick Steps

Insert Page Numbers
1. Click Insert tab.
2. Click Page Number button.
3. Click option at drop-down list.

To change the format of page numbering in a document, double-click the page number, select the page number text, and then apply the formatting. Remove page numbers from a document by clicking the Page Number button and then clicking *Remove Page Numbers* at the drop-down list. Many of the predesigned page number formats insert page numbers in a header or footer pane. As explained in the next section of this chapter, a header pane contains text, such as a page number, that prints at the top of each page and a footer pane contains text that prints at the bottom of each page. If a page number is inserted in a header or footer pane, close the pane by clicking the Close Header and Footer button on the Header & Footer Tools Design tab or by double-clicking in the document, outside the header or footer pane.

Project 3c Inserting Predesigned Page Numbers

Part 3 of 3

1. With **4-CompDevices.docx** open, insert page numbering by completing the following steps:
   a. Move the insertion point so it is positioned anywhere in the title *COMPUTER INPUT DEVICES*.
   b. Click the Insert tab.
   c. Click the Page Number button in the Header & Footer group and then point to *Top of Page*.
   d. Scroll through the drop-down list and then click the *Brackets 2* option.

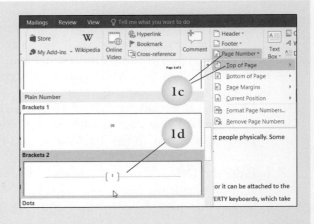

2. Click the Close Header and Footer button on the Header & Footer Tools Design tab.
3. Scroll through the document and notice the page numbering that displays at the top of each page except the cover page. (The cover page and text are divided by a page break. Word does not include the cover page when numbering pages.)
4. Remove the page numbering by clicking the Insert tab, clicking the Page Number button, and then clicking *Remove Page Numbers* at the drop-down list.
5. Click the Page Number button, point to *Bottom of Page*, scroll down the drop-down list, and then click the *Accent Bar 2* option.
6. Click the Close Header and Footer button on the Header & Footer Tools Design tab.
7. Save, print, and then close **4-CompDevices.docx**.

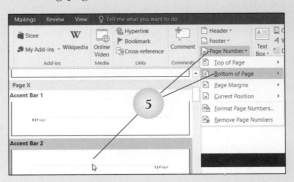

Check Your Work

Tutorial

Inserting and Removing a Predesigned Header and Footer

Inserting Predesigned Headers and Footers

Text that appears in the top margin of a page is called a *header* and text that appears in the bottom margin of a page is referred to as a *footer*. Headers and footers are common in manuscripts, textbooks, reports, and other publications.

 Header

Insert a predesigned header in a document by clicking the Insert tab and then clicking the Header button in the Header & Footer group. This displays the Header button drop-down list. At this list, click a predesigned header option and the header is inserted in the document. Headers and footers are visible in Print Layout view but not Draft view.

A predesigned header or footer may contain location placeholders for entering specific information. For example, a header might contain the *[Document title]* placeholder. Click the placeholder and all the placeholder text is selected. With the placeholder text selected, type the personalized text. Delete a placeholder by clicking the placeholder to select it, clicking the placeholder tab, and then pressing the Delete key.

To return to the document after inserting a header or footer, double-click in the document outside the header or footer pane or click the Close Header and Footer button on the Header & Footer Tools Design tab.

Quick Steps

Insert Predesigned Header or Footer
1. Click Insert tab.
2. Click Header button or Footer button.
3. Click option at drop-down list.
4. Type text in specific placeholders in header or footer.
5. Click Close Header and Footer button.

Project 4a **Inserting a Predesigned Header in a Document**   Part 1 of 3

1. Open **WritingProcess.docx** and then save it with the name **4-WritingProcess**.
2. Press Ctrl + End to move the insertion point to the end of the document.
3. Move the insertion point to the beginning of the heading *REFERENCES* and then insert a page break by clicking the Insert tab and then clicking the Page Break button in the Pages group.

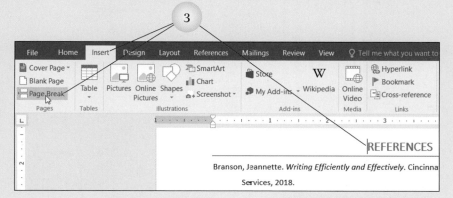

4. Press Ctrl + Home to move the insertion point to the beginning of the document and then insert a header by completing the following steps:
   a. If necessary, click the Insert tab.
   b. Click the Header button in the Header & Footer group.
   c. Scroll to the bottom of the drop-down list and then click the *Sideline* option.

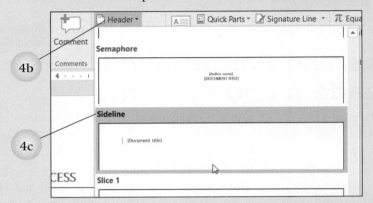

   d. Click the *[Document title]* placeholder and then type The Writing Process.
   e. Double-click in the document text. (This makes the document text active and dims the header.)

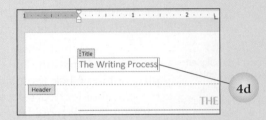

5. Scroll through the document to see how the header will print.
6. Save and then print **4-WritingProcess.docx**.

Check Your Work

 Footer

Insert a predesigned footer in the same manner as inserting a header. Click the Footer button in the Header & Footer group on the Insert tab and a drop-down list displays that is similar to the Header button drop-down list. Click a footer and the predesigned footer is inserted in the document.

Removing a Header or Footer

Remove a header from a document by clicking the Insert tab and then clicking the Header button in the Header & Footer group. At the drop-down list, click the *Remove Header* option. Complete similar steps to remove a footer.

1. With **4-WritingProcess.docx** open, press Ctrl + Home to move the insertion point to the beginning of the document.
2. Remove the header by clicking the Insert tab, clicking the Header button in the Header & Footer group, and then clicking the *Remove Header* option at the drop-down list.
3. Insert a footer in the document by completing the following steps:
   a. Click the Footer button in the Header & Footer group.
   b. Scroll down the drop-down list and then click *Ion (Light)*.

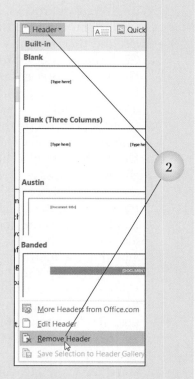

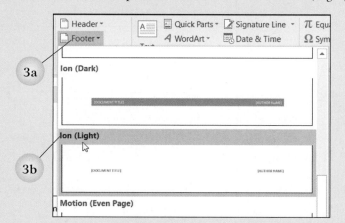

   c. Notice that Word inserted the document title at the left side of the footer. (Word remembered the document title you entered in the header.) Word also inserted your name at the right side of the footer. If the document title does not display, click the *[DOCUMENT TITLE]* placeholder and then type THE WRITING PROCESS. If your name does not display, click the *[AUTHOR NAME]* placeholder and then type your first and last names.
   d. Click the Close Header and Footer button on the Header & Footer Tools Design tab to close the Footer pane and return to the document.
4. Scroll through the document to see how the footer will print.
5. Save and then print **4-WritingProcess.docx**.

> Check Your Work

Editing a Predesigned Header or Footer

Predesigned headers and footers contain elements such as page numbers, a title, and an author's name. The formatting of an element can be changed by clicking the element and then applying formatting. Delete an element from a header or footer by selecting the element and then pressing the Delete key.

1. With **4-WritingProcess.docx** open, remove the footer by clicking the Insert tab, clicking the Footer button, and then clicking *Remove Footer* at the drop-down list.
2. Insert and then format a header by completing the following steps:
    a. Click the Header button in the Header & Footer group on the Insert tab, scroll down the drop-down list, and then click *Grid*. (This header inserts the document title and a date placeholder.)
    b. Delete the date placeholder by clicking the *[Date]* placeholder, clicking the placeholder tab, and then pressing the Delete key.
    c. Double-click in the document text.
3. Insert and then format a footer by completing the following steps:
    a. Click the Insert tab.
    b. Click the Footer button, scroll down the drop-down list, and then click *Retrospect*.
    c. Select the name in the author placeholder at the left side of the footer and then type your first and last names.
    d. Select your name and the page number, apply bold formatting, and then change the font size to 10 point.
    e. Click the Close Header and Footer button.
4. Scroll through the document to see how the header and footer will print.
5. Save, print, and then close **4-WritingProcess.docx**.

Check Your Work

Project 5 Format a Report on Desirable Employee Qualities   2 Parts

You will open a document containing information on desirable employee qualities and then insert a watermark, change the page background color, and insert a page border.

Preview Finished Project

Formatting the Page Background

Quick Steps
Insert a Watermark
1. Click Design tab.
2. Click Watermark button.
3. Click option.

Quick Steps
Apply Page Background Color
1. Click Design tab.
2. Click Page Color button.
3. Click option.

The Page Background group on the Design tab contains three buttons for customizing the page background. Click the Watermark button and choose a predesigned watermark from options at the drop-down list. If a document is going to be viewed on-screen or on the Web, consider adding a page background color. Chapter 3 covered how to apply borders and shading to text at the Borders and Shading dialog box. This dialog box also contains options for inserting a page border. Display the Borders and Shading dialog box with the Page Border tab selected by clicking the Page Borders button in the Page Background group.

Inserting a Watermark

A watermark is a lightened image that displays behind the text in a document. Use a watermark to add visual appeal or to identify a document as a draft, sample, or confidential document. Word provides a number of predesigned watermarks. Display these watermarks by clicking the Watermark button in the Page Background group on the Design tab. Scroll through the list of watermarks and then click an option.

Applying Page Background Color

Use the Page Color button in the Page Background group to apply a background color to a document. This background color is intended for viewing a document on-screen or on the web. The color is visible on the screen but does not print. Insert a page color by clicking the Page Color button and then clicking a color at the drop-down color palette.

Project 5a **Inserting a Watermark and Applying a Page Background Color** Part 1 of 2

1. Open **EmpQualities.docx** and then save it with the name **4-EmpQualities**.
2. Insert a watermark by completing the following steps:
   a. With the insertion point positioned at the beginning of the document, click the Design tab.
   b. Click the Watermark button in the Page Background group.
   c. At the drop-down list, click the *CONFIDENTIAL 1* option.
3. Scroll through the document and notice how the watermark displays behind the text.
4. Remove the watermark and insert a different one by completing the following steps:
   a. Click the Watermark button in the Page Background group and then click *Remove Watermark* at the drop-down list.
   b. Click the Watermark button and then click the *DO NOT COPY 1* option at the drop-down list.
5. Scroll through the document and notice how the watermark displays.
6. Move the insertion point to the beginning of the document.
7. Click the Page Color button in the Page Background group and then click the *Tan, Background 2* color option (third column, first row in the *Theme Colors* section).
8. Save **4-EmpQualities.docx**.

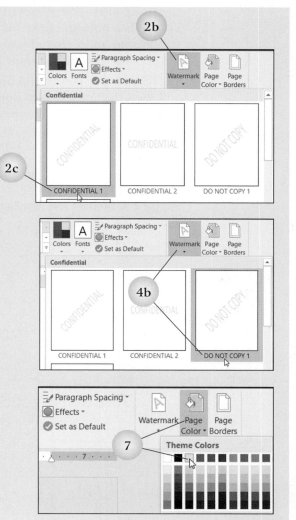

Check Your Work

Inserting a Page Border

To improve the visual appeal of a document, consider inserting a page border. When a page border is inserted in a multiple-page document, it prints on each page. To insert a page border, click the Page Borders button in the Page Background group on the Design tab. This displays the Borders and Shading dialog box with the Page Border tab selected, as shown in Figure 4.5. At this dialog box, specify the border style, color, and width.

The dialog box contains an option for inserting a page border containing an art image. To display the images available, click the *Art* option box arrow, scroll through the drop-down list, and then click an image.

Changing Page Border Options

By default, a page border displays and prints 24 points from the top, left, right, and bottom edges of the page. Some printers, particularly inkjet printers, have a nonprinting area around the outside edges of the page that can interfere with the printing of a border. Before printing a document with a page border, click the File tab and then click the *Print* option. Look at the preview of the page at the right side of the Print backstage area and determine whether the entire border is visible. If a portion of the border is not visible in the preview page (generally at the bottom and right sides of the page), consider changing measurements at the Border and Shading Options dialog box, shown in Figure 4.6.

Display the Border and Shading Options dialog box by clicking the Design tab and then clicking the Page Borders button. At the Borders and Shading dialog box with the Page Border tab selected, click the Options button in the lower right corner of the dialog box. The options at the Border and Shading Options dialog box change depending on whether the Borders tab or the Page Border tab is selected when the Options button is clicked.

Figure 4.5 Borders and Shading Dialog Box with Page Border Tab Selected

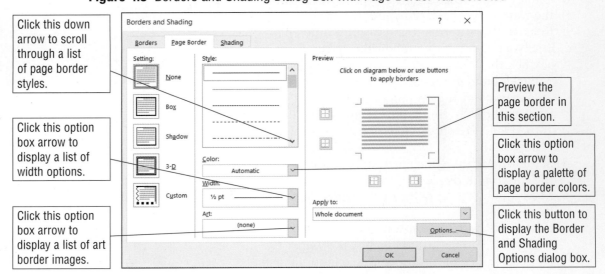

Figure 4.6 Border and Shading Options Dialog Box

Increase these measurements to move the page border away from the edge of the page or decrease the measurements to move the page border closer to the edge of the page.

Change this option to *Text* to specify the distance from the text to the page border.

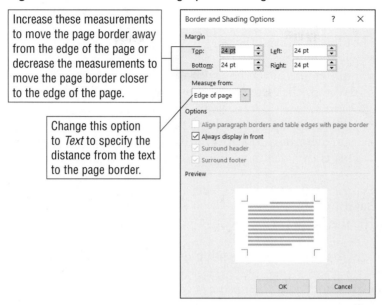

If a printer contains a nonprinting area and the entire page border will not print, consider increasing the spacing from the page border to the edge of the page. Do this with the *Top*, *Left*, *Bottom*, and/or *Right* measurement boxes. The *Measure from* option box has a default setting of *Edge of page*. This option can be changed to *Text*, which changes the top and bottom measurements to *1 pt* and the left and right measurements to *4 pt* and moves the page border into the page. Use the measurement boxes to specify the distances the page border should display and print from the edges of the text in the document.

Project 5b Inserting a Page Border   Part 2 of 2

1. With **4-EmpQualities.docx** open, remove the page color by clicking the Page Color button in the Page Background group on the Design tab and then clicking the *No Color* option.
2. Insert a page border by completing the following steps:
   a. Click the Page Borders button in the Page Background group on the Design tab.
   b. Click the *Box* option in the *Setting* section.
   c. Scroll down the list of line styles in the *Style* list box until the last line style displays and then click the third line from the end.
   d. Click the *Color* option box arrow and then click the *Dark Red, Accent 2* color option (sixth column, first row in the *Theme Colors* section).
   e. Click OK to close the dialog box.

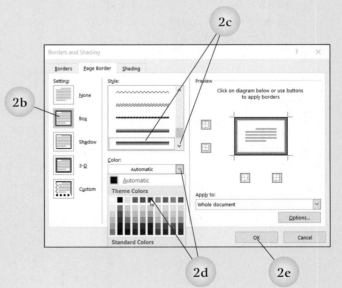

3. Increase the spacing from the page border to the edges of the page by completing the following steps:
   a. Click the Page Borders button in the Page Background group on the Design tab.
   b. At the Borders and Shading dialog box with the Page Border tab selected, click the Options button in the lower right corner.
   c. At the Border and Shading Options dialog box, click the *Top* measurement box up arrow until *31 pt* displays. (This is the maximum measurement allowed.)
   d. Increase the measurements in the *Left, Bottom,* and *Right* measurement boxes to *31 pt*.
   e. Click OK to close the Border and Shading Options dialog box.
   f. Click OK to close the Borders and Shading dialog box.

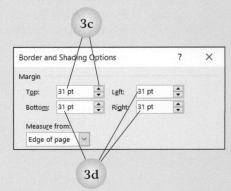

4. Save **4-EmpQualities.docx** and then print page 1.
5. Insert an image page border and change the page border spacing options by completing the following steps:
   a. Click the Page Borders button in the Page Background group on the Design tab.
   b. Click the *Art* option box arrow and then click the border image shown at the right (approximately one-third of the way down the drop-down list).
   c. Click the Options button in the lower right corner of the Borders and Shading dialog box.
   d. At the Border and Shading Options dialog box, click the *Measure from* option box arrow and then click *Text* at the drop-down list.
   e. Click the *Top* measurement box up arrow until *10 pt* displays.
   f. Increase the measurement in the *Bottom* measurement box to *10 pt* and the measurements in the *Left* and *Right* measurement boxes to *14 pt*.
   g. Click the *Surround header* check box to remove the check mark.
   h. Click the *Surround footer* check box to remove the check mark.
   i. Click OK to close the Border and Shading Options dialog box.
   j. Click OK to close the Borders and Shading dialog box.
6. Save, print, and then close **4-EmpQualities.docx**.

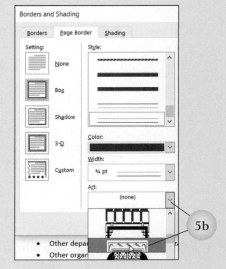

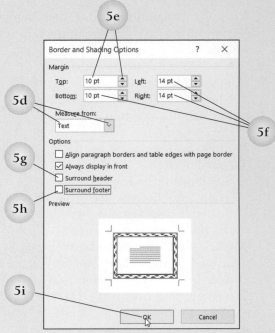

Check Your Work

You will open a lease agreement, search for specific text and replace it with other text, and then search for specific formatting and replace it with other formatting.

Preview Finished Project

Finding and Replacing Text and Formatting

Find

Replace

The Editing group on the Home tab contains the Find button and the Replace button. Use the Find button to search for specific text or formatting in a document and use the Replace button to search for and then replace specific text or formatting.

Finding Text

Tutorial

Finding Text

Click the Find button in the Editing group on the Home tab (or press the keyboard shortcut Ctrl + F) and the Navigation pane displays at the left side of the screen with the Results tab selected. With this tab selected, type search text in the search text box and any occurrence of the text in the document is highlighted. A fragment of the text surrounding the search text also displays in a thumbnail in the Navigation pane. For example, when searching for *Lessee* in **4-LeaseAgrmnt.docx** in Project 6a, the screen displays as shown in Figure 4.7. Any occurrence of *Lessee* displays highlighted in yellow in the document and the Navigation pane displays thumbnails of the text surrounding the occurrences of *Lessee*.

Quick Steps

Find Text
1. Click Find button.
2. Type search text.
3. Click Next button.

Figure 4.7 Navigation Pane Showing Search Results

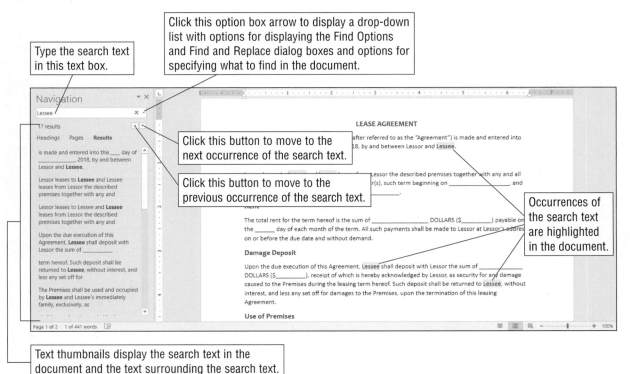

Type the search text in this text box.

Click this option box arrow to display a drop-down list with options for displaying the Find Options and Find and Replace dialog boxes and options for specifying what to find in the document.

Click this button to move to the next occurrence of the search text.

Click this button to move to the previous occurrence of the search text.

Occurrences of the search text are highlighted in the document.

Text thumbnails display the search text in the document and the text surrounding the search text.

Click a text thumbnail in the Navigation pane and the occurrence of the search text is selected in the document. Hover the mouse over a text thumbnail in the Navigation pane and the page number location displays in a small box near the mouse pointer. Move to the next occurrence of the search text by clicking the Next button (contains a down-pointing arrow) below and to the right of the search text box. Click the Previous button (contains an up-pointing arrow) to move to the previous occurrence of the search text.

Click the down arrow at the right side of the search text box and a drop-down list displays. It shows options for displaying dialog boxes, such as the Find Options dialog box and the Find and Replace dialog box. It also shows options for specifying what should be found in the document, such as figures, tables, and equations.

The search text in a document can be highlighted with options at the Find and Replace dialog box with the Find tab selected. Display this dialog box by clicking the Find button arrow in the Editing group on the Home tab and then clicking *Advanced Find* at the drop-down list. Another method for displaying the Find and Replace dialog box is to click the down arrow at the right side of the search text box in the Navigation pane and then click the *Advanced Find* option at the drop-down list. To highlight found text, type the search text in the *Find what* text box, click the Reading Highlight button, and then click *Highlight All* at the drop-down list. All occurrences of the text in the document are highlighted. To remove highlighting, click the Reading Highlight button and then click *Clear Highlighting* at the drop-down list.

Project 6a Finding and Highlighting Text

Part 1 of 4

1. Open **LeaseAgrmnt.docx** and then save it with the name **4-LeaseAgrmnt**.
2. Find all occurrences of *lease* by completing the following steps:
   a. Click the Find button in the Editing group on the Home tab.
   b. If necessary, click the Results tab in the Navigation pane.
   c. Type lease in the search text box in the Navigation pane.
   d. After a moment, all occurrences of *lease* in the document are highlighted and text thumbnails display in the Navigation pane. Click a couple of the text thumbnails in the Navigation pane to select the text in the document.
   e. Click the Previous button (contains an up-pointing arrow) to select the previous occurrence of *lease* in the document.
3. Use the Find and Replace dialog box with the Find tab selected to highlight all occurrences of *Premises* in the document by completing the following steps:
   a. Click in the document and press Ctrl + Home to move the insertion point to the beginning of the document.
   b. Click the search option box arrow in the Navigation pane and then click *Advanced Find* at the drop-down list.

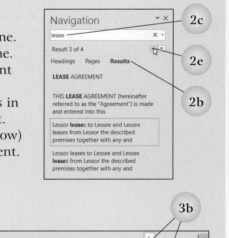

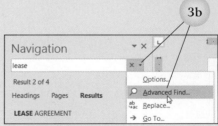

c. At the Find and Replace dialog box with the Find tab selected (and *lease* selected in the *Find what* text box), type Premises.

d. Click the Reading Highlight button and then click *Highlight All* at the drop-down list.

e. Click in the document to make it active and then scroll through the document and notice the occurrences of highlighted text.

f. Click in the dialog box to make it active.

g. Click the Reading Highlight button and then click *Clear Highlighting* at the drop-down list.

h. Click the Close button to close the Find and Replace dialog box.

4. Close the Navigation pane by clicking the Close button in the upper right corner of the pane.

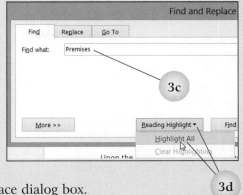

Tutorial ▶

Finding and Replacing Text

Finding and Replacing Text

Quick Steps
Find and Replace Text
1. Click Replace button.
2. Type search text.
3. Press Tab key.
4. Type replacement text.
5. Click Replace or Replace All button.

To find and replace text, click the Replace button in the Editing group on the Home tab or use the keyboard shortcut Ctrl + H. This displays the Find and Replace dialog box with the Replace tab selected, as shown in Figure 4.8. Type the search text in the *Find what* text box, press the Tab key, and then type the replacement text in the *Replace with* text box.

The Find and Replace dialog box contains several command buttons. Click the Find Next button to tell Word to find the next occurrence of the text. Click the Replace button to replace the text and find the next occurrence. If all occurrences of the text in the *Find what* text box are to be replaced with the text in the *Replace with* text box, click the Replace All button.

Figure 4.8 Find and Replace Dialog Box with the Replace Tab Selected

Hint If the Find and Replace dialog box is in the way of specific text, drag it to a different location.

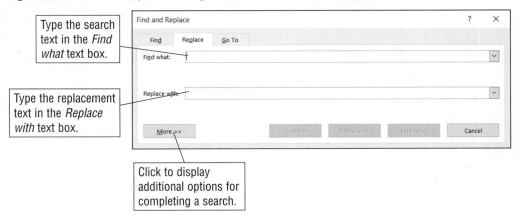

Type the search text in the *Find what* text box.

Type the replacement text in the *Replace with* text box.

Click to display additional options for completing a search.

1. With **4-LeaseAgrmnt.docx** open, make sure the insertion point is positioned at the beginning of the document.
2. Find all occurrences of *Lessor* and replace them with *Tracy Hartford* by completing the following steps:
   a. Click the Replace button in the Editing group on the Home tab.
   b. At the Find and Replace dialog box with the Replace tab selected, type Lessor in the *Find what* text box.
   c. Press the Tab key to move the insertion point to the *Replace with* text box.
   d. Type Tracy Hartford.
   e. Click the Replace All button.
   f. At the message stating that 11 replacements were made, click OK. (Do not close the Find and Replace dialog box.)
3. With the Find and Replace dialog box still open, complete steps similar to those in Step 2 to find all occurrences of *Lessee* and replace them with *Michael Iwami*.
4. Click the Close button to close the Find and Replace dialog box.
5. Save **4-LeaseAgrmnt.docx**.

Check Your Work

Defining Search Parameters

The Find and Replace dialog box contains a variety of check boxes with options for completing a search. To display these options, click the More button in the lower left corner of the dialog box. This causes the Find and Replace dialog box to expand, as shown in Figure 4.9. Each option and what will occur if it is selected

Figure 4.9 Expanded Find and Replace Dialog Box

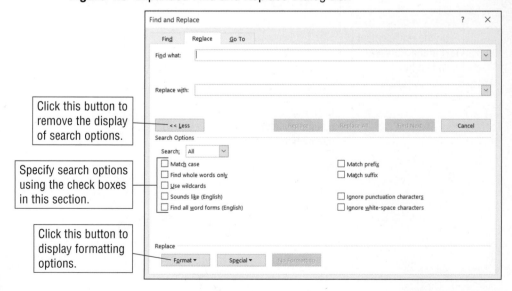

Click this button to remove the display of search options.

Specify search options using the check boxes in this section.

Click this button to display formatting options.

is described in Table 4.2. To remove the display of options, click the Less button. (The Less button was previously the More button.) If a mistake was made when replacing text, close the Find and Replace dialog box and then click the Undo button on the Quick Access Toolbar.

Table 4.2 Options at the Expanded Find and Replace Dialog Box

Choose this option	To
Match case	Exactly match the case of the search text. For example, search for *Book* and select the *Match case* option and Word will stop at *Book* but not *book* or *BOOK*.
Find whole words only	Find a whole word, not a part of a word. For example, search for *her* without selecting *Find whole words only* and Word will stop at *there*, *here*, *hers*, and so on.
Use wildcards	Use special characters as wildcards to search for specific text.
Sounds like (English)	Match words that sound alike but are spelled differently, such as *know* and *no*.
Find all word forms (English)	Find all forms of the word entered in the *Find what* text box. For example, enter *hold* and Word will stop at *held* and *holding*.
Match prefix	Find only those words that begin with the letters in the *Find what* text box. For example, enter *per* and Word will stop at words such as *perform* and *perfect* but skip words such as *super* and *hyperlink*.
Match suffix	Find only those words that end with the letters in the *Find what* text box. For example, enter *ly* and Word will stop at words such as *accurately* and *quietly* but skip words such as *catalyst* and *lyre*.
Ignore punctuation characters	Ignore punctuation within characters. For example, enter *US* in the *Find what* text box and Word will stop at *U.S.*
Ignore white-space characters	Ignore spaces between letters. For example, enter *F B I* in the *Find what* text box and Word will stop at *FBI*.

Project 6c Finding and Replacing Word Forms and Suffixes   Part 3 of 4

1. With **4-LeaseAgrmnt.docx** open, make sure the insertion point is positioned at the beginning of the document.
2. Find all word forms of the word *lease* and replace them with *rent* by completing the following steps:
   a. Click the Replace button in the Editing group on the Home tab.

b. At the Find and Replace dialog box with the Replace tab selected, type lease in the *Find what* text box.

c. Press the Tab key and then type rent in the *Replace with* text box.

d. Click the More button.

e. Click the *Find all word forms (English)* check box. (This inserts a check mark in the check box.)

f. Click the Replace All button.

g. At the message stating that Replace All is not recommended with Find All Word Forms, click OK.

h. At the message stating that six replacements were made, click OK.

i. Click the *Find all word forms* check box to remove the check mark.

3. Find the word *less* and replace it with the word *minus* and specify that you want Word to find only those words that end in *less* by completing the following steps:

a. At the expanded Find and Replace dialog box, select the text in the *Find what* text box and then type less.

b. Select the text in the *Replace with* text box and then type minus.

c. Click the *Match suffix* check box to insert a check mark (telling Word to find only words that end in *less*).

d. Click the Replace All button.

e. Click OK at the message stating that two replacements were made.

f. Click the *Match suffix* check box to remove the check mark.

g. Click the Less button.

h. Close the Find and Replace dialog box.

4. Save **4-LeaseAgrmnt.docx**.

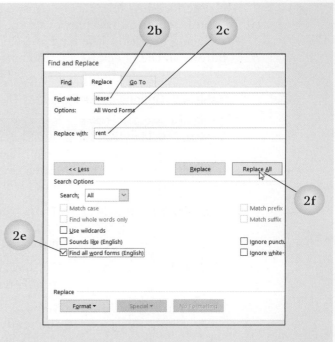

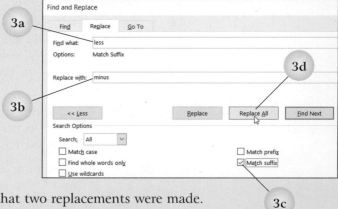

Check Your Work

Tutorial

Finding and Replacing Formatting

Finding and Replacing Formatting

Use options at the Find and Replace dialog box with the Replace tab selected to search for characters containing specific formatting and replace them with other characters or formatting. With the insertion point positioned in the *Find what* text box, specify formatting to be found in the document by clicking the More button, clicking the Format button in the lower left corner of the dialog box, and then clicking the type of formatting at the pop-up list. Click in the *Replace with* text box and then complete similar steps.

1. With **4-LeaseAgrmnt.docx** open, make sure the insertion point displays at the beginning of the document.
2. Find text set in 12-point Candara bold, in the standard dark red color and replace it with text set in 14-point Calibri bold, in the standard dark blue color by completing the following steps:
   a. Click the Replace button in the Editing group on the Home tab.
   b. At the Find and Replace dialog box, press the Delete key. (This deletes any text in the *Find what* text box.)
   c. Click the More button. (If a check mark displays in any of the check boxes, click the option to remove it.)
   d. With the insertion point positioned in the *Find what* text box, click the Format button in the lower left corner of the dialog box and then click *Font* at the pop-up list.
   e. At the Find Font dialog box, choose the *Candara* font and change the font style to *Bold*, the size to *12*, and the font color to *Dark Red* (first color option in the *Standard Colors* section).

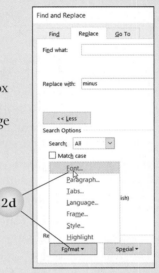

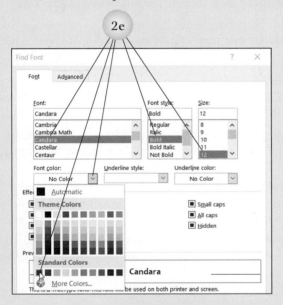

   f. Click OK to close the Find Font dialog box.
   g. At the Find and Replace dialog box, click in the *Replace with* text box and then delete any text that displays.
   h. Click the Format button in the lower left corner of the dialog box and then click *Font* at the pop-up list.
   i. At the Replace Font dialog box, choose the *Calibri* font and change the font style to *Bold*, the size to *14*, and the font color to *Dark Blue* (ninth color option in the *Standard Colors* section).
   j. Click OK to close the Replace Font dialog box.

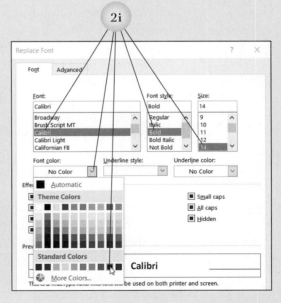

Check Your Work

Chapter Summary

- Change the document view with buttons in the view area on the Status bar or with options in the Views group on the View tab.

- Print Layout is the default view but this can be changed to other views, such as Draft view and Read Mode view.

- Draft view displays the document in a format for efficient editing and formatting.

- Read Mode view displays a document in a format for easy viewing and reading.

- Use the Zoom slider bar or buttons in the Zoom group on the View tab to change the display percentage.

- Use options at the Ribbon Display Options button drop-down list to specify if the Quick Access Toolbar, ribbon, and Status bar should be visible or hidden.

- Navigate in a document using the Navigation pane. Display the pane by inserting a check mark in the *Navigation Pane* check box in the Show group on the View tab.

- By default, a Word document contains 1-inch top, bottom, left, and right margins. Change margins with preset margin settings at the Margins button drop-down list or with options at the Page Setup dialog box with the Margins tab selected.

- The default page layout is portrait orientation, which can be changed to landscape orientation with the Orientation button in the Page Setup group on the Layout tab.

- The default page size is 8.5 inches by 11 inches, which can be changed with options at the Size button drop-down list or options at the Page Setup dialog box with the Paper tab selected.

- A page break that Word inserts automatically is a soft page break. A page break inserted manually is a hard page break. Insert a hard page break using the Page Break button in the Pages group on the Insert tab or by pressing Ctrl + Enter.

- Insert a predesigned and formatted cover page by clicking the Cover Page button in the Pages group on the Insert tab and then clicking an option at the drop-down list.

- Insert predesigned and formatted page numbering by clicking the Page Number button in the Header & Footer group on the Insert tab, specifying the location of the page number, and then clicking a page numbering option.

- Insert predesigned headers and footers in a document with the Header button and the Footer button in the Header & Footer group on the Insert tab.

- A watermark is a lightened image that displays behind the text in a document. Use the Watermark button in the Page Background group on the Design tab to insert a watermark.
- Insert a page background color in a document with the Page Color button in the Page Background group on the Design tab. The page background color is designed for viewing a document on screen and does not print.
- Click the Page Borders button in the Page Background group on the Design tab and the Borders and Shading dialog box with the Page Border tab selected displays. Use options at this dialog box to insert a page border or an art image page border in a document.
- Use the Find button in the Editing group on the Home tab to search for specific characters or formatting. Use the Replace button to search for specific characters or formatting and replace them with other characters or formatting.
- At the Find and Replace dialog box, click the Find Next button to find the next occurrence of the characters and/or formatting. Click the Replace button to replace the characters or formatting and find the next occurrence or click the Replace All button to replace all occurrences of the characters or formatting.
- Click the More button at the Find and Replace dialog box to display additional options for defining search parameters.

Commands Review

FEATURE	RIBBON TAB, GROUP	BUTTON, OPTION	KEYBOARD SHORTCUT
blank page	Insert, Pages		
Borders and Shading dialog box with Page Border tab selected	Design, Page Background		
Border and Shading Options dialog box	Design, Page Background	, Options	
cover page	Insert, Pages		
Draft view	View, Views		
Find and Replace dialog box with Find tab selected	Home, Editing	, Advanced Find	
Find and Replace dialog box with Replace tab selected	Home, Editing		Ctrl + H
footer	Insert, Header & Footer		
header	Insert, Header & Footer		
margins	Layout, Page Setup		
Navigation pane	View, Show	Navigation Pane	Ctrl + F
orientation	Layout, Page Setup		
page break	Insert, Pages		Ctrl + Enter

FEATURE	RIBBON TAB, GROUP	BUTTON, OPTION	KEYBOARD SHORTCUT
page background color	Design, Page Background		
page numbering	Insert, Header & Footer		
Page Setup dialog box with Margins tab selected	Layout, Page Setup	, *Custom Margins* OR	
Page Setup dialog box with Paper tab selected	Layout, Page Setup	, *More Paper Sizes*	
paper size	Layout, Page Setup		
Print Layout view	View, Views		
Read Mode view	View, Views		
ribbon display options			
watermark	Design, Page Background		

Microsoft®
Word Level 1

Unit 2

Enhancing and Customizing Documents

Microsoft®

Word

Applying Formatting and Inserting Objects

Performance Objectives

Precheck

Check your current skills to help focus your study.

Upon successful completion of Chapter 5, you will be able to:

1 Insert section breaks

2 Create and format text in columns

3 Hyphenate words automatically and manually

4 Create a drop cap

5 Insert symbols, special characters, and the date and time

6 Use the Click and Type feature

7 Vertically align text

8 Insert, format, and customize images, text boxes, shapes, and WordArt

9 Create and customize a screenshot

To apply page or document formatting to only a portion of the document, insert a continuous section break or a section break that begins a new page. A section break is useful when formatting text in columns. The hyphenation feature hyphenates words at the ends of lines, creating a less ragged right margin. Use buttons in the Text and Symbols groups on the Insert tab to insert symbols, special characters, the date and time, text boxes, and WordArt. Word includes the Click and Type feature for positioning the insertion point at a particular location in the document and changing the paragraph alignment. Use the *Vertical alignment* option at the Page Setup dialog box with the Layout tab selected to specify how text is aligned vertically on the page. In addition to learning these features, you will learn how to increase the visual appeal of a document by inserting and customizing graphics, such as images, text boxes, shapes, WordArt, and screenshots.

SNAP

If you are a SNAP user, launch the Precheck and Tutorials from your Assignments page.

Data Files

Before beginning chapter work, copy the WL1C5 folder to your storage medium and then make WL1C5 the active folder.

In a document on computer input devices, you will format text into columns, improve the readability by hyphenating long words, and improve the visual appeal by inserting a drop cap, a special character, a symbol, and the date and time.

Preview Finished Project

Tutorial

Inserting and Deleting a Section Break

 Breaks

Quick Steps

Insert a Section Break
1. Click Layout tab.
2. Click Breaks button.
3. Click section break type in drop-down list.

Hint When you delete a section break, the text that follows takes on the formatting of the text preceding the break.

Inserting a Section Break

Insert a section break in a document to change the layout and formatting of specific portions. For example, a section break can be inserted in the document and then the margins can be changed for the text between the section break and the end of the document or to the next section break.

Insert a section break in a document by clicking the Layout tab, clicking the Breaks button in the Page Setup group, and then clicking the desired option in the *Section Breaks* section of the drop-down list. A section break can be inserted that begins a new page or a continuous section break can be inserted. A continuous section break separates the document into sections but does not insert a page break.

A section break inserted in a document is not visible in Print Layout view. Change to Draft view or click the Show/Hide ¶ button on the Home tab to turn on the display of nonprinting characters and a section break displays in the document as a double row of dots with the words *Section Break* in the middle. Word will identify the type of section break. For example, if a continuous section break is inserted, the words *Section Break (Continuous)* display in the middle of the row of dots. To delete a section break, change to Draft view, click anywhere on the section break, and then press the Delete key. Another option is to click the Show/Hide ¶ button to turn on the display of nonprinting characters, click anywhere on the section break, and then press the Delete key.

Project 1a **Inserting a Continuous Section Break** **Part 1 of 8**

1. Open **InputDevices.docx** and then save it with the name **5-InputDevices**.
2. Insert a continuous section break by completing the following steps:
   a. Move the insertion point to the beginning of the *Keyboard* heading.
   b. Click the Layout tab.
   c. Click the Breaks button in the Page Setup group and then click *Continuous* in the *Section Breaks* section of the drop-down list.
3. Click the Home tab, click the Show/Hide ¶ button in the Paragraph group, and then notice the section break at the end of the first paragraph of text.
4. Click the Show/Hide ¶ button to turn off the display of nonprinting characters.

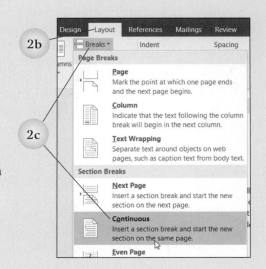

5. With the insertion point positioned at the beginning of the *Keyboard* heading, change the left and right margins to 1.5 inches. (The margin changes affect only the text after the continuous section break.)
6. Save and then print **5-InputDevices.docx**.

Check Your Work

Tutorial

Formatting Text into Columns

Formatting Text into Columns

When preparing a document containing text, an important point to consider is its readability. Readability refers to the ease with which a person can read and understand groups of words. The line length of text in a document can enhance or detract from its readability. If the line length is too long, the reader may lose his or her place and have a difficult time moving to the next line below.

To improve the readability of documents such as newsletters and reports, consider formatting the text in columns. One common type is the newspaper column, which is typically used for text in newspapers, newsletters, and magazines. Newspaper columns contain text in vertical columns.

 Columns

Quick Steps
Create Columns
1. Click Layout tab.
2. Click Columns button.
3. Click number of columns.

Create newspaper columns with the Columns button in the Page Setup group on the Layout tab or with options at the Columns dialog box. Using the Columns button creates columns of equal width. Use the Columns dialog box to create columns with varying widths. A document can include as many columns as will fit the space available on the page. Word determines how many columns can be included on the page based on the page width, the margin widths, and the size and spacing of the columns. Columns must be at least 0.5 inch in width. Changing column widths affects the entire document or the section of the document in which the insertion point is positioned.

Project 1b Formatting Text into Columns   Part 2 of 8

1. With **5-InputDevices.docx** open, make sure the insertion point is positioned below the section break and then change the left and right margins back to 1 inch.
2. Delete the section break by completing the following steps:
   a. Click the Show/Hide ¶ button in the Paragraph group on the Home tab to turn on the display of nonprinting characters.
   b. Click anywhere on *Section Break (Continuous)* at the end of the first paragraph below the title in the document. (This moves the insertion point to the beginning of the section break.)

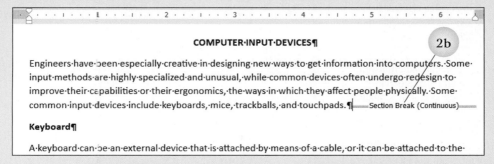

   c. Press the Delete key.
   d. Click the Show/Hide ¶ button to turn off the display of nonprinting characters.

3. Move the insertion point to the beginning of the first paragraph of text below the title and then insert a continuous section break.
4. Format the text into columns by completing the following steps:
   a. Make sure the insertion point is positioned below the section break.
   b. If necessary, click the Layout tab.
   c. Click the Columns button in the Page Setup group.
   d. Click *Two* at the drop-down list.
5. Save **5-InputDevices.docx**.

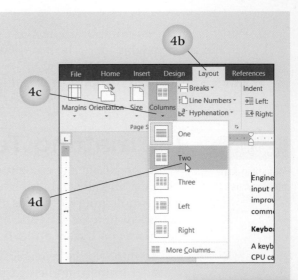

Check Your Work

Creating Columns with the Columns Dialog Box

Quick Steps

Create Columns with the Columns Dialog Box
1. Click Layout tab.
2. Click Columns button.
3. Click *More Columns*.
4. Specify column options.
5. Click OK.

Use the Columns dialog box to create newspaper columns that are equal or unequal in width. To display the Columns dialog box, shown in Figure 5.1, click the Columns button in the Page Setup group on the Layout tab and then click *More Columns* at the drop-down list.

With options at the Columns dialog box, specify the style and number of columns, enter specific column measurements, create unequal columns, and insert a line between columns. By default, column formatting is applied to the whole document. This can be changed to *This point forward* with the *Apply to* option box at the bottom of the Columns dialog box. With the *This point forward* option, a section break is inserted and the column formatting is applied to text from the location of the insertion point to the end of the document or until another column format is encountered. The *Preview* section of the dialog box displays an example of how the columns will appear in the document.

Figure 5.1 Columns Dialog Box

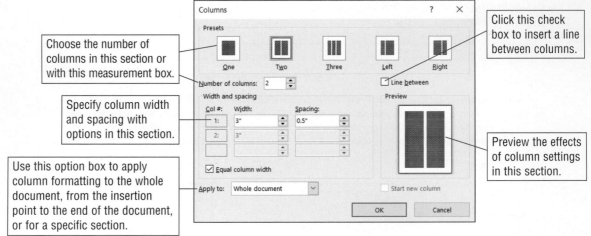

Choose the number of columns in this section or with this measurement box.

Specify column width and spacing with options in this section.

Use this option box to apply column formatting to the whole document, from the insertion point to the end of the document, or for a specific section.

Click this check box to insert a line between columns.

Preview the effects of column settings in this section.

Removing Column Formatting

To remove column formatting using the Columns button, position the insertion point in the section containing columns, click the Layout tab, click the Columns button, and then click *One* at the drop-down list. Column formatting can also be removed at the Columns dialog box by selecting the *One* option in the *Presets* section.

Inserting a Column Break

Hint You can also insert a column break with the keyboard shortcut Ctrl + Shift + Enter.

When formatting text into columns, Word automatically breaks the columns to fit the page. At times, automatic column breaks may appear in undesirable locations. Insert a manual column break by positioning the insertion point where the column is to end, clicking the Layout tab, clicking the Breaks button, and then clicking *Column* at the drop-down list.

Project 1c **Formatting Columns at the Columns Dialog Box**   **Part 3 of 8**

1. With **5-InputDevices.docx** open, delete the section break by completing the following steps:
   a. Click the View tab and then click the Draft button in the Views group.
   b. Click anywhere on *Section Break (Continuous)* and then press the Delete key.
   c. Click the Print Layout button in the Views group on the View tab.
2. Remove column formatting by clicking the Layout tab, clicking the Columns button in the Page Setup group, and then clicking *One* at the drop-down list.
3. Format text in columns by completing the following steps:
   a. Position the insertion point at the beginning of the first paragraph of text below the title.
   b. Click the Columns button in the Page Setup group and then click *More Columns* at the drop-down list.
   c. At the Columns dialog box, click *Two* in the *Presets* section.
   d. Click the *Spacing* measurement box down arrow until *0.3"* displays.
   e. Click the *Line between* check box to insert a check mark.
   f. Click the *Apply to* option box arrow and then click *This point forward* at the drop-down list.
   g. Click OK to close the dialog box.

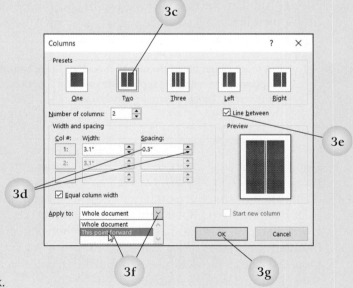

4. Insert a column break by completing the following steps:
   a. Position the insertion point at the beginning of the heading *Mouse*.
   b. Click the Breaks button in the Page Setup group and then click *Column* at the drop-down list.
5. Save and then print **5-InputDevices.docx**.

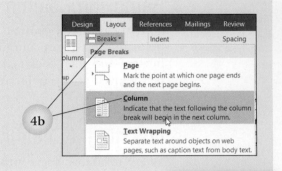

Check Your Work

Balancing Columns on a Page

In a document containing text formatted into columns, Word automatically lines up (balances) the last lines of text at the bottoms of the columns, except on the last page. Text in the first column of the last page may flow to the end of the page, while the text in the second column may end far short of the end of the page. Balance columns by inserting a continuous section break at the end of the text.

Project 1d Formatting and Balancing Columns of Text   Part 4 of 8

1. With **5-InputDevices.docx** open, delete the column break by positioning the insertion point at the beginning of the heading *Mouse* and then pressing the Backspace key.
2. Select the entire document and then change the font to 12-point Constantia.
3. Move the insertion point to the end of the document and then balance the columns by clicking the Layout tab, clicking the Breaks button, and then clicking *Continuous* at the drop-down list.

> A touchscreen allows the user to choose options by pressing the appropriate part of the screen. Touchscreens are widely used | in bank ATMs and in kiosks at retail outlets and in tourist areas.
>
> 3

4. Apply the Green, Accent 6, Lighter 60% paragraph shading (last column, third row) to the title *COMPUTER INPUT DEVICES*.
5. Apply the Green, Accent 6, Lighter 80% paragraph shading (last column, second row) to each heading in the document.
6. Insert page numbering that prints at the bottom center of each page using the Plain Number 2 option.
7. Double-click in the document to make it active.
8. Save **5-InputDevices.docx**.

Check Your Work

Hyphenating Words

In some Word documents, especially those with left and right margins wider than 1 inch or those with text set in columns, the right margin may appear quite ragged. Improve the display of the text by making line lengths more uniform using the hyphenation feature to hyphenate long words that fall at the ends of lines. Use the hyphenation feature to automatically or manually hyphenate words.

Automatically Hyphenating Words

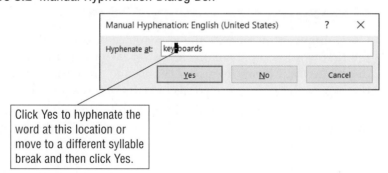

Hyphenation

To automatically hyphenate words in a document, click the Layout tab, click the Hyphenation button in the Page Setup group, and then click *Automatic* at the drop-down list. Scroll through the document and check to see if hyphens display in appropriate locations within the words. To remove all the hyphens after hyphenating words in a document, immediately click the Undo button on the Quick Access Toolbar.

Hint Avoid dividing words at the ends of more than two consecutive lines.

Manually Hyphenating Words

Quick Steps

Automatically Hyphenate a Document
1. Click Layout tab.
2. Click Hyphenation button.
3. Click *Automatic*.

Manually Hyphenate a Document
1. Click Layout tab.
2. Click Hyphenation button.
3. Click *Manual*.
4. Click Yes or No to hyphenate indicated words.
5. When complete, click OK.

To control where hyphens appear in words during hyphenation, choose manual hyphenation. To do this, click the Layout tab, click the Hyphenation button in the Page Setup group, and then click *Manual* at the drop-down list. This displays the Manual Hyphenation dialog box, as shown in Figure 5.2. (The word in the *Hyphenate at* text box will vary.)

At this dialog box, click Yes to hyphenate the word as indicated in the *Hyphenate at* text box, click No if the word should not be hyphenated, or click Cancel to cancel hyphenation. The hyphenation can be repositioned in the *Hyphenate at* text box. Word displays the word with syllable breaks indicated by hyphens. Each place the word will be hyphenated displays as a blinking black bar. To hyphenate the word at a different place, position the blinking black bar where the word is to be hyphenated and then click Yes. Continue clicking Yes or No at the Manual Hyphenation dialog box.

Be careful with words ending in *-ed*. Several two-syllable words can be divided before that final syllable—for example, *noted*. However, one-syllable words ending in *-ed* should not be hyphenated. An example is *served*. Watch for this type of occurrence and click No to cancel the hyphenation. At the hyphenation complete message, click OK.

Figure 5.2 Manual Hyphenation Dialog Box

Manual Hyphenation: English (United States)   ?   X

Hyphenate at: key|boards

Yes   No   Cancel

Click Yes to hyphenate the word at this location or move to a different syllable break and then click Yes.

Remove all hyphens in a document by immediately clicking the Undo button on the Quick Access Toolbar. To delete a few but not all the optional hyphens inserted during hyphenation, use the Find and Replace dialog box. To do this, display the Find and Replace dialog box with the Replace tab selected, insert an optional hyphen symbol in the *Find what* text box (to do this, click the More button, click the Special button, and then click *Optional Hyphen* at the pop-up list), and make sure the *Replace with* text box is empty. Complete the find and replace, clicking the Replace button to replace the hyphen with nothing or clicking the Find Next button to leave the hyphen in the document.

Project 1e Automatically and Manually Hyphenating Words   **Part 5 of 8**

1. With **5-InputDevices.docx** open, hyphenate words automatically by completing the following steps:
   a. Press Ctrl + Home.
   b. Click the Layout tab.
   c. Click the Hyphenation button in the Page Setup group and then click *Automatic* at the drop-down list.
2. Scroll through the document and notice the hyphenation.
3. Click the Undo button to remove the hyphens.
4. Manually hyphenate words by completing the following steps:
   a. Click the Hyphenation button in the Page Setup group and then click *Manual* at the drop-down list.
   b. At the Manual Hyphenation dialog box, make one of the following choices:
      • Click Yes to hyphenate the word as indicated in the *Hyphenate at* text box.
      • Move the hyphen in the word to a more desirable location and then click Yes.
      • Click No if the word should not be hyphenated.
   c. Continue clicking Yes or No at the Manual Hyphenation dialog box.
   d. At the message indicating that hyphenation is complete, click OK.
5. Save **5-InputDevices.docx**.

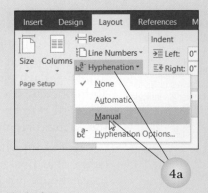

Creating a Drop Cap

Creating and Removing a Drop Cap

Drop Cap

Quick Steps
Create a Drop Cap
1. Click Insert tab.
2. Click Drop Cap button.
3. Click drop cap option.

Use a drop cap to enhance the appearance of text. A drop cap is the first letter of the first word of a paragraph that is set into the paragraph with formatting that differentiates it from the rest of the paragraph. Drop caps can be used to identify the beginnings of major sections or parts of a document.

Create a drop cap with the Drop Cap button in the Text group on the Insert tab. The drop cap can be set in the paragraph or in the margin. At the Drop Cap dialog box, specify a font, the number of lines the letter should drop, and the distance the letter should be positioned from the text of the paragraph. Add a drop cap to the entire first word of a paragraph by selecting the word and then clicking the Drop Cap button.

1. With **5-InputDevices.docx** open, create a drop cap by completing the following steps:
   a. Position the insertion point on the first word of the first paragraph below the title (*Engineers*).
   b. Click the Insert tab.
   c. Click the Drop Cap button in the Text group.
   d. Click *In margin* at the drop-down gallery.
2. Looking at the drop cap, you decide that you do not like it positioned in the margin and want it to be a little smaller. To change the drop cap, complete the following steps:
   a. With the *E* in the word *Engineers* selected, click the Drop Cap button in the Text group and then click *None* at the drop-down gallery.
   b. Click the Drop Cap button and then click *Drop Cap Options* at the drop-down gallery.
   c. At the Drop Cap dialog box, click *Dropped* in the *Position* section.
   d. Click the *Font* option box arrow, scroll up the drop-down list, and then click *Cambria*.
   e. Click the *Lines to drop* measurement box down arrow to change the number to *2*.
   f. Click OK to close the dialog box.
   g. Click outside the drop cap to deselect it.
3. Save **5-InputDevices.docx**.

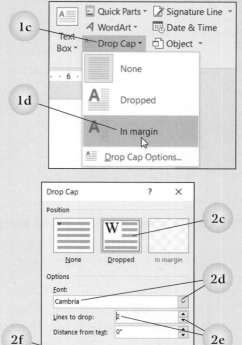

Check Your Work

Inserting Symbols and Special Characters

Use the Symbol button on the Insert tab to insert special symbols in a document. Click the Symbol button in the Symbols group on the Insert tab and a drop-down list displays the most recently inserted symbols along with a *More Symbols* option. Click one of the symbols in the list to insert it in the document or click the *More Symbols* option to display the Symbol dialog box, as shown in Figure 5.3. At the Symbol dialog box, double-click the desired symbol and then click Close or click the symbol, click the Insert button, and then click the Close button. Another method for selecting a symbol at the Symbol dialog box is to type the symbol code in the *Character code* text box.

At the Symbol dialog box with the Symbols tab selected, the font can be changed with the *Font* option box. When the font is changed, different symbols display in the dialog box. Click the Special Characters tab at the Symbol dialog box and a list of special characters displays along with keyboard shortcuts for creating them.

Quick Steps

Insert a Symbol
1. Click Insert tab.
2. Click Symbol button.
3. Click symbol.
OR
1. Click Insert tab.
2. Click Symbol button.
3. Click *More Symbols*.
4. Double-click symbol.
5. Click Close.

Figure 5.3 Symbol Dialog Box with Symbols Tab Selected

Use the *Font* option box to display a specific set of characters.

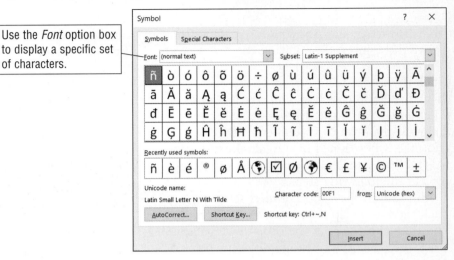

Project 1g Inserting Symbols and Special Characters

1. With **5-InputDevices.docx** open, press Ctrl + End to move the insertion point to the end of the document.
2. Press the Enter key, type Prepared by:, and then press the spacebar.
3. Type the first name Matthew and then press the spacebar.
4. Insert the last name *Viña* by completing the following steps:
   a. Type Vi.
   b. If necessary, click the Insert tab.
   c. Click the Symbol button in the Symbols group.
   d. Click *More Symbols* at the drop-down list.
   e. At the Symbol dialog box, make sure the *Font* option box displays *(normal text)* and then double-click the *ñ* symbol (located in approximately the tenth through twelfth rows).
   f. Click the Close button.
   g. Type a.
5. Press Shift + Enter.
6. Insert the keyboard symbol (⌨) by completing the following steps:
   a. Click the Symbol button and then click *More Symbols*.
   b. At the Symbol dialog box, click the *Font* option box arrow and then click *Wingdings* at the drop-down list. (You will need to scroll down the list to display this option.)
   c. Select the current number in the *Character code* text box and then type 55.
   d. Click the Insert button and then click the Close button.
7. Type SoftCell Technologies.

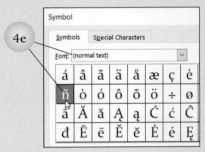

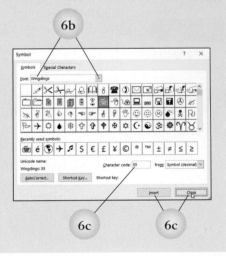

8. Insert the registered trademark symbol (®) by completing the following steps:
   a. Click the Symbol button and then click *More Symbols*.
   b. At the Symbol dialog box, click the Special Characters tab.
   c. Double-click the ® symbol (tenth option from the top).
   d. Click the Close button.
   e. Press Shift + Enter.
9. Select the keyboard symbol (⌨) and then change the font size to 18 points.
10. Save **5-InputDevices.docx**.

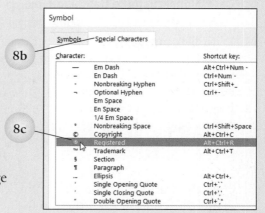

8b

8c

Check Your Work

Tutorial

Inserting the Date and Time

Inserting the Date and Time

 Date & Time

Quick Steps

Insert the Date and Time
1. Click Insert tab.
2. Click Date & Time button.
3. Click desired option in list box.
4. Click OK.

Use the Date & Time button in the Text group on the Insert tab to insert the current date and time in a document. Click this button and the Date and Time dialog box displays, as shown in Figure 5.4. (Your date will vary from what you see in the figure.) At the Date and Time dialog box, click the desired date and/or time format in the *Available formats* list box.

If the *Update automatically* check box does not contain a check mark, the date and/or time are inserted in the document as text that can be edited in the normal manner. The date and/or time can also be inserted as a field. The advantage to using a field is that the date and time are updated when a document is reopened. Insert a check mark in the *Update automatically* check box to insert the date and/or time as a field. The date can also be inserted as a field using the keyboard shortcut Alt + Shift + D, and the time can be inserted as a field with the keyboard shortcut Alt + Shift + T.

A date or time field will automatically update when a document is reopened. The date and time can also be updated in the document by clicking the date or time field and then clicking the Update tab or pressing the F9 function key.

Figure 5.4 Date and Time Dialog Box

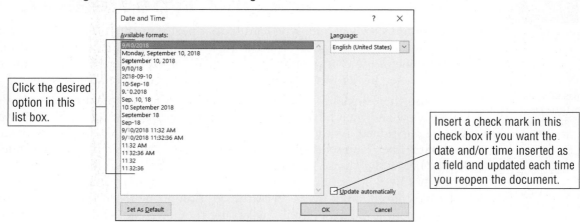

Click the desired option in this list box.

Insert a check mark in this check box if you want the date and/or time inserted as a field and updated each time you reopen the document.

1. With **5-InputDevices.docx** open, press Ctrl + End and make sure the insertion point is positioned below the company name.
2. Insert the current date by completing the following steps:
   a. Click the Insert tab.
   b. Click the Date & Time button in the Text group.
   c. At the Date and Time dialog box, click the third option from the top in the *Available formats* list box. (Your date and time will vary from what you see in the image at the right.)
   d. Click in the *Update automatically* check box to insert a check mark.
   e. Click OK to close the dialog box.
3. Press Shift + Enter.
4. Insert the current time by pressing Alt + Shift + T.
5. Save **5-InputDevices.docx**.
6. Update the time by clicking the time and then pressing the F9 function key.
7. Save, print, and then close **5-InputDevices.docx**.

Check Your Work

Project 2 Create an Announcement about Supervisory Training   **4 Parts**

You will create an announcement about upcoming supervisory training in Australia and use the Click and Type feature to center and right-align text. You will vertically center the text on the page and insert and format an image and an online image to add visual appeal to the announcement.

Preview Finished Project

Quick Steps

Use Click and Type
1. Hover mouse at left margin, between left and right margins, or at right margin.
2. When horizontal lines display next to mouse pointer, double-click left mouse button.

Using the Click and Type Feature

Word contains a Click and Type feature that positions the insertion point at a specific location and alignment in the document. This feature can be used to position one or more lines of text as it is being typed rather than typing the text and then selecting and formatting the text, which requires multiple steps.

To use the Click and Type feature, make sure the document displays in Print Layout view and then hover the mouse pointer at the location the insertion point is to be positioned. As the mouse pointer moves, the pointer displays with varying horizontal lines representing the alignment. When the desired alignment lines display below the mouse pointer, double-click the left mouse button. If the horizontal lines do not display next to the mouse pointer when the mouse button is double-clicked, a left tab is set at the position of the insertion point. To change the alignment and not set a tab, make sure the horizontal lines display near the mouse pointer before double-clicking the mouse button.

1. At a blank document, create the centered text shown in Figure 5.5 by completing the following steps:
   a. Position the I-beam pointer between the left and right margins at about the 3.25-inch mark on the horizontal ruler and at the top of the vertical ruler.
   b. When the center alignment lines display below the I-beam pointer, double-click the left mouse button.
   c. Type the centered text shown in Figure 5.5. Press Shift + Enter to end each line except the last line.
2. Change to right alignment by completing the following steps:
   a. Position the I-beam pointer near the right margin at approximately the 1-inch mark on the vertical ruler until the right alignment lines display at the left side of the I-beam pointer.
   b. Double-click the left mouse button.
   c. Type the right-aligned text shown in Figure 5.5. Press Shift + Enter to end the first line.
3. Select the centered text and then change the font to 14-point Candara bold and the line spacing to double spacing.
4. Select the right-aligned text, change the font to 10-point Candara bold, and then deselect the text.
5. Save the document and name it **5-Training**.

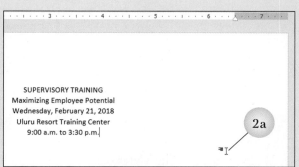

Check Your Work

Figure 5.5 Project 2a

> SUPERVISORY TRAINING
> Maximizing Employee Potential
> Wednesday, February 21, 2018
> Uluru Resort Training Center
> 9:00 a.m. to 3:30 p.m.
>
>   Sponsored by
>   Cell Systems

Tutorial

Vertically Aligning Data

Vertically Aligning Text

Text or items in a Word document are aligned at the top of the page by default. Change this alignment with the *Vertical alignment* option box at the Page Setup dialog box with the Layout tab selected, as shown in Figure 5.6. Display this dialog box by clicking the Layout tab, clicking the Page Setup group dialog box launcher, and then clicking the Layout tab at the Page Setup dialog box.

Figure 5.6 Page Setup Dialog Box with Layout Tab Selected

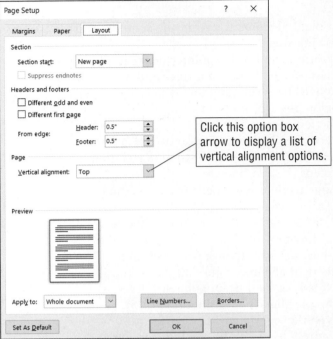

Click this option box arrow to display a list of vertical alignment options.

Quick Steps

Vertically Align Text
1. Click Layout tab.
2. Click Page Setup group dialog box launcher.
3. Click Layout tab.
4. Click *Vertical alignment* option box.
5. Click alignment.
6. Click OK.

The *Vertical alignment* option box in the *Page* section of the Page Setup dialog box contains four choices: *Top*, *Center*, *Justified*, and *Bottom*. The default setting is *Top*, which aligns text and items such as images at the top of the page. Choose *Center* to position the text in the middle of the page vertically. The *Justified* option aligns text between the top and bottom margins. The *Center* option positions text in the middle of the page vertically, while the *Justified* option adds space between paragraphs of text (not within) to fill the page from the top to the bottom margins. If the text is centered or justified, the text does not display centered or justified on the screen in Draft view but it does display centered or justified in Print Layout view. Choose the *Bottom* option to align text at the bottom of the page.

Project 2b   Vertically Centering Text

Part 2 of 4

1. With **5-Training.docx** open, click the Layout tab and then click the Page Setup group dialog box launcher.
2. At the Page Setup dialog box, click the Layout tab.
3. Click the *Vertical alignment* option box arrow and then click *Center* at the drop-down list.
4. Click OK to close the dialog box.
5. Save and then print **5-Training.docx**.

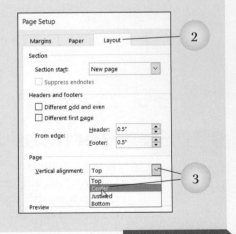

Check Your Work

Inserting and Formatting Images

Insert an image, such as a picture or piece of clip art, in a Word document with buttons in the Illustrations group on the Insert tab. Click the Pictures button to display the Insert Picture dialog box containing the image file or click the Online Pictures button and search online for images, such as pictures and clip art.

Inserting an Image

To insert an image in a document, click the Insert tab and then click the Pictures button in the Illustrations group. At the Insert Picture dialog box, navigate to the folder containing the image and then double-click the image file.

Customizing and Formatting an Image

When an image is inserted in a document the Picture Tools Format tab is active. Use buttons on this tab to format and customize the image. Use options in the Adjust group on the Picture Tools Format tab to remove unwanted portions of the image, correct the brightness and contrast, change the image color, apply artistic effects, compress the size of the image file, change to a different image, and reset the image to the original formatting. Use buttons in the Picture Styles group to apply a predesigned style to the image, change the image border, and apply other picture effects to the image. With options in the Arrange group, position the image on the page, specify how text will wrap around it, align the image with other elements in the document, and rotate the image. Use the Crop button in the Size group to remove any unnecessary parts of the image and specify the image size with the *Shape Height* and *Shape Width* measurement boxes.

An image can also be customized and formatted with options at the shortcut menu. Display this menu by right-clicking the image. Use options at the shortcut menu to replace the image with another image, insert a caption, specify text wrapping, size and position the image, and display the Format Picture task pane.

To move an image, apply a text wrapping style with the Position button or the Wrap Text button on the Picture Tools Format tab and with options from the Layout Options button side menu. The Layout Options button displays just outside the upper right corner of the selected image. Click this button to display a side menu with wrapping options. Click the See more hyperlink text at the bottom of the side menu to display the Layout dialog box containing additional options for positioning the image on the page. Close the Layout Options button side menu by clicking the button or clicking the Close button in the upper right corner of the side menu.

Sizing an Image

Change the size of an image with the *Shape Height* and *Shape Width* measurement boxes in the Size group on the Picture Tools Format tab or with the sizing handles that display around a selected image. To change the image size with a sizing handle, position the mouse pointer on a sizing handle until the pointer turns into a double-headed arrow and then click and hold down the left mouse button. Drag the sizing handle in or out to decrease or increase the size of the image and then release the mouse button. Use the middle sizing handles at the left and right sides of the image to make the image wider or thinner. Use the middle sizing handles at the top and bottom of the image to make the image taller or shorter. Use the sizing handles at the corners of the image to change both the width and height at the same time.

Moving an Image

Move an image to a specific location on the page with options at the Position button drop-down gallery in the Arrange group on the Picture Tools Format tab. Choose an option from this gallery and the image is moved to the specified location and square text wrapping is applied to it.

The image can also be moved by dragging it to the new location. Before dragging an image, specify how the text will wrap around it by clicking the Wrap Text button in the Arrange group and then clicking the desired wrapping style at the drop-down list. After choosing a wrapping style, move the image by positioning the mouse pointer on the image border until the mouse pointer displays with a four-headed arrow attached. Click and hold down the left mouse button, drag the image to the new location, and then release the mouse button. As an image is moved to the top, left, right, or bottom margin or to the center of the document, green alignment guides display. Use these guides to help position the image on the page. Gridlines can be turned on to help position an image precisely. Do this by clicking the Align Objects button in the Arrange group on the Picture Tools Format tab and then clicking *View Gridlines*.

Align Objects

Rotate the image by positioning the mouse pointer on the round rotation handle (circular arrow) above the image until the pointer displays with a black circular arrow attached. Click and hold down the left mouse button, drag in the desired direction, and then release the mouse button. An image can also be rotated with options at the Rotate Objects button drop-down gallery. For example, the image can be rotated left or right or flipped horizontally or vertically.

Rotate Objects

Project 2c Inserting and Customizing an Image

Part 3 of 4

1. With **5-Training.docx** open, return the vertical alignment to top alignment by completing the following steps:
   a. Click the Layout tab.
   b. Click the Page Setup group dialog box launcher.
   c. At the Page Setup dialog box, make sure the Layout tab is selected.
   d. Click the *Vertical alignment* option box arrow and then click *Top* at the drop-down list.
   e. Click OK to close the dialog box.
2. Select and then delete the text *Sponsored by* and *Cell Systems*.
3. Select the remaining text and change the line spacing to single spacing.
4. Move the insertion point to the beginning of the document, press the Enter key, and then move the insertion point back to the beginning of the document.
5. Insert an image by completing the following steps:
   a. Click the Insert tab and then click the Pictures button in the Illustrations group.
   b. At the Insert Picture dialog box, navigate to your WL1C5 folder.
   c. Double-click *Uluru.jpg* in the Content pane.
6. Crop the image by completing the following steps:
   a. Click the Crop button in the Size group on the Picture Tools Format tab.

b. Position the mouse pointer on the bottom middle crop handle (which displays as a short black line) until the pointer turns into the crop tool (which displays as a small black T).

c. Click and hold down the left mouse button, drag up to just below the rock (as shown at the right), and then release the mouse button.

d. Click the Crop button in the Size group to turn the feature off.

7. Change the size of the image by clicking in the *Shape Height* measurement box in the Size group, typing 3.1, and then pressing the Enter key.

8. Move the image behind the text by clicking the Layout Options button outside the upper right corner of the image and then clicking the *Behind Text* option at the side menu (second column, second row in the *With Text Wrapping* section). Close the side menu by clicking the Close button in the upper right corner of the side menu.

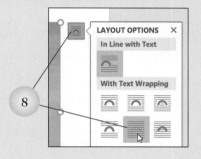

9. Rotate the image by clicking the Rotate Objects button in the Arrange group and then clicking *Flip Horizontal* at the drop-down gallery.

10. Change the image color by clicking the Color button in the Adjust group and then clicking *Saturation: 300%* (sixth option in the *Color Saturation* section).

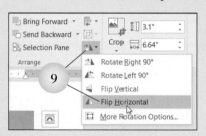

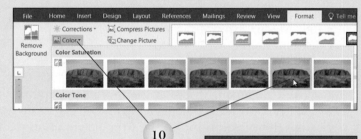

11. Apply an artistic effect by clicking the Artistic Effects button in the Adjust group and then clicking the *Watercolor Sponge* option (second column, third row).

12. Apply a picture effect by clicking the Picture Effects button in the Picture Styles group, pointing to Bevel, and then clicking the *Circle* option (first column, first row in the *Bevel* section).

13. After looking at the new color and artistic effect, you decide to return to the original color and artistic effect and remove the bevel effect by clicking the Reset Picture button in the Adjust group on the Picture Tools Format tab.

14. Sharpen the image by clicking the Corrections button in the Adjust group and then clicking the *Sharpen: 25%* option (fourth option in the *Sharpen/Soften* section).

15. Change the contrast of the image by clicking the Corrections button in the Adjust group and then clicking the *Brightness: 0% (Normal) Contrast: +40%* option (third column, bottom row in the *Brightness/Contrast* section).

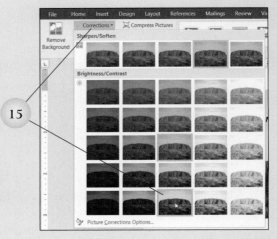

16. Apply a picture style by clicking the More Picture Styles button in the Picture Styles group and then clicking the *Simple Frame, Black* option.

17. Compress the image file by completing the following steps:
    a. Click the Compress Pictures button in the Adjust group.
    b. At the Compress Pictures dialog box, make sure check marks display in both options in the *Compression options* section and then click OK.

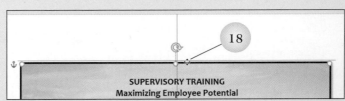

18. Position the mouse pointer on the border of the selected image until the pointer displays with a four-headed arrow attached. Click and hold down the left mouse button, drag the image up and slightly to the left until you

see green alignment guides at the top margin and the center of the page, and then release the mouse button. If the green alignment guides do not display, turn on the guides by clicking the Align button in the Arrange group on the Picture Tools Format tab and then clicking the *Use Alignment Guides* option.

19. Save and then print **5-Training.docx**.
20. With the image selected, remove the background by completing the following steps:
    a. Click the Remove Background button in the Adjust group on the Picture Tools Format tab.
    b. Using the left middle sizing handle, drag the left border to the left border line of the image.
    c. Drag the right middle sizing handle to the right border line of the image.
    d. Drag the bottom middle sizing handle to the bottom border of the image, which displays as a dashed line.
    e. Drag the top middle sizing handle down to just above the top of the rock.

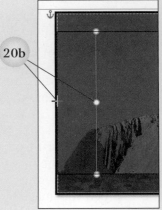

f. Click the Keep Changes button in the Close group on the Background Removal tab. (The image should now display with the sky removed.)

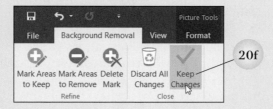

21. Save **5-Training.docx**.

Check Your Work

Inserting an Online Image

 Online Pictures

Use the Bing Image Search feature to search for specific images online. To use this feature, click the Insert tab and then click the Online Pictures button. This displays the Insert Pictures window, shown in Figure 5.7. Click in the search text box, type the search term or topic, and then press the Enter key. Images that match the search term or topic display in the window.

To insert an image, click the image and then click the Insert button or double-click the image. This downloads the image to the document. Customize the image with options and buttons on the Picture Tools Format tab.

When selecting online images to use in documents, be aware that many images are copyrighted and thus may not be available for use without permission. By default, Bing will limit search results to those licensed under Creative Commons. Usually, these images are free to use, but an image may have limitations for its use. For example, it may be necessary to credit the source. Always review the specific license for any image you want to use to ensure you can comply with the specific requirements for that image.

Quick Steps

Insert an Online Image
1. Click Insert tab.
2. Click Online Pictures button.
3. Type search word or topic.
4. Press Enter.
5. Double-click image.

Figure 5.7 Insert Pictures Window

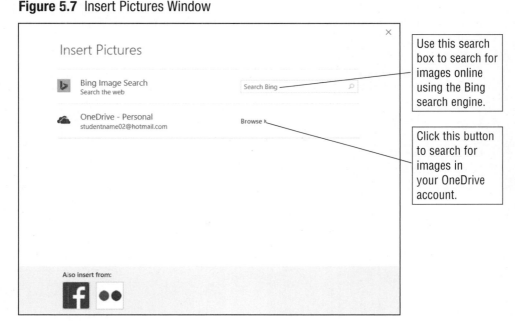

1. With **5-Training.docx** open, insert an image of Australia (with the Northern Territory highlighted) by completing the following steps:
   a. Click the Insert tab.
   b. Click the Online Pictures button in the Illustrations group.
   c. At the Insert Pictures window, type northern territory australia and then press the Enter key.
   d. Double-click the Australia image shown below. (If this image is not available online, click the Pictures button on the Insert tab. At the Insert Picture dialog box, navigate to your WL1C5 folder and then double-click the file *NT-Australia.png*.)

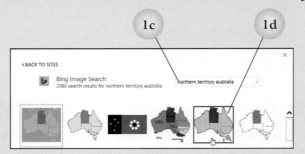

2. Size and position the image by completing the following steps:
   a. Click the Position button in the Arrange group.
   b. Click the *Position in Top Right with Square Text Wrapping* option (third column, first row in the *With Text Wrapping* section).
   c. Click the Wrap Text button.
   d. Click the *Behind Text* option at the drop-down gallery.
   e. Click in the *Shape Height* measurement box in the Size group, type 1, and then press the Enter key.

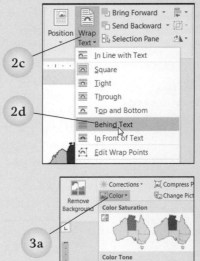

3. Make the white background of the image transparent by completing the following steps:
   a. Click the Color button in the Adjust group.
   b. Click the *Set Transparent Color* option at the bottom of the drop-down list. (The mouse pointer turns into a dropper tool.)
   c. Position the dropper tool on the white background of the image and then click the left mouse button.
4. Click the Color button in the Adjust group and then click the *Orange, Accent color 2 Light* option (third column, third row in the *Recolor* section).
5. Click outside the image to deselect it.
6. Save, print, and then close **5-Training.docx**.

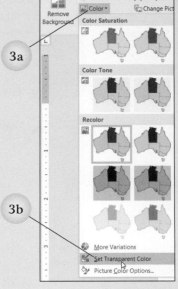

Check Your Work

You will open a report on robots and then add a pull quote using a predesigned text box and insert a drawn text box with information about an upcoming conference.

Preview Finished Project

Inserting a Text Box

Tutorial

Inserting a
Text Box

 Text Box

Add interest or create a location in a document for text by inserting or drawing a text box. Click the Insert tab and then click the Text Box button and a drop-down list displays with predesigned text boxes and the *Draw Text Box* option. Choose one of the predesigned text boxes, which already contain formatting, or draw a text box and then customize or apply formatting to it with options and buttons on the Drawing Tools Format tab.

Inserting a Predesigned Text Box

Quick Steps

Insert a Predesigned Text Box
1. Click Insert tab.
2. Click Text Box button.
3. Click option at drop-down list.

One use for a text box in a document is to insert a pull quote. A pull quote is a quote from the text that is "pulled out" and enlarged and positioned in an attractive location on the page. Some advantages of using pull quotes are that they reinforce important concepts, summarize the message, and break up text blocks to make them easier to read. If a document contains multiple pull quotes, keep them in the order in which they appear in the text to ensure clear comprehension by readers.

A text box for a pull quote can be drawn in a document or a predesigned text box can be inserted in the document. To insert a predesigned text box, click the Insert tab, click the Text Box button, and then click the predesigned text box at the drop-down list.

Formatting a Text Box

Tutorial

Formatting a
Text Box

When a text box is selected, the Drawing Tools Format tab is active. This tab contains buttons for formatting and customizing the text box. Use options in the Insert Shapes group on the Drawing Tools Format tab to insert a shape in the document. Click the Edit Shape button in the Insert Shapes group and a drop-down list displays. Click the *Change Shape* option to change the shape of the selected text box. Click the *Edit Points* option and small black squares display at points around the text box. Use the mouse to drag these points to increase or decrease specific points around the text box.

Apply predesigned styles to a text box and change the shape fill, outline, and effects with options in the Shape Styles group. Change the formatting of the text in the text box with options in the WordArt Styles group. Click the More WordArt Styles button in the WordArt Styles group and then click a style at the drop-down gallery. Customize text in the text box with the Text Fill, Text Outline, and Text Effects buttons in the Text group. Use options in the Arrange group to position the text box on the page, specify text wrapping in relation to the text box, align the text box with other objects in the document, and rotate the text box. Specify the text box size with the *Shape Height* and *Shape Width* measurement boxes in the Size group.

1. Open **Robots.docx** and then save it with the name **5-Robots**.
2. Insert a predesigned text box by completing the following steps:
   a. Click the Insert tab.
   b. Click the Text Box button in the Text group.
   c. Scroll down the drop-down list and then click the *Ion Quote (Dark)* option.
3. Type the following text in the text box: "The task of creating a humanlike body has proven incredibly difficult."
4. Delete the line and the source placeholder in the text box by pressing the F8 function key (which turns on the Selection Mode), pressing Ctrl + End (which selects text from the location of the insertion point to the end of the text box), and then pressing the Delete key.
5. With the Drawing Tools Format tab active, click the More Shape Styles button in the Shape Styles group and then click the *Subtle Effect - Blue, Accent 5* option (sixth column, fourth row in the *Theme Styles* section).
6. Click the Shape Effects button in the Shape Styles group, point to *Shadow*, and then click the *Offset Diagonal Bottom Right* option (first column, first row in the *Outer* section).

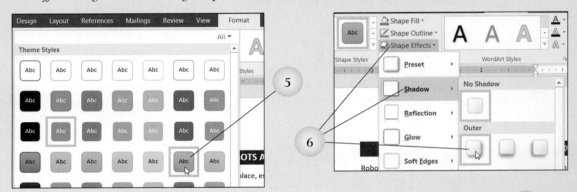

7. Position the mouse pointer on the border of the selected text box until the pointer turns into a four-headed arrow and then drag the text box so it is positioned as shown at the right.
8. Click outside the text box to deselect it.
9. Save **5-Robots.docx**.

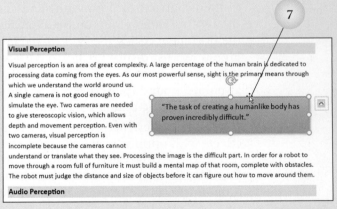

Check Your Work

Drawing and Formatting a Text Box

Quick Steps
Draw a Text Box
1. Click Insert tab.
2. Click Text Box button.
3. Click *Draw Text Box*.
4. Click or drag in document to create box.

In addition to the built-in text boxes provided by Word, a text box can be drawn in a document. To draw a text box, click the Insert tab, click the Text Box button in the Text group, and then click *Draw Text Box* at the drop-down list. With the mouse pointer displaying as crosshairs (a plus [+] symbol), click in the document to insert the text box or position the crosshairs in the document and then drag to create the text box. When a text box is selected, the Drawing Tools Format tab is active. Use buttons on this tab to format drawn text boxes in the same manner as built-in text boxes.

Project 3b Inserting and Formatting a Text Box   Part 2 of 2

1. With **5-Robots.docx** open, press Ctrl + End to move the insertion point to the end of the document.
2. Insert a text box by completing the following steps:
   a. Click the Insert tab.
   b. Click the Text Box button and then click the *Draw Text Box* option.
   c. Position the mouse pointer (displays as crosshairs) immediately right of the insertion point and then click the left mouse button. (This inserts the text box in the document.)
3. Change the text box height and width by completing the following steps:
   a. Click in the *Shape Height* measurement box in the Size group, type 1.2, and then press the Enter key.
   b. Click in the *Shape Width* measurement box in the Size group, type 4.5, and then press the Enter key.
4. Center the text box by clicking the Align button and then clicking *Align Center* at the drop-down list.
5. Apply a shape style by clicking the More Shape Styles button in the Shape Styles group and then clicking the *Subtle Effect - Blue, Accent 1* option (second column, fourth row in the *Theme Styles* section).
6. Apply a bevel shape effect by clicking the Shape Effects button, pointing to the *Bevel* option, and then clicking the *Soft Round* option at the side menu (second column, second row in the *Bevel* section).

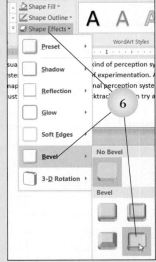

7. Apply a 3-D shape effect by clicking the Shape Effects button, pointing to *3-D Rotation*, and then clicking the *Perspective Above* option (first column, second row in the *Perspective* section).
8. Insert and format text in the text box by completing the following steps:
   a. Press the Enter key two times. (The insertion point should be positioned in the text box.)
   b. Click the Home tab.
   c. Change the font size to 14 points, apply bold formatting, and change the font color to standard *Dark Blue*.
   d. Click the Center button in the Paragraph group.
   e. Type International Conference on Artifical Intelligence Summer 2019.
   f. Click outside the text box to deselect it. (Your text box should appear as shown at the right.)
9. Save, print, and then close **5-Robots.docx**.

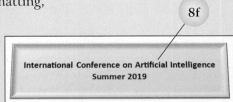

Check Your Work

Project 4 **Prepare a Company Flyer**   **2 Parts**

You will prepare a company flyer by inserting and customizing shapes and WordArt.

Preview Finished Project

Drawing Shapes

Use the Shapes button on the Insert tab to draw shapes in a document, including lines, basic shapes, block arrows, flow chart shapes, stars and banners, and callouts. Click a shape and the mouse pointer displays as crosshairs. Position the crosshairs in the document where the shape is to be inserted and then click the left mouse button or click and hold down the left mouse button, drag to create the shape, and then release the mouse button. The shape is inserted in the document and the Drawing Tools Format tab is active.

A shape selected from the *Lines* section of the drop-down list and then drawn in the document is considered a line drawing. A shape selected from another section of the drop-down list and then drawn in the document is considered an enclosed object. When drawing an enclosed object, maintain the proportions of the shape by pressing and holding down the Shift key while dragging with the mouse to create the shape.

Copying Shapes

To copy a shape, select the shape and then click the Copy button in the Clipboard group on the Home tab. Position the insertion point at the location where the copied shape is to be inserted and then click the Paste button. A selected shape can also be copied by pressing and holding down the Ctrl key while dragging a copy of the shape to the new location.

Project 4a **Drawing Arrow Shapes**   Part 1 of 2

1. At a blank document, press the Enter key two times and then draw an arrow shape by completing the following steps:
   a. Click the Insert tab.
   b. Click the Shapes button in the Illustrations group and then click the *Striped Right Arrow* shape (fifth column, second row) in the *Block Arrows* section.
   c. Position the mouse pointer (which displays as crosshairs) immediately right of the insertion point and then click the left mouse button. (This inserts the arrow shape in the document.)
2. Format the arrow by completing the following steps:
   a. Click in the *Shape Height* measurement box in the Size group, type 2.4, and then press the Enter key.
   b. Click in the *Shape Width* measurement box in the Size group, type 4.5, and then press the Enter key.

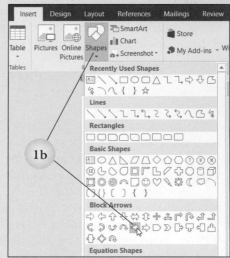

c. Horizontally align the arrow by clicking the Align button in the Arrange group and then clicking *Distribute Horizontally* at the drop-down list.

d. Click the More Shape Styles button in the Shape Styles group and then click the *Intense Effect - Green, Accent 6* option (last option at the drop-down gallery).

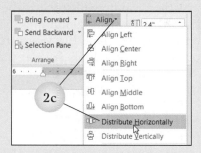

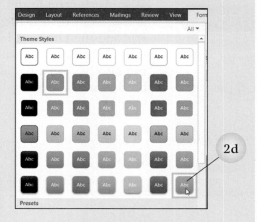

e. Click the Shape Effects button in the Shape Styles group, point to *Bevel*, and then click the *Angle* option (first column, second row in the *Bevel* section).

f. Click the Shape Outline button arrow in the Shape Styles group and then click the *Dark Blue* option (ninth option in the *Standard Colors* section).

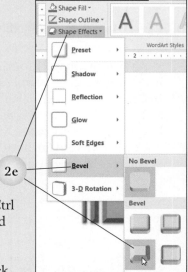

3. Copy the arrow by completing the following steps:

a. With the mouse pointer positioned in the arrow (mouse pointer displays with a four-headed arrow attached), press and hold down the Ctrl key and click and hold down the left mouse button. Drag down until the copied arrow displays just below the top arrow, release the mouse button, and then release the Ctrl key.

b. Click in the document to deselect the arrows and then click the second arrow to select it.

c. Copy the selected arrow by pressing and holding down the Ctrl key and clicking and holding down the left mouse button and then dragging the copied arrow just below the second arrow.

4. Flip the middle arrow by completing the following steps:

a. Click in the document to deselect the arrows and then click the middle arrow to select it.

b. Click the Rotate button in the Arrange group on the Drawing Tools Format tab and then click the *Flip Horizontal* option at the drop-down gallery.

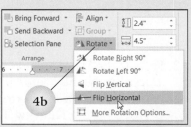

5. Insert the text *Financial* in the top arrow by completing the following steps:

a. Click the top arrow to select it.

b. Type Financial.

c. Select *Financial*.

d. Click the Home tab.

e. Change the font size to 16 points, apply bold formatting, and change the font color to standard *Dark Blue* (ninth option in the *Standard Colors* section).

6. Complete steps similar to those in Step 5 to insert the word *Direction* in the middle arrow.

7. Complete steps similar to those in Step 5 to insert the word *Retirement* in the bottom arrow.

8. Save the document and name it **5-FinConsult**.

9. Print the document.

Check Your Work

Tutorial

Inserting, Sizing,
and Positioning
WordArt

Tutorial

Formatting
WordArt

A | WordArt

Creating and Formatting WordArt

Use the WordArt feature to distort or modify text to conform to a variety of shapes. This is useful for creating company logos, letterheads, flyer titles, and headings.

To insert WordArt in a document, click the Insert tab and then click the WordArt button in the Text group. At the drop-down list, click the desired option and a WordArt text box is inserted in the document containing the words *Your text here* and the Drawing Tools Format tab is active. Type the WordArt text and then format the WordArt with options on the Drawing Tools Format tab. Existing text can also be formatted as WordArt. To do this, select the text, click the WordArt button on the Insert tab and then click the WordArt option at the drop-down list.

Quick Steps
Create WordArt Text
1. Click Insert tab.
2. Click WordArt button.
3. Click option.
4. Type WordArt text.

Project 4b Inserting and Modifying WordArt   Part 2 of 2

1. With **5-FinConsult.docx** open, press Ctrl + Home to move the insertion point to the beginning of the document.
2. Insert WordArt text by completing the following steps:
   a. Type Miller Financial Services and then select *Miller Financial Services*.
   b. Click the Insert tab.
   c. Click the WordArt button in the Text group and then click the *Fill - Orange, Accent 2, Outline - Accent 2* option (third column, first row).

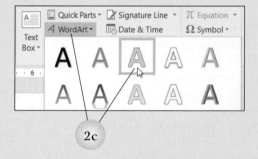

2c

3. Format the WordArt text by completing the following steps:
   a. Make sure the WordArt text border displays as a solid line.
   b. Click the Text Fill button arrow in the WordArt Styles group on the Drawing Tools Format tab and then click the *Light Green* color option (fifth option in the *Standard Colors* section).
   c. Click the Text Outline button arrow in the WordArt Styles group and then click the *Green, Accent 6, Darker 50%* option (last option in *Theme Colors* section).

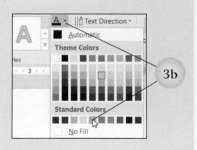

3b

---

d. Click the Text Effects button in the WordArt Styles group, point to *Glow*, and then click the *Blue, 5 pt glow, Accent color 1* option (first option in the *Glow Variations* section).

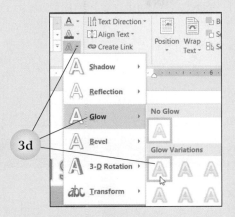

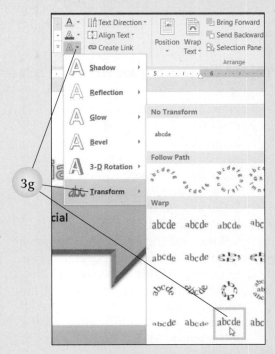

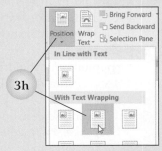

e. Click in the *Shape Height* measurement box in the Size group and then type 1.

f. Click in the *Shape Width* measurement box in the Size group, type 6, and then press the Enter key.

g. Click the Text Effects button in the WordArt Styles group, point to *Transform*, and then click the effect option located in the third column, fourth row in the *Warp* section.

h. Click the Position button in the Arrange group and then click the *Position in Top Center with Square Text Wrapping* option (second column, first row in the *With Text Wrapping* section).

4. Click outside the WordArt to deselect it.

5. Move the arrows as needed to ensure they do not overlap the WordArt or each other and that they all fit on one page.

6. Save, print, and then close **5-FinConsult.docx**.

Check Your Work ▶

Project 5 Create and Format Screenshots   2 Parts

You will create screenshots of the Print and Export backstage areas, screen clippings of cover pages, and a sample cover page document.

Preview Finished Project ▶

Tutorial ▶

Inserting and Formatting Screenshot and Screen Clipping Images

Creating and Inserting a Screenshot

The Illustrations group on the Insert tab contains a Screenshot button, which captures the contents of a screen as an image or captures a portion of a screen. To capture the entire screen, open a new document, click the Insert tab, click the Screenshot button in the Illustrations group, and then click the desired screen thumbnail at the drop-down list. The currently active document does not display

---

Screenshot

as a thumbnail at the drop-down list—only other documents or files that are open. Click the specific thumbnail in the drop-down list and a screenshot of the screen is inserted as an image in the open document. The screenshot image is selected and the Picture Tools Format tab is active. Use buttons on this tab to customize the screenshot image.

Project 5a   Inserting and Formatting Screenshots

Part 1 of 2

1. Press Ctrl + N to open a blank document.
2. Press Ctrl + N to open a second blank document, type Print Backstage Area at the left margin, and then press the Enter key.
3. Save the document and name it **5-BackstageAreas**.
4. Point to the Word button on the taskbar and then click the thumbnail representing the blank document.
5. Display the Print backstage area by clicking the File tab and then clicking the *Print* option.

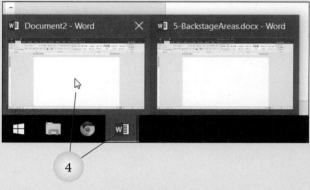

6. Point to the Word button on the taskbar and then click the thumbnail representing **5-BackstageAreas.docx**.
7. Insert and format a screenshot of the Print backstage area by completing the following steps:
   a. Click the Insert tab.
   b. Click the Screenshot button in the Illustrations group and then click the thumbnail in the drop-down list. (This inserts a screenshot of the Print backstage area in the document.)
   c. With the screenshot image selected, click the *Drop Shadow Rectangle* picture style option (fourth option in the picture styles gallery).
   d. Select the measurement in the *Shape Width* measurement box in the Size group, type 5.5, and then press the Enter key.

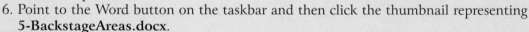
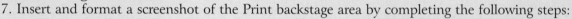

8. Press Ctrl + End and then press the Enter key. (The insertion point should be positioned below the screenshot image.)
9. Type Export Backstage Area at the left margin and then press the Enter key.
10. Point to the Word button on the taskbar and then click the thumbnail representing the blank document.
11. At the backstage area, click the *Export* option. (This displays the Export backstage area.)
12. Point to the Word button on the taskbar and then click the thumbnail representing **5-BackstageAreas.docx**.
13. Insert and format a screenshot of the Export backstage area by completing steps similar to those in Step 7.
14. Press Ctrl + Home to move the insertion point to the beginning of the document.
15. Save, print, and then close **5-BackstageAreas.docx**.
16. At the Export backstage area, press the Esc key to redisplay the blank document.
17. Close the blank document.

Check Your Work

Not only can a screenshot be made of an entire screen, but a screenshot can also be made of a specific portion of a screen by clicking the *Screen Clipping* option at the Screenshot button drop-down list. Click this option and the other open document, file, or Windows Start screen or desktop displays in a dimmed manner and the mouse pointer displays as crosshairs. Using the mouse, draw a border around the specific area of the screen to be captured. The area identified is inserted in the other document as an image, the image is selected, and the Picture Tools Format tab is active.

Project 5b Creating and Formatting a Screen Clipping

1. Open **NSSLtrhd.docx** and then save it with the name **5-NSSCoverPages**.
2. Type the text Sample Cover Pages and then press the Enter key two times.
3. Select the text you just typed, change the font to 18-point Copperplate Gothic Bold, and then center the text.
4. Press Ctrl + End to move the insertion point below the text.
5. Open **NSSCoverPg01.docx** and then change the zoom to 40% by clicking six times on the Zoom Out button at the left side of the Zoom slider bar on the Status bar.
6. Point to the Word button on the taskbar and then click the thumbnail representing **5-NSSCoverPages.docx**.
7. Insert and format a screen clipping image by completing the following steps:
   a. Click the Insert tab.
   b. Click the Screenshot button in the Illustrations group and then click the *Screen Clipping* option.

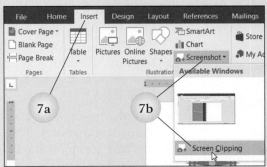

   c. When **NSSCoverPg01.docx** displays in a dimmed manner, position the mouse crosshairs in the upper left corner of the cover page, click and hold down the left mouse button, drag down to the lower right corner of the cover page, and then release the mouse button. (See the image below and to the right.)
   d. With the cover page screen clipping image inserted in **5-NSSCoverPages.docx**, make sure the image is selected. (The sizing handles should display around the cover page image.)
   e. Click the Wrap Text button in the Arrange group on the Picture Tools Format tab and then click *Square* at the drop-down gallery.
   f. Select the current measurement in the *Shape Width* measurement box in the Size group, type 3, and then press the Enter key.
8. Point to the Word button on the Taskbar and then click the thumbnail representing **NSSCoverPg01.docx**.
9. Close **NSSCoverPg01.docx**.
10. Open **NSSCoverPg02.docx** and then, if neccessary, change the zoom to 40%.

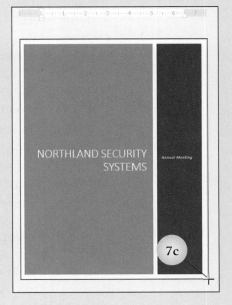

11. Point to the Word button on the Taskbar and then click the thumbnail representing **5-NSSCoverPages.docx**.
12. Insert and format a screen clipping image of the cover page by completing steps similar to those in Step 7.
13. If necessary, position the two cover page screenshot images side by side in the document.
14. Save, print, and then close **5-NSSCoverPages.docx**.
15. Close **NSSCoverPg02.docx**.

Check Your Work

Chapter Summary

- Apply formatting to a portion of a document by inserting a continuous section break or a section break that begins a new page. Turn on the display of nonprinting characters or change to Draft view to display section breaks; they are not visible in Print Layout view.

- Set text in columns to improve the readability of documents such as newsletters and reports. Format text in columns using the Columns button in the Page Setup group on the Layout tab or with options at the Columns dialog box.

- Remove column formatting with the Columns button on the Layout tab or at the Columns dialog box. Balance column text on the last page of a document by inserting a continuous section break at the end of the text.

- Improve the display of text by hyphenating long words that fall at the ends of lines. Use the hyphenation feature to hyphenate words automatically or manually.

- To enhance the appearance of text, use drop caps to identify the beginnings of major sections or paragraphs. Create drop caps with the Drop Cap button in the Text group on the Insert tab.

- Insert symbols with options at the Symbol dialog box with the Symbols tab selected, and insert special characters with options at the Symbol dialog box with the Special Characters tab selected.

- Click the Date & Time button in the Text group on the Insert tab to display the Date and Time dialog box. Insert the date or time with options at this dialog box or with keyboard shortcuts. If the date or time is inserted as a field, update the field with the Update tab or the F9 function key.

- Use the Click and Type feature to center, right-align, and left-align text.

- Vertically align text in a document with the *Vertical alignment* option at the Page Setup dialog box with the Layout tab selected.

- Insert an image such as a picture or clip art with buttons in the Illustrations group on the Insert tab.

- To insert an image from a folder on the computer's hard drive or removable drive, click the Insert tab and then click the Pictures button. At the Insert Picture dialog box, navigate to the specific folder and then double-click the image file.

- To insert an online image, click the Insert tab and then click the Online Pictures button. At the Insert Pictures window, type the search text or topic, press the Enter key, and then double-click the image.

- Customize and format an image with options and buttons on the Picture Tools Format tab. Size an image with the *Shape Height* and *Shape Width* measurement boxes in the Size group or with the sizing handles that display around a selected image.

- Move an image using options from the Position button drop-down gallery on the Picture Tools Format tab, or by choosing a text wrapping style and then moving the image by dragging it with the mouse.

- Insert a predesigned text box using options from the Text Box button drop-down gallery on the Insert tab. A predesigned text box or drawn text box can be used to create a pull quote, which is a quote that is pulled from the document text.

- Draw a text box by clicking the Text Box button in the Text group on the Insert tab, clicking the *Draw Text Box* option at the drop-down list, and then clicking or dragging in the document.

- Customize a text box with buttons on the Drawing Tools Format tab.

- Draw shapes in a document by clicking the Shapes button in the Illustrations group on the Insert tab, clicking a shape at the drop-down list, and then clicking or dragging in the document to draw the shape. Customize a shape with options on the Drawing Tools Format tab.

- Copy a shape by pressing and holding down the Ctrl key while dragging the selected shape.

- Use WordArt to distort or modify text to conform to a variety of shapes. Customize WordArt with options on the Drawing Tools Format tab.

- Use the Screenshot button in the Illustrations group on the Insert tab to capture the contents of a screen or a portion of a screen. Use buttons on the Picture Tools Format tab to customize a screenshot image.

Commands Review

FEATURE	RIBBON TAB, GROUP	BUTTON, OPTION	KEYBOARD SHORTCUT
Column break	Layout, Page Setup	, Columns	Ctrl + Shift + Enter
columns	Layout, Page Setup		
Columns dialog box	Layout, Page Setup	, More Columns	
continuous section break	Layout, Page Setup	, Continuous	
Date and Time dialog box	Insert, Text		
drop cap	Insert, Text		
hyphenate words automatically	Layout, Page Setup	, Automatic	
insert date as field			Alt + Shift + D
Insert Picture dialog box	Insert, Illustrations		
Insert Pictures window	Insert, Illustrations		
insert time as field			Alt + Shift + T
Manual Hyphenation dialog box	Layout, Page Setup	, Manual	
Page Setup dialog box	Layout, Page Setup		
predesigned text box	Insert, Text		
screenshot	Insert, Illustrations		
shapes	Insert, Illustrations		
Symbol dialog box	Insert, Symbols	, More Symbols	
text box	Insert, Text		
update field			F9
WordArt	Insert, Text		

Workbook

Chapter study tools and assessment activities are available in the *Workbook* ebook. These resources are designed to help you further develop and demonstrate mastery of the skills learned in this chapter.

Microsoft®

Word

Maintaining Documents and Printing Envelopes and Labels

CHAPTER

6

Performance Objectives

Upon successful completion of Chapter 6, you will be able to:

1 Create and rename a folder

2 Select, delete, copy, move, rename, and print documents

3 Save documents in different file formats

4 Open, close, arrange, maximize, minimize, and restore documents

5 Split a window, view documents side by side, and open a new window

6 Insert a file into an open document

7 Preview and print specific text and pages in a document

8 Print envelopes and labels

9 Create a document using a template

Precheck

Check your current skills to help focus your study.

Almost every company that conducts business maintains a filing system. The system may consist of documents, folders, and cabinets or it may be a computerized filing system, where information is stored on the computer's hard drive or another storage medium. Whatever type of filing system a business uses, daily maintenance of files is important to its operation. In this chapter, you will learn to maintain files (documents) in Word, performing such activities as creating additional folders and copying, moving, and renaming documents. You will also learn how to create and print documents, envelopes, and labels and create a document using a Word template.

SNAP

If you are a SNAP user, launch the Precheck and Tutorials from your Assignments page.

Data Files

Before beginning chapter work, copy the WL1C6 folder to your storage medium and then make WL1C6 the active folder.

151

Project 1 Manage Documents   8 Parts

You will perform a variety of file management tasks, including creating and
renaming a folder; selecting and then deleting, copying, cutting, pasting, and
renaming documents; deleting a folder; opening multiple documents; and saving a
document in a different format.

Preview Finished Project

Maintaining Documents

Hint Display the
Open dialog box with
the keyboard shortcut
Ctrl + F12.

Many file (document) management tasks can be completed at the Open dialog
box (and some at the Save As dialog box). These tasks can include copying,
moving, printing, and renaming documents; opening multiple documents; and
creating new folders and renaming existing folders.

Directions and projects in this chapter assume that you are managing documents
and folders on a USB flash drive or your computer's hard drive. If you are using your
OneDrive account, some of the document and folder management tasks may vary.

Using Print Screen

Keyboards contain a Print Screen key that will capture the contents of the screen
and insert the image in temporary memory. The image can then be inserted in
a Word document. Press the Print Screen key to capture the entire screen as an
image or press Alt + Print Screen to capture only the dialog box or window open
on the screen. The Print Screen feature is useful for file management because the
folder contents can be printed to help keep track of documents and folders.

To use the Print Screen key, display the desired information on the screen
and then press the Print Screen key on the keyboard (generally located in the top
row) or press Alt + Print Screen to capture the dialog box or window open on the
screen. When the Print Screen key or Alt + Print Screen is pressed, nothing seems
to happen, but in fact, the screen image is captured and inserted in the Clipboard.
To insert this image in a document, display a blank document and then click the
Paste button in the Clipboard group on the Home tab. The image can also be
pasted by right-clicking in a blank location in a document and then clicking the
Paste option at the shortcut menu.

Tutorial

Managing Folders

Creating a Folder

Word documents, like paper documents, should be grouped logically and placed in
folders. The main folder on a storage medium is called the *root folder* and additional
folders can be created within it. At the Open or Save As dialog box, documents
display in the Content pane preceded by document icons and folders display
preceded by folder icons.

New folder

New folder

Create a new folder by clicking the New folder button on the dialog box
toolbar. This inserts a folder in the Content pane that contains the text *New folder*.
Type a name for the folder (the typed name replaces *New folder*) and then press the
Enter key. A folder name can contain a maximum of 255 characters. Folder names
can use numbers, spaces, and symbols, except those symbols explained in the
Naming a Document section on page 8 in Chapter 1.

To make the new folder active, double-click the folder name in the Open dialog box Content pane. The current folder path displays in the Address bar and includes the current folder and any previous folders. If the folder is located on an external storage device, the drive letter and name may display in the path. A right-pointing triangle displays to the right of each folder name in the Address bar. Click this right-pointing triangle and a drop-down list displays the names of any subfolders within the folder.

Project 1a Creating a Folder

Part 1 of 8

1. Open a blank document and then press Ctrl + F12 to display the Open dialog box.
2. In the *This PC* list in the Navigation pane, click the drive containing your storage medium. (You may need to scroll down the list to display the drive.)
3. Double-click the *WL1C6* folder in the Content pane.
4. Click the New folder button on the dialog box toolbar.
5. Type Correspondence and then press the Enter key.
6. Capture the Open dialog box as an image and insert the image in a document by completing the following steps:
   a. With the Open dialog box displayed, hold down the Alt key and then press the Print Screen key on your keyboard (generally located in the top row).
   b. Close the Open dialog box.
   c. At the blank document, click the Paste button in the Clipboard group on the Home tab. (If a blank document does not display on your screen, press Ctrl + N to open a blank document.)
   d. With the print screen image inserted in the document, print the document by clicking the File tab, clicking the *Print* option, and then clicking the Print button at the Print backstage area.
7. Close the document without saving it.
8. Display the Open dialog box and make WL1C6 the active folder.

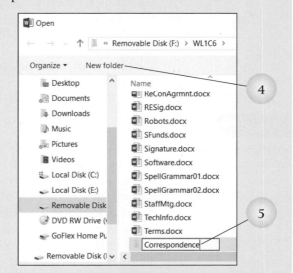

Check Your Work

Renaming a Folder

Organize

When organizing files and folders, a folder may need to be renamed. Rename a folder using the Organize button on the toolbar in the Open or Save As dialog box or using a shortcut menu. To rename a folder using the Organize button, display the Open or Save As dialog box, click the folder to be renamed, click the Organize button on the toolbar in the dialog box, and then click *Rename* at the drop-down list. This selects the folder name and inserts a border around it. Type the new name for the folder and then press the Enter key. To rename a folder using a shortcut menu, display the Open dialog box, right-click the folder name in the Content pane, and then click *Rename* at the shortcut menu. Type a new name for the folder and then press the Enter key.

1. With the Open dialog box open, right-click the *Correspondence* folder name in the Content pane.
2. Click *Rename* at the shortcut menu.
3. Type ComputerDocs and then press the Enter key.

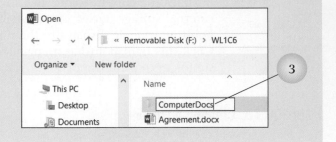

Selecting Documents

Complete document management tasks on one document or selected documents. To select one document, display the Open dialog box and then click the desired document. To select several adjacent documents (documents that display next to each other), click the first document, hold down the Shift key, and then click the last document. To select documents that are not adjacent, click the first document, hold down the Ctrl key, click any other documents, and then release the Ctrl key.

Tutorial

Managing Documents

Deleting Documents

Deleting documents is part of document maintenance. To delete a document, display the Open or Save As dialog box, select the document, click the Organize button on the toolbar, and then click *Delete* at the drop-down list. If documents are being deleted from an external drive, such as a USB flash drive, click the Yes button at the confirmation message. This message does not display if a document is being deleted from the computer's hard drive. To delete a document using the shortcut menu, right-click the document name in the Content pane and then click *Delete* at the shortcut menu. If a confirmation message displays, click Yes.

Quick Steps
Delete a Folder or Document
1. Display Open dialog box.
2. Click folder or document name.
3. Click Organize button.
4. Click *Delete*.
5. Click Yes.

💡 **Hint** Remember to empty the Recycle Bin on a regular basis.

Documents deleted from the hard drive are automatically sent to the Recycle Bin. If a document is accidentally sent to the Recycle Bin, it can be easily restored. To free space on the drive, empty the Recycle Bin on a periodic basis. Restoring a document from or emptying the contents of the Recycle Bin is completed at the Windows desktop (not in Word). To display the Recycle Bin, minimize the Word window, display the Windows desktop, and then double-click the *Recycle Bin* icon on the Windows desktop. At the Recycle Bin, files can be restored and the Recycle Bin can be emptied.

1. Open **FutureHardware.docx** and save it with the name **6-FutureHardware**.
2. Close **6-FutureHardware.docx**.
3. Delete **6-FutureHardware.docx** by completing the following steps:
   a. Display the Open dialog box.
   b. Click *6-FutureHardware.docx* to select it.
   c. Click the Organize button on the toolbar and then click *Delete* at the drop-down list.
   d. At the question asking if you want to delete **6-FutureHardware.docx**, click Yes. (This question will not display if you are deleting the file from your computer's hard drive.)
4. Delete selected documents by completing the following steps:
   a. At the Open dialog box, click *CompCareers.docx*.
   b. Hold down the Shift key and then click *CompEthics.docx*.
   c. Position the mouse pointer on a selected document and then click the right mouse button.
   d. At the shortcut menu, click *Delete*.
   e. At the question asking if you want to delete the items, click Yes.

5. Open **CompKeyboards.docx** and save it with the name **6-CompKeyboards**.
6. Save a copy of the **6-CompKeyboards.docx** file in the ComputerDocs folder by completing the following steps:
   a. With **6-CompKeyboards.docx** open, press the function key F12 to display the Save As dialog box.
   b. At the Save As dialog box, double-click the *ComputerDocs* folder at the top of the Content pane. (Folders are listed before documents.)
   c. Click the Save button in the lower right corner of the dialog box.
7. Close **6-CompKeyboards.docx**.
8. Press Ctrl + F12 to display the Open dialog box and then click *WL1C6* in the Address bar.

Quick Steps

Copy a Document
1. Display Open dialog box.
2. Right-click document name.
3. Click *Copy*.
4. Navigate to folder.
5. Right-click blank area in Content pane.
6. Click *Paste*.

Move a Document
1. Display Open dialog box.
2. Right-click document name.
3. Click *Cut*.
4. Navigate to folder.
5. Right-click blank area in Content pane.
6. Click *Paste*.

Copying and Moving Documents

A document can be copied to another folder without opening the document first. To do this, use the *Copy* and *Paste* options from the Organize button drop-down list or the shortcut menu at the Open dialog box or the Save As dialog box. A document or selected documents also can be copied into the same folder. When a document is copied a second time into the same folder, Word adds to the document name a hyphen followed by the word *Copy*.

Remove a document from one folder and insert it in another folder using the *Cut* and *Paste* options from the Organize button drop-down list or the shortcut menu at the Open dialog box. To do this with the Organize button, display the Open dialog box, select the document to be removed (cut), click the Organize button, and then click *Cut* at the drop-down list. Navigate to the desired folder, click the Organize button, and then click *Paste* at the drop-down list. To do this with the shortcut menu, display the Open dialog box, position the arrow pointer on the document to be removed, click the right mouse button, and then click *Cut* at the shortcut menu. Navigate to the desired folder, position the arrow pointer in a blank area in the Content pane, click the right mouse button, and then click *Paste* at the shortcut menu.

Project 1d Copying and Moving Documents

Note: If you are using your OneDrive account, the steps for copying and moving files will vary from the steps in this project. Check with your instructor.

1. At the Open dialog box with WL1C6 the active folder, copy a document to another folder by completing the following steps:
   a. Click **CompTerms.docx** in the Content pane, click the Organize button, and then click *Copy* at the drop-down list.
   b. Navigate to the ComputerDocs folder by double-clicking *ComputerDocs* at the top of the Content pane.
   c. Click the Organize button and then click *Paste* at the drop-down list.
2. Change back to the WL1C6 folder by clicking *WL1C6* in the Address bar.
3. Copy several documents to the ComputerDocs folder by completing the following steps:
   a. Click **IntelProp.docx**. (This selects the document.)
   b. Hold down the Ctrl key, click **Robots.docx**, click **TechInfo.docx**, and then release the Ctrl key. (You may need to scroll down the Content pane to display the three documents and then select the documents.)
   c. Position the arrow pointer on one of the selected documents, click the right mouse button, and then click *Copy* at the shortcut menu.
   d. Double-click the *ComputerDocs* folder.
   e. Position the arrow pointer in any blank area in the Content pane, click the right mouse button, and then click *Paste* at the shortcut menu.
4. Click *WL1C6* in the Address bar.

5. Move **CompIssues.docx** to the ComputerDocs folder by completing the following steps:
   a. Position the arrow pointer on ***CompIssues.docx***, click the right mouse button, and then click *Cut* at the shortcut menu.
   b. Double-click *ComputerDocs* to make it the active folder.
   c. Position the arrow pointer in any blank area in the Content pane, click the right mouse button, and then click *Paste* at the shortcut menu.
6. Capture the Open dialog box as an image and insert the image in a document by completing the following steps:
   a. With the Open dialog box displayed, press Alt + Print Screen.
   b. Close the Open dialog box.
   c. At a blank document, click the Paste button in the Clipboard group on the Home tab. (If a blank document does not display on your screen, press Ctrl + N to open a blank document.)
   d. With the print screen image inserted in the document, print the document.
7. Close the document without saving it.
8. Display the Open dialog box and make WL1C6 the active folder.

Check Your Work

Renaming Documents

Quick Steps

Rename a Document
1. Display Open dialog box.
2. Click document name.
3. Click Organize button and then click *Rename*.
4. Type new name.
5. Press Enter.

At the Open dialog box, use the *Rename* option from the Organize button drop-down list to give a document a different name. The *Rename* option changes the name of the document and keeps it in the same folder. To rename a document, display the Open dialog box, click the document to be renamed, click the Organize button, and then click *Rename* at the drop-down list. This selects the name and displays a black border around the document name. Type the new name and then press the Enter key. A document can also be renamed by right-clicking the document name at the Open dialog box and then clicking *Rename* at the shortcut menu. Type the new name for the document and then press the Enter key.

Deleting a Folder

As explained earlier in this chapter, a document or selected documents can be deleted. Delete a folder and all of its contents in the same manner as deleting a document.

Hint Open a recently opened document by clicking the File tab, clicking the *Open* option, and then clicking the document in the *Recent* option list.

Opening Multiple Documents

To open more than one document, select the documents in the Open dialog box and then click the Open button. Multiple documents can also be opened by positioning the arrow pointer on one of the selected documents, clicking the right mouse button, and then clicking *Open* at the shortcut menu.

Changing Dialog Box View

Use options in the Change your view button drop-down list at the Open or Save As dialog box to customize the display of folders and documents in the Content pane. Click the Change your view button arrow and a drop-down list displays with options for displaying folders and documents as icons, a list, with specific details, as tiles, or in content form. Change the view by clicking an option at the drop-down list or by clicking the Change your view button until the dialog box displays in the desired view.

1. Rename a document in the ComputerDocs folder by completing the following steps:
   a. At the Open dialog box with the WL1C6 folder open, double-click the *ComputerDocs* folder to make it active.
   b. Click *Robots.docx* to select it.
   c. Click the Organize button.
   d. Click *Rename* at the drop-down list.
   e. Type Androids and then press the Enter key.
2. Capture the Open dialog box as an image and insert the image in a document by completing the following steps:
   a. Press Alt + Print Screen.
   b. Close the Open dialog box.
   c. At a blank document, click the Paste button in the Clipboard group on the Home tab. (If a blank document does not display on your screen, press Ctrl + N to open a blank document.)
   d. With the print screen image inserted in the document, print the document.
3. Close the document without saving it.
4. Display the Open dialog box and make WL1C6 the active folder.
5. Change the dialog box view by clicking the Change your view button arrow and then clicking *Large icons* at the drop-down list.
6. Change the view again by clicking the Change your view button arrow and then clicking *Content* at the drop-down list.
7. Change the view back to a list by clicking the Change your view button and then clicking *List* at the drop-down list.
8. At the Open dialog box, click the *ComputerDocs* folder to select it.
9. Click the Organize button and then click *Delete* at the drop-down list.
10. If a message displays asking if you want to remove the folder and its contents, click Yes.
11. Select *CompKeyboards.docx*, *CompSoftware.docx*, and *CompTerms.docx*.
12. Click the Open button in the lower right corner of the dialog box.
13. Close the open documents.

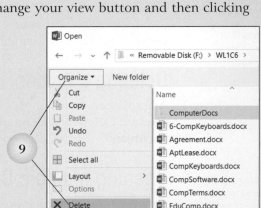

Check Your Work

Tutorial ▶

Saving in a Different Format

Saving in a Different Format

When a document is saved, it is saved as a Word document with the .docx file extension. If the document is to be shared with someone who is using a different word processing program or a different version of Word, consider saving the document in another format. At the Export backstage area, click the *Change File Type* option and the backstage area displays, as shown in Figure 6.1.

Quick Steps

Save in a Different Format

1. Click File tab.
2. Click *Export* option.
3. Click *Change File Type* option.
4. Click format in *Document File Types* or *Other File Types* section.
5. Click Save As button.

Saving in Different Document File Types Use options in the *Document File Types* section, which is below the *Change File Type* heading, to save the Word document with the default file format, in a previous version of Word, in the OpenDocument Text format, or as a template. The OpenDocument Text format is an XML-based file format for displaying, storing, and editing files, such as word processing, spreadsheet, and presentation files. OpenDocument Text format is free from any licensing, royalty payments, or other restrictions. Since technology changes at a rapid pace, saving a document in the OpenDocument Text format ensures that the information in it can be accessed, retrieved, and used now and in the future.

Saving in Other File Types Additional file types are available in the *Other File Types* section. If a document is being sent to a user who does not have access to Microsoft Word, consider saving the document in plain text or rich text file format. Use the *Plain Text (*.txt)* option to save the document with all the formatting stripped, which is good for universal file exchange. Use the *Rich Text Format (*.rtf)* option to save the document with most of the character formatting applied to the text in the document, such as bold, italic, underline, bullets, and fonts, as well as some paragraph formatting. Before the widespread use of Adobe's portable document format (PDF), rich text format was the most portable file format used to exchange files. With the *Single File Web Page (*.mht, *.mhtml)* option, a document can be saved as a single-page web document. Click the *Save as Another File Type* option and the Save As dialog box displays. Click the *Save as type* option box and a drop-down list displays with a variety of available file type options.

Figure 6.1 Export Backstage Area with *Change File Type* Option Selected

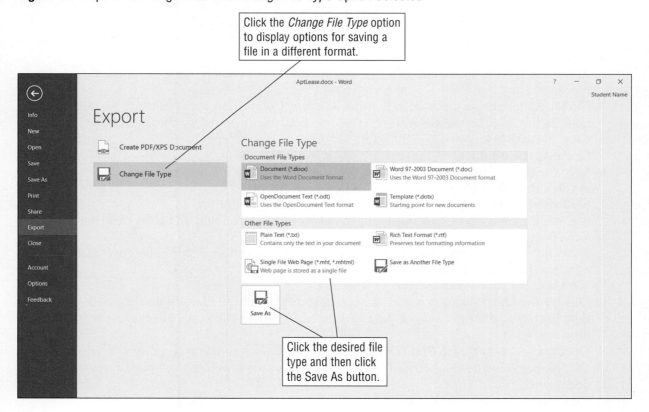

Click the *Change File Type* option to display options for saving a file in a different format.

Click the desired file type and then click the Save As button.

1. Open **AptLease.docx** and then save it in Word 97-2003 format by completing the following steps:
   a. Click the File tab and then click the *Export* option.
   b. At the Export backstage area, click the *Change File Type* option.
   c. Click the *Word 97-2003 Document (*.doc)* option in the *Document File Types* section and then click the Save As button.

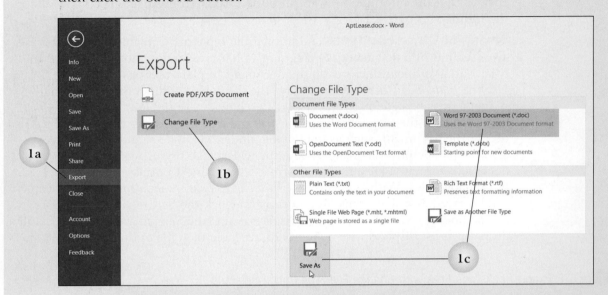

   d. At the Save As dialog box with the *Save as type* option changed to *Word 97-2003 Document (*.doc)*, type 6-AptLease-Word97-2003 in the *File name* text box and then press the Enter key.
2. At the document, notice that the title bar displays *[Compatibility Mode]* after the document name.
3. Click the Design tab and notice that the Themes, Colors, and Fonts buttons are dimmed. (This is because the themes features were not available in Word 97 through 2003.)
4. Close **6-AptLease-Word97-2003.doc**.
5. Open **AptLease.docx**.
6. Save the document in plain text format by completing the following steps:
   a. Click the File tab and then click the *Export* option.
   b. At the Export backstage area, click the *Change File Type* option.
   c. Click the *Plain Text (*.txt)* option in the *Other File Types* section and then click the Save As button.
   d. At the Save As dialog box, type 6-AptLease-PlainTxt and then press the Enter key.
   e. At the File Conversion dialog box, click OK.
7. Close **6-AptLease-PlainTxt.txt**.
8. Display the Open dialog box and, if necessary, display all the files. To do this, click the file type button at the right side of the *File name* text box and then click *All Files (*.*)* at the drop-down list.
9. Double-click *6-AptLease-PlainTxt.txt*. (If a File Conversion dialog box displays, click OK. Notice that the character and paragraph formatting have been removed from the document.)
10. Close **6-AptLease-PlainTxt.txt**.

Check Your Work

Saving in a Different File Type at the Save As Dialog Box In addition to saving a document using options in the Export backstage area with the *Change File Type* option selected, a document can be saved in a different format using the *Save as type* option box at the Save As dialog box. Click the *Save as type* option box and a drop-down list displays containing all the available file formats for saving a document. Click the desired format and then click the Save button.

Project 1g Saving in a Different Format at the Save As Dialog Box

Part 7 of 8

1. Open **AptLease.docx**.
2. Save the document in rich text format by completing the following steps:
   a. Press the function key F12 to display the Save As dialog box.
   b. At the Save As dialog box, type 6-AptLease-RichTxt in the *File name* text box.
   c. Click the *Save as type* option box.
   d. Click *Rich Text Format (*.rtf)* at the drop-down list.
   e. Click the Save button.
3. Close the document.
4. Display the Open dialog box and, if necessary, display all the files.
5. Double-click *6-AptLease-RichTxt.rtf*. (Notice that the formatting has been retained in the document.)
6. Close the document.

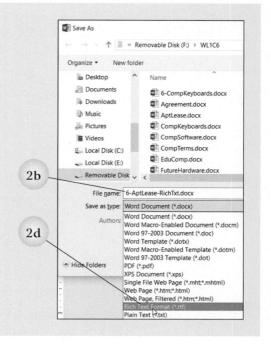

Saving in PDF/XPS Format A Word document can be saved in PDF or XPS file format. PDF stands for *portable document format* and is a file format that preserves fonts, formatting, and images in a printer-friendly version that looks the same on most computers. A person who receives a Word file saved in PDF format does not need to have the Word application on his or her computer to open, read, and print the file. Exchanging PDF files is a popular method for collaborating, since this file type has cross-platform compatibility, allowing users to open PDF files on Windows-based personal computers, Macintosh computers, tablets, and smartphones. The XML paper specification (XPS) format, which was developed by Microsoft, is a fixed-layout format with all the formatting preserved (similar to PDF).

To save a document in PDF or XPS format, click the File tab, click the *Export* option, and then click the Create PDF/XPS button. This displays the Publish as PDF or XPS dialog box with the *PDF (*.pdf)* option selected in the *Save as type* option box. To save the document in XPS format, click the *Save as type* option box and then click *XPS Document (*.xps)* at the drop-down list. At the Save As dialog box, type a name in the *File name* text box and then click the Publish button.

Quick Steps
Save in PDF/XPS Format
1. Click File tab.
2. Click *Export* option.
3. Click Create PDF/XPS button.
4. At Publish as PDF or XPS dialog box, specify PDF or XPS format.
5. Click Publish button.

A PDF file will open in Adobe Acrobat Reader, Microsoft Edge, and Word 2016. An XPS file will open in Internet Explorer and XPS Viewer. One method for opening a PDF or XPS file is to open File Explorer navigate, to the folder containing the file, right-click the file, and then point to *Open with*. This displays a side menu with the programs that can be used to open the file. A PDF file can be opened and edited in Word but an XPS file cannot.

Project 1h Saving in PDF Format and Editing a PDF File in Word

Part 8 of 8

1. Open **NSS.docx** and then save the document in PDF format by completing the following steps:
   a. Click the File tab and then click the *Export* option.
   b. At the Export backstage area, click the Create PDF/XPS button.
   c. At the Publish as PDF or XPS dialog box, make sure that *PDF (*.pdf)* is selected in the *Save as type* option box and that the *Open file after publishing* check box contains a check mark. After confirming both selections, click the Publish button.

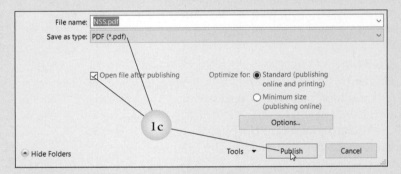

2. Scroll through the document in Adobe Acrobat Reader and then close Acrobat Reader by clicking the Close button in the upper right corner of the window.
3. Close **NSS.docx**.
4. In Word, open the **NSS.pdf** file you saved to your WL1C6 folder. At the message telling you that Word will convert the file to an editable Word document, click the OK button.
5. Notice that the formatting of the text is slightly different from the original formatting and that the graphic has been moved to the second page. Edit the file by completing the following steps:
   a. Click the Design tab and then click the *Lines (Distinctive)* style set.
   b. Delete the text *We are* in the text below the first heading and replace it with Northland Security Systems is.
6. Save the file with Save As and name it **6-NSS**. (The file will be saved in the .docx file format.)
7. Print and then close **6-NSS.docx**.
8. Display the Open dialog box, capture the Open dialog box as an image, and then close the Open dialog box. Press Ctrl + N to open a blank document, paste the image in the document, print the document, and then close the document without saving it.

Check Your Work

Project 2 Manage Multiple Documents   7 Parts

You will arrange, maximize, restore, and minimize windows; move selected text between split windows; compare formatting of documents side by side; and print specific text, pages, and multiple copies.

Preview Finished Project

Working with Windows

Multiple documents can be opened in Word. The insertion point can be moved between the documents and information can be moved or copied from one document and pasted into another. When a new document is opened, it displays on top of any previously opened document. With multiple documents open, the window containing each document can be resized to see all or a portion of it on the screen.

When a document is open, a Word button displays on the taskbar. Hover the mouse pointer over this button and a thumbnail of the document displays above the button. If more than one document is open, another Word button displays behind the first button in a cascading manner with only a portion of the button displaying at the right side of the first button. If multiple documents are open, hovering the mouse pointer on the Word button or clicking the Word button on the taskbar will display thumbnails of all the documents above the buttons. To make a change to a document, click the thumbnail that represents the document.

Another method for determining what documents are open is to click the View tab and then click the Switch Windows button in the Window group. The document name in the list with the check mark in front of it is the active document. The active document contains the insertion point. To make a different document active, click the document name. To switch to another document using the keyboard, type the number shown in front of the desired document.

Arranging Windows

If several documents are open, they can be arranged so a portion of each displays. The portion that displays includes the title (if present) and the opening paragraph of each document. To arrange a group of open documents, click the View tab and then click the Arrange All button in the Window group.

Maximizing, Restoring, and Minimizing Documents

Use the Maximize and Minimize buttons in the upper right corner of the active document to change the size of the window. The two buttons are at the left of the Close button. (The Close button is in the upper right corner of the screen and contains an X.)

If all of the open documents are arranged on the screen, clicking the Maximize button in the active document causes that document to expand to fill the screen. In addition, the Maximize button changes to the Restore button. To return the active document back to its original size, click the Restore button. Click the Minimize button in the active document and the document is reduced and a button displays on the taskbar representing it. To maximize a document that has been minimized, click the button on the taskbar representing it.

Note: If you are using Word on a network system that contains a virus checker, you may not be able to open multiple documents at once. Continue by opening each document individually.

1. Open the following documents: **AptLease.docx**, **CompSoftware.docx**, **IntelProp.docx**, and **NSS.docx**.
2. Arrange the windows by clicking the View tab and then clicking the Arrange All button in the Window group.

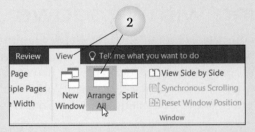

3. Make **AptLease.docx** the active document by clicking the Switch Windows button in the Window group on the View tab of the document at the top of your screen and then clicking *AptLease.docx* at the drop-down list.
4. Close **AptLease.docx**.
5. Make **IntelProp.docx** active and then close it.
6. Make **CompSoftware.docx** active and minimize it by clicking the Minimize button in the upper right corner of the active window.

7. Maximize **NSS.docx** by clicking the Maximize button immediately left of the Close button.
8. Close **NSS.docx**.
9. Restore **CompSoftware.docx** by clicking the button on the taskbar that represents the document.
10. Maximize **CompSoftware.docx**.

Splitting a Window

A window can be split into two panes, which is helpful for viewing different parts of a document at one time. For example, display an outline for a report in one pane and the part of the report to be edited in the other pane. The original window is split into two panes that extend horizontally across the screen.

Split a window by clicking the View tab and then clicking the Split button in the Window group. This splits the window in two with a split bar and another horizontal ruler. The location of the split bar can be changed by positioning the mouse pointer on the split bar until it displays as an up-and-down-pointing arrow with two small lines in the middle, holding down the left mouse button, dragging to the new location, and then releasing the mouse button.

When a window is split, the insertion point is positioned in the bottom pane. To move the insertion point to the other pane with the mouse, position the I-beam pointer in the other pane and then click the left mouse button. To remove the split bar from the document, click the View tab and then click the Remove Split button in the Window group. The split bar can also be double-clicked or dragged to the top or bottom of the screen.

Project 2b Moving Selected Text between Split Windows

Part 2 of 7

1. With **CompSoftware.docx** open, save the document and name it **6-CompSoftware**.
2. Click the View tab and then click the Split button in the Window group.

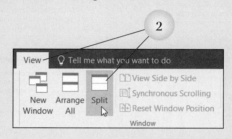

3. Move the first section below the second section by completing the following steps:
   a. Click in the top pane and then click the Home tab.
   b. Select the section *SECTION 1: PERSONAL-USE SOFTWARE* from the title to right above *SECTION 2: GRAPHICS AND MULTIMEDIA SOFTWARE*.
   c. Click the Cut button in the Clipboard group in the Home tab.
   d. Click in the bottom pane and then move the insertion point to the end of the document.
   e. Click the Paste button in the Clipboard group on the Home tab.
   f. Reverse the numbers in the two titles to *SECTION 1: GRAPHICS AND MULTIMEDIA SOFTWARE* and *SECTION 2: PERSONAL-USE SOFTWARE*.
4. Remove the split from the window by clicking the View tab and then clicking the Remove Split button in the Window group.
5. Press Ctrl + Home to move the insertion point to the beginning of the document.
6. Save **6-CompSoftware.docx**.

Check Your Work

Viewing Documents Side by Side

View Side by Side

Synchronous Scrolling

Quick Steps

View Documents Side by Side
1. Open two documents.
2. Click View tab.
3. Click View Side by Side button.

The contents of two documents can be compared on screen by opening both documents, clicking the View tab, and then clicking the View Side by Side button in the Window group. Both documents are arranged on the screen side by side, as shown in Figure 6.2. By default, synchronous scrolling is active. With this feature active, scrolling in one document causes the same scrolling in the other document. This feature is useful for comparing the text, formatting, or another feature between documents. To scroll in one document and not the other, click the Synchronous Scrolling button in the Window group to turn it off.

Figure 6.2 Viewing Documents Side by Side

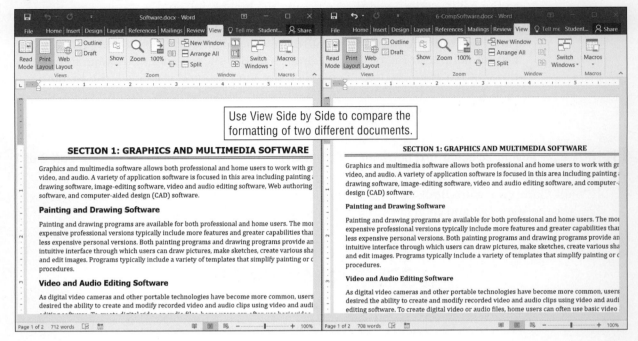

Use View Side by Side to compare the formatting of two different documents.

Project 2c Viewing Documents Side by Side

Part 3 of 7

1. With **6-CompSoftware.docx** open, open **Software.docx**.
2. Click the View tab and then click the View Side by Side button in the Window group.
3. Scroll through both documents simultaneously. Notice the difference between the two documents. (The titles and headings are set in different fonts and colors.) Select and then format the title and headings in **6-CompSoftware.docx** so they match the formatting in **Software.docx**. *Hint: Use the Format Painter button to copy the formats.*
4. Turn off synchronous scrolling by clicking the Synchronous Scrolling button in the Window group on the View tab.
5. Scroll through the document and notice that no scrolling occurs in the other document.
6. Make **Software.docx** the active document and then close it.
7. Save **6-CompSoftware.docx**.

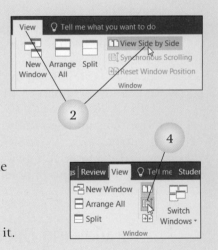

Check Your Work

Quick Steps

Open a New Window
1. Open document.
2. Click View tab.
3. Click New Window button.

 New Window

Opening a New Window

In addition to splitting a document to view two locations of the same document, a new window can be opened that contains the same document. When a new window is opened, the document name in the Title bar displays followed by *:2*. The document name in the original window displays followed by *:1*. Any change made to the document in one window is reflected in the document in the other window.

1. With **6-CompSoftware.docx** open, open a new window by clicking the New Window button in the Window group on the View tab. (Notice that the document name in the Title bar displays followed by *:2*.)
2. Click the View tab and then click the View Side by Side button in the Window group.
3. Click the Synchronous Scrolling button to turn off synchronous scrolling.
4. With the **6-CompSoftware.docx:2** window active, look at the first paragraph of text and notice the order in which the software is listed in the last sentence (painting and drawing software, image-editing software, video and audio editing software, and computer-aided design [CAD] software).
5. Click in the **6-CompSoftware.docx:1** window and then cut and paste the headings and text so the software displays in the order listed in the paragraph.
6. Click the Save button on the Quick Access Toolbar.
7. Close the second version of the document by clicking the Word buttons on the taskbar and then clicking the Close button in the upper right corner of the **6-CompSoftware. docx:2** thumbnail (above the Word button on the taskbar).

Check Your Work

 Object

Inserting a File

The contents of one document can be inserted into another using the Object button in the Text group on the Insert tab. Click the Object button arrow and then click *Text from File* and the Insert File dialog box displays. This dialog box contains similar features as the Open dialog box. Navigate to the desired folder and then double-click the document to be inserted in the open document.

Quick Steps
Insert a File
1. Click Insert tab.
2. Click Object button arrow.
3. Click *Text from File.*
4. Navigate to folder.
5. Double-click document.

1. With **6-CompSoftware.docx** open, move the insertion point to the end of the document.
2. Insert a file into the open document by completing the following steps:
   a. Click the Insert tab.
   b. Click the Object button arrow in the Text group and then click *Text from File* at the drop-down list.
   c. At the Insert File dialog box, navigate to the WL1C6 folder and then double-click ***EduComp.docx***.
3. Save **6-CompSoftware.docx**.

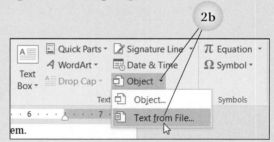

Check Your Work

Previewing and Printing

Use options at the Print backstage area, shown in Figure 6.3, to specify what is to be printed and to preview pages before printing them. To display the Print backstage area, click the File tab and then click the *Print* option.

Previewing Pages

💡 **Hint** Display the
Print backstage area
with the keyboard
shortcut Ctrl + P.

🔲 Zoom to Page

At the Print backstage area, a preview of the page where the insertion point is positioned displays at the right side (see Figure 6.3). Click the Next Page button (right-pointing triangle) below and to the left of the page, to view the next page in the document and click the Previous Page button (left-pointing triangle) to display the previous page in the document. Use the Zoom slider bar to increase or decrease the size of the page and click the Zoom to Page button to fit the page in the viewing area in the Print backstage area.

Figure 6.3 Print Backstage Area

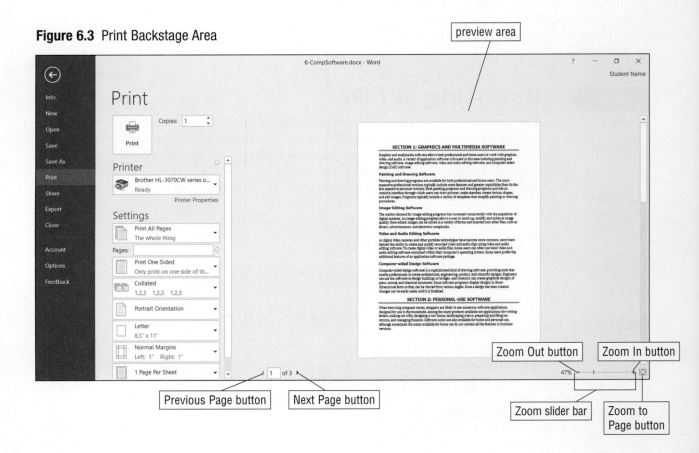

1. With **6-CompSoftware.docx** open, press Ctrl + Home to move the insertion point to the beginning of the document.
2. Preview the document by clicking the File tab and then clicking the *Print* option.
3. Click the Zoom In button (plus symbol) at the right side of the Zoom slider bar two times. (This increases the size of the preview page.)
4. At the Print backstage area, click the Next Page button below and to the left of the preview page. (This displays page 2 in the preview area.)
5. Click the Zoom Out button (minus [-] symbol) at the left side of the Zoom slider bar, until two pages of the document display in the preview area.
6. Change the zoom at the Zoom dialog box by completing the following steps:
   a. Click the percentage number at the left side of the Zoom slider bar.
   b. At the Zoom dialog box, click the *Many pages* option in the *Zoom to* section.
   c. Click OK to close the dialog box. (Notice that all pages in the document display as thumbnails in the preview area.)
7. Click the Zoom to Page button at the right side of the Zoom slider bar. (This returns the page to the default size.)
8. Click the Back button to return to the document.

Printing Specific Text and Pages

Control what prints in a document with options at the Print backstage area. Click the first gallery in the *Settings* category and a drop-down list displays with options for printing all the pages in the document, selected text, the current page, or a custom range of pages.

Print a portion of a document by selecting the text and then choosing the *Print Selection* option at the Print backstage area. With this option, only the selected text in the document prints. (This option is dimmed unless text is selected in the document.) Click the *Print Current Page* option to print only the page on which the insertion point is located. Use the *Custom Print* option to identify a specific page, multiple pages, or a range of pages to print. To print specific pages, use a comma (,) to indicate *and* and use a hyphen (-) to indicate *through*. For example, to print pages 2 and 5, type 2,5 in the *Pages* text box and to print pages 6 through 10, type 6-10.

With the other galleries available in the *Settings* category of the Print backstage area, specify whether to print on one or both sides of the page, change the page orientation (portrait or landscape), specify how the pages are collated, choose a paper size, and specify margins of a document. The last gallery contains options for printing 1, 2, 4, 6, 8, or 16 pages of a multiple-page document on one sheet of paper. This gallery also contains the *Scale to Paper Size* option. Click this option and then use the side menu to choose the paper size to scale the document.

To print more than one copy of a document, use the *Copies* measurement box to the right of the Print button. If several copies of a multiple-page document are printed, Word collates the pages as they print. For example, if two copies of a three-page document are printed, pages 1, 2, and 3 print and then the pages print a second time. Printing collated pages is helpful for assembling them but takes more printing time. To reduce printing time, tell Word *not* to print collated pages by clicking the *Collated* gallery in the *Settings* category and then clicking *Uncollated*.

To send a document directly to the printer without displaying the Print backstage area, consider adding the Quick Print button to the Quick Access Toolbar. To do this, click the Customize Quick Access Toolbar button at the right side of the toolbar, and then click *Quick Print* at the drop-down gallery. Click the Quick Print button and all the pages of the active document print.

Project 2g Printing Specific Text and Pages

1. With **6-CompSoftware.docx** open, print selected text by completing the following steps:
   a. Select the heading *Painting and Drawing Software* and the paragraph of text that follows it.
   b. Click the File tab and then click the *Print* option.
   c. At the Print backstage area, click the first gallery in the *Settings* category (displays with *Print All Pages*) and then click *Print Selection* at the drop-down list.
   d. Click the Print button.
2. Change the margins and page orientation and then print only the first page by completing the following steps:
   a. Press Ctrl + Home to move the insertion point to the beginning of the document.

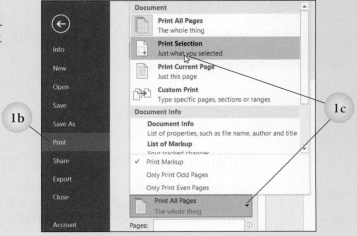

b. Click the File tab and then click the *Print* option.

c. At the Print backstage area, click the fourth gallery (displays with *Portrait Orientation*) in the *Settings* category and then click *Landscape Orientation* at the drop-down list.

d. Click the sixth gallery (displays with *Normal Margins*) in the *Settings* category and then click *Narrow* at the drop-down list.

e. Click the first gallery (displays with *Print All Pages*) in the *Settings* category and then click *Print Current Page* at the drop-down list.

f. Click the Print button. (The first page of the document prints in landscape orientation with 0.5-inch margins.)

3. Print all the pages as thumbnails on one page by completing the following steps:

a. Click the File tab and then click the *Print* option.

b. At the Print backstage area, click the bottom gallery (displays with *1 Page Per Sheet*) in the *Settings* category and then click *4 Pages Per Sheet* at the drop-down list.

c. Click the first gallery (displays with *Print Current Page*) in the *Settings* category and then click *Print All Pages* at the drop-down list.

d. Click the Print button.

4. Select the entire document, change the line spacing to 1.5 lines, and then deselect the text.

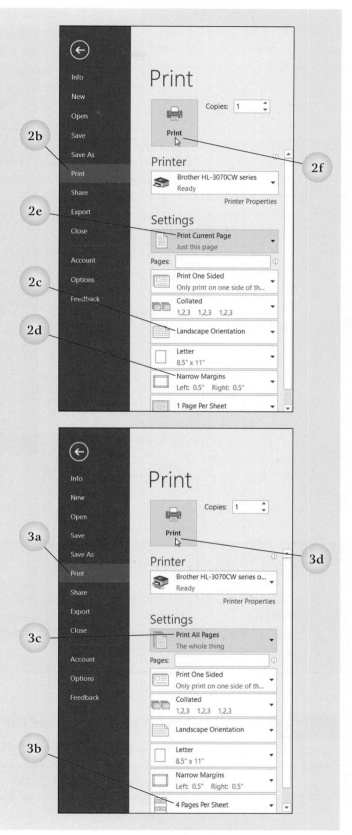

5. Print two copies of specific pages by completing the following steps:

   a. Click the File tab and then click the *Print* option.

   b. Click the fourth gallery (displays with *Landscape Orientation*) at the *Settings* category and then click *Portrait Orientation* in the drop-down list.

   c. Click in the *Pages* text box below the first gallery in the *Settings* category, and then type 1,3.

   d. Click the *Copies* measurement box up arrow (located to the right of the Print button) to display *2*.

   e. Click the third gallery (displays with *Collated*) in the *Settings* category and then click *Uncollated* at the drop-down list.

   f. Click the bottom gallery (displays with *4 Pages Per Sheet*) in the *Settings* category and then click *1 Page Per Sheet* at the drop-down list.

   g. Click the Print button. (The first page of the document will print two times and then the third page will print two times.)

6. Save and then close **6-CompSoftware.docx**.

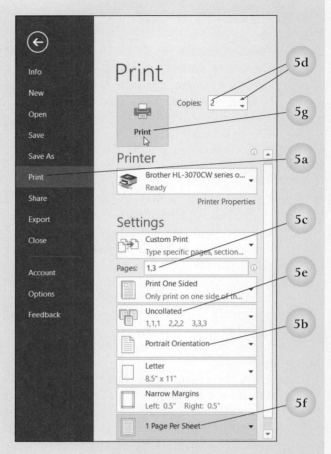

Check Your Work

Project 3 Create and Print Envelopes   2 Parts

You will create an envelope document and type the return address and delivery address using envelope addressing guidelines issued by the United States Postal Service. You will also open a letter document and then create an envelope using the inside address.

Preview Finished Project

Tutorial

Preparing an Envelope

 Envelopes

Creating and Printing Envelopes

Word automates the creation of envelopes with options at the Envelopes and Labels dialog box with the Envelopes tab selected, as shown in Figure 6.4. Display this dialog box by clicking the Mailings tab and then clicking the Envelopes button in the Create group. At the dialog box, type the delivery address in the *Delivery address* text box and the return address in the *Return address* text box. Send the envelope directly to the printer by clicking the Print button or insert the envelope in the current document by clicking the Add to Document button.

Figure 6.4 Envelopes and Labels Dialog Box with Envelopes Tab Selected

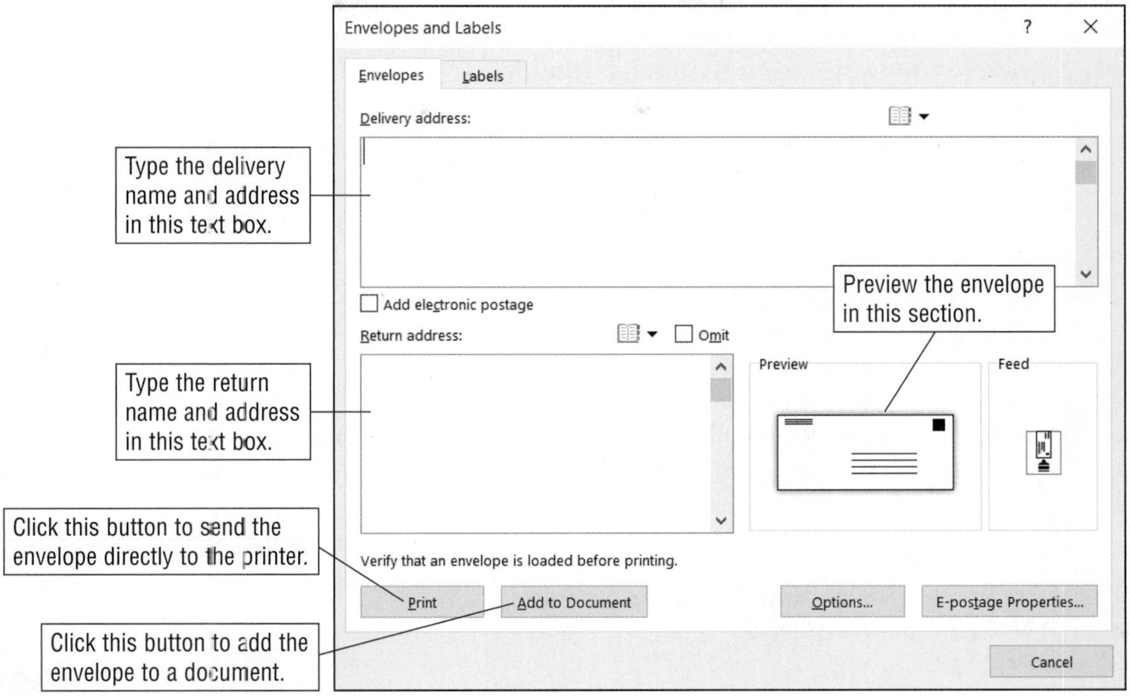

Type the delivery name and address in this text box.

Preview the envelope in this section.

Type the return name and address in this text box.

Click this button to send the envelope directly to the printer.

Click this button to add the envelope to a document.

Quick Steps

Create an Envelope
1. Click Mailings tab.
2. Click Envelopes button.
3. Type delivery address.
4. Click in *Return address* text box.
5. Type return address.
6. Click Add to Document button or Print button.

If a return address is entered before printing the envelope, Word will display the question *Do you want to save the new return address as the default return address?* At this question, click Yes to save the current return address for future envelopes or click No if the return address should not be used as the default. By default, the return address in the *Return address* text box will print on the envelope. To omit the printing of the return address, insert a check mark in the *Omit* check box.

The Envelopes and Labels dialog box contains a *Preview* sample box and a *Feed* sample box. The *Preview* sample box shows how the envelope will appear when printed and the *Feed* sample box shows how the envelope should be inserted into the printer.

When addressing envelopes, consider following general guidelines issued by the United States Postal Service (USPS). The USPS guidelines suggest using all capital letters with no commas or periods for return and delivery addresses. Figure 6.5 shows envelope addresses that follow the USPS guidelines. Use abbreviations for street suffixes (such as *ST* for *Street* and *AVE* for *Avenue*). For a complete list of address abbreviations, visit the USPS.com website and then search for *Official USPS Abbreviations*.

Project 3a Printing an Envelope

Part 1 of 2

1. At a blank document, create an envelope that prints the delivery address and return address shown in Figure 6.5. Begin by clicking the Mailings tab.
2. Click the Envelopes button in the Create group.

3. At the Envelopes and Labels dialog box with the Envelopes tab selected, type the delivery address shown in Figure 6.5 (the one containing the name *GREGORY LINCOLN*). (Press the Enter key to end each line in the name and address.)
4. Click in the *Return address* text box. (If any text displays in the *Return address* text box, select and then delete it.)
5. Type the return address shown in Figure 6.5 (the one containing the name *WENDY STEINBERG*). (Press the Enter key to end each line in the name and address.)
6. Click the Add to Document button.
7. At the message *Do you want to save the new return address as the default return address?*, click No.
8. Save the document and name it **6-Env**.
9. Print and then close **6-Env.docx**. *Note: Manual feed of the envelope may be required. Please check with your instructor.*

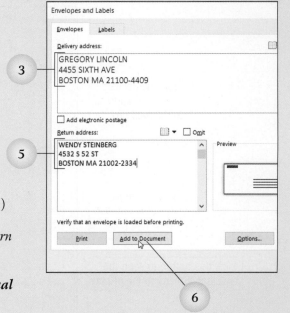

Check Your Work

Figure 6.5 Project 3a

WENDY STEINBERG
4532 S 52 ST
BOSTON MA 21002-2334

GREGORY LINCOLN
4455 SIXTH AVE
BOSTON MA 21100-4409

If the Envelopes and Labels dialog box opens in a document containing a name and address (each name and address line must end with a press of the Enter key and not Shift + Enter), the name and address are automatically inserted in the *Delivery address* text box in the dialog box. The name and address are inserted in the *Delivery address* text box as they appear in the document and may not conform to the USPS guidelines. The USPS guidelines for addressing envelopes are only suggestions, not requirements. Word automatically inserts the first name and address in a document in the *Delivery address* text box if the name and address lines end with a press of the Enter key. A different name and address in a document with each line ending in a press of the Enter key can be inserted in the *Delivery address* text box by selecting the name and address and then displaying the Envelopes and Labels dialog box.

1. Open **LAProg.docx**.
2. Click the Mailings tab.
3. Click the Envelopes button in the Create group.
4. At the Envelopes and Labels dialog box (with the Envelopes tab selected), make sure the delivery address displays properly in the *Delivery address* text box.
5. If any text displays in the *Return address* text box, insert a check mark in the *Omit* check box (located to the right of the *Return address* option). (This tells Word not to print the return address on the envelope.)
6. Click the Print button.
7. Close **LAProg.docx** without saving the changes.

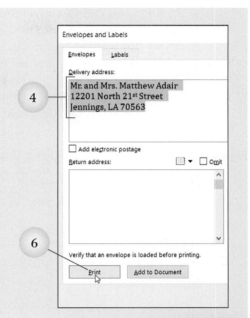

Check Your Work

Project 4 Create Labels   **2 Parts**

You will create mailing labels containing different names and addresses, labels with the same name and address, and labels with an image.

Preview Finished Project

Creating and Printing Labels

Use Word's labels feature to print text on mailing labels, file labels, disc labels, and other types of labels. Word includes a variety of predefined formats for the brands and sizes of labels that can be purchased at most office supply stores. Use the Labels feature to create a sheet of mailing labels with different names and addresses on each label or the same name and address or image on each label.

Tutorial

Creating Mailing Labels with Different Names and Addresses

Labels

Creating Mailing Labels with Different Names and Addresses

To create a sheet of mailing labels with different names and addresses on each label, click the Labels button in the Create group on the Mailings tab. At the Envelopes and Labels dialog box with the Labels tab selected, as shown in Figure 6.6, leave the *Address* text box empty and then click the New Document button to insert the labels in a new document. The insertion point is positioned in the first label. Type the name and address in the label and then press the Tab key one or two times (depending on the label) to move the insertion point to the next label. Pressing Shift + Tab will move the insertion point to the preceding label.

Changing Label Options

Click the Options button at the Envelopes and Labels dialog box with the Labels tab selected and the Label Options dialog box displays, as shown in Figure 6.7. At the Label Options dialog box, choose the type of printer, the label product, and the product number. This dialog box also displays information about the selected label, such as type, height, width, and paper size. When a label is selected, Word automatically determines the label margins. To customize these default settings, click the Details button at the Label Options dialog box.

Figure 6.6 Envelopes and Labels Dialog Box with Labels Tab Selected

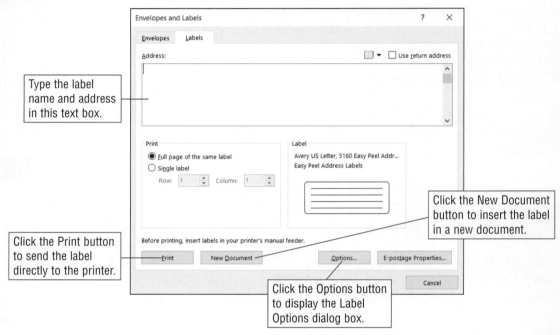

Type the label name and address in this text box.

Click the Print button to send the label directly to the printer.

Click the New Document button to insert the label in a new document.

Click the Options button to display the Label Options dialog box.

Figure 6.7 Label Options Dialog Box

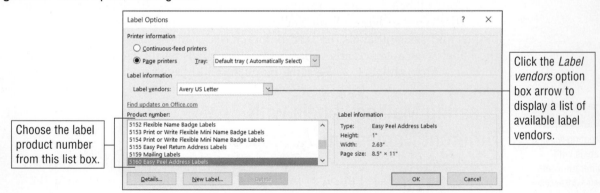

Click the *Label vendors* option box arrow to display a list of available label vendors.

Choose the label product number from this list box.

1. At a blank document, click the Mailings tab.
2. Click the Labels button in the Create group.
3. At the Envelopes and Labels dialog box with the Labels tab selected, click the Options button.
4. At the Label Options dialog box, click the *Label vendors* option box arrow and then click *Avery US Letter* at the drop-down list.
5. Scroll down the *Product number* list box and then click *5160 Easy Peel Address Labels*.
6. Click OK or press the Enter key.
7. At the Envelopes and Labels dialog box, click the New Document button.
8. At the document screen, type the first name and address shown in Figure 6.8 in the first label.
9. Press the Tab key two times to move the insertion point to the next label and then type the second name and address shown in Figure 6.8.
10. Continue in this manner until all the names and addresses shown in Figure 6.8 have been typed. (After typing the third name and address, you only need to press the Tab key once to move the insertion point to the first label in the second row.)
11. Save the document and name it **6-Labels**.
12. Print and then close **6-Labels.docx**.
13. Close the blank document without saving changes.

Check Your Work

Tutorial

Creating Mailing Labels with the Same Name and Address and an Image

Creating Mailing Labels with the Same Name and Address

To create labels with the same name and address on each label, open a document containing the desired name and address, click the Mailings tab, and then click the Labels button. At the Envelopes and Labels dialog box, make sure the desired label vendor and product number are selected and then click the New Document button. Another method for creating labels with the same name and address is to display the Envelopes and Labels dialog box with the Labels tab selected, type the name and address in the *Address* text box, and then click the New Document button.

Creating Mailing Labels with an Image

Labels can be created with a graphic image, such as a company's logo and address or a company's slogan. To create labels with an image, insert the image in a

Figure 6.8 Project 4a

DAVID LOWRY 12033 S 152 ST HOUSTON TX 77340	MARCELLA SANTOS 394 APPLE BLOSSOM FRIENDSWOOD TX 77533	KEVIN DORSEY 26302 PRAIRIE DR HOUSTON TX 77316
AL AND DONNA SASAKI 1392 PIONEER DR BAYTOWN TX 77903	JACKIE RHYNER 29039 107 AVE E HOUSTON TX 77302	MARK AND TINA ELLIS 607 FORD AVE HOUSTON TX 77307

document, select the image, click the Mailings tab. and then click the Labels button. At the Envelopes and Labels dialog box, make sure the desired label vendor and product number are selected and then click the New Document button.

Project 4b **Creating Mailing Labels with the Same Name and Address and an Image** **Part 2 of 2**

1. Open **LAProg.docx** and create mailing labels with the delivery address. Begin by clicking the Mailings tab.
2. Click the Labels button in the Create group.
3. At the Envelopes and Labels dialog box with the Labels tab selected, make sure the delivery address displays properly in the *Address* text box as shown at the right.
4. Make sure *Avery US Letter, 5160 Easy Peel Address Labels* displays in the *Label* section; if not, refer to Steps 3 through 6 of Project 4a to select the label type.
5. Click the New Document button.
6. Save the mailing label document and name it **6-LAProg.docx**.
7. Print and then close **6-LAProg.docx**.
8. Close **LAProg.docx**.
9. At a blank document, insert an image by completing the following steps:
   a. Click the Insert tab and then click the Pictures button in the Illustrations group.
   b. At the Insert Picture dialog box, make sure the WL1C6 folder on your storage medium is active and then double-click **BGCLabels.png**.
10. With the image selected in the document, click the Mailings tab and then click the Labels button.
11. At the Envelopes and Labels dialog box, make sure *Avery US Letter, 5160 Easy Peel Address Labels* displays in the *Label* section and then click the New Document button.
12. Save the document and name it **6-BGCLabels**.
13. Print and then close **6-BGCLabels.docx**.
14. Close the document containing the image without saving changes.

Check Your Work

Project 5 **Use a Template to Create a Business Letter** **1 Part**

You will use a letter template provided by Word to create a business letter.

Preview Finished Project

Tutorial

Creating a Document Using a Template

Creating a Document Using a Template

Word includes a number of template documents that are formatted for specific uses. Each Word document is based on a template document and the Normal template is the default. Use Word templates to create a variety of documents with special formatting, such as letters, calendars, and awards.

Figure 6.9 New Backstage Area

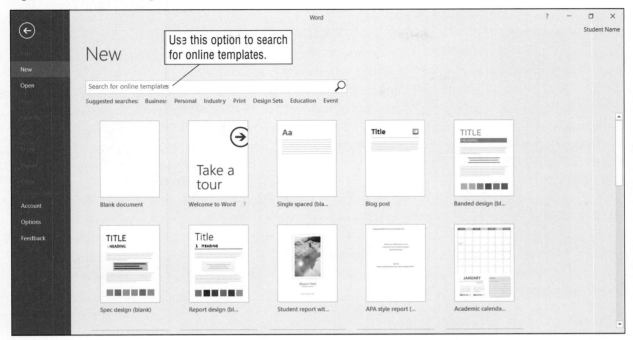

Use this option to search for online templates.

Quick Steps

Create a Document Using a Template
1. Click File tab.
2. Click *New* option.
3. Click template.
OR
1. Click File tab.
2. Click *New* option.
3. Click in search text box.
4. Type search text.
5. Press Enter.
6. Double-click template.

Display templates by clicking the File tab and then clicking the *New* option. This displays the New backstage area, as shown in Figure 6.9. Open one of the templates in the New backstage area by clicking the template. This opens a document based on the template, not the template file.

In addition to the templates that display at the New backstage area, templates can be downloaded from the Internet. To do this, click in the search text box, type the search text or category, and then press the Enter key. Templates that match the search text or category display in the New backstage area. Click the desired template and then click the Create button or double-click the template. This downloads the template and opens a document based on it. Locations for personalized text may display in placeholders in the document. Click the placeholder text and then type the personalized text.

If a template is used on a regular basis, consider pinning it to the New backstage area. To do this, search for the template, hover the mouse pointer over it, and then click the left-pointing stick pin (Pin to list) to the right of the template name. To unpin a template, click the down-pointing stick pin (Unpin from list).

Project 5 Creating a Letter Using a Template

Part 1 of 1

1. Click the File tab and then click the *New* option.
2. At the New backstage area, click in the search text box, type letter, and then press the Enter key.
3. When templates display that match *letter*, notice the *Category* list box at the right side of the New backstage area.
4. Click the *Business* option in the *Category* list box. (This displays only business letter templates.)

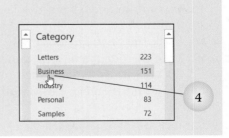

Category	
Letters	223
Business	151
Industry	114
Personal	83
Samples	72

4

5. Scroll down the template list and then double-click the *Letter (Equity theme)* template.

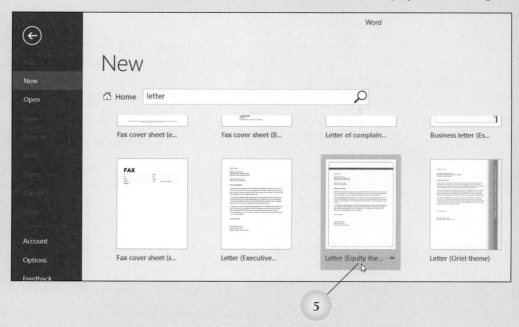

6. When the letter document displays on the screen, click the *[Pick the date]* placeholder, click the placeholder down arrow, and then click the Today button at the bottom of the calendar.
7. Click in the name below the date, select the name, and then type your first and last names.
8. Click the *[Type the sender company name]* placeholder and then type Sorenson Funds.
9. Click the *[Type the sender company address]* placeholder, type 6250 Aurora Boulevard, press the Enter key, and then type Baltimore, MD 20372.
10. Click the *[Type the recipient name]* placeholder and then type Ms. Jennifer Gonzalez.
11. Click the *[Type the recipient address]* placeholder, type 12990 Boyd Street, press the Enter key, and then type Baltimore, MD 20375.
12. Click the *[Type the salutation]* placeholder and then type Dear Ms. Gonzalez:.
13. Insert a file in the document by completing the following steps:
    a. Click anywhere in the three paragraphs of text in the body of the letter and then press the Delete key.
    b. Click the Insert tab.
    c. Click the Object button arrow in the Text group and then click *Text from File* at the drop-down list.
    d. At the Insert File dialog box, navigate to the WL1C6 folder on your storage medium and then double-click **SFunds.docx**.
    e. Press the Backspace key to delete a blank line.
14. Click the *[Type the closing]* placeholder and then type Sincerely,.
15. If your name does not display above the *[Type the sender title]* placeholder, select the name and then type your first and last names.
16. Click the *[Type the sender title]* placeholder and then type Financial Consultant.
17. Save the document and name it **6-SFunds**. (If a message displays notifying you that the document will be upgraded to the newest file format, click OK.)
18. Print and then close **6-SFunds.docx**.

Check Your Work

Chapter Summary

- Group Word documents logically into folders. Create a new folder at the Open or Save As dialog box.

- One document or several documents can be selected at the Open dialog box. Copy, move, rename, delete, or open a document or selected documents.

- Use the *Cut*, *Copy*, and *Paste* options from the Organize button drop-down list or the Open dialog box shortcut menu to move or copy a document from one folder to another.

- Delete documents and/or folders with the *Delete* option from the Organize button drop-down list or shortcut menu.

- Click the *Change File Type* option at the Export backstage area and options display for saving the document in a different file format. Documents can also be saved in different file formats with the *Save as type* option box at the Save As dialog box.

- Move among open documents by hovering the mouse pointer over the Word button on the taskbar and then clicking the thumbnail of the document or by clicking the View tab, clicking the Switch Windows button in the Window group, and then clicking the document name.

- View portions of all open documents by clicking the View tab and then clicking the Arrange All button in the Window group.

- Use the Minimize, Restore, and Maximize buttons in the upper right corner of the window to reduce or increase the size of the active window.

- Divide a window into two panes by clicking the View tab and then clicking the Split button in the Window group.

- View the contents of two open documents side by side by clicking the View tab and then clicking the View Side by Side button in the Window group.

- Open a new window containing the same document by clicking the View tab and then clicking the New Window button in the Window group.

- Insert a document into the open document by clicking the Insert tab, clicking the Object button arrow, and then clicking *Text from File* at the drop-down list. At the Insert File dialog box, double-click the document.

- Preview a document at the Print backstage area. Scroll through the pages in the document with the Next Page and the Previous Page buttons, which display below the preview page. Use the Zoom slider bar to increase or decrease the display size of the preview page.

- Use options at the Print backstage area to customize the print job by changing the page orientation, size, and margins; specify how many pages to print on one page; indicate the number of copies and whether to collate the pages; and specify the printer.

- Create and print an envelope at the Envelopes and Labels dialog box with the Envelopes tab selected.

- If the Envelopes and Labels dialog box is opened in a document containing a name and address (with each line ending with a press of the Enter key), that information is automatically inserted in the *Delivery address* text box in the dialog box.

- Use Word's labels feature to print text on mailing labels, file labels, disc labels, and other types of labels. Create labels at the Envelopes and Labels dialog box with the Labels tab selected.

- Available templates display in the New backstage area. Double-click a template to open a document based on it. Search for templates online by typing in the search text or category in the search text box and then pressing the Enter key.

Commands Review

FEATURE	RIBBON TAB, GROUP	BUTTON, OPTION	KEYBOARD SHORTCUT
arrange documents	View, Window		
Envelopes and Labels dialog box with Envelopes tab selected	Mailings, Create		
Envelopes and Labels dialog box with Labels tab selected	Mailings, Create		
Export backstage area	File, *Export*		
Insert File dialog box	Insert, Text	, *Text from File*	
maximize document			Ctrl + F10
minimize document			
New backstage area	File, *New*		
new window	View, Window		
Open dialog box	File, *Open*	*Browse*	Ctrl + F12
Print backstage area	File, *Print*		Ctrl + P
restore document to previous size			
Save As dialog box	File, *Save As*	*Browse*	F12
split window	View, Window		Alt + Ctrl + S
switch windows	View, Window		
synchronous scrolling	View, Window		
view documents side by side	View, Window		

Workbook

Chapter study tools and assessment activities are available in the *Workbook* ebook. These resources are designed to help you further develop and demonstrate mastery of the skills learned in this chapter.

Microsoft®

Word

Creating Tables and SmartArt

Performance Objectives

Upon successful completion of Chapter 7, you will be able to:

1 Create a table

2 Change the table design and layout

3 Convert text to a table and a table to text

4 Draw a table

5 Insert a Quick Table

6 Perform calculations on data in a table

7 Insert an Excel spreadsheet

8 Create, format, and modify a SmartArt graphic

Some Word data can be organized in a table, which is a combination of columns and rows. Use the Tables feature to insert data in columns and rows. This data can consist of text, values, and formulas. In this chapter, you will learn how to create and format a table and insert and format data in it. Word also includes a SmartArt feature that provides a number of predesigned graphics. In this chapter, you will learn how to use these graphics to create diagrams and organizational charts.

Data Files

Before beginning chapter work, copy the WL1C7 folder to your storage medium and then make WL1C7 the active folder.

SNAP

If you are a SNAP user, launch the Precheck and Tutorials from your Assignments page.

Project 1　Create and Format Tables with Company Information　8 Parts

You will create one table containing contact information and another containing information on plans offered by the company. You will then change the design and layout of each table.

Preview Finished Project

Tutorial

Creating a Table

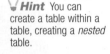
Table

⏱ *Quick Steps*

Create a Table
1. Click Insert tab.
2. Click Table button.
3. Point to create number of columns and rows.
4. Click mouse button.
OR
1. Click Insert tab.
2. Click Table button.
3. Click *Insert Table*.
4. Specify number of columns and rows.
5. Click OK.

💡 *Hint* You can create a table within a table, creating a *nested* table.

Creating a Table

Use the Tables feature to create boxes of information called *cells*. A cell is the intersection between a row and a column. A cell can contain text, characters, numbers, data, graphics, or formulas. Create a table by clicking the Insert tab, clicking the Table button, moving the mouse pointer down and to the right in the drop-down grid until the correct numbers of rows and columns display, and then clicking the mouse button. A table can also be created with options at the Insert Table dialog box. Display this dialog box by clicking the Table button in the Tables group on the Insert tab and then clicking *Insert Table* at the drop-down list.

Figure 7.1 shows an example of a table with four columns and four rows. Various parts of the table are identified in Figure 7.1, such as the gridlines, move table column marker, end-of-cell marker, end-of-row marker, table move handle, and resize handle. In a table, nonprinting characters identify the ends of cells and the ends of rows. To view these characters, click the Show/Hide ¶ button in the Paragraph group on the Home tab. The end-of-cell marker displays inside each cell and the end-of-row marker displays at the end of each row of cells. These markers are identified in Figure 7.1.

When a table is created, the insertion point is positioned in the cell in the upper left corner of the table. Each cell in a table has a cell designation. Columns in a table are lettered from left to right beginning with *A*. Rows in a table are numbered from top to bottom beginning with *1*. The cell in the upper left corner of the table is cell A1. The cell to the right of A1 is B1, the cell to the right of B1 is C1, and so on.

When the insertion point is positioned in a cell in the table, move table column markers display on the horizontal ruler. These markers represent the ends of columns and are useful in changing the widths of columns. Figure 7.1 identifies a move table column marker.

Figure 7.1 Table with Nonprinting Characters Displayed

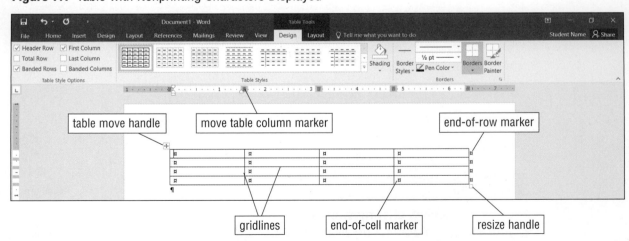

Entering Text in Cells

Hint Pressing the Tab key in a table moves the insertion point to the next cell. Pressing Ctrl + Tab moves the insertion point to the next tab within a cell.

With the insertion point positioned in a cell, type or edit text. Move the insertion point to another cell with the mouse by clicking in the cell. To move the insertion point to another cell using the keyboard, press the Tab key to move to the next cell or press Shift + Tab to move to the preceding cell.

If the text typed in a cell does not fit on one line, it wraps to the next line within the same cell, or if the Enter key is pressed within a cell, the insertion point moves to the next line within the same cell. The cell vertically lengthens to accommodate the text and all cells in that row also lengthen. Pressing the Tab key in a table causes the insertion point to move to the next cell in the table. To move the insertion point to a tab within a cell, press Ctrl + Tab. If the insertion point is in the last cell of the table, pressing the Tab key adds another row to the table. Insert a page break within a table by pressing Ctrl + Enter. The page break is inserted between rows, not within a row.

Moving the Insertion Point within a Table

To use the mouse to move the insertion point to a different cell within the table, click in the specific cell. To use the keyboard to move the insertion point to a different cell within the table, refer to the information shown in Table 7.1.

Table 7.1 Insertion Point Movement within a Table Using the Keyboard

To move the insertion point	Press
to next cell	Tab
to preceding cell	Shift + Tab
forward one character	Right Arrow key
backward one character	Left Arrow key
to previous row	Up Arrow key
to next row	Down Arrow key
to first cell in row	Alt + Home
to last cell in row	Alt + End
to top cell in column	Alt + Page Up
to bottom cell in column	Alt + Page Down

1. At a blank document, turn on bold formatting and then type the title CONTACT INFORMATION, as shown in Figure 7.2.
2. Turn off bold formatting and then press the Enter key.
3. Create the table shown in Figure 7.2 by completing the following steps:
   a. Click the Insert tab.
   b. Click the Table button in the Tables group.
   c. Move the mouse pointer down and to the right in the drop-down grid until the label above the grid displays as *3x5 Table* and then click the left mouse button.

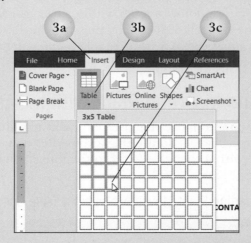

4. Type the text in the cells as indicated in Figure 7.2. Press the Tab key to move to the next cell and press Shift + Tab to move to the preceding cell. (If you accidentally press the Enter key within a cell, immediately press the Backspace key. Do not press the Tab key after typing the text in the last cell. If you do, another row is inserted in the table. If this happens, immediately click the Undo button on the Quick Access Toolbar.)
5. Save the table and name it **7-Tables**.

Check Your Work

Figure 7.2 Project 1a

CONTACT INFORMATION

Maggie Rivera	First Trust Bank	(203) 555-3440
Les Cromwell	Madison Trust	(602) 555-4900
Cecilia Nordyke	American Financial	(509) 555-3995
Regina Stahl	United Fidelity	(301) 555-1201
Justin White	Key One Savings	(360) 555-8963

Using the Insert Table Dialog Box

A table can also be created with options at the Insert Table dialog box, shown in Figure 7.3. To display this dialog box, click the Insert tab, click the Table button in the Tables group, and then click *Insert Table*. At the Insert Table dialog box, enter the numbers of columns and rows and then click OK.

Figure 7.3 Insert Table Dialog Box

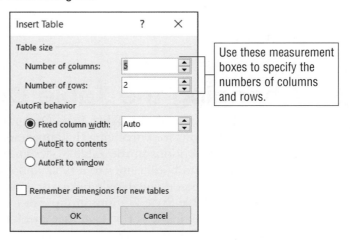

Use these measurement boxes to specify the numbers of columns and rows.

Project 1b Creating a Table with the Insert Table Dialog Box   Part 2 of 8

1. With **7-Tables.docx** open, press Ctrl + End to move the insertion point below the table.
2. Press the Enter key two times.
3. Turn on bold formatting and then type the title OPTIONAL PLAN PREMIUM RATES, as shown in Figure 7.4.
4. Turn off bold formatting and then press the Enter key.
5. Click the Insert tab, click the Table button in the Tables group, and then click *Insert Table* at the drop-down list.
6. At the Insert Table dialog box, type 3 in the *Number of columns* measurement box. (The insertion point is automatically positioned in this measurement box.)
7. Press the Tab key (this moves the insertion point to the *Number of rows* measurement box) and then type 5.
8. Click OK.
9. Type the text in the cells as indicated in Figure 7.4. Press the Tab key to move to the next cell and press Shift + Tab to move to the preceding cell. To indent the text in cells B2 through B5 and cells C2 through C5, press Ctrl + Tab to move the insertion point to a tab within a cell and then type the text.
10. Save **7-Tables.docx**.

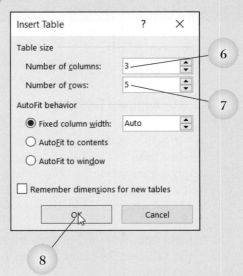

Check Your Work

Figure 7.4 Project 1b

OPTIONAL PLAN PREMIUM RATES

Waiting Period	Basic Plan Employees	Plan 2018 Employees
60 days	0.67%	0.79%
90 days	0.49%	0.59%
120 days	0.30%	0.35%
180 days	0.23%	0.26%

Tutorial

Changing the
Table Design

Changing the Table Design

When a table is created, the Table Tools Design tab is active. This tab contains a number of options for enhancing the appearance of the table, as shown in Figure 7.5. With options in the Table Styles group, apply a predesigned style that adds color and border lines to a table and shading to cells. Maintain further control over the predesigned style formatting applied to columns and rows with options in the Table Style Options group. For example, if the table contains a total row, insert a check mark in the *Total Row* check box. Apply a predesigned table style with options in the Table Styles group.

Border Styles

Border
Painter

Use options in the Borders group to customize the borders of cells in a table. Click the Border Styles button to display a drop-down list of predesigned border lines. Use other buttons in the Borders group to change the line style, width, and color; add or remove borders; and apply the same border style to other cells with the Border Painter button.

Figure 7.5 Table Tools Design Tab

Project 1c Applying Table Styles

Part 3 of 8

1. With **7-Tables.docx** open, click in any cell in the top table.
2. Apply a table style by completing the following steps:
   a. Make sure the Table Tools Design tab is active.
   b. Click the More Table Styles button in the table styles gallery in the Table Styles group.
   c. Click the *Grid Table 5 Dark - Accent 5* table style (sixth column, fifth row in the *Grid Tables* section).

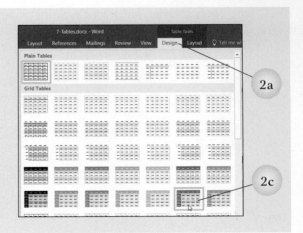

3. After looking at the table, you realize that the first row is not a header row and the first column should not be formatted differently from the other columns. To format the first row and the first column in the same manner as the other rows and columns, click the *Header Row* check box and the *First Column* check box in the Table Style Options group to remove the check marks.

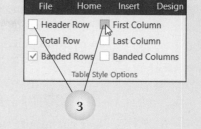

4. Click in any cell in the bottom table and then apply the List Table 6 Colorful - Accent 5 table style (sixth column, sixth row in the *List Tables* section).

5. Add color borders to the top table by completing the following steps:
   a. Click in any cell in the top table.
   b. Click the Pen Color button arrow in the Borders group on the Table Tools Design tab and then click the *Orange, Accent 2, Darker 50%* color option (sixth column, bottom row in the *Theme Colors* section).
   c. Click the *Line Weight* option box arrow in the Borders group and then click *1 ½ pt* at the drop-down list. (When you choose a line weight, the Border Painter button is automatically activated.)

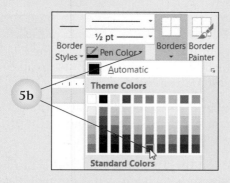
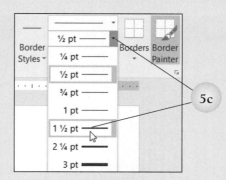

   d. Using the mouse (the mouse pointer displays as a pen), drag along all four sides of the table. (As you drag with the mouse, a thick brown line is inserted. If you make a mistake or the line does not display as you intended, click the Undo button and then continue drawing along each side of the table.)

6. Click the Border Styles button arrow and then click the *Double solid lines, 1/2 pt, Accent 2* option (third column, third row in the *Theme Borders* section).

7. Drag along all four sides of the bottom table.

8. Click the Border Painter button to turn off the feature.

9. Save **7-Tables.docx**.

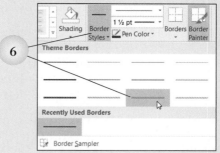

Check Your Work

Selecting Cells

Data within a table can be formatted in several ways. For example, the alignment of text within cells or rows can be changed, rows or columns can be selected and then moved or copied, and character formatting can be applied to text, such as bold, italic, and underlining. To format specific cells, rows, or columns, select the cells.

Selecting in a Table with the Mouse

Use the mouse pointer to select a cell, row, or column or to select an entire table. Table 7.2 describes methods for selecting in a table with the mouse. The left edge of each cell, between the left column border and the end-of-cell marker or first character in the cell, is called the cell selection bar. Position the mouse pointer in the cell selection bar and it turns into a small black arrow that points up and to the right. Each row in a table contains a row selection bar, which is the space just left of the left edge of the table. Position the mouse pointer in the row selection bar and the mouse pointer turns into a white arrow that points up and to the right.

Table 7.2 Selecting in a Table with the Mouse

To select this	Do this
cell	Position the mouse pointer in the cell selection bar at the left edge of the cell until it turns into a small black arrow that points up and to the right and then click the left mouse button.
row	Position the mouse pointer in the row selection bar at the left edge of the table until it turns into an arrow that points up and to the right and then click the left mouse button.
column	Position the mouse pointer on the uppermost horizontal gridline of the table in the appropriate column until it turns into a small black arrow that points down and then click the left mouse button.
adjacent cells	Position the mouse pointer in the first cell to be selected, click and hold down the left mouse button, drag the mouse pointer to the last cell to be selected, and then release the mouse button.
all cells in a table	Click the table move handle or position the mouse pointer in the row selection bar for the first row at the left edge of the table until it turns into an arrow that points up and to the right, click and hold down the left mouse button, drag down to select all the rows in the table, and then release the left mouse button.
text within a cell	Position the mouse pointer at the beginning of the text, click and hold down the left mouse button, and then drag the mouse across the text. (When a cell is selected, its background color changes to gray. When the text within a cell is selected, only those lines containing text are selected.)

Selecting in a Table with the Keyboard

In addition to the mouse, the keyboard can be used to select specific cells within a table. Table 7.3 displays the commands for selecting specific elements of a table.

To select only the text within a cell, rather than the entire cell, press the F8 function key to turn on the Extend mode and then move the insertion point with an arrow key. When a cell is selected, its background color changes to gray. When the text within a cell is selected, only those lines containing text are selected.

Table 7.3 Selecting in a Table with the Keyboard

To select	Press
next cell's contents	Tab
preceding cell's contents	Shift + Tab
entire table	Alt + 5 (on numeric keypad with Num Lock off)
adjacent cells	Press and hold down the Shift key and then press an arrow key repeatedly.
column	Position the insertion point in the top cell of the column, click and hold down the Shift key, and then press the Down Arrow key until the column is selected.

Project 1d Selecting, Moving, and Formatting Cells in a Table

1. With **7-Tables.docx** open, move two rows in the top table by completing the following steps:
   a. Position the mouse pointer in the row selection bar at the left side of the row containing the name *Cecilia Nordyke*, click and hold down the left mouse button, and then drag down to select two rows (the *Cecilia Nordyke* row and the *Regina Stahl* row).
   b. Click the Home tab and then click the Cut button in the Clipboard group.
   c. Move the insertion point so it is positioned at the beginning of the name *Les Cromwell* and then click the Paste button in the Clipboard group.
2. Move the third column in the bottom table by completing the following steps:
   a. Position the mouse pointer on the top border of the third column in the bottom table until the pointer turns into a short black arrow that points down and then click the left mouse button. (This selects the entire column.)
   b. Click the Cut button in the Clipboard group on the Home tab.
   c. With the insertion point positioned at the beginning of the text *Basic Plan Employees*, click the Paste button in the Clipboard group. (Moving the column removed the right border.)
   d. Insert the right border by clicking the Table Tools Design tab, clicking the Border Styles button arrow, and then clicking the *Double solid lines, 1/2 pt, Accent 2* option at the drop-down list (third column, third row in the *Theme Borders* section).

e. Drag along the right border of the bottom table.

f. Click the Border Painter button to turn off the feature.

3. Apply shading to a row by completing the following steps:

a. Position the mouse pointer in the row selection bar at the left edge of the first row in the bottom table until the pointer turns into an arrow that points up and to the right and then click the left mouse button. (This selects the entire first row of the bottom table.)

b. Click the Shading button arrow in the Table Styles group and then click the *Orange, Accent 2, Lighter 80%* color option (sixth column, second row in the *Theme Colors* section).

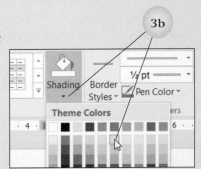

4. Apply a border line to the right sides of two columns by completing the following steps:

a. Position the mouse pointer on the top border of the first column in the bottom table until the pointer turns into a short black arrow that points down and then click the left mouse button.

b. Click the *Line Style* option box arrow and then click the top line option (a single line).

c. Click the Borders button arrow and then click *Right Border* at the drop-down list.

d. Select the second column in the bottom table.

e. Click the Borders button arrow and then click *Right Border* at the drop-down list.

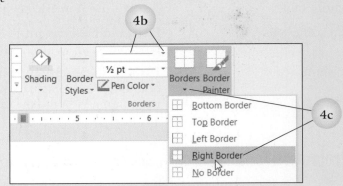

5. Apply italic formatting to a column by completing the following steps:

a. Click in the first cell of the first row in the top table.

b. Press and hold down the Shift key and then press the Down Arrow key four times. (This should select all the cells in the first column.)

c. Press Ctrl + I.

6. Save **7-Tables.docx**.

Check Your Work

Tutorial

Changing the Table Layout

Changing the
Table Layout

To further customize a table, consider changing the layout by inserting or deleting columns and rows and specifying cell alignments. Change the table layout with options at the Table Tools Layout tab, shown in Figure 7.6. Use options and buttons on the tab to select specific cells, delete and insert rows and columns, merge and split cells, specify cell height and width, sort data in cells, and insert formulas.

Figure 7.6 Table Tools Layout Tab

Selecting with the Select Button

Select

Along with selecting cells with the keyboard and mouse, specific cells can be selected with the Select button in the Table group on the Table Tools Layout tab. To select with this button, position the insertion point in the specific cell, column, or row and then click the Select button. At the drop-down list, specify what is to be selected: the entire table or a column, row, or cell.

💡**Hint** Some table layout options are available at a shortcut menu that can be viewed by right-clicking in a table.

Viewing Gridlines

In a table, cell borders are identified by horizontal and vertical thin black gridlines. A cell border gridline can be removed but the cell border is maintained. If cell border gridlines are removed or a table style is applied that removes gridlines, the display of nonprinting gridlines can be turned on to help visually determine cell borders. These nonprinting gridlines display as dashed lines. Turn on or off the display of nonprinting dashed gridlines with the View Gridlines button in the Table group on the Table Tools Layout tab.

View Gridlines

Inserting and Deleting Rows and Columns

Insert Above

Insert Below

Insert Left

Insert Right

Delete

Insert a row or column and delete a row or column with buttons in the Rows & Columns group on the Table Tools Layout tab. Click the button in the group that inserts the row or column in the desired location, such as above, below, to the left, or to the right. To delete a table, row, or column, click the Delete button and then click the option identifying what is to be deleted.

In addition to using options on the Table Tools Layout tab, rows or columns can be inserted using icons. Display the insert row icon by positioning the mouse pointer just outside the left border of the table at the left of the row border. When the insert row icon displays (a plus symbol in a circle and a border line), click the icon and a row is inserted below the insert icon border line. To insert a column, position the mouse pointer above the column border line until the insert column icon displays and then click the icon. This inserts a new column immediately left of the insert column icon border line.

Project 1e **Selecting, Inserting, and Deleting Columns and Rows**   **Part 5 of 8**

1. Make sure **7-Tables.docx** is open.
2. The table style applied to the bottom table removed row border gridlines. If you do not see dashed row border gridlines in the bottom table, turn on the display of nonprinting gridlines by positioning your insertion point in the table, clicking the Table Tools Layout tab, and then clicking the View Gridlines button in the Table group. (The button should display with a gray background, indicating it is active.)
3. Select a column and apply formatting by completing the following steps:
   a. Click in any cell in the first column in the top table.
   b. Make sure the Table Tools Layout tab is active, click the Select button in the Table group, and then click *Select Column* at the drop-down list.
   c. With the first column selected, press Ctrl + I to remove italic formatting and then press Ctrl + B to apply bold formatting.

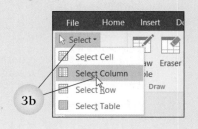

---

4. Select a row and apply formatting by completing the following steps:
   a. Click in any cell in the first row in the bottom table.
   b. Click the Select button in the Table group and then click *Select Row* at the drop-down list.
   c. With the first row selected in the bottom table, press Ctrl + I to apply italic formatting.
5. Insert a new row in the bottom table and type text in the new cells by completing the following steps:
   a. Click in the cell containing the text *60 days*.
   b. Click the Insert Above button in the Rows & Columns group.
   c. Type 30 days in the first cell of the new row. Press the Tab key, press Ctrl + Tab, and then type 0.85% in the second cell of the new row. Press the Tab key, press Ctrl + Tab, and then type 0.81% in the third cell of the new row.

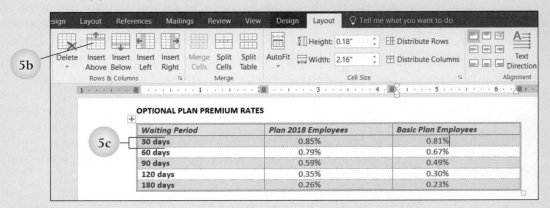

6. Insert two new rows in the top table by completing the following steps:
   a. Select the two rows of cells that begin with the names *Cecilia Nordyke* and *Regina Stahl*.
   b. Click the Insert Below button in the Rows & Columns group.
   c. Click in any cell of the top table to deselect the new rows.
7. Insert a new row in the top table by positioning the mouse pointer at the left side of the table next to the border line below *Regina Stahl* until the insert row icon displays and then clicking the icon.
8. Type the following text in the new cells:

Teresa Getty	Meridian Bank	(503) 555-9800
Michael Vazquez	New Horizon Bank	(702) 555-2435
Samantha Roth	Cascade Mutual	(206) 555-6788

CONTACT INFORMATION

Maggie Rivera	First Trust Bank	(203) 555-3440
Cecilia Nordyke	American Financial	(509) 555-3995
Regina Stahl	United Fidelity	(301) 555-1201
Teresa Getty	Meridian Bank	(503) 555-9800
Michael Vazquez	New Horizon Bank	(702) 555-2435
Samantha Roth	Cascade Mutual	(206) 555-6788
Les Cromwell	Madison Trust	(602) 555-4900
Justin White	Key One Savings	(360) 555-8963

9. Delete a row by completing the following steps:
   a. Click in the cell containing the name *Les Cromwell*.
   b. Click the Delete button in the Rows & Columns group and then click *Delete Rows* at the drop-down list.
10. Insert a new column in the top table by completing the following steps:
    a. Position the mouse pointer immediately above the border line between the first and second columns in the top table until the insert column icon displays.
    b. Click the insert column icon.
11. Type the following text in the new cells:
    B1 = Vice President
    B2 = Loan Officer
    B3 = Account Manager
    B4 = Branch Manager
    B5 = President
    B6 = Vice President
    B7 = Regional Manager
12. Save **7-Tables.docx**.

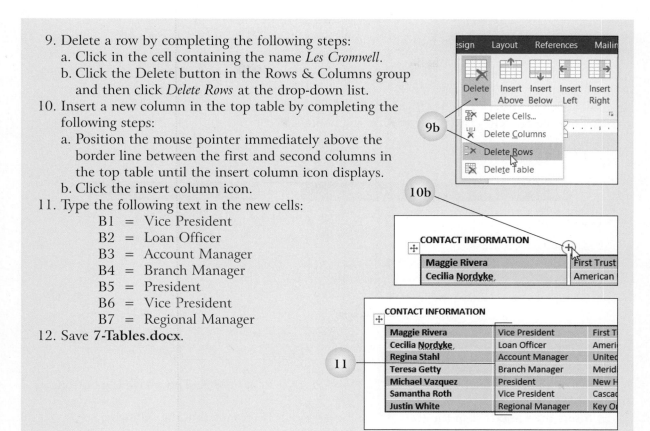

Check Your Work

Merging and Splitting Cells and Tables

Merge Cells

Split Cells

Split Table

Click the Merge Cells button in the Merge group on the Table Tools Layout tab to merge selected cells and click the Split Cells button to split the currently active cell. Click the Split Cells button and the Split Cells dialog box displays with options for specifying the number of columns or rows into which the active cell should be split. To split one table into two tables, position the insertion point in a cell in the row that will be the first row in the new table and then click the Split Table button.

Project 1f Merging and Splitting Cells and Splitting a Table   Part 6 of 8

1. With **7-Tables.docx** open, insert a new row and merge cells in the row by completing the following steps:
   a. Click in the cell containing the text *Waiting Period* (in the bottom table).

b. Click the Insert Above button in the Rows & Columns group on the Table Tools Layout tab.

c. With all of the cells in the new row selected, click the Merge Cells button in the Merge group.

d. Type OPTIONAL PLAN PREMIUM RATES and then press Ctrl + E to center-align the text in the cell. (The text you type will be italicized.)

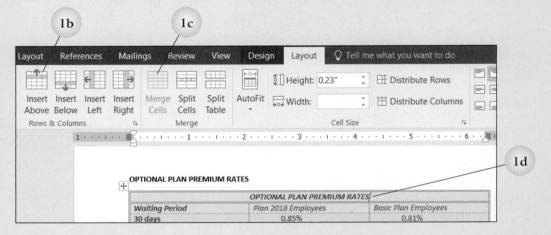

2. Select and then delete the text *OPTIONAL PLAN PREMIUM RATES* above the bottom table.

3. Insert rows and text in the top table and merge cells by completing the following steps:
   a. Click in the cell containing the text *Maggie Rivera*.
   b. Click the Table Tools Layout tab.
   c. Click the Insert Above button two times. (This inserts two rows at the top of the table.)
   d. With the cells in the top row selected, click the Merge Cells button in the Merge group.
   e. Type CONTACT INFORMATION, NORTH and then press Ctrl + E to center-align the text in the cell.
   f. Type the following text in the four cells in the new second row.

   Name   Title   Company   Telephone

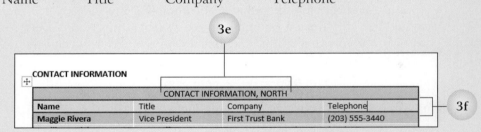

4. Apply heading formatting to the new top row by completing the following steps:
   a. Click the Table Tools Design tab.
   b. Click the *Header Row* check box in the Table Style Options group to insert a check mark.

5. Select and then delete the text *CONTACT INFORMATION* above the top table.

6. Split a cell by completing the following steps:
   a. Click in the cell containing the telephone number *(301) 555-1201*.
   b. Click the Table Tools Layout tab.
   c. Click the Split Cells button in the Merge group.
   d. At the Split Cells dialog box, click OK. (The telephone number will wrap to a new line. You will change this in the next project.)
   e. Click in the new cell.

f. Type x453 in the new cell. If AutoCorrect automatically capitalizes the *x*, hover the mouse pointer over the *X* until the AutoCorrect Options button displays. Click the AutoCorrect Options button and then click *Undo Automatic Capitalization* or click *Stop Auto-capitalizing First Letter of Table Cells*.

Telephone	
(203) 555-3440	
(509) 555-3995	
(301) 555-1201	x453
(503) 555-9800	

6f

7. Split the cell containing the telephone number *(206) 555-6788* and then type x2310 in the new cell. (If necessary, make the *x* lowercase.)
8. Split the top table into two tables by completing the following steps:
   a. Click in the cell containing the name *Teresa Getty*.
   b. Click the Split Table button in the Merge group.
   c. Click in the cell containing the name *Teresa Getty* (in the first row of the new table).
   d. Click the Insert Above button in the Rows and Columns group on the Table Tools Layout tab.
   e. With the new row selected, click the Merge Cells button.
   f. Type CONTACT INFORMATION, SOUTH in the new row and then press Ctrl + E to center-align the text.
9. Save and then print **7-Tables.docx**.
10. Delete the middle table by completing the following steps:
    a. Click in any cell in the middle table.
    b. Click the Table Tools Layout tab.
    c. Click the Delete button in the Rows & Columns group and then click *Delete Table* at the drop-down list.
11. Draw a dark-orange border at the bottom of the top table by completing the following steps:
    a. Click in any cell in the top table and then click the Table Tools Design tab.
    b. Click the *Line Weight* option box arrow in the Borders group and then click *1½ pt* at the drop-down list. (This activates the Border Painter button.)
    c. Click the Pen Color button and then click the *Orange, Accent 2, Darker, 50%* color option (sixth column, bottom row in the *Theme Colors* section).
    d. Using the mouse, drag along the bottom border of the top table.
    e. Click the Border Painter button to turn off the feature.
12. Save **7-Tables.docx**.

Check Your Work

Tutorial

Customizing Cell Size

Customizing Cells in a Table

 Distribute Rows

 Distribute Columns

When a table is created, the column width and row height are equal. Both can be customized with buttons in the Cell Size group on the Table Tools Layout tab. Use the *Table Row Height* measurement box to increase or decrease the heights of rows and use the *Table Column Width* measurement box to increase or decrease the widths of columns. The Distribute Rows button will make all the selected rows the same height and the Distribute Columns button will make all the selected columns the same width.

Column width can also be changed using the move table column markers on the horizontal ruler or using the table gridlines. To change column width using the horizontal ruler, position the mouse pointer on a move table column marker until it turns into a left-and-right-pointing arrow and then drag the marker on the horizontal ruler to the desired position. Press and hold down the Shift key while dragging a table column marker and the horizontal ruler remains stationary while the table column marker moves. Press and hold down the Alt key while dragging a table column marker and measurements display on the horizontal ruler. To change column width using gridlines, position the arrow pointer on the gridline separating columns until the insertion point turns into a left-and-right-pointing arrow with a vertical double-line in the middle and then drag the gridline to the desired position. Press and hold down the Alt key while dragging the gridline and column measurements display on the horizontal ruler.

Adjust row height in a manner similar to adjusting column width. Drag the adjust table row marker on the vertical ruler or drag the gridline separating rows. Press and hold down the Alt key while dragging the adjust table row marker or the row gridline and measurements display on the vertical ruler.

Use the AutoFit button in the Cell Size group to make the column widths in a table automatically fit the contents. To do this, position the insertion point in any cell in the table, click the AutoFit button in the Cell Size group, and then click *AutoFit Contents* at the drop-down list.

 AutoFit

Project 1g Changing Column Width and Row Height

1. With **7-Tables.docx** open, change the width of the first column in the top table by completing the following steps:
   a. Click in the cell containing the name *Maggie Rivera*.
   b. Position the mouse pointer on the move table column marker just right of the 1.5-inch mark on the horizontal ruler until the pointer turns into a left-and-right-pointing arrow.
   c. Press and hold down the Shift key and then click and hold down the left mouse button.
   d. Drag the marker to the 1.25-inch mark, release the mouse button, and then release the Shift key.

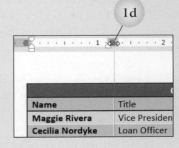

2. Complete steps similar to those in Step 1 to drag the move table column marker just right of the 3-inch mark on the horizontal ruler to the 2.75-inch mark. (Make sure the text *Account Manager* in the second column does not wrap to the next line. If it does, slightly increase the width of the column.)

3. Change the width of the third column in the top table by completing the following steps:
   a. Position the mouse pointer on the gridline separating the third and fourth columns until the pointer turns into a left-and-right-pointing arrow with a vertical double-line in the middle.
   b. Press and hold down the Alt key and then click and hold down the left mouse button, drag the gridline to the left until the measurement for the third column on the horizontal ruler displays as *1.31"*, and then release the Alt key followed by the mouse button.

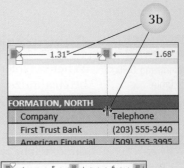

4. Position the mouse pointer on the gridline that separates the telephone number *(301) 555-1201* from the extension *x453* and then drag the gridline to the 5.25-inch mark on the horizontal ruler. (Make sure the phone number does not wrap down to the next line.)

5. Drag the right border of the top table to the 5.75-inch mark on the horizontal ruler.

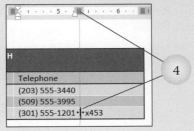

6. Automatically fit the columns in the bottom table by completing the following steps:
   a. Click in any cell in the bottom table.
   b. Click the AutoFit button in the Cell Size group on the Table Tools Layout tab and then click *AutoFit Contents* at the drop-down list.

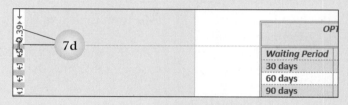

7. Increase the height of the first row in the bottom table by completing the following steps:
   a. Make sure the insertion point is positioned in one of the cells in the bottom table.
   b. Position the mouse pointer on the top adjust table row marker on the vertical ruler.
   c. Press and hold down the Alt key and then click and hold down the left mouse button.
   d. Drag the adjust table row marker down until the first row measurement on the vertical ruler displays as *0.39"*, release the mouse button, and then release the Alt key.

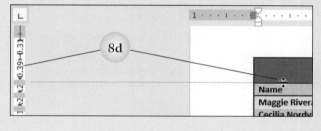

8. Increase the height of the first row in the top table by completing the following steps:
   a. Click in any cell in the top table.
   b. Position the arrow pointer on the gridline at the bottom of the top row until the arrow pointer turns into an up-and-down-pointing arrow with a vertical double-line in the middle.
   c. Click and hold down the left mouse button and then press and hold down the Alt key.
   d. Drag the gridline down until the first row measurement on the vertical ruler displays as *0.39"*, release the mouse button, and then release the Alt key.
9. Save **7-Tables.docx**.

Check Your Work

Changing Cell Alignment

The Alignment group on the Table Tools Layout tab contains a number of buttons for specifying the horizontal and vertical alignment of text in cells. Each button contains a visual representation of the alignment. Hover the mouse pointer over a button to display a ScreenTip with the button name and description.

Quick Steps

Repeat a Header Row
1. Click in header row or select rows.
2. Click Table Tools Layout tab.
3. Click Repeat Header Rows button.

Repeat Header Rows

Repeating a Header Row

If a table is divided between two pages, consider adding the header row at the beginning of the table that continues on the second page. This helps the reader understand the data in each column. To repeat a header row, click in the first row (header row) and then click the Repeat Header Rows button in the Data group on the Table Tools Layout tab. To repeat more than one header row, select the rows and then click the Repeat Header Rows button.

1. With **7-Tables.docx** open, click in the top cell in the top table (the cell containing the title *CONTACT INFORMATION, NORTH*).
2. Click the Align Center button in the Alignment group on the Table Tools Layout tab.

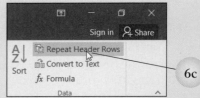

3. Format and align the text in the second row in the top table by completing the following steps:
   a. Select the second row.
   b. Press Ctrl + B to turn off bold formatting for the entry in the first cell and then press Ctrl + B again to turn on bold formatting for all the entries in the second row.
   c. Click the Align Top Center button in the Alignment group.
4. Click in the top cell in the bottom table and then click the Align Center button in the Alignment group.
5. Press Ctrl + End to move the insertion point to the end of the document, press the Enter key four times, and then insert a table into the current document by completing the following steps:
   a. Click the Insert tab.
   b. Click the Object button arrow in the Text group and then click *Text from File* at the drop-down list.
   c. At the Insert File dialog box, navigate to the WL1C7 folder on your storage medium and then double-click ***ContactsWest.docx***.
6. Repeat the header row by completing the following steps:
   a. Select the first two rows in the table you just inserted.
   b. Click the Table Tools Layout tab.
   c. Click the Repeat Header Rows button in the Data group.
7. Save, print, and then close **7-Tables.docx**.

Check Your Work

Project 2 Create and Format Tables with Employee Information   **6 Parts**

You will create and format a table containing information on the names and departments of employees of Tri-State Products, a table containing additional information on employees, and a calendar quick table.

Preview Finished Project

Changing Cell Margin Measurements

Cell Margins

By default, the cells in a table contain specific margin measurements. The top and bottom margins in a cell have a default measurement of 0 inch and the left and right margins have a default measurement of 0.08 inch. Change these default measurements with options at the Table Options dialog box, shown in Figure 7.7. Display this dialog box by clicking the Cell Margins button in the Alignment group on the Table Tools Layout tab. Use the measurement boxes in the *Default cell margins* section to change the top, bottom, left, and/or right cell margin measurements.

Figure 7.7 Table Options Dialog Box

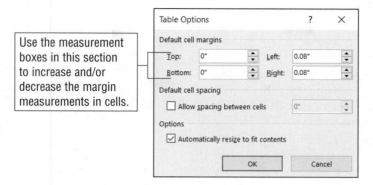

Use the measurement boxes in this section to increase and/or decrease the margin measurements in cells.

 Properties

Changes to cell margins will affect all the cells in a table. To change the cell margin measurements for one cell or selected cells, position the insertion point in the cell or select the cells and then click the Properties button in the Table group on the Table Tools Layout tab (or click the Cell Size group dialog box launcher). At the Table Properties dialog box, click the Cell tab and then the Options button in the lower right corner of the dialog box. This displays the Cell Options dialog box, shown in Figure 7.8.

Before setting the new cell margin measurements, remove the check mark from the *Same as the whole table* check box. With the check mark removed, the cell margin options become available. Specify the new cell margin measurements and then click OK to close the dialog box.

Figure 7.8 Cell Options Dialog Box

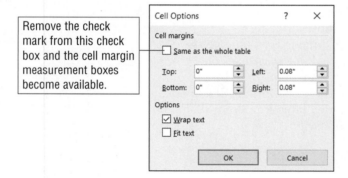

Remove the check mark from this check box and the cell margin measurement boxes become available.

Project 2a Changing Cell Margin Measurements

1. Open **TSPTables.docx** and then save it with the name **7-TSPTables**.
2. Change the top and bottom cell margin measurements for all the cells in the table by completing the following steps:
   a. Position the insertion point in any cell in the table and then click the Table Tools Layout tab.
   b. Click the Cell Margins button in the Alignment group.

c. At the Table Options dialog box, change the *Top* and *Bottom* measurements to 0.05 inch.

d. Click OK to close the Table Options dialog box.

3. Change the top and bottom cell margin measurements for the first row of cells by completing the following steps:

   a. Select the first row of cells (the cells containing *Name* and *Department*).

   b. Click the Properties button in the Table group.

   c. At the Table Properties dialog box, click the Cell tab.

   d. Click the Options button in the lower right corner of the dialog box.

   e. At the Cell Options dialog box, click the *Same as the whole table* check box to remove the check mark.

   f. Change the *Top* and *Bottom* measurements to 0.1 inch.

   g. Click OK to close the Cell Options dialog box.

   h. Click OK to close the Table Properties dialog box.

4. Change the left cell margin measurement for specific cells by completing the following steps:

   a. Select all of the rows in the table *except* the top row.

   b. Click the Cell Size group dialog box launcher.

   c. At the Table Properties dialog box, make sure the Cell tab is active.

   d. Click the Options button.

   e. At the Cell Options dialog box, remove the check mark from the *Same as the whole table* check box.

   f. Change the *Left* measurement to 0.3 inch.

   g. Click OK to close the Cell Options dialog box.

   h. Click OK to close the Table Properties dialog box.

5. Save **7-TSPTables.docx**.

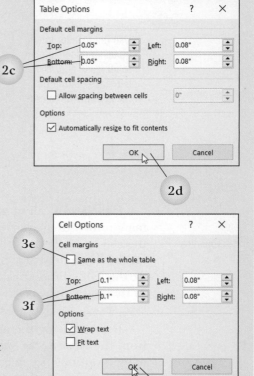

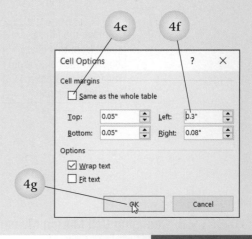

Check Your Work

Changing Cell Direction

 Text Direction   Change the direction of text in a cell using the Text Direction button in the Alignment group on the Table Tools Layout tab. Each time the Text Direction button is clicked, the text in the cell rotates 90 degrees.

Changing Table Alignment and Dimensions

By default, a table aligns at the left margin. Change this alignment with options at the Table Properties dialog box with the Table tab selected, as shown in Figure 7.9. To change the alignment, click the desired alignment option in the *Alignment* section of the dialog box. Change table dimensions by clicking the *Preferred width* check box to insert a check mark. This makes active both the width measurement box and the *Measure in* option box. Type a width measurement in the measurement box and specify whether the measurement type is inches or a percentage with the *Measurement in* option box.

Figure 7.9 Table Properties Dialog Box with Table Tab Selected

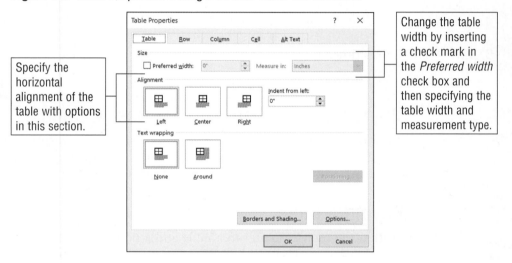

Specify the horizontal alignment of the table with options in this section.

Change the table width by inserting a check mark in the *Preferred width* check box and then specifying the table width and measurement type.

Project 2b Changing Table Alignment and Dimensions

Part 2 of 6

1. With **7-TSPTables.docx** open, insert a new column and change text direction by completing the following steps:
   a. Click in any cell in the first column.
   b. Click the Insert Left button in the Rows & Columns group.
   c. With the cells in the new column selected, click the Merge Cells button in the Merge group.
   d. Type Tri-State Products.
   e. Click the Align Center button in the Alignment group.
   f. Click two times on the Text Direction button in the Alignment group.
   g. With *Tri-State Products* selected, click the Home tab and then increase the font size to 16 points.
2. Automatically fit the contents by completing the following steps:
   a. Click in any cell in the table.
   b. Click the Table Tools Layout tab.
   c. Click the AutoFit button in the Cell Size group and then click *AutoFit Contents* at the drop-down list.

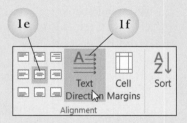

3. Change the table width and alignment by completing the following steps:
   a. Click the Properties button in the Table group on the Table Tools Layout tab.
   b. At the Table Properties dialog box, click the Table tab.
   c. Click the *Preferred width* check box to insert a check mark.
   d. Select the measurement in the measurement box and then type 4.5.
   e. Click the *Center* option in the *Alignment* section.
   f. Click OK.
4. Select the two cells containing the text *Name* and *Department* and then click the Align Center button in the Alignment group.
5. Save **7-TSPTables.docx**.

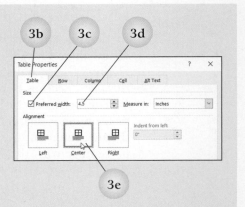

Check Your Work

Quick Steps
Move a Table
1. Position mouse pointer on table move handle until pointer displays with four-headed arrow attached.
2. Click and hold down left mouse button.
3. Drag table to new location.
4. Release mouse button.

Changing Table Size with the Resize Handle

Hover the mouse pointer over a table and a resize handle displays in the lower right corner. The resize handle displays as a small white square. Drag this resize handle to increase and/or decrease the size and proportion of the table.

Moving a Table

Position the mouse pointer in a table and a table move handle displays in the upper left corner. Use this handle to move the table in the document. To move a table, position the mouse pointer on the table move handle until the pointer displays with a four-headed arrow attached, click and hold down the left mouse button, drag the table to the new location, and then release the mouse button.

Project 2c Resizing and Moving Tables   Part 3 of 6

1. With **7-TSPTables.docx** open, insert a table into the current document by completing the following steps:
   a. Press Ctrl + End to move the insertion point to the end of the document and then press the Enter key.
   b. Click the Insert tab.
   c. Click the Object button arrow in the Text group and then click *Text from File* at the drop-down list.
   d. At the Insert File dialog box, navigate to the WL1C7 folder and then double-click **TSPEmps.docx**.
2. Automatically fit the bottom table by completing the following steps:
   a. Click in any cell in the bottom table.
   b. Click the Table Tools Layout tab.
   c. Click the AutoFit button in the Cell Size group and then click *AutoFit Contents* at the drop-down list.

3. Format the bottom table by completing the following steps:
   a. Click the Table Tools Design tab.
   b. Click the More Table Styles button in the table styles gallery and then click the *List Table 4 - Accent 6* table style (last column, fourth row in the *List Tables* section).
   c. Click the *First Column* check box in the Table Style Options group to remove the check mark.
   d. Select the first and second rows, click the Table Tools Layout tab, and then click the Align Center button in the Alignment group.
   e. Select the second row and then press Ctrl + B to turn on bold formatting.
4. Resize the bottom table by completing the following steps:
   a. Position the mouse pointer on the resize handle in the lower right corner of the bottom table.
   b. Click and hold down the left mouse button, drag down and to the right until the width and height of the table increase approximately 1 inch, and then release the mouse button.
5. Move the bottom table by completing the following steps:
   a. Move the mouse pointer over the bottom table and then position the mouse pointer on the table move handle until the pointer displays with a four-headed arrow attached.
   b. Click and hold down the left mouse button, drag the table so it is positioned equally between the left and right margins, and then release the mouse button.

3b

TRI-STATE PRODUCTS		
Name	**Employee #**	**Department**
Whitaker, Christine	1432-323-09	Financial Services
Higgins, Dennis	1230-933-21	Public Relations
Coffey, Richard	1321-843-22	Research and Development
Lee, Yong	1411-322-76	Human Resources
Fleishmann, Jim	1246-432-90	Public Relations
Schaffer, Mitchell	1388-340-44	Purchasing
Porter, Robbie	1122-361-38	Public Relations
Buchanan, Lillian	1432-857-87	Research and Development
Kensington, Jacob	1112-473-31	Human Resources

4a-4b

5b

TRI-STATE PRODUCTS		
Name	**Employee #**	**Department**
Whitaker, Christine	1432-323-09	Financial Services

6. Select the cells in the column below the heading *Employee #* and then click the Align Top Center button in the Alignment group.
7. Save **7-TSPTables.docx**.

Check Your Work

Converting Text to a Table and a Table to Text

Create a table and then enter text in the cells or create the text and then convert it to a table. Converting text to a table provides formatting and layout options available on the Table Tools Design tab and the Table Tools Layout tab. When typing the text to be converted to a table, separate units of information using separator characters, such as commas or tabs. These characters identify where the text is divided into columns. To convert text, select the text, click the Insert tab, click the Table button in the Tables group, and then click *Convert Text to Table* at the drop-down list. At the Convert Text to Table dialog box, specify the separator and then click OK.

Convert a table to text by positioning the insertion point in any cell of the table, clicking the Table Tools Layout tab, and then clicking the Convert to Text button in the Data group. At the Convert Table To dialog box, specify the separator and then click OK.

Tutorial
Converting Text to a Table and a Table to Text

Quick Steps

Convert Text to Table
1. Select text.
2. Click Insert tab.
3. Click Table button.
4. Click *Convert Text to Table*.
5. Click OK.

Convert Table to Text
1. Click Table Tools Layout tab.
2. Click Convert to Text button.
3. Specify separator.
4. Click OK.

Convert to Text

Project 2d Converting Text to a Table

1. With **7-TSPTables.docx** open, press Ctrl + End to move the insertion point to the end of the document. (If the insertion point does not display below the second table, press the Enter key until the insertion point displays there.)
2. Insert the document named **TSPExecs.docx** into the current document.
3. Convert the text to a table by completing the following steps:
   a. Select the text you just inserted.
   b. Make sure the Insert tab is active.
   c. Click the Table button in the Tables group and then click *Convert Text to Table* at the drop-down list.
   d. At the Convert Text to Table dialog box, type 2 in the *Number of columns* measurement box.
   e. Click the *AutoFit to contents* option in the *AutoFit behavior* section.
   f. Click the *Commas* option in the *Separate text at* section.
   g. Click OK.

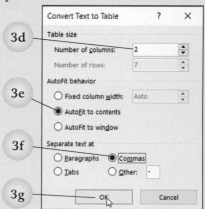

4. Select and merge the cells in the top row (the row containing the title *TRI-STATE PRODUCTS*) and then center-align the text in the merged cell.
5. Apply the List Table 4 - Accent 6 style (last column, fourth row in the *List Tables* section) and remove the check mark from the *First Column* check box in the Table Style Options group on the Table Tools Design tab.
6. Drag the table so it is centered below the table above it.
7. Apply the List Table 4 - Accent 6 style to the top table. Increase the widths of the columns so the text *Tri-State Products* is visible and the text in the second and third columns displays on one line.
8. Drag the table so it is centered above the middle table. Make sure the three tables fit on one page.

9. Click in the middle table and then convert the table to text by completing the following steps:
   a. Click the Table Tools Layout tab and then click the Convert to Text button in the Data group.
   b. At the Convert Table To dialog box, make sure *Tabs* is selected and then click OK.
10. Print **7-TSPTables.docx**.
11. Click the Undo button to return the text to a table.
12. Save **7-TSPTables.docx**.

Check Your Work

Drawing a Table

In Project 1, options in the Borders group on the Table Tools Design tab were used to draw borders around an existing table. These options can also be used to draw an entire table. To draw a table, click the Insert tab, click the Table button in the Tables group, and then click *Draw Table* at the drop-down list. Or click the Draw Table button in the Draw group on the Table Tools Layout tab; this turns the mouse pointer into a pen. Drag the pen pointer in the document to create the table. To correct an error when drawing a table, click the Eraser button in the Draw group on the Table Tools Layout tab (which changes the mouse pointer to an eraser) and then drag over any border lines to be erased. Clicking the Undo button will also undo the most recent action.

 Eraser

Project 2e   Drawing and Formatting a Table   Part 5 of 6

1. With **7-TSPTables.docx** open, select and then delete three rows in the middle table from the row that begins with the name *Lee, Yong* through the row that begins with the name *Schaffer, Mitchell*.
2. Move the insertion point to the end of the document (outside any table) and then press the Enter key. (Make sure the insertion point is positioned below the third table.)
3. Click the Insert tab, click the Table button, and then click the *Draw Table* option at the drop-down list. (This turns the insertion point into a pen.)
4. Using the mouse, drag in the document (below the bottom table) to create the table shown at the right, drawing the outside border first. If you make a mistake, click the Undo button. You can also click the Eraser button in the Draw group on the Table Tools Layout tab and drag over a border line to erase it. Click the Draw Table button in the Draw group to turn off the pen feature.

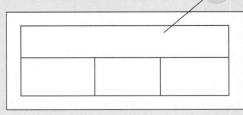

5. After drawing the table, type Tri-State Products in the top cell, Washington Division in the cell at the left, Oregon Division in the middle bottom cell, and California Division in the cell at the right.
6. Apply the Grid Table 4 - Accent 6 table style (last column, fourth row in the *Grid Tables* section).
7. Select the table, change the font size to 12 points, apply bold formatting, and then center-align the text in the cells using the Align Center button in the Alignment group.
8. Make any adjustments needed to the border lines so the text in each cell displays on one line.
9. Drag the table so it is centered and positioned below the bottom table.
10. Save **7-TSPTables.docx**.

Check Your Work

Inserting a Quick Table

Quick Steps
Insert a Quick Table
1. Click Insert tab.
2. Click Table button.
3. Point to *Quick Tables*.
4. Click table.

Word includes a Quick Tables feature for inserting predesigned tables in a document. To insert a quick table, click the Insert tab, click the Table button, point to *Quick Tables*, and then click a table at the side menu. A quick table has formatting applied but additional formatting can be applied with options on the Table Tools Design tab and the Table Tools Layout tab.

Project 2f Inserting a Quick Table   Part 6 of 6

1. With **7-TSPTables.docx** open, press Ctrl + End to move the insertion point to the end of the document and then press Ctrl + Enter to insert a page break.
2. Insert a quick table by clicking the Insert tab, clicking the Table button, pointing to *Quick Tables*, and then clicking the *Calendar 3* option at the side menu.

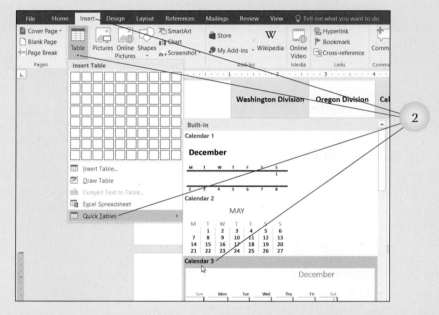

3. Edit the text in each cell so the calendar reflects the current month. (If the bottom row is empty, select and then delete the row.)
4. Select the entire table by clicking the Table Tools Layout tab, clicking the Select button in the Table group, and then clicking the *Select Table* option. With the table selected, change the font to Copperplate Gothic Light.
5. Save, print, and then close **7-TSPTables.docx**.

> **Check Your Work**

Project 3 Calculate Sales Data   1 Part

You will insert formulas in a Tri-State Products sales table to calculate total sales, average sales, and top sales.

> **Preview Finished Project**

Performing Calculations in a Table

Use the Formula button in the Data group on the Table Tools Layout tab to insert formulas that perform calculations on the data in a table. The numbers in cells can be added, subtracted, multiplied, and divided. In addition, other calculations can be performed, such as determining averages, counting items, and identifying minimum and maximum values. Data can be calculated in a Word table, but for complex calculations consider using an Excel worksheet.

To perform a calculation on the data in a table, position the insertion point in the cell where the result of the calculation is to be inserted and then click the Formula button in the Data group on the Table Tools Layout tab. This displays the Formula dialog box, as shown in Figure 7.10. At this dialog box, accept the default formula in the *Formula* text box or type a calculation and then click OK.

fx Formula

Quick Steps

Insert a Formula in a Table
1. Click in cell.
2. Click Table Tools Layout tab.
3. Click Formula button.
4. Type formula in Formula dialog box.
5. Click OK.

Figure 7.10 Formula Dialog Box

Four basic operators are available for writing a formula, including the plus symbol (+) for addition, the minus symbol (–) for subtraction, the asterisk (*) for multiplication, and the forward slash (/) for division. If a calculation contains two or more operators, Word performs the operations from left to right. To change the order of operations, put parentheses around the part of the calculation to be performed first.

In the default formula, the SUM part of the formula is called a *function*. Word also provides other functions for inserting formulas. These functions are available in the *Paste function* option box in the Formula dialog box. For example, use the AVERAGE function to average numbers in cells.

Specify the numbering format with the *Number format* option box in the Formula dialog box. For example, when calculating amounts of money, specify that the numbers display with no numbers or two numbers following the decimal point.

If changes are made to the values in a formula, the result of the formula needs to be updated. To do this, right-click the formula result and then click *Update Field* at the shortcut menu. Or click the formula result and then press the F9 function key, which is the Update Field keyboard shortcut. To update the results of all the formulas in a table, select the entire table and then press the F9 function key.

Hint Use the Update Field keyboard shortcut, F9, to update the selected field.

1. Open **TSPSalesTable.docx** and then save it with the name **7-TSPSalesTable**.
2. Insert a formula in the table by completing the following steps:
   a. Click in cell B9. (Cell B9 is the empty cell immediately below the cell containing the amount *$375,630.*)
   b. Click the Table Tools Layout tab.
   c. Click the Formula button in the Data group.
   d. At the Formula dialog box, make sure *=SUM(ABOVE)* displays in the *Formula* text box.
   e. Click the *Number format* option box arrow and then click *#,##0* at the drop-down list (the top option in the list).
   f. Click OK to close the Formula dialog box.

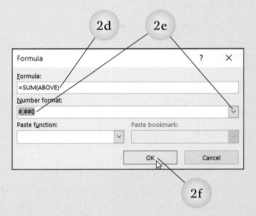

   g. In the table, type a dollar symbol ($) before the number just inserted in cell B9.
3. Complete steps similar to those in Steps 2c through 2g to insert a formula in cell C9. (Cell C9 is the empty cell immediately below the cell containing the amount *$399,120.*)
4. Insert a formula that calculates the average of amounts by completing the following steps:
   a. Click in cell B10. (Cell B10 is the empty cell immediately right of the cell containing the word *Average.*)
   b. Click the Formula button in the Data group.
   c. At the Formula dialog box, delete the formula in the *Formula* text box *except* for the equals (=) sign.
   d. With the insertion point positioned immediately right of the equals sign, click the *Paste function* option box arrow and then click *AVERAGE* at the drop-down list.
   e. With the insertion point positioned between the left and right parentheses, type B2:B8. (When typing cell designations in a formula, you can type either uppercase or lowercase letters.)
   f. Click the *Number format* option box arrow and then click *#,##0* at the drop-down list (the top option in the list).
   g. Click OK to close the Formula dialog box.
   h. Type a dollar symbol ($) before the number just inserted in cell B10.
5. Complete steps similar to those in Steps 4b through 4h to insert a formula in cell C10 that calculates the average of the amounts in cells C2 through C8.

6. Insert a formula that calculates the maximum number by completing the following steps:
   a. Click in cell B11. (Cell B11 is the empty cell immediately right of the cell containing the words *Top Sales*.)
   b. Click the Formula button in the Data group.
   c. At the Formula dialog box, delete the formula in the *Formula* text box *except* for the equals sign.
   d. With the insertion point positioned immediately right of the equals sign, click the *Paste function* option box arrow and then click *MAX* at the drop-down list. (You will need to scroll down the list to display the *MAX* option.)
   e. With the insertion point positioned between the left and right parentheses, type B2:B8.
   f. Click the *Number format* option box arrow and then click *#,##0* at the drop-down list (the top option in the list).
   g. Click OK to close the Formula dialog box.
   h. Type a dollar symbol ($) before the number just inserted in cell B11.
7. Complete steps similar to those in Steps 6b through 6h to insert the maximum number in cell C11.
8. Save and then print **7-TSPSalesTable.docx**.
9. Change the amount in cell B2 from *$543,241* to *$765,700*.
10. Recalculate all the formulas in the table by completing the following steps:
    a. Make sure the Table Tools Layout tab is active and then click the Select button in the Table group.
    b. Click the *Select Table* option.
    c. Press the F9 function key.
11. Save, print, and then close **7-TSPSalesTable.docx**.

Check Your Work

Project 4 Insert an Excel Worksheet   1 Part

You will insert an Excel worksheet in a blank document, decrease the number of rows and columns in the worksheet, insert data on sales increases in the worksheet from a Word document, and calculate data in the worksheet.

Preview Finished Project

Inserting an Excel Spreadsheet

An Excel spreadsheet (usually referred to as a *worksheet*) can be inserted into a Word document, which provides some Excel functions for modifying and formatting the data. To insert an Excel worksheet, click the Insert tab, click the Table button in the Tables group, and then click the *Excel Spreadsheet* option at the drop-down list. This inserts a worksheet in the document with seven columns and ten rows visible. Increase or decrease the number of visible cells by dragging the sizing handles that display around the worksheet. Use buttons on the Excel ribbon tabs to format the worksheet. Click outside the worksheet and the Excel ribbon tabs are removed. Double-click the table to redisplay the Excel ribbon tabs.

1. Open **SalesIncrease.docx**.
2. Press Ctrl + N to open a blank document.
3. Insert an Excel spreadsheet into the blank document by clicking the Insert tab, clicking the Table button in the Tables group, and then clicking *Excel Spreadsheet* at the drop-down list.

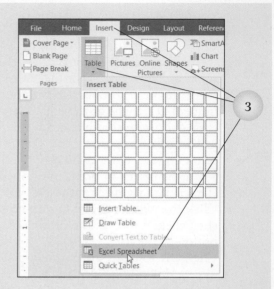

4. Decrease the size of the worksheet by completing the following steps:
   a. Position the mouse pointer on the sizing handle (small black square) located in the lower right corner of the worksheet until the pointer displays as a black, diagonal, two-headed arrow.
   b. Click and hold down the left mouse button, drag up and to the left, and release the mouse button. Continue dragging the sizing handles until columns A, B, and C and rows 1 through 7 are visible.
5. Copy a table into the Excel worksheet by completing the following steps:
   a. Position the mouse pointer on the Word button on the taskbar and then click the *SalesIncrease.docx* thumbnail.
   b. Position the mouse pointer over the table and then click the table move handle (small square containing a four-headed arrow) that displays in the upper left corner of the table. (This selects all of the cells in the table.)
   c. Click the Copy button in the Clipboard group on the Home tab.
   d. Close **SalesIncrease.docx**.
   e. With the first cell in the worksheet active, click the Paste button in the Clipboard group.
6. Format the worksheet and insert a formula by completing the following steps:
   a. Increase the width of the second column by positioning the mouse pointer on the column boundary between columns B and C and double-clicking the left mouse button.

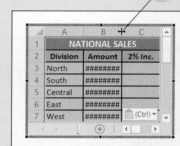

   b. Click in cell C3, type the formula =B3*1.02, and then press the Enter key.
7. Copy the formula in cell C3 to the range C4:C7 by completing the following steps:
   a. Position the mouse pointer (white plus symbol) in cell C3, click and hold down the left mouse button, drag down into cell C7, and then release the mouse button.
   b. Click the Fill button in the Editing group on the Home tab and then click *Down* at the drop-down list.

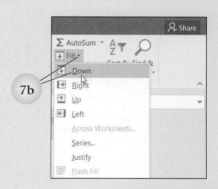

8. Click outside the worksheet to remove the Excel ribbon tabs.
9. Save the document and name it **7-Worksheet**.
10. Print and then close **7-Worksheet.docx**.

Check Your Work

You will prepare a SmartArt process graphic that identifies steps in the production process and then apply formatting to enhance the graphic.

Preview Finished Project

Creating SmartArt

Use Word's SmartArt feature to insert graphics such as diagrams and organizational charts in a document. SmartArt offers a variety of predesigned graphics that are available at the Choose a SmartArt Graphic dialog box, as shown in Figure 7.11. At this dialog box, *All* is selected by default in the left panel and all of the available predesigned SmartArt graphics display in the middle panel.

Inserting and Formatting a SmartArt Graphic

To insert a SmartArt graphic, click the Insert tab and then click the SmartArt button in the Illustrations group to open the Choose a SmartArt Graphic dialog box. Predesigned SmartArt graphics display in the middle panel of the dialog box. Use the scroll bar at the right side of the middle panel to scroll down the list of choices. Click a graphic in the middle panel and its name displays in the right panel along with a description. SmartArt includes graphics for presenting a list of data; showing data processes, cycles, and relationships; and presenting data in a matrix or pyramid. Double-click a graphic in the middle panel of the dialog box and the graphic is inserted in the document.

When a SmartArt graphic is inserted in a document, a text pane displays at the left side of the graphic. Type text in the text pane or type directly in the graphic. Apply formatting to a graphic with options on the SmartArt Tools Design tab. This

Figure 7.11 Choose a SmartArt Graphic Dialog Box

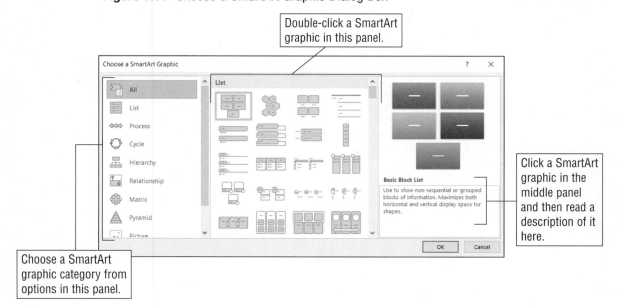

Double-click a SmartArt graphic in this panel.

Click a SmartArt graphic in the middle panel and then read a description of it here.

Choose a SmartArt graphic category from options in this panel.

Hint Limit the number of shapes and amount of text in your SmartArt graphic.

tab becomes active when the graphic is inserted in the document. Use options and buttons on this tab to add objects, change the graphic layout, apply a style to the graphic, and reset the graphic to the original formatting.

Apply formatting to a SmartArt graphic with options on the SmartArt Tools Format tab. Use options and buttons on this tab to change the sizes and shapes of objects in the graphic; apply shape styles and WordArt styles; change the shape fill, outline, and effects; and arrange and size the graphic.

Project 5a Inserting and Formatting a SmartArt Graphic

Part 1 of 2

1. At a blank document, insert the SmartArt graphic shown in Figure 7.12 by completing the following steps:
   a. Click the Insert tab.
   b. Click the SmartArt button in the Illustrations group.
   c. At the Choose a SmartArt Graphic dialog box, click *Process* in the left panel and then double-click the *Alternating Flow* graphic.
   d. If a *Type your text here* text pane does not display at the left side of the graphic, click the Text Pane button in the Create Graphic group to display it.
   e. With the insertion point positioned after the top bullet in the *Type your text here* text pane, type Design.
   f. Click the *[Text]* placeholder below *Design* and then type Mock-up.
   g. Continue clicking occurrences of the *[Text]* placeholder and typing text so the text pane displays as shown at the right.
   h. Close the text pane by clicking the Close button in the upper right corner of the pane. (You can also click the Text Pane button in the Create Graphic group.)

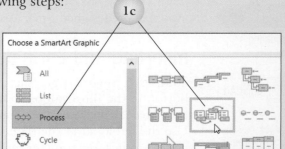

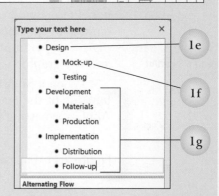

2. Change the graphic colors by clicking the Change Colors button in the SmartArt Styles group and then clicking the *Colorful Range - Accent Colors 5 to 6* option (last option in the *Colorful* section).

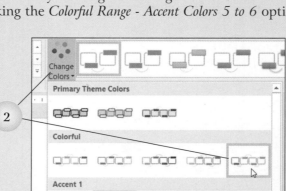

3. Apply a style by clicking the More SmartArt Styles button in the gallery in the SmartArt Styles group and then clicking the *Inset* option (second column, first row in the *3-D* section).

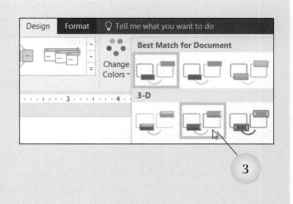

4. Copy the graphic and then change the layout by completing the following steps:
    a. Click inside the SmartArt graphic border but outside any shapes.
    b. Click the Home tab and then click the Copy button in the Clipboard group.
    c. Press Ctrl + End, press the Enter key, and then press Ctrl + Enter to insert a page break.
    d. Click the Paste button in the Clipboard group.
    e. Click inside the SmartArt graphic border but outside any shapes.
    f. Click the SmartArt Tools Design tab.
    g. Click the More Layouts button in the Layouts gallery and then click the *Continuous Block Process* layout (second column, second row).
    h. Click outside the graphic to deselect it.

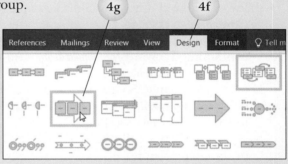

5. Save the document and name it **7-SAGraphics**.

Check Your Work

Figure 7.12 Project 5a

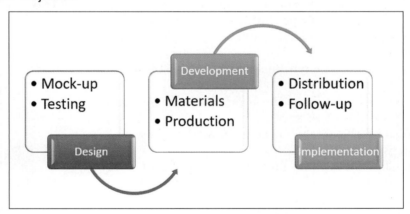

Arranging and Moving a SmartArt Graphic

Position a SmartArt graphic by clicking the Arrange button on the SmartArt Tools Format tab, clicking the Position button, and then clicking the desired position option at the drop-down gallery. Along with positioning the SmartArt graphic, the options at the Position button drop-down gallery apply square text wrapping, which means text wraps around the border of an object. Text wrapping can also be applied by clicking the Arrange button, clicking the Wrap Text button, and then clicking a wrapping style at the drop-down gallery. Or it can be applied with options from

Position

Arrange

Wrap Text

the Layout Options button outside the upper right corner of the selected SmartArt graphic. Move a SmartArt graphic by positioning the arrow pointer on the graphic border until the pointer displays with a four-headed arrow attached, clicking and holding down the left mouse button, and then dragging the graphic to the new location. Nudge the SmartArt graphic or a shape or selected shapes in the graphic using the up, down, left, and right arrow keys on the keyboard.

Project 5b Formatting SmartArt Graphics

Part 2 of 2

1. With **7-SAGraphics.docx** open, format shapes by completing the following steps:
   a. Click the graphic on the first page to select it (a border surrounds the graphic).
   b. Click the SmartArt Tools Format tab.
   c. In the graphic, click the rectangle shape containing the word *Design*.
   d. Press and hold down the Shift key and then click the shape containing the word *Development*.
   e. With the Shift key still held down, click the shape containing the word *Implementation*. (All three shapes should now be selected.)
   f. Click the Change Shape button in the Shapes group.
   g. Click the *Pentagon* shape (seventh column, second row in the *Block Arrows* section).
   h. With the shapes still selected, click the Larger button in the Shapes group.
   i. With the shapes still selected, click the Shape Outline button arrow in the Shape Styles group and then click the *Dark Blue* color option (ninth option in the *Standard Colors* section).
   j. Click inside the graphic border but outside any shape. (This deselects the shapes but keeps the graphic selected.)

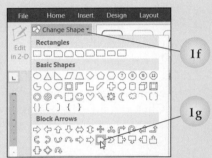

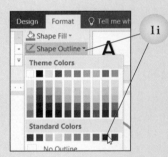

2. Change the size of the graphic by completing the following steps:
   a. Click the Size button at the right side of the SmartArt Tools Format tab.
   b. Click in the *Shape Height* measurement box, type 4, and then press the Enter key.
3. Position the graphic by completing the following steps:
   a. Click the Arrange button on the SmartArt Tools Format tab and then click the Position button at the drop-down list.
   b. Click the *Position in Middle Center with Square Text Wrapping* option (second column, second row in the *With Text Wrapping* section).
   c. Click outside the graphic to deselect it.
4. Format the bottom SmartArt graphic by completing the following steps:
   a. Press Ctrl + End to move to the end of the document and then click in the bottom SmartArt graphic to select it.

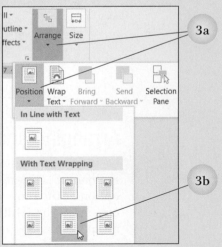

b. Press and hold down the Shift key and then click each of the three shapes.

c. Click the More WordArt Styles button in the WordArt styles gallery on the SmartArt Tools Format tab.

d. Click the *Fill - Black, Text 1, Shadow* option (first column, first row).

e. Click the Text Outline button arrow in the WordArt Styles group and then click the *Dark Blue* color option (ninth color in the *Standard Colors* section).

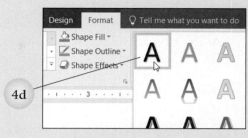

f. Click the Text Effects button in the WordArt Styles group, point to *Glow* at the drop-down list, and then click the *Orange, 5 pt glow, Accent color 2* option (second column, first row in the *Glow Variations* section).

g. Click inside the SmartArt graphic border but outside any shape.

5. Arrange the graphic by clicking the Arrange button, clicking the Position button, and then clicking the *Position in Middle Center with Square Text Wrapping* option (second column, second row in the *With Text Wrapping* section).

6. Click outside the graphic to deselect it.

7. Save, print, and then close **7-SAGraphics.docx**.

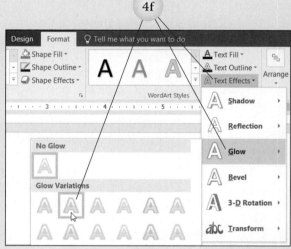

Check Your Work

Project 6 Prepare and Format a Company Organizational Chart   1 Part

You will prepare an organizational chart for a company and then apply formatting to enhance the visual appeal of the chart.

Preview Finished Project

Creating an Organizational Chart with SmartArt

Ǫuick Steps

Insert an Organizational Chart
1. Click Insert tab.
2. Click SmartArt button.
3. Click *Hierarchy*.
4. Double-click organizational chart.

To visually illustrate hierarchical data, consider creating an organizational chart with a SmartArt option. To display organizational chart SmartArt options, click the Insert tab and then click the SmartArt button in the Illustrations group. At the Choose a SmartArt Graphic dialog box, click *Hierarchy* in the left panel. Organizational chart options display in the middle panel of the dialog box. Double-click an organizational chart and the chart is inserted in the document. Type text in a SmartArt graphic by selecting the shape and then typing text in it or type text in the *Type your text here* window at the left side of the graphic. Format a SmartArt organizational chart with options and buttons on the SmartArt Tools Design tab, the SmartArt Tools Format tab, and the Layout Options button.

1. At a blank document, create the organizational chart shown in Figure 7.13. To begin, click the Insert tab.
2. Click the SmartArt button in the Illustrations group.
3. At the Choose a SmartArt Graphic dialog box, click *Hierarchy* in the left panel of the dialog box and then double-click the *Organization Chart* option (first option in the middle panel).

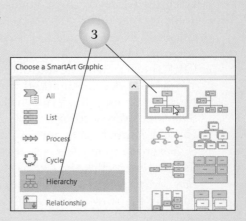

4. If a *Type your text here* pane displays at the left side of the organizational chart, close it by clicking the Text Pane button in the Create Graphic group.
5. Delete one of the boxes in the organizational chart by clicking the border of the box in the lower right corner to select it and then pressing the Delete key. (Make sure that the selection border surrounding the box is a solid line and not a dashed line. If a dashed line displays, click the box border again. This should change the border to a solid line.)
6. With the bottom right box selected, click the Add Shape button arrow in the Create Graphic group and then click the *Add Shape Below* option.

7. Click the *[Text]* placeholder in the top box, type Blaine Willis, press Shift + Enter, and then type President. Click in each of the remaining boxes and type the text as shown in Figure 7.13. (Press Shift + Enter after typing the name.)
8. Click the More SmartArt Styles button in the gallery in the SmartArt Styles group and then click the *Inset* style (second column, first row in the *3-D* section).
9. Click the Change Colors button in the SmartArt Styles group and then click the *Colorful Range - Accent Colors 4 to 5* option (fourth option in the *Colorful* section).

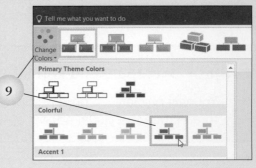

10. Click the SmartArt Tools Format tab.
11. Click the text pane control (displays with a left-pointing arrow) at the left side of the graphic border. (This displays the *Type your text here* window.)
12. Using the mouse, select all the text in the *Type your text here* window.
13. Click the Change Shape button in the Shapes group and then click the *Round Same Side Corner Rectangle* option (eighth option in the *Rectangles* section).

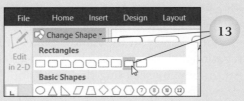

14. Click the Shape Outline button arrow in the Shape Styles group and then click the *Dark Blue* color option (ninth option in the *Standard Colors* section).
15. Close the *Type your text here* window by clicking the Close button in the upper right corner of the window.
16. Click inside the organizational chart border but outside any shape.
17. Click the Size button at the right side of the SmartArt Tools Format tab, click in the *Shape Height* measurement box, and then type 4. Click in the *Shape Width* measurement box, type 6.5, and then press the Enter key.
18. Click outside the chart to deselect it.
19. Save the document and name it **7-OrgChart**.
20. Print and then close the document.

Check Your Work

Figure 7.13 Project 6

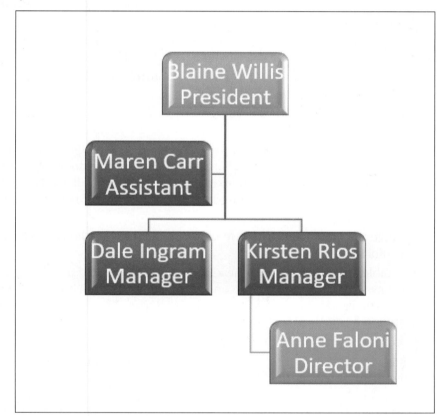

Chapter Summary

- Use the Tables feature to create columns and rows of information. Create a table with the Table button in the Tables group on the Insert tab or with options at the Insert Table dialog box.

- A cell is the intersection between a row and a column. The lines that form the cells of the table are called *gridlines*.

- Move the insertion point to cells in a table using the mouse by clicking in a cell or using the keyboard commands shown in Table 7.1.

- Change the table design with options and buttons on the Table Tools Design tab.

- Refer to Table 7.2 for a list of mouse commands for selecting specific cells in a table and Table 7.3 for a list of keyboard commands for selecting specific cells in a table.

- Change the layout of a table with options and buttons on the Table Tools Layout tab.

- Select a table, column, row, or cell using the Select button in the Table group on the Table Tools Layout tab.

- Turn on and off the display of gridlines by clicking the View Gridlines button in the Table group on the Table Tools Layout tab.

- Insert and delete columns and rows with buttons in the Rows & Columns group on the Table Tools Layout tab.

- Merge selected cells with the Merge Cells button and split cells with the Split Cells button, both in the Merge group on the Table Tools Layout tab.

- Change the column width and row height using the height and width measurement boxes in the Cell Size group on the Table Tools Layout tab; by dragging move table column markers on the horizontal ruler, adjust table row markers on the vertical ruler, or gridlines in the table; or using the AutoFit button in the Cell Size group.

- Change the alignment of text in cells with buttons in the Alignment group on the Table Tools Layout tab.

- If a table spans two pages, a header row can be inserted at the beginning of the rows that extend to the second page. To do this, click in the header row or select the header rows and then click the Repeat Header Rows button in the Data group on the Table Tools Layout tab.

- Change cell margins with options in the Table Options dialog box.

- Change text direction in a cell with the Text Direction button in the Alignment group on the Table Tools Layout tab.

- Change the table dimensions and alignment with options at the Table Properties dialog box with the Table tab selected.

- Use the resize handle to change the size of the table and the table move handle to move the table.

- Convert text to a table with the *Convert Text to Table* option at the Table button drop-down list. Convert a table to text with the Convert to Text button in the Data group on the Table Tools Layout tab.

- Draw a table in a document by clicking the Insert tab, clicking the Table button, and then clicking *Draw Table*. Using the mouse, drag in the document to create the table.

- Quick tables are predesigned tables that can be inserted in a document by clicking the Insert tab, clicking the Table button, pointing to *Quick Tables*, and then clicking a table at the side menu.
- Perform calculations on data in a table by clicking the Formula button in the Data group on the Table Tools Layout tab and then specifying the formula and number format at the Formula dialog box.
- Insert an Excel spreadsheet (worksheet) into a Word document to provide Excel functions by clicking the Insert tab, clicking the Table button in the Tables group, and then clicking Excel Spreadsheet at the drop-down list.
- Use the SmartArt feature to insert predesigned graphics and organizational charts in a document. Click the SmartArt button on the Insert tab to display the Choose a SmartArt Graphic dialog box.
- Format a SmartArt graphic with options and buttons on the SmartArt Tools Design tab and the SmartArt Tools Format tab.
- Choose a position or a text wrapping style for a SmartArt graphic with the Arrange button on the SmartArt Tools Format tab or the Layout Options button outside the upper right corner of the selected SmartArt graphic.

Commands Review

FEATURE	RIBBON TAB, GROUP	BUTTON, OPTION
AutoFit table contents	Table Tools Layout, Cell Size	
cell alignment	Table Tools Layout, Alignment	
Choose a SmartArt Graphic dialog box	Insert, Illustrations	
convert table to text	Table Tools Layout, Data	
convert text to table	Insert, Tables	, *Convert Text to Table*
delete column	Table Tools Layout, Rows & Columns	, *Delete Columns*
delete row	Table Tools Layout, Rows & Columns	, *Delete Rows*
delete table	Table Tools Layout, Rows & Columns	, *Delete Table*
draw table	Insert, Tables	, *Draw Table*
Formula dialog box	Table Tools Layout, Data	
insert column left	Table Tools Layout, Rows & Columns	
insert column right	Table Tools Layout, Rows & Columns	
Insert Excel spreadsheet	Insert, Tables	, *Excel Spreadsheet*
insert row above	Table Tools Layout, Rows & Columns	

FEATURE	RIBBON TAB, GROUP	BUTTON, OPTION
insert row below	Table Tools Layout, Rows & Columns	
Insert Table dialog box	Insert, Tables	, *Insert Table*
merge cells	Table Tools Layout, Merge	
Quick Table	Insert, Tables	, *Quick Tables*
repeat header row	Table Tools Layout, Data	
Split Cells dialog box	Table Tools Layout, Merge	
table	Insert, Tables	
Table Options dialog box	Table Tools Layout, Alignment	
text direction	Table Tools Layout, Alignment	
view gridlines	Table Tools Layout, Table	

Workbook

Chapter study tools and assessment activities are available in the *Workbook* ebook. These resources are designed to help you further develop and demonstrate mastery of the skills learned in this chapter.

Microsoft®

Word

Merging Documents

Performance Objectives

Upon successful completion of Chapter 8, you will be able to:

1 Create a data source file

2 Create a main document and merge it with a data source file

3 Preview a merge and check for errors before merging

4 Create an envelope, a labels, and a directory main document and then merge it with a data source file

5 Edit a data source file

6 Select specific records for merging

7 Input text during a merge

8 Use the Mail Merge wizard to merge a letter main document with a data source file

Precheck

Check your current skills to help focus your study.

Word includes a Mail Merge feature for creating customized letters, envelopes, labels, directories, email messages, and faxes. The Mail Merge feature is useful for situations where the same letter is to be sent to a number of people and an envelope needs to be created for each letter. Use Mail Merge to create a main document that contains a letter, an envelope, or other data and then merge it with a data source file. In this chapter, you will use Mail Merge to create letters, envelopes, labels, and directories.

Data Files

Before beginning chapter work, copy the WL1C8 folder to your storage medium and then make WL1C8 the active folder.

SNAP

If you are a SNAP user, launch the Precheck and Tutorials from your Assignments page.

You will create a data source file and a letter main document and then merge the main document with the records in the data source file.

Preview Finished Project

Completing a Merge

Use buttons and options on the Mailings tab to complete a merge. A merge generally takes two files: the data source file and the main document. The main document contains the standard text along with fields identifying where variable information is inserted during the merge. The data source file contains the variable information that will be inserted in the main document.

Start Mail
Merge

Select
Recipients

Use the Start Mail Merge button on the Mailings tab to identify the type of main document to be created and use the Select Recipients button to create a data source file or specify an existing data source file. The Mail Merge Wizard is also available to provide guidance on the merge process.

Tutorial

Creating a Data
Source File

Creating a Data Source File

Before creating a data source file, determine what type of correspondence will be created and what type of information is needed to insert in the correspondence. Word provides predesigned field names when creating the data source file. Use these field names if they represent the desired data. Variable information in a data source file is saved as a record. A record contains all the information for one unit (for example, a person, family, customer, client, or business). A series of fields makes one record and a series of records makes a data source file.

Quick Steps

**Create a Data Source
File**
1. Click Mailings tab.
2. Click Select
   Recipients button.
3. Click *Type a New List*
   at drop-down list.
4. Type data in
   predesigned or
   custom fields.
5. Click OK.

Create a data source file by clicking the Select Recipients button in the Start Mail Merge group on the Mailings tab and then clicking *Type a New List* at the drop-down list. At the New Address List dialog box, shown in Figure 8.1, use the predesigned fields offered by Word or edit the fields by clicking the Customize Columns button. At the Customize Address List dialog box, insert new fields or delete existing fields and then click OK. With the fields established, type the required data. Note that fields in the main document correspond to the column headings in the data source file. When all the records have been entered, click OK.

Figure 8.1   New Address List Dialog Box

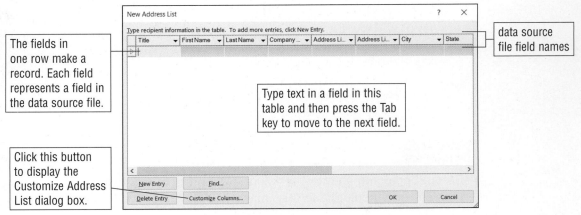

The fields in one row make a record. Each field represents a field in the data source file.

Type text in a field in this table and then press the Tab key to move to the next field.

data source file field names

Click this button to display the Customize Address List dialog box.

At the Save Address List dialog box, navigate to the desired folder, type a name for the data source file, and then click OK. Word saves a data source file as an Access database. Having Access is not required on the computer to complete a merge with a data source file.

Project 1a Creating a Data Source File

1. At a blank document, click the Mailings tab.
2. Click the Start Mail Merge button in the Start Mail Merge group and then click *Letters* at the drop-down list.
3. Click the Select Recipients button in the Start Mail Merge group and then click *Type a New List* at the drop-down list.

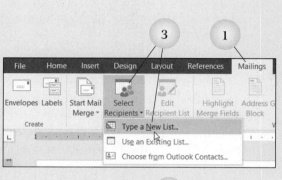

4. At the New Address List dialog box, Word provides a number of predesigned fields. Delete the fields you do not need by completing the following steps:
   a. Click the Customize Columns button.
   b. At the Customize Address List dialog box, click *Company Name* to select it and then click the Delete button.
   c. At the message that displays, click Yes.
   d. Complete steps similar to those in 4b and 4c to delete the following fields:
      Country or Region
      Home Phone
      Work Phone
      E-mail Address

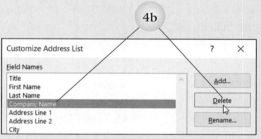

5. Insert a custom field by completing the following steps:
   a. With the *ZIP Code* field selected in the *Field Names* list in the Customize Address List dialog box, click the Add button.
   b. At the Add Field dialog box, type Fund and then click OK.
   c. Click OK to close the Customize Address List dialog box.

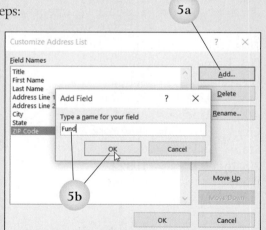

6. At the New Address List dialog box, enter the information for the first client shown in Figure 8.2 by completing the following steps:
   a. Type Mr. in the field in the *Title* column and then press the Tab key. (This moves the insertion point to the field in the *First Name* column. Pressing Shift + Tab will move the insertion point to the previous field. When typing text, do not press the spacebar after the last word in the field and proofread all entries to ensure that the data is accurate.)
   b. Type Kenneth and then press the Tab key.
   c. Type Porter and then press the Tab key.
   d. Type 7645 Tenth Street and then press the Tab key.
   e. Type Apt. 314 and then press the Tab key.

f. Type New York and then press the Tab key.

g. Type NY and then press the Tab key.

h. Type 10192 and then press the Tab key.

i. Type Mutual Investment Fund and then press the Tab key. (This makes the field in the *Title* column active in the next row.)

j. With the insertion point positioned in the field in the *Title* column, complete steps similar to those in 6a through 6i to enter the information for the three other clients shown in Figure 8.2 (reading the records from left to right).

7. After entering all the information for the last client in Figure 8.2 (Mrs. Wanda Houston), click OK in the bottom right corner of the New Address List dialog box.

8. At the Save Address List dialog box, navigate to the WL1C8 folder on your storage medium, type 8-MFDS in the *File name* text box, and then click the Save button.

Figure 8.2 Project 1a

Title	= Mr.		Title	= Ms.
First Name	= Kenneth		First Name	= Carolyn
Last Name	= Porter		Last Name	= Renquist
Address Line 1	= 7645 Tenth Street		Address Line 1	= 13255 Meridian Street
Address Line 2	= Apt. 314		Address Line 2	= (leave this blank)
City	= New York		City	= New York
State	= NY		State	= NY
Zip Code	= 10192		Zip Code	= 10435
Fund	= Mutual Investment Fund		Fund	= Quality Care Fund
Title	= Dr.		Title	= Mrs.
First Name	= Amil		First Name	= Wanda
Last Name	= Ranna		Last Name	= Houston
Address Line 1	= 433 South 17th Street		Address Line 1	= 566 North 22nd Avenue
Address Line 2	= Apt. 17-D		Address Line 2	= (leave this blank)
City	= New York		City	= New York
State	= NY		State	= NY
Zip Code	= 10322		Zip Code	= 10634
Fund	= Priority One Fund		Fund	= Quality Care Fund

Tutorial

Creating a Main Document

Creating a Main Document

After creating and typing the records in the data source file, type the main document. Insert in the main document fields that identify where variable information is to be inserted when the document is merged with the data source file. Use buttons in the Write & Insert Fields group to insert fields in the main document.

Quick Steps

Create a Main Document
1. Click Mailings tab.
2. Click Start Mail Merge button.
3. Click document type at drop-down list.
4. Type main document text and insert fields as needed.

Insert all of the fields required for the inside address of a letter with the Address Block button in the Write & Insert Fields group. Click this button and the Insert Address Block dialog box displays with a preview of how the fields will be inserted in the document to create the inside address; the dialog box also contains buttons and options for customizing the fields. Click OK and the «AddressBlock» field is inserted in the document. The «AddressBlock» field is an example of a composite field, which groups a number of fields (such as *Title, First Name, Last Name, Address Line 1*, and so on).

Click the Greeting Line button and the Insert Greeting Line dialog box displays with options for customizing how the fields are inserted in the document to create the greeting line. Click OK at the dialog box and the «GreetingLine» composite field is inserted in the document.

To insert an individual field from the data source file, click the Insert Merge Field button. This displays the Insert Merge Field dialog box with a list of fields from the data source file. Click the Insert Merge Field button arrow and a drop-down list displays containing the fields in the data source file.

A field or composite field is inserted in the main document surrounded by chevrons (« and »). The chevrons distinguish fields in the main document and do not display in the merged document. Formatting can be applied to merged data by formatting the merge field in the main document.

Address Block

Greeting Line

Insert Merge Field

Project 1b Creating a Main Document

Part 2 of 3

1. At a blank document, create the letter shown in Figure 8.3. Begin by clicking the *No Spacing* style in the styles gallery on the Home tab.
2. Press the Enter key six times and then type February 23, 2018.
3. Press the Enter key four times and then insert the «AddressBlock» composite field by completing the following steps:
   a. Click the Mailings tab and then click the Address Block button in the Write & Insert Fields group.
   b. At the Insert Address Block dialog box, click OK.
   c. Press the Enter key two times.
4. Insert the «GreetingLine» composite field by completing the following steps:
   a. Click the Greeting Line button in the Write & Insert Fields group.
   b. At the Insert Greeting Line dialog box, click the option box arrow for the option box containing the comma (the box to the right of the box containing *Mr. Randall*).
   c. At the drop-down list, click the colon.
   d. Click OK to close the Insert Greeting Line dialog box.
   e. Press the Enter key two times.

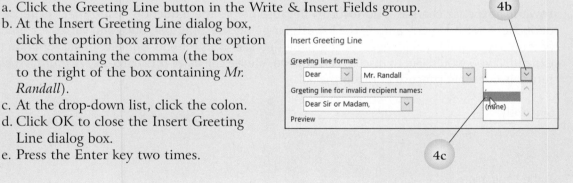

5. Type the letter shown in Figure 8.3 to the point where «Fund» displays and then insert the «Fund» field by clicking the Insert Merge Field button arrow and then clicking *Fund* at the drop-down list.
6. Type the letter to the point where the «Title» field displays and then insert the «Title» field by clicking the Insert Merge Field button arrow and then clicking *Title* at the drop-down list.
7. Press the spacebar and then insert the «Last_Name» field by clicking the Insert Merge Field button arrow and then clicking *Last_Name* at the drop-down list.
8. Type the remainder of the letter shown in Figure 8.3. (Insert your initials instead of *XX* at the end of the letter.)
9. Save the document and name it **8-MFMD**.

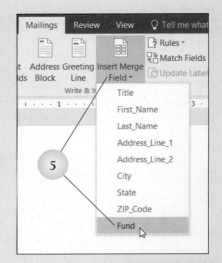

Check Your Work

Figure 8.3 Project 1b

February 23, 2018

«AddressBlock»

«GreetingLine»

McCormack Funds is lowering its expense charges beginning May 1, 2018. The reduction in expense charges means that more of your account investment performance in the «Fund» is returned to you, «Title» «Last_Name». The reductions are worth your attention because most of our competitors' fees have gone up.

Lowering expense charges is noteworthy because before the reduction, McCormack expense deductions were already among the lowest, far below most mutual funds and variable annuity accounts with similar objectives. At the same time, services for you, our client, will continue to expand. If you would like to discuss this change, please call us at (212) 555-2277. Your financial future is our main concern at McCormack.

Sincerely,

Jodie Langstrom
Director, Financial Services

XX
8-MFMD.docx

Preview
Results

 First
Record

 Previous
Record

 Next
Record

 Last
Record

 Find
Recipient

Previewing a Merge

To view how the main document will appear when merged with the first record in the data source file, click the Preview Results button on the Mailings tab. View the main document merged with other records by using the navigation buttons in the Preview Results group. This group contains the First Record, Previous Record, Next Record, and Last Record buttons and the *Go to Record* text box. Click the button that will display the main document merged with the desired record. Viewing the merged document before printing is helpful to ensure that the merged data is correct. To use the *Go to Record* text box, click in the text box, type the number of the record, and then press the Enter key. Turn off the preview feature by clicking the Preview Results button.

The Preview Results group on the Mailings tab also includes a Find Recipient button. To search for and preview merged documents with specific entries, click the Preview Results button and then click the Find Recipient button. At the Find Entry dialog box, type the specific field entry in the *Find* text box and then click the Find Next button. Continue clicking the Find Next button until Word displays a message indicating that there are no more entries that contain the typed text.

Checking for Errors

 Check for
Errors

Before merging documents, check for errors using the Check for Errors button in the Preview Results group on the Mailings tab. Click this button and the Checking and Reporting Errors dialog box, shown in Figure 8.4, displays containing three options. Click the first option, *Simulate the merge and report errors in a new document,* and Word will test the merge, not make any changes, and report errors in a new document. Choose the second option, *Complete the merge, pausing to report each error as it occurs,* and Word will merge the documents and display errors as they occur during the merge. Choose the third option, *Complete the merge without pausing. Report errors in a new document,* and Word will complete the merge without pausing and insert any errors in a new document.

Merging Documents

 Finish &
Merge

To complete the merge, click the Finish & Merge button in the Finish group on the Mailings tab. At the drop-down list, merge the records and create a new document, send the merged documents directly to the printer, or send the merged documents by email.

Figure 8.4 Checking and Reporting Errors Dialog Box

Choose an option at this dialog box to tell Word to simulate the merge and then check for errors; complete the merge and then pause to report errors; or report errors without pausing.

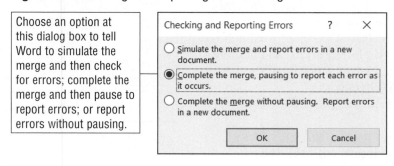

Merge Documents
1. Click Finish & Merge button.
2. Click *Edit Individual Documents* at drop-down list.
3. Make sure *All* is selected in Merge to New Document dialog box.
4. Click OK.

💡 **Hint** Press Alt + Shift + N to display the Merge to New Document dialog box and press Alt + Shift + M to display the Merge to Printer dialog box.

To merge the documents and create a new document with the merged records, click the Finish & Merge button and then click *Edit Individual Documents* at the drop-down list. At the Merge to New Document dialog box, make sure *All* is selected in the *Merge records* section and then click OK. This merges the records in the data source file with the main document and inserts the merged documents in a new document.

Identify specific records to be merged with options at the Merge to New Document dialog box. Display this dialog box by clicking the Finish & Merge button on the Mailings tab and then clicking the *Edit Individual Documents* option at the drop-down list. Click the *All* option in the Merge to New Document dialog box to merge all the records in the data source file and click the *Current record* option to merge only the current record. To merge specific adjacent records, click in the *From* text box, type the beginning record number, press the Tab key, and then type the ending record number in the *To* text box.

Project 1c **Merging the Main Document with the Data Source File** Part 3 of 3

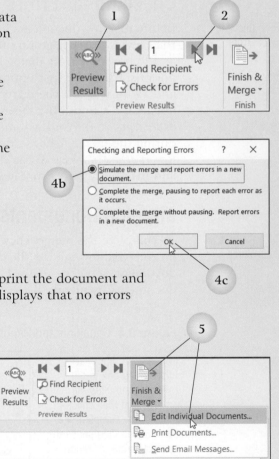

1. With **8-MFMD.docx** open, preview the main document merged with the first record in the data source file by clicking the Preview Results button on the Mailings tab.
2. Click the Next Record button to view the main document merged with the second record in the data source file.
3. Click the Preview Results button to turn off the preview feature.
4. Automatically check for errors by completing the following steps:
   a. Click the Check for Errors button in the Preview Results group on the Mailings tab.
   b. At the Checking and Reporting Errors dialog box, click the first option, *Simulate the merge and report errors in a new document*.
   c. Click OK.
   d. If a new document displays with any errors, print the document and then close it without saving it. If a message displays that no errors were found, click OK.
5. Click the Finish & Merge button in the Finish group and then click *Edit Individual Documents* at the drop-down list.
6. At the Merge to New Document dialog box, make sure *All* is selected and then click OK.
7. Save the merged letters and name the document **8-MFLtrs**.
8. Print **8-MFLtrs.docx**. (This document will print four letters.)
9. Close **8-MFLtrs.docx**.
10. Save and then close **8-MFMD.docx**.

Check Your Work

Project 2 **Merge Envelopes**   **1 Part**

You will use Mail Merge to prepare envelopes with customer names and addresses.

Preview Finished Project

Merging with Other Main Documents

In addition to merging letters, a data source file can be merged with an envelope, label, or directory main document. Create an envelope main document with the *Envelopes* option at the Start Mail Merge button drop-down list and create a label main document with the *Labels* option. Create a directory, which merges fields to the same page, with the *Directory* option at the Start Mail Merge button drop-down list.

Merging Envelopes

A letter created as a main document and then merged with a data source file will more than likely need properly addressed envelopes in which to send the letters. To prepare an envelope main document that is merged with a data source file, click the Mailings tab, click the Start Mail Merge button, and then click *Envelopes* at the drop-down list. This displays the Envelope Options dialog box, as shown in Figure 8.5. At this dialog box, specify the envelope size, make any other changes, and then click OK.

The next step in the envelope merge process is to create the data source file or identify an existing data source file. To identify an existing data source file, click the Select Recipients button in the Start Mail Merge group and then click *Use an Existing List* at the drop-down list. At the Select Data Source dialog box, navigate to the folder containing the data source file and then double-click the file.

With the data source file attached to the envelope main document, the next step is to insert the appropriate fields. Click in the envelope in the approximate location the recipient's address will appear and a box with a dashed gray border displays. Click the Address Block button in the Write & Insert Fields group and then click OK at the Insert Address Block dialog box.

Figure 8.5 Envelope Options Dialog Box

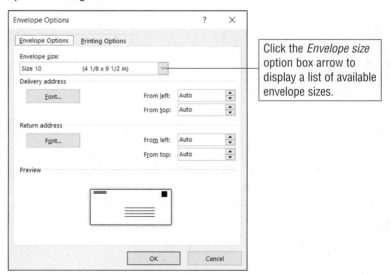

1. At a blank document, click the Mailings tab.
2. Click the Start Mail Merge button in the Start Mail Merge group and then click *Envelopes* at the drop-down list.

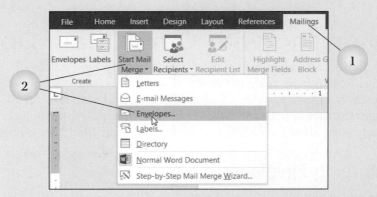

3. At the Envelope Options dialog box, make sure the envelope size is Size 10 and then click OK.
4. Click the Select Recipients button in the Start Mail Merge group and then click *Use an Existing List* at the drop-down list.

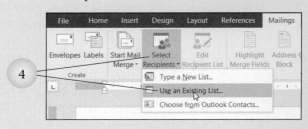

5. At the Select Data Source dialog box, navigate to the WL1C8 folder on your storage medium and then double-click the data source file named **8-MFDS.mdb**.
6. Click in the approximate location in the envelope document where the recipient's address will appear. (This causes a box with a dashed gray border to display. If you do not see this box, try clicking in a different location on the envelope.)

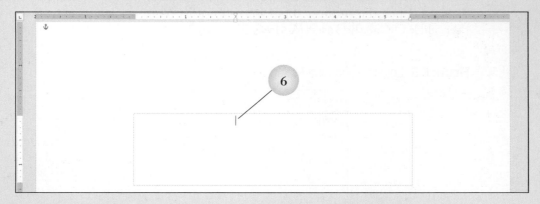

7. Click the Address Block button in the Write & Insert Fields group.
8. At the Insert Address Block dialog box, click OK.
9. Click the Preview Results button to see how the envelope appears merged with the first record in the data source file.
10. Click the Preview Results button to turn off the preview feature.
11. Click the Finish & Merge button in the Finish group and then click *Edit Individual Documents* at the drop-down list.

12. At the Merge to New Document dialog box, specify that you want only the first two records to merge by completing the following steps:
    a. Click in the *From* text box and then type 1.
    b. Click in the *To* text box and then type 2.
    c. Click OK. (This merges only the first two records and opens a document with two merged envelopes.)
13. Save the merged envelopes and name the document **8-MFEnvs**.
14. Print **8-MFEnvs.docx**. (This document will print two envelopes. Manual feeding of the envelopes may be required. Please check with your instructor.)
15. Close **8-MFEnvs.docx**.
16. Save the envelope main document and name it **8-EnvMD**.
17. Close **8-EnvMD.docx**.

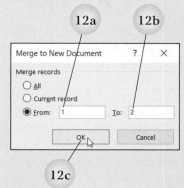

Check Your Work

Project 3 Merge Mailing Labels
1 Part

You will use Mail Merge to prepare mailing labels with customer names and addresses.

Preview Finished Project

Merging Labels

Mailing labels for records in a data source file are created in much the same way that envelopes are created. Click the Start Mail Merge button and then click *Labels* at the drop-down list. This displays the Label Options dialog box, as shown in Figure 8.6. Make sure the desired label is selected and then click OK to close the dialog box. The next step is to create the data source file or identify an existing data source file. With the data source file attached to the label main document, insert the appropriate fields and then complete the merge.

Figure 8.6 Label Options Dialog Box

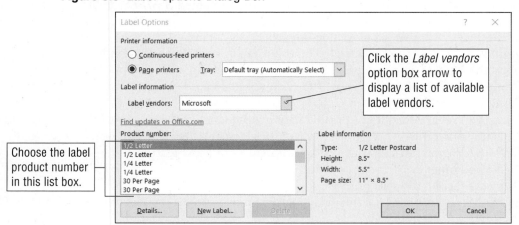

1. At a blank document, change the document zoom to 100% and then click the Mailings tab.
2. Click the Start Mail Merge button in the Start Mail Merge group and then click *Labels* at the drop-down list.
3. At the Label Options dialog box, complete the following steps:
   a. If necessary, click the *Label vendors* option box arrow and then click *Avery US Letter* at the drop-down list. (If this option is not available, choose a vendor that offers labels that print on a full page.)
   b. Scroll in the *Product number* list box and then, if necessary, click *5160 Easy Peel Address Labels*. (If this option is not available, choose a label number that prints labels in two or three columns down a full page.)
   c. Click OK to close the dialog box.

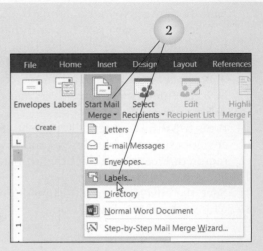

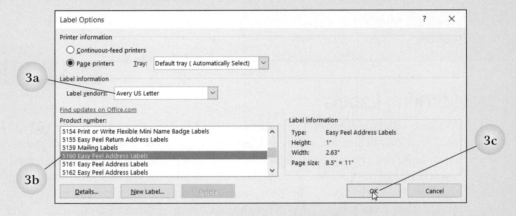

4. Click the Select Recipients button in the Start Mail Merge group and then click *Use an Existing List* at the drop-down list.
5. At the Select Data Source dialog box, navigate to the WL1C8 folder on your storage medium and then double-click the data source file named *8-MFDS.mdb*.
6. At the labels document, click the Address Block button in the Write & Insert Fields group.
7. At the Insert Address Block dialog box, click OK. (This inserts the «AddressBlock» composite field in the first label. The other labels contain the «Next Record» field.)
8. Click the Update Labels button in the Write & Insert Fields group. (This adds the «AddressBlock» composite field after each «Next Record» field in the second and subsequent labels.)
9. Click the Preview Results button to see how the labels appear merged with the records in the data source file.
10. Click the Preview Results button to turn off the preview feature.
11. Click the Finish & Merge button in the Finish group and then click *Edit Individual Documents* at the drop-down list.
12. At the Merge to New Document dialog box, make sure *All* is selected and then click OK.

13. Format the labels by completing the following steps:
   a. Click the Table Tools Layout tab.
   b. Click the Select button in the Table group and then click the *Select Table* option.
   c. Click the Align Center Left button in the Alignment group.
   d. Click the Home tab and then click the Paragraph group dialog box launcher.
   e. At the Paragraph dialog box, click the *Before* measurement box up arrow to change the measurement to 0 points.
   f. Click the *After* measurement box up arrow to change the measurement to 0 points.
   g. Click the *Inside* measurement box up arrow three times to change the measurement to 0.3 inch.
   h. Click OK.

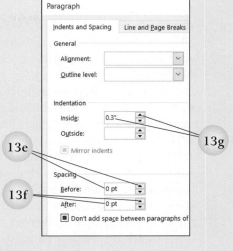

14. Save the merged labels and name the document **8-MFLabels**.
15. Print and then close **8-MFLabels.docx**.
16. Save the label main document and name it **8-LabelsMD**.
17. Close **8-LabelsMD.docx**.

Check Your Work

Project 4 Merge a Directory   1 Part

You will use Mail Merge to prepare a directory list containing customer names and types of financial investment funds.

Preview Finished Project

Tutorial

Merging a Directory

Merging a Directory

When merging letters, envelopes, or mailing labels, a new form is created for each record. For example, if the data source file merged with the letter contains eight records, eight letters are created, each on a separate page. If the data source file merged with a mailing label contains 20 records, 20 labels are created. In some situations, merged information should remain on the same page. This is useful, for example, when creating a list such as a directory or address list.

Begin creating a merged directory by clicking the Start Mail Merge button and then clicking *Directory* at the drop-down list. Create or identify an existing data source file and then insert the desired fields in the directory document. To display the merged data in columns, set tabs for all of the columns.

1. At a blank document, click the Mailings tab.
2. Click the Start Mail Merge button in the Start Mail Merge group and then click *Directory* at the drop-down list.
3. Click the Select Recipients button in the Start Mail Merge group and then click *Use an Existing List* at the drop-down list.
4. At the Select Data Source dialog box, navigate to the WL1C8 folder on your storage medium and then double-click the data source file named *8-MFDS.mdb*.

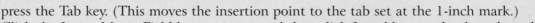

5. At the document screen, set left tabs at the 1-inch mark, the 2.5-inch mark, and the 4-inch mark on the horizontal ruler and then press the Tab key. (This moves the insertion point to the tab set at the 1-inch mark.)
6. Click the Insert Merge Field button arrow and then click *Last_Name* at the drop-down list.
7. Press the Tab key to move the insertion point to the tab set at the 2.5-inch mark.
8. Click the Insert Merge Field button arrow and then click *First_Name* at the drop-down list.
9. Press the Tab key to move the insertion point to the tab set at the 4-inch mark.
10. Click the Insert Merge Field button arrow and then click *Fund* at the drop-down list.
11. Press the Enter key.
12. Click the Finish & Merge button in the Finish group and then click *Edit Individual Documents* at the drop-down list.
13. At the Merge to New Document dialog box, make sure *All* is selected and then click OK. (This merges the fields in the document.)
14. Press Ctrl + Home, press the Enter key, and then press the Up Arrow key.
15. Press the Tab key, turn on bold formatting, and then type Last Name.
16. Press the Tab key and then type First Name.
17. Press the Tab key and then type Fund.

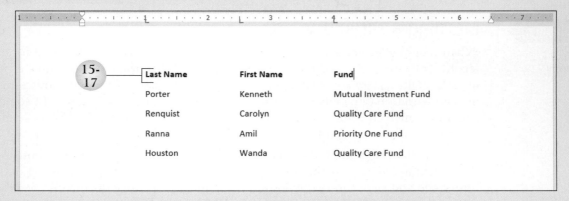

18. Save the directory document and name it **8-Directory**.
19. Print and then close the document.
20. Close the directory main document without saving it.

Check Your Work

You will use Mail Merge to prepare mailing labels with the names and addresses of customers living in Baltimore.

Preview Finished Project

Tutorial

Editing a Data Source File

Editing a Data
Source File

 Edit Recipient
List

Edit a main document in the normal manner. Open the document, make the required changes, and then save the document. Since a data source file is actually an Access database file, it cannot be opened in the normal manner. Open a data source file for editing using the Edit Recipient List button in the Start Mail Merge group on the Mailings tab. Click the Edit Recipient List button and the Mail Merge Recipients dialog box displays, as shown in Figure 8.7. Select or edit records at this dialog box.

Selecting Specific Records

Each record in the Mail Merge Recipients dialog box contains a check mark before the first field. To select specific records, remove the check marks from those records that should not be included in a merge. This way, only certain records in the data source file will be merged with the main document.

Figure 8.7 Mail Merge Recipients Dialog Box

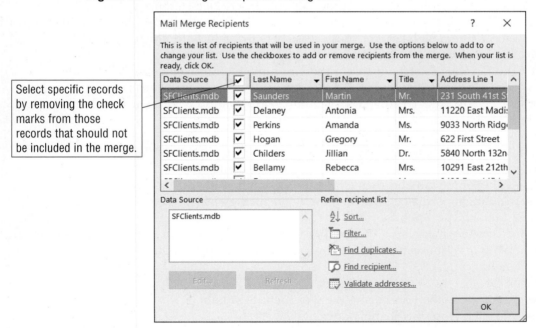

Select specific records by removing the check marks from those records that should not be included in the merge.

1. At a blank document, create mailing labels for customers living in Baltimore. Begin by clicking the Mailings tab.
2. Click the Start Mail Merge button in the Start Mail Merge group and then click *Labels* at the drop-down list.
3. At the Label Options dialog box, make sure *Avery US Letter* displays in the *Label vendors* option box and *5160 Easy Peel Address Labels* displays in the *Product number* list box and then click OK.
4. Click the Select Recipients button in the Start Mail Merge group and then click *Use an Existing List* at the drop-down list.
5. At the Select Data Source dialog box, navigate to the WL1C8 folder on your storage medium and then double-click the data source file named **SFClients.mdb**.
6. Click the Edit Recipient List button in the Start Mail Merge group.
7. At the Mail Merge Recipients dialog box, complete the following steps:
   a. Click the check box immediately left of the *Last Name* field column heading to remove the check mark. (This removes all the check marks from the check boxes.)
   b. Click the check box immediately left of each of the following last names: *Saunders*, *Perkins*, *Dutton*, *Fernandez*, and *Stahl*. (These are the customers who live in Baltimore.)
   c. Click OK to close the dialog box.

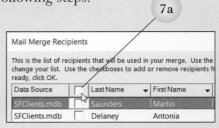

8. At the labels document, click the Address Block button in the Write & Insert Fields group.
9. At the Insert Address Block dialog box, click OK.
10. Click the Update Labels button in the Write & Insert Fields group.
11. Click the Preview Results button and then click the Previous Record button to display each label. Make sure only labels for those customers living in Baltimore display.
12. Click the Preview Results button to turn off the preview feature.
13. Click the Finish & Merge button in the Finish group and then click *Edit Individual Documents* at the drop-down list.
14. At the Merge to New Document dialog box, make sure *All* is selected and then click OK.
15. Format the labels by completing the following steps:
    a. Click the Table Tools Layout tab.
    b. Click the Select button in the Table group and then click *Select Table*.
    c. Click the Align Center Left button in the Alignment group.
    d. Click the Home tab and then click the Paragraph group dialog box launcher.
    e. At the Paragraph dialog box, click the *Before* measurement box up arrow to change the measurement to 0 points.
    f. Click the *After* measurement box up arrow to change the measurement to 0 points.
    g. Click the *Inside* measurement box up arrow three times to change the measurement to 0.3 inch.
    h. Click OK.
16. Save the merged labels and name the document **8-SFLabels**.
17. Print and then close **8-SFLabels.docx**.
18. Close the main labels document without saving it.

Check Your Work

You will edit records in a data source file and then use Mail Merge to prepare a directory with the edited records that contains customer names, telephone numbers, and cell phone numbers.

Preview Finished Project

Editing Records

Quick Steps

Edit a Data Source File
1. Open main document.
2. Click Mailings tab.
3. Click Edit Recipient List button.
4. Click data source file name in *Data Source* list box.
5. Click Edit button.
6. Make changes at Edit Data Source dialog box.
7. Click OK.
8. Click OK.

A data source file may need editing on a periodic basis to add or delete customer names, update fields, insert new fields, or delete existing fields. To edit a data source file, click the Edit Recipient List button in the Start Mail Merge group. At the Mail Merge Recipients dialog box, click the data source file name in the *Data Source* list box and then click the Edit button below the list box. This displays the Edit Data Source dialog box, as shown in Figure 8.8. At this dialog box, add a new entry, delete an entry, find a particular entry, and customize columns.

Figure 8.8 Edit Data Source Dialog Box

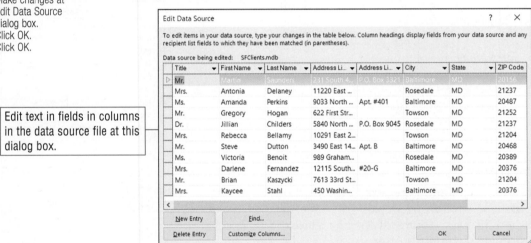

Edit text in fields in columns in the data source file at this dialog box.

Project 6 Editing Records in a Data Source File Part 1 of 1

1. Make a copy of the **SFClients.mdb** file by completing the following steps:
   a. Display the Open dialog box and make WL1C8 the active folder.
   b. If necessary, change the file type option to *All Files (*.*)*.
   c. Right-click **SFClients.mdb** and then click *Copy* at the shortcut menu.
   d. Position the mouse pointer in a white portion of the Open dialog box Content pane (outside any file name), click the right mouse button, and then click *Paste* at the shortcut menu. (This inserts a copy of the file in the dialog box Content pane and names the file **SFClients - Copy.mdb**.)
   e. Right-click **SFClients - Copy.mdb** and then click *Rename* at the shortcut menu.
   f. Type 8-DS and then press the Enter key.
   g. Close the Open dialog box.

2. At a blank document, click the Mailings tab.
3. Click the Select Recipients button and then click *Use an Existing List* from the drop-down list.
4. At the Select Data Source dialog box, navigate to the WL1C8 folder on your storage medium and then double-click the data source file named **8-DS.mdb**.
5. Click the Edit Recipient List button in the Start Mail Merge group.
6. At the Mail Merge Recipients dialog box, click *8-DS.mdb* in the *Data Source* list box and then click the Edit button.

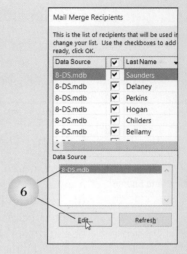

7. Delete the record for Steve Dutton by completing the following steps:
   a. Click the square at the beginning of the row for *Mr. Steve Dutton*.
   b. Click the Delete Entry button.
   c. At the message asking if you want to delete the entry, click Yes.
8. Insert a new record by completing the following steps:
   a. Click the New Entry button in the dialog box.
   b. Type the following text in the new record in the specified fields:

Title	Ms.
First Name	Jennae
Last Name	Davis
Address Line 1	3120 South 21st
Address Line 2	(none)
City	Rosedale
State	MD
ZIP Code	20389
Home Phone	410-555-5774

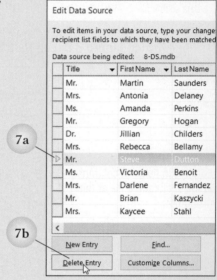

9. Insert a new field and type text in the field by completing the following steps:
   a. At the Edit Data Source dialog box, click the Customize Columns button.
   b. At the message asking if you want to save the changes made to the data source file, click Yes.
   c. At the Customize Address List dialog box, click *ZIP Code* in the *Field Names* list box. (A new field is inserted below the selected field.)
   d. Click the Add button.
   e. At the Add Field dialog box, type Cell Phone and then click OK.
   f. You decide that you want the *Cell Phone* field to display after the *Home Phone* field. To move the *Cell Phone* field, make sure it is selected and then click the Move Down button.
   g. Click OK to close the Customize Address List dialog box.

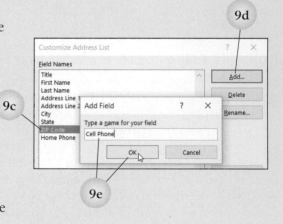

h. At the Edit Data Source dialog box, scroll to the right to display the *Cell Phone* field (last field in the file) and then type the following cell phone numbers (after typing each cell phone number except the last number, press the Down Arrow key to make the next field below active):

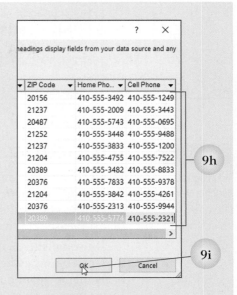

Record 1	410-555-1249
Record 2	410-555-3443
Record 3	410-555-0695
Record 4	410-555-9488
Record 5	410-555-1200
Record 6	410-555-7522
Record 7	410-555-8833
Record 8	410-555-9378
Record 9	410-555-4261
Record 10	410-555-9944
Record 11	410-555-2321

9h

9i

i. Click OK to close the Edit Data Source dialog box.
j. At the message asking if you want to update the recipient list and save changes, click Yes.
k. At the Mail Merge Recipients dialog box, click OK.

10. Create a directory by completing the following steps:
   a. Click the Start Mail Merge button and then click *Directory* at the drop-down list.
   b. At the blank document, set left tabs on the horizontal ruler at the 1-inch mark, the 3-inch mark, and the 4.5-inch mark.
   c. Press the Tab key. (This moves the insertion point to the first tab set at the 1-inch mark.)
   d. Click the Insert Merge Field button arrow and then click *Last_Name* at the drop-down list.
   e. Type a comma and then press the spacebar.
   f. Click the Insert Merge Field button arrow and then click *First_Name* at the drop-down list.
   g. Press the Tab key, click the Insert Merge Field button arrow, and then click *Home_Phone* at the drop-down list.
   h. Press the Tab key, click the Insert Merge Field button arrow, and then click *Cell_Phone* at the drop-down list.
   i. Press the Enter key.
   j. Click the Finish & Merge button in the Finish group and then click *Edit Individual Documents* at the drop-down list.
   k. At the Merge to New Document dialog box, make sure *All* is selected and then click OK. (This merges the fields in the document.)
11. Press Ctrl + Home, press the Enter key, and then press the Up Arrow key.
12. Press the Tab key, turn on bold formatting, and then type Name.
13. Press the Tab key and then type Home Phone.
14. Press the Tab key and then type Cell Phone.

12-14

Name	Home Phone	Cell Phone
Saunders	Martin	410-555-1249
Delaney	Antonia	410-555-3443

15. Save the directory document and name it **8-Directory-P6**.
16. Print and then close the document.
17. Close the directory main document without saving it.

Check Your Work

You will edit a form letter and insert sales representative contact information during a merge.

Preview Finished Project

 Rules

Inputting Text during a Merge

Word's Merge feature contains a large number of merge fields that can be inserted in a main document. The fill-in field is used to identify information that will be entered at the keyboard during a merge. For more information on the other merge fields, please refer to the on-screen help.

In some situations, keeping all the variable information in a data source file may not be necessary. For example, variable information that changes on a regular basis might include a customer's monthly balance, a product price, and so on. Insert a fill-in field in the main document and when the main document is merged with the data source file, variable information can be inserted in the document using the keyboard. Insert a fill-in field in a main document by clicking the Rules button in the Write & Insert Fields group on the Mailings tab and then clicking *Fill-in* at the drop-down list. This displays the Insert Word Field: fill-in dialog box, shown in Figure 8.9. At this dialog box, type a short message indicating what should be entered at the keyboard and then click OK. At the Microsoft Word dialog box with the message entered displayed in the upper left corner, type the text to display in the document and then click OK. When the fill-in field or fields are added, save the main document in the normal manner. A document can contain any number of fill-in fields.

Quick Steps

Insert a Fill-in Field in a Main Document
1. Click Mailings tab.
2. Click Rules button.
3. Click *Fill-in*.
4. Type prompt text.
5. Click OK.
6. Type text to be inserted.
7. Click OK.

When the main document is merged with the data source file, the first record is merged with the main document and the Microsoft Word dialog box displays with the message entered displayed in the upper left corner. Type the required information for the first record in the data source file and then click OK. Word displays the dialog box again. Type the required information for the second record in the data source file and then click OK. Continue in this manner until the required information has been entered for each record in the data source file. Word then completes the merge.

Figure 8.9 Insert Word Field: Fill-in Dialog Box

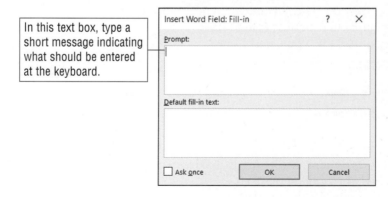

In this text box, type a short message indicating what should be entered at the keyboard.

1. Open the document **8-MFMD.docx**. (At the message asking if you want to continue, click Yes.) Save the document with the name **8-MFMD-P7**.
2. Edit the second paragraph in the body of the letter to the paragraph shown in Figure 8.10. Insert the first fill-in field (representative's name) by completing the following steps:
   a. Click the Mailings tab.
   b. Click the Rules button in the Write & Insert Fields group and then click *Fill-in* at the drop-down list.
   c. At the Insert Word Field: Fill-in dialog box, type Insert rep name in the *Prompt* text box and then click OK.
   d. At the Microsoft Word dialog box with *Insert rep name* displayed in the upper left corner, type (representative's name) and then click OK.

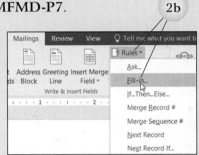

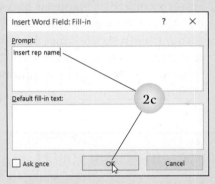

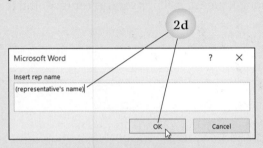

3. Complete steps similar to those in Step 2 to insert the second fill-in field (phone number), except type Insert phone number in the *Prompt* text box at the Insert Word Field: Fill-in dialog box and type (phone number) at the Microsoft Word dialog box.
4. Save **8-MFMD-P7.docx**.
5. Merge the main document with the data source file by completing the following steps:
   a. Click the Finish & Merge button and then click *Edit Individual Documents* at the drop-down list.
   b. At the Merge to New Document dialog box, make sure *All* is selected and then click OK.
   c. When Word merges the main document with the first record, a dialog box displays with the message *Insert rep name* and the text *(representative's name)* selected. At this dialog box, type Marilyn Smythe and then click OK.

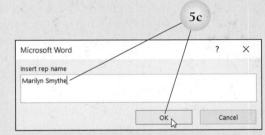

   d. At the dialog box with the message *Insert phone number* and *(phone number)* selected, type (646) 555-8944 and then click OK.
   e. At the dialog box with the message *Insert rep name*, type Anthony Mason (over *Marilyn Smythe*) and then click OK.
   f. At the dialog box with the message *Insert phone number*, type (646) 555-8901 (over the previous number) and then click OK.
   g. At the dialog box with the message *Insert rep name*, type Faith Ostrom (over *Anthony Mason*) and then click OK.
   h. At the dialog box with the message *Insert phone number*, type (646) 555-8967 (over the previous number) and then click OK.

    i. At the dialog box with the message *Insert rep name*, type Thomas Rivers (over *Faith Ostrom*) and then click OK.

    j. At the dialog box with the message *Insert phone number*, type (646) 555-0793 (over the previous number) and then click OK.

6. Save the merged document and name it **8-MFLtrs**.

7. Print and then close **8-MFLtrs.docx**.

8. Save and then close **8-MFMD-P7.docx**.

Check Your Work

Figure 8.10 Project 7

> Lowering expense charges is noteworthy because before the reduction, McCormack expense deductions were already among the lowest, far below most mutual funds and variable annuity accounts with similar objectives. At the same time, services for you, our client, will continue to expand. If you would like to discuss this change, please call our service representative, **(representative's name)**, at **(phone number)**.

Project 8 Use Mail Merge Wizard   1 Part

You will use the Mail Merge wizard to merge a main document with a data source file and create letters for clients of Sorenson Funds.

Preview Finished Project

Tutorial

Using the Mail Merge Wizard

Merging Using the Mail Merge Wizard

The Mail Merge feature includes a Mail Merge wizard with steps for completing the merge process. To access the wizard, click the Mailings tab, click the Start Mail Merge button, and then click the *Step-by-Step Mail Merge Wizard* option at the drop-down list. The first of six Mail Merge task panes displays at the right side of the screen. The options in each task pane may vary depending on the type of merge being performed. Generally, one of the following steps is completed at each task pane:

- Step 1: Select the type of document to be created, such as a letter, email message, envelope, label, or directory.
- Step 2: Specify whether the current document is to be used to create the main document, a template, or an existing document.
- Step 3: Specify whether a new list will be created or an existing list or Outlook contacts list will be used.
- Step 4: Use the items in this task pane to help prepare the main document by performing tasks such as inserting fields.
- Step 5: Preview the merged documents.
- Step 6: Complete the merge.

1. At a blank document, click the Mailings tab, click the Start Mail Merge button in the Start Mail Merge group, and then click *Step-by-Step Mail Merge Wizard* at the drop-down list.
2. At the first Mail Merge task pane, make sure *Letters* is selected in the *Select document type* section and then click the Next: Starting document hyperlink at the bottom of the task pane.
3. At the second Mail Merge task pane, click the *Start from existing document* option in the *Select starting document* section.
4. Click the Open button in the *Start from existing* section of the task pane.
5. At the Open dialog box, navigate to the WL1C8 folder on your storage medium and then double-click *SFLtrMD.docx*.
6. Click the Next: Select recipients hyperlink at the bottom of the task pane.
7. At the third Mail Merge task pane, click the Browse hyperlink in the *Use an existing list* section of the task pane.
8. At the Select Data Source dialog box, navigate to the WL1C8 folder on your storage medium and then double-click *SFClients.mdb*.
9. At the Mail Merge Recipients dialog box, click OK.
10. Click the Next: Write your letter hyperlink at the bottom of the task pane.
11. At the fourth Mail Merge task pane, enter fields in the form letter by completing the following steps:
    a. Position the insertion point a double space above the first paragraph of text in the letter.
    b. Click the Address block hyperlink in the *Write your letter* section of the task pane.
    c. At the Insert Address Block dialog box, click OK.
    d. Press the Enter key two times and then click the Greeting line hyperlink in the *Write your letter* section of the task pane.
    e. At the Insert Greeting Line dialog box, click the option box arrow at the right of the option box containing the comma (the box to the right of the box containing *Mr. Randall*).
    f. At the drop-down list, click the colon.
    g. Click OK to close the Insert Greeting Line dialog box.
12. Click the Next: Preview your letters hyperlink at the bottom of the task pane.
13. At the fifth Mail Merge task pane, look over the letter in the document window and make sure the information merged properly. If you want to see the letters for the other recipients, click the Next button (button containing two right-pointing arrows) in the Mail Merge task pane.
14. Click the Preview Results button in the Preview Results group to turn off the preview feature.
15. Click the Next: Complete the merge hyperlink at the bottom of the task pane.

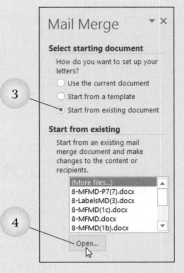

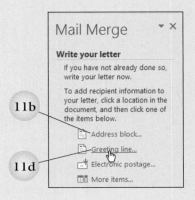

16. At the sixth Mail Merge task pane, click the <u>Edit individual letters</u> hyperlink in the *Merge* section of the task pane.
17. At the Merge to New Document dialog box, make sure *All* is selected and then click OK.
18. Save the merged letters document with the name **8-SFLtrs**.
19. Print only the first two pages of **8-SFLtrs.docx**.
20. Close the document.
21. Close the letter main document without saving it.

Check Your Work

Chapter Summary

- Use the Mail Merge feature to create documents such as letters, envelopes, labels, and directories with personalized information.

- Generally, a merge takes two documents: the data source file containing the variable information and the main document containing standard text along with fields identifying where variable information is inserted during the merge process.

- Variable information in a data source file is saved as a record. A record contains all the information for one unit. A series of fields makes a record and a series of records makes a data source file.

- A data source file is saved as an Access database but having Access on the computer is not required to complete a merge with a data source file.

- Use predesigned fields when creating a data source file or create custom fields at the Customize Address List dialog box.

- Use the Address Block button in the Write & Insert Fields group on the Mailings tab to insert all of the fields required for the inside address of a letter. This inserts the «AddressBlock» field, which is considered a composite field because it groups together a number of fields.

- Click the Greeting Line button in the Write & Insert Fields group on the Mailings tab to insert the «GreetingLine» composite field in the document.

- Click the Insert Merge Field button arrow in the Write & Insert Fields group on the Mailings tab to display a drop-down list of the fields contained in the data source file.

- Click the Preview Results button on the Mailings tab to view the main document merged with the first record in the data source file. Use the navigation buttons in the Preview Results group on the Mailings tab to display the main document merged with the desired record.

- Before merging documents, check for errors by clicking the Check for Errors button in the Preview Results group on the Mailings tab. This displays the Checking and Reporting Errors dialog box with three options for checking errors.

- Click the Finish & Merge button on the Mailings tab to complete the merge.

- Select specific records for merging by inserting or removing check marks from the records in the Mail Merge Recipients dialog box. Display this dialog box by clicking the Edit Recipient List button on the Mailings tab.

- Edit specific records in a data source file at the Edit Data Source dialog box. Display this dialog box by clicking the Edit Recipient List button on the Mailings tab, clicking the data source file name in the *Data Source* list box, and then clicking the Edit button.

- Use the fill-in field in a main document to insert variable information at the keyboard during a merge.
- Word includes a Mail Merge wizard that provides guidance through the process of creating letters, envelopes, labels, directories, and email messages with personalized information.

Commands Review

FEATURE	RIBBON TAB, GROUP	BUTTON, OPTION
Address Block field	Mailings, Write & Insert Fields	
Checking and Reporting Errors dialog box	Mailings, Preview Results	
directory main document	Mailings, Start Mail Merge	, *Directory*
envelopes main document	Mailings, Start Mail Merge	, *Envelopes*
fill-in merge field	Mailings, Write & Insert Fields	, *Fill-in*
Greeting Line field	Mailings, Write & Insert Fields	
insert merge fields	Mailings, Write & Insert Fields	
labels main document	Mailings, Start Mail Merge	, *Labels*
letter main document	Mailings, Start Mail Merge	, *Letters*
Mail Merge Recipients dialog box	Mailings, Start Mail Merge	
Mail Merge wizard	Mailings, Start Mail Merge	, *Step-by-Step Mail Merge Wizard*
New Address List dialog box	Mailings, Start Mail Merge	, *Type a New List*
preview merge results	Mailings, Preview Results	

Workbook

Chapter study tools and assessment activities are available in the *Workbook* ebook. These resources are designed to help you further develop and demonstrate mastery of the skills learned in this chapter.

Unit assessment activities are also available in the *Workbook*. These activities are designed to help you demonstrate mastery of the skills learned in this unit.

Index

Microsoft® Word Level 2

Unit 1

Formatting and Customizing Documents

Word
Customizing Paragraphs and Pages

CHAPTER

1

Performance Objectives

Upon successful completion of Chapter 1, you will be able to:

1 Apply custom numbering and bulleting formatting to text

2 Define and insert custom bullets

3 Define and insert multilevel list numbering

4 Insert, format, and customize images and text boxes

5 Group and ungroup objects

6 Edit points and wrap points in a shape

7 Link and unlink text boxes

8 Insert headers and footers in documents

9 Format, edit, and remove headers and footers

10 Insert and print sections

11 Control widows/orphans and keep text together on a page

Precheck

Check your current skills to help focus your study.

Word contains a variety of options for formatting text in paragraphs and applying page formatting. In this chapter, you will learn how to insert custom numbers and bullets, define new numbering formats, define picture and symbol bullets, apply multilevel numbering to text, and define a new multilevel list. You will also learn about customizing objects, inserting and editing headers and footers, printing specific sections of a document, and controlling text flow on pages.

Data Files

Before beginning chapter work, copy the WL2C1 folder to your storage medium and then make WL2C1 the active folder.

SNAP

If you are a SNAP user, launch the Precheck and Tutorials from your Assignments page.

Project 1 **Apply Number Formatting to an Agenda**

2 Parts

You will open an agenda document, apply formatting that includes number formatting, and then define and apply custom numbering.

Preview Finished Project

Inserting Custom Numbers and Bullets

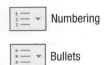

Numbering

Bullets

Number paragraphs or insert bullets before paragraphs using buttons in the Paragraph group on the Home tab. Use the Numbering button to insert numbers before specific paragraphs and use the Bullets button to insert bullets. To insert custom numbering or bullets, click the button arrow and then choose from the drop-down gallery that displays.

Inserting Custom Numbers

Insert numbers as text is typed or select text and then apply a numbering format. Type *1.* and then press the spacebar and Word indents the number approximately 0.25 inch. Type text after the number and then press the Enter key and Word indents all the lines in the paragraph 0.5 inch from the left margin (called a *hanging indent*). At the beginning of the next paragraph, Word inserts the number 2 followed by a period 0.25 inch from the left margin. Continue typing items and Word numbers successive paragraphs in the list. To number existing paragraphs of text, select the paragraphs and then click the Numbering button in the Paragraph group on the Home tab.

Click the Numbering button in the Paragraph group and arabic numbers (1., 2., 3., etc.) are inserted in the document. This default numbering can be changed by clicking the Numbering button arrow and then clicking an option at the Numbering drop-down gallery.

> **Hint** If the automatic numbering or bulleting feature is on, press Shift + Enter to insert a line break without inserting a number or bullet.

To change list levels, click the Numbering button arrow, point to the *Change List Level* option at the bottom of the drop-down gallery, and then click a list level at the side menu. Set the numbering value with options at the Set Numbering Value dialog box, shown in Figure 1.1. Display this dialog box by clicking the Numbering button arrow and then clicking the *Set Numbering Value* option at the bottom of the drop-down gallery.

Figure 1.1 Set Numbering Value Dialog Box

Choose this option to continue numbering from a previous list.

Change the starting value for the numbered list with this measurement box.

Set Numbering Va...   ?   ✕

◉ Start new list
◯ Continue from previous list

☐ Advance value (skip numbers)

Set value to:

1

Preview: 1.

OK   Cancel

1. Open **FDAgenda.docx** and then save it with the name **1-FDAgenda**.
2. Restart the list numbering at 1 by completing the following steps:
   a. Select the numbered paragraphs.
   b. Click the Numbering button arrow in the Paragraph group on the Home tab and then click *Set Numbering Value* at the drop-down gallery.
   c. At the Set Numbering Value dialog box, select the number in the *Set value to* measurement box, type 1, and then press the Enter key.

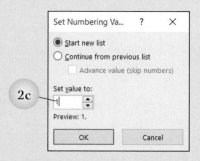

3. Change the paragraph numbers to letters by completing the following steps:
   a. With the numbered paragraphs selected, click the Numbering button arrow.
   b. At the Numbering drop-down gallery, click the option that uses capital letters (second column, second row in the *Numbering Library* section [this location may vary]).

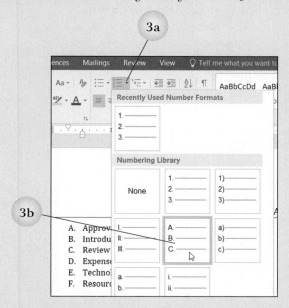

4. Add text by positioning the insertion point immediately right of the text *Introductions*, pressing the Enter key, and then typing Organizational Overview.

5. Demote the lettered list by completing the following steps:
   a. Select the lettered paragraphs.
   b. Click the Numbering button arrow, point to the *Change List Level* option, and then click the *a.* option at the side menu (*Level 2*).

6. With the paragraphs still selected, promote the list by clicking the Decrease Indent button in the Paragraph group on the Home tab. (The lowercase letters change back to capital letters.)

7. Move the insertion point to the end of the document and then type The meeting will stop for lunch, which is catered and will be held in the main conference center from 12:15 to 1:30 p.m.

8. Press the Enter key and then click the Numbering button.

9. Click the AutoCorrect Options button next to the *A.* inserted in the document and then click *Continue Numbering* at the drop-down list. (This changes the letter from *A.* to *H.*)

10. Type Future Goals, press the Enter key, type Proposals, press the Enter key, and then type Adjournment.

11. Press the Enter key and *K.* is inserted in the document. Turn off the list formatting by clicking the Numbering button arrow and then clicking the *None* option at the drop-down gallery.

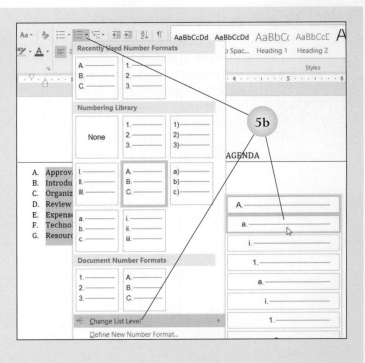

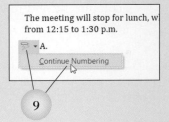

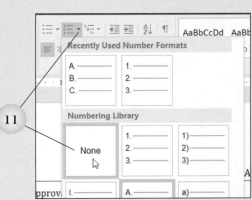

12. Save and then print **1-FDAgenda.docx**.

13. Select and then delete the paragraph of text in the middle of the list (the paragraph that begins *The meeting will stop*). (All the lettered items should be listed consecutively and the same amount of space should appear between them.)

14. Save **1-FDAgenda.docx**.

Check Your Work

Creating Custom Numbering

Along with default and custom numbers, custom numbering formats can be created with options at the Define New Number Format dialog box, shown in Figure 1.2. Display this dialog box by clicking the Numbering button arrow and then clicking *Define New Number Format* at the drop-down gallery. Use options at the dialog box to specify the number style, font, and alignment. Preview the formatting in the *Preview* section.

Any number format created at the Define New Number Format dialog box is automatically included in the *Numbering Library* section of the Numbering button drop-down list. Remove a number format from the drop-down list by right-clicking the format and then clicking *Remove* at the shortcut menu.

Figure 1.2 Define New Number Format Dialog Box

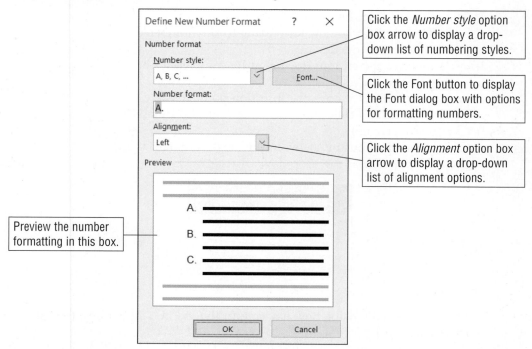

Click the *Number style* option box arrow to display a drop-down list of numbering styles.

Click the Font button to display the Font dialog box with options for formatting numbers.

Click the *Alignment* option box arrow to display a drop-down list of alignment options.

Preview the number formatting in this box.

Project 1b Defining a Numbering Format

Part 2 of 2

1. With **1-FDAgenda.docx** open, define a new numbering format by completing the following steps:
   a. With the insertion point positioned anywhere in the numbered paragraphs, click the Numbering button arrow in the Paragraph group on the Home tab.
   b. Click *Define New Number Format* at the drop-down list.
   c. At the Define New Number Format dialog box, click the *Number style* option box arrow and then click the *I, II, III, …* option.
   d. Click the Font button at the right side of the *Number style* list box.

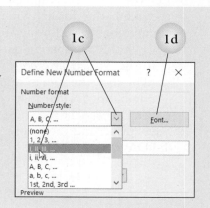

e. At the Font dialog box, scroll down the *Font* list box and then click *Calibri*.

f. Click *Bold* in the *Font style* list box.

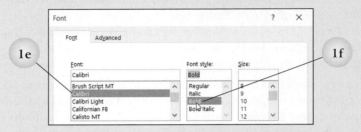

1e   1f

g. Click OK to close the Font dialog box.

h. Click the *Alignment* option box arrow and then click *Right* at the drop-down list.

i. Click OK to close the Define New Number Format dialog box. (This applies the new formatting to the numbered paragraphs in the document.)

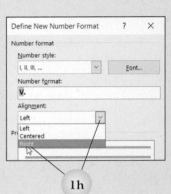

1h

2. Insert a file into the current document by completing the following steps:

a. Press Ctrl + End to move the insertion point to the end of the document and then press the Enter key two times.

b. Click the Insert tab.

c. Click the Object button arrow in the Text group and then click *Text from File* at the drop-down list.

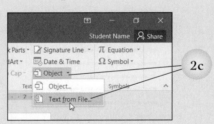

2c

d. At the Insert File dialog box, navigate to the WL2C1 folder and then double-click **PDAgenda.docx**.

3. Select the text below the title *PRODUCTION DEPARTMENT AGENDA*, click the Home tab, click the Numbering button arrow, and then click the roman numeral style created in Step 1.

4. Remove from the Numbering Library the numbering format you created by completing the following steps:

a. Click the Numbering button arrow.

b. In the *Numbering Library* section, right-click the roman numeral numbering format that you created.

c. Click *Remove* at the shortcut menu.

5. Save, print, and then close **1-FDAgenda.docx**.

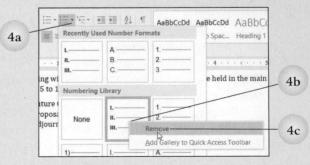

4a

4b

4c

Check Your Work

Project 2 **Apply Custom Bullets to a Travel Document** **1 Part**

You will open a travel document and then define and insert custom picture and symbol bullets.

Preview Finished Project

Creating Custom Bullets

Click the Bullets button in the Paragraph group and a round bullet is inserted in the document. Insert custom bullets by clicking the Bullets button arrow and then clicking a bullet type at the drop-down gallery. This drop-down gallery displays the most recently used bullets along with an option for defining a new bullet.

Click the *Define New Bullet* option and the Define New Bullet dialog box displays, as shown in Figure 1.3. Use options at the dialog box to choose a symbol or picture bullet, change the font size of the bullet, and specify the alignment of the bullet. When creating a custom bullet, consider matching the theme or mood of the document to maintain a consistent look or creating a picture bullet to add visual interest.

A bullet created at the Define New Bullet dialog box is automatically included in the *Bullet Library* section of the Bullets button drop-down gallery. Remove a custom bullet from the drop-down gallery by right-clicking the bullet and then clicking *Remove* at the shortcut menu.

As with the level of a numbered list, the level of a bulleted list can be changed. To do this, click the item or select the items to be changed, click the Bullets button arrow, and then point to *Change List Level*. At the side menu of bullet options that displays, click a bullet. To insert a line break in the list while the automatic bullets feature is on without inserting a bullet, press Shift + Enter. (A line break can also be inserted in a numbered list without inserting a number by pressing Shift + Enter.)

Figure 1.3 Define New Bullet Dialog Box

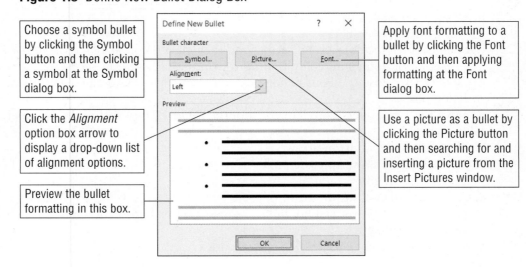

Choose a symbol bullet by clicking the Symbol button and then clicking a symbol at the Symbol dialog box.

Apply font formatting to a bullet by clicking the Font button and then applying formatting at the Font dialog box.

Click the *Alignment* option box arrow to display a drop-down list of alignment options.

Use a picture as a bullet by clicking the Picture button and then searching for and inserting a picture from the Insert Pictures window.

Preview the bullet formatting in this box.

1. Open **TTSHawaii.docx** and then save it with the name **1-TTSHawaii**.
2. Define and insert a picture bullet by completing the following steps:

   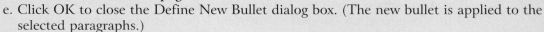

   a. Select the four paragraphs of text below the heading *Rainy Day Activities*.
   b. Click the Bullets button arrow in the Paragraph group on the Home tab and then click *Define New Bullet* at the drop-down gallery.
   c. At the Define New Bullet dialog box, click the Picture button.
   d. At the Insert Picture dialog box, click the *Browse* option, navigate to the WL2C1 folder on your storage medium, and then double-click the ***Flower.png*** file.
   e. Click OK to close the Define New Bullet dialog box. (The new bullet is applied to the selected paragraphs.)
3. Define and insert a symbol bullet by completing the following steps:
   a. Select the six paragraphs below the heading *Kauai Sights*.
   b. Click the Bullets button arrow and then click *Define New Bullet* at the drop-down gallery.
   c. At the Define New Bullet dialog box, click the Symbol button.

   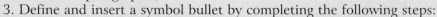

   d. At the Symbol dialog box, click the *Font* option box arrow, scroll down the drop-down list, and then click *Wingdings*.
   e. Click the flower symbol shown at the right.
   f. Click OK to close the Symbol dialog box.
   g. At the Define New Bullet dialog box, click the Font button.
   h. At the Font dialog box, click *11* in the *Size* list box.
   i. Click the *Font color* option box arrow and then click the *Light Blue, Background 2, Darker 25%* color option (third column, third row in the *Theme Colors* section).
   j. Click OK to close the Font dialog box and then click OK to close the Define New Bullet dialog box.
4. Remove the two bullets you defined from the *Bullet Library* section by completing the following steps:
   a. Click the Bullets button arrow.
   b. Right-click the flower picture bullet in the *Bullet Library* section and then click *Remove* at the shortcut menu.
   c. Click the Bullets button arrow.
   d. Right-click the flower symbol bullet in the *Bullet Library* section and then click *Remove* at the shortcut menu.
5. Save, print, and then close **1-TTSHawaii.docx**.

Check Your Work

Project 3 Apply Multilevel List Numbering to a Job Search Document

2 Parts

You will open a document containing a list of job search terms, apply multilevel list numbering to the text, and then define and apply a new multilevel list numbering style.

Preview Finished Project

Tutorial

Applying Multilevel List Numbering

Applying
Multilevel List
Numbering

 Multilevel
List

Quick Steps

Insert Multilevel List Numbering
1. Click Multilevel List button.
2. Click style at drop-down gallery.

Use the Multilevel List button in the Paragraph group on the Home tab to specify the type of numbering for paragraphs of text at the left margin, first tab, second tab, and so on. To apply predesigned multilevel numbering to text in a document, click the Multilevel List button and then click a numbering style at the drop-down gallery.

Some options at the Multilevel List button drop-down gallery display with *Heading 1*, *Heading 2*, and so on after the numbers. Click one of these options and Word inserts the numbering and applies the heading styles to the text.

Project 3a Inserting Multilevel List Numbering

Part 1 of 2

1. Open **JSList.docx** and then save it with the name **1-JSList(3a)**.
2. Select the paragraphs of text below the title and then apply multilevel list numbering by completing the following steps:
   a. Click the Multilevel List button in the Paragraph group on the Home tab.
   b. At the drop-down gallery, click the middle option in the top row of the *List Library* section.

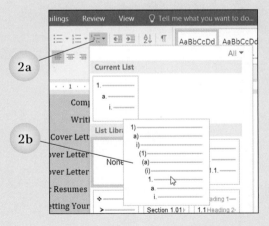

   c. Deselect the text.
3. Save, print, and then close **1-JSList(3a).docx**.

Check Your Work

Tutorial

Creating a
Custom Multilevel
List Option

Ö̇uick Steps

Define a Multilevel List
1. Click Multilevel List button.
2. Click *Define New Multilevel List*.
3. Choose level, number format, and/or position.
4. Click OK.

♡ Hint When defining a multilevel list style, you can mix numbers and bullets in the same list.

Creating a Custom Multilevel List

The Multilevel List button drop-down gallery contains predesigned level numbering options. If the gallery does not contain the type of numbering required, custom numbering can be created. To do this, click the Multilevel List button and then click *Define New Multilevel List*. This displays the Define new Multilevel list dialog box, shown in Figure 1.4. At this dialog box, click a level in the *Click level to modify* list box and then specify the number format, style, position, and alignment.

Typing a Multilevel List

Select text and then apply a multilevel list or apply the list and then type the text. When typing the text, press the Tab key to move to the next level or press Shift + Tab to move to the previous level.

Figure 1.4 Define New Multilevel List Dialog Box

Click a level to modify in this list box.

Specify the number format, style, position, and alignment for the selected level.

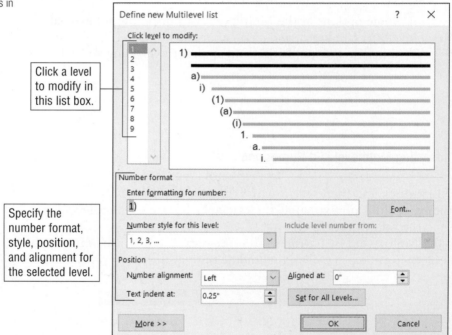

1. Open **JSList.docx** and then save it with the name **1-JSList(3b)**.
2. Select the paragraphs of text below the title.
3. Click the Multilevel List button in the Paragraph group on the Home tab.
4. Click the *Define New Multilevel List* option at the drop-down gallery.
5. At the Define new Multilevel list dialog box, make sure *1* is selected in the *Click level to modify* list box.
6. Click the *Number style for this level* option box arrow and then click *A, B, C, …* at the drop-down list.
7. Click in the *Enter formatting for number* text box, delete any text that displays after *A*, and then type a period (.). (The entry in the text box should now display as *A*.)
8. Click the *Aligned at* measurement box up arrow until *0.3"* displays in the measurement box.
9. Click the *Text indent at* measurement box up arrow until *0.6"* displays in the measurement box.

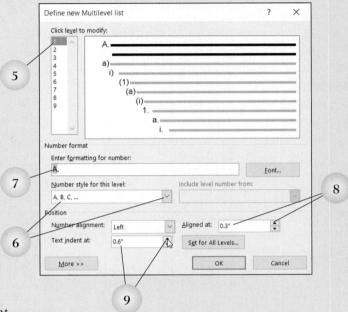

10. Click *2* in the *Click level to modify* list box.
11. Click the *Number style for this level* option box arrow and then click *1, 2, 3, …* at the drop-down list.
12. Click in the *Enter formatting for number* text box, delete any text that displays after the *1*, and then type a period (.).
13. Click the *Aligned at* measurement box up arrow until *0.6"* displays in the measurement box.
14. Click the *Text indent at* measurement box up arrow until *0.9"* displays in the measurement box.

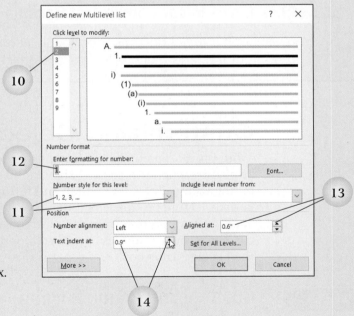

15. Click *3* in the *Click level to modify* list box.
16. Click the *Number style for this level* option box arrow and then click *a, b, c, …* at the drop-down list.
17. Make sure that *a)* displays in the *Enter formatting for number* text box. (If not, delete any text that displays after the *a* and then type a right parenthesis.)
18. Click the *Aligned at* measurement box up arrow until *0.9"* displays in the measurement box.
19. Click the *Text indent at* measurement box up arrow until *1.2"* displays in the measurement box.
20. Click OK to close the dialog box. (This applies the new multilevel list numbering to the selected text.)
21. Deselect the text.
22. Save, print, and then close **1-JSList(3b).docx**.

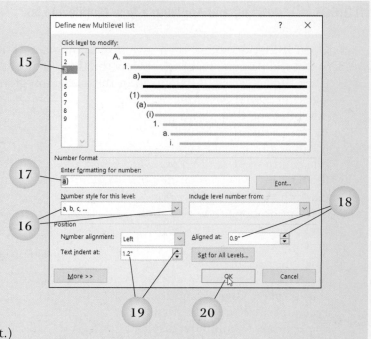

Check Your Work

Project 4 Insert Images and a Text Box in a Travel Document   3 Parts

You will open a travel document on Maui, insert and customize a clip art image and photograph, and then insert and customize a text box.

Preview Finished Project

Customizing Objects

Word provides a number of methods for formatting and customizing objects, such as pictures, clip art images, shapes and text boxes. Format images with buttons on the Picture Tools Format tab and further customize images with options at the Format Picture task pane and the Layout dialog box. Use buttons on the Drawing Tools Format tab to format and customize shapes and text boxes and further customize shapes and text boxes with options at the Format Shape task pane and the Layout dialog box.

Tutorial

Formatting an Image at the Layout Dialog Box

Customizing Image Layout

Customize the layout of images with options at the Layout dialog box. Display the Layout dialog box by clicking the Size group dialog box launcher on the Picture Tools Format tab. The Layout dialog box contains three tabs. Click the Position tab and the dialog box displays as shown in Figure 1.5.

Figure 1.5 Layout Dialog Box with Position Tab Selected

Use options in this section to specify the horizontal position of the image.

Use options in this section to specify the vertical position of the image.

Use options in this section to specify whether the image should move with the text and whether images should overlap.

Use options at the Layout dialog box with the Position tab selected to specify horizontal and vertical layout options. In the *Horizontal* section, choose the *Alignment* option to specify left, center, or right alignment relative to the margin, page, column, or character. Choose the *Book layout* option to align the image with the inside or outside margin of the page. Use the *Absolute position* option to align the image horizontally with the specified amount of space between the left edge of the image and the left edge of the page, column, left margin, or character. In the *Vertical* section of the dialog box, use the *Alignment* option to align the image at the top, bottom, center, inside, or outside relative to the page, margin, or line. In the *Options* section, attach (anchor) the image to a paragraph so that the image and paragraph move together. Choose the *Move object with text* option to move the image up or down on the page with the paragraph it is anchored to. Keep the image anchored in the same place on the page by choosing the *Lock anchor* option. Choose the *Allow overlap* option to overlap images with the same wrapping style.

Use options at the Layout dialog box with the Text Wrapping tab selected to specify the wrapping style for the image. Specify which sides of the image the text is to wrap around and the amounts of space between the text and the top, bottom, left, and right edges of the image.

Click the Size tab at the Layout dialog box to display options for specifying the height and width of the image relative to the margin, page, top margin, bottom margin, inside margin, or outside margin. Use the *Rotation* measurement box to rotate the image by degrees and use options in the *Scale* section to change the percentage of the height and width scales. By default, the *Lock aspect ratio* check box contains a check mark, which means that if a change is made to the height measurement of an image, the width measurement is automatically changed to maintain the proportional relationship between the height and width. Change the width measurement and the height measurement is automatically changed.

To change the height measurement of an image without changing the width or to change the width measurement without changing the height, remove the check mark from the *Lock aspect ratio* check box. To reset the image size, click the Reset button in the lower right corner of the dialog box.

Project 4a Inserting and Customizing the Layout of an Image Part 1 of 3

1. Open **TTSMaui.docx** and then save it with the name **1-TTSMaui**.
2. Insert an image by completing the following steps:
   a. Click the Insert tab and then click the Pictures button in the Illustrations group.
   b. At the Insert Picture dialog box, navigate to the WL2C1 folder on your storage medium and then double-click *HawaiiBanner.png*.
3. Select the current measurement in the *Shape Height* measurement box in the Size group on the Picture Tools Format tab, type 2, and then press the Enter key.

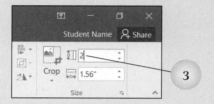

4. Click the *Beveled Matte, White* style in the Picture Styles group (second style from the left).

5. Click the Corrections button in the Adjust group and then click the *Brightness: –20% Contrast: +20%* option (second column, fourth row in the *Brightness/Contrast* section).
6. After looking at the image, you decide to reset it. Do this by clicking the Reset Picture button arrow in the Adjust group and then clicking *Reset Picture & Size* at the drop-down list.

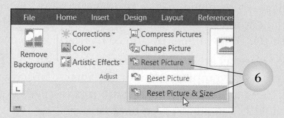

7. Select the current measurement in the *Shape Height* measurement box, type 1.3, and then press the Enter key.
8. Click the Wrap Text button in the Arrange group and then click *In Front of Text* at the drop-down gallery.

9. Position the image precisely on the page by completing the following steps:
   a. With the image selected, click the Size group dialog box launcher.
   b. At the Layout dialog box, click the Position tab.
   c. Make sure the *Absolute position* option in the *Horizontal* section is selected.
   d. Press the Tab key two times and then type 6.2 in the *Absolute position* measurement box.
   e. Click the *to the right of* option box arrow and then click *Page* at the drop-down list.
   f. Click the *Absolute position* option in the *Vertical* section.
   g. Select the current measurement in the box to the right of the *Absolute position* option and then type 2.
   h. Click the *below* option box arrow and then click *Page* at the drop-down list.
   i. Click OK to close the Layout dialog box.

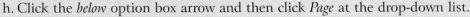

10. Click the *Drop Shadow Rectangle* style in the Picture Styles group (fourth style from the left).
11. Click the Color button in the Adjust group and then click the *Blue, Accent color 1 Light* option (second column, third row in the *Recolor* section).
12. Compress the image by clicking the Compress Pictures button in the Adjust group and then clicking OK at the Compress Pictures dialog box.
13. Click outside the image to deselect it.
14. Save **1-TTSMaui.docx**.

Check Your Work

Tutorial

Formatting an Image at the Format Picture Task Pane

Applying Formatting at the Format Picture Task Pane

Options for formatting an image are available at the Format Picture task pane, shown in Figure 1.6. Display this task pane by clicking the Picture Styles group task pane launcher on the Picture Tools Format tab.

The options in the Format Picture task pane vary depending on the icon selected. The formatting options may need to be expanded within the icons. For example, click *Shadow* in the task pane with the Effects icon selected to display options for applying shadow effects to an image. Many of the options available at the Format Picture task pane are also available on the Picture Tools Format tab. The task pane is a central location for formatting options and also includes some additional advanced formatting options.

Figure 1.6 Format Picture Task Pane

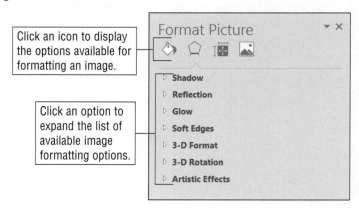

Click an icon to display the options available for formatting an image.

Click an option to expand the list of available image formatting options.

Applying Artistic Effects to Images

 Artistic Effects

Apply an artistic effect to a selected image with the Artistic Effects button in the Adjust group on the Picture Tools Format tab. Click this button and a drop-down gallery displays with effect options. Hover the mouse over an option in the drop-down gallery to see the effect applied to the selected image. An artistic effect can also be applied to an image with options at the Format Picture task pane with the Effects icon selected.

Project 4b   **Inserting and Customizing a Photograph**   Part 2 of 3

1. With **1-TTSMaui.docx** open, press Ctrl + End to move the insertion point to the end of the document and then insert a photograph by completing the following steps:
   a. Click the Insert tab and then click the Pictures button in the Illustrations group.
   b. At the Insert Picture dialog box, navigate to the WL2C1 folder on your storage medium and then double-click *Surfing.png*.
2. With the surfing photograph selected, click the Picture Effects button in the Picture Styles group, point to *Bevel*, and then click the *Circle* option (first column, first row in the *Bevel* section).

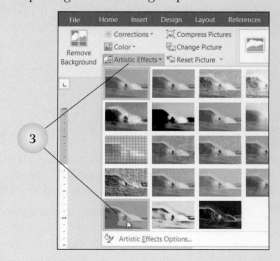

3. Click the Artistic Effects button in the Adjust group and then click the *Cutout* option (first column, bottom row).
4. After looking at the formatting, you decide to remove it from the image by clicking the Reset Picture button in the Adjust group.
5. Select the current measurement in the *Shape Height* measurement box, type 1.4, and then press the Enter key.

6. Format the photograph by completing the following steps:
   a. Click the Picture Styles group task pane launcher.
   b. At the Format Picture task pane, click *Reflection* to expand the reflection options in the task pane.
   c. Click the Presets button and then click the *Tight Reflection, touching* option (first column, first row in the *Reflection Variations* section).
   d. Click *Artistic Effects* in the task pane to expand the artistic effect options.
   e. Click the Artistic Effects button and then click the *Paint Brush* option (third column, second row).
   f. Close the task pane by clicking the Close button in the upper right corner of the task pane.

7. Click the Wrap Text button in the Arrange group on the Picture Tools Format tab and then click *Tight* at the drop-down list.

8. Position the photograph precisely on the page by completing the following steps:
   a. With the photograph selected, click the Position button in the Arrange group and then click *More Layout Options* at the bottom of the drop-down gallery.
   b. At the Layout dialog box with the Position tab selected, select the current measurement in the *Absolute position* measurement box in the *Horizontal* section and then type 5.3.
   c. Click the *to the right of* option box arrow and then click *Page* at the drop-down list.
   d. Select the current measurement in the *Absolute position* measurement box in the *Vertical* section and then type 6.6.
   e. Click the *below* option box arrow and then click *Page* at the drop-down list.
   f. Click OK to close the Layout dialog box.

9. Click outside the photograph to deselect it.

10. Save **1-TTSMaui.docx**.

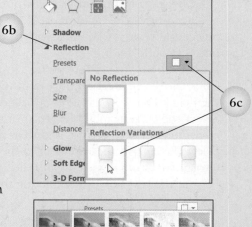

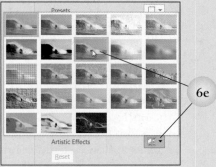

Check Your Work

Customizing and Formatting Objects

When an object such as a text box or shape is inserted in a document, the Drawing Tools Format tab is active. Use options on this tab to format and customize a text box or shape or use options at the Format Shape task pane.

Customizing a Text Box Display the Format Shape task pane by clicking the Shape Styles group task pane launcher. The task pane displays with three icons: Fill & Line, Effects, and Layout & Properties. The Format Shape task pane can also be displayed by clicking the WordArt Styles group task pane launcher. The Format Shape task pane displays with different icons than the Format Shape task pane that displays when the Shape Styles group task pane launcher is clicked. Click the WordArt Styles group task pane launcher and the task pane displays with *Text Options* selected and with three icons: Text Fill & Outline, Text Effects, and Layout & Properties.

1. With **1-TTSMaui.docx** open, insert a text box by completing the following steps:
   a. Click the Insert tab, click the Text Box button in the Text group, and then click the *Draw Text Box* option at the drop-down list.
   b. Click above the heading *MAUI SITES* and then type Hawaii, the Aloha State.
2. Select the text box by clicking its border. (This changes the text box border from a dashed line to a solid line.)
3. Press Ctrl + E to center the text in the text box.
4. Click the Text Direction button in the Text group and then click *Rotate all text 270°* at the drop-down list.

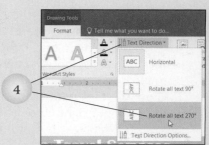

5. Select the current measurement in the *Shape Height* measurement box, type 6, and then press the Enter key.
6. Select the current measurement in the *Shape Width* measurement box, type 0.8, and then press the Enter key.
7. Format the text box by completing the following steps:
   a. Click the Shape Styles group task pane launcher.
   b. At the Format Shape task pane with the Fill & Line icon selected, click *Fill* to expand the options.
   c. Click the Fill Color button (displays to the right of the *Color* option) and then click the *Blue, Accent 1, Lighter 80%* option (fifth column, second row).
   d. Click the Effects icon and then click *Shadow* to expand the options.
   e. Click the Presets button and then click the *Offset Bottom* option (second column, first row in the *Outer* section).
   f. Scroll down the task pane and then click *Glow* to display the glow options.
   g. Click the Presets button in the *Glow* section and then click the *Blue, 5 pt glow, Accent color 1* option (first column, first row in the *Glow Variations* section).

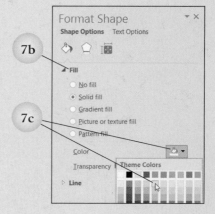

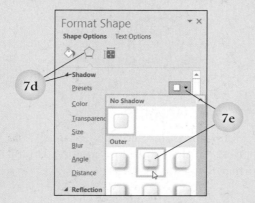

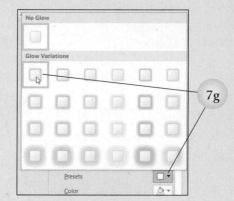

   h. Close the Format Shape task pane by clicking the Close button in the upper right corner of the task pane.
8. Click the More WordArt Styles button in the WordArt Styles group and then click the *Fill - Blue, Accent 5, Outline - Background 1, Hard Shadow - Accent 5* option (third column, third row).

9. Position the text box precisely on the page by completing the following steps:
   a. With the text box selected, click the Size group dialog box launcher.
   b. At the Layout dialog box, click the Position tab.
   c. Select the current measurement in the *Absolute position* measurement box in the *Horizontal* section and then type 1.
   d. Click the *to the right of* option box arrow and then click *Page* at the drop-down list.
   e. Select the current measurement in the *Absolute position* measurement box in the *Vertical* section and then type 2.7.
   f. Click the *below* option box arrow and then click *Page* at the drop-down list.
   g. Click OK to close the Layout dialog box.
10. Click the Home tab, click the *Font Size* option arrow, and then click *36* at the drop-down gallery.
11. Click outside the text box to deselect it.
12. Save **1-TTSMaui.docx**.

> **Check Your Work**

Project 5 Customize Shapes and an Image in a Financial Document and Link and Unlink Text Boxes
4 Parts

You will open a financial document, format, group, customize, ungroup, and edit points of a shape. You will also edit wrap points around an image and link and unlink text boxes.

> **Preview Finished Project**

Customizing Shapes Like a text box, a shape can be customized with buttons and options on the Drawing Tools Format tab or with options at the Format Shape task pane. Customize or format one shape or select multiple shapes and then customize and apply formatting to all of the selected shapes. Display the Format Shape task pane for a shape by clicking the Shape Styles group task pane launcher. When a shape is selected, the WordArt Styles group task pane launcher is dimmed and unavailable.

Tutorial

Grouping and Ungrouping Objects

Quick Steps
Group Objects
1. Select objects.
2. Click Picture Tools Format tab (or Drawing Tools Format tab).
3. Click Group button.
4. Click *Group*.

Hint Group multiple objects to work with them as if they are a single object.

Grouping and Ungrouping Objects Objects in a document such as an image, text box, or shape can be grouped so that the objects in the group can be sized, moved, or formatted as one object. To group objects, select the objects, click the Picture Tools Format tab (or Drawing Tools Format tab), click the Group button in the Arrange group, and then click *Group* at the drop-down list. With the objects grouped, move, size, or apply formatting to all of the objects in the group at once.

To select objects, click the first object, press and hold down the Shift key, click each remaining object to be included in the group, and then release the Shift key. Another method for grouping objects is to click the Select button in the Editing group on the Home tab, click the *Select Objects* option, and then use the mouse to draw a border around all of the objects. Turn off selecting objects by clicking the Select button and then clicking the *Select Objects* option.

Hint To group objects, a text wrapping other than *In Line with Text* must be applied to each object.

Hint A group can be created within a group.

Grouped objects can be sized, moved, and formatting as one object. However, an object within a group of objects can be sized, moved, or formatted individually. To do this, click the specific object and then make the changes to the individual object.

To ungroup grouped objects, click the group to select it, and then click the Picture Tools Format tab (or Drawing Tools Format tab). Click the Group button in the Arrange group and then click the *Ungroup* option at the drop-down list.

Project 5a Customizing and Formatting Shapes

1. Open **Leland.docx** and then save it with the name **1-Leland**.
2. Rotate the middle arrow shape by completing the following steps:
   a. Scroll down the document and then click the middle arrow shape to select it (on the first page).
   b. Click the Drawing Tools Format tab.
   c. Click the Rotate button and then click *Flip Horizontal* at the drop-down list.

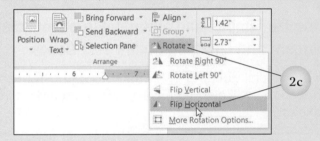

3. Align and format the arrow shapes by completing the following steps:
   a. With the middle arrow shape selected, press and hold down the Shift key.
   b. Click the top arrow shape, click the bottom arrow shape, and then release the Shift key.
   c. With all three arrow shapes selected, click the Align button and then click *Align Left* at the drop-down list.
   d. Click the Shape Styles group task pane launcher.
   e. At the Format Shape task pane with the Fill & Line icon selected, click *Fill* to display the fill options.
   f. Click the *Gradient fill* option.
   g. Click the Preset gradients button and then click the *Top spotlight - Accent 2* option (second column, second row).

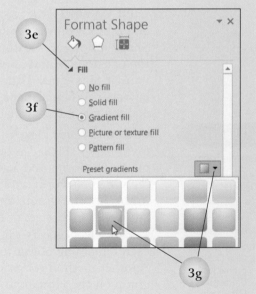

h. Scroll down the task pane and then click *Line* to display the line options.

i. If necessary, scroll down the task pane and then click the *No line* option.

j. Click the Effects icon (at the top of the task pane).

k. Click *Shadow* to display shadow options.

l. Click the Presets button and then click the *Inside Diagonal Top Right* option (third column, first row in the *Inner* section).

m. Close the Format Shape task pane.

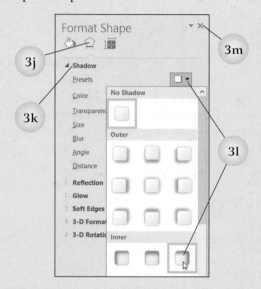

4. With the three arrow shapes still selected, group the shapes, size and move the group, and then ungroup the shapes by completing the following steps:

a. Click the Group button and then click *Group* at the drop-down list.

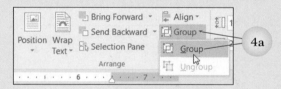

b. Click in the *Shape Height* measurement box and then type 6.

c. Click in the *Shape Width* measurement box, type 3.7, and then press the Enter key.

d. Click the Position button in the Arrange group and then click the *Position in Bottom Center with Square Text Wrapping* option (second column, third row in the *With Text Wrapping* section).

e. Click the Group button and then click *Ungroup* at the drop-down list.

f. Click outside the arrow shapes to deselect the shapes.

5. Delete the bottom arrow shape by clicking the shape and then pressing the Delete key.

6. Save **1-Leland.docx**.

Check Your Work

Editing Points in a Shape Sizing handles are small, white circles that display around a selected shape. Depending on the shape, small, yellow circles might also display. Use the yellow circles to change the width or height of a specific element of the shape.

Another method for customizing specific elements is to display and then use edit points. Display edit points by selecting the shape, clicking the Edit Shape button in the Insert Shapes group on the Drawing Tools Format tab, and then clicking the *Edit Points* option. Edit points display as small, black squares at the intersecting points in the shape. A red line also displays between edit points in the shape. Position the mouse pointer on an edit point and the pointer displays as a box surrounded by four triangles. Click and hold down the left mouse button, drag to change the specific element in the shape, and then release the mouse button.

Create a custom editing point by pressing and holding down the Ctrl key, clicking a specific location on a red line, and then releasing the Ctrl key. Position the mouse pointer on a red line and the pointer displays as a box inside a cross.

Project 5b Editing Points in a Shape

1. With **1-Leland.docx** open, press Ctrl + End to move the insertion point to the end of the document (page 2).
2. Click the shape on the second page to select the shape.
3. With the shape selected, edit points by completing the following steps:
   a. Position the mouse pointer on the top yellow circle, click and hold down the left mouse button, drag to the right approximately one-half inch (use the horizontal ruler as a guide and drag to approximately the 2.5-inch mark on the ruler), and then release the mouse button.

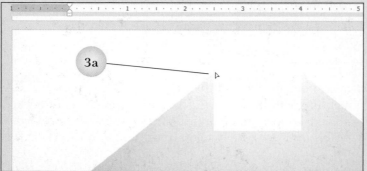

   b. Click the Drawing Tools Format tab, click the Edit Shape button in the Insert Shapes group, and then click *Edit Points* at the drop-down list.

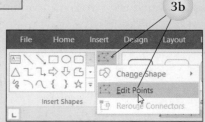

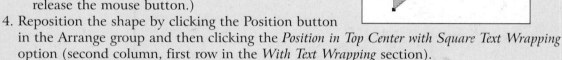

c. Position the mouse pointer on the edit point that displays at the tip of the arrow at the right side of the shape. Click and hold down the left mouse button, drag to the left approximately one inch (use the horizontal ruler as a guide), and then release the mouse button. (The shape will move when you release the mouse button.)

d. Position the mouse pointer on the edit point that displays at the tip of the arrow at the left side of the shape. Click and hold down the left mouse button, drag to the right approximately one inch (use the horizontal ruler as a guide), and then release the mouse button. (The shape will move when you release the mouse button.)

4. Reposition the shape by clicking the Position button in the Arrange group and then clicking the *Position in Top Center with Square Text Wrapping* option (second column, first row in the *With Text Wrapping* section).

5. Insert and format text in the shape by completing the following steps:
   a. With the shape selected, type Free seminar!, press the Enter key, and then type 1-888-555-4588.
   b. Select the text you just typed.
   c. Click the Text Fill button arrow in the WordArt Styles group and then click the *Orange, Accent 2, Darker 50%* color option (sixth column, bottom row in the *Theme Colors* section).
   d. Click the Home tab and then click the Bold button in the Font group.
   e. Click the *Font Size* option box arrow and then click *24* at the drop-down gallery.

6. Press Ctrl + Home to move the insertion point to the beginning of the document.

7. Save **1-Leland.docx**.

Check Your Work

Editing Wrap Points in a Shape When an object such as an image or shape is inserted in a document, a series of wrap points are defined around the object. These wrap points display in a manner similar to the editing points that display around an object. The difference between editing points and wrap points is that editing points change the shape of specific elements in an object while wrap points wrap text closer or farther away from an object.

To display wrap points in a shape, select the shape, click the Drawing Tools Format tab, click the Wrap Text button in the Arrange group, and then click the *Edit Wrap Points* option. Display wrap points for an image in a similar manner except click the Wrap Text button on the Picture Tools Format tab. Use wrap points to change how text or other data wraps around an object by dragging specific wrap points.

When wrap points are displayed in an object, red lines display between wrap points. Create a custom wrap point by clicking and holding down the mouse pointer on a location on a red line and then dragging to a specific position.

1. With **1-Leland.docx** open, click the border of the banner shape that displays in the paragraph of text below the title.
2. Edit wrap points in the shape by completing the following steps:
   a. Click the Drawing Tools Format tab.
   b. Click the Wrap Text button and then click *Edit Wrap Points* at the drop-down list.
   c. Drag the wrap point at the left side of the shape into the shape as shown below.

   d. Drag the wrap point at the right side of the shape into the shape as shown below.

3. Click outside the shape to remove the wrap points.
4. Save **1-Leland.docx**.

Check Your Work

Tutorial

Linking and
Unlinking Text
Boxes

 Create Link

 Break Link

Quick Steps

Link Text Boxes
1. Select text box.
2. Click Drawing Tools Format tab.
3. Click Create Link button.
4. Click in another text box.

Inserting a Text Box on a Shape In addition to typing text directly in a shape, a text box can be drawn on a shape. When a text box is drawn on a shape, it is actually added as a layer on top of the shape. To format or move the text box with the shape, select or group the shape with the text box.

Linking and Unlinking Text Boxes Text in text boxes can flow from one text box to another by linking the text boxes. To do this, draw the text boxes, and then click in the first text box. Click the Create Link button in the Text group on the Drawing Tools Format tab and the mouse pointer displays with a pouring jug icon attached. Click an empty text box to link it with the selected text box. Type text in the first text box and the text will flow to the linked text box.

More than two text boxes can be linked. To link several text boxes, click the first text box, click the Create Link button on the Drawing Tools Format tab, and then click in the second text box. Select the second text box, click the Create Link button, and then click the third text box. Continue in this manner until all desired text boxes are linked.

To break a link between two boxes, select the first text box in the link and then click the Break Link button in the Text group. When a link is broken, all of the text is placed in the first text box.

Project 5d Linking and Unlinking Text Boxes

1. With **1-Leland.docx** open, scroll down the document to display the first arrow shape on the first page.
2. Insert, size, and format a text box by completing the following steps:
   a. Click the Insert tab.
   b. Click the Text Box button in the Text group and then click *Draw Text Box* at the drop-down list.
   c. Click in the document near the first shape.
   d. With the text box selected, click in the *Shape Height* measurement box and then type 0.73.
   e. Click in the *Shape Width* measurement box and then type 2.
   f. Click the Shape Fill button arrow and then click *No Fill* at the drop-down list.
   g. Drag the text box so it is positioned on the first arrow (see image below).

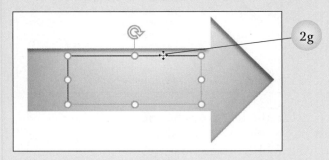

   h. Copy the text box to the second arrow shape by pressing and holding down the Ctrl key, clicking the text box border and holding down the left mouse button, dragging the copy of the text box so it is positioned on top of the second arrow shape, and then releasing the mouse button and the Ctrl key.
3. Link the text boxes by completing the following steps:
   a. Click the border of the text box on the first arrow shape to select the text box.
   b. Click the Create Link button in the Text group on the Drawing Tools Format tab.
   c. Click in the text box on the second arrow shape.
4. Insert text in the text box on the first arrow shape by completing the following steps:
   a. Click in the text box in the first arrow shape.
   b. Click the Home tab, change the font size to 12 points, apply the Orange, Accent 2, Darker 50% font color (sixth column, bottom row in the *Theme Colors* section), and apply bold formatting.

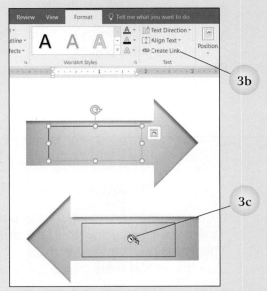

c. Click the Center button in the Paragraph group.

d. Click the Line and Paragraph Spacing button in the Paragraph group and then click *Remove Space After Paragraph*.

e. Click the Line and Paragraph Spacing button and then click *1.0*.

f. Type Let Leland Financial Services help you plan for retirement and provide you with information to determine your financial direction. (The text will flow to the text box on the second arrow.)

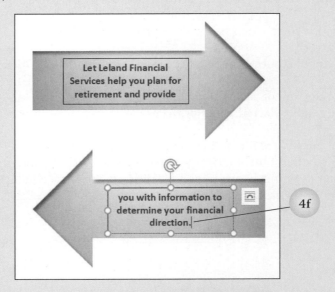

5. Break the link between the text boxes by completing the following steps:

a. Select the text box in the first arrow shape by clicking the text box border.

b. Click the Drawing Tools Format tab.

c. Click the Break Link button in the Text group (previously the Create Link button).

6. Relink the text boxes by clicking the Create Link button and then clicking in the text box on the second arrow shape.

7. Remove the outline around the two text boxes by completing the following steps:

a. With the text box on the first arrow shape selected, press and hold down the Shift key and then click the text box border of the second arrow shape.

b. With both text boxes selected, click the Shape Outline button and then click *No Outline* at the drop-down list.

8. Save, print, and then close **1-Leland.docx**.

Check Your Work

Project 6 Insert Headers and Footers in a Computer Software Report
8 Parts

You will open a report on productivity and graphics and multimedia software and then create and position headers and footers in the document. You will also create headers and footers for different pages in a document, divide a document into sections, and then create footers for specific sections.

Preview Finished Project

Tutorial

Creating a
Custom Header
and Footer

Inserting Headers and Footers

Text that appears in the top margin of a page is called a *header* and text that appears in the bottom margin of a page is called a *footer*. Headers and footers are commonly used in manuscripts, textbooks, reports, and other publications to display the page numbers and section or chapter titles. For example, see the footer at the bottom of this page.

Insert a predesigned header by clicking the Insert tab and then clicking the Header button. This displays a drop-down list of header choices. Click the predesigned header and the formatted header is inserted in the document. Complete similar steps to insert a predesigned footer.

If the predesigned headers and footers do not meet specific needs, create a custom header or footer. To create a custom header, click the Insert tab, click the Header button in the Header & Footer group, and then click *Edit Header* at the drop-down list. This displays a Header pane in the document along with the Header & Footer Tools Design tab, as shown in Figure 1.7. Use options on this tab to insert elements such as page numbers, pictures, and images; to navigate to other headers or footers in the document; and to position headers and footers on different pages in a document.

♀ *Hint* One method for formatting a header or footer is to select the header or footer text and then use the options on the Mini toolbar.

 Header

 Footer

Figure 1.7 Header & Footer Tools Design Tab

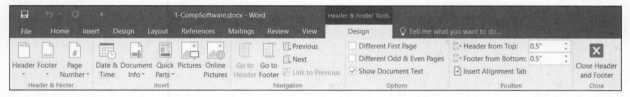

Inserting Elements in Headers and Footers

Use buttons in the Insert group on the Header & Footer Tools Design tab to insert elements into the header or footer, such as the date and time, Quick Parts, pictures, and images.

Click the Date & Time button in the Insert group and the Date and Time dialog box displays. This is the same dialog box that displays when the Date & Time button in the Text group on the Insert tab is clicked. Choose a date and time option in the *Available formats* list box of the dialog box and then click OK.

Click the Document Info button to display a drop-down list of document information fields that can be inserted into the document. Hover the mouse pointer over the *Document Property* option in the Document Info button drop-down list to display a side menu of document properties such as *Author*, *Comments*, and *Company* that can be inserted in the header or footer.

The Quick Parts button in the Insert group on the Header & Footer Tools Design tab displays the same options at the drop-down list as the Quick Parts button on the Insert tab. Click the Pictures button to display the Insert Picture dialog box and insert an image from the computer's hard drive or removable drive. Click the Online Pictures button and the Insert Pictures window displays with options for searching for and then downloading an image into the header or footer.

1. Open **CompSoftware.docx** and then save it with the name **1-CompSoftware**.
2. Insert a header by completing the following steps:
   a. Click the Insert tab.
   b. Click the Header button in the Header & Footer group and then click *Edit Header* at the drop-down list.
   c. With the insertion point positioned in the Header pane, click the Pictures button in the Insert group on the Header & Footer Tools Design tab.

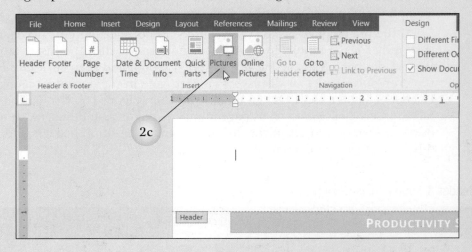

   d. At the Insert Picture dialog box, navigate to the WL2C1 folder on your storage medium and then double-click **Worldwide.jpg**.
   e. With the image selected, click in the *Shape Height* measurement box, type 0.4, and then press the Enter key.
   f. Click the Wrap Text button in the Arrange group and then click *Behind Text* at the drop-down list.
   g. Drag the image up approximately one-third of an inch.
   h. Click outside the image to deselect it.
   i. Press the Tab key two times. (This moves the insertion point to the right margin.)
   j. Click the Header & Footer Tools Design tab and then click the Date & Time button in the Insert group.
   k. At the Date and Time dialog box, click the twelfth option from the top (the option that displays the date in numbers and the time) and then click OK to close the dialog box.
   l. Select the date and time text and then click the Home tab. Click the Bold button in the Font group, click the *Font Size* option box arrow, and then click *9* at the drop-down gallery.
   m. Double-click in the document to make the document active and dim the header.
3. Save **1-CompSoftware.docx**.

Check Your Work

Positioning Headers and Footers

Word inserts a header 0.5 inch from the top of the page and a footer 0.5 inch from the bottom of the page. These default positions can be changed with buttons in the Position group on the Header & Footer Tools Design tab. Use the *Header from Top* and the *Footer from Bottom* measurement boxes to adjust the position of the header and the footer, respectively, on the page.

By default, headers and footers contain two tab settings. A center tab is set at 3.25 inches and a right tab is set at 6.5 inches. If the document contains default left and right margin settings of 1 inch, the center tab set at 3.25 inches is the center of the document and the right tab set at 6.5 inches is at the right margin. If the default margins are changed, the default center tab may need to be changed before inserting header or footer text at the center tab. Position tabs with the Insert Alignment Tab button in the Position group. Click this button and the Alignment Tab dialog box displays. Use options at this dialog box to change tab alignment and set tabs with leaders.

Project 6b Positioning Headers and Footers

1. With **1-CompSoftware.docx** open, change the margins by completing the following steps:
   a. Click the Layout tab, click the Margins button in the Page Setup group, and then click the *Custom Margins* option at the bottom of the drop-down list.
   b. At the Page Setup dialog box with the Margins tab selected, select the measurement in the *Left* measurement box and then type 1.25.
   c. Select the measurement in the *Right* measurement box and then type 1.25.
   d. Click OK to close the dialog box.
2. Create a footer by completing the following steps:
   a. Click the Insert tab.
   b. Click the Footer button in the Header & Footer group and then click *Edit Footer* at the drop-down list.
   c. With the insertion point positioned in the Footer pane, type your first and last names at the left margin.
   d. Press the Tab key. (This moves the insertion point to the center tab position.)
   e. Click the Page Number button in the Header & Footer group, point to *Current Position*, and then click *Accent Bar 2* at the drop-down list.

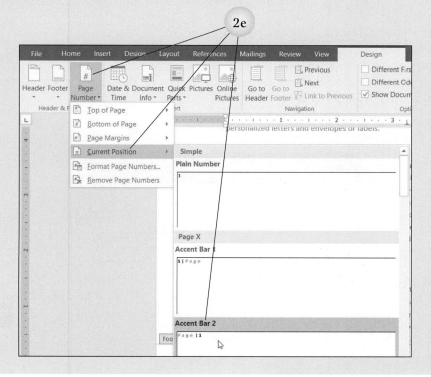

f. Press the Tab key.
g. Click the Document Info button in the Insert group and then click *File Name* at the drop-down list.

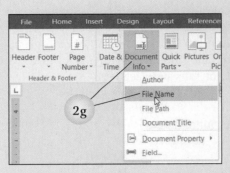

h. You notice that the center tab and right tab are slightly off, because the left and right margins in the document are set at 1.25 inches instead of 1 inch. To align the tabs correctly, drag the center tab marker to the 3-inch mark on the horizontal ruler and drag the right tab marker to the 6-inch mark on the horizontal ruler.

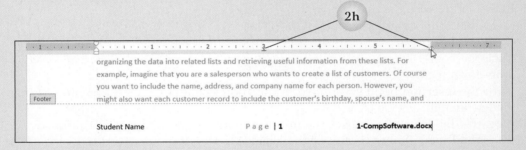

i. Select all the footer text and then change the font to 9-point Calibri and apply bold formatting.
3. Change the position of the header and footer by completing the following steps:
a. With the Header & Footer Tools Design tab active, click the *Header from Top* measurement box up arrow until *0.8″* displays.
b. Click in the *Footer from Bottom* measurement box, type 0.6, and then press the Enter key.
c. Click the Close Header and Footer button.

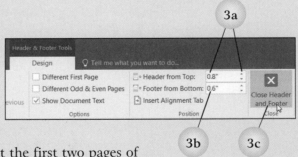

4. Save and then print the first two pages of **1-CompSoftware.docx**.

Check Your Work

Creating a Different First Page Header or Footer

A header and/or footer inserted in a document will display and print on every page in the document by default. However, different headers and footers can be created within one document. For example, a unique header or footer can be created for the first page of a document and a different header or footer can be created for the subsequent pages.

To create a different first page header, click the Insert tab, click the Header button, and then click *Edit Header* at the drop-down list. Click the *Different First Page* check box to insert a check mark and the First Page Header pane displays with the insertion point inside it. Insert elements or type text to create the first page header and then click the Next button in the Navigation group. This displays the Header pane with the insertion point positioned inside it. Insert elements and/or type text to create the header. Complete similar steps to create a different first page footer.

In some situations, the first page header or footer should be blank. This is particularly useful if a document contains a title page and the header or footer should not print on it.

Project 6c Creating a Header That Prints on All Pages Except the First Page Part 3 of 8

1. With **1-CompSoftware.docx** open, press Ctrl + A to select the entire document and then press Ctrl + 2 to change to double-line spacing.
2. Remove the header and footer by completing the following steps:
   a. Click the Insert tab.
   b. Click the Header button in the Header & Footer group and then click *Remove Header* at the drop-down list.
   c. Click the Footer button in the Header & Footer group and then click *Remove Footer* at the drop-down list.
3. Press Ctrl + Home and then create a header that prints on all pages except the first page by completing the following steps:
   a. With the Insert tab active, click the Header button in the Header & Footer group.
   b. Click *Edit Header* at the drop-down list.
   c. Click the *Different First Page* check box in the Options group on the Header & Footer Tools Design tab to insert a check mark.
   d. With the insertion point positioned in the First Page Header pane, click the Next button in the Navigation group. (This tells Word that the first page header should be blank.)
   e. With the insertion point positioned in the Header pane, click the Page Number button in the Header & Footer group, point to *Top of Page*, and then click *Accent Bar 2* at the drop-down gallery.
   f. Click the Close Header and Footer button.
4. Scroll through the document and notice that the header appears on the second, third, fourth, and fifth pages.
5. Save and then print the first two pages of **1-CompSoftware.docx**.

Check Your Work

Creating Odd and Even Page Headers or Footers

If a document will be read in book form, consider inserting odd and even page headers or footers. When presenting pages in a document in book form with facing pages, the outside margins are the left side of the left page and the right side of the right page. Also, when a document has facing pages, the right-hand page is generally numbered with an odd number and the left-hand page is generally numbered with an even number.

Create even and odd headers or footers to insert this type of page numbering. Use the *Different Odd & Even Pages* check box in the Options group on the Header & Footer Tools Design tab to create odd and even headers and/or footers.

Project 6d **Creating Odd and Even Page Footers**   Part 4 of 8

1. With **1-CompSoftware.docx** open, remove the header from the document by completing the following steps:
   a. Click the Insert tab.
   b. Click the Header button in the Header & Footer group and then click *Edit Header* at the drop-down list.
   c. Click the *Different First Page* check box in the Options group on the Header & Footer Tools Design tab to remove the check mark.
   d. Click the Header button in the Header & Footer group and then click *Remove Header* at the drop-down list. (This displays the insertion point in an empty Header pane.)
2. Create one footer that prints on odd pages and another that prints on even pages by completing the following steps:
   a. Click the Go to Footer button in the Navigation group on the Header & Footer Tools Design tab.
   b. Click the *Different Odd & Even Pages* check box in the Options group to insert a check mark. (This displays the Odd Page Footer pane with the insertion point inside it.)
   c. Click the Page Number button in the Header & Footer group, point to *Bottom of Page*, and then click *Plain Number 3* at the drop-down list.

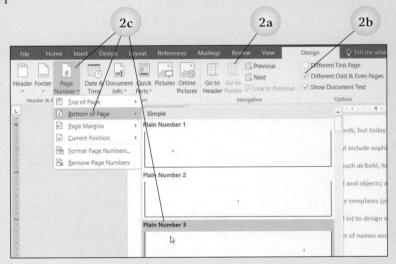

   d. Click the Next button in the Navigation group. (This displays the Even Page Footer pane with the insertion point inside it.)

e. Click the Page Number button in the Header & Footer group, point to *Current Position*, and then click *Plain Number* at the drop-down list.

f. Click the Close Header and Footer button.

3. Scroll through the document and notice the page numbers at the right sides of the odd page footers and the page numbers at the left sides of the even page footers.

4. Save and then print the first two pages of **1-CompSoftware.docx**.

> Check Your Work

Creating Headers and Footers for Different Sections

Quick Steps

Create Headers or Footers for Different Sections

1. Insert section break.
2. Click Insert tab.
3. Click Header or Footer button.
4. Click *Edit Header* or *Edit Footer*.
5. Click Link to Previous button to deactivate.
6. Insert elements and/or text.
7. Click Next button.
8. Insert elements and/or text.

A document can be divided into sections and then different formatting can be applied to each section. Insert a section break to divide the document into sections. A section break can be inserted that begins a new page or a section break can be inserted that allows the sections to be formatted differently but does not begin a new page. A section break can also be inserted that starts a new section on the next even-numbered page or the next odd-numbered page.

To insert different headers and/or footers on pages in a document, divide the document into sections. For example, if a document contains several chapters, each chapter can be a separate section and a different header and footer can be created for each section. When dividing a document into sections by chapter, insert section breaks that also begin new pages.

Breaking a Section Link

Link to Previous

When a header or footer is created for a specific section in a document, it can be created for all the previous and following sections or only the following sections. By default, each section in a document is linked to the other sections. To print a header or footer only on the pages within a section and not the previous section, deactivate the Link to Previous button. This tells Word not to print the header or footer on previous sections. Word will, however, print the header or footer on following sections. To specify that the header or footer should not print on following sections, create a blank header or footer at the next section. When creating a header or footer for a specific section in a document, preview the document to determine if the header or footer appears on the correct pages.

Project 6e Creating Footers for Different Sections and Breaking a Section Link   Part 5 of 8

1. With **1-CompSoftware.docx** open, remove the odd and even page footers by completing the following steps:

a. Click the Insert tab.

b. Click the Footer button in the Header & Footer group and then click *Edit Footer* at the drop-down list.

c. Click the *Different Odd & Even Pages* check box in the Options group on the Header & Footer Tools Design tab to remove the check mark.

d. Click the Footer button in the Header & Footer group and then click *Remove Footer* at the drop-down list.

e. Click the Close Header and Footer button.

2. Remove the page break before the second title in the document by completing the following steps:

   a. Move the insertion point immediately right of the period that ends the paragraph in the section PRESENTATION SOFTWARE (near the top of page 3).

   b. Press the Delete key two times. (The title GRAPHICS AND MULTIMEDIA SOFTWARE should now display below the paragraph on the third page.)

3. Insert an odd page section break (a section break that starts a section on the next odd page) by completing the following steps:

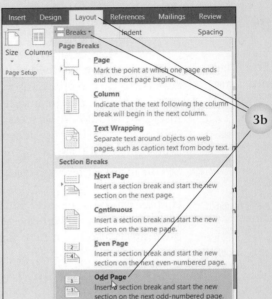

   a. Position the insertion point at the beginning of the title GRAPHICS AND MULTIMEDIA SOFTWARE.

   b. Click the Layout tab, click the Breaks button in the Page Setup group, and then click Odd Page at the drop-down list.

4. Create section titles and footers with page numbers for the two sections by completing the following steps:

   a. Position the insertion point at the beginning of the document.

   b. Click the Insert tab.

   c. Click the Footer button in the Header & Footer group and then click Edit Footer at the drop-down list.

   d. At the Footer -Section 1- pane, type Section 1 Productivity Software and then press the Tab key two times. (This moves the insertion point to the right margin.)

   e. Type Page and then press the spacebar.

   f. Click the Page Number button in the Header & Footer group, point to *Current Position*, and then click *Plain Number* at the side menu.

   g. Click the Next button in the Navigation group.

   h. Click the Link to Previous button to deactivate it. (This removes the message *Same as Previous* from the top right side of the footer pane.)

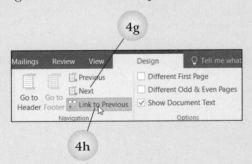

   i. Change the text *Section 1 Productivity Software* to *Section 2 Graphics and Multimedia Software* in the footer.

   j. Click the Close Header and Footer button.

5. Scroll through the document and notice the page numbering in the sections.

6. Save **1-CompSoftware.docx**.

Check Your Work

Customizing Page Numbers

By default, Word inserts arabic numbers (1, 2, 3, and so on) and numbers pages sequentially beginning with 1. These default settings can be customized with options at the Page Number Format dialog box shown in Figure 1.8. To display this dialog box, click the Insert tab, click the Page Number button in the Header & Footer group, and then click *Format Page Numbers* at the drop-down list. Another method for displaying the dialog box is to click the Page Number button in the Header & Footer group on the Header & Footer Tools Design tab and then click the *Format Page Numbers* option.

Use the *Number format* option at the Page Number Format dialog box to change from arabic numbers to arabic numbers preceded and followed by hyphens, lowercase letters, uppercase letters, lowercase roman numerals, or uppercase roman numerals. By default, page numbering begins with 1 and continues sequentially from 1 through all the pages and sections in a document. Change the beginning page number with the *Start at* option by clicking the *Start at* option and then typing the beginning page number in the measurement box. The number in the *Start at* measurement box can also be changed by clicking the measurement box up or down arrow.

If section breaks are inserted in a document and then a header and footer is inserted with page numbering for each section, the page numbering is sequential throughout the document. The document used in Project 6f has a section break but the pages are numbered sequentially. If the page numbering in a section should start with a new number, use the *Start at* option at the Page Number Format dialog box.

Figure 1.8 Customizing Page Numbering

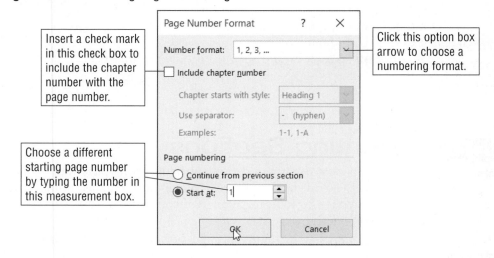

Insert a check mark in this check box to include the chapter number with the page number.

Click this option box arrow to choose a numbering format.

Choose a different starting page number by typing the number in this measurement box.

1. With **1-CompSoftware.docx** open, change page numbering to lowercase roman numerals and change the starting page number by completing the following steps:
   a. Press Ctrl + Home.
   b. Click the Insert tab.
   c. Click the Page Number button in the Header & Footer group and then click *Format Page Numbers* at the drop-down list.
   d. At the Page Number Format dialog box, click the *Number format* option box arrow and then click *i, ii, iii, …* at the drop-down list.
   e. Click the *Start at* option and then type 4.
   f. Click OK to close the dialog box.
2. Scroll through the document and notice the lowercase roman numeral page numbers (beginning with *iv*) that display at the right margin at the bottom of the pages.
3. Scroll to the bottom of the page containing the title *GRAPHICS AND MULTIMEDIA SOFTWARE* and notice that the page numbers did not change. (This is because the sections were unlinked.)
4. Position the insertion point in the first paragraph of text below the title *GRAPHICS AND MULTIMEDIA SOFTWARE* and then change page numbering by completing the following steps:
   a. Click the Page Number button in the Header & Footer group and then click *Format Page Numbers* at the drop-down list.
   b. At the Page Number Format dialog box, click the *Number format* option box arrow and then click *i, ii, iii, …* at the drop-down list.
   c. Click the *Start at* option and then type 7.
   d. Click OK to close the dialog box.
5. Save **1-CompSoftware.docx** and then print only the first page.

Page Number Format dialog box:

Number format: i, ii, iii, …   **1d**

☐ Include chapter number

Chapter starts with style: Heading 1

Use separator: - (hyphen)

Examples: 1-1, 1-A   **1e**

Page numbering

○ Continue from previous section

● Start at: 4

OK   Cancel   **1f**

Check Your Work

Printing Sections

Printing Sections

Print specific pages in a document by inserting page numbers in the *Pages* text box at the Print backstage area. When entering page numbers in this text box, use a hyphen to indicate a range of consecutive pages or a comma to specify nonconsecutive pages.

In a document that contains sections, use the *Pages* text box at the Print backstage area to specify the section and pages within the section to be printed. For example, if a document is divided into three sections, print only section 2 by typing *s2* in the *Pages* text box. If a document contains six sections, print sections 3 through 5 by typing *s3-s5* in the *Pages* text box. Specific pages within or between sections can also be identified for printing. For example, to print pages 2 through 5 of section 4, type *p2s4-p5s4*; to print from page 3 of section 1 through page 5 of section 4, type *p3s1-p5s4*; to print page 1 of section 3, page 4 of section 5, and page 6 of section 8, type *p1s3,p4s5,p6s8*.

 Quick Steps

Print a Section
1. Click File tab.
2. Click *Print* option.
3. Click in *Pages* text box.
4. Type s followed by section number.
5. Click Print button.

1. With **1-CompSoftware.docx** open, change the starting page number for section 2 to *1* by completing the following steps:
   a. Click the Insert tab, click the Footer button in the Header & Footer group, and then click *Edit Footer* at the drop-down list.
   b. At the Footer -Section 1- footer pane, click the Page Number button in the Header & Footer group and then click the *Format Page Numbers* option at the drop-down list.
   c. Click the *Number format* option box arrow and then click the *1, 2, 3, ...* option at the drop-down list.
   d. Select the current number in the *Start at* measurement box and then type 1.
   e. Click OK to close the dialog box.
   f. Display the section 2 footer by clicking the Next button in the Navigation group on the Header & Footer Tools Design tab.
   g. At the Footer -Section 2- footer pane, click the Page Number button in the Header & Footer group and then click the *Format Page Numbers* option at the drop-down list.
   h. At the Page Number Format dialog box, click the *Number format* option box arrow and then click the *1, 2, 3, ...* option at the drop-down list.
   i. Select the current number in the *Start at* measurement box and then type 1.
   j. Click OK to close the dialog box.
   k. Click the Close Header and Footer button.
2. Print only page 1 of section 1 and page 1 of section 2 by completing the following steps:
   a. Click the File tab and then click the *Print* option.
   b. At the Print backstage area, click in the *Pages* text box in the *Settings* category and then type p1s1,p1s2.
   c. Click the Print button.

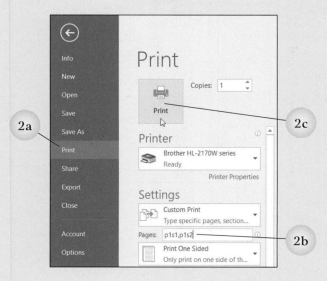

3. Save **1-CompSoftware.docx**.

Check Your Work

Keeping Text Together

In a multipage document, Word automatically inserts soft page breaks, which are page breaks that adjust when data is added or deleted from the document. However, a soft page break may occur in an undesirable location. For example, a soft page break may cause a heading to display at the bottom of a page while the text related to the heading displays at the top of the next page. A soft page break may also create a widow or orphan. A widow is the last line of text in a paragraph that appears by itself at the top of a page and an orphan is the first line of text in a paragraph that appears by itself at the bottom of a page.

Use options at the Paragraph dialog box with the Line and Page Breaks tab selected, as shown in Figure 1.9, to control widows and orphans and keep a paragraph, group of paragraphs, or group of lines together. Display this dialog box by clicking the Paragraph group dialog box launcher on the Home tab and then clicking the Line and Page Breaks tab at the dialog box.

By default, the *Widow/Orphan control* option is active and Word tries to avoid creating widows and orphans when inserting soft page breaks. The other three options in the *Pagination* section of the dialog box are not active by default. Use the *Keep with next* option to keep a line together with the next line. This is useful for keeping a heading together with the first line of text below it. To keep a group of selected lines together, use the *Keep lines together* option. Use the *Page break before* option to insert a page break before selected text.

Quick Steps

Keep Text Together
1. Click Paragraph group dialog box launcher.
2. Click Line and Page Breaks tab.
3. Click *Keep with next, Keep lines together,* and/or *Page break before.*
4. Click OK.

💡 *Hint* Text formatted with *Keep with next* option applied to it is identified with a ■ nonprinting character in the left margin.

Figure 1.9 Paragraph Dialog Box with Line and Page Breaks Tab Selected

Use options in this section to control the locations of soft page breaks in a document.

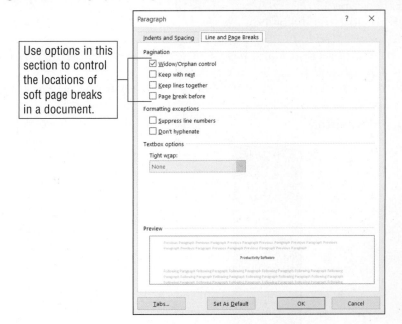

1. With **1-CompSoftware.docx** open, scroll through the document and notice that the heading *SPREADSHEET SOFTWARE* displays at the bottom of page 1 and the paragraph that follows the heading displays at the top of page 2. Keep the heading and paragraph together by completing the following steps:
   a. Position the insertion point on any character in the heading *SPREADSHEET SOFTWARE*.
   b. Make sure the Home tab is active and then click the Paragraph group dialog box launcher.
   c. At the Paragraph dialog box, click the Line and Page Breaks tab.
   d. Click the *Keep with next* check box to insert a check mark.
   e. Click OK to close the dialog box.
2. Scroll through the document and notice the heading *MULTIMEDIA SOFTWARE* near the end of the document. Insert a soft page break at the beginning of the heading by completing the following steps:
   a. Move the insertion point to the beginning of the heading *MULTIMEDIA SOFTWARE*.
   b. Click the Paragraph group dialog box launcher.
   c. At the Paragraph dialog box with the Line and Page Breaks tab selected, click the *Page break before* check box to insert a check mark.
   d. Click OK to close the dialog box.
3. Save, print, and then close **1-CompSoftware.docx**.

Check Your Work

Chapter Summary

- Use the Bullets button to insert bullets before specific paragraphs of text and use the Numbering button to insert numbers.
- Insert custom numbers by clicking the Numbering button arrow and then clicking an option at the drop-down gallery.
- Define custom numbering formatting with options at the Define New Number Format dialog box. Display this dialog box by clicking the Numbering button arrow and then clicking *Define New Number Format* at the drop-down gallery.
- Insert custom bullets by clicking the Bullets button arrow and then clicking an option at the drop-down gallery.
- Define custom bullets with options at the Define New Bullet dialog box. Display this dialog box by clicking the Bullets button arrow and then clicking *Define New Bullet* at the drop-down gallery.
- Apply numbering to multilevel paragraphs of text by clicking the Multilevel List button in the Paragraph group on the Home tab.
- Define custom multilevel list numbering with options at the Define New Multilevel List dialog box. Display this dialog box by clicking the Multilevel List button and then clicking *Define New Multilevel List* at the drop-down gallery.
- When typing a multilevel list, press the Tab key to move to the next level and press Shift + Tab to move to the previous level.

- Customize the layout of images with options at the Layout dialog box. Display this dialog box by clicking the Size group dialog box launcher on the Picture Tools Format tab.

- The Layout dialog box contains three tabs. Click the Position tab to specify the position of an image in the document, click the Text Wrapping tab to specify a wrapping style for an image, and click the Size tab to display options for specifying the height and width of an image.

- Format an image with options at the Format Picture task pane. Display this task pane by clicking the Picture Styles group task pane launcher.

- Apply artistic effects to an image with the Artistic Effects button in the Adjust group on the Picture Tools Format tab or with options at the Format Picture task pane with the Effects icon selected.

- Use the yellow circles that display around certain selected shapes to change the width and height of a specific element in a shape.

- Use edit points to customize specific elements in a shape. Display edit points around a shape by clicking the Edit Shape button in the Insert Shapes group on the Drawing Tools Format tab, and then clicking *Edit Points*.

- Display wrap points around an object by clicking the Wrap Text button on the Picture Tools Format tab or Drawing Tools Format tab and then clicking *Edit Wrap Points*. Use wrap points to wrap text closer or father away from an object.

- Link text boxes with the Create Link button in the Text group on the Drawing Tools Format tab. Break a link with the Break Link button in the Text group.

- Text that appears at the top of every page is called a *header*; text that appears at the bottom of every page is called a *footer*.

- Insert predesigned headers and footers in a document or create custom headers and footers.

- To create a custom header, click the Header button in the Header & Footer group on the Insert tab and then click *Edit Header*. At the Header pane, insert elements or text. Complete similar steps to create a custom footer.

- Use buttons in the Insert group on the Header & Footer Tools Design tab to insert elements such as the date and time, Quick Parts, pictures, and images into a header or footer.

- Word inserts headers and footers 0.5 inch from the top and bottom of the page, respectively. Reposition a header or footer with buttons in the Position group on the Header & Footer Tools Design tab.

- A unique header or footer can be created on the first page; a header or footer can be omitted on the first page; different headers or footers can be created for odd and even pages; and different headers or footers can be created for sections in a document. Use options in the Options group on the Header & Footer Tools Design tab to specify the type of header or footer to be created.

- Insert page numbers in a document in a header or footer or with options from the Page Number button drop-down list in the Header & Footer group on the Insert tab.

- Remove page numbers with the *Remove Page Numbers* option from the Page Number button drop-down list.

- Format page numbers with options at the Page Number Format dialog box.

- To print specific sections or pages within a section, use the *Pages* text box at the Print backstage area. When specifying sections and pages, use the letter *s* before a section number and the letter *p* before a page number.
- Word attempts to avoid creating widows and orphans when inserting soft page breaks. Turn on or off the widow/orphan control feature at the Paragraph dialog box with the Line and Page Breaks tab selected. This dialog box also contains options for keeping a paragraph, group of paragraphs, or group of lines together.

Commands Review

FEATURE	RIBBON TAB, GROUP	BUTTON, OPTION
bulleting	Home, Paragraph	
create footer	Insert, Header & Footer	, *Edit Footer*
create header	Insert, Header & Footer	, *Edit Header*
Define New Bullet dialog box	Home, Paragraph	, *Define New Bullet*
Define New Multilevel List dialog box	Home, Paragraph	, *Define New Multilevel List*
Define New Number Format dialog box	Home, Paragraph	, *Define New Number Format*
edit points	Drawing Tools Format, Insert Shapes	, *Edit Points*
footer	Insert, Header & Footer	
header	Insert, Header & Footer	
multilevel list	Home, Paragraph	
numbering	Home, Paragraph	
Paragraph dialog box	Home, Paragraph	
text box	Insert, Text	
wrap points	Picture Tools Format, Arrange OR Drawing Tools Format, Arrange	, *Edit Wrap Points*

> **Workbook**
>
> Chapter study tools and assessment activities are available in the *Workbook* ebook. These resources are designed to help you further develop and demonstrate mastery of the skills learned in this chapter.

Microsoft®

Word
Proofing Documents and Creating Charts

CHAPTER

2

Performance Objectives

Upon successful completion of Chapter 2, you will be able to:

1 Complete a spelling check and a grammar check on the text in a document

2 Display readability statistics

3 Create a custom dictionary and change the default dictionary

4 Display synonyms and antonyms for specific words using the thesaurus

5 Display document word, paragraph, and character counts

6 Insert line numbers

7 Use the Smart Lookup feature

8 Use the translation feature to translate words from English to other languages

9 Insert and format charts

Microsoft Word includes proofing tools to help you create well-written, error-free documents. These tools include a spelling checker, grammar checker, and thesaurus. Word also provides tools for translating words from English to other languages, as well as a Mini Translator that will translate specific words in a document. In this chapter, you will learn how to use these proofing tools and how to create a custom dictionary. You will also learn how to present text visually in a chart and apply formatting to the chart.

Data Files

Before beginning chapter work, copy the WL2C2 folder to your storage medium and then make WL2C2 the active folder.

SNAP

If you are a SNAP user, launch the Precheck and Tutorials from your Assignments page.

Project 1 **Check Spelling and Grammar in an Investment Plan Document**

1 Part

You will open an investment plan document and then complete a spelling and grammar check on it.

Preview Finished Project

Checking the Spelling and Grammar

Word provides proofing tools to help create professional, polished documents. Two of these tools are the spelling checker and grammar checker.

The spelling checker works by finding misspelled words and offering replacement words. It also finds duplicate words and words with irregular capitalization. When checking a document, the spelling checker compares the words in the document with the words in its dictionary. If the spelling checker finds a match, it passes over the word. If the spelling checker does not find a match, it stops. The spelling checker stops when it discovers the following types of errors and unfamiliar words:

- a misspelled word (when it does not match another word in the dictionary)
- typographical errors (such as transposed letters)
- double occurrences of a word (such as *the the*)
- irregular capitalization
- some proper names
- jargon and some technical terms

Quick Steps

Check Spelling and Grammar
1. Click Review tab.
2. Click Spelling & Grammar button.
   OR
   Press F7.
3. Change or ignore errors.
4. Click OK.

ABC✓ Spelling & Grammar

The grammar checker searches a document for errors in grammar, punctuation, and word usage. Using the spelling checker and grammar checker can help create well-written documents but does not replace the need for proofreading.

Begin a spelling and grammar check by clicking the Review tab and then clicking the Spelling & Grammar button or pressing the F7 function key. If Word detects a possible spelling error, it selects the text containing the error and displays the Spelling task pane, similar to the one shown in Figure 2.1. Possible corrections for the word display in the Spelling task pane list box along with buttons for changing or ignoring the spelling error, as described in Table 2.1. The Spelling task pane also displays a definition of the selected word in the task pane list box.

Figure 2.1 Spelling Task Pane with Error Selected

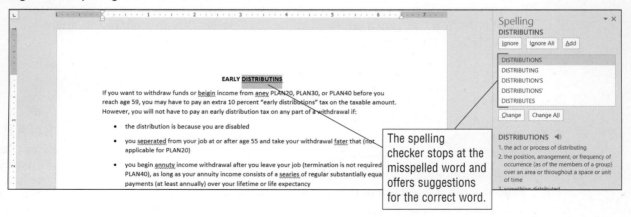

Table 2.1 Spelling Task Pane and Grammar Task Pane Buttons

Button	Function
Ignore	during spell checking, skips that occurrence of the word; during grammar checking, leaves the currently selected text as written
Ignore All	during spell checking, skips that occurrence of the word and all other occurrences of it
Add	adds the selected word to the main spelling check dictionary
Delete	deletes the currently selected word
Change	replaces the selected word with the selected word in the task pane list box
Change All	replaces the selected word and all other occurrences of it with the selected word in the task pane list box

Hint Complete a spelling and grammar check on part of a document by first selecting the text and then clicking the Spelling & Grammar button.

If Word detects a grammar error, it selects the word(s) or the sentence containing the error and displays possible corrections in the Grammar task pane. Depending on the error selected, some of the buttons described in Table 2.1 may display in the Grammar task pane. A description of the grammar rule, with suggestions on how to correct an error, may display in the lower half of the Grammar task pane. Choose to ignore or change errors found by the grammar checker by clicking the Change, Change All, Ignore, or Ignore All button.

Editing During a Spelling and Grammar Check

When checking the spelling and grammar in a document, edits or corrections can be made in the document. Do this by clicking in the document outside the task pane, making the changes or edits, and then clicking the Resume button in the task pane.

Tutorial

Customizing Spelling and Grammar Checking

Customizing Spell Checking

Customize the spelling checker with options at the Word Options dialog box with the *Proofing* option selected, as shown in Figure 2.2. Display this dialog box by clicking the File tab and then clicking *Options*. At the Word Options dialog box, click *Proofing* in the left panel. Use options at this dialog box to specify what the spelling checker should review or ignore.

A custom dictionary can be created for use when spell checking a document. Click the Custom Dictionaries button in the Word Options dialog box to display the Custom Dictionaries dialog box with options for creating a new dictionary or editing an existing dictionary.

Figure 2.2 Word Options Dialog Box with *Proofing* Selected

Click *Proofing* to display spelling check and grammar check options.

Customize spell checking with options in this section.

Click this button to create a custom dictionary.

Insert a check mark in this check box to tell Word to display words that sound similar to other words.

Word Options   ?   ×

General	ABC✓ Change how Word corrects and formats your text.
Display	
Proofing	**AutoCorrect options**
Save	Change how Word corrects and formats text as you type: AutoCorrect Options...
Language	
Advanced	**When correcting spelling in Microsoft Office programs**
Customize Ribbon	☑ Ignore words in UPPERCASE
Quick Access Toolbar	☑ Ignore words that contain numbers
Add-ins	☑ Ignore Internet and file addresses
Trust Center	☑ Flag repeated words
	☐ Enforce accented uppercase in French
	☐ Suggest from main dictionary only
	Custom Dictionaries...
	French modes: Traditional and new spellings ▾
	Spanish modes: Tuteo verb forms only ▾
	When correcting spelling and grammar in Word
	☑ Check spelling as you type
	☑ Mark grammar errors as you type
	☑ Frequently confused words
	☑ Check grammar with spelling
	☐ Show readability statistics
	Writing Style: Grammar ▾ Settings...
	Recheck Document

OK   Cancel

Project 1 Spell Checking a Document with Uppercase Words and Numbers   Part 1 of 1

1. Open **PlanDists.docx** and then save it with the name **2-PlanDists**.
2. Change a spell checking option by completing the following steps:
   a. Click the File tab.
   b. Click *Options*.
   c. At the Word Options dialog box, click the *Proofing* option in the left panel.
   d. Click the *Ignore words in UPPERCASE* check box to remove the check mark.
   e. Click OK to close the dialog box.
3. Complete a spelling check on the document by completing the following steps:
   a. Click the Review tab.
   b. Click the Spelling & Grammar button in the Proofing group.

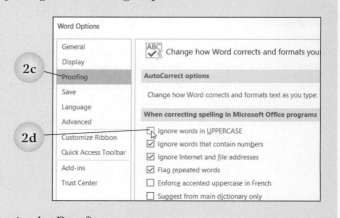

c. The spelling checker selects the word *DISTRIBUTINS* and displays the Spelling task pane. The proper spelling, *DISTRIBUTIONS*, is selected in the Spelling task pane list box and a defintion of *DISTRIBUTIONS* displays below the list box. Click the Change button (or Change All button).

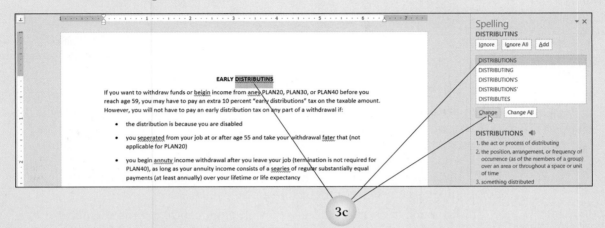

3c

d. The spelling checker selects the word *beigin*. The proper spelling of the word is selected in the task pane list box, so click the Change button.
e. The spelling checker selects the word *aney*. The proper spelling of the word is selected in the task pane list box, so click the Change button.
f. The spelling checker selects *seperated*. The proper spelling is selected in the task pane list box, so click the Change button.
g. The spelling checker selects *fater*. The proper spelling *after* is not selected in the task pane list box but it is one of the words suggested. Click *after* in the task pane list box and then click the Change button.
h. The spelling checker selects *annuty*. The proper spelling is selected in the task pane list box, so click the Change button.
i. The spelling checker selects *searies*. The proper spelling is selected in the task pane list box, so click the Change button.
j. The spelling checker selects *to*. (This is a double word occurrence.) Click the Delete button to delete the second occurrence of *to*.
k. The spelling checker selects *Haverson*. This is a proper name, so click the Ignore button.
l. When the message displays that the spelling and grammar check is complete, click OK.

3g

3j

4. Complete steps similar to those in Step 2 to insert a check mark in the *Ignore words in UPPERCASE* check box.
5. Save, print, and then close **2-PlanDists.docx**.

Check Your Work

Project 2 Check the Grammar in a Medical Document

2 Parts

You will check the grammar in a medical document, change the grammar settings, and then check the grammar again. You will also display readability statistics for the document.

Preview Finished Project

Checking the Grammar

When performing a spelling check and grammar check, Word stops and highlights text that may contain grammatical errors and displays the Grammar task pane, similar to the one shown in Figure 2.3. Like the spelling checker, the grammar checker does not find every error in a document and may stop at correct sentences. Using the grammar checker can help create well-written documents but using it does not eliminate the need for proofreading.

Hint Read grammar suggestions carefully. Some may not be valid in a specific context and a problem identified by the grammar checker may not actually be an issue.

If the grammar checker detects a possible grammatical error in the document, Word selects the sentence containing the possible error and inserts a possible correction in the Grammar task pane list box. The Grammar task pane may also display information on the grammar rule that may have been broken and offer possible methods for correcting the error. Choose to ignore or change a possible error found by the grammar checker by clicking the Change, Change All, Ignore, or Ignore All button.

The Spelling task pane and the Grammar task pane include a pronunciation feature that will speak the word currently selected in the task pane list box. To hear the word pronounced, click the speaker icon to the right of the word below the task pane list box. For this feature to work, the computer speakers must be turned on.

Figure 2.3 Grammar Task Pane with Grammar Error Selected

The grammar checker selects a sentence containing a possible error and offers a suggestion to correct the grammar.

Nationwide Medical Databases

The medical community looks forward to the day when medical records change from manila folders full of dusty document's to a nationwide registry off electronic medical records available to medical personnel anywhere. With these new medical database systems, doctor's located anywhere in the world could pull up charts immediately, with a few clicks of the mouse. Full color 3-D X-rays could be included in electronic patient records. People receiving care away from home would no longer have to worry that there doctor did not have all of their medical records.

At this point some obstacles may obstruct the widespread use of this new technology. Medical systems tend to cost much more than other systems due to legalities and the need for complicated approval processes. Everyone involved must have medical training, raising costs even further. Data validation is critical, as lives may be lost if data is faulty. Privacy issues are another roadblock. Medical records are as private and closely guarded as financial ones. Should any doctor be able to see a record? Can patients access their own records? How would incapacetated patients grant permission?

Some medical providers are embracing such databases with a more limited scope, only sharing information about patients in the same HBO, for example. So far no nationwide system exists, but such systems may appear within the next few years.

Grammar
document's
Ignore

documents

Change

Possessive and Plural Forms
Possessive nouns require an apostrophe. The possessive pronoun "its" does not; the form "it's" is a contraction of "it is" exclusively.

• Instead of: As long as it's doing it's job, we're happy.
• Consider: As long as it's doing its job, we're happy.

• Instead of: He is taking his brothers car to the wash.
• Consider: He is taking his brother's car to the wash.

The lower portion of the Grammar task pane displays information about the grammar error.

1. Open **MedData.docx** and then save it with the name **2-MedData**.
2. Check the grammar in the document by completing the following steps:
   a. Click the Review tab.
   b. Click the Spelling & Grammar button in the Proofing group.
   c. The grammar checker selects the first sentence in the first paragraph and displays *documents* in the list box. Read the information on possessive and plural forms below the list box in the task pane.
   d. Click the Change button to change *document's* to *documents*.
   e. The grammar checker selects *there* in the document and displays *their* in the list box. Read the definitions of *there* and *their* in the task pane.
   f. Click the Change button.
   g. The spelling checker selects the word *incapacetated* and displays the proper spelling in the task pane list box. Listen to the pronunciation of the word *incapacitated* by clicking the speaker icon at the right of the word *incapacitated* below the list box. (Your computer speakers must be turned on to hear the pronunciation.)
   h. With the proper spelling of *incapacitated* selected in the task pane list box, click the Change button.
   i. At the message telling you that the spelling and grammar check is complete, click OK.
3. Save **2-MedData.docx**.

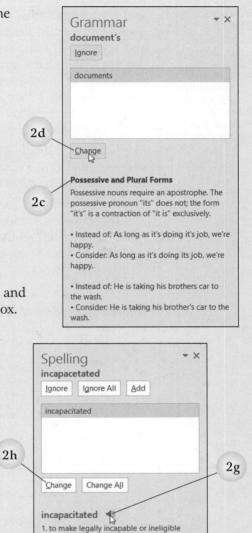

Check Your Work

Setting the Proofing Language

Language

Microsoft provides a number of dictionaries for proofing text in various languages. To change the language used for proofing a document, click the Review tab, click the Language button in the Language group, and then click *Set Proofing Language* at the drop-down list. At the Language dialog box, click a language in the *Mark selected text as* list box. To make the selected language the default, click the Set As Default button in the lower left corner of the dialog box. Click OK to close the Language dialog box.

Quick Steps
Choose Proofing Language
1. Click Review tab.
2. Click Language button.
3. Click *Set Proofing Language*.
4. Click language in list box.
5. Click OK.

Displaying Readability Statistics

Quick Steps

Show Readability Statistics
1. Click File tab.
2. Click *Options.*
3. Click *Proofing.*
4. Click *Show readability statistics* check box.
5. Click OK.
6. Complete spelling and grammar check.

Readability statistics about a document can be displayed when completing a spelling and grammar check of it. Figure 2.4 lists the readability statistics for the document used in Project 2b. The statistics include word, character, paragraph, and sentence counts; average number of sentences per paragraph, words per sentence, and characters per word; and readability information such as the percentage of passive sentences in the document, the Flesch Reading Ease score, and the Flesch-Kincaid Grade Level score. Control the display of readability statistics with the *Show readability statistics* check box in the Word Options dialog box with *Proofing* selected.

The Flesch Reading Ease score is based on the average number of syllables per word and the average number of words per sentence. The higher the score, the greater the number of people who will be able to understand the text in the document. Standard writing generally scores in the 60 to 70 range.

The Flesch-Kincaid Grade Level score is based on the average number of syllables per word and the average number of words per sentence. The score indicates a grade level. Standard writing is generally scored at the seventh or eighth grade level.

Figure 2.4 Readability Statistics Dialog Box

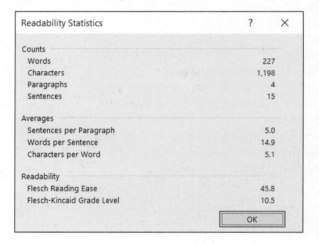

Project 2b Displaying Readability Statistics

Part 2 of 2

1. With **2-MedData.docx** open, display readability statistics about the document by completing the following steps:
   a. Click the File tab and then click *Options.*
   b. At the Word Options dialog box, click *Proofing* in the left panel.
   c. Click the *Show readability statistics* check box to insert a check mark.
   d. Click OK to close the Word Options dialog box.
   e. At the document, make sure the Review tab is selected and then click the Spelling & Grammar button.

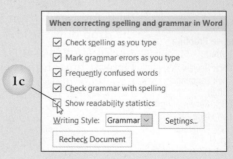

f. Look at the readability statistics that display in the Readability Statistics dialog box and then click OK to close the dialog box.

2. Stop the display of readability statistics after completing a spelling check by completing the following steps:
   a. Click the File tab and then click *Options*.
   b. At the Word Options dialog box, click *Proofing* in the left panel.
   c. Click the *Show readability statistics* check box to remove the check mark.
   d. Click OK to close the Word Options dialog box.

3. Save and then close **2-MedData.docx**.

Project 3   Check the Spelling in an Online Banking Document   4 Parts

You will open an online banking document, create a custom dictionary, add specific terms to the custom dictionary, and then complete a spelling check. You will also display word count, use the Thesaurus feature to replace a word with a synonym, insert line numbers, and display the Smart Lookup task pane and review information about selected text.

Preview Finished Project

Tutorial

Creating a Custom Dictionary

Q̃uick Steps

Create a Custom Dictionary
1. Click File tab.
2. Click *Options*.
3. Click *Proofing*.
4. Click Custom Dictionaries button.
5. Click New button.
6. Type name for dictionary; press Enter.

Hint When you change the custom dictionary settings in one Microsoft Office program, the changes affect all the other programs in the suite.

Creating a Custom Dictionary

When completing a spelling check on a document, Word uses the main dictionary, named RoamingCustom.dic, to compare words. This main dictionary contains most common words but may not include specific proper names, medical terminology, technical terms, acronyms, or other text related to a specific field or business. If documents will be created with specific words, terms, or acronyms not found in the main dictionary, consider creating a custom dictionary. When completing a spelling check, the spelling checker will compare words in a document with the main dictionary as well as a custom dictionary.

To create a custom dictionary, display the Word Options dialog box with *Proofing* selected and then click the Custom Dictionaries button. This displays the Custom Dictionaries dialog box, as shown in Figure 2.5. To create a new dictionary, click the New button. At the Create Custom Dictionary dialog box, type a name for the dictionary in the *File name* text box and then press the Enter key. The new dictionary name displays in the *Dictionary List* list box in the Custom Dictionaries dialog box. More than one dictionary can be used when spell checking a document. Insert a check mark in the check box next to each dictionary to be used when spell checking.

Changing the Default Dictionary

At the Custom Dictionaries dialog box, the default dictionary displays in the *Dictionary List* list box followed by *(Default)*. Change this default by clicking the dictionary name in the list box and then clicking the Change Default button.

Removing a Dictionary

Quick Steps

Remove a Custom Dictionary
1. Click File tab.
2. Click *Options*.
3. Click *Proofing*.
4. Click Custom Dictionaries button.
5. Click custom dictionary name.
6. Click Remove button.
7. Click OK.

Remove a custom dictionary with the Remove button at the Custom Dictionaries dialog box. To do this, display the Custom Dictionaries dialog box, click the dictionary name in the *Dictionary List* list box, and then click the Remove button. No prompt will display confirming the deletion, so make sure the correct dictionary name is selected before clicking the Remove button.

Figure 2.5 Custom Dictionaries Dialog Box

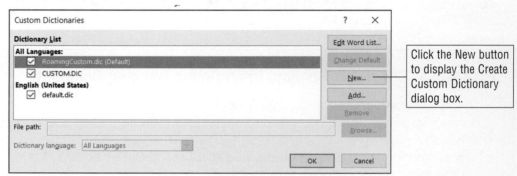

Click the New button to display the Create Custom Dictionary dialog box.

Project 3a   Creating a Custom Dictionary and Changing the Default Dictionary   Part 1 of 4

1. Open **BankBrazil.docx**, notice the wavy red lines indicating words not recognized by the spelling checker (words not in the main dictionary), and then close the document.
2. Create a custom dictionary, add words to the dictionary, and then change the default dictionary by completing the following steps:
   a. Click the File tab and then click *Options*.
   b. At the Word Options dialog box, click *Proofing* in the left panel.
   c. Click the Custom Dictionaries button.

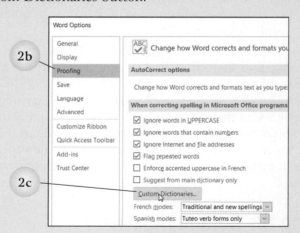

   d. At the Custom Dictionaries dialog box, click the New button.
   e. At the Create Custom Dictionary dialog box, type your first and last names (without a space between them) in the *File name* text box and then press the Enter key.

f. At the Custom Dictionaries dialog box, add a word to your dictionary by completing the following steps:

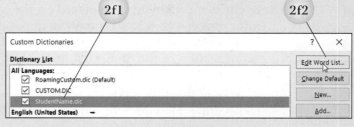

1) Click the name of your dictionary in the *Dictionary List* list box.
2) Click the Edit Word List button.
3) At the dialog box for your custom dictionary, type Abreu in the *Word(s)* text box.
4) Click the Add button.

g. Complete steps similar to those in Steps 2f3 and 2f4 to add the following words:

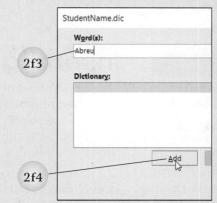

    Banco
    Itau
    Bradesco
    Unibanco
    Monteiro
    Lipschultz

h. When you have added all the words, click OK to close the dialog box.
i. At the Custom Dictionaries dialog box with the name of your dictionary selected in the *Dictionary List* list box, click the Change Default button. (Notice that the word *(Default)* displays after your custom dictionary.)
j. Click OK to close the Custom Dictionaries dialog box.
k. Click OK to close the Word Options dialog box.
3. Open **BankBrazil.docx** and then save it with the name **2-BankBrazil**.
4. Complete a spelling and grammar check on the document and correct misspelled words. (The spelling checker will not stop at the words you added to your custom dictionary.)
5. Save and then print **2-BankBrazil.docx**.
6. Change the default dictionary and then remove your custom dictionary by completing the following steps:
a. Click the File tab and then click *Options*.
b. At the Word Options dialog box, click *Proofing* in the left panel.
c. Click the Custom Dictionaries button.
d. At the Custom Dictionaries dialog box, click *RoamingCustom.dic* in the *Dictionary List* list box.
e. Click the Change Default button. (This changes the default back to the RoamingCustom.dic dictionary.)
f. Click the name of your dictionary in the *Dictionary List* list box.
g. Click the Remove button.
h. Click OK to close the Custom Dictionaries dialog box.
i. Click OK to close the Word Options dialog box.

Check Your Work

Displaying the Word Count

Words are counted as they are typed in a document and the total number of words in a document is displayed on the Status bar. To display more information—such as the numbers of pages, paragraphs, and lines—display the Word Count dialog box. Display the Word Count dialog box by clicking the word count section of the Status bar or by clicking the Review tab and then clicking the Word Count button in the Proofing group.

Quick Steps

Display the Word Count Dialog Box
Click word count
section of Status bar.
OR
1. Click Review tab.
2. Click Word Count button.

 Word Count

Count words in a portion of the document, rather than the entire document, by selecting the portion of text and then displaying the Word Count dialog box. To determine the total word count of several sections throughout a document, select the first section, press and hold down the Ctrl key, and then select the other sections.

Inserting Line Numbers

Use the Line Numbers button in the Page Setup group on the Layout tab to insert line numbers in a document. Numbering lines has practical applications for certain legal papers and reference purposes. To number lines in a document, click the Layout tab, click the Line Numbers button in the Page Setup group, and then click a line number option at the drop-down list.

Quick Steps

Insert Line Numbers
1. Click Layout tab.
2. Click Line Numbers button.
3. Click line number option.

To have more control over inserting line numbers in a document, click the Line Numbers button and then click *Line Numbering Options* at the drop-down list. At the Page Setup dialog box with the Layout tab selected, click the Line Numbering button at the bottom of the dialog box and the Line Numbers dialog box displays as shown in Figure 2.6. Use options at this dialog box to insert line numbering and to specify the starting number, the location line numbers are printed, the interval between printed line numbers, and whether line numbers are consecutive or start over at the beginning of each page.

Figure 2.6 Line Numbers Dialog Box

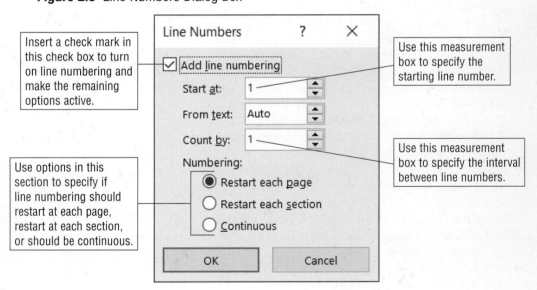

Using the Thesaurus

Word offers a Thesaurus feature for finding synonyms, antonyms, and related words for a particular word. Synonyms are words that have the same or nearly the same meaning. When the Thesaurus feature is used, antonyms may display for some words, which are words with opposite meanings.

📖 Thesaurus

Quick Steps
Use the Thesaurus
1. Click Review tab.
2. Click Thesaurus button.
3. Type word in search text box.
4. Press Enter.

To use the Thesaurus feature, click the Review tab and then click the Thesaurus button in the Proofing group or use the keyboard shortcut Shift + F7. At the Thesaurus task pane that displays, click in the search text box at the top of the task pane, type a word, and then press the Enter key or click the Start searching button (which contains a magnifying glass icon). A list of synonyms and antonyms for the typed word displays in the task pane list box. Another method for finding synonyms and antonyms is to select a word and then display the Thesaurus task pane. Figure 2.7 shows the Thesaurus task pane with synonyms and antonyms for the word *normally* displayed.

Depending on the word typed in the search text box, the words in the Thesaurus task pane list box may display followed by *(n.)* for *noun, (adj.)* for *adjective,* or *(adv.)* for *adverb.* Any antonyms that display at the end of the list of related synonyms will be followed by *(Antonym).* If a dictionary is installed on the computer, a definition of the selected word will display below the task pane list box.

The Thesaurus feature provides synonyms for the selected word as well as a list of related synonyms. For example, in the Thesaurus task pane list box shown in Figure 2.7, the main synonym *usually* displays for *normally* and is preceded by a collapse triangle (a right-and-down-pointing triangle). The collapse triangle indicates that the list of related synonyms is displayed. Click the collapse triangle

Figure 2.7 Thesaurus Task Pane

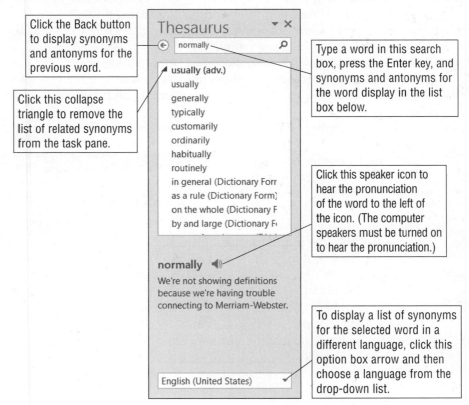

and the list of related synonyms is removed from the task pane list box and the collapse triangle changes to an expand triangle (a right-pointing triangle). Click a word in the Thesaurus task pane list box to see synonyms for it.

When reviewing synonyms and antonyms for words within a document, display the list of synonyms and antonyms for the previous word by clicking the Back button (left-pointing arrow) at the left side of the search text box. Click the down-pointing triangle at the left side of the Close button in the upper right corner of the task pane and a drop-down list displays with options for moving, sizing, and closing the task pane.

To replace a selected word in the document with a synonym in the Thesaurus task pane, hover the mouse pointer over the synonym in the task pane list box until a down arrow displays. Click the down arrow and then click *Insert* at the drop-down list.

The Thesaurus task pane, like the Spelling task pane and Grammar task pane, includes a pronunciation feature that will speak the word currently selected in the task pane. To hear the word pronounced, click the speaker icon at the right side of the word below the task pane list box. (For this feature to work, the computer speakers must be turned on.)

The Thesaurus task pane also includes a language option for displaying synonyms of the selected word in a different language. To use this feature, click the option box arrow at the bottom of the task pane and then click a language at the drop-down list.

Project 3b Displaying Word Count, Inserting Line Numbers, and Using the Thesaurus   Part 2 of 4

1. With **2-BankBrazil.docx** open, click the word count section of the Status bar.
2. After reading the statistics in the Word Count dialog box, click the Close button.
3. Display the Word Count dialog box by clicking the Review tab and then clicking the Word Count button in the Proofing group.
4. Click the Close button to close the Word Count dialog box.
5. Press Ctrl + A to select the entire document, click the Home tab, click the Line and Paragraph Spacing button in the Paragraph group, and then click *2.0* at the drop-down gallery.
6. Insert line numbering by completing the following steps:
   a. Click the Layout tab.
   b. Click the Line Numbers button in the Page Setup group and then click *Continuous* at the drop-down list.

   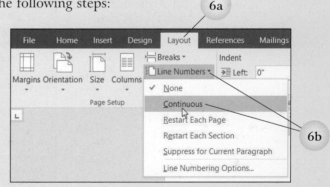

   c. Scroll through the document and notice the line numbers that display at the left side of the document.
   d. With the document selected, click the Line Numbers button and then click the *Restart Each Page* option.
   e. Scroll through the document and notice that the line numbers start over again at the beginning of page 2.

f. With the document selected, click the Line Numbers button and then click *Line Numbering Options* at the drop-down list.

g. At the Page Setup dialog box, click the Line Numbers button toward the bottom of the dialog box.

h. At the Line Numbers dialog box, select the current number in the *Start at* measurement box and then type 30.

i. Click the *Count by* measurement box up arrow. (This displays *2* in the measurement box.)

j. Click the *Continuous* option in the *Numbering* section.

k. Click OK to close the Line Numbers dialog box.

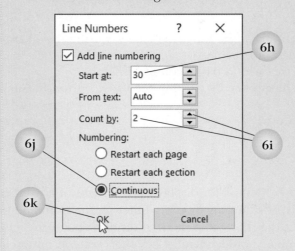

l. Click OK to close the Page Setup dialog box.

m. Scroll through the document and notice the line numbers that display at the left side of the document. The numbers start with *30* and increment by two.

n. Click the Line Numbers button and then click *None* at the drop-down list.

7. With the document selected, click the Home tab, click the Line and Paragraph Spacing button in the Paragraph group, and then click *1.0* at the drop-down gallery.

8. Use the Thesaurus feature to change the word *normally* in the first paragraph to *generally* by completing the following steps:

a. Select the word *normally* in the first paragraph (first word in the seventh line of text).

b. Click the Review tab.

c. Click the Thesaurus button in the Proofing group.

d. At the Thesaurus task pane, hover the mouse pointer over the synonym *generally*, click the down arrow at the right of the word, and then click *Insert* at the drop-down list.

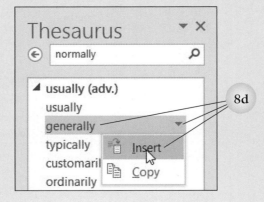

e. Click the word *generally* in the Thesaurus task pane.

f. If your computer speakers are turned on, listen to the pronunciation of the word *generally* by clicking the speaker icon next to the word below the task pane list box.

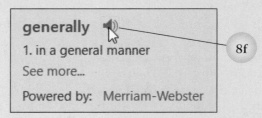

9. Follow similar steps to make the following changes using the Thesaurus feature:

a. Change *acquaintances* in the first paragraph to *friends*.

b. Change *combat* in the second paragraph to *battle*.

10. Close the Thesaurus task pane by clicking the Close button in the upper right corner of the task pane.

11. Save **2-BankBrazil.docx**.

Check Your Work

Another method for displaying synonyms of a word is to use a shortcut menu. To do this, position the mouse pointer on the word and then click the right mouse button. At the shortcut menu that displays, point to *Synonyms* and then click the a synonym at the side menu. Click the *Thesaurus* option at the bottom of the side menu to display synonyms and antonyms for the word in the Thesaurus task pane.

Project 3c Replacing Synonyms Using the Shortcut Menu

Part 3 of 4

1. With **2-BankBrazil.docx** open, position the mouse pointer on the word *vogue* in the second sentence of the third paragraph.

2. Click the right mouse button.

3. At the shortcut menu, point to *Synonyms* and then click *fashion* at the side menu.

4. Save **2-BankBrazil.docx**.

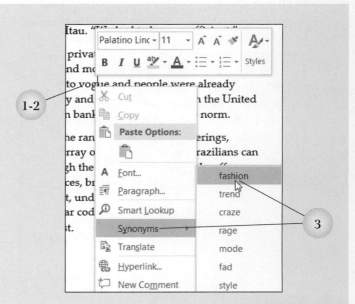

Check Your Work

Using Smart Lookup

The Smart Lookup feature provides information on selected text from a variety of sources on the web, such as Wikipedia, Bing, and the Oxford Dictionary. To use the Smart Lookup feature, select text and then click the Smart Lookup button in the Insights group on the Review tab. This opens the Smart Lookup task pane at the right side of the screen.

The Smart Lookup task pane contains the *Explore* and *Define* options. With the *Explore* option selected, the task pane displays information about the selected text from sources on the web, as shown in Figure 2.8. Click the *Define* option and a definition from the Oxford Dictionary website displays for the selected text, as shown in Figure 2.9.

The Smart Lookup task pane, like the Spelling, Grammar, and Thesaurus task panes, includes a pronunciation feature that will speak the word displayed in the task pane. To hear the word pronounced, click the speaker icon in the task pane. For this feature to work, the computer speakers must be turned on.

The Smart Lookup feature can also be accessed through the Tell Me feature. To use Tell Me for Smart Lookup, click in the *Tell Me* text box, type text or a function, and then click the *Smart Lookup* option at the drop-down list.

Figure 2.8 Smart Lookup Task Pane with the *Explore* Option Selected

With the *Explore* option selected, the Smart Lookup task pane displays information about the selected text (*e-commerce*, in this example) from sources on the web such as *Wikipedia*.

Figure 2.9 Smart Lookup Task Pane with the *Details* Option Selected

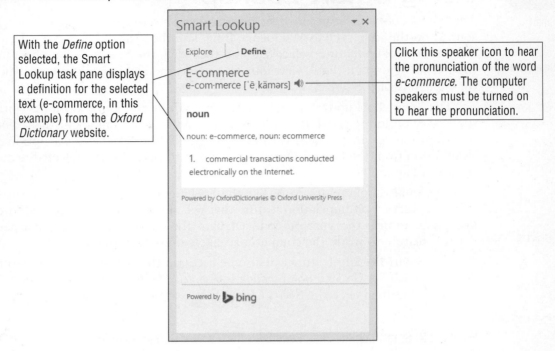

With the *Define* option selected, the Smart Lookup task pane displays a definition for the selected text (e-commerce, in this example) from the *Oxford Dictionary* website.

Click this speaker icon to hear the pronunciation of the word *e-commerce*. The computer speakers must be turned on to hear the pronunciation.

Project 3d Using the Smart Lookup Feature

Part 4 of 4

1. With **2-BankBrazil.docx** open, display information about and definitions for words by completing the following steps:
   a. Select the word *e-commerce* in the third sentence of the first paragraph.
   b. Click the Review tab, if necessary, and then click the Smart Lookup button in the Insights group.
   c. Look at the information about e-commerce in the Smart Lookup task pane with the *Explore* option selected.
   d. Click the *Define* option.
   e. Read the definition in the task pane.
   f. If the computer speakers are turned on, click the speaker icon at the top of the task pane.
   g. Click the Close button in the upper right corner of the Smart Lookup task pane.
   h. Select the word *economy* in the second sentence of the second paragraph.
   i. Click the Smart Lookup button in the Insights group.
   j. Look at the information that displays in the Smart Lookup task pane and then click the *Define* option.
   k. Read the definition in the task pane.
   l. Click the Close button to close the Smart Lookup task pane.
2. Save, print, and then close **2-BankBrazil.com**.

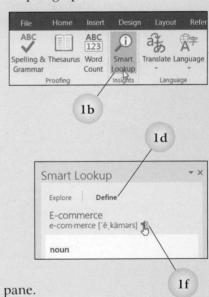

Check Your Work

You will use the translation feature to translate text from English to Spanish and English to French.

Preview Finished Project

Tutorial

Translating Text to and from Different Languages

 Translate

Translating Text to and from Different Languages

Word provides several methods of translating text from one language into another. One method is provided at the Thesaurus task pane. The Translate button in the Language group on the Review tab provides additional translation methods. Click the Translate button and a drop-down list displays with options for translating the entire document or selected text and for turning on the Mini Translator.

Translating Text

Quick Steps

Translate an Entire Document
1. Open document.
2. Click Review tab.
3. Click Translate button.
4. Click *Translate Document*.
5. Click Yes button.

Translate Selected Text
1. Select text.
2. Click Review tab.
3. Click Translate button.
4. Click *Translate Selected Text*.
5. Click Yes button.

Click the first option, *Translate Document*, and a message displays indicating that the document will be sent over the Internet in a secured format to Microsoft or a third-party translation service provider. To continue to the translator, click the Yes button. The computer must be connected to the Internet for the document to be sent to Microsoft or a third-party translation service provider.

Click the second option, *Translate Selected Text*, and Microsoft Translator or a third-party translation service provider will translate the selected text in the document and insert the translation in the Research task pane. The Research task pane displays at the right side of the screen and includes options for translating text to and from different languages.

Click the third option, *Mini Translator*, to turn on this feature. With the Mini Translator turned on, point to a word or select a phrase in the document and the translation of the text displays in a box above the text. To turn off the Mini Translator, click the *Mini Translator* option at the Translate button drop-down list. When the Mini Translator is turned on, the icon positioned to the left of the *Mini Translator* option displays with a light-gray background.

Hint Press and hold down the Alt key and then click anywhere in the document to display the Research task pane.

Choosing a Translation Language

Quick Steps

Turn on Mini Translator
1. Click Review tab.
2. Click Translate button.
3. Click *Mini Translator*.

Click the fourth option in the Translate button drop-down list, *Choose Translation Language*, and the Translation Language Options dialog box displays, as shown in Figure 2.10. At this dialog box, specify the translate-from language and the translate-to language and also the translate-to language for the Mini Translator.

Figure 2.10 Translation Language Options Dialog Box

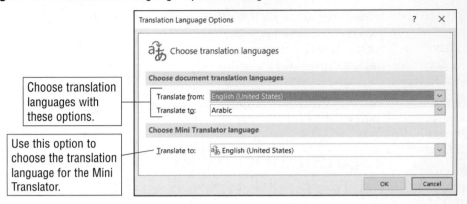

Choose translation languages with these options.

Use this option to choose the translation language for the Mini Translator.

Preparing Documents for Translation

The translation features in Word are considered machine translations because a machine rather than a person is translating text from one language to another. While machine translation is useful for basic information, important or sensitive information should be translated by a person to ensure that the translation reflects the full meaning of the information.

When using Word's translation features, consider the following content standards and guidelines when translating information to reduce confusion or errors and optimize the translation:

1. Use standard, formal language
2. Use proper punctuation and grammar
3. Spell words correctly
4. Avoid abbreviations and acronyms
5. Avoid using slang, colloquialisms, and idioms
6. Avoid ambiguities and vague references
7. Write sentences that are direct and express only one idea
8. Use articles (such as *the*) in sentences whenever possible
9. Repeat the noun in a sentence instead of using a pronoun
10. Apply predesigned heading styles to headings in a document

Project 4 Translating Text   Part 1 of 1

Note: Check with your instructor before completing this project to make sure you have access to the Internet.

1. Open **ChapQuestions.docx** and then save it with the name **2-ChapQuestions**.
2. Change the translation language to Spanish by completing the following steps:
   a. Click the Review tab.
   b. Click the Translate button in the Language group and then click the *Choose Translation Language* option at the drop-down list.

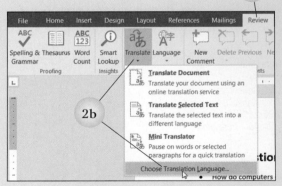

c. At the Translation Language Options dialog box, make sure that *English (United States)* displays in the *Translate from* option box.

d. Click the *Translate to* option box arrow in the *Choose document translation languages* section and then click *Spanish (Spain)* at the drop-down list. (Skip this step if *Spanish (Spain)* is already selected.)

e. Click OK to close the dialog box.

3. Translate the entire document to Spanish by completing the following steps:

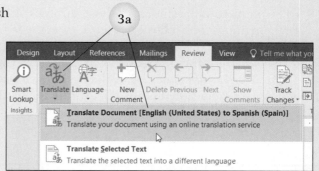

a. Click the Translate button and then click the *Translate Document [English (United States) to Spanish (Spain)]* option.

b. At the message indicating that the document will be sent over the Internet in a secured format to Microsoft or a third-party translation service provider, click the Yes button.

c. In a few moments, the Microsoft Translator window will open (or a window from a third-party translation service provider).

d. Select the translated text.

e. Press Ctrl + C to copy the text.

f. Close the Microsoft Translator window.

g. At the **2-ChapQuestions.docx** document, press Ctrl + End to move the insertion point to the end of the document and then press Ctrl + V to insert the copied text.

4. Save, print, and then close **2-ChapQuestions.docx**.

5. Open **TranslateTerms.docx** and then save it with the name **2-TranslateTerms**.

6. Translate the word *Central* into Spanish by completing the following steps:

a. Click the Review tab.

b. Click the Translate button and then click the *Choose Translation Language* option at the drop-down list.

c. At the Translation Language Options dialog box, click the *Translate to* option box arrow in the *Choose Mini Translator language* section and then click *Spanish (Spain)* at the drop-down list. (Skip this step if *Spanish (Spain)* is already selected.)

d. Click OK to close the dialog box.

e. Click the Translate button and then click *Mini Translator [Spanish (Spain)]* at the drop-down list.

f. At the message that displays, click the Yes button.

g. Hover the mouse pointer over the word *Central* in the table. (The Mini Translator displays dimmed above the word.) Move the mouse pointer to the Mini Translator and then look at the translation in the box above the term. Type one of the Spanish terms in the *Spanish* column.

h. Complete steps similar to those in Step 6g to display Spanish translations for the remaining terms. For each term, type the corresponding Spanish term in the appropriate location in the table. Type the terms without any accents or special symbols.

7. Use the Mini Translator to translate terms into French by completing the following steps:
   a. Click the Translate button and then click the *Choose Translation Language* option at the drop-down list.
   b. At the Translation Language Options dialog box, click the *Translate to* option box arrow in the *Choose Mini Translator lanuguage* section and then click *French (France)* at the drop-down list.
   c. Click OK to close the dialog box.
   d. With the Mini Translator turned on, hover the mouse pointer over the word *Central* in the table. (The Mini Translator displays dimmed above the term.)
   e. Move the mouse pointer to the Mini Translator and then choose one of the French terms and type it in the *French* column.
   f. Complete steps similar to those in Steps 7d and 7e to display French translations for the remaining terms. For each term, type the corresponding French term in the appropriate location in the table. Type the terms without any accents or special symbols.
8. Turn off the Mini Translator by clicking the Translate button and then clicking *Mini Translator [French (France)]* at the drop-down list.
9. Save, print, and then close **2-TranslateTerms.docx**.

Check Your Work

Project 5 Create and Format a Column Chart and Pie Chart

5 Parts

You will use the Chart feature to create and format a column chart and then create and format a pie chart.

Preview Finished Project

Tutorial

Creating a Chart

 Chart

Quick Steps

Insert a Chart
1. Click Insert tab.
2. Click Chart button.
3. Enter data in Excel worksheet.
4. Close Excel.

Hint You can copy a chart from Excel to Word and embed it as static data or link it to the worksheet.

Creating a Chart

A chart is a visual presentation of data. In Word, a variety of charts can be created, including bar and column charts, pie charts, area charts, and many more. To create a chart, click the Insert tab and then click the Chart button in the Illustrations group. This displays the Insert Chart dialog box, as shown in Figure 2.11. At this dialog box, choose the chart type in the list at the left side, click the chart style, and then click OK.

Click OK at the Insert Chart dialog box and a chart is inserted in the document and Excel opens with sample data, as shown in Figure 2.12. Type specific data in the Excel worksheet cells over the existing data. As data is typed in the Excel worksheet, it appears in the chart in the Word document. To type data in the Excel worksheet, click in a cell and type the data; then press the Tab key to make the next cell active, press Shift + Tab to make the previous cell active, or press the Enter key to make the cell below active.

The sample worksheet contains a data range of four columns and five rows and the cells in the data range display with a light fill color. Excel uses the data in the range to create the chart in the document. The sample worksheet is not limited to four columns and five rows. Simply type data in cells outside the data range and Excel expands the data range and incorporates the new data in the chart. This occurs because the table AutoExpansion feature is turned on by

Figure 2.11 Insert Chart Dialog Box

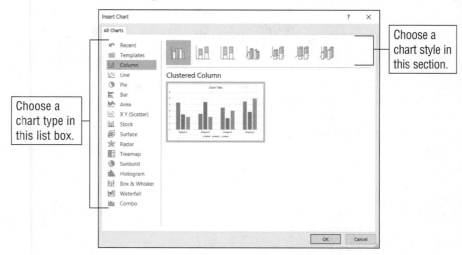

Choose a chart type in this list box.

Choose a chart style in this section.

Figure 2.12 Sample Chart

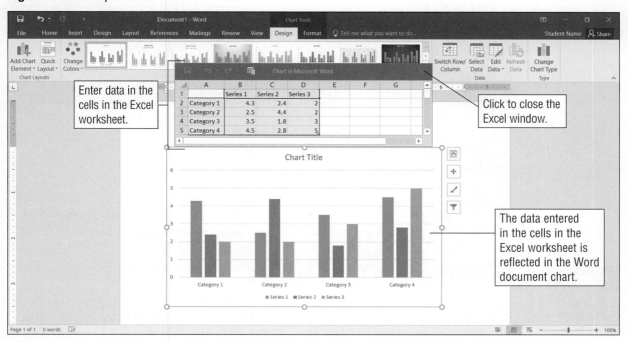

Enter data in the cells in the Excel worksheet.

Click to close the Excel window.

The data entered in the cells in the Excel worksheet is reflected in the Word document chart.

default. If data is typed in a cell outside the data range, an AutoCorrect Options button displays in the lower right corner of the cell. Use this button to turn off AutoExpansion.

If data is not typed in all four columns and five rows, decrease the size of the data range. To do this, position the mouse pointer on the small, square, blue icon in the lower right corner of cell E5 until the pointer displays as a diagonally pointing two-headed arrow and then drag up to decrease the number of rows in the range and/or drag left to decrease the number of columns.

When all the data is typed in the worksheet, click the Close button in the upper right corner of the Excel window. This closes the Excel window, expands the Word document window, and displays the chart in the document.

1. At a blank document, click the Insert tab and then click the Chart button in the Illustrations group.
2. At the Insert Chart dialog box, click OK.
3. Type Sales 2016 in cell B1 in the Excel worksheet.
4. Press the Tab key and then type Sales 2017 in cell C1.
5. Press the Tab key and then type Sales 2018 in cell D1.
6. Press the Tab key. (This makes cell A2 active.)
7. Continue typing the remaining data in cells, as indicated in Figure 2.13. After typing the last entry, click in cell A1.
8. Click the Close button in the upper right corner of the Excel window.
9. Save the document and name it **2-Charts**.

Check Your Work

Figure 2.13 Project 5a

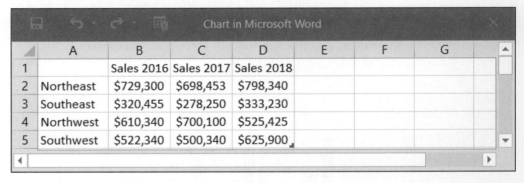

	A	B	C	D	E	F	G
1		Sales 2016	Sales 2017	Sales 2018			
2	Northeast	$729,300	$698,453	$798,340			
3	Southeast	$320,455	$278,250	$333,230			
4	Northwest	$610,340	$700,100	$525,425			
5	Southwest	$522,340	$500,340	$625,900			

Tutorial

Formatting with Chart Buttons

Formatting with Chart Buttons

When a chart is inserted in a document, four buttons display at the right side of the chart border, as shown in Figure 2.14. These buttons contain options for applying formatting to the chart.

Click the top button, Layout Options, and a side menu displays with text wrapping options. Click the next button, Chart Elements, and a side menu displays with chart elements, such as axis title, chart title, data labels, data table, gridlines, and legend. Elements with check marks inserted in the check boxes are included in the chart. To include other elements, insert check marks in the check boxes for them.

Click the Chart Styles button at the right side of the chart and a side menu gallery of styles displays. Scroll down the gallery and hover the mouse over an option and the style formatting is applied to the chart. In addition to providing options for chart styles, the Chart Styles button side menu gallery provides options for chart colors. Click the Chart Styles button, click the Color tab to the right of the Style tab, and then click a color option at the color palette that displays. Hover the mouse over a color option to view how the color change affects the elements in the chart.

Figure 2.14 Chart Buttons

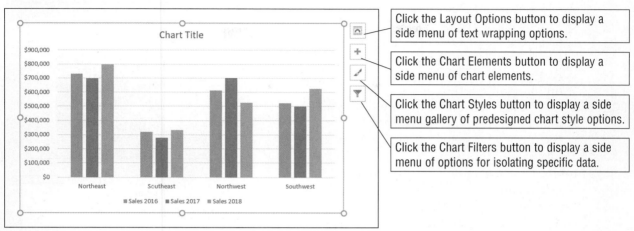

Click the Layout Options button to display a side menu of text wrapping options.

Click the Chart Elements button to display a side menu of chart elements.

Click the Chart Styles button to display a side menu gallery of predesigned chart style options.

Click the Chart Filters button to display a side menu of options for isolating specific data.

Hint Use a pie chart if the data series you want to plot has seven categories or less and the categories represent parts of a whole.

Use the bottom button, Chart Filters, to isolate specific data in the chart. Click the button and a side menu displays. Specify the series or categories to display in the chart. To do this, remove check marks from those elements that should not appear in the chart. After removing any check marks, click the Apply button in the lower left corner of the side menu. Click the Names tab at the Chart Filters button side menu and options display for turning on and off the display of column and row names.

Project 5b Formatting with Chart Buttons

1. With **2-Charts.docx** open, make sure the chart is selected.
2. Click the Layout Options button that displays outside the upper right side of the chart and then click the *Square* option in the side menu (first option in the *With Text Wrapping* section).
3. Remove and add chart elements by completing the following steps:
   a. Click the Chart Elements button that displays below the Layout Options button outside the upper right side of the chart.
   b. At the side menu, click the *Chart Title* check box to remove the check mark.
   c. Click the *Data Table* check box to insert a check mark.

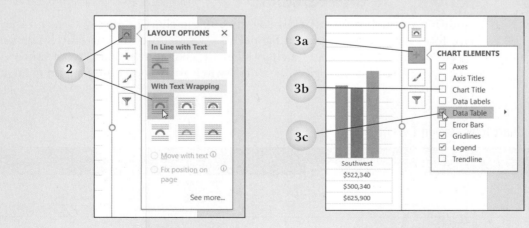

4. Apply a different chart style by completing the following steps:
   a. Click the Chart Styles button below the Chart Elements button.
   b. At the side menu gallery, click the *Style 3* option (third option in the gallery).
   c. Click the Color tab at the top of the side menu and then click the *Color 4* option at the drop-down gallery (fourth row in the *Colorful* section).
   d. Click the Chart Styles button to close the side menu.

5. Display only Northeast and Southeast sales by completing the following steps:
   a. Click the Chart Filters button that displays below the Chart Styles button.
   b. Click the *Northwest* check box in the *Categories* section to remove the check mark.
   c. Click the *Southwest* check box in the *Categories* section to remove the check mark.
   d. Click the Apply button in the lower left corner of the side menu.
   e. Click the Chart Filters button to close the side menu.
   f. After viewing only Northeast and Southeast sales, redisplay the other regions by clicking the Chart Filters button, clicking the *Northwest* and *Southwest* check boxes, and then clicking the Apply button.
   g. Click the Chart Filters button to close the side menu.

6. Save **2-Charts.docx**.

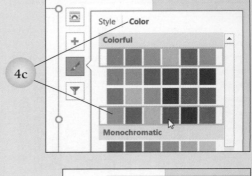

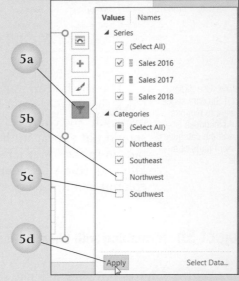

Check Your Work

Tutorial

Changing the Chart Design

Changing the Chart Design

In addition to the buttons that display outside the chart border, options on the Chart Tools Design tab, shown in Figure 2.15, can be used to customize a chart. Use options on this tab to add a chart element, change the chart layout and colors, apply a chart style, select data and switch rows and columns, and change the chart type.

Figure 2.15 Chart Tools Design Tab

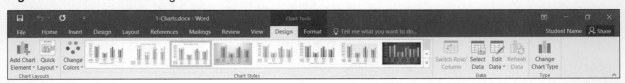

1. With **2-Charts.docx** open, make sure the chart is selected and the Chart Tools Design tab is active.
2. Change to a different layout by clicking the Quick Layout button in the Chart Layouts group and then clicking the *Layout 3* option (third column, first row in the drop-down gallery).
3. Click the *Style 7* chart style in the Chart Styles group (seventh option from the left).
4. Click the Add Chart Element button in the Chart Layouts group, point to *Chart Title* at the drop-down list, and then click *Centered Overlay* at the side menu.

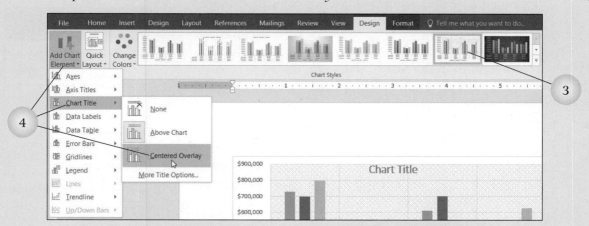

5. Select the words *Chart Title* and then type Regional Sales.
6. Click the chart border to deselect the chart title.
7. Edit the data by completing the following steps:
    a. Click the Edit Data button in the Data group.
    b. Click in cell C3 in the Excel worksheet.
    c. Type 375250. (Typing this text replaces the original amount, *$278,250*.)
    d. Click in cell C5, type 550300, and then press the Tab key.
    e. Click the Close button in the upper right corner of the Excel window.
8. Save **2-Charts.docx**.

Check Your Work

Tutorial

Changing Chart Formatting

Changing Chart Formatting

Use buttons on the Chart Tools Format tab, shown in Figure 2.16, to format and customize a chart and chart elements. To format or modify a specific element in a chart, select the element. Do this by clicking the element or by clicking the *Chart Elements* option box in the Current Selection group and then clicking the element at the drop-down list. Use other options on the Chart Tools Format tab to apply a shape style and WordArt style and arrange and size the chart or chart element.

Figure 2.16 Chart Tools Format Tab

Project 5d Formatting a Chart and Chart Elements

1. With **2-Charts.docx** open and the chart selected, click the Chart Tools Format tab.
2. Apply a shape style to the chart title by completing the following steps:
    a. Click the *Chart Elements* option box arrow in the Current Selection group and then click *Chart Title* at the drop-down list.
    b. Click the *Colored Outline - Blue, Accent 1* style option (second option in the Shape Styles group).
3. Change the color of the Sales 2018 series by completing the followings steps:
    a. Click the *Chart Elements* option box arrow in the Current Selection group and then click *Series "Sales 2018"* at the drop-down list.
    b. Click the Shape Fill button arrow in the Shape Styles group and then click the *Dark Red* option (first color option in the *Standard Colors* section).

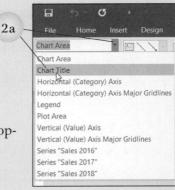

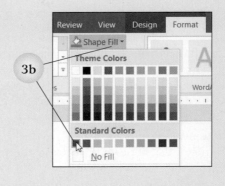

4. Apply a WordArt style to all the text in the chart by completing the following steps:
    a. Click the *Chart Elements* option box arrow.
    b. Click *Chart Area* at the drop-down list.
    c. Click the first WordArt style in the WordArt Styles group (*Fill - Black, Text 1, Shadow*).

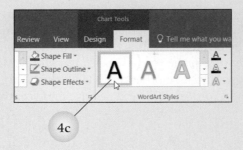

Chapter 2 | Proofing Documents and Creating Charts

5. Change the size of the chart by completing the following steps:
   a. Click in the *Shape Height* measurement box and then type 3.
   b. Click in the *Shape Width* measurement box, type 5.5, and then press the Enter key.
6. With the chart selected (not a chart element), change its position by clicking the Position button in the Arrange group and then clicking the *Position in Top Center with Square Text Wrapping* option (second column, first row in the *With Text Wrapping* section).
7. Save and then print **2-Charts.docx**.

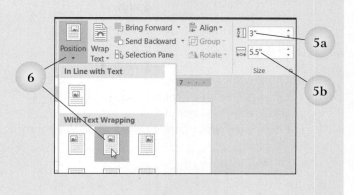

Check Your Work

Formatting a Chart with Task Pane Options

Format Selection

Additional formatting options are available at various task panes. Display a task pane by clicking the Format Selection button in the Current Selection group on the Chart Tools Format tab or a group task pane launcher. The Shape Styles and WordArt Styles groups on the Chart Tools Format tab contain task pane launchers. Which task pane opens at the right side of the screen depends on which chart or chart element is selected.

Project 5e Creating and Formatting a Pie Chart   Part 5 of 5

1. With **2-Charts.docx** open, press Ctrl + End (which deselects the chart) and then press the Enter key 12 times to move the insertion point below the chart.
2. Click the Insert tab and then click the Chart button in the Illustrations group.
3. At the Insert Chart dialog box, click *Pie* in the left panel and then click OK.
4. Type the data in the Excel worksheet cells as shown in Figure 2.17. After typing the last entry, click in cell A1.
5. Click the Close button in the upper right corner of the Excel window.
6. Click in the title *Percentage* and then type Investments.
7. Add data labels to the pie chart by completing the following steps:
   a. Click the Add Chart Element button in the Chart Layouts group on the Chart Tools Design tab.
   b. Point to *Data Labels* at the drop-down list and then click *Inside End* at the side menu.
8. Click on the chart border to select the chart (not a chart element).
9. Click the Chart Tools Format tab.

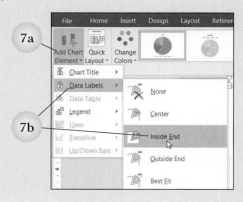

10. Apply formatting to the chart with options at the Format Chart Area task pane by completing the following steps:
   a. With the chart selected, click the Shape Styles group task pane launcher.
   b. At the Format Chart Area task pane with the Fill & Line icon selected, click *Fill*. (This expands the options below *Fill*.)
   c. Click the *Gradient fill* option.
   d. Click the Effects icon at the top of the task pane.
   e. Click *Shadow* to expand the shadow options.
   f. Click the Presets button.
   g. Click the *Offset Bottom* option (second column, first row in the *Outer* section).

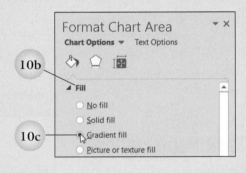

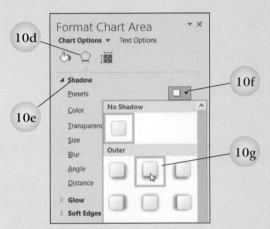

   h. Click the Text Options tab at the top of the task pane.
   i. Click *Text Outline* to expand the options.
   j. Click the *Solid line* option.
   k. Click the Color button and then click the *Blue, Accent 1, Darker 50%* option (fifth column, last row in the *Theme Colors* section).

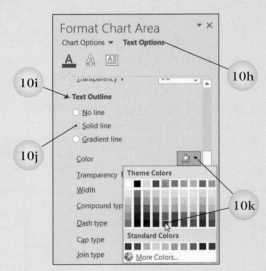

11. Format the pie chart by completing the following steps:
   a. Click in any piece of the pie. (This selects all the pieces of the pie. Notice that the name of the task pane has changed to *Format Data Series*.)

b. Click the Effects icon at the top of the task pane.

c. Click *3-D Format* to expand the options.

d. Click the Top bevel button and then click the *Soft Round* option at the drop-down gallery (second column, second row in the *Bevel* section).

e. Close the task pane by clicking the Close button in the upper right corner.

12. Click the chart border to select the chart (not a chart element).

13. Change the size of the chart by completing the following steps:

a. Click in the *Shape Height* measurement box and then type 3.

b. Click in the *Shape Width* measurement box, type 5.5, and then press the Enter key.

14. Change the position of the chart by clicking the Position button in the Arrange group and then clicking the *Position in Bottom Center with Square Text Wrapping* option (second column, third row in the *With Text Wrapping* section).

15. Save, print, and then close **2-Charts.docx**.

Check Your Work

Figure 2.17 Project 5

	A	B
1	Assets	Percentage
2	Loans	34%
3	Bonds	22%
4	Mutuals	20%
5	Stocks	17%
6	Other	7%
7		

Chapter Summary

- The spelling checker matches the words in the document with the words in its dictionary. If a match is not found, the word is selected and possible corrections are suggested.

- When checking the spelling and grammar in a document, changes can be made by clicking in the document outside the task pane, making the changes, and then clicking the Resume button in the task pane to continue checking.

- Customize spell checking options at the Word Options dialog box with *Proofing* selected in the left panel.

- Use the grammar checker to search a document for correct grammar, punctuation, and word usage.

- To display readability statistics for a document, insert a check mark in the *Show readability statistics* check box in the Word Options dialog box with *Proofing* selected and then complete a spelling and grammar check.

- Word uses the RoamingCustom.dic dictionary when spell checking a document. A custom dictionary can be added at the Custom Dictionaries dialog box. Display this dialog box by clicking the Custom Dictionaries button at the Word Options dialog box with *Proofing* selected.

- The Word Count dialog box displays the numbers of pages, words, characters, paragraphs, and lines in a document. Display this dialog box by clicking the word count section of the Status bar or by clicking the Word Count button in the Proofing group on the Review tab.

- Number lines in a document with options at the Line Numbers button drop-down list or the Line Numbers dialog box.

- Use the Thesaurus feature to find synonyms and antonyms for words in a document. Display synonyms and antonyms at the Thesaurus task pane or by right-clicking a word and then pointing to *Synonyms* at the shortcut menu.

- The Smart Lookup feature provides information on selected text from a variety of sources on the web, such as Wikipedia, Bing, and the Oxford Dictionary. To use the Smart Lookup feature, select text and then click the Smart Lookup button in the Insights group on the Review tab. This displays the Smart Lookup task pane at the right side of the screen.

- Use the Translate button in the Language group on the Review tab to translate a document, a selected section of text, or a word from one language to another.

- To present data visually, create a chart with the Chart button on the Insert tab. Choose a chart type at the Insert Chart dialog box. Enter chart data in an Excel worksheet.

- Four buttons display at the right side of a selected chart. Use the Layout Options button to apply text wrapping, the Chart Elements button to add or remove chart elements, the Chart Styles button to apply a predesigned chart style, and the Chart Filters button to isolate specific data in the chart.

- Modify a chart design with options and buttons on the Chart Tools Design tab.

- The cells in an Excel worksheet used to create a chart are linked to the chart in the document. To edit the chart data, click the Edit Data button on the Chart Tools Design tab and then make changes to the data in the Excel worksheet.

- Customize the format of a chart and chart elements with options and buttons on the Chart Tools Format tab. Select the chart or a specific chart element and then apply a style to a shape, apply a WordArt style to the text, and arrange and size the chart.

- Apply formatting to a chart with options in task panes. Display a task pane by clicking the Format Selection button on the Chart Tools Format tab or a group task pane launcher. The options in the task pane vary depending on the chart or chart element selected.

Commands Review

FEATURE	RIBBON TAB, GROUP	BUTTON, OPTION	KEYBOARD SHORTCUT
Insert Chart dialog box	Insert, Illustrations		
line numbers	Layout, Page Setup		
Mini Translator	Review, Language	, Mini Translator	
Smart Lookup task pane	Review, Insights		
spelling and grammar checker	Review, Proofing		F7
Thesaurus task pane	Review, Proofing		Shift + F7
translate selected text	Review, Language	, Translate Selected Text	
translate text in document	Review, Language	, Translate Document	
Translation Language Options dialog box	Review, Language	, Choose Translation Language	
Word Count dialog box	Review, Proofing		

Microsoft®
Word

Automating and Customizing Formatting

Performance Objectives

Precheck

Check your
current skills to
help focus your
study.

Upon successful completion of Chapter 3, you will be able to:

1 Specify AutoCorrect exceptions

2 Add and delete AutoCorrect text

3 Use the AutoCorrect Options button

4 Customize AutoFormatting

5 Insert and sort building blocks

6 Create, edit, modify, and delete custom building blocks

7 Insert document property placeholders from Quick Parts

8 Insert and update fields from Quick Parts

9 Customize the Quick Access Toolbar

10 Customize the ribbon

11 Export Quick Access Toolbar and ribbon customizations

Microsoft Word offers a number of features to help you customize documents and streamline the formatting of documents. In this chapter, you will learn how to customize the AutoCorrect feature and use the AutoCorrect Options button. You will also learn how to build a document using building blocks; create, save, and edit your own building blocks; and customize the Quick Access Toolbar and the ribbon.

SNAP

If you are a SNAP user, launch the Precheck and Tutorials from your Assignments page.

Data Files

Before beginning chapter work, copy the WL2C3 folder to your storage medium and then make WL2C3 the active folder.

Project 1 **Create a Travel Document Using AutoCorrect**   **4 Parts**

You will create several AutoCorrect entries, open a letterhead document, and then use the AutoCorrect entries to type text in the document.

Preview Finished Project

Customizing AutoCorrect

Tutorial

Customizing
AutoCorrect

Word's AutoCorrect feature corrects certain text automatically as it is typed. The types of corrections that can be made are specified with options at the AutoCorrect dialog box with the AutoCorrect tab selected, as shown in Figure 3.1.

Display this dialog box by clicking the File tab, clicking *Options*, clicking *Proofing*, clicking the AutoCorrect Options button, and then clicking the AutoCorrect tab. At the dialog box, turn AutoCorrect features on or off by inserting or removing check marks from the check boxes. In addition, specify AutoCorrect exceptions, replace frequently misspelled words with the correctly spelled words, add frequently used words, and specify keys to quickly insert the words in a document.

Quick Steps

Display the AutoCorrect Exceptions Dialog Box
1. Click File tab.
2. Click *Options*.
3. Click *Proofing*.
4. Click AutoCorrect Options button.
5. Click AutoCorrect tab.
6. Click Exceptions button.

Specifying AutoCorrect Exceptions

The check box options at the AutoCorrect dialog box with the AutoCorrect tab selected identify the types of corrections made by AutoCorrect. Specify which corrections should not be made with options at the AutoCorrect Exceptions dialog box, shown in Figure 3.2. Display this dialog box by clicking the Exceptions button at the AutoCorrect dialog box with the AutoCorrect tab selected.

Figure 3.1 AutoCorrect Dialog Box with AutoCorrect Tab Selected

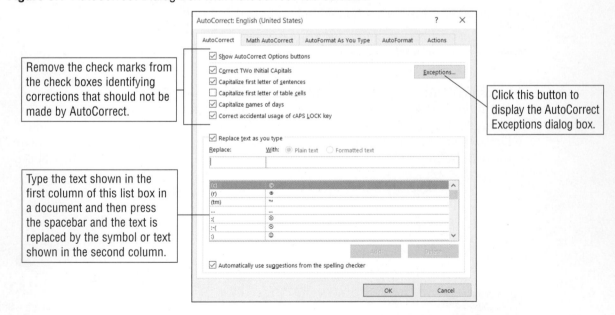

Remove the check marks from the check boxes identifying corrections that should not be made by AutoCorrect.

Click this button to display the AutoCorrect Exceptions dialog box.

Type the text shown in the first column of this list box in a document and then press the spacebar and the text is replaced by the symbol or text shown in the second column.

Figure 3.2 AutoCorrect Exceptions Dialog Box

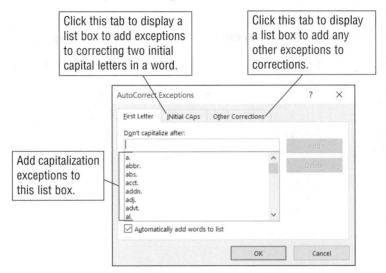

AutoCorrect usually capitalizes a word that comes after an abbreviation ending in a period, since a period usually ends a sentence. Exceptions to this general practice display in the AutoCorrect Exceptions dialog box with the First Letter tab selected. Many exceptions already display in the dialog box but additional exceptions can be added by typing each exception in the *Don't capitalize after* text box and then clicking the Add button.

By default, AutoCorrect corrects the use of two initial capital letters in a word. If AutoCorrect should not correct these instances, display the AutoCorrect Exceptions dialog box with the INitial CAps tab selected and then type the exception text in the *Don't correct* text box. At the AutoCorrect Exceptions dialog box with the Other Corrections tab selected, type the text that should not be corrected in the *Don't correct* text box. Delete an exception from the dialog box with any of the tabs selected by clicking the text in the list box and then clicking the Delete button.

Adding and Deleting an AutoCorrect Entry

Tutorial

Adding and
Deleting an
AutoCorrect Entry

Q̃uick Steps

Add a Word to AutoCorrect
1. Click File tab.
2. Click *Options*.
3. Click *Proofing*.
4. Click AutoCorrect Options button.
5. Click AutoCorrect tab.
6. Type misspelled or abbreviated word.
7. Press Tab.
8. Type correctly spelled or complete word.
9. Click Add button.
10. Click OK.

Commonly misspelled words and/or typographical errors can be added to AutoCorrect. For example, if a user consistently types *relavent* instead of *relevant*, *relavent* can be added to AutoCorrect with the direction to correct it to *relevant*. The AutoCorrect dialog box also contains a few symbols that can be inserted in a document. For example, type *(c)* and AutoCorrect changes the text to © (copyright symbol). Type *(r)* and AutoCorrect changes the text to ® (registered trademark symbol). The symbols display at the beginning of the AutoCorrect dialog box list box.

An abbreviation can be added to AutoCorrect that will insert the entire word (or words) in the document when it is typed. For example, in Project 1a, the abbreviation *fav* will be added to AutoCorrect and *Family Adventure Vacations* will be inserted when *fav* is typed followed by a press of the spacebar. The capitalization of the abbreviation can also be controlled. For example, in Project 1a, the abbreviation *Na* will be added to AutoCorrect and *Namibia* will be inserted when *Na* is typed and *NAMIBIA* will be inserted when *NA* is typed.

AutoCorrect text can be deleted from the AutoCorrect dialog box. To do this, display the AutoCorrect dialog box with the AutoCorrect tab selected, click the word or words in the list box, and then click the Delete button.

1. At a blank document, click the File tab and then click *Options*.
2. At the Word Options dialog box, click *Proofing* in the left panel.
3. Click the AutoCorrect Options button in the *AutoCorrect options* section.
4. At the AutoCorrect dialog box with the AutoCorrect tab selected, add an exception to AutoCorrect by completing the following steps:
   a. Click the Exceptions button.
   b. At the AutoCorrect Exceptions dialog box, click the INitial CAps tab.
   c. Click in the *Don't correct* text box, type STudent, and then click the Add button.
   d. Click in the *Don't correct* text box, type STyle, and then click the Add button.
   e. Click OK.
5. At the AutoCorrect dialog box with the AutoCorrect tab selected, click in the *Replace* text box and then type fav.
6. Press the Tab key (which moves the insertion point to the *With* text box) and then type Family Adventure Vacations.
7. Click the Add button. (This adds *fav* and *Family Adventure Vacations* to AutoCorrect and also selects *fav* in the *Replace* text box.)
8. Type Na in the *Replace* text box. (The text *fav* is automatically removed when the typing of *Na* begins.)
9. Press the Tab key and then type Namibia.
10. Click the Add button.
11. With the insertion point positioned in the *Replace* text box, type vf.
12. Press the Tab key and then type Victoria Falls.
13. Click the Add button.
14. With the insertion point positioned in the *Replace* text box, type tts.
15. Press the Tab key and then type Terra Travel Services.
16. Click the Add button.
17. Click OK to close the AutoCorrect dialog box and then click OK to close the Word Options dialog box.
18. Open **TTSLtrhd.docx** and then save it with the name **3-TTSAfrica**.
19. Type the text shown in Figure 3.3. Type the text exactly as shown (including applying bold formatting and centering *fav* at the beginning of the document). AutoCorrect will correct the words as they are typed.
20. Save **3-TTSAfrica.docx**.

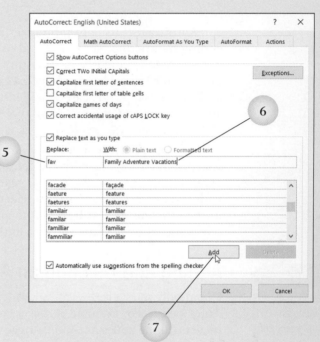

Check Your Work

Figure 3.3 Project 1a

<hr>

fav

Na and vf Adventure

tts is partnering with fav to provide adventurous and thrilling family vacations. Our first joint adventure is a holiday trip to Na. Na is one of the most fascinating holiday destinations in Africa and offers comfortable facilities, great food, cultural interaction, abundant wildlife, and a wide variety of activities to interest people of all ages.

During the 12-day trip, you and your family will travel across Na through national parks, enjoying the beautiful and exotic scenery and watching wildlife in natural habitats. You will cruise along the Kwando and Chobe rivers and spend time at the Okapuka Lodge located near Windhoek, the capital of Na.

If you or your family member is a college student, contact one of our college travel adventure consultants to learn more about the newest Student Travel package titled "STudent STyle" that offers a variety of student discounts, rebates, and free travel accessories for qualifying participants.

tts and fav are offering a 15 percent discount if you sign up for this once-in-a-lifetime trip to Na. This exciting adventure is limited to twenty people, so don't wait to sign up.

<hr>

Using the AutoCorrect Options Button

Tutorial

Undoing an
AutoCorrect
Correction

 AutoCorrect Options

After AutoCorrect corrects a portion of text, hover the mouse pointer near the text and a small blue box displays below it. Move the mouse pointer to this blue box and the AutoCorrect Options button displays. Click this button to display a drop-down list with the options to change the text back to the original version, stop automatically correcting the specific text, and display the AutoCorrect dialog box.

If the AutoCorrect Options button does not display, turn on the feature. To do this, display the AutoCorrect dialog box with the AutoCorrect tab selected, click the *Show AutoCorrect Options buttons* check box to insert a check mark, and then click OK to close the dialog box.

Project 1b   Using the AutoCorrect Options Button   Part 2 of 4

1. With **3-TTSAfrica.docx** open, select and then delete the last paragraph.
2. With the insertion point positioned on the blank line below the last paragraph of text (you may need to press the Enter key), type the following text. (AutoCorrect will automatically change *Ameria* to *America*, which you will change in the next step.) Through the sponsorship of Ameria Resorts, we are able to offer you a 15 percent discount for groups of twelve or more people.
3. Change the spelling of *America* back to *Ameria* by completing the following steps:
   a. Position the mouse pointer over *America* until a blue box displays below it.
   b. Position the mouse pointer on the blue box until the AutoCorrect Options button displays.

c. Click the AutoCorrect Options
   button and then click the
   Change back to "Ameria" option.
4. Save and then print
   3-TTSAfrica.docx.

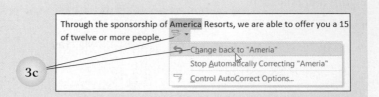

3c

Check Your Work

Inserting Symbols Automatically

AutoCorrect recognizes and replaces symbols as well as text. Several symbols
included in AutoCorrect display in the AutoCorrect dialog box and are listed first
in the *Replace* text box. Table 3.1 lists these symbols along with the characters to
insert them. Along with the symbols provided by Word, other symbols can be
inserted in the AutoCorrect dialog box with the AutoCorrect button in the Symbol
dialog box. To insert a symbol in the AutoCorrect dialog box, click the Insert tab,
click the Symbol button in the Symbols group, and then click *More Symbols* at the
drop-down list. At the Symbol dialog box, click the specific symbol and then click
the AutoCorrect button that displays in the lower left corner of the dialog box.
This displays the AutoCorrect dialog box with the symbol inserted in the *With*
text box and the insertion point positioned in the *Replace* text box. Type the text
that will insert the symbol, click the Add button, and then click OK to close the
AutoCorrect dialog box. Click the Close button to close the Symbol dialog box.

Table 3.1 AutoCorrect Symbols Available at the AutoCorrect Dialog Box

Type	To Insert
(c)	©
(r)	®
(tm)	™
...	. . .
:) or :-)	☺
:l or :-l	☺
:(or :-(	☹
-->	→
<--	←
==>	→
<==	←
<=>	⇔

1. With **3-TTSAfrica.docx** open, move the insertion point so it is positioned immediately right of the last *s* in *Resorts* (located in the last paragraph) and then type (r). (This inserts the registered trademark symbol.)
2. Move the insertion point immediately left of the *1* in *15* and then type ==>. (This inserts the ➔symbol.)
3. Move the insertion point immediately right of the *t* in *discount* and then type <==. (This inserts the ⬅ symbol.)
4. Insert the pound (£) currency unit symbol in AutoCorrect by completing the following steps:
   a. Click the Insert tab.
   b. Click the Symbol button and then click *More Symbols* at the drop-down list.
   c. At the Symbol dialog box, make sure that *(normal text)* displays in the *Font* option box. If it does not, click the *Font* option box arrow and then click *(normal text)* at the drop-down list (first option in the list).
   d. Scroll through the list of symbols and then click the pound (£) currency unit symbol (located in approximately the sixth or seventh row; character code *00A3*).
   e. Click the AutoCorrect button in the lower left corner of the dialog box.
   f. At the AutoCorrect dialog box, type pcu in the *Replace* text box and then click the Add button.
   g. Click OK to close the AutoCorrect dialog box.

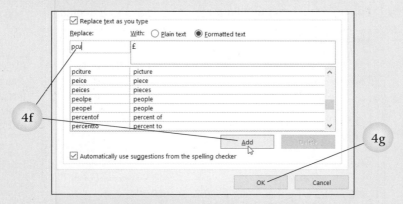

   h. Click the Close button to close the Symbol dialog box.
5. Press Ctrl + End to move the insertion point to the end of the document and then press the Enter key.
6. Type the text shown in Figure 3.4. (Press Shift + Enter or the Enter key as indicated in the figure.) Create the pound currency unit symbol by typing pcu and then pressing the spacebar. Press the Backspace key once and then type 1,999. (Complete similar steps when typing *£1,599 (UK)*.)
7. Save **3-TTSAfrica.docx**.

Check Your Work

Figure 3.4 Project 1c

> **Individual price:** *(press Shift+ Enter)*
> $3,299 (US) *(press Shift+ Enter)*
> £1,999 (UK) *(press Enter)*
>
> **Individual price for groups of twenty or more:** *(press Shift+ Enter)*
> $3,999 (US) *(press Shift+ Enter)*
> £1,599 (UK)

Tutorial ▶

Customizing
AutoFormatting

Customizing AutoFormatting

When typing text, Word provides options to automatically apply some formatting, such as changing a fraction to a fraction character (1/2 to ½), changing numbers to ordinals (1st to 1st), changing an Internet or network path to a hyperlink (www.emcp.net to www.emcp.net), and applying bullets or numbers to text. The autoformatting options display in the AutoCorrect dialog box with the AutoFormat As You Type tab selected, as shown in Figure 3.5.

Display this dialog box by clicking the File tab and then clicking *Options*. At the Word Options dialog box, click *Proofing* in the left panel and then click the AutoCorrect Options button. At the AutoCorrect dialog box, click the AutoFormat As You Type tab. At the dialog box, remove the check marks from those options to be turned off and insert check marks for those options to be formatted automatically.

Figure 3.5 AutoCorrect Dialog Box with the AutoFormat As You Type Tab Selected

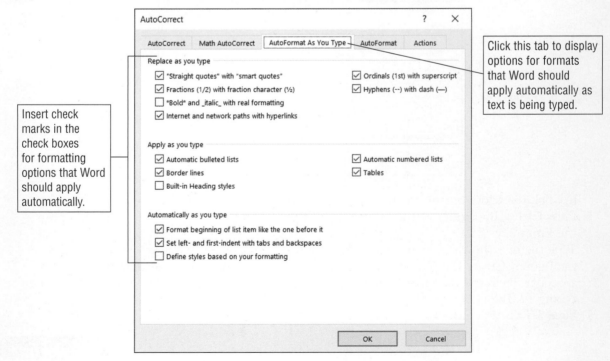

Insert check marks in the check boxes for formatting options that Word should apply automatically.

Click this tab to display options for formats that Word should apply automatically as text is being typed.

1. Make sure **3-TTSAfrica.docx** is open.
2. Suppose that you need to add a couple of web addresses to a document and do not want the addresses automatically formatted as hyperlinks (since you are sending the document as hard copy rather than electronically). Turn off the autoformatting of web addresses by completing the following steps:
   a. Click the File tab and then click *Options*.
   b. At the Word Options dialog box, click *Proofing* in the left panel.
   c. Click the AutoCorrect Options button.
   d. At the AutoCorrect dialog box, click the AutoFormat As You Type tab.
   e. Click the *Internet and network paths with hyperlinks* check box to remove the check mark.

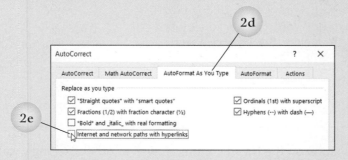

   f. Click OK to close the AutoCorrect dialog box.
   g. Click OK to close the Word Options dialog box.
3. Press Ctrl + End to move the insertion point to the end of the document, press the Enter key, and then type the text shown in Figure 3.6.
4. Turn on the autoformatting of web addresses that was turned off in Step 2 by completing Steps 2a through 2g (except in Step 2e, insert the check mark rather than remove it).
5. Delete *fav* from AutoCorrect by completing the following steps:
   a. Click the File tab and then click *Options*.
   b. At the Word Options dialog box, click *Proofing* in the left panel.
   c. Click the AutoCorrect Options button.
   d. At the AutoCorrect dialog box, click the AutoCorrect tab.
   e. Click in the *Replace* text box and then type fav. (This selects the entry in the list box.)
   f. Click the Delete button.
6. Complete steps similar to those in Steps 5e-5f to delete the *Na*, *tts*, and *vf* AutoCorrect entries.

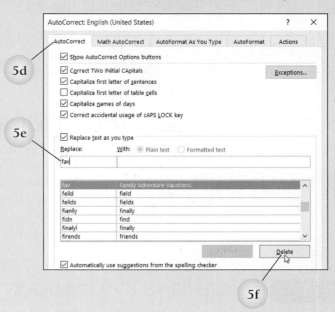

7. Delete the exceptions added to the AutoCorrect Exceptions dialog box by completing the following steps:
   a. At the AutoCorrect dialog box with the AutoCorrect tab selected, click the Exceptions button.
   b. At the AutoCorrect Exceptions dialog box, if necessary, click the INitial CAps tab.
   c. Click *STudent* in the list box and then click the Delete button.
   d. Click *STyle* in the list box and then click the Delete button.
   e. Click OK to close the AutoCorrect Exceptions dialog box.
8. Click OK to close the AutoCorrect dialog box.
9. Click OK to close the Word Options dialog box.
10. Save, print, and then close **3-TTSAfrica.docx**.

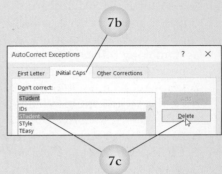

Check Your Work

Figure 3.6 Project 1d

For additional information on the Na adventure, as well as other exciting vacation specials, please visit our website at www.emcp.net/terratravel or visit www.emcp.net/famadv.

Project 2 **Build a Document with Predesigned and Custom Building Blocks**   **1 Part**

You will open a report document and then add elements to it by inserting predesigned building blocks.

Preview Finished Project

Managing Building Blocks

Quick Parts

Word includes a variety of tools for inserting data such as text, fields, objects, and other items to help build a document. To view some of the tools available, click the Quick Parts button in the Text group on the Insert tab. This displays a drop-down list of choices for inserting document properties, fields, and building blocks. Building blocks are tools for developing a document. Word provides a number of building blocks that can be inserted in a document or custom building blocks can be created.

Tutorial

Inserting and Sorting Building Blocks

Inserting a Building Block

To insert a building block into a document, click the Insert tab, click the Quick Parts button in the Text group, and then click *Building Blocks Organizer* at the drop-down list. This displays the Building Blocks Organizer dialog box, shown in

Quick Steps

Insert a Building Block

1. Click Insert tab.
2. Click Quick Parts button.
3. Click *Building Blocks Organizer*.
4. Click building block.
5. Click Insert button.
6. Click Close.

Figure 3.7. The dialog box displays columns of information about the building blocks. The columns in the dialog box display information about the building block, including its name, the gallery that contains it, the template in which it is stored, its behavior, and a brief description of it.

The Building Blocks Organizer dialog box is a central location for viewing all the predesigned building blocks available in Word. Some of the building blocks were used in previous chapters when a predesigned header or footer, cover page, page number, or watermark were inserted in a document. Other galleries in the Building Blocks Organizer dialog box contain predesigned building blocks such as bibliographies, equations, tables of contents, tables, and text boxes. The Building Blocks Organizer dialog box provides a convenient location for viewing and inserting building blocks.

Sorting Building Blocks

Quick Steps

Sort Building Blocks

1. Click Insert tab.
2. Click Quick Parts button.
3. Click *Building Blocks Organizer*.
4. Click column heading.

The Building Blocks Organizer dialog box displays the building blocks in the list box sorted by the *Gallery* column. The building blocks can be sorted by another column by clicking that column heading. For example, to sort the building blocks alphabetically by name, click the *Name* column heading.

Figure 3.7 Building Blocks Organizer Dialog Box

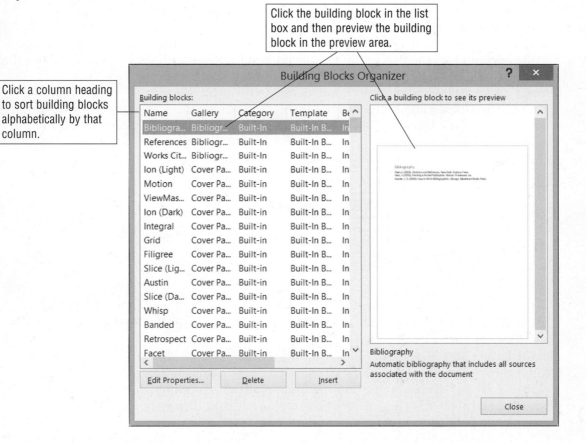

1. Open **CompViruses.docx** and then save it with the name **3-CompViruses**.
2. Sort the building blocks and then insert a table of contents building block by completing the following steps:
   a. Press Ctrl + Home to move the insertion point to the beginning of the document, press Ctrl + Enter to insert a page break, and then press Ctrl + Home again.
   b. Click the Insert tab, click the Quick Parts button in the Text group, and then click *Building Blocks Organizer* at the drop-down list.

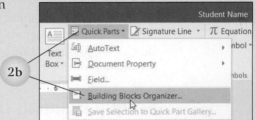

   c. At the Building Blocks Organizer dialog box, notice the arrangement of building blocks in the list box. (The building blocks are most likely organized alphabetically by the *Gallery* column.)
   d. Click the *Name* column heading. (This sorts the building blocks alphabetically by name. However, some blank building blocks may display at the beginning of the list box.)

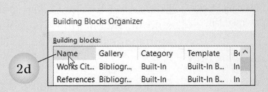

   e. Scroll down the list box and then click *Automatic Table 1*. (You may see only a portion of the name. Click the name and the full name as well as a description display in the dialog box below the preview of the table of contents building block.)
   f. Click the Insert button at the bottom of the dialog box. (This inserts a contents page at the beginning of the document and creates a table of contents that includes the headings with styles applied.)
3. Insert a footer building block by completing the following steps:
   a. Click the Quick Parts button on the Insert tab and then click *Building Blocks Organizer*.
   b. Scroll down the Building Blocks Organizer list box, click the *Sempahore* footer, and then click the Insert button.

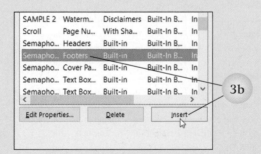

   c. Decrease the *Footer from Bottom* measurement to 0.3 inch (in the Position group on the Header & Footer Tools Design tab).
   d. Click the Close Header and Footer button.
4. Insert a cover page building block by completing the following steps:
   a. Press Ctrl + Home to move the insertion point to the beginning of the document.
   b. Click the Insert tab, click the Quick Parts button, and then click *Building Blocks Organizer*.
   c. Scroll down the Building Blocks Organizer list box, click the *Semaphore* cover page, and then click the Insert button.
   d. Click the *[DATE]* placeholder and then type today's date.

e. Click the *[DOCUMENT TITLE]* placeholder and then type Northland Security Systems. (The text will be converted to all uppercase letters.)

f. Click the *[DOCUMENT SUBTITLE]* placeholder and then type Computer Viruses and Security Strategies.

g. Select the name above the *[COMPANY NAME]* placeholder and then type your first and last names.

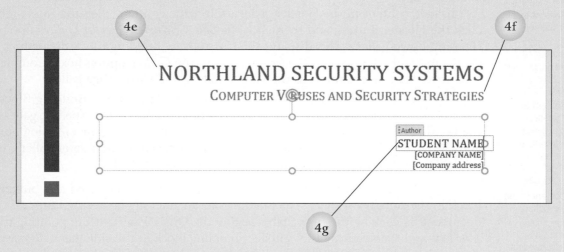

h. Select and then delete the *[COMPANY NAME]* placeholder.

i. Select and then delete the *[Company address]* placeholder.

5. Scroll through the document and look at each page. The semaphore footer and cover page building blocks that were inserted have similar formatting and are part of the Semaphore group. Using building blocks from the same group provides consistency in the document and gives it a polished and professional appearance.

6. Save, print, and then close **3-CompViruses.docx**.

Check Your Work

Project 3 **Create a Letter Document Using Custom Building Blocks**   **3 Parts**

You will create custom building blocks and then use them to prepare a business letter.

Preview Finished Project

Tutorial

Saving Content as a Building Block

Saving Content as a Building Block

Consider saving data that is typed and formatted on a regular basis as a building block. Saving commonly created data as a building block saves time and reduces errors that might occur each time the data is typed or formatting is applied. The data can be saved as a building block in a specific gallery, such as the Text Box, Header, or Footer gallery, or saved to the AutoText gallery or Quick Part gallery.

Save Content to a Text Box Gallery
1. Select content.
2. Click Insert tab.
3. Click Text Box button.
4. Click *Save Selection to Text Box Gallery*.

Save Content to a Header Gallery
1. Select content.
2. Click Insert tab.
3. Click Header button.
4. Click *Save Selection to Header Gallery*.

Save Content to a Footer Gallery
1. Select content.
2. Click Insert tab.
3. Click Footer button.
4. Click *Save Selection to Footer Gallery*.

Save Content to the AutoText Gallery
1. Select content.
2. Click Insert tab.
3. Click Quick Parts button.
4. Point to *AutoText*.
5. Click *Save Selection to AutoText Gallery*.

Saving Content to a Specific Gallery To save content in a specific gallery, use the button for the gallery. For example, to save a text box in the Text Box gallery, use the Text Box button. To do this, select the text box, click the Insert tab, click the Text Box button, and then click the *Save Selection to Text Box Gallery* option at the drop-down gallery. At the Create New Building Block dialog box as shown in Figure 3.8, type a name for the text box building block, type a description of it, and then click OK.

To save content in the Header gallery, select the content, click the Insert tab, click the Header button, and then click the *Save Selection to Header Gallery* option at the drop-down gallery. This displays the Create New Building Block dialog box, as shown in Figure 3.8 (except *Headers* displays in the *Gallery* option box). Complete similar steps to save content to the Footer gallery and Cover Page gallery.

When data is saved as a building block, it is available in the Building Blocks Organizer dialog box. If content is saved as a building block in a specific gallery, the building block is available at both the Building Blocks Organizer dialog box and the gallery. For example, if a building block is saved in the Footer gallery, it is available when the Footer button on the Insert tab is clicked.

Saving Content to the AutoText Gallery Content can be saved as a building block in the AutoText gallery. The building block can easily be inserted into a document by clicking the Insert tab, clicking the Quick Parts button, pointing to *AutoText*, and then clicking the AutoText building block at the side menu. To save content in the AutoText gallery, type and format the content and then select it. Click the Insert tab, click the Quick Parts button, point to *AutoText*, and then click the *Save Selection to AutoText Gallery* option at the side menu or use the keyboard shortcut Alt + F3. At the Create New Building Block dialog box, type a name for the building block, type a description of it, and then click OK.

Saving Content to the Quick Part Gallery Not only can content be saved in the AutoText gallery, but selected content can also be saved in the Quick Part gallery. To do this, select the content, click the Insert tab, click the Quick Parts button, and then click the *Save Selection to Quick Part Gallery* option at the drop-down gallery. This displays the Create New Building Block dialog box with *Quick Parts* specified in the *Gallery* option box and *Building Blocks.dotx* specified in the *Save in* option box. Type a name for the building block, type a description of it, and then click OK.

Figure 3.8 Create New Building Block Dialog Box

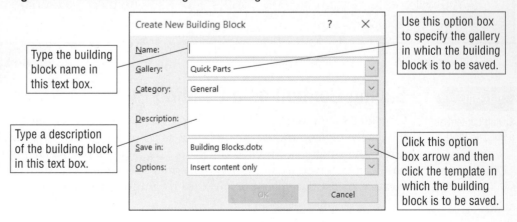

Type the building block name in this text box.

Use this option box to specify the gallery in which the building block is to be saved.

Type a description of the building block in this text box.

Click this option box arrow and then click the template in which the building block is to be saved.

Quick Steps

Save a Template
1. Click File tab.
2. Click *Save As* option.
3. Click *Browse* option.
4. Click *Save as type* option.
5. Click *Word Template (*.dotx)*.
6. Type a name for the template.
7. Click Save button.

Quick Steps

Open a Document Based on a Template
1. Click File tab.
2. Click *New* option.
3. Click *PERSONAL* option.
4. Click template thumbnail.
OR
1. Click File Explorer icon on taskbar.
2. Navigate to folder containing template.
3. Double-click template.

Saving Building Blocks in a Specific Template By default, building block content is saved in one of two templates, either Building Blocks.dotx or Normal.dotm. The template location depends on the gallery selected at the Create New Building Block dialog box. A building block saved in either of these templates is available each time a document is opened in Word. In a public environment, such as a school, saving to one of these templates may not be possible. To create a new personal template, display the Save As dialog box and then change the *Save as type* option to *Word Template (*.dotx)*. Choosing this option automatically selects the Custom Office Templates folder. Type a name for the template, click the Save button, and the template is saved in the Custom Office Templates folder.

To open a document based on a personal template, click the File tab and then click the *New* option. At the New backstage area, click the *PERSONAL* option that displays below the search text box. This displays thumbnails of the templates saved in the Custom Office Templates folder. Click the thumbnail of a specific template and a blank document opens based on the selected template.

Another option for opening a document based on a template is to save a template to a location other than the Custom Office Templates folder, such as the WL2C3 folder on your storage medium, and then use File Explorer to open a document based on the template. To do this, click the File Explorer icon on the taskbar, navigate to the folder containing the template, and then double-click the template. Instead of the template opening, a blank document opens that is based on the template.

To specify the template in which a building block is to be saved, click the *Save in* option box arrow in the Create New Building Block dialog box and then click the specific template. A document must be opened based on a personal template for the template name to display in the drop-down list.

Project 3a Saving a Template and Saving Content to the Text Box, Footer, AutoText, and Quick Part Galleries

Part 1 of 3

1. Press Ctrl + N to display a blank document and then save the document as a template by completing the following steps:
   a. Press the F12 function key to display the Save As dialog box.
   b. At the Save As dialog box, type FAVTemplate in the *File name* text box.
   c. Click the *Save as type* option box and then click *Word Template (*.dotx)* at the drop-down list.
   d. Navigate to the WL2C3 folder on your storage medium.
   e. Click the Save button.
2. Close **FAVTemplate.dotx**.
3. Open a document based on the template by completing the following steps:
   a. Click the File Explorer icon on the taskbar. (The taskbar displays along the bottom of the screen.)
   b. Navigate to the WL2C3 folder on your storage medium.
   c. Double-click *FAVTemplate.dotx*.
4. Insert **FAVContent.docx** into the current document. (Do this with the Object button arrow on the Insert tab. This document is located in your WL2C3 folder.)

5. Save the text box as a building block in the Text Box gallery by completing the following steps:
   a. Select the text box by clicking in it and then clicking its border.
   b. With the Insert tab active, click the Text Box button, and then click *Save Selection to Text Box Gallery* at the drop-down list.

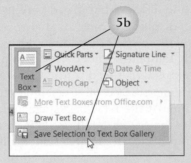

   c. At the Create New Building Block dialog box, type FAVTextBox in the *Name* text box.
   d. Click the *Save in* option box arrow and then click *FAVTemplate.dotx* at the drop-down list.
   e. Click OK to close the Create New Building Block dialog box.

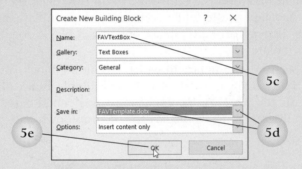

6. Save content as a building block in the Footer gallery by completing the following steps:
   a. Select the text *"Making your vacation dreams a reality"* below the text box. (Be sure to select the paragraph mark at the end of the text. If necessary, click the Show/Hide ¶ button in the Paragraph group on the Home tab to display the paragraph mark.)
   b. Click the Footer button in the Header & Footer group on the Insert tab and then click *Save Selection to Footer Gallery* at the drop-down list.
   c. At the Create New Building Block dialog box, type FAVFooter in the *Name* text box.
   d. Click the *Save in* option box and then click *FAVTemplate.dotx* at the drop-down list.
   e. Click OK to close the Create New Building Block dialog box.

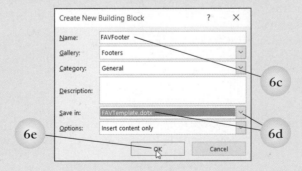

7. Save the company name *Pacific Sky Cruise Lines* and the address below it as a building block in the AutoText gallery by completing the following steps:
   a. Select the company name and address (the two lines below the company name). (Be sure to include the paragraph mark at the end of the last line of the address).
   b. Click the Quick Parts button in the Text group on the Insert tab, point to *AutoText*, and then click *Save Selection to AutoText Gallery* at the side menu.

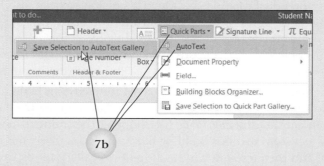

7b

   c. At the Create New Building Block dialog box, type PacificSky in the *Name* text box.
   d. Click the *Save in* option box arrow and then click *FAVTemplate.dotx* at the drop-down list.
   e. Click OK to close the dialog box.
8. Type your name and company title and then save the text as a building block in the AutoText gallery by completing the following steps:
   a. Move the insertion point to a blank line one double space below the address for Pacific Sky Cruise Lines.
   b. Type your first and last names and then press the spacebar.
   c. Press the Down Arrow key to move the insertion point to the next line and then type Travel Consultant. (Do not press the Enter key.)
   d. Select your first and last names and the title *Travel Consultant*. (Include the paragraph mark at the end of the title.)
   e. Press Alt + F3.
   f. At the Create New Building Block dialog box, type Title in the *Name* text box.
   g. Click the *Save in* option box arrow and then click *FAVTemplate.dotx* at the drop-down list.
   h. Click OK to close the dialog box.
9. Save the letterhead as a building block in the Quick Part gallery by completing the following steps:
   a. Select the letterhead text (the company name *FAMILY ADVENTURE VACATIONS*, the address below the name, and the paragraph mark at the end of the address and telephone number).
   b. Click the Quick Parts button in the Text group on the Insert tab and then click *Save Selection to Quick Part Gallery* at the drop-down list.
   c. At the Create New Building Block dialog box, type FAV in the *Name* text box and change the *Save in* option to *FAVTemplate.dotx*.
   d. Click OK to close the dialog box.
10. Close the document without saving it.
11. At the message that displays indicating that you have modified styles, building blocks, or other content stored in FAVTemplate.dotx and asking if you want to save changes to the template, click the Save button.

Editing Building Block Properties

Changes can be made to the properties of a building block with options at the Modify Building Block dialog box. This dialog box contains the same options as the Create New Building Block dialog box.

Display the Modify Building Block dialog box by opening the Building Blocks Organizer dialog box, clicking the specific building block in the list box, and then clicking the Edit Properties button. This dialog box can also be displayed for a building block in the Quick Parts button drop-down gallery. To do this, click the Quick Parts button, right-click the building block in the drop-down gallery, and then click *Edit Properties* at the shortcut menu. Make changes to the Modify Building Block dialog box and then click OK. At the confirmation message, click Yes.

The dialog box can also be displayed for a custom building block in a button drop-down gallery by clicking the button, right-clicking the custom building block, and then clicking the *Edit Properties* option at the shortcut menu. For example, to modify a custom text box building block, click the Insert tab, click the Text Box button, and then scroll down the drop-down gallery to display the custom text box building block. Right-click the custom text box building block and then click *Edit Properties* at the shortcut menu.

Quick Steps

Edit a Building Block
1. Click Insert tab.
2. Click Quick Parts button.
3. Click *Building Blocks Organizer*.
4. Click building block.
5. Click Edit Properties button.
6. Make changes.
7. Click OK.
OR
1. Click button.
2. Right-click custom building block.
3. Click *Edit Properties*.
4. Make changes.
5. Click OK.

Project 3b Editing Building Block Properties

Part 2 of 3

1. Open a blank document based on your template **FAVTemplate.dotx** by completing the following steps:
   a. Click the File Explorer icon on the taskbar.
   b. Navigate to the WL2C3 folder on your storage medium.
   c. Double-click **FAVTemplate.dotx**.
2. Edit the PacificSky building block by completing the following steps:
   a. Click the Insert tab, click the Quick Parts button, and then click *Building Blocks Organizer* at the drop-down list.
   b. At the Building Blocks Organizer dialog box, click the *Gallery* heading to sort the building blocks by gallery. (This displays the *AutoText* galleries at the beginning of the list.)
   c. Using the horizontal scroll bar at the bottom of the *Building blocks* list box, scroll to the right and notice that the PacificSky building block does not contain a description.
   d. Click the *PacificSky* building block in the list box.
   e. Click the Edit Properties button at the bottom of the dialog box.

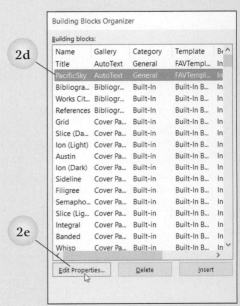

f. At the Modify Building Block dialog box, click in the *Name* text box and then type Address at the end of the name.

g. Click in the *Description* text box and then type Inserts the Pacific Sky name and address.

h. Click OK to close the dialog box.

i. At the message asking if you want to redefine the building block entry, click Yes.

j. Close the Building Blocks Organizer dialog box.

3. Edit the letterhead building block by completing the following steps:

a. Click the Quick Parts button in the Text group on the Insert tab, right-click the Family Adventure Vacations letterhead building block, and then click *Edit Properties* at the shortcut menu.

b. At the Modify Building Block dialog box, click in the *Name* text box and then type Letterhead at the end of the name.

c. Click in the *Description* text box and then type Inserts the Family Adventure Vacations letterhead including the company name and address.

d. Click OK to close the dialog box.

e. At the message asking if you want to redefine the building block entry, click Yes.

4. Close the document.

5. At the message that displays, click the Save button.

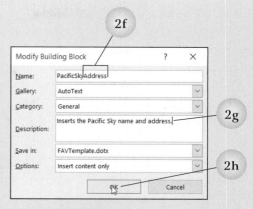

Tutorial ▶

Inserting a Custom Building Block

Inserting a Custom Building Block

Inserting a Custom Building Block

Any content saved as a building block can be inserted in a document using options at the Building Blocks Organizer dialog box. Some content can also be inserted using specific drop-down galleries. For example, insert a custom text box building block by clicking the Text Box button on the Insert tab and then clicking the text box at the drop-down gallery. Insert a custom header at the Header button drop-down gallery, a custom footer at the Footer button drop-down gallery, a custom cover page at the Cover Page button drop-down gallery, and so on.

Use the button drop-down gallery to specify where the custom building block content should be inserted in a document. To do this, display the button drop-down gallery, right-click the custom building block, and then click the location at the shortcut menu. For example, click the Insert tab, click the Quick Parts button, and then right-click the *FAVLetterhead* building block, and a shortcut menu displays, as shown in Figure 3.9.

Figure 3.9 Quick Parts Button Drop-Down Gallery Shortcut Menu

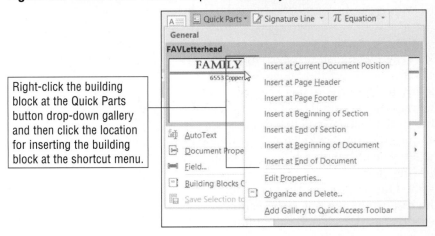

Right-click the building block at the Quick Parts button drop-down gallery and then click the location for inserting the building block at the shortcut menu.

Project 3c   Inserting Custom Building Blocks

1. Open File Explorer, navigate to your WL2C3 folder, and then double-click *FAVTemplate.dotx*.
2. At the blank document, click the *No Spacing* style in the Styles group on the Home tab and then change the font to Candara.
3. Insert the letterhead building block as a header by completing the following steps:
   a. Click the Insert tab.
   b. Click the Quick Parts button, right-click the *FAVLetterhead* building block, and then click the *Insert at Page Header* option at the shortcut menu.

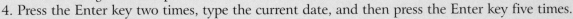

4. Press the Enter key two times, type the current date, and then press the Enter key five times.
5. Type Mrs. Jody Lancaster and then press the Enter key.
6. Insert the Pacific Sky Cruise Lines name and address building block by clicking the Quick Parts button, pointing to *AutoText*, and then clicking the *PacificSkyAddress* building block at the side menu.

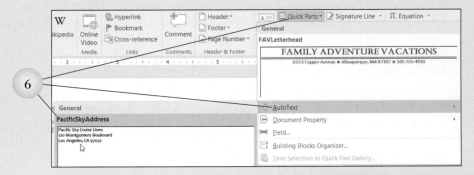

7. Press the Enter key and then insert a letter document by completing the following steps:
   a. Click the Object button arrow in the Text group on the Insert tab and then click *Text from File* at the drop-down list.
   b. At the Insert File dialog box, navigate to the WL2C3 folder on your storage medium and then double-click *PSLetter01.docx*.

8. With the insertion point positioned one double space below the last paragraph of text in the body of the letter, type Sincerely, and then press the Enter key four times.

9. Insert your name and title building block by clicking the Quick Parts button, pointing to *AutoText*, and then clicking the *Title* building block at the side menu.

10. Press the Enter key and then type 3-PSLtr01.docx.

11. Press the Enter key five times and then insert the custom text box you saved as a building block by completing the following steps:

   a. Click the Text Box button in the Text group on the Insert tab.

   b. Scroll to the end of the drop-down gallery and then click the *FAVTextBox* building block. (Your custom text box will display in the *General* section of the drop-down gallery.)

   c. Click in the document to deselect the text box.

12. Insert the custom footer you created by completing the following steps:

   a. Click the Insert tab.

   b. Click the Footer button in the Header & Footer group.

   c. Scroll to the end of the drop-down gallery and then click the *FAVFooter* building block. (Your custom footer will display in the *General* section.)

   d. Close the footer pane by double-clicking in the document.

13. Save the completed letter and name it **3-PSLtr01**.

14. Print and then close **3-PSLtr01.docx**.

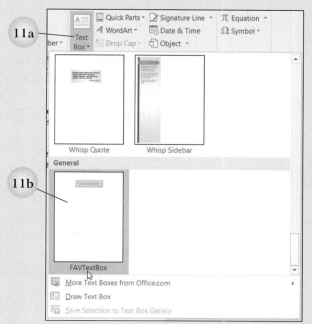

Check Your Work

Project 4 Create a Letter Document with Modified Building Blocks and Save Building Blocks to a Different Template 3 Parts

You will modify your custom building blocks and use them to prepare a business letter. You will also save building blocks to a different template, use the building blocks to format an announcement, and then delete your custom building blocks.

Preview Finished Project

Tutorial

Modifying and
Deleting Building
Blocks

Modifying a Custom Building Block

A building block can be inserted in a document, corrections or changes can be made to the building block, and then the building block can be saved with the same name or a different name. Save a building block with the same name when updating the building block to reflect any changes. Save the building block with a new name when using an existing building block as the foundation for creating a new building block.

To save a modified building block with the same name, insert the building block into the document and then make modifications. Select the building block data and then specify the gallery. At the Create New Building Block dialog box, type the original name and description and then click OK. At the confirmation message that displays, click Yes.

Inserting a Building Block Gallery as a Button on the Quick Access Toolbar

Quick Steps

Insert Building Block Gallery as a Button on Quick Access Toolbar
1. Click specific button.
2. Right-click building block.
3. Click *Add Gallery to Quick Access Toolbar.*

To make building blocks more accessible, insert a building block gallery as a button on the Quick Access Toolbar. To do this, right-click a building block and then click *Add Gallery to Quick Access Toolbar*. For example, to add the *Quick Part* gallery to the Quick Access Toolbar, click the Quick Parts button on the Insert tab, right-click a building block at the drop-down gallery, and then click *Add Gallery to Quick Access Toolbar*.

To remove a button from the Quick Access Toolbar, right-click the button and then click *Remove from Quick Access Toolbar* at the shortcut menu. Removing a button containing a building block gallery does not delete the building block.

Project 4a Modifying Building Blocks and Inserting Custom Building Blocks
as Buttons on the Quick Access Toolbar
Part 1 of 3

1. Open File Explorer, navigate to your WL2C3 folder, and then double-click ***FAVTemplate.dotx***.
2. Modify your name and title building block to reflect a title change by completing the following steps:
   a. At the blank document, click the Insert tab, click the Quick Parts button in the Text group, point to *AutoText*, and then click the *Title* building block at the side menu.
   b. Edit your title so it displays as *Senior Travel Consultant*.
   c. Select your name and title, click the Quick Parts button, point to *AutoText*, and then click the *Save Selection to AutoText Gallery* option.
   d. At the Create New Building Block dialog box, type Title in the *Name* text box.
   e. Click the *Save in* option box arrow and then click *FAVTemplate.dotx* at the drop-down list.
   f. Click OK.
   g. At the message asking if you want to redefine the building block entry, click Yes.
   h. With your name and title selected, press the Delete key to remove them from the document.

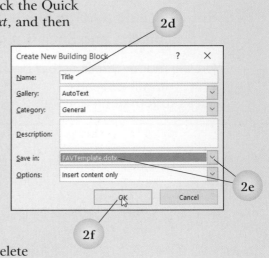

3. Since most of the correspondence you send to Pacific Sky Cruise Lines is addressed to Jody Lancaster, you decide to include her name at the beginning of the company name and address by completing the following steps:
   a. With the Insert tab active, click the Quick Parts button, point to *AutoText*, and then click the *PacificSkyAddress* building block at the side menu.
   b. Type Mrs. Jody Lancaster above the name of the cruise line.
   c. Select the name, company name, and address.
   d. Click the Quick Parts button, point to *AutoText*, and then click the *Save Selection to AutoText Gallery* option.
   e. At the Create New Building Block dialog box, type PacificSkyAddress (the original name) in the *Name* text box.
   f. Click the *Save in* option box arrow and then click *FAVTemplate.dotx* at the drop-down list.
   g. Click OK.
   h. At the message asking if you want to redefine the building block entry, click Yes.

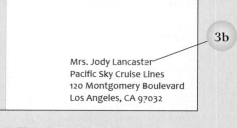

4. Press Ctrl + End and then add the FAVFooter building block to the Quick Part gallery by completing the following steps:
   a. Click the Footer button on the Insert tab, scroll down the drop-down gallery, and then click the *FAVFooter* custom building block.
   b. Press the Backspace key to delete the extra space below the footer and then press Ctrl + A to select the footer.
   c. Click the Insert tab, click the Quick Parts button, and then click *Save Selection to Quick Part Gallery*.
   d. At the Create New Building Block dialog box, type FAVFooter in the *Name* text box.
   e. Click the *Save in* option box arrow and then click *FAVTemplate.dotx* at the drop-down list.
   f. Click OK to close the Create New Building Block dialog box. (You now have the footer saved in the Footer gallery and Quick Part gallery.)
   g. Double-click in the document.

5. Insert the Quick Part gallery as a button on the Quick Access Toolbar by completing the following steps:
   a. Click the Insert tab, click the Quick Parts button, and then right-click one of your custom building blocks.
   b. At the shortcut menu, click the *Add Gallery to Quick Access Toolbar* option. (Notice the Explore Quick Parts button that appears at the right side of the Quick Access Toolbar.)

6. Insert the AutoText gallery as a button on the Quick Access Toolbar by completing the following steps:
   a. Click the Quick Parts button, point to *AutoText*, and then right-click one of your custom building blocks.
   b. At the shortcut menu, click the *Add Gallery to Quick Access Toolbar* option. (Notice the AutoText button that appears at the right side of the Quick Access Toolbar.)

7. Close the document without saving it. At the message that displays, click the Save button.
8. Create a business letter by completing the following steps:
   a. Use File Explorer to open a blank document based on **FAVTemplate.dotx** in the WL2C3 folder on your storage medium.
   b. Click the *No Spacing* style in the Styles group on the Home tab, and then change the font to Candara.
   c. Insert the FAVLetterhead building block as a page header.
   d. Press the Enter key two times, type today's date, and then press the Enter key four times.
   e. Insert the building block that includes Jody Lancaster's name as well as the cruise line name and address by clicking the AutoText button on the Quick Access Toolbar and then clicking the *PacificSkyAddress* building block at the drop-down list.
   f. Press the Enter key and then insert the file named **PSLetter02.docx** in the WL2C3 folder on your storage medium. *Hint: Do this with the Object button arrow in the Text group on the Insert tab.*
   g. Type Sincerely, and then press the Enter key four times.
   h. Click the AutoText button on the Quick Access Toolbar and then click the *Title* building block.
   i. Press the Enter key and then type 3-PSLtr02.docx.
   j. Insert the footer building block by clicking the Explore Quick Parts button on the Quick Access Toolbar, right-clicking *FAVFooter*, and then clicking *Insert at Page Footer* at the shortcut menu.

9. Save the completed letter and name it **3-PSLtr02**.
10. Print and then close **3-PSLtr02.docx**.
11. Use File Explorer to open a blank document based on your template **FAVTemplate.dotx**.
12. Click the AutoText button on the Quick Access Toolbar, press the Print Screen button on your keyboard, and then click in the document to remove the drop-down list.
13. At the blank document, click the Paste button. (This pastes the screen capture in your document.)
14. Print the document and then close it without saving it.
15. Remove the Explore Quick Parts button you added to the Quick Access Toolbar by right-clicking the Explore Quick Parts button and then clicking *Remove from Quick Access Toolbar* at the shortcut menu. Complete similar steps to remove the AutoText button from the Quick Access Toolbar. (The buttons will display dimmed if no documents are open.)

Check Your Work

Saving Building Blocks in a Different Template

Building blocks saved to a personal template are available only when a document is opened based on the template. To make building blocks available for all documents, save them in Building Block.dotx or Normal.dotm. Use the *Save in* option at the Create New Building Block or Modify Building Block dialog box to save building blocks to one of these two templates.

If an existing building block in a personal template is modified and saved in Normal.dotm or Building Block.dotx, the building block is no longer available in the personal template. It is available only in documents based on the default template Normal.dotm. To keep a building block in a personal template and also make it available for other documents, insert the building block content in the document, select the content, and then create a new building block.

Project 4b Saving Building Blocks in a Different Template

1. Use File Explorer to open a blank document based on your template **FAVTemplate.dotx**.
2. Create a new FAVLetterhead building block and save it in Building Block.dotx so it is available for all documents by completing the following steps:
   a. Click the Insert tab.
   b. Click the Quick Parts button and then click the *FAVLetterhead* building block to insert the content in the document.
   c. Select the letterhead (company name, address, and telephone number including the paragraph mark at the end of the line containing the address and telephone number).
   d. Click the Quick Parts button on the Insert tab and then click *Save Selection to Quick Part Gallery* at the drop-down list.
   e. At the Create New Building Block dialog box, type XXX-FAVLetterhead. (Type your initials in place of the *XXX*.)
   f. Make sure *Building Blocks.dotx* displays in the *Save in* option box and then click OK. (The FAVLetterhead building block is still available in your template FAVTemplate.dotx and the new XXX-FAVLetterhead building block is available in all documents, including documents based on FAVTemplate.dotx.)

   g. Delete the selected letterhead text.
3. Create a new FAVFooter building block and then save it in Building Blocks.dotx so it is available for all documents by completing the following steps:
   a. Click the Quick Parts button on the Insert tab and then click the *FAVFooter* building block to insert the content in the document.
   b. Select the footer text *"Making your travel dreams a reality"* and make sure you select the paragraph mark at the end of the text.
   c. Click the Quick Parts button on the Insert tab and then click *Save Selection to Quick Part Gallery* at the drop-down list.
   d. At the Create New Building Block dialog box, type XXX-FAVFooter. (Type your initials in place of the *XXX*.)
   e. Make sure *Building Blocks.dotx* displays in the *Save in* option box and then click OK.
4. Close the document without saving it.
5. Open **FAVContent.docx**.
6. Create a new FAVTextBox building block and save it in Building Blocks.dotx so it is available for all documents by completing the following steps:
   a. Select the text box by clicking the text box and then clicking the text box border.
   b. Click the Insert tab, click the Text Box button, and then click *Save Selection to Text Box Gallery* at the drop-down list.
   c. At the Create New Building Block dialog box, type XXX-FAVTextBox. (Type your initials in place of the *XXX*.)
   d. Make sure *Building Blocks.dotx* displays in the *Save in* option box and then click OK.

7. Close **FAVContent.docx**.
8. Insert in a document the building blocks you created by completing the following steps:
   a. Open **PSAnnounce.docx** and then save it with the name **3-PSAnnounce**.
   b. Insert the XXX-FAVLetterhead building block by clicking the Insert tab, clicking the Quick Parts button, right-clicking *XXX-FAVLetterhead* (where your initials display in place of the *XXX*), and then clicking *Insert at Page Header* at the shortcut menu.

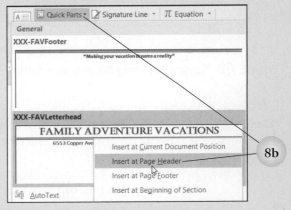

   c. Insert the XXX-FAVFooter building block by clicking the Quick Parts button, right-clicking *XXX-FAVFooter* (where your initials display in place of the *XXX*), and then clicking *Insert at Page Footer* at the shortcut menu.
   d. Press Ctrl + End to move the insertion point to the end of the document.
   e. Insert the XXX-FAVTextBox building block by clicking the Text Box button, scrolling down the drop-down gallery, and then clicking *XXX-FAVTextBox* (where your initials display in place of the *XXX*).
   f. Horizontally align the text box by clicking the Align button in the Arrange group on the Drawing Tools Format tab and then clicking *Distribute Horizontally* at the drop-down list.

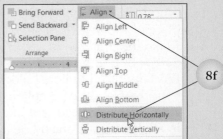

9. Save, print, and then close **3-PSAnnounce.docx**.
10. At the message that displays, click the Save button.

Check Your Work

Deleting a Building Block

A custom building block that is no longer needed can be deleted by displaying the Building Blocks Organizer dialog box, clicking the building block, and then clicking the Delete button. At the confirmation message that displays, click Yes.

Another method for deleting a custom building block is to right-click the building block at the drop-down gallery and then click the *Organize and Delete* option at the shortcut menu. This displays the Building Blocks Organizer dialog box with the building block selected. Click the Delete button and then click Yes at the confirmation message box.

1. At a blank document, delete the XXX-FAVLetterhead building block by completing the following steps:
   a. Click the Insert tab and then click the Quick Parts button in the Text group.
   b. Right-click the *XXX-FAVLetterhead* building block and then click *Organize and Delete* at the shortcut menu.

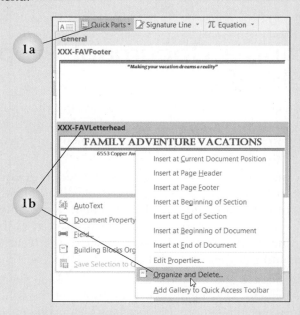

   c. At the Building Blocks Organizer dialog box with the building block selected, click the Delete button.
   d. At the message that displays asking if you are sure you want to delete the selected building block, click Yes.
   e. Close the Building Blocks Organizer dialog box.
2. Delete the XXX-FAVFooter building block by completing the following steps:
   a. Click the Quick Parts button, right-click the *XXX-FAVFooter* building block, and then click *Organize and Delete* at the shortcut menu.
   b. At the Building Blocks Organizer dialog box with the building block selected, click the Delete button.
   c. At the message asking if you are sure you want to delete the selected building block, click Yes.
   d. Close the Building Blocks Organizer dialog box.
3. Delete the *XXX-FAVTextBox* (in the Text Box gallery) by completing the following steps:
   a. Click the Text Box button in the Text group on the Insert tab.
   b. Scroll down the drop-down gallery to display your custom text box.
   c. Right-click your text box and then click *Organize and Delete* at the shortcut menu.
   d. At the Building Blocks Organizer dialog box with the building block selected, click the Delete button.
   e. At the message asking if you are sure you want to delete the selected building block, click Yes.
   f. Close the Building Blocks Organizer dialog box.
4. Close the document without saving it.

You will open a testing agreement document and then insert and update document properties and fields.

Preview Finished Project

Inserting a Document Property Placeholder

Click the Quick Parts button on the Insert tab and then point to *Document Property* at the drop-down list and a side menu displays with document property options. Click an option at this side menu and a document property placeholder is inserted in the document. Text can be typed in the placeholder.

If a document property placeholder is inserted in multiple locations in a document, updating one of the placeholders will automatically update all occurrences of that placeholder in the document. For example, in Project 5a, a Company document property placeholder is inserted in six locations in a document. The content of the first occurrence of the placeholder will be changed and the remaining placeholders will update to reflect the change.

Click the File tab and the Info backstage area displays containing information about the document. Document properties display at the right side of the Info backstage area, including information such as the document size, number of pages, title, and comments.

Project 5a Inserting Document Property Placeholders   Part 1 of 2

1. Open **TestAgrmnt.docx** and then save it with the name **3-TestAgrmnt**.
2. Select the first occurrence of *FP* in the document (in the first line of text after the title) and then insert a document property placeholder by completing the following steps:
   a. Click the Insert tab, click the Quick Parts button in the Text group, point to *Document Property*, and then click *Company* at the side menu.
   b. Type Frontier Productions in the company placeholder.
   c. Press the Right Arrow key to move the insertion point outside the company placeholder.
3. Select each remaining occurrence of *FP* in the document (it appears five more times) and insert the company document property placeholder. (The company name, *Frontier Productions,* will automatically be inserted in the placeholder.)

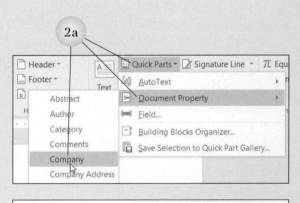

4. Press Ctrl + End to move the insertion point to the end of the document and then insert a comments document property placeholder by completing the following steps:

   a. Click the Quick Parts button, point to *Document Property*, and then click *Comments* at the side menu.

   b. Type First Draft in the comments placeholder.

   c. Press the Right Arrow key.

   d. Press Shift + Enter.

5. Click the File tab, make sure the *Info* option is selected, and then notice that the comment typed in the comments document property placeholder displays at the right side of the backstage area. Click the Back button to display the document.

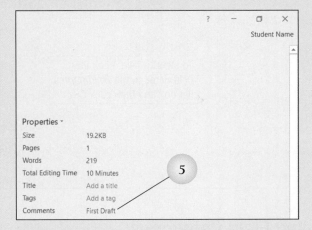

6. Save and then print **3-TestAgrmnt.docx**.

7. Click in the first occurrence of the company name *Frontier Productions* and then click the company placeholder tab. (This selects the company placeholder.)

8. Type Frontier Video Productions.

9. Press the Right Arrow key. (Notice that the other occurrences of the Company document property placeholder automatically updated to reflect the new name.)

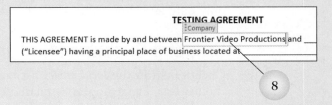

10. Save **3-TestAgrmnt.docx**.

Check Your Work

Tutorial

Inserting and Updating Fields

Inserting, Formatting, and Updating Fields

Quick Steps

Insert a Field
1. Click Insert tab.
2. Click Quick Parts button.
3. Click *Field* at drop-down list.
4. Click field.
5. Click OK.

Fields are placeholders for data that varies. Word provides buttons for many of the types of fields that can be inserted in a document as well as options at the Field dialog box, shown in Figure 3.10. This dialog box contains a list of all available fields. Just as the Building Blocks Organizer dialog box is a central location for building blocks, the Field dialog box is a central location for fields.

To display the Field dialog box, click the Insert tab, click the Quick Parts button in the Text group, and then click *Field* at the drop-down list. At the Field dialog box, click a field in the *Field names* list box and then click OK.

Figure 3.10 Field Dialog Box

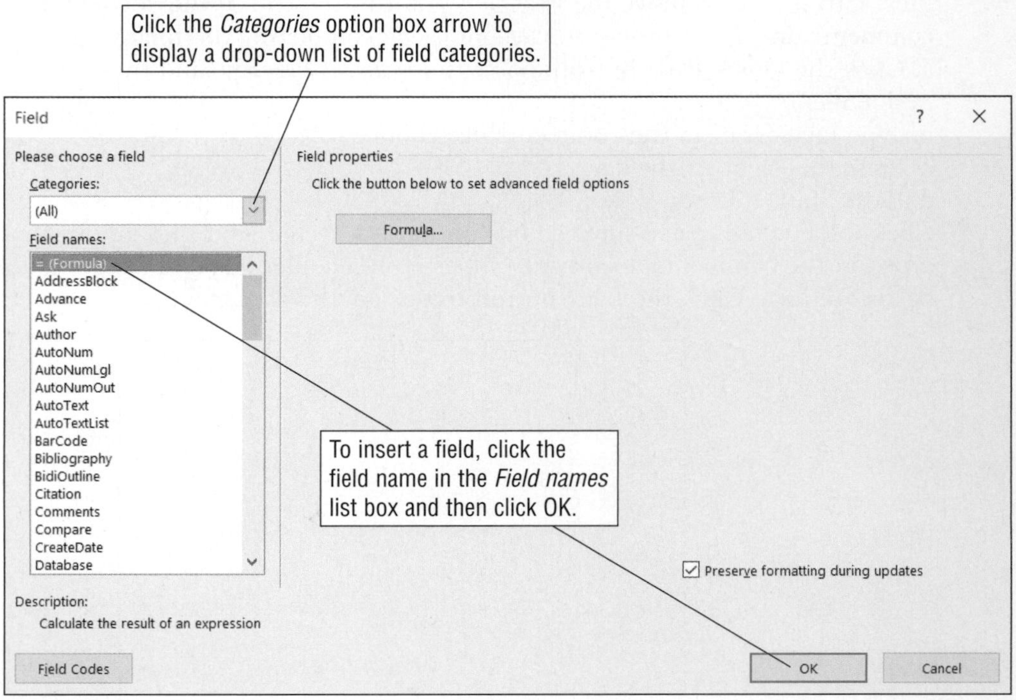

Click the *Categories* option box arrow to display a drop-down list of field categories.

To insert a field, click the field name in the *Field names* list box and then click OK.

Choosing Field Categories

All available fields display in the *Field names* list box at the Field dialog box. Narrow the list of fields to a specific category by clicking the *Categories* option box arrow and then clicking a specific category at the drop-down list. For example, to display only date and time fields, click the *Date and Time* category at the drop-down list.

Creating Custom Field Formats

Click a field in the *Field names* list box and a description of the field displays below the list box. Field properties related to the selected field also display in the dialog box. A custom field format can be created for some fields. For example, click the *NumWords* field in the *Field names* list box and custom formatting options display in the *Format* list box and the *Numeric format* list box.

By default, the *Preserve formatting during updates* check box contains a check mark. With this option active, the custom formatting specified for a field will be preserved if the field is updated.

Updating Fields

Quick Steps
Update a Field
1. Click field.
2. Click Update tab.
OR
1. Click field.
2. Press F9.
OR
1. Right-click field.
2. Click *Update Field*.

Some fields, such as the date and time field, update automatically when a document is opened. Other fields can be updated manually. A field can be updated manually by clicking the field and then clicking the Update tab; by clicking the field and then pressing the F9 function key; and by right-clicking the field and then clicking *Update Field* at the shortcut menu. Update all fields in a document (except headers, footers, and text boxes) by pressing Ctrl + A to select the document and then pressing the F9 function key.

1. With **3-TestAgrmnt.docx** open, press Ctrl + End to move the insertion point to the end of the document.
2. Type Current date and time:, press the spacebar, and then insert a field that inserts the current date and time by clicking the following steps:
   a. Click the Insert tab.
   b. Click the Quick Parts button and then click *Field* at the drop-down list.
   c. At the Field dialog box, click the *Categories* option box arrow and then click *Date and Time* at the drop-down list. (This displays only fields in the Date and Time category in the *Field names* list box.)
   d. Click *Date* in the *Field names* list box.
   e. Click the twelfth option in the *Date formats* list box (the option that will insert the date in figures followed by the time [hours and minutes]).
   f. Click OK to close the dialog box.
3. Press Shift + Enter, type File name and path:, press the spacebar, and then insert a field for the current file name with custom field formatting by completing the following steps:
   a. With the Insert tab active, click the Quick Parts button and then click *Field* at the drop-down list.
   b. At the Field dialog box, click the *Categories* option box arrow and then click *Document Information* at the drop-down list.
   c. Click *FileName* in the *Field names* list box.
   d. Click the *Uppercase* option in the *Format* list box.
   e. Click the *Add path to filename* check box to insert a check mark.

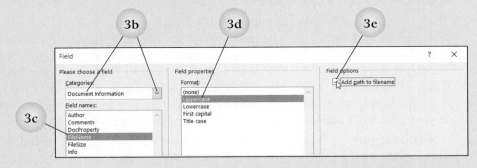

   f. Click OK to close the dialog box. (The current file name is inserted in the document in uppercase letters and includes the path to the file name.)
4. Insert a header and then insert a custom field in the header by completing the following steps:
   a. Click the Header button in the Header & Footer group and then click *Edit Header* at the drop-down list.
   b. In the header pane, press the Tab key two times. (This moves the insertion point to the right tab at the right margin.)

c. Click the Quick Parts button in the Insert group on the Header & Footer Tools Design tab and then click *Field* at the drop-down list.

d. At the Field dialog box, click the *Categories* option box arrow and then click *Date and Time* at the drop-down list.

e. Click in the *Date formats* text box and then type MMMM yyyy. (This tells Word to insert the month as text followed by the four-digit year.)

f. Click OK to close the dialog box.

g. Double-click in the document.

5. Update the time in the date and time field at the end of the document by clicking the date and time and then clicking the Update tab.

6. Save, print, and then close **3-TestAgrmnt.docx**.

4d   **4e**

Field	
Please choose a field	Field properties
Categories:	Date formats:
Date and Time	MMMM yyyy
Field names:	10/22/2018
CreateDate	Monday, October 22, 2018
Date	October 22, 2018
EditTime	10/22/18
PrintDate	2018-10-22
SaveDate	22-Oct-18
Time	10.22.2018
	Oct. 22, 18
	22 October 2018

Check Your Work

Project 6   Customize the Quick Access Toolbar and Ribbon   4 Parts

You will open a document, customize the Quick Access Toolbar by inserting and removing buttons, customize the ribbon by inserting a new tab, and export ribbon and Quick Access Toolbar customizations.

Preview Finished Project

Tutorial

Customizing the Quick Access Toolbar

 Customize Quick Access Toolbar

Quick Steps
Customize the Quick Access Toolbar
1. Click Customize Quick Access Toolbar button.
2. Insert check mark before each button to insert.
3. Remove check mark before each button to remove.

Customizing the Quick Access Toolbar

The Quick Access Toolbar contains buttons for some of the most commonly performed tasks. By default, the toolbar contains the Save, Undo, and Redo buttons. Some basic buttons can be easily inserted on or removed from the Quick Access Toolbar with options at the Customize Quick Access Toolbar drop-down list. Display this list by clicking the Customize Quick Access Toolbar button at the right side of the toolbar. Insert a check mark before each button to be inserted on the toolbar and remove the check mark from each button to be removed from the toolbar.

The Customize Quick Access Toolbar button drop-down list includes an option for moving the location of the Quick Access Toolbar. By default, the Quick Access Toolbar is positioned above the ribbon. To move the toolbar below the ribbon, click the *Show Below the Ribbon* option at the drop-down list.

Buttons or commands from a tab can be inserted on the Quick Access Toolbar. To do this, click the tab, right-click the button or command, and then click *Add to Quick Access Toolbar* at the shortcut menu.

1. Open **InterfaceApps.docx** and then save it with the name **3-InterfaceApps**.
2. Insert the New button on the Quick Access Toolbar by clicking the Customize Quick Access Toolbar button at the right of the toolbar and then clicking *New* at the drop-down list.
3. Insert the Open button on the Quick Access Toolbar by clicking the Customize Quick Access Toolbar button and then clicking *Open* at the drop-down list.
4. Click the New button on the Quick Access Toolbar. (This displays a new blank document.)
5. Close the document.
6. Click the Open button on the Quick Access Toolbar to display the Open backstage area.
7. Press the Esc key to return to the document.
8. Move the Quick Access Toolbar by clicking the Customize Quick Access Toolbar button and then clicking *Show Below the Ribbon* at the drop-down list.
9. Move the Quick Access Toolbar back to the default position by clicking the Customize Quick Access Toolbar button and then clicking *Show Above the Ribbon* at the drop-down list.
10. Insert the Margins and the Themes buttons on the Quick Access Toolbar by completing the following steps:
    a. Click the Layout tab.
    b. Right-click the Margins button in the Page Setup group and then click *Add to Quick Access Toolbar* at the shortcut menu.

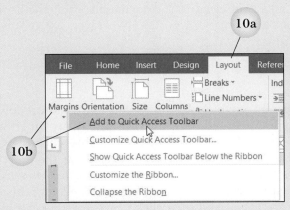

   c. Click the Design tab.
   d. Right-click the Themes button in the Themes group and then click *Add to Quick Access Toolbar* at the shortcut menu.
11. Change the top margin by completing the following steps:
    a. Click the Margins button on the Quick Access Toolbar and then click *Custom Margins* at the drop-down list.
    b. At the Page Setup dialog box, change the top margin to 1.5 inches and then click OK.
12. Change the theme by clicking the Themes button on the Quick Access Toolbar and then clicking *View* at the drop-down gallery.

13. Create a screenshot of the Quick Access Toolbar by completing the following steps:
    a. Click the New button on the Quick Access Toolbar. (This displays a new blank document.)
    b. Click the Insert tab, click the Screenshot button in the Illustrations group, and then click *Screen Clipping* at the drop-down list.

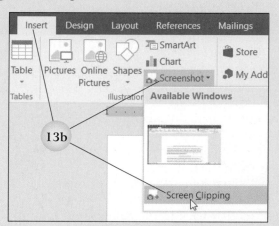

    c. In a few moments, **3-InterfaceApps.docx** displays in a dimmed manner. Using the mouse, drag down and to the right from the upper left corner of the screen to capture the Quick Access Toolbar and then release the mouse button.

    d. With the screenshot image inserted in the document, print the document and then close the document without saving it.
14. Save **3-InterfaceApps.docx**.

Check Your Work

Quick Steps

Add Buttons to the Quick Access Toolbar from the Word Options Dialog Box

1. Click Customize Quick Access Toolbar button.
2. Click *More Commands* at drop-down list.
3. Click desired command in left list box.
4. Click Add button.
5. Click OK.

The Customize Quick Access Toolbar button drop-down list contains 11 of the most commonly used buttons. However, many other buttons can be inserted on the toolbar. To display the buttons available, click the Customize Quick Access Toolbar button and then click *More Commands* at the drop-down list. This displays the Word Options dialog box with *Quick Access Toolbar* selected in the left panel, as shown in Figure 3.11. Another method for displaying this dialog box is to click the File tab, click *Options*, and then click *Quick Access Toolbar* in the left panel of the Word Options dialog box.

To reset the Quick Access Toolbar to the default (Save, Undo, and Redo buttons), click the Reset button in the lower right corner of the dialog box and then click *Reset only Quick Access Toolbar* at the drop-down list. At the message that displays asking if the Quick Access Toolbar shared between all documents should be restored to its default contents, click Yes.

Figure 3.11 Word Options Dialog Box with *Quick Access Toolbar* Selected

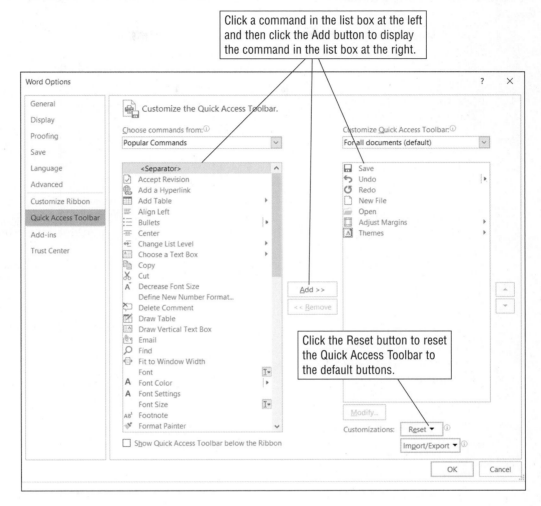

Click a command in the list box at the left and then click the Add button to display the command in the list box at the right.

Click the Reset button to reset the Quick Access Toolbar to the default buttons.

The Quick Access Toolbar can be customized for all documents or for a specific document. To customize the toolbar for the currently open document, display the Word Options dialog box with *Quick Access Toolbar* selected, click the *Customize Quick Access Toolbar* option box arrow, and then click the *For (document name)* option, where the name of the currently open document displays.

The *Choose commands from* option has a default setting of *Popular Commands*. At this setting, the list box below the option displays only a portion of all the commands available to insert as buttons on the Quick Access Toolbar. To display all the commands available, click the *Choose commands from* option box arrow and then click *All Commands*. The drop-down list also contains options for specifying commands that are not currently available on the ribbon, as well as commands on the File tab and various other tabs.

To insert a button on the Quick Access Toolbar, click the command in the list box at the left side of the dialog box and then click the Add button between the two list boxes. Continue inserting buttons and then click OK to close the dialog box.

1. With **3-InterfaceApps.docx** open, reset the Quick Access Toolbar by completing the following steps:
   a. Click the Customize Quick Access Toolbar button at the right of the Quick Access Toolbar and then click *More Commands* at the drop-down list.
   b. At the Word Options dialog box, click the Reset button at the bottom of the dialog box and then click *Reset only Quick Access Toolbar* at the drop-down list.

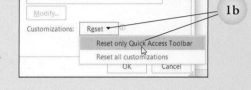

   c. At the message asking if you are sure you want to restore the Quick Access Toolbar shared between all documents to its default contents, click Yes.
   d. Click OK to close the dialog box.
2. Insert buttons on the Quick Access Toolbar for the currently open document by completing the following steps:
   a. Click the Customize Quick Access Toolbar button and then click *More Commands*.
   b. At the Word Options dialog box, click the *Customize Quick Access Toolbar* option box arrow and then click *For 3-InterfaceApps.docx* at the drop-down list.

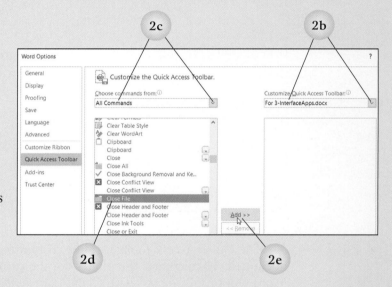

   c. Click the *Choose commands from* option box arrow and then click *All Commands*.
   d. Scroll down the list box and then click the *Close File* command. (Commands are listed in alphabetical order.)
   e. Click the Add button between the two list boxes.
   f. Scroll up the list box and then click *Add a Footer*.
   g. Click the Add button.
   h. Click OK to close the dialog box.
   i. Check the Quick Access Toolbar and notice that the two buttons display along with the default buttons.
3. Insert a footer by completing the following steps:
   a. Click the Add a Footer button on the Quick Access Toolbar.
   b. Click *Integral* at the drop-down list.
   c. Select the name in the footer and then type your first and last names.
   d. Double-click in the document.
4. Save and then print **3-InterfaceApps.docx**.
5. Close the document by clicking the Close button on the Quick Access Toolbar.

Check Your Work

Customizing the Ribbon

Just as the Quick Access Toolbar can be customized, the ribbon can be customized by creating a new tab and inserting groups with buttons on the tab. To customize the ribbon, click the File tab and then click *Options*. At the Word Options dialog box, click *Customize Ribbon* in the left panel and the dialog box displays as shown in Figure 3.12.

With options at the *Choose commands from* drop-down list, choose to display only popular commands, which is the default, or choose to display all commands, commands not on the ribbon, and all tabs or commands on the File tab, main tabs, tool tabs, and custom tabs and groups. The commands in the list box vary depending on the option selected at the *Choose commands from* option drop-down list. Click the *Customize the Ribbon* option box arrow and a drop-down list displays with options for customizing all tabs, only main tabs, or only tool tabs. By default, *Main Tabs* is selected.

Figure 3.12 Word Options Dialog Box with *Customize Ribbon* Selected

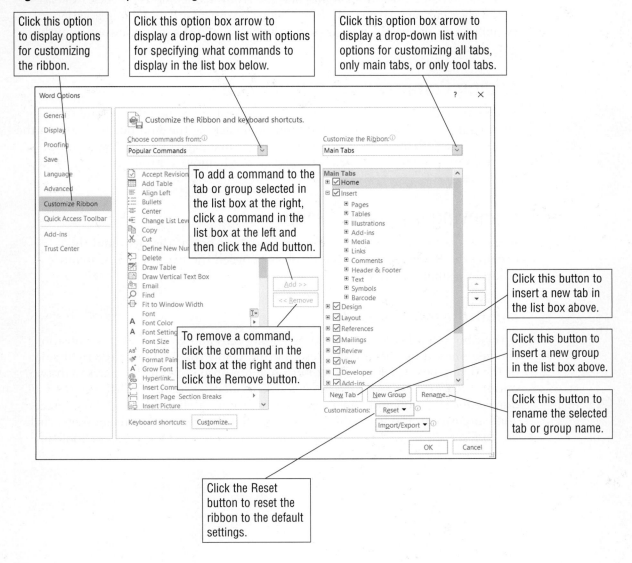

Creating a New Tab

Add a command to an existing tab or create a new tab and then add commands in groups on it. To create a new tab, click the tab name in the list box at the right side of the Word Options dialog box that will precede the new tab and then click the New Tab button below the list box. This inserts a new tab in the list box along with a new group below the new tab. Move the new tab up or down in the list box by clicking the new tab and then clicking the Move Up or Move Down button. Both buttons display to the right of the list box.

Renaming a Tab and Group

Rename a tab by clicking the tab in the list box and then clicking the Rename button below the list box at the right. At the Rename dialog box, type a new name for the tab and then click OK. The Rename dialog box also can be displayed by right-clicking the tab name and then clicking *Rename* at the shortcut menu.

Complete similar steps to rename a group. Click the group name and then click the Rename button (or right-click the group name and then click *Rename* at the shortcut menu) and a Rename dialog box displays containing a variety of symbols. Use the symbols to identify new buttons in the group, rather than the group name.

Adding Commands to a Tab Group

Add commands to a tab by clicking the group name on the tab, clicking the command in the list box at the left, and then clicking the Add button between the two list boxes. Remove commands in a similar manner. Click the command to be removed from the tab group and then click the Remove button between the two list boxes.

Removing a Tab and Group

Remove a tab by clicking the tab name in the list box at the right and then clicking the Remove button that displays between the two list boxes. Remove a group in a similar manner.

Resetting the Ribbon

If the ribbon has been customized by adding tabs and groups, all customizations can be removed by clicking the Reset button below the list box at the right side of the dialog box. Click the Reset button and a drop-down list displays with two options: *Reset only selected Ribbon tab* and *Reset all customizations*. Click the *Reset all customizations* option and a message displays asking if all ribbon and Quick Access Toolbar customizations for this program should be deleted. At this message, click Yes to reset all the customizations to the ribbon and the Quick Access Toolbar.

1. Open **3-InterfaceApps.docx** and then add a new tab and group by completing the following steps:
   a. Click the File tab and then click *Options*.
   b. At the Word Options dialog box, click *Customize Ribbon* in the left panel.
   c. Click *View* in the list box at the right side of the dialog box. (Do not click the check box before *View*.)
   d. Click the New Tab button below the list box. (This inserts a new tab below *View*.)

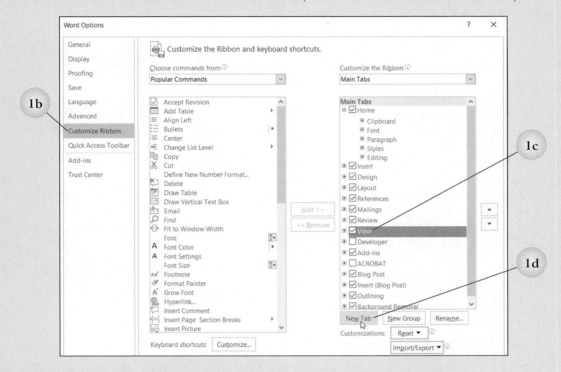

2. Rename the tab and group by completing the following steps:
   a. Click *New Tab (Custom)*. (Do not click the check box.)
   b. Click the Rename button below the list box.
   c. At the Rename dialog box, type your initials and then click OK.
   d. Click *New Group (Custom)* below your initials tab.
   e. Click the Rename button.
   f. At the Rename dialog box, type IP Movement and then click OK. (Use *IP* to stand for *insertion point*.)

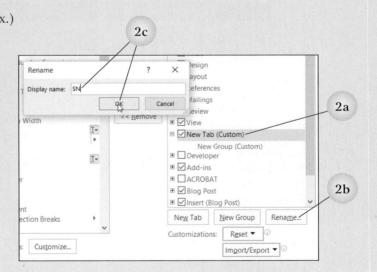

3. Add buttons to the IP Movement (Custom) group by completing the following steps:
   a. Click *IP Movement (Custom)* in the list box at the right side.
   b. Click the *Choose commands from* option box arrow and then click *Commands Not in the Ribbon* at the drop-down list.
   c. Scroll down the list box at the left side of the dialog box (which displays alphabetically), click the *End of Document* command, and then click the Add button. (This inserts the command below the *IP Movement (Custom)* group name.)
   d. With the *End of Line* command selected in the list box at the left side of the dialog box, click the Add button.
   e. Scroll down the list box at the left side of the dialog box, click the *Page Down* command, and then click the Add button.
   f. Click the *Page Up* command in the list box and then click the Add button.
   g. Scroll down the list box, click the *Start of Document* command, and then click the Add button.
   h. With the *Start of Line* command selected in the list box, click the Add button.
4. Click OK to close the Word Options dialog box.
5. Move the insertion point in the document by completing the following steps:
   a. Click the tab containing your initials.
   b. Click the End of Document button in the IP Movement group on the tab.
   c. Click the Start of Document button in the IP Movement group.
   d. Click the End of Line button.
   e. Click the Start of Line button.

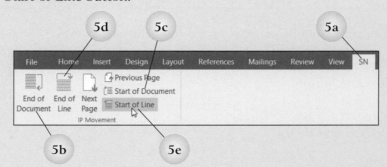

6. Create a screenshot of the ribbon with the tab containing your initials the active tab by completing the following steps:
   a. Make sure your tab is active and then press Ctrl + N to display a new blank document.
   b. Click the Insert tab, click the Screenshot button in the Illustrations group, and then click *Screen Clipping* at the drop-down list.

c. In a few moments, the **3-InterfaceApps.docx** document displays in a dimmed manner. Using the mouse, drag from the upper left corner of the screen down and to the right to capture the Quick Access Toolbar and the buttons on the tab containing your initials and then release the mouse button.

d. With the screenshot image inserted in the document, print the document and then close the document without saving it.

7. Reset the Quick Access Toolbar and ribbon by completing the following steps:
   a. Click the File tab and then click *Options*.
   b. At the Word Options dialog box, click *Customize Ribbon* in the left panel.
   c. Click the Reset button below the list box at the right side of the dialog box and then click *Reset all customizations* at the drop-down list.

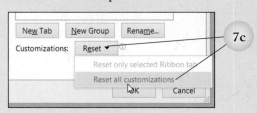

   d. At the message asking if you want to delete all the ribbon and Quick Access Toolbar customizations, click Yes.
   e. Click OK to close the Word Options dialog box. (The buttons you added to the Quick Access Toolbar will display while this document is open.)

8. Save **3-InterfaceApps.docx**.

Check Your Work

Quick Steps

Export Customizations
1. Click File tab.
2. Click *Options*.
3. Click *Customize Ribbon*.
4. Click Import/Export button.
5. Click *Export all customizations*.
6. At File Save dialog box, navigate to folder.
7. Click in *File name* text box.
8. Type name.
9. Press Enter.

Import Customizations
1. Click File tab.
2. Click *Options*.
3. Click *Customize Ribbon* or *Quick Access Toolbar*.
4. Click Import/Export button.
5. Click *Import customization file*.
6. At File Open dialog box, navigate to folder.
7. Double-click file.
8. Click Yes.

Importing and Exporting Customizations

If the ribbon and/or Quick Access Toolbar are customized, the customizations can be exported to a file and then that file can be used on other computers. To export the customized ribbon and/or Quick Access Toolbar, display the Word Options dialog box with *Customize Ribbon* or *Quick Access Toolbar* selected in the left panel, click the Import/Export button that displays below the list box at the right side of the dialog box, and then click *Export all customizations* at the drop-down list. At the File Save dialog box that displays, navigate to the desired folder, type a name for the file in the *File name* text box, and then press the Enter key or click the Save button. By default, Word saves the file type as *Exported Office UI file (*.exportedUI)* with the *.exportedUI* file extension.

To import a ribbon and Quick Access Toolbar customization file, display the Word Options dialog box with *Customize Ribbon* or *Quick Access Toolbar* selected in the left panel, click the Import/Export button, and then click *Import customization file* at the drop-down list. At the File Open dialog box, navigate to the folder containing the customization file and then double-click the file. (The file name will display with the *.exportedUI* file extension.) At the message that displays asking if all existing ribbon and Quick Access Toolbar customizations for this program should be replaced, click Yes.

1. With **3-InterfaceApps.docx** open, export your ribbon and Quick Access Toolbar customizations to a file by completing the following steps:
   a. Click the File tab and then click *Options*.
   b. Click *Customize Ribbon* in the left panel at the Word Options dialog box.
   c. Click the Import/Export button that displays below the list box at the right side of the dialog box and then click *Export all customizations* at the drop-down list.

   d. At the File Save dialog box, navigate to your WL2C3 folder.
   e. Click in the *File name* text box. (This selects the file name.)
   f. Type CustomRibbon&QAT and then press the Enter key.
2. Reset the Quick Access Toolbar and ribbon by completing the following steps:
   a. Click the Reset button that displays below the list box at the right side of the dialog box and then click *Reset all customizations* at the drop-down list.
   b. At the message asking if you want to delete all ribbon and Quick Access Toolbar customizations, click Yes.
   c. Click OK to close the Word Options dialog box.
3. Save and then close **3-InterfaceApps.docx**.

Chapter Summary

- Words can be added to AutoCorrect during a spelling check and at the AutoCorrect dialog box. Display the AutoCorrect dialog box by clicking the File tab, clicking *Options*, clicking *Proofing*, and then clicking the AutoCorrect Options button.

- Display the AutoCorrect Exceptions dialog box by clicking the Exceptions button at the AutoCorrect dialog box with the AutoCorrect tab selected. Specify AutoCorrect exceptions at this dialog box.

- Use the AutoCorrect Options button, which displays when the mouse pointer is hovered over corrected text, to change corrected text back to the original spelling, stop automatically correcting specific text, or display the AutoCorrect dialog box.

- The AutoCorrect dialog box contains several symbols that can be inserted in a document by typing specific text or characters.

- A symbol can be inserted from the Symbol dialog box into the AutoCorrect dialog box. To do this, display the Symbol dialog box, click the specific symbol, and then click the AutoCorrect button.

- When typing text, control what Word formats automatically with options at the AutoCorrect dialog box with the AutoFormat As You Type tab selected.

- Word provides a number of predesigned building blocks that can be used to help build a document.

- Insert building blocks at the Building Blocks Organizer dialog box. Display the dialog box by clicking the Quick Parts button on the Insert tab and then clicking *Building Blocks Organizer* at the drop-down list. Sort building blocks in the dialog box by clicking the column heading.

- Content can be saved as building blocks to specific galleries, such as the Text Box, Header, Footer, and Cover Page galleries.

- Save content to the AutoText gallery by selecting the content, clicking the Insert tab, clicking the Quick Parts button, pointing to *AutoText*, and then clicking the *Save Selection to AutoText Gallery* option.

- Save content to the Quick Part gallery by selecting the content, clicking the Insert tab, clicking the Quick Parts button, and then clicking *Save Selection to Quick Part Gallery* at the drop-down gallery.

- By default, building block content is saved in one of two templates, either Building Block.dotx or Normal.dotm, depending on the gallery selected. Change where a building block is saved with the *Save in* option box at the Create New Building Block dialog box.

- Create and save a personal template to the Custom Office Templates folder by changing the *Save as type* option at the Save As dialog box to *Word Template (*.dotx)*, typing a name for the template, and then clicking the Save button.

- Open a personal template from the Custom Office Templates folder by displaying the New backstage area, clicking the *PERSONAL* option, and then clicking the personal template thumbnail.

- A personal template can be saved to a location other than the Custom Office Templates folder. To open a document based on a personal template that is saved in a location other than the Custom Office Templates folder, open File Explorer, navigate to the folder containing the personal template, and then double-click the template.

- Edit a building block with options at the Modify Building Block dialog box. Display this dialog box by displaying the Building Blocks Organizer dialog box, clicking the building block, and then clicking the Edit Properties button.

- Insert a custom building block from a gallery using a button by clicking the specific button (such as the Text Box, Header, Footer, or Cover Page button), scrolling down the drop-down gallery, and then clicking the custom building block near the end of the gallery.

- Insert a custom building block saved to the AutoText gallery by clicking the Insert tab, clicking the Quick Parts button, pointing to *AutoText*, and then clicking the building block at the side menu.

- Insert a custom building block saved to the Quick Part gallery by clicking the Insert tab, clicking the Quick Parts button, and then clicking the building block at the drop-down list.

- A building block gallery can be inserted as a button on the Quick Access Toolbar by clicking a button, such as the Quick Parts button, right-clicking a building block and then clicking *Add Gallery to Quick Access Toolbar* at the shortcut menu.

- Remove a button from the Quick Access Toolbar by right-clicking the button and then clicking *Remove from Quick Access Toolbar* at the shortcut menu.

- Delete a building block at the Building Blocks Organizer dialog box by clicking the building block, clicking the Delete button, and then clicking Yes at the confirmation question.

- Insert a document property placeholder by clicking the Insert tab, clicking the Quick Parts button, pointing to *Document Property*, and then clicking the document property placeholder at the side menu.

- Fields are placeholders for data and can be inserted with options at the Field dialog box, which is a central location for all the fields provided by Word. Display the Field dialog box by clicking the Quick Parts button on the Insert tab and then clicking *Field*.

- Some fields in a document update automatically when a document is opened. A field can also be updated manually by clicking the field and then clicking the Update tab, by pressing the F9 function key, or by right-clicking the field and then clicking *Update Field*.

- Customize the Quick Access Toolbar with options from the Customize Quick Access Toolbar button drop-down list and options at the Word Options dialog box with *Quick Access Toolbar* selected.

- Insert a button or command on the Quick Access Toolbar by right-clicking the button or command and then clicking *Add to Quick Access Toolbar* at the shortcut menu.

- Use options at the Word Options dialog box with *Quick Access Toolbar* selected to display all the options and buttons available for adding to the Quick Access Toolbar and to reset the Quick Access Toolbar. The Quick Access Toolbar can be customized for all documents or for a specific document.

- Use options at the Word Options dialog box with *Customize Ribbon* selected to add a new tab and group, rename a tab or group, add a command to a new group, remove a command from a tab group, and reset the ribbon.

- Export a file containing customizations to the ribbon and/or Quick Access Toolbar with the Import/Export button at the Word Options dialog box with *Customize Ribbon* or *Quick Access Toolbar* selected.

Commands Review

FEATURE	RIBBON TAB, GROUP/OPTION	BUTTON, OPTION	KEYBOARD SHORTCUT
AutoCorrect dialog box	File, *Options*	*Proofing*, AutoCorrect Options	
Building Blocks Organizer dialog box	Insert, Text	, *Building Blocks Organizer*	
Create New Building Block dialog box	Insert, Text	, *Save Selection to Quick Part Gallery*	Alt + F3
Document Property side menu	Insert, Text	, *Document Property*	
Field dialog box	Insert, Text	, *Field*	
Word Options dialog box	File, *Options*		

Microsoft®

Word
Customizing Themes, Creating Macros, and Navigating in a Document

CHAPTER

4

Performance Objectives

Upon successful completion of Chapter 4, you will be able to:

1 Create custom theme colors, theme fonts, and theme effects

2 Save a custom theme

3 Apply, edit, and delete custom themes

4 Reset the template theme

5 Apply styles and modify existing styles

6 Record, run, and delete macros

7 Assign a macro to a keyboard command

8 Navigate in a document using the Navigation pane, bookmarks, hyperlinks, and cross-references

9 Insert hyperlinks to a location in the same document, a different document, a file in another program, and an email address

Precheck

Check your current skills to help focus your study.

The Microsoft Office suite offers themes that provide consistent formatting and help create documents with a professional and polished look. Apply formatting with the themes provided by Office or create custom themes. Word provides a number of predesigned styles, grouped into style sets, for applying consistent formatting to text in documents. Word also allows you to build macros to automate the formatting of a document.

In this chapter, you will learn how to customize themes; how to modify an existing style; how to record and run macros; and how to insert hyperlinks, bookmarks, and cross-references to provide additional information for readers and to allow for more efficient navigation within a document.

Data Files

Before beginning chapter work, copy the WL2C4 folder to your storage medium and then make WL2C4 the active folder.

SNAP

If you are a SNAP user, launch the Precheck and Tutorials from your Assignments page.

Project 1 **Apply Custom Themes to Company Documents**   **5 Parts**

You will create custom theme colors and theme fonts and then apply theme effects. You will save the changes as a custom theme, which you will apply to a company services document and a company security document.

Preview Finished Project

Customizing Themes

A document created in Word is based on the template Normal.dotm. This template provides a document with default layout, formatting, styles, and themes. The default template provides a number of built-in or predesigned themes. Some of these built-in themes have been used in previous chapters to apply colors, fonts, and effects to content in documents. The same built-in themes are available in Microsoft Word, Excel, Access, PowerPoint, and Outlook. Because the same themes are available across these applications, business files—such as documents, workbooks, databases, and presentations—can be branded with a consistent and professional appearance.

Hint Every document created in Word 2016 has a theme applied to it.

A theme is a combination of theme colors, theme fonts, and theme effects. Within a theme, any of these three elements can be changed with the additional buttons in the Document Formatting group on the Design tab. Apply one of the built-in themes or create a custom theme. A custom theme will display in the *Custom* section of the Themes drop-down gallery. To create a custom theme, change the theme colors, theme fonts, and/or theme effects.

 Themes

 Colors

 Fonts

The Themes, Colors, and Fonts buttons in the Document Formatting group on the Design tab display representations of the current theme. For example, the Themes button displays an uppercase and lowercase A with colored squares below it. When the theme colors are changed, the changes are reflected in the small colored squares on the Themes button and the four squares on the Colors button. If the theme fonts are changed, the letters on the Themes button and the Fonts button reflect the change.

Creating Custom Theme Colors

Tutorial

Creating and Applying Custom Theme Colors

Quick Steps

Create Custom Theme Colors
1. Click Design tab.
2. Click Colors button.
3. Click *Customize Colors*.
4. Type name for custom theme colors.
5. Change background, accent, and hyperlink colors.
6. Click Save button.

To create custom theme colors, click the Design tab, click the Colors button, and then click *Customize Colors* at the drop-down gallery. This displays the Create New Theme Colors dialog box, similar to the one shown in Figure 4.1. Type a name for the custom theme colors in the *Name* text box and then change colors. Theme colors contain four text and background colors, six accent colors, and two hyperlink colors, as shown in the *Theme colors* section of the dialog box. Change a color in the list box by clicking the color button at the right side of the color option and then clicking a color at the color palette.

After making all the changes to the colors, click the Save button. This saves the custom theme colors and also applies the color changes to the active document. Display the custom theme by clicking the Colors button. The custom theme will display at the top of the drop-down gallery in the *Custom* section.

Figure 4.1 Create New Theme Colors Dialog Box

Type a name for the custom theme in the *Name* text box.

Click the Reset button to reset the colors back to the defult.

Change a theme color by clicking the color button and then clicking a color at the drop-down palette.

Resetting Custom Theme Colors

If changes have been made to colors at the Create New Theme Colors dialog box, the colors can be reset to the default colors by clicking the Reset button in the lower left corner of the dialog box. Clicking this button restores the colors to the default Office theme colors.

Project 1a Creating Custom Theme Colors   Part 1 of 5

Note: If you are running Word 2016 on a computer connected to a network in a public environment, such as a school, you may need to complete all five parts of Project 1 during the same session. Network system software may delete your custom themes when you exit Word. Check with your instructor.

1. At a blank document, click the Design tab.
2. Click the Colors button in the Document Formatting group and then click *Customize Colors* at the drop-down gallery.
3. At the Create New Theme Colors dialog box, click the color button to the right of the *Text/Background - Light 1* option and then click the *Dark Red* color (first option in the *Standard Colors* section).
4. Click the color button to the right of the *Accent 1* option and then click the *Yellow* color (fourth option in the *Standard Colors* section).

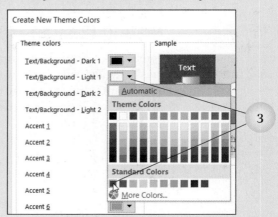

---

5. You decide that you do not like the colors you have chosen and want to start over. To do this, click the Reset button in the lower left corner of the dialog box.
6. Click the color button to the right of the *Text/Background - Dark 2* option and then click the *Blue* color (eighth option in the *Standard Colors* section).
7. Change the color for the *Accent 1* option by completing the following steps:
   a. Click the color button to the right of the *Accent 1* option.
   b. Click the *More Colors* option below the color palette.
   c. At the Colors dialog box, click the Standard tab.
   d. Click the dark green color, as shown below.
   e. Click OK to close the dialog box.

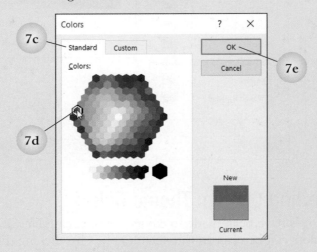

8. Save the custom colors by completing the following steps:
   a. Select the current text in the *Name* text box.
   b. Type your first and last names.
   c. Click the Save button.
9. Close the document without saving it.

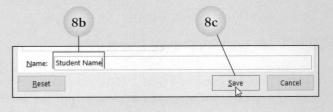

Tutorial

Creating and Applying Custom Theme Fonts

Creating Custom Fonts

To create a custom theme font, click the Design tab, click the Fonts button, and then click *Customize Fonts* at the drop-down gallery. This displays the Create New Theme Fonts dialog box. At this dialog box, choose a font for headings and a font for body text. Type a name for the custom fonts in the *Name* text box and then click the Save button.

Quick Steps

Create Custom Fonts
1. Click Design tab.
2. Click Fonts button.
3. Click *Customize Fonts*.
4. Choose fonts.
5. Type name for custom theme fonts.
6. Click Save button.

1. At a blank document, click the Design tab.
2. Click the Fonts button in the Document Formatting group and then click the *Customize Fonts* option at the drop-down gallery.
3. At the Create New Theme Fonts dialog box, click the *Heading font* option box arrow, scroll up the drop-down list, and then click *Arial*.
4. Click the *Body font* option box arrow, scroll down the drop-down list, and then click *Cambria*.
5. Save the custom fonts by completing the following steps:
    a. Select the current text in the *Name* text box.
    b. Type your first and last names.
    c. Click the Save button.
6. Close the document without saving it.

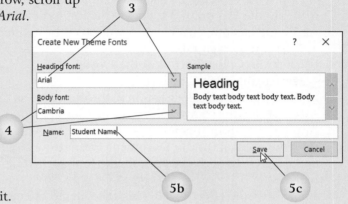

Applying Custom Theme Colors and Fonts

Apply custom theme colors to a document by clicking the Colors button in the Document Formatting group on the Design tab and then clicking the custom theme colors option at the top of the drop-down gallery in the *Custom* section. Complete similar steps to apply custom theme fonts.

Applying Theme Effects

The options in the Theme Effects button drop-down gallery apply sets of line and fill effects to the graphics in a document. Custom theme effects cannot be created but a theme effect can be applied to a document and the formatting can then be saved in a custom theme.

Tutorial

Saving a Custom Document Theme

Saving a Custom Document Theme

A custom document theme containing custom theme colors and fonts and effects can be saved. To do this, create and apply custom theme colors and fonts and theme effects to a document, click the Themes button on the Design tab, and then click *Save Current Theme* at the drop-down gallery. This displays the Save Current Theme dialog box, which has many of the same options as the Save As dialog box. Type a name for the custom document theme in the *File name* text box and then click the Save button.

Quick Steps

Save a Custom
Document Theme
1. Click Design tab.
2. Click Themes button.
3. Click *Save Current Theme*.
4. Type name for theme.
5. Click Save button.

1. Open **NSSServices.docx** and then save it with the name **4-NSSServices**.
2. Make the following changes to the document:
   a. Apply the Title style to the company name *Northland Security Systems.*
   b. Apply the Heading 1 style to the heading *Northland Security Systems Mission.*
   c. Apply the Heading 2 style to the remaining headings, *Security Services* and *Security Software.*
   d. Apply the Word 2010 style set (the last option in the expanded style sets gallery).
3. Apply the custom theme colors you saved by completing the following steps:
   a. Click the Design tab.
   b. Click the Colors button in the Document Formatting group.
   c. Click the theme colors option with your name at the top of the drop-down gallery in the *Custom* group.
4. Apply the custom theme fonts you saved by clicking the Fonts button in the Document Formatting group and then clicking the custom theme font with your name.
5. Apply a theme effect by clicking the Theme Effects button in the Document Formatting group and then clicking *Glossy* at the drop-down gallery (last option).
6. Make the following changes to the SmartArt graphic:
   a. Click near the graphic to select it. (When the graphic is selected, a gray border displays around it.)
   b. Click the SmartArt Tools Design tab.
   c. Click the Change Colors button and then click *Colorful Range - Accent Colors 5 to 6* (last option in the *Colorful* section).
   d. Click the More SmartArt Styles button in the SmartArt Styles group and then click *Cartoon* (third column, first row in the *3-D* section).
   e. Click outside the SmartArt graphic to deselect it.

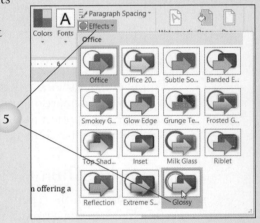

7. Save the custom theme colors and fonts, as well as the Glossy theme effect, as a custom document theme by completing the following steps:
   a. Click the Design tab.
   b. Click the Themes button in the Document Formatting group.
   c. Click the *Save Current Theme* option at the bottom of the drop-down gallery.
   d. At the Save Current Theme dialog box, type your first and last names in the *File name* text box and then click the Save button.

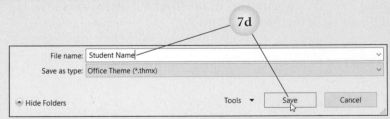

8. Save and then print **4-NSSServices.docx**.

Check Your Work ▶

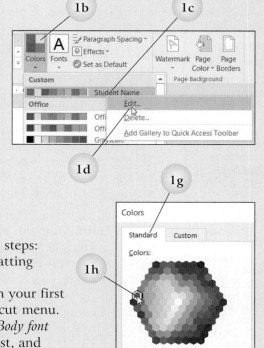

Editing Custom Themes

Custom theme colors and theme fonts can be edited. To edit custom theme colors, click the Design tab and then click the Colors button in the Document Formatting group. At the drop-down gallery of custom and built-in theme colors, right-click the custom theme colors and then click *Edit* at the shortcut menu. This displays the Edit Theme Colors dialog box, which contains the same options as the Create New Theme Colors dialog box. Make changes to the theme colors and then click the Save button.

Quick Steps
Edit Custom Theme Colors or Fonts
1. Click Design tab.
2. Click Colors button or Fonts button.
3. Right-click custom theme colors or fonts.
4. Click *Edit*.
5. Make changes.
6. Click Save button.

To edit custom theme fonts, click the Fonts button in the Document Formatting group on the Design tab, right-click the custom theme fonts, and then click *Edit* at the shortcut menu. This displays the Edit Theme Fonts dialog box, which contains the same options as the Create New Theme Fonts dialog box. Make changes to the theme fonts and then click the Save button.

Project 1d Editing Custom Themes

Part 4 of 5

1. With **4-NSSServices.docx** open, edit the theme colors by completing the following steps:
   a. If necessary, click the Design tab.
   b. Click the Colors button.
   c. Right-click the custom theme colors named with your first and last names.
   d. Click *Edit* at the shortcut menu.
   e. At the Edit Theme Colors dialog box, click the color button to the right of the *Text/Background - Dark 2* option.
   f. Click the *More Colors* option below the color palette.
   g. At the Colors dialog box, click the Standard tab.
   h. Click the dark green color. (This is the same color you chose for *Accent 1* in Project 1a.)
   i. Click OK to close the dialog box.
   j. Click the Save button.
2. Edit the theme fonts by completing the following steps:
   a. Click the Fonts button in the Document Formatting group.
   b. Right-click the custom theme fonts named with your first and last names and then click *Edit* at the shortcut menu.
   c. At the Edit Theme Fonts dialog box, click the *Body font* option box arrow, scroll down the drop-down list, and then click *Constantia*.
   d. Click the Save button.

3. Apply a different theme effect by clicking the Theme Effects button in the Document Formatting group and then clicking *Extreme Shadow* at the drop-down gallery. (This applies a shadow behind each shape.)
4. Save the changes to the custom theme by completing the following steps:
   a. Click the Themes button and then click *Save Current Theme* at the drop-down gallery.
   b. At the Save Current Theme dialog box, click the theme named with your first and last names in the content pane.
   c. Click the Save button.
   d. At the message telling you that the theme already exists and asking if you want to replace it, click Yes.
5. Save, print, and then close **4-NSSServices.docx**.

Check Your Work

Resetting a Template Theme

If a built-in theme other than the Office default theme or a custom theme is applied to a document, the theme can be reset to the default by clicking the Themes button and then clicking the *Reset to Theme from Template* at the drop-down gallery. If the document is based on the default template provided by Word, clicking this option resets the theme to the Office default theme.

Tutorial

Deleting Custom Themes

Deleting Custom Themes

Delete custom theme colors from the Colors button drop-down gallery, delete custom theme fonts from the Fonts drop-down gallery, and delete custom themes from the Save Current Theme dialog box.

To delete custom theme colors, click the Colors button, right-click the theme to be deleted, and then click *Delete* at the shortcut menu. At the confirmation message, click Yes. To delete custom theme fonts, click the Fonts button, right-click the theme to be deleted, and then click *Delete* at the shortcut menu. At the confirmation message, click Yes.

Delete a custom theme (including custom colors, fonts, and effects) at the Themes button drop-down gallery or the Save Current Theme dialog box. To delete a custom theme from the drop-down gallery, click the Themes button, right-click the custom theme, click *Delete* at the shortcut menu, and then click Yes at the confirmation message. To delete a custom theme from the Save Current Theme dialog box, click the Themes button and then click *Save Current Theme* at the drop-down gallery. At the dialog box, click the custom theme document name, click the Organize button on the dialog box toolbar, and then click *Delete* at the drop-down list. If a confirmation message displays, click Yes.

Changing Default Settings

If formatting is applied to a document—such as a specific style set, theme, and paragraph spacing—it can be saved as the default formatting. To do this, click the Set as Default button in the Document Formatting group on the Design tab. At the message asking if the current style set and theme should be set as the default and indicating that the settings will be applied to new documents, click Yes.

1. Open **NSSSecurity.docx** and then save it with the name **4-NSSSecurity**.
2. Apply the Title style to the company name, apply the Heading 1 style to the two headings in the document, and then apply the Word 2010 style set.
3. Apply your custom theme by completing the following steps:
   a. If necessary, click the Design tab.
   b. Click the Themes button.
   c. Click the custom theme named with your first and last names at the top of the drop-down gallery in the *Custom* section.
4. Save and then print **4-NSSSecurity.docx**.
5. Reset the theme to the Office default theme by clicking the Themes button and then clicking *Reset to Theme from Template* at the drop-down gallery.
6. Save and then close **4-NSSSecurity.docx**.
7. Press Ctrl + N to display a new blank document.
8. Delete the custom theme colors by completing the following steps:
   a. Click the Design tab.
   b. Click the Colors button in the Document Formatting group.
   c. Right-click the custom theme colors named with your first and last names.
   d. Click *Delete* at the shortcut menu.

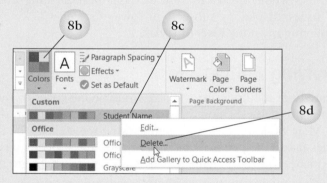

   e. At the message that displays asking if you want to delete the theme colors, click Yes.
9. Complete steps similar to those in Step 8 to delete the custom theme fonts named with your first and last names.
10. Delete the custom theme by completing the following steps:
    a. Click the Themes button.
    b. Right-click the custom theme named with your first and last names.
    c. Click *Delete* at the shortcut menu.
    d. At the message asking if you want to delete the theme, click Yes.
11. Close the document without saving it.

Check Your Work

Project 2 Format a Travel Document with Styles   1 Part

You will open a travel document, change the style set, and apply styles.

Preview Finished Project

Formatting with Styles

A style is a set of formatting instructions that can be applied to text. Word provides a number of predesigned styles and groups those that apply similar formatting into style sets. Whereas a theme changes the overall colors, fonts, and effects used in a document, a style set changes the font and paragraph formatting for the document. Using the styles within a style set, formatting can be applied to a document to give it a uniform and professional appearance.

Displaying Styles in a Style Set

The styles in a style set are available in the Styles group on the Home tab. Generally, the visible styles include Normal, No Spacing, Heading 1, Heading 2, Title, Subtitle, and Subtitle Emphasis. (Depending on the monitor and screen resolution, more or fewer styles may display in the Styles group.) The styles change to reflect the style set that has been applied to the active document. Click the More Styles button in the Styles group and a drop-down gallery displays containing all the styles available in the default style set. Hover the mouse pointer over a style in the drop-down gallery to see how the style will format the text in the document.

Another method for displaying additional styles is to click either the up arrow or the down arrow at the right of the styles. Clicking the down arrow scrolls down the styles, displaying subsequent rows of styles. Clicking the up arrow scrolls up, displaying previous rows of styles.

Tutorial

Applying and
Modifying a Style

Applying a Style

A variety of methods are available for applying styles to the text in a document. Apply a style by clicking the style in the Styles group on the Home tab or by clicking the More Styles button and then clicking the style at the drop-down gallery. The Styles task pane provides another method for applying a style. Display the Styles task pane, shown in Figure 4.2, by clicking the Styles group task pane launcher.

The styles in the currently selected style set display in the task pane followed by the paragraph symbol (¶), indicating that the style applies paragraph formatting, or the character symbol (a), indicating that the style applies character formatting. If both characters display to the right of a style, the style applies both paragraph and character formatting. In addition to displaying styles that apply formatting, the Styles task pane also displays a *Clear All* option that removes all formatting from the selected text.

Hover the mouse pointer over a style in the Styles task pane and a ScreenTip displays with information about the formatting applied by the style. Apply a style in the Styles task pane by clicking the style. Close the Styles task pane by clicking the Close button in the upper right corner of the task pane.

Quick Steps

Apply a Style
Click style in Styles group on Home tab.
OR
1. Click More Styles button in Styles group on Home tab.
2. Click style.
OR
1. Display Styles task pane.
2. Click style in task pane.

Hint You can also display the Styles task pane by pressing Alt + Ctrl + Shift + S.

Modifying a Style

If a predesigned style contains most but not all the desired formatting, consider modifying the style. To modify a predesigned style, right-click the style in the Styles group or in the Styles task pane and then click *Modify* at the shortcut menu. This displays the Modify Style dialog box, shown in Figure 4.3. Use options at this dialog box to make changes such as renaming the style, applying or changing the formatting, and specifying whether the modified style should be available only in the current document or in all new documents.

The *Formatting* section of the Modify Style dialog box contains a number of buttons and options for applying formatting. Additional options are available by clicking the Format button in the lower left corner of the dialog box and then clicking an option at the drop-down list. For example, display the Font dialog box by clicking the Format button and then clicking *Font* at the drop-down list.

Hint You can also apply styles at the Apply Styles window. Display this window with the keyboard shortcut Ctrl + Shift + S or by clicking the More Styles button at the right side of the styles in the Styles group on the Home tab and then clicking *Apply Styles* at the drop-down gallery.

Figure 4.2 Styles Task Pane

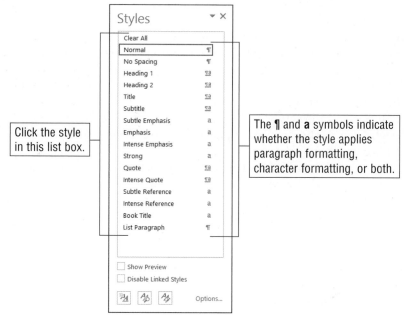

Click the style in this list box.

The ¶ and **a** symbols indicate whether the style applies paragraph formatting, character formatting, or both.

Figure 4.3 Modify Style Dialog Box

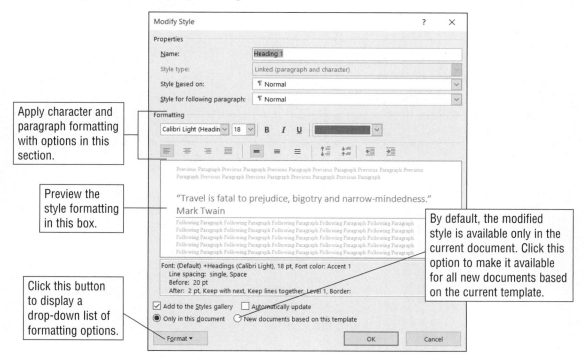

Apply character and paragraph formatting with options in this section.

Preview the style formatting in this box.

By default, the modified style is available only in the current document. Click this option to make it available for all new documents based on the current template.

Click this button to display a drop-down list of formatting options.

1. Open **BTAdventures.docx** and then save it with the name **4-BTAdventures**.
2. Apply styles using the Styles task pane by completing the following steps:
   a. Move the insertion point to the end of the document and then select the last paragraph.
   b. With the Home tab active, click the Styles group task pane launcher. (This displays the Styles task pane.)
   c. Click the *Subtle Reference* style in the Styles task pane. (Notice that the style is followed by the character symbol **a**, indicating that the style applies character formatting.)
   d. Select the bulleted text below the heading *Disneyland Adventure* and then click the *Subtle Emphasis* style in the Styles task pane.
   e. Apply the Subtle Emphasis style to the bulleted text below the heading *Florida Adventure* and the heading *Cancun Adventure*.
   f. Select the quote by Mark Twain and his name at the beginning of the document and then click *Quote* in the Styles task pane.
   g. After noticing the formatting of the quote, remove the formatting by making sure the text is selected and then clicking *Clear All* at the top of the Styles task pane.
   h. With the Mark Twain quote still selected, click the *Intense Quote* style in the Styles task pane.
   i. Click anywhere in the document to deselect the text.
3. Modify the Heading 1 style by completing the following steps:
   a. Right-click the *Heading 1* style in the Styles group.
   b. Click *Modify* at the shortcut menu.

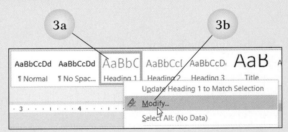

   c. At the Modify Style dialog box, click the Bold button in the *Formatting* section.
   d. Click the Center button in the *Formatting* section.

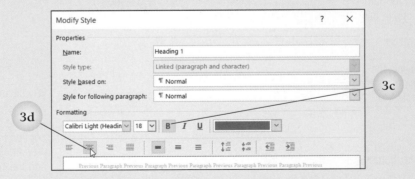

   e. Click OK to close the Modify Style dialog box.

4. Modify the Heading 2 style by completing the following steps:
   a. Right-click the *Heading 2* style in the Styles task pane and then click *Modify* at the shortcut menu.
   b. At the Modify Style dialog box, click the Format button in the lower left corner and then click *Font* at the drop-down list.
   c. At the Font dialog box, click the *Font color* option box arrow and then click *Dark Red* (first option in the *Standard Colors* section).
   d. Click the *Small caps* check box to insert a check mark.
   e. Click OK to close the Font dialog box.
   f. Click the Format button in the dialog box and then click *Paragraph* at the drop-down list.
   g. At the Paragraph dialog box, click the *After* measurement box up arrow. (This displays *6 pt* in the measurement box.)
   h. Click OK to close the Paragraph dialog box and then click OK to close the Modify Style dialog box.
5. Close the Styles task pane.
6. Save, print, and then close **4-BTAdventures.docx**.

Check Your Work

Project 3 Record and Run Macros in Documents   4 Parts

You will record several macros, run the macros in a document on writing resumes, assign a macro to a keyboard command, run macros in a business letter, and delete a macro.

Preview Finished Project

Tutorial

Recording and Running a Macro

Creating a Macro

A macro is a time-saving tool that automates the formatting of Word documents. The word *macro* was coined by computer programmers for a collection of commands used to make a large programming job easier and thus save time. Two basic steps are involved in working with macros: recording a macro and running a macro. When recording a macro, all the keys pressed and dialog boxes displayed are recorded and become part of the macro. After a macro is recorded, running it carries out the recorded actions.

Recording a Macro

Recording a macro involves turning on the macro recorder, performing the steps to be recorded, and then turning off the recorder. Both the View tab and Developer tab contain buttons for recording a macro. If the Developer tab does not appear on the ribbon, turn on the display of this tab by opening the Word Options dialog box with *Customize Ribbon* selected in the left panel, inserting a check mark in the *Developer* check box in the list box at the right, and then clicking OK to close the dialog box.

Figure 4.4 Record Macro Dialog Box

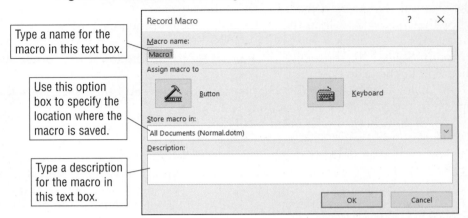

Type a name for the macro in this text box.

Use this option box to specify the location where the macro is saved.

Type a description for the macro in this text box.

 Record Macro

 Macros

Quick Steps

Record a Macro
1. Click Developer tab.
2. Click Record Macro button.
OR
1. Click View tab.
2. Click Macros button arrow.
3. Click *Record Macro*.
4. Make changes at Record Macro dialog box.
5. Click OK.
6. Complete macro steps.
7. Click Stop Recording button.
OR
7. Click macro icon on Status bar.

 Stop Recording

💡 **Hint** A macro can record mouse clicks but not selections made with the mouse.

To record a macro, click the Record Macro button in the Code group on the Developer tab. Or click the View tab, click the Macros button arrow in the Macros group, and then click *Record Macro* at the drop-down list. This displays the Record Macro dialog box, shown in Figure 4.4. At the Record Macro dialog box, type a name for the macro in the *Macro name* text box. A macro name must begin with a letter and can contain only letters and numbers.

By default, Word stores macros in the Normal.dotm template. Macros stored here are available for any document based on this template. In a company or school setting, where computers may be networked, consider storing macros in personalized documents or templates. Specify the location for a macro with the *Store macro in* option box at the Record Macro dialog box (shown in Figure 4.4).

Type a description of the macro in the *Description* text box at the dialog box. A macro description can contain a maximum of 255 characters and may include spaces. After typing the macro name, specifying where the macro is to be stored, and typing a description of the macro, click OK to close the Record Macro dialog box. At the open document, a macro icon displays near the left side of the Status bar and the mouse displays with a cassette icon attached. In the document, perform the actions to be recorded. A macro can record mouse clicks and key presses. However, if part of the macro is selecting text, use the keyboard to select text because a macro cannot record selections made by the mouse. When all the steps have been completed, click the Stop Recording button (previously the Record Macro button) in the Code group on the Developer tab or click the macro icon near the left side of the Status bar.

When you record macros in Project 3a, you will be instructed to name the macros beginning with your initials. Recorded macros are stored in the Normal.dotm template by default and display in the Macros dialog box. If the computer you are using is networked, macros recorded by other students will also display at the Macros dialog box. Naming macros with your initials will enable you to distinguish your macros from those of other users.

1. Turn on the display of the Developer tab by completing the following steps. (Skip to Step 2 if the Developer tab is already visible.)
   a. Click the File tab and then click *Options*.
   b. At the Word Options dialog box, click *Customize Ribbon* in the left panel.
   c. In the list box at the right, click the *Developer* check box to insert a check mark.
   d. Click OK to close the dialog box.

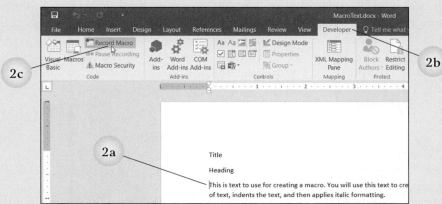

2. Record a macro that selects text, indents a paragraph of text, and then applies italic formatting by completing the following steps:
   a. Open **MacroText.docx** and then position the insertion point at the left margin of the paragraph that begins with *This is text to use for creating a macro.*
   b. Click the Developer tab.
   c. Click the Record Macro button in the Code group on the Developer tab.

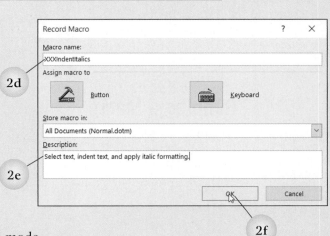

   d. At the Record Macro dialog box, type XXXIndentItalics in the *Macro name* text box. (Type your initials in place of *XXX*.)
   e. Click inside the *Description* text box and then type Select text, indent text, and apply italic formatting. (If text displays in the *Description* text box, select it and then type the description.)
   f. Click OK.
   g. At the document, press the F8 function key to turn on the Extend mode.
   h. Press and hold down the Shift key and the Ctrl key, press the Down Arrow key, and then release the Shift and Ctrl keys. (Shift + Ctrl + Down Arrow is the keyboard shortcut to select a paragraph.)

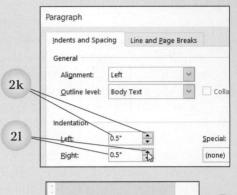

i. Click the Home tab.
j. Click the Paragraph group dialog box launcher.
k. At the Paragraph dialog box, click the *Left* measurement box up arrow until *0.5"* displays.
l. Click the *Right* measurement box up arrow until *0.5"* displays.
m. Click OK.
n. Press Ctrl + I to apply italic formatting.
o. Press the Esc key and then press the Left Arrow key. (This deselects the text.)
p. Click the macro icon on the Status bar to turn off the macro recording.

3. Record a macro that applies formatting to a heading by completing the following steps:
   a. Move the insertion point to the beginning of the text *Heading*.
   b. Click the Developer tab and then click the Record Macro button in the Code group.
   c. At the Record Macro dialog box, type XXXHeading in the *Macro name* text box. (Type your initials in place of *XXX*.)
   d. Click inside the *Description* text box and then type Select text, change font size, turn on bold and italic, and insert bottom border line. (If text displays in the *Description* text box, select it and then type the description.)
   e. Click OK.
   f. At the document, press the F8 function key and then press the End key.
   g. Click the Home tab.
   h. Click the Bold button in the Font group.
   i. Click the Italic button in the Font group.
   j. Click the *Font Size* option box arrow in the Font group and then click *12* at the drop-down gallery.
   k. Click the Borders button arrow in the Paragraph group and then click *Bottom Borde*r at the drop-down list.
   l. Press the Home key. (This moves the insertion point back to the beginning of the heading and deselects the text.)
   m. Click the macro icon on the Status bar to turn off the macro recording.
4. Close the document without saving it.

Running a Macro

Quick Steps

Run a Macro
1. Click Developer tab.
2. Click Macros button.
3. At Macros dialog box, double-click macro in list box.
OR
1. Click View tab.
2. Click Macros button.
3. At Macros dialog box, double-click macro in list box.

To run a recorded macro, click the Macros button in the Code group on the Developer tab or click the Macros button on the View tab. This displays the Macros dialog box, shown in Figure 4.5. At this dialog box, double-click a macro in the list box or click a macro and then click the Run button.

Figure 4.5 Macros Dialog Box

In this list box, click the macro to be run.

Click to run the macro selected in the list box.

Project 3b Running Macros

1. Open **WriteResumes.docx** and then save it with the name **4-WriteResumes**.
2. With the insertion point positioned at the beginning of the heading *Resume Strategies*, run the XXXHeading macro by completing the following steps:
   a. Click the View tab.
   b. Click the Macros button in the Macros group.
   c. At the Macros dialog box, click *XXXHeading* in the list box.
   d. Click the Run button.

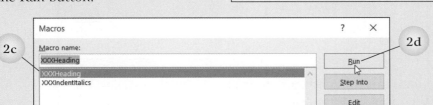

3. Complete steps similar to those in Steps 2a–2d to run the macro for the two other headings in the document: *Writing Style* and *Phrases to Avoid*.
4. Move the insertion point to the beginning of the paragraph below *First Person* and then complete the following steps to run the XXXIndentItalics macro:
   a. Click the Developer tab.
   b. Click the Macros button in the Code group.
   c. At the Macros dialog box, double-click *XXXIndentItalics* in the list box.
5. Complete steps similar to those in Step 4a–4c to run the XXXIndentItalics macro for the paragraph below *Third Person*, the paragraph that begins *Responsible for all marketing and special events*, and the paragraph that begins *Orchestrated a series of marketing and special-event programs*.
6. Save, print, and then close **4-WriteResumes.docx**.

Check Your Work

Pausing and Resuming a Macro

When recording a macro, the recording can be suspended temporarily to perform actions that should not be included in the recording. To pause the recording of a macro, click the Pause Recording button in the Code group on the Developer tab or click the Macros button on the View tab and then click *Pause Recording* at the drop-down list. To resume recording the macro, click the Resume Recorder button (previously the Pause Recording button).

Deleting a Macro

If a macro is no longer needed, delete it. To delete a macro, display the Macros dialog box, click the macro name in the list box, and then click the Delete button. At the confirmation message, click Yes. Click the Close button to close the Macros dialog box.

Project 3c Deleting a Macro Part 3 of 4

1. At a blank document, delete the XXXIndentItalics macro by completing the following steps:
   a. Click the Developer tab and then click the Macros button in the Code group.
   b. At the Macros dialog box, click *XXXIndentItalics* in the list box.
   c. Click the Delete button.

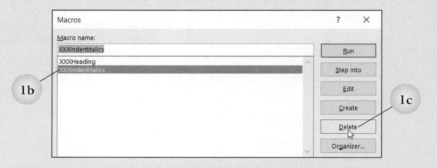

   d. At the message asking if you want to delete the macro, click Yes.
   e. Click the Close button to close the Macros dialog box.
2. Close the document without saving it.

Tutorial

Assigning a Macro to a Keyboard Command

Assigning a Macro to a Keyboard Command

Consider assigning regularly used macros to keyboard commands. To run a macro that has been assigned to a keyboard command, simply press the assigned keys. A macro can be assigned to a keyboard command with the following combinations:

> Alt + letter
> Ctrl + letter
> Alt + Ctrl + letter
> Alt + Shift + letter
> Ctrl + Shift + letter
> Alt + Ctrl + Shift + letter

Word already uses many combinations for Word functions. For example, pressing Alt + Ctrl + C inserts the copyright symbol (©).

Assign a macro to a keyboard command at the Customize Keyboard dialog box, shown in Figure 4.6. Specify the keyboard command by pressing the keys, such as Alt + D. The keyboard command entered displays in the *Press new shortcut key* text box. Word inserts the message *Currently assigned to:* below the *Current keys* list box. If the keyboard command is already assigned to a command, the command is listed after the *Currently assigned to:* message. If Word has not used the keyboard command, *[unassigned]* displays after the *Currently assigned to:* message. When assigning a keyboard command to a macro, use an unassigned keyboard command.

In Project 3d, you will record a macro and then assign it to a keyboard command. When you delete a macro, the keyboard command is no longer assigned to that action. This allows using the key combination again.

Figure 4.6 Customize Keyboard Dialog Box

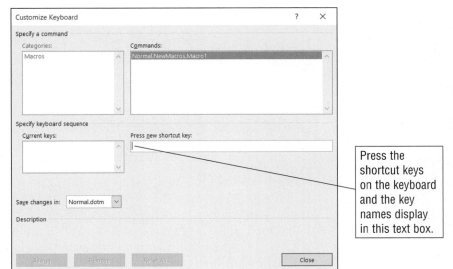

Press the shortcut keys on the keyboard and the key names display in this text box.

Project 3d Assigning a Macro to a Keyboard Command   **Part 4 of 4**

1. Record a macro named *XXXFont* that selects text and applies font formatting and assign it to the keyboard command Alt + Ctrl + A by completing the following steps:
   a. At a blank document, click the Developer tab and then click the Record Macro button in the Code group.
   b. At the Record Macro dialog box, type XXXFont in the *Macro name* text box. (Type your initials in place of *XXX*.)
   c. Click inside the *Description* text box and then type Select text and change the font and font color.
   d. Click the Keyboard button.

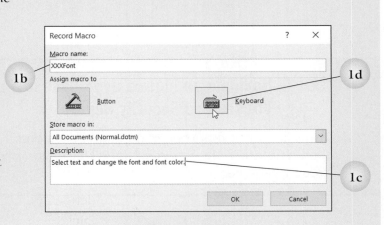

e. At the Customize Keyboard dialog box with the insertion point positioned in the *Press new shortcut key* text box, press Alt + Ctrl + A.

f. Check to make sure *[unassigned]* displays after *Currently assigned to:*.

g. Click the Assign button.

h. Click the Close button.

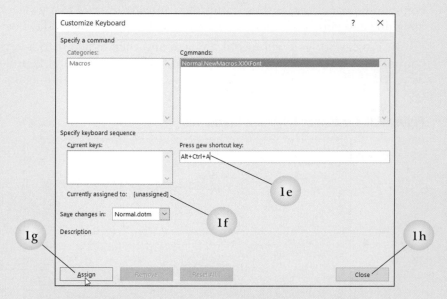

i. At the document, click the Home tab.

j. Press Ctrl + A.

k. Click the Font group dialog box launcher.

l. At the Font dialog box, click *Cambria* in the *Font* list box and click the *Dark Blue* font color (ninth option in the *Standard Colors* section).

m. Click OK to close the Font dialog box.

n. At the document, press the Down Arrow on the keyboard.

o. Click the macro icon on the Status bar to turn off the macro recording.

2. Close the document without saving it.

3. Open **GSHLtr.docx** and then save it with the name **4-GSHLtr**.

4. Run the XXXFont macro by pressing Alt + Ctrl + A.

5. Run the XXXHeading macro for the heading *Procedural* and the heading *Teaching*.

6. Save, print, and then close **4-GSHLtr.docx**.

Check Your Work

Project 4 Navigate and Insert Hyperlinks in a Computer Viruses and Security Report

6 Parts

You will open a report on computer viruses and computer security and insert and then navigate in the report with the Navigation pane, bookmarks, hyperlinks, and cross-references.

Preview Finished Project

Navigating in a Document

Word provides a number of features for navigating in a document. Navigate in a document using the Navigation pane or using bookmarks, hyperlinks, or cross-references.

Navigating Using the Navigation Pane

Tutorial

Review:
Navigating Using
the Navigation
Pane

Quick Steps

**Display the
Navigation Pane**
1. Click View tab.
2. Click *Navigation
   Pane* check box.

As explained in Level 1, Chapter 4, the Navigation pane can be used to navigate in a document. To navigate with the Navigation pane, click the View tab and then click the *Navigation Pane* check box in the Show group to insert a check mark. The Navigation pane displays at the left side of the screen and includes a search text box and a pane with three tabs.

Click the first Navigation pane tab, Headings, and titles and headings with certain styles applied display in the Navigation pane. Click a title or heading and the insertion point moves to it. Click the Pages tab and a thumbnail of each page displays in the pane. Click a thumbnail to move the insertion point to that specific page. Click the Results tab to browse the current search results in the document.

Close the Navigation pane by clicking the *Navigation Pane* check box in the Show group on the View tab to remove the check mark. Another option is to click the Close button in the upper right corner of the pane.

Project 4a Navigating Using the Navigation Pane   Part 1 of 6

1. Open **Security.docx** and then save it with the name **4-Security**.
2. Since this document has heading styles applied, you can easily navigate in the document with the Navigation pane by completing the following steps:
   a. Click the View tab.
   b. Click the *Navigation Pane* check box in the Show group to insert a check mark. (This displays the Navigation pane at the left side of the screen.)
   c. With the Headings tab active, click the heading *CHAPTER 2: INFORMATION THEFT* in the Navigation pane.

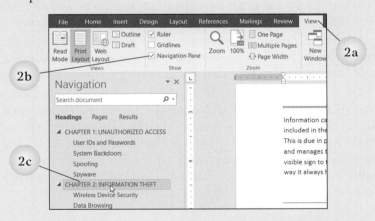

   d. Click *CHAPTER 3: COMPUTER VIRUSES* in the Navigation pane.
   e. Click *Systems Failure* in the Navigation pane.

3. Navigate in the document using thumbnails by completing the following steps:
   a. Click the Pages tab in the Navigation pane. (This displays thumbnails of the pages in the pane.)
   b. Click the page 1 thumbnail in the Navigation pane. (You may need to scroll up the Navigation pane to display this thumbnail.)

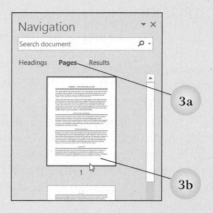

   c. Click the page 3 thumbnail in the Navigation pane.
4. Close the Navigation pane by clicking the Close button in the upper right corner of the Navigation pane.
5. Save **4-Security.docx**.

Tutorial

Inserting and Navigating with Bookmarks

 Bookmark

Quick Steps
Insert a Bookmark
1. Position insertion point at specific location.
2. Click Insert tab.
3. Click Bookmark button.
4. Type name for bookmark.
5. Click Add button.

Inserting and Navigating with Bookmarks

When working in a long document, marking a place in it with a bookmark may be useful for moving the insertion point to that specific location. Create bookmarks for locations in a document at the Bookmark dialog box.

To create a bookmark, position the insertion point at the specific location, click the Insert tab, and then click the Bookmark button in the Links group. This displays the Bookmark dialog box, as shown in Figure 4.7. Type a name for the bookmark in the *Bookmark name* text box and then click the Add button. Repeat these steps as many times as needed to insert additional bookmarks.

Give each bookmark a unique name. A bookmark name must begin with a letter and can contain numbers but not spaces. To separate words in a bookmark name, use the underscore character.

By default, the bookmarks inserted in a document are not visible. Turn on the display of bookmarks at the Word Options dialog box with *Advanced* selected. Display this dialog box by clicking the File tab and then clicking *Options*. At the Word Options dialog box, click *Advanced* in the left panel. Click the *Show bookmarks* check box in the *Show document content* section to insert a check mark. Complete similar steps to turn off the display of bookmarks. A bookmark displays in the document as an I-beam marker.

Figure 4.7 Bookmark Dialog Box

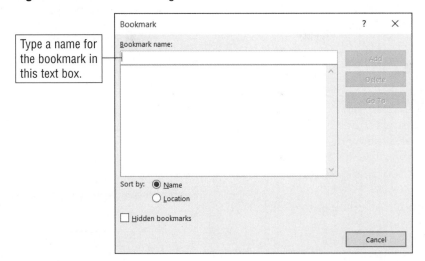

Type a name for the bookmark in this text box.

💡*Hint* Bookmark brackets do not print.

A bookmark can be created for selected text. To do this, first select the text and then complete the steps to create a bookmark. A bookmark created with selected text displays a left bracket ([) indicating the beginning of the selected text and a right bracket (]) indicating the end of the selected text.

Quick Steps

Navigate with Bookmarks
1. Click Insert tab.
2. Click Bookmark button.
3. Double-click bookmark name.

Navigate in a document by moving the insertion point to a specific bookmark. To do this, display the Bookmark dialog box and then double-click the bookmark name or click the bookmark name and then click the Go To button. When Word stops at the location of the bookmark, click the Close button to close the dialog box. When moving to a bookmark created with selected text, Word moves the insertion point to the bookmark and then selects the text. Delete a bookmark in the Bookmark dialog box by clicking the bookmark name in the list box and then clicking the Delete button.

Project 4b **Inserting and Navigating with Bookmarks** Part 2 of 6

1. With **4-Security.docx** open, turn on the display of bookmarks by completing the following steps:
   a. Click the File tab and then click *Options*.
   b. At the Word Options dialog box, click *Advanced* in the left panel.
   c. Scroll down the dialog box and then click the *Show bookmarks* check box in the *Show document content* section to insert a check mark.
   d. Click OK to close the dialog box.
2. Insert a bookmark by completing the following steps:
   a. Move the insertion point to the beginning of the paragraph in the section *TYPES OF VIRUSES* (the paragraph that begins *Viruses can be categorized*).
   b. Click the Insert tab.
   c. Click the Bookmark button in the Links group.

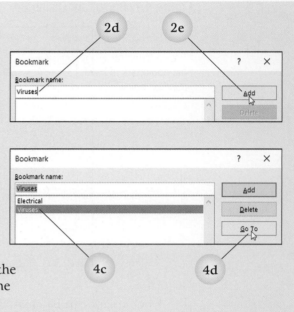

d. At the Bookmark dialog box, type Viruses in the *Bookmark name* text box.

e. Click the Add button.

3. Using steps similar to those in Steps 2a–2e, insert a bookmark named *Electrical* at the beginning of the paragraph in the section *SYSTEMS FAILURE*.

4. Navigate to the Viruses bookmark by completing the following steps:

   a. If necessary, click the Insert tab.

   b. Click the Bookmark button in the Links group.

   c. At the Bookmark dialog box, click *Viruses* in the list box.

   d. Click the Go To button.

5. With the Bookmark dialog box open, delete the Electrical bookmark by clicking *Electrical* in the list box and then clicking the Delete button.

6. Click the Close button to close the Bookmark dialog box.

7. Save **4-Security.docx**.

Inserting Hyperlinks

Tutorial

Inserting and Editing a Hyperlink

 Hyperlink

Quick Steps

Insert a Hyperlink
1. Click Insert tab.
2. Click Hyperlink button.
3. Make changes at Insert Hyperlink dialog box.
4. Click OK.

Hyperlinks can serve a number of purposes in a document. They can be used to navigate to a specific location in the document, to display a different document, to open a file in a different program, to create a new document, and to link to an email address.

Insert a hyperlink by clicking the Hyperlink button in the Links group on the Insert tab. This displays the Insert Hyperlink dialog box, as shown in Figure 4.8. This dialog box can also be displayed by pressing Ctrl + K. At the Insert Hyperlink dialog box, identify what to link to and where to find the link. Click the ScreenTip button to customize the ScreenTip for the hyperlink.

Figure 4.8 Insert Hyperlink Dialog Box

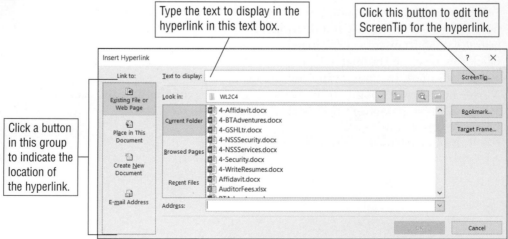

Linking to a Place in the Document To create a hyperlink to another location in the document, first mark the location by applying a heading style to the text or inserting a bookmark. To hyperlink to that heading or bookmark, display the Insert Hyperlink dialog box and then click the Place in This Document button in the *Link to* section. This displays text with heading styles applied and bookmarks in the *Select a place in this document* list box. Click the heading style or bookmark name and the heading or bookmark name displays in the *Text to display* text box. Leave the text as displayed or select the text and then type the text that will appear in the document.

Navigating Using Hyperlinks Navigate to a hyperlink by hovering the mouse pointer over the hyperlink text, pressing and holding down the Ctrl key, clicking the left mouse button, and then releasing the Ctrl key. When hovering the mouse pointer over the hyperlink text, a ScreenTip displays with the name of the heading or bookmark. To display specific information in the ScreenTip, click the ScreenTip button in the Insert Hyperlink dialog box, type the text in the Set Hyperlink ScreenTip dialog box, and then click OK.

Project 4c **Inserting and Navigating with Hyperlinks**   **Part 3 of 6**

1. With **4-Security.docx** open, insert a hyperlink to a bookmark in the document by completing the following steps:
   a. Position the insertion point at the immediate right of the period that ends the first paragraph of text in the section *CHAPTER 4: SECURITY RISKS* (located on page 4).
   b. Press the spacebar.
   c. If necessary, click the Insert tab.
   d. Click the Hyperlink button in the Links group.
   e. At the Insert Hyperlink dialog box, click the Place in This Document button in the *Link to* section.
   f. Scroll down the *Select a place in this document* list box and then click *Viruses,* which displays below *Bookmarks* in the list box.
   g. Select the text in the *Text to display* text box and then type Click to view types of viruses.
   h. Click the ScreenTip button in the upper right corner of the dialog box.
   i. At the Set Hyperlink ScreenTip dialog box, type View types of viruses and then click OK.
   j. Click OK to close the Insert Hyperlink dialog box.
2. Navigate to the hyperlinked location by hovering the mouse pointer over the <u>Click to view types of viruses</u> hyperlink, pressing and holding down the Ctrl key, clicking the left mouse button, and then releasing the Ctrl key.

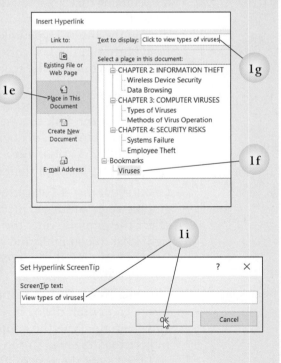

3. Insert a hyperlink to a heading in the document by completing the following steps:

a. Press Ctrl + Home to move the insertion point to the beginning of the document.

b. Move the insertion point to the immediate right of the period that ends the second paragraph in the document and then press the spacebar.

c. Click the Hyperlink button on the Insert tab.

d. At the Insert Hyperlink dialog box with Place in This Document button active in the *Link To* section, click the *Methods of Virus Operation* heading in the *Select a place in this document* list box.

e. Click OK to close the Insert Hyperlink dialog box.

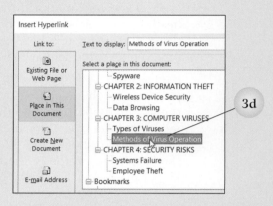

4. Navigate to the hyperlinked heading by hovering the mouse pointer over the 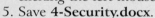 Methods of Virus Operation hyperlink, pressing and holding down the Ctrl key, clicking the left mouse button, and then releasing the Ctrl key.

5. Save **4-Security.docx**.

Check Your Work

Linking to a File in Another Application A hyperlink can be inserted in a document that links to another Word document, an Excel worksheet, or a PowerPoint presentation. To link a Word document to a file in another application, display the Insert Hyperlink dialog box and then click the Existing File or Web Page button in the *Link to* section. Use the *Look in* option box to navigate to the folder that contains the specific file and then click the file name. Make other changes in the Insert Hyperlink dialog box as needed and then click OK.

Linking to a New Document In addition to linking to an existing document, a hyperlink can link to a new document. To insert this kind of hyperlink, display the Insert Hyperlink dialog box and then click the Create New Document button in the *Link to* section. Type a name for the new document in the *Name of new document* text box and then specify if the document is to be edited now or later.

Linking Using a Graphic A hyperlink to a file or website can be inserted in a graphic such an image, picture, or text box. To create a hyperlink with a graphic, select the graphic, click the Insert tab, and then click the Hyperlink button or right-click the graphic and then click *Hyperlink* at the shortcut menu. At the Insert Hyperlink dialog box, specify where to link to and what text to display in the hyperlink.

Linking to an Email Address Insert a hyperlink to an email address at the Insert Hyperlink dialog box. To do this, click the E-Mail Address button in the *Link to* group, type the address in the *E-mail address* text box, and then type a subject for the email in the *Subject* text box. Click in the *Text to display* text box and then type the text to display in the document. To use this feature, the email address must be set up in Outlook.

1. The **4-Security.docx** document contains information used by Northland Security Systems. The company also has a PowerPoint presentation that contains similar information. Link the document with the presentation by completing the following steps:
   a. Move the insertion point to the immediate right of the period that ends the first paragraph in the section *CHAPTER 3: COMPUTER VIRUSES* and then press the spacebar.
   b. If necessary, click the Insert tab.
   c. Click the Hyperlink button in the Links group.
   d. At the Insert Hyperlink dialog box, click the Existing File or Web Page button in the *Link to* section.
   e. Click the *Look in* option box arrow, at the drop-down list that displays, navigate to the WL2C4 folder on your storage medium, and then click the folder.
   f. Click **NSSPres.pptx** in the list box.
   g. Select the text in the *Text to display* text box and then type Computer Virus Presentation.
   h. Click OK to close the Insert Hyperlink dialog box.

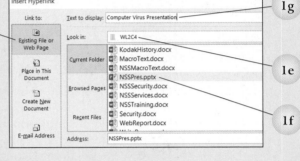

2. View the PowerPoint presentation by completing the following steps:
   a. Position the mouse pointer over the <u>Computer Virus Presentation</u> hyperlink, press and hold down the Ctrl key, click the left mouse button, and then release the Ctrl key.
   b. At the PowerPoint presentation, click the Slide Show button in the view area on the Status bar.
   c. Click the left mouse button to advance each slide.
   d. Click the left mouse button at the black screen that displays the message *End of slide show, click to exit*.
   e. Close the presentation and PowerPoint by clicking the Close button (which contains an X) in the upper right corner of the screen.
3. Insert a hyperlink with a graphic by completing the following steps:
   a. Press Ctrl + End to move the insertion point to the end of the document.
   b. Click the compass image to select it.
   c. Click the Hyperlink button on the Insert tab.
   d. At the Insert Hyperlink dialog box, make sure the Existing File or Web Page button is active in the *Link to* group.
   e. Navigate to the WL2C4 folder on your storage medium and then double-click **NSSTraining.docx**. (This selects the document name and closes the dialog box.)
   f. Click outside the compass image to deselect it.
4. Navigate to **NSSTraining.docx** by hovering the mouse pointer over the compass image, pressing and holding down the Ctrl key, clicking the left mouse button, and then releasing the Ctrl key.
5. Close the document by clicking the File tab and then clicking the *Close* option.

6. Insert a hyperlink to a new document by completing the following steps:
   a. Move the insertion point to the immediate right of the period that ends the paragraph in the section *USER IDS AND PASSWORDS* and then press the spacebar.
   b. Click the Hyperlink button on the Insert tab.
   c. Click the Create New Document button in the *Link to* section.
   d. In the *Name of new document* text box, type 4-PasswordSuggestions.
   e. Edit the text in the *Text to display* text box so it displays as *Password Suggestions*.
   f. Make sure the *Edit the new document now* option is selected.
   g. Click OK.
   h. At the blank document, turn on bold formatting, type Please type any suggestions you have for creating secure passwords:, turn off bold formatting, and then press the Enter key.
   i. Save and then close the document.
7. Press Ctrl + End to move the insertion point to the end of the document and then press the Enter key four times.
8. Insert a hyperlink to your email address or your instructor's email address by completing the following steps:
   a. Click the Hyperlink button.
   b. At the Insert Hyperlink dialog box, click the E-mail Address button in the *Link to* group.
   c. Type your email address or your instructor's email address in the *E-mail address* text box.
   d. Select the current text in the *Text to display* text box and then type Click to send an email.
   e. Click OK to close the dialog box.

Optional: If you have Outlook set up, press and hold down the Ctrl key, click the Click to send an email hyperlink, release the Ctrl key, and then send a message indicating that you have completed inserting hyperlinks in 4-Security.docx.

9. Save **4-Security.docx**.

Check Your Work

Editing a Hyperlink

The hyperlink or the hyperlink destination can be edited with options at the Edit Hyperlink dialog box. The Edit Hyperlink dialog box contains the same options as the Insert Hyperlink dialog box. Display the Edit Hyperlink dialog box by selecting the hyperlinked text and then clicking the Hyperlink button on the Insert tab or by right-clicking the hyperlinked text and then clicking *Edit Hyperlink* at the shortcut menu. In addition to editing the hyperlink, the hyperlinked text can be edited. For example, a different font, font size, text color, or text effect can be applied to the hyperlink text. Remove a hyperlink from a document by right-clicking the hyperlinked text and then clicking *Remove Hyperlink* at the shortcut menu.

1. With **4-Security.docx** open, edit a hyperlink by completing the following steps:
   a. Display the hyperlink that displays at the end of the paragraph below the title CHAPTER 3: COMPUTER VIRUSES.
   b. Right-click the <u>Computer Virus Presentation</u> hyperlink and then click *Edit Hyperlink* at the shortcut menu.

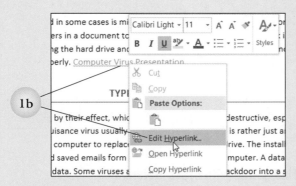

   c. At the Edit Hyperlink dialog box, select the text in the *Text to display* text box and then type Click to view a presentation on computer viruses.
   d. Click the ScreenTip button in the upper right corner of the dialog box.
   e. At the Set Hyperlink ScreenTip dialog box, type View the Computer Viruses PowerPoint presentation and then click OK.
   f. Click OK to close the Edit Hyperlink dialog box.
2. Remove a hyperlink by completing the following steps:
   a. Press Ctrl + Home to move the insertion point to the beginning of the document.
   b. Right-click the <u>Methods of Virus Operation</u> hyperlink that displays at the end of the second paragraph below the title *CHAPTER 1: UNAUTHORIZED ACCESS.*
   c. At the shortcut menu that displays, click the *Remove Hyperlink* option.
3. Save **4-Security.docx**.

> **Check Your Work**

Tutorial

Creating a Cross-Reference

Creating a
Cross-Reference

Quick Steps

**Insert a
Cross-Reference**

1. Type text or position insertion point.
2. Click Insert tab.
3. Click Cross-reference button.
4. Identify reference type, location, and text.
5. Click Insert.
6. Click Close.

Cross-reference

A *cross-reference* in a Word document refers readers to another location within the document. Providing cross-references is useful in a long document or a document containing related information. References to items such as headings, figures, and tables are helpful to readers. For example, a cross-reference can be inserted that refers readers to a location with more information about the topic, to a specific table, or to a specific page. Cross-references are inserted in a document as hyperlinks.

To insert a cross-reference, type introductory text or position the insertion point at a specific location, click the Insert tab, and then click the Cross-reference button in the Links group. This displays the Cross-reference dialog box similar to the one shown in Figure 4.9. At the Cross-reference dialog box, identify the type of reference, the location to reference, and the specific text to reference.

The reference identified in the Cross-reference dialog box displays immediately after the introductory text. To move to the specified reference, press and hold down the Ctrl key, position the mouse pointer over the text (the pointer turns into a hand), click the left mouse button, and then release the Ctrl key.

Figure 4.9 Cross-reference Dialog Box

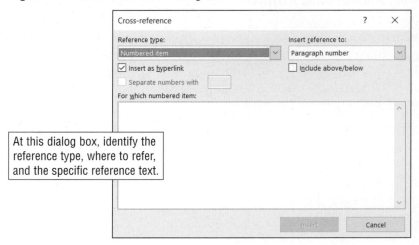

At this dialog box, identify the reference type, where to refer, and the specific reference text.

Project 4f Inserting and Navigating with Cross-References

1. With **4-Security.docx** open, insert a cross-reference in the document by completing the following steps:

   a. Move the insertion point immediately right of the period that ends the paragraph in the section *TYPES OF VIRUSES*.

   b. Press the spacebar and then type (For more information, refer to.

   c. Press the spacebar.

   d. If necessary, click the Insert tab.

   e. Click the Cross-reference button in the Links group.

   f. At the Cross-reference dialog box, click the *Reference type* option box arrow and then click *Heading* at the drop-down list.

   g. Click *Spyware* in the *For which heading* list box.

   h. Click the Insert button.

   i. Click the Close button to close the dialog box.

   j. At the document, type a period followed by a right parenthesis.

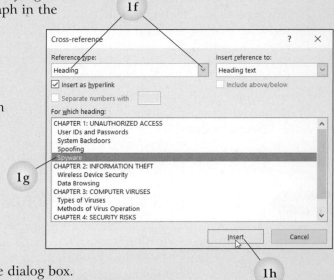

2. Move to the referenced text by pressing and holding down the Ctrl key, positioning the mouse pointer over *Spyware* until the pointer turns into a hand, clicking the left mouse button, and then releasing the Ctrl key.

3. Save and then print **4-Security.docx**.

4. Turn off the display of bookmarks by completing the following steps:

   a. Click the File tab and then click *Options*.

   b. At the Word Options dialog box, click *Advanced* in the left panel.

   c. Click the *Show bookmarks* check box in the *Show document content* section to remove the check mark.

   d. Click OK to close the dialog box.

5. Close **4-Security.docx**.

Check Your Work

Chapter Summary

- Create custom theme colors with options at the Create New Theme Colors dialog box and create custom theme fonts with options at the Create New Theme Fonts dialog box.

- Click the Reset button in the Create New Theme Colors dialog box to reset the colors back to the default Office theme colors.

- Create custom theme colors and custom theme fonts, apply a theme effect, and then save the changes in a custom theme. Save a custom theme at the Save Current Theme dialog box. Display this dialog box by clicking the Themes button in the Document Formatting group on the Design tab and then clicking *Save Current Theme* at the drop-down gallery.

- Apply custom theme colors by clicking the Colors button and then clicking the custom theme at the top of the drop-down gallery. Complete similar steps to apply custom theme fonts and a custom theme.

- Delete a custom theme at the Themes button drop-down gallery or at the Save Current Theme dialog box.

- Click the *Reset to Theme from Template* option at the Themes button drop-down gallery to reset the theme to the template default.

- A style is a set of formatting instructions that can be applied to text in a document. Word provides a number of predesigned styles grouped into style sets.

- Styles within a style set are available in the Styles group on the Home tab or the Styles task pane.

- Apply a style by clicking the style in the Styles group on the Home tab or clicking a style in the Styles task pane. Display the Styles task pane by clicking the Styles group task pane launcher.

- Modify a predesigned style with options at the Modify Style dialog box. Display this dialog box by right-clicking the style in the Styles group or in the Styles task pane and then clicking *Modify* at the shortcut menu.

- A macro automates the formatting of a document. Recording a macro involves turning on the macro recorder, performing the steps to be recorded, and then turning off the recorder.

- Both the View tab and the Developer tab contain buttons for recording a macro. Turn on the display of the Developer tab by inserting a check mark in the *Developer* check box at the Word Options dialog box with *Customize Ribbon* selected in the left panel.

- Name and describe a macro at the Record Macro dialog box. Display the dialog box by clicking the Record Macro button on the Developer tab or clicking the Macros button arrow on the View tab and then clicking *Record Macro* at the drop-down list.

- Run a macro by displaying the Macros dialog box and then double-clicking the macro name or clicking the macro name and then clicking the Run button.

- Temporarily suspend the recording of a macro by clicking the Pause Recording button in the Code group on the Developer tab.

- Delete a macro by displaying the Macros dialog box, clicking the macro name, and then clicking the Delete button.

- Assign a macro to a keyboard command at the Customize Keyboard dialog box. Display this dialog box by clicking the Keyboard button at the Record Macro dialog box. To run a macro that has been assigned a keyboard command, press the combination of keys assigned to the macro.
- Navigate in a document using the Navigation pane or by inserting bookmarks, hyperlinks, or cross-references.
- Insert bookmarks with options at the Bookmark dialog box.
- Insert hyperlinks in a document with options at the Insert Hyperlink dialog box. Insert a hyperlink to an existing file or web page, a location in the current document, a new document, or an email. A graphic can also be used to link to a file or website.
- Create a cross-reference with options at the Cross-reference dialog box.

Commands Review

FEATURE	RIBBON TAB, GROUP	BUTTON, OPTION	KEYBOARD SHORTCUT
Bookmark dialog box	Insert, Links		
Create New Theme Colors dialog box	Design, Document Formatting	, *Customize Colors*	
Create New Theme Fonts dialog box	Design, Document Formatting	, *Customize Fonts*	
Cross-reference dialog box	Insert, Links		
Insert Hyperlink dialog box	Insert, Links		Ctrl + K
Macros dialog box	Developer, Code OR View, Macros		Alt + F8
Record Macro dialog box	Developer, Code OR View, Macros		
Save Current Theme dialog box	Design, Document Formatting	, *Save Current Theme*	
Styles task pane	Home, Styles		Alt + Ctrl + Shift + S
theme effects	Design, Document Formatting		

Workbook

Chapter study tools and assessment activities are available in the *Workbook* ebook. These resources are designed to help you further develop and demonstrate mastery of the skills learned in this chapter.

Unit assessment activities are also available in the *Workbook*. These activities are designed to help you demonstrate mastery of the skills learned in this unit.

Microsoft
Word Level 2

Unit 2

Editing and Formatting Documents

Microsoft®
Word

CHAPTER 5

Inserting Special Features and References

Performance Objectives

Upon successful completion of Chapter 5, you will be able to:

1 Sort text in paragraphs, columns, and tables

2 Sort records in a data source file

3 Select specific records in a data source file

4 Find specific records in a data source file

5 Create and use specialized templates

6 Insert footnotes and endnotes

7 Insert and edit sources and citations

8 Insert, modify, and format source lists

Precheck

Check your current skills to help focus your study.

In Word, you can sort text in paragraphs, columns, tables, and records in a data source file. You can also select specific records in a data source file and merge them with a main document. Use the default template provided by Word to create a document or create and use your own specialized template. When you prepare research papers and reports, citing sources of information properly is important. In this chapter, you will learn to reference documents and acknowledge sources using footnotes, endnotes, citations, and source lists.

Data Files

Before beginning chapter work, copy the WL2C5 folder to your storage medium and then make WL2C5 the active folder.

SNAP

If you are a SNAP user, launch the Precheck and Tutorials from your Assignments page.

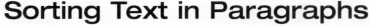

Project 1 Sort Company Information   2 Parts

You will open a document containing information on company employees and then sort data in paragraphs, columns, and tables.

Preview Finished Project

Preview Finished Project

Tutorial

Sorting Text in Paragraphs

Sorting Text in Paragraphs

Paragraphs of text in a document can be sorted alphanumerically, numerically, or chronologically. For example, a list of company employees can be sorted to create an internal telephone directory or a list for a company-wide mailing. Sorting items in a Word document is also an effective way to organize a list of customers by zip code or by product purchased.

In an alphanumeric sort, punctuation marks and special symbols are sorted first, followed by numbers, and then text. If paragraphs are sorted alphanumerically or numerically, dates are treated as regular text. During a paragraph sort, blank lines in a document are moved to the beginning of the sorted text.

 Sort

To sort text, select the text and then click the Sort button in the Paragraph group on the Home tab. This displays the Sort Text dialog box, which contains sorting options. The *Sort by* option box has a default setting of *Paragraphs*. This setting changes depending on the text in the document. For example, when items within a table are being sorted, the *Sort by* option box has a default setting of *Column 1*. The *Sort by* options also vary depending on selections at the Sort Options dialog box, shown in Figure 5.1. To display this dialog box, click the Options button in the Sort Text dialog box. At the Sort Options dialog box, specify how fields are separated.

Quick Steps

Sort Text in Paragraphs
1. Click Sort button.
2. Make changes at Sort Text dialog box.
3. Click OK.

Display the Sort Options Dialog Box
1. Click Sort button.
2. Click Options button.

Figure 5.1 Sort Options Dialog Box

Sorting Text in Columns

To sort text set in columns, the text must be separated with tabs. When sorting text in columns, Word considers the left margin *Field 1*, text typed at the first tab *Field 2*, and so on. When sorting text in columns, make sure the columns are separated with only one tab because Word recognizes each tab as beginning a separate column. Thus, using more than one tab may result in field numbers that correspond to empty columns.

Sorting on More Than One Field

Text can be sorted on more than one field. For example, in Project 1a, Step 6, the department entries will be sorted alphabetically and then the employee names will be sorted alphabetically within the departments. To do this, specify the *Department* column in the *Sort by* option box and then specify the *Employee* column in the *Then by* option box. If a document contains columns with heading text, click the *Header row* option in the *My list has* section.

Project 1a   Sorting Text

Part 1 of 2

1. Open **Sorting.docx** and then save it with the name **5-Sorting**.
2. Sort the text alphabetically by first name by completing the following steps:
   a. Select the seven lines of text at the beginning of the document.
   b. Click the Sort button in the Paragraph group on the Home tab.
   c. At the Sort Text dialog box, click OK.
3. Sort the text by last name by completing the following steps:
   a. With the seven lines of text still selected, click the Sort button.
   b. At the Sort Text dialog box, click the Options button.
   c. At the Sort Options dialog box, click *Other* and then press the spacebar. (This indicates that the first and last names are separated by a space.)
   d. Click OK.
   e. At the Sort Text dialog box, click the *Sort by* option box arrow and then click *Word 2* at the drop-down list.
   f. Click OK.

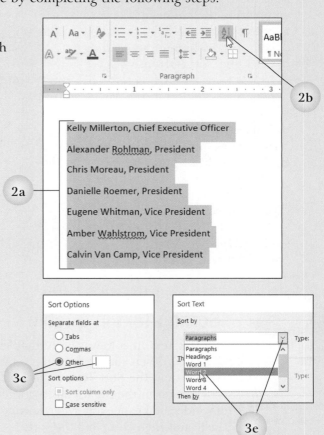

4. Sort text in columns by completing the
following steps:
a. Select the six lines of text below each
of these column headings: *Employee*,
Department, and *Ext*.
b. Click the Sort button in the
Paragraph group on the Home tab.
c. At the Sort Text dialog box, click the
Options button.
d. At the Sort Options dialog box, make
sure the *Tabs* option is selected in the
Separate fields at section and then click
OK to close the dialog box.
e. At the Sort Text dialog box, click the *Sort by* option box arrow and then click *Field 2* at
the drop-down list. (The left margin is *Field 1* and the first tab is *Field 2*.)
f. Click OK.

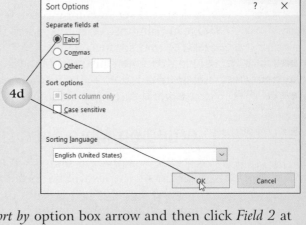

5. With the six lines of text still selected, sort the third column of text numerically by
completing the following steps:
a. Click the Sort button.
b. Click the *Sort by* option box arrow and then click *Field 4* at the drop-down list.
c. Click OK.
6. Sort the text in the first two columns by
completing the following steps:
a. Select the seven lines of text set in the
columns, including the headings.
b. Click the Sort button.
c. At the Sort Text dialog box, click the
Header row option in the *My list has*
section.
d. If necessary, click the *Sort by* option
box arrow and then click *Department*.
e. Click the *Type* option box arrow in the
Sort by section and then click *Text*.
f. Click the *Then by* option box arrow
and then click *Employee* at the drop-
down list.
g. Click OK.
7. Save **5-Sorting.docx**.

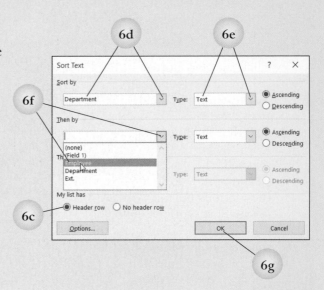

Check Your Work

Tutorial

Sorting Text in
a Table

Quick Steps
Sort Text in a Table
1. Position insertion
   point in table.
2. Click Sort button.
3. Make changes at
   Sort dialog box.
4. Click OK.

Sorting Text in a Table

Sorting text in columns within tables is similar to sorting columns of text separated
by tabs. When sorting text in a table, the dialog box is named the Sort dialog box
rather than the Sort Text dialog box. If a table contains a header, click the *Header
row* option in the *My list has* section of the Sort dialog box to tell Word not to
include the header row when sorting. To sort only specific cells in a table, select the
cells and then complete the sort.

160   Word Level 2 | Unit 2   Chapter 5 | Inserting Special Features and References

1. With **5-Sorting.docx** open, sort the text in the first column of the table by completing the following steps:
   a. Position the insertion point in any cell in the table.
   b. Click the Sort button.
   c. At the Sort dialog box, make sure the *Header row* option is selected in the *My list has* section.
   d. Click the *Sort by* option box arrow and then click *Sales, First Half* at the drop-down list.
   e. Click OK.
2. Sort the numbers in the third column in descending order by completing the following steps:
   a. Select all the cells in the table except the cells in the first row.
   b. Click the Sort button.
   c. Click the *Sort by* option box arrow and then click *Column 3* at the drop-down list.
   d. Click *Descending*.
   e. Click OK.
3. Save, print, and then close **5-Sorting.docx**.

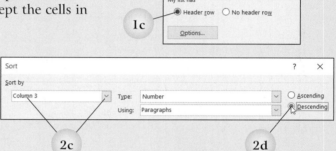

Check Your Work

Project 2 **Sort, Select, and Find Records in a Data Source File**   **4 Parts**

You will sort data in a data source file and create a labels main document. You will select and merge records and find specific records in a data source file.

Preview Finished Project

Sorting, Selecting, and Finding Records in a Data Source File

If a project requires sorting or selecting data and merging documents, consider the order in which the merged documents are to be printed or which records are to be merged and then sort and select the data before merging.

Tutorial

Sorting Records in a Data Source File

Sorting Records in a Data Source File

To sort records in a data source file, click the Mailings tab, click the Select Recipients button, and then click *Use an Existing List*. At the Select Data Source dialog box, navigate to the folder containing the data source file and then double-click the file. Click the Edit Recipient List button in the Start Mail Merge group on the Mailings tab and the Mail Merge Recipients dialog box displays, similar to the one shown in Figure 5.2.

Quick Steps

Sort Records in a Data Source File
1. Click Mailings tab.
2. Click Select Recipients button.
3. Click *Use an Existing List.*
4. Double-click file.
5. Click Edit Recipient List button.
6. At Mail Merge Recipients dialog box, sort by specific field by clicking field column heading.
7. Click OK.

Click the column heading to sort data in a specific column in ascending order. To perform an additional sort, click the down arrow at the right side of the column heading and then click the sort order. Another method for performing an additional sort is to click the <u>Sort</u> hyperlink in the *Refine recipient list* section of the Mail Merge Recipients dialog box. Clicking this hyperlink displays the Filter and Sort dialog box with the Sort Records tab selected, as shown in Figure 5.3. The options at the dialog box are similar to the options available at the Sort Text (and Sort) dialog box.

Figure 5.2 Mail Merge Recipients Dialog Box

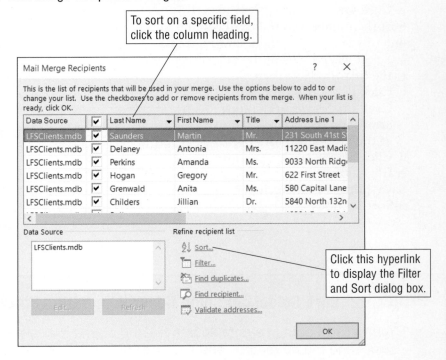

Figure 5.3 Filter and Sort Dialog Box with Sort Records Tab Selected

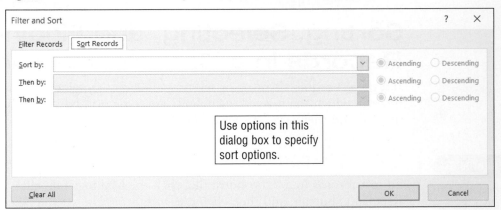

1. At a blank document, click the Mailings tab, click the Start Mail Merge button in the Start Mail Merge group, and then click *Labels* at the drop-down list.
2. At the Label Options dialog box, click the *Label vendors* option box arrow and then click *Avery US Letter* at the drop-down list.
3. Scroll down the *Product number* list box, click *5160 Easy Peel Address Labels*, and then click OK.

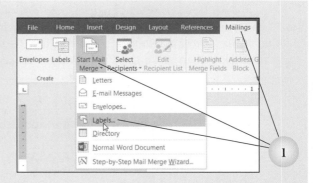

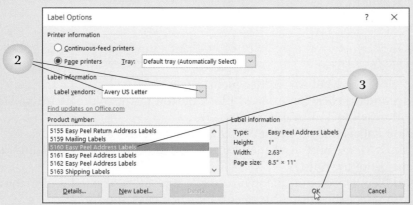

4. Click the Select Recipients button in the Start Mail Merge group and then click *Use an Existing List* at the drop-down list.
5. At the Select Data Source dialog box, navigate to the WL2C5 folder on your storage medium and then double-click the data source file named **LFSClients.mdb**.
6. Click the Edit Recipient List button in the Start Mail Merge group on the Mailings tab.
7. At the Mail Merge Recipients dialog box, click the *Last Name* column heading. (This sorts the last names in ascending alphabetical order.)
8. Scroll right to display the *City* field and then click the *City* column heading.
9. Sort records by zip code and then by last name by completing the following steps:
   a. Click the <u>Sort</u> hyperlink in the *Refine recipient list* section of the Mail Merge Recipients dialog box.

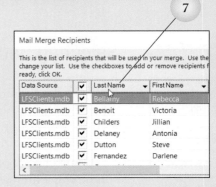

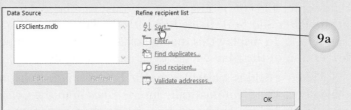

b. At the Filter and Sort dialog box with the Sort Records tab selected, click the *Sort by* option box arrow and then click *ZIP Code* at the drop-down list. (You will need to scroll down the list to display the *ZIP Code* field.)

c. Make sure *Last Name* displays in the *Then by* option box.

d. Click OK to close the Filter and Sort dialog box.

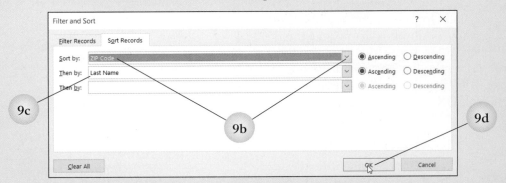

e. Click OK to close the Mail Merge Recipients dialog box.

10. At the labels document, click the Address Block button in the Write & Insert Fields group.

11. At the Insert Address Block dialog box, click OK.

12. Click the Update Labels button in the Write & Insert Fields group.

13. Click the Finish & Merge button in the Finish group and then click *Edit Individual Documents* at the drop-down list.

14. At the Merge to New Document dialog box, make sure *All* is selected and then click OK.

15. Press Ctrl + A to select the entire document and then click the *No Spacing* style in the Styles group on the Home tab.

16. Save the merged labels and name the document **5-Lbls01**.

17. Print and then close **5-Lbls01.docx**.

18. Close the labels main document without saving it.

Check Your Work

Tutorial

Selecting Records in a Data Source File

Selecting Specific Records for Merging

Hint Including or excluding certain records from a merge is referred to as *filtering*.

If a data source file contains numerous records, specific records can be selected from the data source file and then merged with a main document. For example, records with a specific zip code or city can be selected from a data source file. One method for selecting records is to display the Mail Merge Recipients dialog box and then insert or remove check marks from specific records.

Using check boxes to select specific records is useful in a data source file containing a limited number of records; however, it may not be practical in a data source file containing many records. In a large data source file, use options at the Filter and Sort dialog box with the Filter Records tab selected, as shown in Figure 5.4. To display this dialog box, click the <u>Filter</u> hyperlink in the *Refine recipient list* section of the Mail Merge Recipients dialog box.

When a field is selected from the *Field* drop-down list at the Filter and Sort dialog box, Word automatically inserts *Equal to* in the *Comparison* option box but other comparisons can be made. Clicking the *Comparison* option box arrow displays a drop-down list with these additional options: *Not equal to*, *Less than*, *Greater than*, *Less than or equal*, *Greater than or equal*, *Is blank*, and *Is not blank*. Use one of these options to create a select equation.

Figure 5.4 Filter and Sort Dialog Box with Filter Records Tab Selected

Click this option box arrow to specify the field to select on.

Use the *Comparison* and *Compare to* options to specify records that match certain criteria.

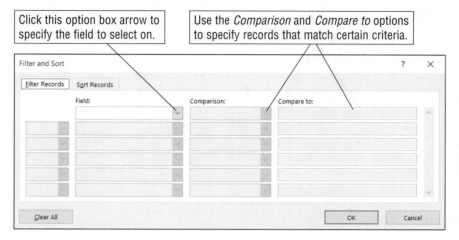

Project 2b Selecting Records in a Data Source File

1. At a blank document, click the Mailings tab, click the Start Mail Merge button in the Start Mail Merge group, and then click *Labels* at the drop-down list.
2. At the Label Options dialog box, make sure *Avery US Letter* displays in the *Label vendors* option box and *5160 Easy Peel Address Labels* displays in the *Product number* list box and then click OK.
3. Click the Select Recipients button in the Start Mail Merge group and then click *Use an Existing List* at the drop-down list.
4. At the Select Data Source dialog box, navigate to the WL2C5 folder on your storage medium and then double-click the data source file named ***LFSClients.mdb***.
5. Click the Edit Recipient List button.
6. At the Mail Merge Recipients dialog box, click the <u>Filter</u> hyperlink in the *Refine recipient list* section.
7. At the Filter and Sort dialog box with the Filter Records tab selected, click the *Field* option box arrow and then click *ZIP Code* at the drop-down list. (You will need to scroll down the list to display *ZIP Code*. When *ZIP Code* is inserted in the *Field* option box, *Equal to* is inserted in the *Comparison* option box, and the insertion point is positioned in the *Compare to* text box.)

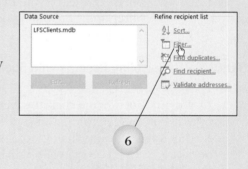

8. Type 21000 in the *Compare to* text box.
9. Click the *Comparison* option box arrow and then click *Greater than* at the drop-down list.

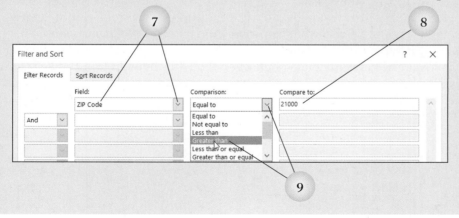

10. Click OK to close the Filter and Sort dialog box.
11. Click OK to close the Mail Merge Recipients dialog box.
12. At the labels document, click the Address Block button in the Write & Insert Fields group and then click OK at the Insert Address Block dialog box.
13. Click the Update Labels button in the Write & Insert Fields group.
14. Click the Finish & Merge button in the Finish group and then click *Edit Individual Documents* at the drop-down list.
15. At the Merge to New Document dialog box, make sure *All* is selected and then click OK.
16. Press Ctrl + A to select the entire document and then click the *No Spacing* style in the Styles group on the Home tab.
17. Save the merged labels and name the document **5-Lbls02**.
18. Print and then close **5-Lbls02.docx**.
19. Close the labels main document without saving it.

Check Your Work

When a field is selected from the *Field* option box, Word automatically inserts *And* in the first box at the left side of the dialog box but this can be changed to *Or* if necessary. With the *And* and *Or* options, more than one condition for selecting records can be specified. For example, in Project 2c, all the records of clients living in the cities Rosedale or Towson will be selected. If the data source file contained another field, such as a specific financial plan for each customer, all the customers living in these two cities that subscribe to a specific financial plan could be selected. In this situation, the *And* option would be used.

To clear the current options at the Filter and Sort dialog box with the Filter Records tab selected, click the Clear All button. This clears all the text from text boxes and leaves the dialog box on the screen. Click the Cancel button to close the Filter and Sort dialog box without specifying any records.

Project 2c Selecting Records with Specific Cities in a Data Source File   Part 3 of 4

1. At a blank document, click the Mailings tab, click the Start Mail Merge button in the Start Mail Merge group, and then click *Labels* at the drop-down list.
2. At the Label Options dialog box, make sure *Avery US Letter* displays in the *Label vendors* option box and *5160 Easy Peel Address Labels* displays in the *Product number* list box and then click OK.
3. Click the Select Recipients button in the Start Mail Merge group and then click *Use an Existing List* at the drop-down list.
4. At the Select Data Source dialog box, navigate to the WL2C5 folder on your storage medium and then double-click the data source file named *LFSClients.mdb*.
5. Click the Edit Recipient List button.
6. At the Mail Merge Recipients dialog box, click the Filter hyperlink in the *Refine recipient list* section.

7. At the Filter and Sort dialog box with the Filter Records tab selected, click the *Field* option box arrow and then click *City* at the drop-down list. (You will need to scroll down the list to display this field.)
8. Type Rosedale in the *Compare to* text box.
9. Click the option box arrow for the option box containing the word *And* (at the left side of the dialog box) and then click *Or* at the drop-down list.
10. Click the second *Field* option box arrow and then click *City* at the drop-down list. (You will need to scroll down the list to display this field.)
11. With the insertion point positioned in the second *Compare to* text box (the one below the box containing *Rosedale*), type Towson.
12. Click OK to close the Filter and Sort dialog box.

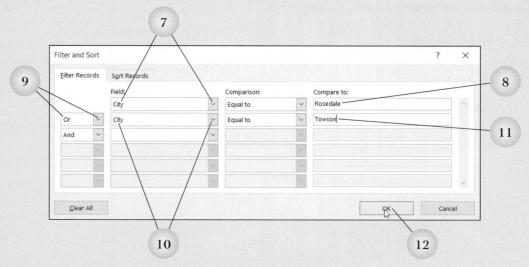

13. Click OK to close the Mail Merge Recipients dialog box.
14. At the labels document, click the Address Block button in the Write & Insert Fields group and then click OK at the Insert Address Block dialog box.
15. Click the Update Labels button in the Write & Insert Fields group.
16. Click the Finish & Merge button in the Finish group and then click *Edit Individual Documents* at the drop-down list.
17. At the Merge to New Document dialog box, make sure *All* is selected and then click OK.
18. Press Ctrl + A to select the entire document and then click the *No Spacing* style in the Styles group on the Home tab.
19. Save the merged labels and name the document **5-Lbls03**.
20. Print and then close **5-Lbls03.docx**.
21. Save the labels main document and name it **5-LblsMD**.

Check Your Work

Tutorial

Finding Records in a Data Source File

Finding Records
in a Data Source
File

Hint Visit the Microsoft Office website to find more information about address validation software.

The <u>Find duplicates</u> and <u>Find recipient</u> hyperlinks in the *Refine recipient list* section of the Mail Merge Recipients dialog box can be useful for finding records in an extensive data source file. Use the <u>Find duplicates</u> hyperlink to locate duplicate records that appear in the data source file. Use the <u>Find recipient</u> hyperlink to find a record or records that meet a specific criterion. The <u>Validate addresses</u> hyperlink in the *Refine recipient list* section is available only if address validation software has been installed.

Click the <u>Find duplicates</u> hyperlink and any duplicate records display in the Find Duplicates dialog box. At this dialog box, remove the check mark from the duplicate record check box that should not be included in the merge. To find a specific record in a data source file, click the <u>Find recipient</u> hyperlink. At the Find Entry dialog box, type the find text and then click the Find Next button. Continue clicking the Find Next button until a message displays indicating that there are no more entries that contain the text. By default, Word searches for the specified text in all of the fields of all of the records in the data source file. The search can be limited by clicking the *This field* option box arrow and then clicking the specific field. Type the text to find in the *Find* text box and then click OK.

Project 2d Finding Records in a Data Source File Part 4 of 4

1. With **5-LblsMD.docx** open, remove the filter by completing the following steps:
   a. With the Mailings tab active, click the Edit Recipient List button in the Start Mail Merge group.
   b. At the Mail Merge Recipients dialog box, click the <u>Filter</u> hyperlink in the *Refine recipient list* section.
   c. At the Filter and Sort dialog box, click the Clear All button.

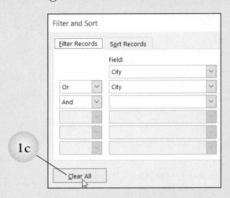

   d. Click OK to close the Filter and Sort dialog box.
   e. At the Mail Merge Recipients dialog box, click the <u>Find duplicates</u> hyperlink in the *Refine recipient list* section.
   f. At the Find Duplicates dialog box, which indicates that there are no duplicate items, click OK.
2. Find all records containing the zip code *20376* by completing the following steps:
   a. At the Mail Merge Recipients dialog box, click the <u>Find recipient</u> hyperlink in the *Refine recipient list* section.
   b. At the Find Entry dialog box, type 20376 in the *Find* text box.
   c. Click the *This field* option box arrow and then click *ZIP Code* at the drop-down list. (You will need to scroll down the list to display this option.)
   d. Click the Find Next button.
   e. When the first record is selected containing the zip code *20376*, click the Find Next button.
   f. When the second record is selected containing the zip code *20376*, click the Find Next button.

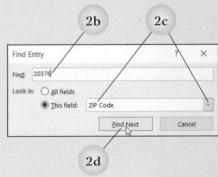

g. At the message indicating that there are no more entries that contain the text you typed, click OK.

h. Click the Cancel button to close the Find Entry dialog box.

3. Select and then merge records of those clients with a zip code of *20376* by completing the following steps:

a. At the Mail Merge Recipients dialog box, click the <u>Filter</u> hyperlink in the *Refine recipient list* section of the dialog box.

b. At the Filter and Sort dialog box, click the *Field* option box arrow and then click *ZIP Code* at the drop-down list. (You will need to scroll down the list to display this field.)

c. Type 20376 in the *Compare to* text box.

d. Click OK to close the Filter and Sort dialog box.

e. Click OK to close the Mail Merge Recipients dialog box.

4. At the label document, click the Finish & Merge button in the Finish group and then click *Edit Individual Documents* at the drop-down list.

5. At the Merge to New Document dialog box, make sure that *All* is selected and then click OK.

6. Save the merged labels and name the document **5-Lbls-04**.

7. Print and then close **5-Lbls-04.docx**.

8. Save and then close **5-LblsMD.docx**.

> **Check Your Work**

Project 3 Save and Use a Summons Template 2 Parts

You will open a summons legal document, save it as a template, and then use it to create other summons documents.

> **Preview Finished Project**

> **Tutorial**
>
> Saving and Using a Template

> **Quick Steps**
>
> **Save a Template**
> 1. Display Save As dialog box.
> 2. Change *Save as type* to *Word Template (*.dotx)*.
> 3. Type template name in *File name* text box.
> 4. Click Save.

Saving and Using a Template

If the content of a document is used to create other documents, consider saving the document as a template. Save a personal template in the Custom Office Templates folder in the Documents folder on the hard drive. A template saved in the Custom Office Templates folder will display in the New backstage area with the *PERSONAL* option selected.

To save a document as a template, display the Save As dialog box, change the *Save as type* option to *Word Template (*.dotx)*, type a name for the template, and then press the Enter key. When the *Save as type* option is changed to *Word Template (*.dotx)*, Word automatically makes Custom Office Templates the active folder. Word templates are saved with the .dotx file extension. A template also can be saved as a macro-enabled template with the .dotm file extension.

Another method for saving a template is to display the Export backstage area, click the *Change File Type* option, click the *Template (*.dotx)* option, and then click the Save As button. At the Save As dialog box, type a name for the template, and then click the Save button.

Note: Before completing this project, check to make sure you can save a template in the Custom Office Templates folder in the Documents folder on the hard drive. If not, please check with your instructor.

1. Open **Summons.docx**.
2. Save the document as a template in the Custom Office Templates folder by completing the following steps:
   a. Press the F12 function key.
   b. At the Save As dialog box, click the *Save as type* option box and then click *Word Template (*.dotx)*. (When the *Save as type* option is changed to *Word Template (*.dotx)*, Word automatically makes Custom Office Templates the active folder.)
   c. Select the name in the *File name* text box and then type your last name followed by *Summons*.
   d. Press the Enter key or click the Save button.
3. Close the summons template.

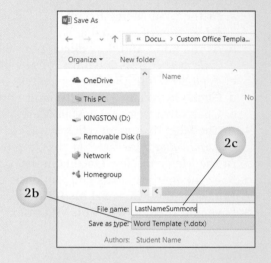

To open a document based on a template saved in the Custom Office Templates folder, click the File tab and then click the *New* option. At the New backstage area, click the *PERSONAL* option. This displays the templates available in the Custom Office Templates folder. Click a template to open a document based on that template.

1. Open a document based on the summons template by completing the following steps:
   a. Click the File tab.
   b. Click the *New* option.
   c. At the New backstage area, click the *PERSONAL* option.
   d. Click the summons template that is preceded by your last name.
2. With the summons document open, find and replace text as follows:
   a. Find *NAME1* and replace all occurrences with *AMY GARCIA*.
   b. Find *NAME2* and replace all occurrences with *NEIL CARLIN*.
   c. Find *NUMBER* and replace with *C-98002*.
3. Save the document in the WL2C5 folder on your storage medium and name it **5-Summons**.

4. Print and then close **5-Summons.docx**.

5. Delete the summons template from the hard drive by completing the following steps:

   a. Press Ctrl + F12 to display the Open dialog box.

   b. At the Open dialog box, click *Documents* in the Navigation pane.

   c. Double-click the *Custom Office Templates* folder in the Content pane.

   d. Click the summons template that begins with your last name.

   e. Click the Organize button and then click *Delete* at the drop-down list.

   f. At the message asking if you want to move the file to the Recycle Bin, click the Yes button.

6. Close the Open dialog box.

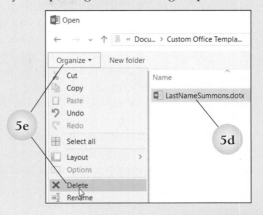

Check Your Work

Project 4 Insert Footnotes and Endnotes in Reports   3 Parts

You will open a report on pioneers of computing intelligence and then insert, format, and modify footnotes. You will also open a report on technology visionaries and then insert endnotes.

Preview Finished Project

Tutorial

Inserting Footnotes and Endnotes

💡 **Hint** Ctrl + Alt + F is the keyboard shortcut to insert a footnote and Ctrl + Alt + D is the keyboard shortcut to insert an endnote.

 Insert Footnote

 Insert Endnote

Quick Steps

Insert a Footnote
1. Click References tab.
2. Click Insert Footnote button.
3. Type footnote text.

Insert an Endnote
1. Click References tab.
2. Click Insert Endnote button.
3. Type endnote text.

Inserting Footnotes and Endnotes

A research paper or report contains information from a variety of sources. To give credit to those sources, footnotes or endnotes can be inserted in a document formatted in a specific reference style, such as that of the *Chicago Manual of Style*. (You will learn more about different reference styles in the next project.) A footnote is an explanatory note or source reference that is printed at the bottom of the page on which the corresponding information appears. An endnote is also an explanatory note or reference but it is printed at the end of the document.

Two steps are involved in creating a footnote or endnote. First, the note reference number is inserted in the document where the corresponding information appears. Second, the note entry text is typed. Footnotes and endnotes are created in a similar manner.

To create a footnote, position the insertion point where the reference number is to appear, click the References tab, and then click the Insert Footnote button in the Footnotes group. This inserts a number in the document along with a separator line at the bottom of the page and a superscript number below it. With the insertion point positioned immediately right of the superscript number, type the note entry text. By default, Word numbers footnotes with superscript arabic numbers and endnotes with superscript lowercase roman numerals.

1. Open **CompPioneers.docx** and then save it with the name **5-CompPioneers**.
2. Create the first footnote shown in Figure 5.7 by completing the following steps:
   a. Position the insertion point at the end of the first paragraph of text below the heading *Konrad Zuse* (immediately following the period).
   b. Click the References tab.
   c. Click the Insert Footnote button in the Footnotes group.
   d. With the insertion point positioned at the bottom of the page immediately following the superscript number, type the first footnote shown in Figure 5.7.

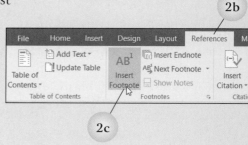

3. Move the insertion point to the end of the third paragraph below the heading *Konrad Zuse*. Using steps similar to those in Steps 2c and 2d, create the second footnote shown in Figure 5.7.
4. Move the insertion point to the end of the last paragraph below the heading *Konrad Zuse* and then create the third footnote shown in Figure 5.7.
5. Move the insertion point to the end of the third paragraph below the heading *William Hewlett and David Packard* and then create the fourth footnote shown in Figure 5.7.
6. Move the insertion point to the end of the last paragraph in the document and then create the fifth foonote shown in Figure 5.7.
7. Save, print, and then close **5-CompPioneers.docx**.

Check Your Work

Figure 5.7 Project 5a

Natalie Sanberg, *Technology: Pioneers of Computing* (Chicago: Home Town, 2018), 45-51.

Miguel Whitworth and Danielle Reyes, "Development of Computing," *Design Technologies* (2017): 24-26.

Sam Wells, *Biographies of Computing Pioneers* (San Francisco: Laurelhurst, 2018), 20-23.

Terrell Montgomery, *History of Computers* (Boston: Langley-Paulsen, 2018), 13-15.

Justin Evans, "Hewlett-Packard's Impact on Computing," *Computing Technologies* (2018): 7-12.

Printing Footnotes and Endnotes

When printing a document containing footnotes, Word automatically reduces the number of lines of text on each page to create the space needed for the footnotes and separator line. If a page does not have enough space, the footnote number and entry text are moved to the next page. Word separates the footnotes from the text with a 2-inch separator line that begins at the left margin. When endnotes are created in a document, Word prints all the endnote references at the end of the document, separated from the text by a 2-inch line.

1. Open **TechVisionaries.docx** and then save it with the name **5-TechVisionaries**.
2. Create the first endnote shown in Figure 5.8 by completing the following steps:
   a. Position the insertion point at the end of the second paragraph below the heading *Gordon E. Moore*.
   b. Click the References tab.
   c. Click the Insert Endnote button in the Footnotes group.
   d. Type the first endnote shown in Figure 5.8.
3. Move the insertion point to the end of the fourth paragraph below the heading *Jack S. Kilby* and then complete steps similar to those in Steps 2c and 2d to create the second endnote shown in Figure 5.8.
4. Move the insertion point to the end of the first paragraph below the heading *Linus Torvalds* and then create the third endnote shown in Figure 5.8.
5. Move the insertion point to the end of the last paragraph in the document and then create the fourth endnote shown in Figure 5.8.
6. Save **5-TechVisionaries.docx**.

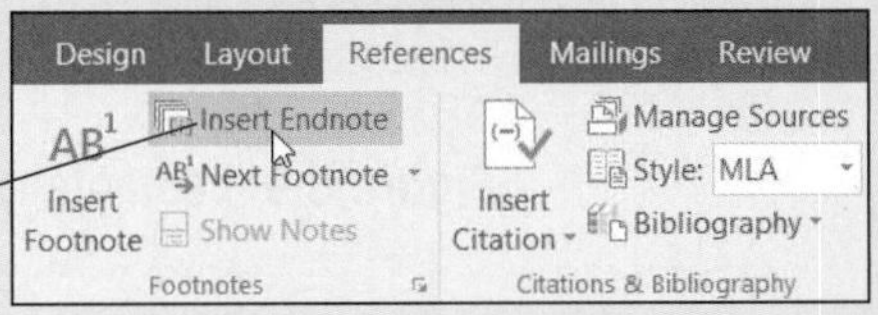

Check Your Work

Figure 5.8 Project 4b

Gina Shaw, *History of Computing Technologies* (Los Angeles: Gleason Rutherford, 2018), 11-14.

Ellen Littleton, "Jack Kilby: Nobel Prize Winner," *Horizon Computing* (Boston: Robison, 2018): 23-51.

Eric Ventrella, "Computer Nerd Hero," *Computing Today* (2018): 5-10.

Joseph Daniels, "Linus Torvalds: Technology Visionary," *Connections* (2018): 13-17.

Viewing and Editing Footnotes and Endnotes

Tutorial

Viewing and Editing Footnotes and Endnotes

 Next Footnote

 Show Notes

Hint To view the entry text for a footnote or endnote where the note occurs within the document, position the mouse pointer on the note reference number. The footnote or endnote text displays in a box above the number.

To view the footnotes in a document, click the Next Footnote button in the Footnotes group on the References tab. This moves the insertion point to the first footnote reference number following the insertion point. To view the endnotes in a document, click the Next Footnote button arrow and then click *Next Endnote* at the drop-down list. Use other options at the Next Footnote button drop-down list to view the previous footnote, next endnote, or previous endnote. Move the insertion point to specific footnote text with the Show Notes button.

If a footnote or endnote reference number is moved, copied, or deleted, all the remaining footnotes or endnotes automatically renumber. To move a footnote or endnote, select the reference number and then click the Cut button in the Clipboard group on the Home tab. Position the insertion point at the new location and then click the Paste button in the Clipboard group. To delete a footnote or endnote, select the reference number and then press the Delete key. This deletes the reference number as well as the footnote or endnote text.

Click the Footnotes group dialog box launcher and the Footnote and Endnote dialog box displays, as shown in Figure 5.9. Use options at this dialog box to convert footnotes to endnotes and endnotes to footnotes; change the locations of footnotes or endnotes; change the number formatting; start footnote or endnote numbering with a specific number, letter, and symbol; or change numbering within sections in a document.

Figure 5.9 Footnote and Endnote Dialog Box

Click this button to display the Convert Notes dialog box with options for converting footnotes to endnotes or endnotes to footnotes

Use these option boxes to specify locations for footnotes or endnotes.

Specify the formatting of the footnote or endnote number with options in this section of the dialog box.

Project 4c Editing Endnotes, Converting Endnotes to Footnotes, and Editing Footnotes   Part 3 of 3

1. With **5-TechVisionaries.docx** open, press Ctrl + Home to move the insertion point to the beginning of the document and then edit the endnotes by completing the following steps:
   a. If necessary, click the References tab.
   b. Click the Next Footnote button arrow and then click *Next Endnote* at the drop-down list.
   c. Click the Show Notes button to display the endnote text.
   d. Change the page numbers for the Gina Shaw entry from *11-14* to *6-10*.
   e. Click the Show Notes button again to return to the reference number in the document.

2. Press Ctrl + A to select the document (but not the endnote entry text) and then change the font to Constantia.
3. Change the font for the endnotes by completing the following steps:
   a. Press Ctrl + End to move the insertion point to the end of the document.
   b. Click in any endnote entry and then press Ctrl + A to select all the endnote entries.
   c. Change the font to Constantia.
   d. Press Ctrl + Home.

4. Convert the endnotes to footnotes by completing the following steps:
   a. Click the References tab and then click the Footnotes group dialog box launcher.
   b. At the Footnote and Endnote dialog box, click the Convert button.
   c. At the Convert Notes dialog box with the *Convert all endnotes to footnotes* option selected, click OK.
   d. Click the Close button to close the Footnote and Endnote dialog box.
5. Change the footnote number format by completing the following steps:
   a. Click the Footnotes group dialog box launcher.
   b. Click the *Footnotes* option in the *Location* section of the dialog box.
   c. Click the *Footnotes* option box arrow and then click *Below text* at the drop-down list.
   d. Click the *Number format* option box arrow in the *Format* section and then click *a, b, c, …* at the drop-down list.
   e. Change the starting number by clicking the *Start at* measurement box up arrow until *d* displays in the measurement box.
   f. Click the Apply button and then scroll through the document and notice the renumbering of the footnotes.

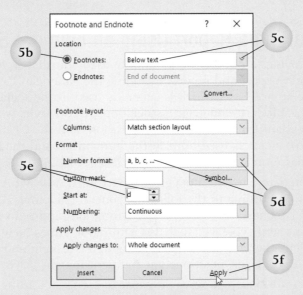

6. Change the footnote number format back to arabic numbers by completing the following steps:
   a. With the References tab active, click the Footnotes group dialog box launcher.
   b. At the Footnote and Endnote dialog box, click the *Footnotes* option in the *Location* section.
   c. Click the *Number format* option box arrow in the *Format* section and then click *1, 2, 3, …* at the drop-down list.
   d. Change the starting number back to 1 by clicking the *Start at* measurement box down arrow until *1* displays in the measurement box.
   e. Click the Apply button.
7. Delete the third footnote by completing the following steps:
   a. Press Ctrl + Home.
   b. Make sure the References tab is active and then click the Next Footnote button in the Footnotes group three times.
   c. Select the third footnote reference number (superscript number) and then press the Delete key.
8. Save, print, and then close **5-TechVisionaries.docx**.

Check Your Work

You will open a report on securing mobile devices, add information and insert source citations and a bibliography, and then modify and customize citation styles.

Preview Finished Project

Citing and Editing Sources

In addition to using footnotes and endnotes to credit sources in a research paper or manuscript, consider inserting in-text citations and a works cited page to identify sources of quotations, facts, theories, and other borrowed or summarized material. An in-text citation acknowledges that information is being borrowed from a source. Not acknowledging someone else's words or ideas is called *plagiarizing*.

Tutorial

Formatting a Report in MLA Style

Formatting a Report Using an Editorial Style

Word provides a number of commonly used editorial styles for citing references in research papers and reports including the American Psychological Association (APA) reference style, which is generally used in the social sciences and research fields; the Modern Language Association (MLA) style, which is generally used in the humanities and English composition; and the *Chicago Manual of Style* (Chicago), which is used both in the humanities and the social sciences and is considered more complex than either APA or MLA style.

To prepare a research paper or report in APA or MLA style, format the document according to the following general guidelines: Use standard-sized paper (8.5 × 11 inches); set 1-inch top, bottom, left, and right margins; format text in a 12-point serif typeface (such as Cambria or Times New Roman); double-space text; indent the first line of each paragraph 0.5 inch; and insert page numbers in the header of pages, positioned at the right margin.

When formatting a research paper or report according to the MLA or APA style, follow certain guidelines for properly formatting the first page of the document. With MLA style, at the beginning of the first page, at the left margin, insert the author's name (person writing the report), the instructor's name, the course title, and the current date. Double space after each of the four lines. Type the title of the document a double-space below the current date and then center the title. Also double-space between the title and the first line of text. The text should be left aligned and double spaced. Finally, insert a header in the upper right corner of the document that includes the author's last name and page number.

When using APA style, create a title page that is separate from the body of the document. On this page, include the title of the paper, the author's name, and the school's name, all double-spaced, centered, and positioned on the upper half of the page. Also include a header with the text *Running Head:* followed by the title of the paper in uppercase letters at the left margin and the page number at the right margin.

1. Open **MobileSecurity.docx** and then save it with the name **5-MobileSecurity**.
2. Format the document in MLA Style by completing the following steps:
   a. Press Ctrl + A to select the entire document.
   b. Change the font to Cambria and the font size to 12 points.
   c. Change the line spacing to double spacing (2.0).
   d. Remove extra spacing after paragraphs by clicking the Layout tab, clicking in the *After* measurement box in the *Spacing* section in the Paragraph group, typing 0, and then pressing the Enter key.
   e. Press Ctrl + Home to position the insertion point at the beginning of the document. Type your first and last names and then press the Enter key.
   f. Type your instructor's name and then press the Enter key.
   g. Type your course title and then press the Enter key.
   h. Type the current date and then press the Enter key.
   i. Type the document title Mobile Security and then center it.

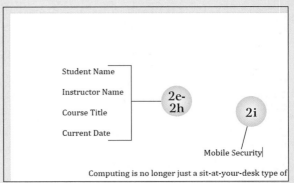

3. Insert a header in the document by completing the following steps:
   a. Click the Insert tab.
   b. Click the Header button in the Header & Footer group and then click *Edit Header* at the drop-down list.
   c. Press the Tab key two times to move the insertion point to the right margin in the Header pane.
   d. Type your last name and then press the spacebar.
   e. Click the Page Number button in the Header & Footer group on the Header & Footer Tools Design tab, point to *Current Position*, and then click the *Plain Number* option.

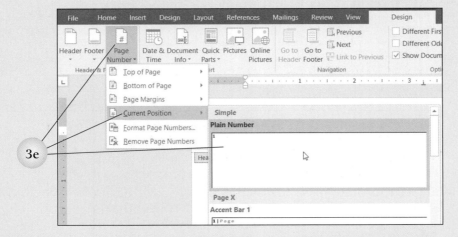

   f. Select the header text and change the font to 12-point Cambria.
   g. Double-click in the body of the document.
4. Save **5-MobileSecurity.docx**.

Check Your Work

Inserting Source Citations

When creating an in-text source citation, enter the information about the source in fields at the Create Source dialog box. To insert a citation in a document, click the References tab, click the Insert Citation button in the Citations & Bibliography group, and then click *Add New Source* at the drop-down list. At the Create Source dialog box, shown in Figure 5.10, select the type of source to be cited (such as a book, journal article, or report) and then type the bibliographic information in the required fields. To include more information than required in the displayed fields, click the *Show All Bibliography Fields* check box to insert a check mark and then type the additional bibliographic details in the extra fields. After filling in the necessary source information, click OK. The citation is automatically inserted in the document at the location of the insertion point.

Inserting Citation Placeholders

If information for an in-text source citation will be inserted later, insert a citation placeholder. To do this, click the Insert Citation button in the Citations & Bibliography group and then click *Add New Placeholder* at the drop-down list. At the Placeholder Name dialog box, type a name for the citation placeholder and then press the Enter key or click OK. Insert the citation text later at the Edit Source dialog box, which contains the same options as the Create Source dialog box.

Quick Steps

Insert a New Citation
1. Click References tab.
2. Click Insert Citation button.
3. Click *Add New Source*.
4. Type source information.
5. Click OK.

Insert a Citation Placeholder
1. Click References tab.
2. Click Insert Citation button.
3. Click *Add New Placeholder*.
4. Type citation name.
5. Click OK.

Figure 5.10 Create Source Dialog Box

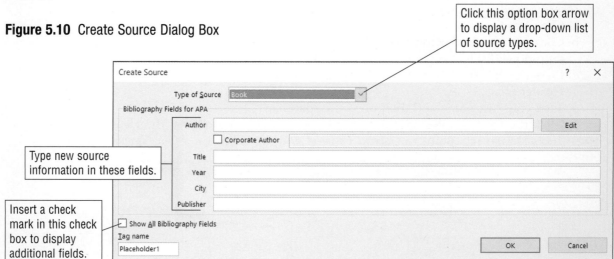

Click this option box arrow to display a drop-down list of source types.

Type new source information in these fields.

Insert a check mark in this check box to display additional fields.

Project 5b Inserting Sources and a Citation Placeholder

1. With **5-MobileSecurity.docx** open, press Ctrl + End to move the insertion point to the end of the document. Type the text shown in Figure 5.11 up to the first citation—the text *(Jefferson)*. To insert the citation, complete these steps:
   a. Press the spacebar once after typing the text *laptop*.

b. Click the References tab.

c. Make sure the *Style* option box in the Citations & Bibliography group is set to *MLA*. If not, click the *Style* option box arrow and then click *MLA* at the drop-down list.

d. Click the Insert Citation button in the Citations & Bibliography group and then click *Add New Source* at the drop-down list.

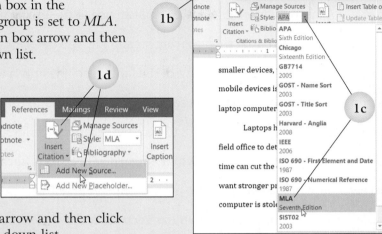

e. At the Create Source dialog box, click the *Type of Source* option box arrow and then click *Journal Article* at the drop-down list.

f. In the *Bibliography Fields for MLA* section, click in the *Author* text box, type Gabe Jefferson, and then press the Tab key three times.

g. In the *Title* text box, type Securing Laptops and Mobile Devices and then press the Tab key.

h. In the *Journal Name* text box, type Computing Technologies and then press the Tab key.

i. In the *Year* text box, type 2018 and then press the Tab key.

j. In the *Pages* text box, type 8-10.

k. Click OK.

l. Type a period to end the sentence in the document.

2. Continue typing the text up to the next citation—the text *(Lopez)*—and then insert the following source information for a book. (Click the *Type of Source* option box arrow and then click *Book* at the drop-down list.)

Author	Rafael Lopez
Title	Technology World
Year	2018
City	Chicago
Publisher	Great Lakes

3. Continue typing the text up to the next citation—the text *(Nakamura)*—and then insert a citation placeholder by completing the following steps. (You will create the citation and fill in the source information in the next project.)

a. Click the Insert Citation button in the Citations & Bibliography group.

b. Click *Add New Placeholder* at the drop-down list.

c. At the Placeholder Name dialog box, type Nakamura and then press the Enter key.

4. Type the remaining text shown in Figure 5.11.

5. Save **5-MobileSecurity.docx**.

Check Your Work

Figure 5.11 Project 5b

A laptop has a cable device you can use to tie it to an airport chair or desk in a field office to deter potential thieves from stealing it. The determined thief with enough time can cut the cable and get away with the laptop, so it is only a slight deterrent. If you want stronger protection, consider a service that allows you to remotely delete data if your computer is stolen and uses GPS to track your laptop (Jefferson).

Many newer laptops include fingerprint readers. Because fingerprints are unique to each individual, being able to authenticate yourself with your own set of prints to gain access to your computer is a popular security feature. If somebody without a fingerprint match tries to get into the computer data, the system locks up. If you travel with a laptop, activating password protection and creating a secure password is a good idea. If somebody steals your laptop and cannot get past the password feature, he or she cannot immediately get at your valuable data (Lopez).

Stopping thieves is one concern when you are on the road, but stopping employees from making costly mistakes regarding company data is another area in which companies must take precautions. Making sure that employees who take company laptops outside the office are responsible for safe and secure storage offsite is vital to company security (Nakamura). Policies might require them to keep backups of data on physical storage media or to back up data to a company network.

Quick Steps

Insert a Citation with an Existing Source
1. Click References tab.
2. Click Insert Citation button.
3. Click source.

Inserting a Citation with an Existing Source

Once source information is inserted at the Create Source dialog box, Word automatically saves it. To insert a citation in a document for source information that has already been saved, click the Insert Citation button in the Citations & Bibliography group and then click the source at the drop-down list.

Tutorial

Editing a Citation and Source

Editing a Citation and Source

After source information is inserted in a document, it may need to be edited to correct errors or change data. Or perhaps the citation needs to be edited to add page numbers or suppress specific fields. Edit a citation at the Edit Citation dialog box. Display this dialog box by clicking the citation, clicking the Citations Options arrow, and then clicking the *Edit Citation* option.

In addition to the citation, the source information of a citation can be edited. Edit a source at the Edit Source dialog box. Display this dialog box by clicking the citation in the document, clicking the Citations Options arrow, and then clicking the *Edit Source* option.

Project 5c Editing an Existing Source and Inserting a Citation with an Existing Source   Part 3 of 8

1. With **5-MobileSecurity.docx** open, add the Nakamura source information by completing the following steps:
   a. Click the *Nakamura* citation in the document.
   b. Click the Citation Options arrow that displays at the right side of the selected citation.
   c. Click *Edit Source* at the drop-down list.
   d. At the Edit Source dialog box, click the *Type of Source* option box arrow and then click *Journal Article*.
   e. Type the following information in the specified text boxes:

Author	Janet Nakamura
Title	Computer Security
Journal Name	Current Technology Times
Year	2018
Pages	20-28
Volume	6

   (Display the *Volume* field by clicking the *Show All Bibliography Fields* check box and then scrolling down the options list.)
   f. Click OK to close the Edit Source dialog box.
2. Press Ctrl + End to move the insertion point to the end of the document and then press the Enter key. Type the text shown in Figure 5.12 up to the citation text *(Jefferson)* and then insert a citation from an existing source by completing the following steps:
   a. If necessary, click the References tab.
   b. Click the Insert Citation button in the Citations & Bibliography group.
   c. Click the *Jefferson, Gabe* reference at the drop-down list.
   d. Type the remaining text in Figure 5.12.
3. Save **5-MobileSecurity.docx**.

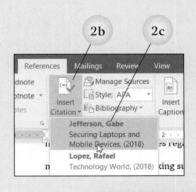

Check Your Work

Figure 5.12 Project 5c

> If you travel and access the Internet using a public location, you have to be very careful not to expose private information (Jefferson). Anything you send over a public network can be accessed by malicious hackers and cybercriminals. Limit your use of online accounts to times when it is essential.

Quick Steps

Insert a Page Number in a Citation
1. Click citation to display placeholder.
2. Click Citation Options arrow.
3. Click *Edit Citation*.
4. Type page number(s).
5. Click OK.

Inserting Page Numbers in a Citation

If a direct quote from a source is included in a report, insert quotation marks around the text used from that source and insert in the citation the page number or numbers of the quoted material. To insert specific page numbers in a citation, click the citation to select the citation placeholder. Click the Citation Options arrow and then click *Edit Citation* at the drop-down list. At the Edit Citation dialog box, type the page number or numbers of the source from which the quote was borrowed and then click OK.

Tutorial

Managing Sources

 Manage Sources

Quick Steps

Manage Sources
1. Click References tab.
2. Click Manage Sources button.
3. Edit, add, and/or delete sources.
4. Click Close.

💡 **Hint** Click the Browse button in the Source Manager dialog box to select another master list.

Managing Sources

All the sources cited in the current document and in previous documents display in the Source Manager dialog box, as shown in Figure 5.13. Display this dialog box by clicking the References tab and then clicking the Manage Sources button in the Citations & Bibliography group. The *Master List* list box in the Source Manager dialog box displays all the sources that have been created in Word. The *Current List* list box displays all the sources used in the currently open document.

Use options at the Source Manager dialog box to copy a source from the master list to the current list, delete a source, edit a source, and create a new source. To copy a source from the master list to the current list, click the source in the *Master List* list box and then click the Copy button between the two list boxes. Click the Delete button to delete a source. Edit a source by clicking the source, clicking the Edit button, and then making changes at the Edit Source dialog box that displays. Click the New button to create a new source at the Create Source dialog box.

If the *Master List* list box contains a large number of sources, search for a specific source by typing keywords in the *Search* text box. As text is typed, the list narrows to sources that match the text. After making all the changes at the Source Manager dialog box, click the Close button.

Figure 5.13 Source Manager Dialog Box

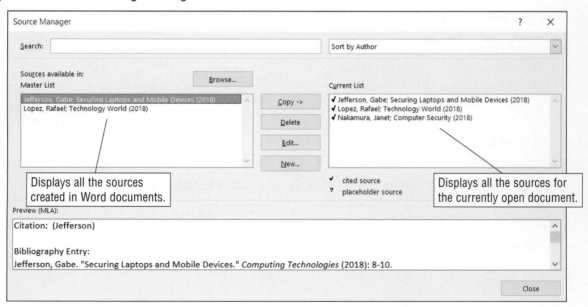

1. With **5-MobileSecurity.docx** open, edit a source by completing the following steps:
   a. If necessary, click the References tab.
   b. Click the Manage Sources button in the Citations & Bibliography group.
   c. At the Source Manager dialog box, click the *Jefferson, Gabe* source entry in the *Master List* list box.
   d. Click the Edit button.
   e. At the Edit Source dialog box, delete the text in the *Author* text box and then type Gabriel Jackson.
   f. Click OK to close the Edit Source dialog box.
   g. At the message asking if you want to update both the master list and current list with the changes, click Yes.
   h. Click the Close button to close the Source Manager dialog box. (Notice that the last name changed in both of the Jefferson citations to reflect the edit.)

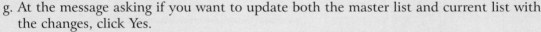

2. Delete a source by completing the following steps:
   a. Select and then delete the last sentence in the fourth paragraph in the document (the sentence beginning *If somebody steals your laptop*), including the citation.
   b. Click the Manage Sources button in the Citations & Bibliography group.
   c. At the Source Manager dialog box, click the *Lopez, Rafael* entry in the *Current List* list box. (This entry will not contain a check mark because you deleted the citation from the document.)
   d. Click the Delete button.

   e. Click the Close button to close the Source Manager dialog box.
3. Create and insert a new source in the document by completing the following steps:
   a. Click the Manage Sources button in the Citations & Bibliography group.
   b. Click the New button in the Source Manager dialog box.
   c. Type the following book information in the Create Source dialog box. (Change the *Type of Source* option to *Book*.)

Author	Georgia Miraldi
Title	Evolving Technology
Year	2018
City	Houston
Publisher	Rio Grande

d. Click OK to close the Create Source dialog box.

e. Click the Close button to close the Source Manager dialog box.

f. Position the insertion point one space after the period that ends the last sentence in the document and then type this sentence: "Be especially on guard when accessing your bank accounts, investment accounts, and retail accounts that store your credit card for purchases, and avoid entering your social security number" (Press the spacebar after typing the quotation mark that follows the word *number*.)

g. Insert a citation for Georgia Miraldi at the end of the sentence by clicking the Insert Citation button in the Citations & Bibliography group and then clicking *Miraldi, Georgia* at the drop-down list.

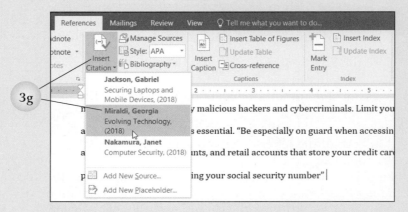

h. Type a period (.) to end the sentence.

4. To correctly acknowledge the direct quote from Georgia Miraldi, the page on which the quote appears in the book needs to be added. Insert the page number in the citation by completing the following steps:

a. Click the *Miraldi* citation in the document.

b. Click the Citation Options arrow that displays at the right of the citation placeholder and then click *Edit Citation* at the drop-down list.

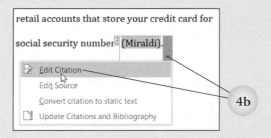

c. At the Edit Citation dialog box, type 19 in the *Pages* text box.

d. Click OK.

5. Save **5-MobileSecurity.docx**.

Check Your Work

Inserting a Sources List

If citations are included in a report or research paper, a sources list needs to be inserted as a separate page at the end of the document. A sources list is an alphabetical list of the books, journal articles, reports, and other sources referenced in the report or paper. Depending on the reference style applied to the document, the sources list may be a bibliography, a references page, or a works cited page.

Quick Steps

Insert a Sources List
1. Insert new page at end of document.
2. Click References tab.
3. Click Bibliography button.
4. Click works cited, reference, or bibliography option.

When source information for citations is typed in the document, Word automatically saves the information from all the fields and compiles a sources list. The sources are alphabetized by the authors' last names and/or the titles of the works. To include the sources list in a report or research paper, insert a works cited page for a document formatted in MLA style, insert a references page for a document formatted in APA style, and insert a bibliography for a document formatted in Chicago style.

To insert a works cited page, move the insertion point to the end of the document and then insert a new page. Click the References tab and make sure the *Style* option box is set to *MLA*. Click the Bibliography button in the Citations & Bibliography group and then click the *Works Cited* option. Complete similar steps to insert a bibliography in an APA-style document, except click the *Bibliography* option.

Bibliography

Project 5e Inserting a Works Cited Page

Part 5 of 8

1. With **5-MobileSecurity.docx** open, insert a works cited page at the end of the document by completing these steps:
   a. Press Ctrl + End to move the insertion point to the end of the document.
   b. Press Ctrl + Enter to insert a page break.
   c. If necessary, click the References tab.
   d. Click the Bibliography button in the Citations & Bibliography group.
   e. Click the *Works Cited* option in the *Built-In* section of the drop-down list.
2. Save **5-MobileSecurity.docx**.

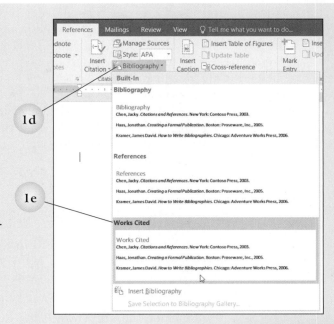

Check Your Work

Modifying and Updating a Sources List

Quick Steps

Update a Sources List
1. Click in sources list.
2. Click Update Citations and Bibliography tab.

If a new source is inserted at the Source Manager dialog box or an existing source is modified, Word automatically inserts the source information in the sources list. If a new citation requires a new source to be added, Word will not automatically update the sources list. To update the sources list, click in the list and then click the Update Citations and Bibliography tab. The updated sources list reflects any changes made to the citations and source information in the document.

1. With **5-MobileSecurity.docx** open, create a new source and citation by completing the following steps:
   a. Position the insertion point immediately left of the period that ends the last sentence in the first paragraph of the document (after the word *safer*).
   b. Press the spacebar.
   c. If necessary, click the References tab.
   d. Click the Insert Citation button in the Citations & Bibliography group and then click *Add New Source* at the drop-down list.
   e. At the Create Source dialog box, insert the following source information for a website. (Change the *Type of Source* option to *Web site* and click the *Show All Bibliography Fields* check box to display all the fields.)

Author	Chay Suong
Name of Web Page	Securing and Managing Mobile Devices
Year	2018
Month	April
Day	20
Year Accessed	(type current year in numbers)
Month Accessed	(type current month in letters)
Day Accessed	(type current day in numbers)
URL	www.emcp.net/publishing

   f. Click OK to close the Create Source dialog box.
2. Update the works cited page to include the new source by completing the following steps:
   a. Press Ctrl + End to move the insertion point to the end of the document.
   b. Click in the works cited text.
   c. Click the Update Citations and Bibliography tab above the heading *Works Cited*. (Notice that the updated sources list includes the Suong reference.)
3. Save **5-MobileSecurity.docx**.

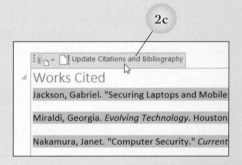

Check Your Work

Formatting a Sources List

The formatting applied by Word to the sources list may need to be changed to meet the specific guidelines of MLA, APA, or Chicago style. For example, MLA and APA styles require the following formats for a sources list:

- Begin the sources list on a separate page after the last page of text in the report.
- Include the title *Works Cited*, *References*, or *Bibliography* at the top of the page and center it on the width of the page.
- Use the same font for the sources list as for the main document.
- Double-space between and within entries.
- Begin each entry at the left margin and format subsequent lines in each entry with a hanging indent.
- Alphabetize the entries.

The general formatting requirements for Chicago style are similar except that single spacing is applied within entries and double spacing is applied between entries.

1. With **5-MobileSecurity.docx** open, make the following formatting changes to the works cited page:
   a. Select the *Works Cited* title and the entries below the title.
   b. Click the Home tab and then click the *No Spacing* style in the Styles group.
   c. With the text still selected, change the font to Cambria, the font size to 12 points, and the line spacing to double spacing (2.0).

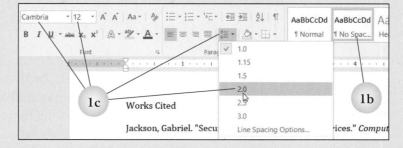

   d. Click in the title *Works Cited* and then click the Center button in the Paragraph group.
   e. Select only the works cited entries and then press Ctrl + T. (This formats the entries with a hanging indent.)
2. Press Ctrl + Home to move the insertion point to the beginning of the document.
3. Save and then print **5-MobileSecurity.docx**.

Check Your Work

Choosing a Citation Style

Different subjects and different instructors or professors may require different forms of citation or reference styles. The citation or reference style can be changed before beginning a new document or while working in an existing document. To change the reference style of an existing document, click the References tab, click the *Style* option box arrow, and then click the style at the drop-down list.

1. With **5-MobileSecurity.docx** open, change the document and works cited page from MLA style to APA style by completing the following steps:
   a. With the insertion point positioned at the beginning of the document, click the References tab.
   b. Click the *Style* option box arrow in the Citations & Bibliography group and then click *APA* at the drop-down list.
   c. Scroll to the last page in the document (notice the changes to the citations), change the title *Works Cited* to *References*, select the four references, change the font to 12-point Cambria, remove the extra spacing after paragraphs, and then change the line spacing to double spacing (2.0).

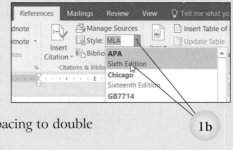

2. Save the document and then print only the references page.
3. Close **5-MobileSecurity.docx**.
4. Display a blank document, click the References tab, change the style to *MLA*, and then close the document without saving it.

Check Your Work

Chapter Summary

- Text in paragraphs, columns, and tables can be sorted alphabetically, numerically, and chronologically. Use the Sort button in the Paragraph group on the Home tab to sort text in paragraphs, columns, and tables.

- When sorting text set in columns, Word considers text typed at the left margin *Field 1*, text typed at the first tab *Field 2*, and so on.

- Sort on more than one field with the *Sort by* and *Then by* options at the Sort dialog box.

- Use the *Header row* option in the *My list has* section in the Sort Text dialog box to sort all the text in columns except the first row.

- Sort records in a data source file at the Mail Merge Recipients dialog box. Sort by clicking the column heading or using options at the Filter and Sort dialog box with the Sort Records tab selected.

- Select specific records in a data source file with options at the Filter and Sort dialog box with the Filter Records tab selected.

- Use the *Comparison* option box at the Filter and Sort dialog box to refine a search to records that meet specific criteria.

- Use the <u>Find duplicates</u> hyperlink in the *Refine recipient list* section of the Mail Merge Recipients dialog box to find duplicate records in a data source file, and use the <u>Find recipient</u> hyperlink to search for records that match a specific criterion.

- Save a document as a template by changing the *Save as type* option at the Save As dialog box to *Word Template (*.dotx)*. Or display the Export backstage area, click the *Change File Type* option, click the *Template (*.dotx)* option, and then click the Save As button.

- Word adds the file extension *.dotx* to a template.

- Open a document based on a template from the Custom Office Templates folder by displaying the New backstage area, clicking the *PERSONAL* option, and then clicking the template.

- Footnotes and endnotes provide explanatory notes and source citations. Footnotes are inserted and printed at the bottoms of pages and endnotes are inserted and printed at the end of the document.

- By default, footnotes are numbered with arabic numbers and endnotes are numbered with lowercase roman numerals.

- When printing a document containing footnotes, Word automatically reduces the number of lines on each page to create space for the footnotes and the separator line. In a document containing endnotes, the notes are separated from the last line of text by a separator line.

- Move, copy, or delete a footnote/endnote reference number in a document and all the other footnotes/endnotes automatically renumber.

- Delete a footnote or endnote by selecting the reference number and then pressing the Delete key.

- Use options at the Footnote and Endnote dialog box to convert footnotes to endnotes and endnotes to footnotes and to change note numbering and number formatting.

- Consider using in-text citations to acknowledge sources in a report or research paper. Commonly used citation and reference styles include American Psychological Association (APA), Modern Language Association (MLA), and *Chicago Manual of Style* (Chicago).

- Insert a citation using the Insert Citation button in the Citations & Bibliography group on the References tab. Specify source information at the Create Source dialog box.

- Insert a source citation placeholder in a document if the source information will be added later.

- When source information is inserted at the Create Source dialog box, Word automatically saves it. New citations can be added using this saved source information.

- Edit a citation at the Edit Citation dialog box—for instance, to add the page numbers of quoted material. To display this dialog box, click the citation, click the Citation Options arrow, and then click the *Edit Citation* option.

- Edit a source at the Edit Source dialog box. Display this dialog box by clicking the source citation in the document, clicking the Citation Options arrow, and then clicking *Edit Source* at the drop-down list. Another option is to display the Source Manager dialog box, click the source to be edited, and then click the Edit button.

- Use options at the Source Manager dialog box to copy, delete, and edit existing sources and create new sources. Display this dialog box by clicking the Manage Sources button in the Citations & Bibliography group on the References tab.

- Insert a sources list—such as a works cited page, references page, or bibliography—at the end of the document on a separate page. To do so, use the Bibliography button in the Citations & Bibliography group on the References tab.

- To update a sources list, click in the list and then click the Update Citations and Bibliography tab.

- Apply APA, MLA, or Chicago style to the sources list in a new or existing document using the *Style* option box in the Citations & Bibliography group on the References tab.

Commands Review

FEATURE	RIBBON TAB, GROUP/OPTION	BUTTON, OPTION	KEYBOARD SHORTCUT
bibliography or works cited	References, Citations & Bibliography		
citation style	References, Citations & Bibliography		
Create Source dialog box	References, Citations & Bibliography	, Add New Source	
Filter and Sort dialog box with Select Records tab selected	Mailings, Start Mail Merge	, Filter	
Filter and Sort dialog box with Sort Records tab selected	Mailings, Start Mail Merge	, Sort	
endnote	References, Footnotes		Alt + Ctrl + D
footnote	References, Footnotes	AB¹	Alt + Ctrl + F
Footnote and Endnote	References, Footnotes		dialog box
next footnote	References, Footnotes	AB¹	
personal template	File, *New*, *PERSONAL*		
show footnotes and endnotes	References, Footnotes		
Sort Options dialog box	Home, Paragraph	, Options	
Sort Text dialog box	Home, Paragraph		
Source Manager dialog box	References, Citations & Bibliography		

Microsoft®

Word

Creating Specialized Tables and Indexes

Performance Objectives

Precheck

Check your current skills to help focus your study.

Upon successful completion of Chapter 6, you will be able to:

1   Create, insert, and update a table of contents

2   Create, insert, and update a table of figures

3   Create and customize captions

4   Create, insert, and update an index

A book, textbook, report, or manuscript often includes sections such as a table of contents, table of figures, and index. Creating these sections manually can be tedious. However, using Word's automated features, these sections can be created quickly and easily. In this chapter, you will learn how to mark text for a table of contents, table of figures, and index and then insert the table or index in a document.

SNAP

If you are a SNAP user, launch the Precheck and Tutorials from your Assignments page.

Data Files

Before beginning chapter work, copy the WL2C6 folder to your storage medium and then make WL2C6 the active folder.

Project 1 **Create a Table of Contents for a Computer** **2 Parts**
Interface Report

You will open a report on computer interfaces, mark text for a table of contents, and then insert the table of contents in the document. You will also customize and update the table of contents.

Preview Finished Project

Creating a Table of Contents

Table of Contents

A table of contents appears at the beginning of a book, manuscript, or report and contains headings and subheadings with page numbers. In Chapter 3, a table of contents was created using the Quick Parts button in the Text group on the Insert tab. A table of contents can also be created using the Table of Contents button in the Table of Contents group on the References tab. Identify the text to be included in a table of contents by applying built-in heading styles or custom styles, assigning levels, or marking text.

Applying Styles

Hint If you apply heading styles to the text in a document, you can easily insert a table of contents later.

To create a table of contents with built-in styles, open the document and then apply the styles. All the text with the Heading 1 style applied is used for the first level of the table of contents, all the text with the Heading 2 style applied is used for the second level, and so on. Apply built-in styles with options in the Styles group on the Home tab.

Tutorial

Inserting a Table of Contents

Inserting a Table of Contents

After applying styles to the headings, insert the table of contents in the document. To do this, position the insertion point where the table of contents is to appear, click the References tab, click the Table of Contents button, and then click the specific option at the drop-down list.

Quick Steps

Insert a Table of Contents
1. Apply heading styles.
2. Click References tab.
3. Click Table of Contents button.
4. Click option at drop-down list.

Number the Table of Contents Page
1. Click Insert tab.
2. Click Page Number button.
3. Click *Format Page Numbers*.
4. Change number format to lowercase roman numerals at Page Number Format dialog box.
5. Click OK.

Page Number

Numbering the Table of Contents Page

Generally, the pages that contain the table of contents are numbered with lowercase roman numerals (*i, ii, iii*). Change the format of the page number to lowercase roman numerals at the Page Number Format dialog box, shown in Figure 6.1. Display this dialog box by clicking the Insert tab, clicking the Page Number button in the Header & Footer group, and then clicking *Format Page Numbers* at the drop-down list.

The first page of text in the main document, which usually comes immediately after the table of contents, should begin with arabic number 1. To change from roman to arabic page numbers within the same document, separate the table of contents from the first page of the document with a section break that begins a new page.

Figure 6.1 Page Number Format Dialog Box

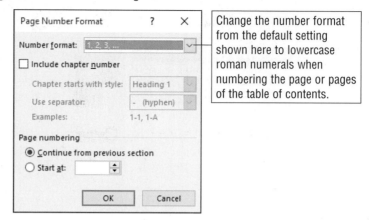

Change the number format from the default setting shown here to lowercase roman numerals when numbering the page or pages of the table of contents.

Navigating Using a Table of Contents

Hint You can use a table of contents to navigate quickly in a document and to get an overview of the topics it covers.

When a table of contents is inserted in a document, the headings contained in the table of contents can be used to navigate within the document. The headings in the table of contents are hyperlinks that connect to the headings where they appear within the document.

To navigate in a document using the table of contents headings, click in the table of contents to select it. Position the mouse pointer over a heading and a box displays with the path and file name as well as the text *Ctrl+Click to follow link*. Press and hold down the Ctrl key, click the left mouse button, and release the Ctrl key and the insertion point is positioned in the document at the location of the heading.

Project 1a   Inserting a Table of Contents   Part 1 of 2

1. Open **AIReport.docx** and then save it with the name **6-AIReport**. (This document contains headings with heading styles applied.)
2. Position the insertion point immediately left of the first *N* in *NATURAL INTERFACE APPLICATIONS* and then insert a section break by completing the following steps:
   a. Click the Layout tab.
   b. Click the Breaks button in the Page Setup group.
   c. Click the *Next Page* option in the *Section Breaks* section.
3. With the insertion point positioned below the section break, insert page numbers and change the beginning number to 1 by completing the following steps:
   a. Click the Insert tab.
   b. Click the Page Number button in the Header & Footer group, point to *Bottom of Page*, and then click *Plain Number 2*.

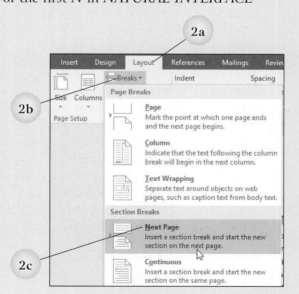

c. Click the Page Number button in the Header & Footer group on the Header & Footer Tools Design tab and then click *Format Page Numbers* at the drop-down list.

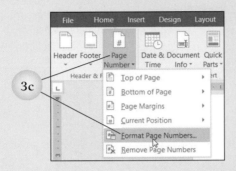

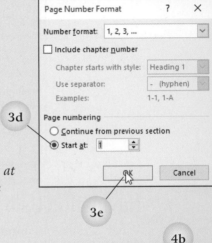

d. At the Page Number Format dialog box, click *Start at* in the *Page numbering* section. (This inserts *1* in the *Start at* measurement box.)

e. Click OK to close the Page Number Format dialog box.

f. Double-click in the document to make it active.

4. Insert a table of contents at the beginning of the document by completing the following steps:

a. Press Ctrl + Home to move the insertion point to the beginning of the document.

b. Click the References tab.

c. Click the Table of Contents button in the Table of Contents group and then click the *Automatic Table 1* option in the *Built-In* section of the drop-down list.

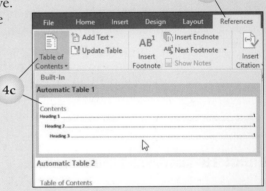

5. Insert a page number on the table of contents page by completing the following steps:

a. Scroll up the document and then click in the heading *Contents*.

b. Click the Insert tab.

c. Click the Page Number button in the Header & Footer group and then click *Format Page Numbers* at the drop-down list.

d. At the Page Number Format dialog box, click the *Number format* option box arrow and then click *i, ii, iii, …* at the drop-down list.

e. Click OK to close the dialog box.

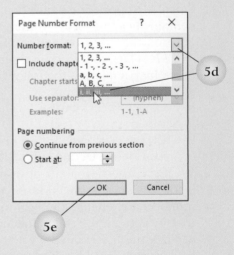

6. Navigate in the document using the table of contents by completing the following steps:

a. Click in the table of contents.

b. Position the mouse pointer on the heading *Virtual Reality*, press and hold down the Ctrl key, click the left mouse button, and then release the Ctrl key. (This moves the insertion point to the beginning of the heading *Virtual Reality* in the document.)

c. Press Ctrl + Home to move the insertion point to the beginning of the document.

7. Save **6-AIReport.docx** and then print only page 1 (the table of contents page).

Check Your Work

Customizing a Table of Contents

Customize an existing table of contents in a document with options at the Table of Contents dialog box, shown in Figure 6.2. Display this dialog box by clicking the Table of Contents button on the References tab and then clicking *Custom Table of Contents* at the drop-down list.

At the Table of Contents dialog box, a sample table of contents displays in the *Print Preview* section. Change the table of contents format by clicking the *Formats* option box arrow in the *General* section. At the drop-down list that displays, click a format. When a different format is selected, that format displays in the *Print Preview* section.

Page numbers in a table of contents will display after the text or aligned at the right margin, depending on what option is selected. Page number alignment can also be specified with the *Right align page numbers* option. The possible number of levels in the contents list that display in a table of contents depends on the number of heading levels in the document. Control the number of levels that display with the *Show levels* measurement box in the *General* section. Tab leaders help guide readers' eyes from the table of contents heading to the page number. The default tab leader is a period. To choose a different leader, click the *Tab leader* option box arrow and then click a character at the drop-down list.

Figure 6.2 Table of Contents Dialog Box

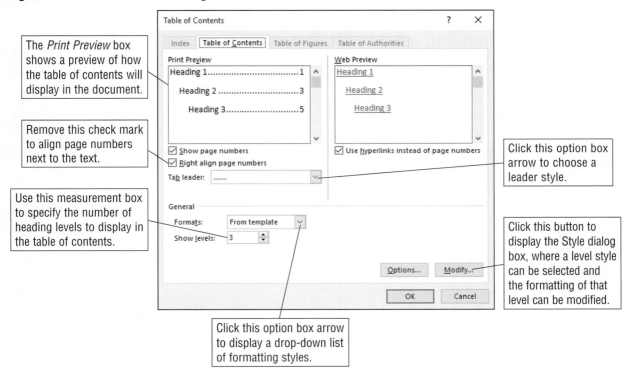

Word automatically formats the headings in a table of contents as hyperlinks and inserts page numbers. Each hyperlink can be used to move the insertion point to a specific location in the document. Word automatically inserts a check mark in the *Use hyperlinks instead of page numbers* check box so that if the document is posted to the web, readers will only need to click the hyperlink to view a specific page. Therefore readers of the document on the web do not need page numbers. Remove page numbering in the printed document by removing the check mark from the *Show page numbers* check box in the Table of Contents dialog box.

If changes are made to the options at the Table of Contents dialog box, clicking OK will cause a message to display asking if the selected table of contents should be replaced. At this message, click Yes.

Updating a Table of Contents

If headings or other text in a document is deleted, moved, or edited after the table of contents is inserted, the table of contents will need to be updated. To do this, click in the current table of contents and then click the Update Table button in the Table of Contents group, the Update Table tab, or press the F9 function key (the Update Field key). At the Update Table of Contents dialog box, shown in Figure 6.3, click *Update page numbers only* if changes were made that only affected page numbers or click *Update entire table* if changes were made to the headings or subheadings in the document. Click OK or press the Enter key to close the dialog box.

Removing a Table of Contents

Remove a table of contents from a document by clicking the Table of Contents button on the References tab and then clicking *Remove Table of Contents* at the drop-down list. Another way to remove a table of contents is to click in the table of contents, click the Table of Contents tab in the upper left corner of the table of contents (immediately left of the Update Table tab), and then click *Remove Table of Contents* at the drop-down list.

Update Table

Quick Steps

Update a Table of Contents
1. Click in table of contents.
2. Click References tab.
3. Click Update Table button, Update Table tab, or press F9.
4. Click *Update page numbers only* or *Update entire table.*
5. Click OK.

Remove a Table of Contents
1. Click References tab.
2. Click Table of Contents button.
3. Click *Remove Table of Contents.*
OR
1. Click in table of contents.
2. Click Table of Contents tab.
3. Click *Remove Table of Contents.*

Figure 6.3 Update Table of Contents Dialog Box

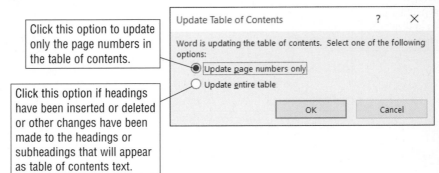

Click this option to update only the page numbers in the table of contents.

Click this option if headings have been inserted or deleted or other changes have been made to the headings or subheadings that will appear as table of contents text.

1. With **6-AIReport.docx** open and the insertion point positioned at the beginning of the document, apply a different formatting style to the table of contents by completing the following steps:

   a. Click the References tab, click the Table of Contents button, and then click *Custom Table of Contents* at the drop-down list.

   b. At the Table of Contents dialog box with the Table of Contents tab selected, click the *Formats* option box arrow in the *General* section and then click *Formal* at the drop-down list.

   c. Click the *Tab leader* option box arrow and then click the solid line option (bottom option) at the drop-down list.

   d. Click the *Show levels* measurement box down arrow to change the number to *2*.

   e. Click OK to close the dialog box.

   f. At the message asking if you want to replace the selected table of contents, click the Yes button.

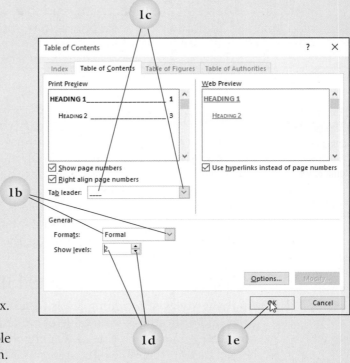

2. Use the table of contents to move the insertion point to the beginning of the heading *Navigation* at the bottom of page 3.

3. Press Ctrl + Enter to insert a page break.

4. Update the table of contents by completing the following steps:

   a. Press Ctrl + Home and then click in the table of contents.

   b. Click the Update Table tab.

   c. At the Update Table of Contents dialog box, make sure *Update page numbers only* is selected and then click OK.

5. Save the document, print only the table of contents page, and then close **6-AIReport.docx**.

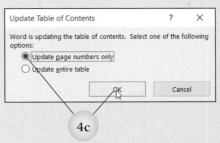

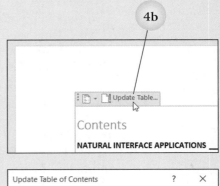

Check Your Work

You will open a document that contains employee pay and evaluation information, mark text as table of contents fields, and then insert a table of contents. You will also insert a file containing additional information on employee classifications and then update the table of contents.

Preview Finished Project

Assigning Levels to Table of Contents Entries

Another method for identifying text for a table of contents is to use the Add Text button in the Table of Contents group on the References tab. Click this button and a drop-down list of level options displays. Click a level for the currently selected text and a heading style is applied to the text. For example, click the *Level 2* option and the Heading 2 style is applied to the selected text. After specifying levels, insert the table of contents by clicking the Table of Contents button and then clicking an option at the drop-down list.

Marking Table of Contents Entries as Fields

Applying styles or assigning levels to text applies specific formatting. To identify titles and/or headings for a table of contents without applying heading style formatting, mark each title or heading as a field entry. To do this, select the text to be included in the table of contents and then press Alt + Shift + O. This displays the Mark Table of Contents Entry dialog box, shown in Figure 6.4.

In the dialog box, the selected text displays in the *Entry* text box. Specify the text level using the *Level* measurement box and then click the Mark button. This turns on the display of nonprinting characters in the document and also inserts a field code immediately after the selected text.

For example, when the title is selected in Project 2a, the following code is inserted immediately after the title *COMPENSATION*: { TC "COMPENSATION" \f C \l "1" }. The Mark Table of Contents Entry dialog box also remains open. To mark the next entry for the table of contents, select the text and then click the Title bar of the Mark Table of Contents Entry dialog box. Specify the level and then click the Mark button. Continue in this manner until all the table of contents entries have been marked.

If the table of contents entries are marked as fields, the *Table entry fields* option will need to be activated when inserting the table of contents. To do this, display the Table of Contents dialog box and then click the Options button. At the Table of Contents Options dialog box, shown in Figure 6.5, click the *Table entry fields* check box to insert a check mark and then click OK.

Figure 6.4 Mark Table of Contents Entry Dialog Box

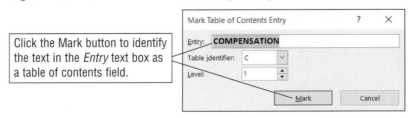

Click the Mark button to identify the text in the *Entry* text box as a table of contents field.

Figure 6.5 Table of Contents Options Dialog Box

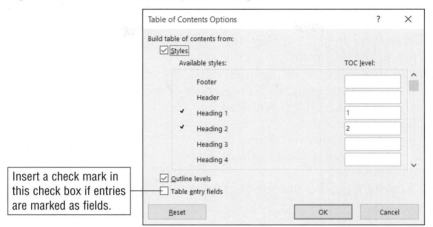

Insert a check mark in this check box if entries are marked as fields.

Project 2a Marking Headings as Fields

1. Open **CompEval.docx** and then save it with the name **6-CompEval**.
2. Position the insertion point immediately left of the *C* in *COMPENSATION* and then insert a section break that begins a new page by clicking the Layout tab, clicking the Breaks button in the Page Setup group, and then clicking the *Next Page* option.
3. Mark the titles and headings as fields for insertion in a table of contents by completing the following steps:
   a. Select the title *COMPENSATION*.
   b. Press Alt + Shift + O.
   c. At the Mark Table of Contents Entry dialog box, make sure the *Level* measurement box is set at *1* and then click the Mark button. (This turns on the display of nonprinting characters.)
   d. Click in the document, scroll down, and then select the title *EVALUATION*.
   e. Click the dialog box Title bar and then click the Mark button.
   f. Click in the document, scroll up, and then select the heading *Rate of Pay*.
   g. Click the dialog box Title bar and then click the *Level* measurement box up arrow in the Mark Table of Contents Entry dialog box until *2* displays.
   h. Click the Mark button.
   i. Mark the following headings as level 2:

      Direct Deposit Option
      Pay Progression
      Overtime
      Work Performance Standards
      Performance Evaluation
      Employment Records

   j. Click the Close button to close the Mark Table of Contents Entry dialog box.

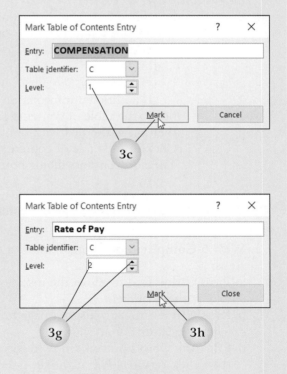

4. Position the insertion point at the beginning of the title *COMPENSATION*. Insert a page number at the bottom center of each page of the section and change the starting number to 1. ***Hint: Refer to Project 1a, Step 3.***
5. Double-click in the document.
6. Insert a table of contents at the beginning of the document by completing the following steps:
   a. Position the insertion point at the beginning of the document (on the new page).
   b. Type the title TABLE OF CONTENTS and then press the Enter key.
   c. Click the References tab.
   d. Click the Table of Contents button and then click *Custom Table of Contents* at the drop-down list.
   e. At the Table of Contents dialog box, click the Options button.
   f. At the Table of Contents Options dialog box, click the *Table entry fields* check box to insert a check mark.
   g. Click OK to close the Table of Contents Options dialog box.
   h. Click OK to close the Table of Contents dialog box.
   i. Apply bold formatting to and center the heading *TABLE OF CONTENTS*.

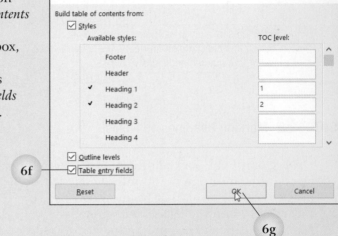

7. Insert a lowercase roman numeral page number on the table of contents page. ***Hint: Refer to Project 1a, Step 5.***
8. Click the Show/Hide ¶ button to turn off the display of nonprinting characters.
9. Save **6-CompEval.docx** and then print only page 1 (the table of contents page).

Check Your Work

If additional information is inserted in a document with headings marked as fields, the table of contents can be easily updated. To do this, insert the text and then mark the text with options at the Mark Table of Contents Entry dialog box. Click in the table of contents and then click the Update Table tab. At the Update Table of Contents dialog box, click the *Update entire table* option and then click OK.

Project 2b Updating an Entire Table of Contents   Part 2 of 2

1. With **6-CompEval.docx** open, insert a file into the document by completing the following steps:
   a. Press Ctrl + End to move the insertion point to the end of the document.
   b. Press Ctrl + Enter to insert a page break.
   c. Click the Insert tab.
   d. Click the Object button arrow in the Text group and then click *Text from File* at the drop-down list.
   e. At the Insert File dialog box, navigate to the WL2C6 folder on your storage medium and then double-click **PosClass.docx**.

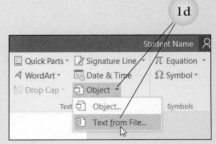

2. Select and then mark text for inclusion in the table of contents by completing the following steps:
   a. Select the title *POSITION CLASSIFICATION*.
   b. Press Alt + Shift + O.
   c. At the Mark Table of Contents Entry dialog box, make sure that *1* displays in the *Level* measurement box and then click the Mark button.
   d. Click the Close button to close the Mark Table of Contents Entry dialog box.
3. Update the table of contents by completing the following steps:
   a. Select the entire table of contents (excluding the title).
   b. Click the References tab.
   c. Click the Update Table button in the Table of Contents group.
   d. At the Update Table of Contents dialog box, click the *Update entire table* option.
   e. Click OK.
4. Turn off the display of nonprinting characters.
5. Save the document, print only the table of contents page, and then close **6-CompEval.docx**.

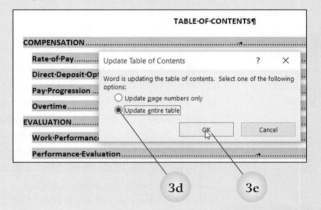

Check Your Work

Project 3 **Create a Table of Figures for a Technology Report**   **3 Parts**
                    and a Travel Document

You will open a report containing information on software, output devices, and the software development cycle, as well as images and a SmartArt diagram; insert captions; and then create a table of figures. You will also create and customize captions and insert a table of figures for an adventure document.

Preview Finished Project

Creating a Table of Figures

Insert Caption

Insert Table of Figures

A document that contains figures should include a table of figures so readers can quickly locate specific figures, images, tables, equations, and charts. Figure 6.6 shows an example of a table of figures. Create a table of figures by marking text or images with captions and then using the caption names to create the table. The Captions group on the References tab includes the Insert Caption button for creating captions and the Insert Table of Figures button for inserting a table of figures in a document.

Figure 6.6 Sample Table of Figures

> **TABLE OF FIGURES**
>

Tutorial

Creating and Customizing Captions

Quick Steps

Create a Caption
1. Select text or image.
2. Click References tab.
3. Click Insert Caption button.
4. Type caption name.
5. Click OK.

Creating a Caption

A caption is text that describes an item such as a figure, image, table, equation, or chart. The caption generally displays below the item. Create a caption by selecting the figure text or image, clicking the References tab, and then clicking the Insert Caption button in the Captions group. This displays the Caption dialog box, shown in Figure 6.7. At the dialog box, *Figure 1* displays in the *Caption* text box and the insertion point is positioned after *Figure 1*. Type a name for the figure and then press the Enter key. Word inserts *Figure 1* followed by the typed caption below the selected text or image. If the insertion point is positioned in a table when the Caption dialog box is displayed, *Table 1* displays in the *Caption* text box instead of *Figure 1*.

Tutorial

Inserting a Table of Figures

Quick Steps

Insert a Table of Figures
1. Click References tab.
2. Click Insert Table of Figures button.
3. Select format.
4. Click OK.

Inserting a Table of Figures

After marking figures, images, tables, equations, or charts with captions in a document, insert the table of figures. A table of figures generally displays at the beginning of the document after the table of contents and on a separate page. To insert the table of figures, click the Insert Table of Figures button in the Captions group on the References tab. At the Table of Figures dialog box, shown in Figure 6.8, make any necessary changes and then click OK.

The options at the Table of Figures dialog box are similar to the options at the Table of Contents dialog box. They include choosing a format for the table of figures from the *Formats* option box, changing the alignment of the page numbers, and adding leaders before page numbers.

Figure 6.7 Caption Dialog Box

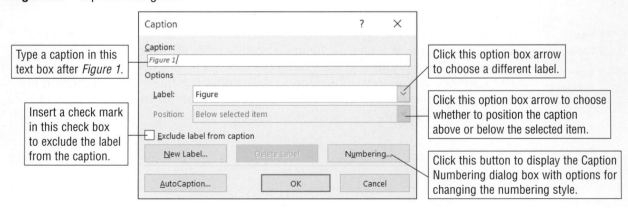

Type a caption in this text box after *Figure 1*.

Insert a check mark in this check box to exclude the label from the caption.

Click this option box arrow to choose a different label.

Click this option box arrow to choose whether to position the caption above or below the selected item.

Click this button to display the Caption Numbering dialog box with options for changing the numbering style.

Figure 6.8 Table of Figures Dialog Box

The *Print Preview* box shows a preview of how the table of figures will display in the document.

Click this option box arrow to display table of figures formatting styles.

Click this option box arrow to specify the caption labels of items to be included in the table of figures.

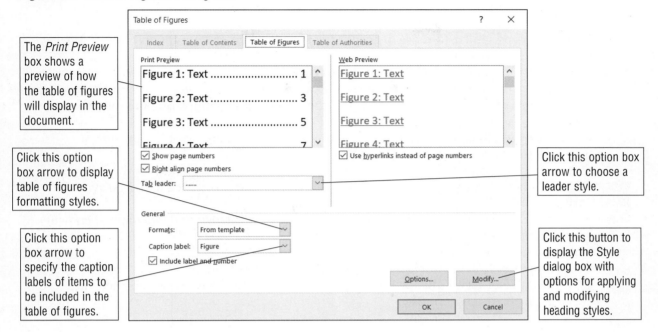

Click this option box arrow to choose a leader style.

Click this button to display the Style dialog box with options for applying and modifying heading styles.

Project 3a Creating a Table of Figures

Part 1 of 3

1. Open **TechRpt.docx** and then save it with the name **6-TechRpt**.
2. Add the caption *Figure 1 Word Document* to an image by completing the following steps:
   a. Click the screen image in the WORD PROCESSING SOFTWARE section.
   b. Click the References tab.
   c. Click the Insert Caption button in the Captions group.
   d. At the Caption dialog box with the insertion point positioned after *Figure 1* in the *Caption* text box, press the spacebar and then type Word Document.
   e. Click OK or press the Enter key.

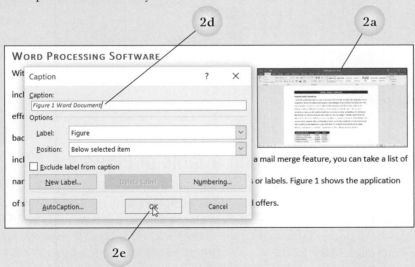

   f. Press Ctrl + E to center the caption in the text box.

3. Complete steps similar to those in Step 2 to create and center the caption *Figure 2 Excel Worksheet* for the image in the *SPREADSHEET SOFTWARE* section.
4. Complete steps similar to those in Step 2 to create and center the caption *Figure 3 Monitor* for the image in the *MONITOR* section.
5. Complete steps similar to those in Step 2 to create and center the caption *Figure 4 Software Life Cycle* for the SmartArt graphic in the *Developing Software* section.
6. Insert a table of figures at the beginning of the document by completing the following steps:
   a. Press Ctrl + Home to move the insertion point to the beginning of the document.
   b. Press Ctrl + Enter to insert a page break.
   c. Press Ctrl + Home to move the insertion point back to the beginning of the document, turn on bold formatting, change the paragraph alignment to center, and then type the title TABLE OF FIGURES.
   d. Press the Enter key, turn off bold formatting, and then change the paragraph alignment back to left alignment.
   e. If necessary, click the References tab.
   f. Click the Insert Table of Figures button in the Captions group.
   g. At the Table of Figures dialog box, click the *Formats* option box arrow and then click *Formal* at the drop-down list.

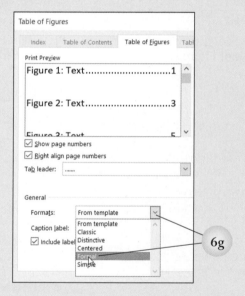

   h. Click OK.
7. Save **6-TechRpt.docx**.

Check Your Work

Updating or Deleting a Table of Figures

Quick Steps
Update a Table of Figures
1. Click in table of figures.
2. Click References tab.
3. Click Update Table button or press F9.
4. Click OK.

Delete a Table of Figures
1. Select entire table of figures.
2. Press Delete key.

If changes are made to a document after a table of figures is inserted, update the table. To do this, click in the table of figures and then click the Update Table button in the Captions group on the References tab or press the F9 function key. At the Update Table of Figures dialog box, click *Update page numbers only* if changes were made only to the page numbers or click *Update entire table* if changes were made to caption text. Click OK or press the Enter key to close the dialog box. To delete a table of figures, select the entire table using the mouse or keyboard and then press the Delete key.

1. With **6-TechRpt.docx** open, insert an image of a laser printer by completing the following steps:
   a. Move the insertion point to the beginning of the second paragraph of text in the *PRINTERS* section.
   b. Click the Insert tab and then click the Pictures button in the Illustrations group.
   c. At the Insert Picture dialog box, navigate to the WL2C6 folder on your storage medium and then double-click the file named ***LaserPrinter.png***.
   d. Change the height of the image to 1.5 inches.
   e. Change to square text wrapping.
2. Add the caption *Figure 4 Laser Printer* to the printer image and then center the caption.
3. Click in the table of figures.
4. Press the F9 function key.
5. At the Update Table of Figures dialog box, click the *Update entire table* option and then click OK.
6. Save, print, and then close **6-TechRpt.docx**.

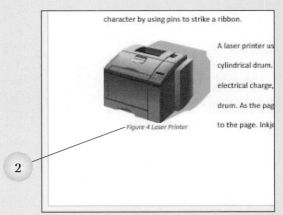

Check Your Work

Customizing a Caption

The Caption dialog box contains a number of options for customizing captions. Click the *Label* option box arrow to specify the caption label. The default is *Figure*, which can be changed to *Equation* or *Table*. The caption is positioned below the selected item. Use the *Position* option to change the position of the caption so it is above the selected item by default. A caption contains a label, such as *Figure*, *Table*, or *Equation*. To insert only a caption number and not a caption label, insert a check mark in the *Exclude label from caption* check box.

Click the New Label button and the Label dialog box displays. At this dialog box, type a custom label for the caption. Word automatically inserts an arabic number (*1, 2, 3,* and so on) after each caption label. To change the caption numbering style, click the Numbering button. At the Caption Numbering dialog box that displays, click the *Format* option box arrow and then click a numbering style at the drop-down list. For example, caption numbering can be changed to uppercase or lowercase letters or to roman numerals.

If items such as tables are inserted in a document on a regular basis, a caption can be inserted automatically with each item. To do this, click the AutoCaption button. At the AutoCaption dialog box, insert a check mark before the item (such as *Microsoft Word Table*) in the *Add caption when inserting* list box and then click OK. Each time a table is inserted in a document, Word inserts a caption above it.

1. Open **TTSAdventures.docx** and then save it with the name **6-TTSAdventures**.
2. Insert a custom caption for the first table by completing the following steps:
    a. Click in any cell in the table.
    b. Click the References tab.
    c. Click the Insert Caption button.
    d. At the Caption dialog box, press the spacebar and then type Antarctic Zenith Adventures in the *Caption* text box.
    e. Remove the label (*Figure*) from the caption by clicking the *Exclude label from caption* check box to insert a check mark.
    f. Click the Numbering button.
    g. At the Caption Numbering dialog box, click the *Format* option box arrow and then click the *A, B, C, …* option at the drop-down list.
    h. Click OK to close the Caption Numbering dialog box.
    i. At the Caption dialog box, click the *Position* option box arrow and then click *Below selected item* at the drop-down list. (Skip this step if *Below selected item* is already selected.)
    j. Click OK to close the Caption dialog box.

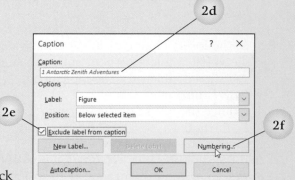

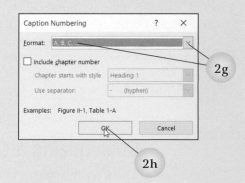

3. After looking at the caption, you decide to add a custom label and change the numbering. Do this by completing the following steps:
    a. Select the caption *A Antarctic Zenith Adventures*.
    b. Click the Insert Caption button in the Captions group on the References tab.
    c. At the Caption dialog box, click the *Exclude label from caption* check box to remove the check mark.
    d. Click the New Label button.
    e. At the New Label dialog box, type Adventure and then click OK.
    f. Click OK to close the Caption dialog box.
4. Format the caption by completing the following steps:
    a. Select the caption *Adventure 1 Antarctic Zenith Adventures*.
    b. Click the Home tab.
    c. Click the Font Color button arrow.
    d. Click the *Dark Blue* color (ninth color in the *Standard Colors* section).
    e. Click the Bold button.
5. Insert a custom caption for the second table by completing the following steps:
    a. Click in any cell in the table.
    b. Click the References tab and then click the Insert Caption button.
    c. At the Caption dialog box, press the spacebar and then type Tall-Ship Adventures.
    d. Make sure *Below selected item* displays in the *Position* option box and then click OK to close the Caption dialog box.
6. Select the caption *Adventure 2 Tall-Ship Adventures*, apply the standard dark blue font color, and apply bold formatting.

7. Insert a table of figures by completing the following steps:
   a. Press Ctrl + Home and then press Ctrl + Enter to insert a page break.
   b. Press Ctrl + Home to move the insertion point above the page break.
   c. Turn on bold formatting, type TABLES, turn off bold formatting, and then press the Enter key.
   d. Click the References tab and then click the Insert Table of Figures button in the Captions group.
   e. At the Table of Figures dialog box, click OK.
8. Save, print, and then close **6-TTSAdventures.docx**.

Check Your Work

Project 4 Create an Index for a Desktop Publishing Report　　　**2 Parts**

You will open a report containing information on desktop publishing, mark specific text for an index, and then insert the index in the document. You will also make changes to the document and then update the index.

Preview Finished Project

Creating an Index

An index is a list of the topics in a publication that includes the numbers of the pages those topics are discussed on. In Word, the process of creating an index is automated similarly to the process of creating a table of contents. When creating an index, single words and groups of words are marked to be included.

Creating an index takes careful thought and consideration. The author of the book, manuscript, or report must determine the main entries to be included, as well as the subentries to be added under the main entries. An index may include entries such as the main subject of a document, the main subjects of chapters and sections, variations of headings and subheadings, and abbreviations. Figure 6.9 shows an example of a portion of an index.

Figure 6.9 Sample Index

INDEX

A
Alignment, 12, 16
ASCII, 22, 24, 35
　　data processing, 41
　　word processing, 39

B
Backmatter, 120
　　page numbering, 123
Balance, 67-69
Banners, 145

C
Callouts, 78
Captions, 156
Color, 192-195
　　　ink for offset printing, 193
　　　process color, 195

D
Databases, 124-129
　　fields, 124
　　records, 124
Directional flow, 70-71

Marking Text for an Index

A selected word or group of words can be marked for inclusion in an index. Before marking the text for an index, determine what main entries and subentries are to be included. Selected text is marked as an index entry at the Mark Index Entry dialog box.

To mark text for an index, select the word or group of words, click the References tab, and then click the Mark Entry button in the Index group. Another option is to use the keyboard shortcut Alt + Shift + X. At the Mark Index Entry dialog box, shown in Figure 6.10, the selected word or group of words appears in the *Main entry* text box. Click the Mark button to mark the word or groups of words and then click the Close button. Word automatically turns on the display of nonprinting characters and displays the index field code.

At the Mark Index Entry dialog box, if the selected word or group of words displayed in the *Main entry* text box is to be a main entry, leave it as displayed. However, if the selected text is to be a subentry, type the main entry in the *Main entry* text box, click in the *Subentry* text box, and then type the selected text. For example, suppose a publication includes the terms *Page layout* and *Portrait*. The group of words *Page layout* is to be marked as a main entry for the index and the word *Portrait* is to be marked as a subentry below *Page layout*. Marking these terms for use in an index would involve completing these steps:

1. Select *Page layout*.
2. Click the References tab and then click the Mark Entry button or press Alt + Shift + X.
3. At the Mark Index Entry dialog box, click the Mark button. (This turns on the display of nonprinting characters.)
4. With the Mark Index Entry dialog box still displayed, click in the document to make it active and then select the word *Portrait*.
5. Click the Mark Index Entry dialog box Title bar to make it active.
6. Select *Portrait* in the *Main entry* text box and then type Page layout.
7. Click in the *Subentry* text box and then type Portrait.
8. Click the Mark button.
9. Click the Close button.

Figure 6.10 Mark Index Entry Dialog Box

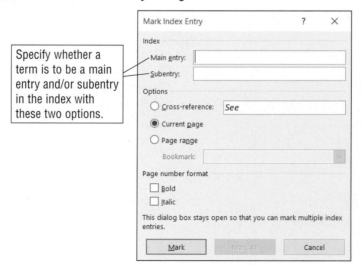

Specify whether a term is to be a main entry and/or subentry in the index with these two options.

The main entry and subentry do not have to be the same as the selected text. Select text for an index, type specific text to be displayed in the document in the *Main entry* or *Subentry* text box, and then click the Mark button. At the Mark Index Entry dialog box, bold and/or italic formatting can be applied to the page numbers that will appear in the index. In the *Page number format* section, click *Bold* and/or *Italic* to insert a check mark in the check box.

In the *Options* section of the Mark Index Entry dialog box, *Current page* is the default. At this setting, the current page number will be provided in the index for the main entry and/or subentry. Click the *Cross-reference* option to cross reference specific text. To do this, type the text to be used as a cross-reference for the index entry in the *Cross-reference* text box. For example, the word *Serif* can be marked and cross referenced to *Typefaces*.

Click the Mark All button at the Mark Index Entry dialog box to mark all occurrences of the term in the document as index entries. Word marks only those entries whose uppercase and lowercase letters match the index entries.

Project 4a Marking Text for an Index   Part 1 of 2

1. Open **DTP.docx** and then save it with the name **6-DTP**.
2. Insert a page number at the bottom center of each page.
3. In the first paragraph, mark *software* for the index as a main entry and mark *word processing* as a subentry below *software* by completing the following steps:
   a. Select *software* (located in the second sentence of the first paragraph).
   b. Click the References tab and then click the Mark Entry button in the Index group.
   c. At the Mark Index Entry dialog box, click the Mark All button. (This turns on the display of nonprinting characters.)

   d. With the Mark Index Entry dialog box still displayed, click in the document to make it active and then select *word processing* (located in the last sentence of the first paragraph). (You may want to drag the dialog box down the screen so more of the document text is visible.)
   e. Click the Title bar of the Mark Index Entry dialog box to make the dialog box active.

f. Select *word processing* in the *Main entry* text box and then type software.

g. Click in the *Subentry* text box and then type word processing.

h. Click the Mark All button.

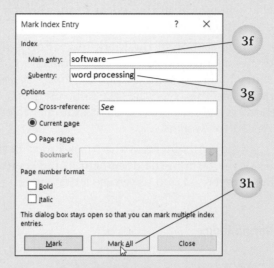

i. With the Mark Index Entry dialog box still displayed, complete steps similar to those in Steps 3d through 3h to select the first occurrence of each of the following words and then mark the word as a main entry or subentry for the index (click the Mark All button at the Mark Index Entry dialog box):

1) In the first paragraph in the *Defining Desktop Publishing* section:

   spreadsheets = subentry (main entry = *software*)
   database = subentry (main entry = *software*)

2) In the second paragraph in the *Defining Desktop Publishing* section:

   publishing = main entry
   desktop = subentry (main entry = *publishing*)
   printer = main entry
   laser = subentry (main entry = *printer*)

3) In the third paragraph in the *Defining Desktop Publishing* section:

   design = main entry

4) In the fourth paragraph in the *Defining Desktop Publishing* section:

   traditional = subentry (main entry = *publishing*)

5) In the only paragraph in the *Initiating the Process* section:

   publication = main entry
   planning = subentry (main entry = *publication*)
   creating = subentry (main entry = *publication*)
   intended audience = subentry (main entry = *publication*)
   content = subentry (main entry = *publication*)

6) In the third paragraph in the *Planning the Publication* section:

   message = main entry

j. Click Close to close the Mark Index Entry dialog box.

4. Turn off the display of nonprinting characters.

5. Save **6-DTP.docx**.

Figure 6.11 Index Dialog Box

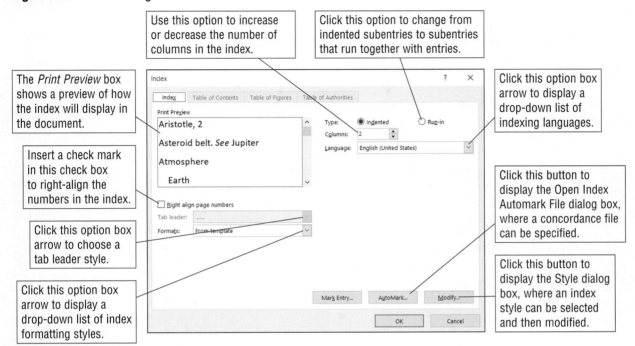

The *Print Preview* box shows a preview of how the index will display in the document.

Use this option to increase or decrease the number of columns in the index.

Click this option to change from indented subentries to subentries that run together with entries.

Click this option box arrow to display a drop-down list of indexing languages.

Insert a check mark in this check box to right-align the numbers in the index.

Click this option box arrow to choose a tab leader style.

Click this option box arrow to display a drop-down list of index formatting styles.

Click this button to display the Open Index Automark File dialog box, where a concordance file can be specified.

Click this button to display the Style dialog box, where an index style can be selected and then modified.

Inserting an Index

After marking all the terms to be included in an index as main entries or subentries, the next step is to insert the index. The index should appear at the end of the document and generally begins on a separate page.

 Insert Index

To insert the index, position the insertion point at the end of the document and then insert a page break. With the insertion point positioned below the page break, type *INDEX*, center it, apply bold formatting, and then press the Enter key. With the insertion point positioned at the left margin, click the References tab and then click the Insert Index button in the Index group. At the Index dialog box, shown in Figure 6.11, select formatting options and then click OK. Word inserts the index at the location of the insertion point with the formatting selected at the Index dialog box. Word also inserts section breaks above and below the index text.

Quick Steps

Insert an Index
1. Click References tab.
2. Click Insert Index button.
3. Select format.
4. Click OK.

At the Index dialog box, specify how the index entries are to appear. The *Print Preview* section shows how the index will display in the document. The *Columns* measurement box has a default setting of *2*. With this setting applied, the index will display in two columns; this number can be increased or decreased.

Insert a check mark in the *Right align page numbers* check box and the *Tab leader* options become active. Use these options to apply leaders before page numbers. The default tab leader is a period. To choose a different leader, click the *Tab leader* option box arrow and then click a character at the drop-down list.

In the *Type* section, the *Indented* option is selected by default. With this setting applied, subentries will appear indented below main entries. Click *Run-in* and subentries will display on the same lines as main entries.

Click the *Formats* option box arrow and a list of formatting choices displays. At this list, click a formatting choice and the *Print Preview* box displays how the index will appear in the document.

1. With **6-DTP.docx** open, insert the index in the document by completing the following steps:
   a. Press Ctrl + End to position the insertion point at the end of the document.
   b. Insert a page break.
   c. With the insertion point positioned below the page break, type INDEX and then press the Enter key.
   d. Click the References tab.
   e. Click the Insert Index button in the Index group.
   f. At the Index dialog box, click the *Formats* option box arrow and then click *Modern* at the drop-down list.
   g. Click OK to close the dialog box.
   h. Click in the title *INDEX*, apply the Heading 1 style (located in the Styles group on the Home tab), and then press Ctrl + E to center the title.
2. Save **6-DTP.docx** and then print the index page (the last page) of the document.
3. Close **6-DTP.docx**.

1f

Check Your Work

Project 5 Mark Index Entries and Insert an Index   1 Part

You will create bookmarks in a document on computers, mark entries for an index, and then insert an index in the document.

Preview Finished Project

Marking Index Entry Options

The *Options* section of the Mark Index Entry dialog box provides additional options for marking text for an index. A bookmark can be marked as an index entry or text can be marked that refers readers to another index entry.

Marking Text That Spans a Range of Pages To use more than a few words as a single index entry, consider identifying the text as a bookmark and then marking the bookmark as an index entry. This option is especially useful when the text for an entry spans a range of pages. To mark text identified as a bookmark, position the insertion point at the end of the text, click the References tab, and then click the Mark Entry button in the Index group.

At the Mark Index Entry dialog box, type the index entry for the text and then click the *Page range* option in the *Options* section. Click the *Bookmark* option box arrow and then click the bookmark name at the drop-down list. Click the Mark button to mark the bookmark text and then close the dialog box.

Marking an Entry as a Cross-Reference Text that refers readers to another entry can be marked for inclusion in an index. For example, if the acronym *MIS* is used in a document to refer to *Management Information Systems*, *MIS* can be marked as an index entry that refers readers to the entry for *Management Information Systems*. To do this, select *MIS*, click the References tab, and then click the Mark Entry button in the Index group. At the Mark Index Entry dialog box, click *Cross-reference* in the *Options* section of the dialog box (to move the insertion point inside the text box), type *Management Information Systems*, and then click the Mark button.

Project 5   Marking Entries and Inserting an Index   Part 1 of 1

1. Open **Computers.docx** and then save it with the name **6-Computers**.
2. Make the following changes to the document:
   a. Apply the Heading 1 style to the title *COMPUTERS*.
   b. Apply the Heading 2 style to the five headings in the document (*Speed*, *Accuracy*, *Versatility*, *Storage*, and *Communications*).
   c. Apply the Lines (Stylish) style set.
   d. Apply the Blue theme colors.
   e. Change the theme fonts to Candara.
3. Create a bookmark for the *Speed* section of the document by completing the following steps:
   a. Select text from the beginning of the heading *Speed* through the paragraph of text that follows the heading.
   b. Click the Insert tab.
   c. Click the Bookmark button in the Links group.
   d. At the Bookmark dialog box, type Speed in the *Bookmark name* text box.
   e. Click the Add button.

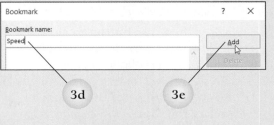

4. Complete steps similar to those in Step 3 to create the following bookmarks:
   a. Select text from the beginning of the *Accuracy* heading through the paragraph of text that follows the heading and then create a bookmark named *Accuracy*.
   b. Select text from the beginning of the *Versatility* heading through the paragraph of text that follows the heading and then create a bookmark named *Versatility*.
   c. Select text from the beginning of the *Storage* heading through the paragraph of text that follows the heading and then create a bookmark named *Storage*.
   d. Select text from the beginning of the *Communications* heading through the two paragraphs of text that follow the heading and then create a bookmark named *Communications*.
5. Mark the *Speed* bookmark as an index entry that spans multiple pages by completing the following steps:
   a. Move the insertion point so it is positioned immediately following the only paragraph of text in the *Speed* section.
   b. Click the References tab.
   c. Click the Mark Entry button in the Index group.
   d. At the Mark Index Entry dialog box, type Speed in the *Main entry* text box.
   e. Click the *Page range* option.
   f. Click the *Bookmark* option box arrow and then click *Speed* at the drop-down list.
   g. Click the Mark button.

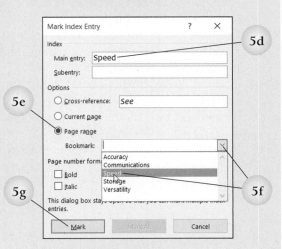

6. Complete steps similar to those in Step 5 to mark the following bookmarks as index entries: *Accuracy, Versatility, Storage*, and *Communications*.
7. With the Mark Index Entry dialog box open, mark the *first* occurrences of the following words (click the Mark All button) as main entries or subentries for the index:
   a. Mark *computers*, located in the first sentence of the first paragraph of text in the document as a main entry.
   b. Mark *personal computers*, located in the second paragraph of text in the document, as a main entry.
   c. Mark *supercomputers*, located in the *Speed* section of the document, as a main entry.
   d. Mark *GIGO*, located in the *Accuracy* section of the document, as a main entry.
   e. Mark the following text located in the *Versatility* section:

   > *Human Genome Project:* main entry
   > *DNA:* main entry

   f. Mark the following text located in the *Communications* section:

   > *wireless devices:* main entry
   > *notebook computers:* subentry (main entry: *wireless devices*)
   > *cell phones:* subentry (main entry: *wireless devices*)
   > *local area network:* main entry
   > *wide area network:* main entry

   g. Click the Close button to close the Mark Index Entry dialog box.
8. Mark *microcomputers* as a cross-reference by completing the following steps:
   a. Press Ctrl + Home to move the insertion point to the beginning of the document.
   b. Select the word *microcomputers* that is located in the first sentence of the second paragraph of text.
   c. If necessary, click the References tab.
   d. Click the Mark Entry button in the Index group.
   e. At the Mark Index Entry dialog box, click the *Cross-reference* option in the *Options* section (after the word *See*) and then type personal computers.
   f. Click the Mark button.
   g. Click the Close button to close the Mark Index Entry dialog box.

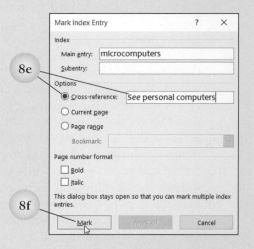

9. Complete steps similar to those in Step 8 to mark the following text as cross-references:
   a. Select *LAN* in the second paragraph of text in the *Communications* section and cross-reference it to *local area network*.
   b. Select *WAN* in the second paragraph of text in the *Communications* section and cross-reference it to *wide area network*.
10. Close the Mark Index Entry dialog box and then turn off the display of nonprinting characters.
11. Insert the index in the document by completing the following steps:
    a. Position the insertion point at the end of the document.
    b. Insert a page break.
    c. With the insertion point positioned below the page break, type INDEX, and then press the Enter key.
    d. Click the References tab.
    e. Click the Insert Index button in the Index group.

f. At the Index dialog box, click the *Formats* option box arrow, scroll down the drop-down list, and then click *Formal*.

g. Make sure *3* displays in the *Columns* measurement box.

h. Click OK to close the dialog box.

i. Apply the Heading 1 style to the title *INDEX*.

12. Save and then print the last page (the index page) of the document.

13. Close **6-Computers.docx**.

Project 6 **Create an Index with a Concordance File for a Newsletter**   **3 Parts**

You will create and then save a concordance file. You will then open a report containing information on designing newsletters and use the concordance file to create an index.

Preview Finished Project

Creating and Using a Concordance File

Tutorial

Creating and Using a Concordance File

Quick Steps

Create a Concordance File

1. Click Insert tab.
2. Click Table button and drag to create table.
3. In first column, type word or words for index.
4. In second column, type corresponding main entry and subentry.
5. Save document.

Another method for creating an index is to create a concordance file and use the information in it to create the index. Creating a concordance file avoids the need to mark each word or group of words in a document.

A concordance file is a Word document that contains a two-column table with no text outside the table. In the first column of the table, enter the word or group of words to be included in the index. In the second column, enter the corresponding main entry and subentry, if applicable, that should appear in the index. To create a subentry, type the main entry followed by a colon, a space, and then the subentry. Figure 6.12 shows an example of a completed concordance file.

In the concordance file shown in Figure 6.12, the word or group of words as it appears in the document text is inserted in the first column (such as *World War I*, *Technology*, and *technology*). The second column contains what is to appear in the index, identifying each item as a main entry or subentry. For example, the words *motion pictures* in the concordance file will appear in the index as a subentry under the main entry *Technology*.

Use a concordance file to quickly mark text for an index in a document. To do this, open the document containing the text to be marked for the index, display the Index dialog box with the Index tab selected, and then click the AutoMark button. At the Open Index AutoMark File dialog box, double-click the concordance file name in the list box. Word turns on the display of nonprinting characters, searches the document for text that matches the text in the concordance file, and then marks it accordingly. After marking text for the index, insert the index at the end of the document, as described earlier.

When creating the concordance file in Project 5a, Word's AutoCorrect feature will automatically capitalize the first letter of the first word entered in each cell. In Figure 6.12, several of the first words in the first column do not begin with capital letters. Before beginning the project, consider turning off this AutoCorrect capitalization feature. To do this, click the File tab and then click *Options*. At the Word Options dialog box, click *Proofing* in the left panel and then click the AutoCorrect Options button. At the AutoCorrect dialog box with the AutoCorrect tab selected, click the *Capitalize first letter of table cells* check box to remove the check mark. Click OK to close the dialog box and then click OK to close the Word Options dialog box.

Figure 6.12 Sample Concordance File

World War I	World War I
Technology	Technology
technology	Technology
Teletypewriters	Technology: teletypewriters
motion pictures	Technology: motion pictures
Television	Technology: television
Radio Corporation of America	Radio Corporation of America
coaxial cable	Coaxial cable
Telephone	Technology: telephone
Communications Act of 1934	Communications Act of 1934
World War II	World War II
radar system	Technology: radar system
Computer	Computer
Atanasoff Berry Computer	Computer: Atanasoff Berry Computer
Korean War	Korean War
Columbia Broadcasting System	Columbia Broadcasting System
Cold War	Cold War
Vietnam	Vietnam
artificial satellite	Technology: artificial satellite
Communications Satellite Act of 1962	Communications Satellite Act of 1962

Project 6a Creating a Concordance File   Part 1 of 3

1. At a blank document, create the text shown in Figure 6.13 as a concordance file by completing the following steps:
   a. Click the Insert tab.
   b. Click the Table button in the Tables group.
   c. Drag down and to the right until *2×1 Table* displays at the top of the grid and then click the left mouse button.

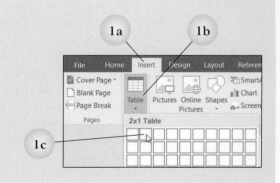

d. Type the text in the cells as shown in Figure 6.13. As you type the text shown in the figure, press the Tab key to move to the next cell. (If you did not remove the check mark before the *Capitalize first letter of table cells* option at the AutoCorrect dialog box, the *n* in the first word in the first cell, *newsletters*, is automatically capitalized. Hover the mouse pointer over the *N*, click the blue rectangle that displays below the *N*, and then click *Stop Auto-capitalizing First Letter of Table Cells*.)

2. Save the document and name it **6-CFile**.
3. Print and then close **6-CFile.docx**.

Check Your Work

Figure 6.13 Project 6a

newsletters	Newsletters
Newsletters	Newsletters
software	Software
desktop publishing	Software: desktop publishing
word processing	Software: word processing
printers	Printers
laser	Printers: laser
Design	Design
communication	Communication
consistency	Design: consistency
ELEMENTS	Elements
Elements	Elements
elements	Elements
Nameplate	Elements: nameplate
nameplate	Elements: nameplate
Logo	Elements: logo
logo	Elements: logo
Subtitle	Elements: subtitle
subtitle	Elements: subtitle
Folio	Elements: folio
folio	Elements: folio
Headlines	Elements: headlines
headlines	Elements: headlines
Subheads	Elements: subheads
subheads	Elements: subheads
Byline	Elements: byline
byline	Elements: byline
Body Copy	Elements: body copy
body copy	Elements: body copy

continues

Figure 6.13 Project 6a—*Continued*

Graphics Images	Elements: graphics images
Graphics images	Elements: graphics images
audience	Newsletters: audience
Purpose	Newsletters: purpose
purpose	Newsletters: purpose
focal point	Newsletters: focal point

If the check mark was removed from the *Capitalize first letter of table cells* option at the AutoCorrect dialog box, this feature may need to be turned back on. To do this, click the File tab and then click *Options*. At the Word Options dialog box, click *Proofing* in the left panel and then click the AutoCorrect Options button. At the AutoCorrect dialog box with the AutoCorrect tab selected, click the *Capitalize first letter of table cells* check box to insert a check mark. Click OK to close the dialog box and then click OK to close the Word Options dialog box.

Project 6b Inserting an Index Using a Concordance File   Part 2 of 3

1. Open **PlanNwsltr.docx** and then save it with the name **6-PlanNwsltr**.
2. Mark text for the index using the concordance file you created in Project 6a by completing the following steps:
   a. Click the References tab.
   b. Click the Insert Index button in the Index group.
   c. At the Index dialog box, click the AutoMark button.

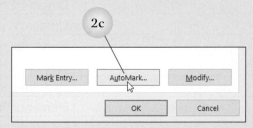

   d. At the Open Index AutoMark File dialog box, double-click **6-CFile.docx** in the Content pane. (This turns on the display of nonprinting characters.)
3. Insert the index in the document by completing the following steps:
   a. Position the insertion point at the end of the document.
   b. Insert a page break.
   c. Type INDEX and then press the Enter key.
   d. Click the Insert Index button in the Index group.
   e. At the Index dialog box, click the *Formats* option box arrow and then click *Formal* at the drop-down list.
   f. Click OK to close the dialog box.
4. Apply the Heading 1 style to the title *INDEX* and then center the title.
5. Turn off the display of nonprinting characters.
6. Save **6-PlanNwsltr.docx** and then print only the Index page.

Check Your Work

Updating and Deleting an Index

 Update Index

If changes are made to a document after the index is inserted, update the index. To do this, click in the index and then click the Update Index button in the Index group or press the F9 function key. To delete an index, select the entire index using the mouse or keyboard and then press the Delete key.

Quick Steps

Update an Index
1. Click in index.
2. Click Update Index button or press F9.

Delete an Index
1. Select entire index.
2. Press Delete key.

Project 6c Updating an Index   Part 3 of 3

1. With **6-PlanNwsltr.docx** open, insert a page break at the beginning of the title *PLANNING A NEWSLETTER*.
2. Update the index by clicking in the index, clicking the References tab, and then clicking the Update Index button in the Index group.
3. Save **6-PlanNwsltr.docx** and then print only the index page.
4. Close **6-PlanNwsltr.docx**.

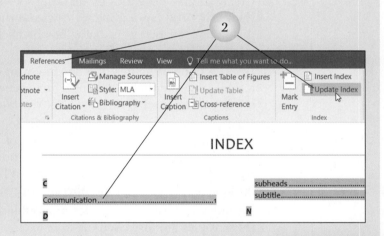

Check Your Work

Chapter Summary

- Word provides options for automating the creation of a table of contents, table of figures, and index.
- Identify the text to be included in a table of contents by applying heading styles, assigning levels, or marking text as field entries.
- Mark text as a field entry at the Mark Table of Contents dialog box. Display this dialog box by pressing Alt + Shift + O.
- Creating a table of contents using heading styles involves two steps: applying the appropriate styles to mark the text to be included and inserting the table of contents in the document.
- To insert a table of contents, position the insertion point where the table is to appear, click the References tab, click the Table of Contents button, and then click a specific option at the drop-down list.
- Generally, the pages containing the table of contents are numbered with lowercase roman numerals.
- The headings in a table of contents in a document are hyperlinks and these hyperlinks can be used to navigate within the document.

- If changes are made to a document after the table of contents is inserted, update the table of contents. To do this, click in the current table of contents and then click the Update Table button on the References tab click the Update Table tab, or press the F9 function key. Update a table of figures or index in a similar manner.

- Remove a table of contents by clicking the Table of Contents button on the References tab and then clicking *Remove Table of Contents* at the drop-down list.

- Another method for identifying text for a table of contents is to select the text, click the Add Text button on the References tab, and then click a specific level for the selected text.

- To identify text for a table of contents without applying styles, mark the text at the Mark Table of Contents Entry dialog box. Display this dialog box by pressing Alt + Shift + O.

- Create a table of figures by marking specific text or images with captions and then using the caption names to create the table. Mark captions at the Caption dialog box. Display this dialog box by clicking the Insert Caption button in the Captions group on the References tab.

- Insert a table of figures in a document in a manner similar to that for inserting a table of contents. A table of figures generally displays at the beginning of the document on a separate page after the table of contents.

- Customize captions at the Caption dialog box. Customizations include specifying a caption label, the position of the caption, and whether or not the label should be included in the caption. Click the Numbering button at the Caption dialog box and the Caption Numbering dialog box displays with options for specifying a numbering format and style.

- An index is a list of the topics in a publication and the numbers of the pages those topics are discussed on.

- Mark the words and groups of words to be included in an index at the Mark Index Entry dialog box. Display this dialog box by clicking the Mark Entry button in the Index group on the References tab or using the keyboard shortcut Alt + Shift + X.

- After all the words and groups of words have been marked as main entries and subentries, insert the index. Place it on a separate page at the end of the document.

- Insert an index in a document by clicking the Insert Index button on the References tab, selecting formatting at the Index dialog box, and then clicking OK.

- Text can be identified as a bookmark and then the bookmark can be marked as an index entry. This is especially useful when the text for an entry spans a range of pages.

- Mark text as a cross-reference to refer readers to another index entry.

- Words that appear frequently in a document can be saved in a concordance file and used in creating an index. A concordance file is a Word document that contains a two-column table. Using this table to create the index eliminates the need to mark all the words and groups of words in a document.

Commands Review

FEATURE	RIBBON TAB, GROUP	BUTTON, OPTION	KEYBOARD SHORTCUT
Caption dialog box	References, Captions		
Index dialog box	References, Index		
Mark Index Entry dialog box	References, Index		Alt + Shift + X
Mark Table of Contents Entry dialog box			Alt + Shift + O
Open Index AutoMark File dialog box	References, Index	, AutoMark button	
Page Number Format dialog box	Insert, Header & Footer	, *Format Page Numbers*	
Table of Contents dialog box	References, Table of Contents	, *Custom Table of Contents*	
Table of Contents Options dialog box	References, Table of Contents	, *Custom Table of Contents*, Options button	
Table of Figures dialog box	References, Captions		
update index	References, Index		F9
update table of contents	References, Table of Contents		F9

Workbook

Chapter study tools and assessment activities are available in the *Workbook* ebook. These resources are designed to help you further develop and demonstrate mastery of the skills learned in this chapter.

Microsoft®
Word

Working with Shared Documents

Performance Objectives

Precheck

Check your current skills to help focus your study.

Upon successful completion of Chapter 7, you will be able to:

1 Insert, edit, show, reply to, print, and delete comments

2 Navigate between comments

3 Distinguish comments from different users

4 Edit a document using the Track Changes feature

5 Customize the display of changes, markups, and review information

6 Navigate to and accept/reject revisions

7 Compare documents

8 Combine documents and show source documents

9 Embed and link data between Excel and Word

In a workplace environment, you may need to share documents with and distribute them to coworkers and associates. You may be part of a workgroup, which is a networked collection of computers that share files, printers, and other resources. As a member of a workgroup, you can collaborate with other members and distribute documents for their review and/or revision. In this chapter, you will perform workgroup activities such as inserting comments, tracking changes, comparing documents, and combining documents from multiple users.

If a Word 2016 document (.docx format) is located on a server running Microsoft SharePoint Server, multiple users can edit it concurrently. Concurrent editing allows a group of users to work on a document at the same time or a single user to work on the same document from different computers. If a document is not located on a server running SharePoint Server, Word 2016 supports only single-user editing. Projects and assessments in this chapter assume that the files you are editing are not located on a server running SharePoint Server.

SNAP

If you are a SNAP user, launch the Precheck and Tutorials from your Assignments page.

Data Files

Before beginning chapter work, copy the WL2C7 folder to your storage medium and then make WL2C7 the active folder.

You will open a report containing company information for new employees and then insert and edit comments from multiple users.

Preview Finished Project

Tutorial

Inserting
Comments

Inserting and Managing Comments

Use Word's comment feature to provide feedback on and suggest changes to a document that someone else has written. Similarly, get feedback on a document by distributing it electronically to others and having them insert comments in it.

Quick Steps

Insert a Comment
1. Select text.
2. Click Review tab.
3. Click New Comment button.
4. Type comment.

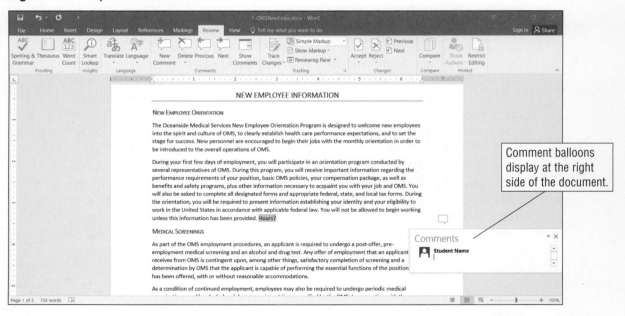

New
Comment

💡 **Hint** Use comments to add notes, suggestions, and explanations and to communicate with members of your workgroup.

To insert a comment in a document, select the text or item the comment pertains to or position the insertion point at the end of the text, click the Review tab, and then click the New Comment button in the Comments group. This displays a comment balloon at the right margin, as shown in Figure 7.1.

Depending on what settings have been applied, clicking the New Comment button may cause the Reviewing pane to display at the left side of the document, rather than the comment balloon. If this happens, click the Show Markup button in the Tracking group on the Review tab, point to *Balloons*, and then click *Show Only Comments and Formatting in Balloons* at the side menu. Also check to make sure the *Display for Review* option box in the Tracking group is set to *Simple Markup*. If it is not, click the *Display for Review* option box arrow and then click *Simple Markup* at the drop-down list.

Figure 7.1 Sample Comment Balloon

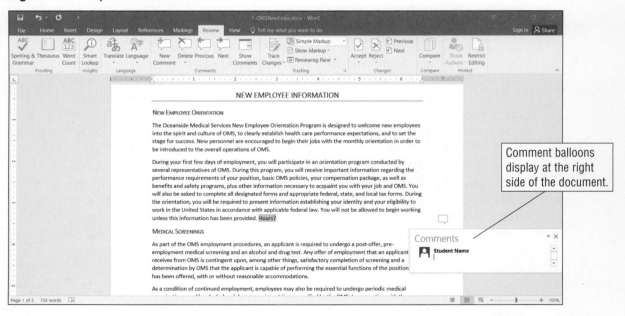

1. Open **OMSNewEmps.docx** and then save it with the name **7-OMSNewEmps**.
2. Insert a comment by completing the following steps:
   a. Position the insertion point at the end of the second paragraph in the *New Employee Orientation* section.
   b. Press the spacebar and then type Hours?.
   c. Select *Hours?*.
   d. Click the Review tab.
   e. Make sure *Simple Markup* displays in the *Display for Review* option box. If it does not, click the *Display for Review* option box arrow and then click *Simple Markup* at the drop-down list.
   f. If the Show Comments button in the Comments group is active (displays with a gray background), click the button to deactivate it.
   g. Click the New Comment button in the Comments group.
   h. Type Please include the total number of orientation hours. in the comment balloon.

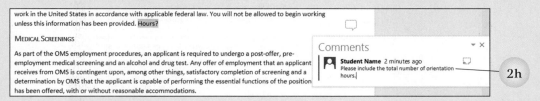

3. Insert another comment by completing the following steps:
   a. Move the insertion point to the end of the third (last) paragraph in the *Medical Screenings* section.
   b. Click the New Comment button in the Comments group.
   c. Type Specify the locations where drug tests are administered. in the comment balloon. (Since you did not select any text before clicking the New Comment button, Word selects the word immediately left of the insertion point.)
   d. Click in the document to close the comment balloons.
4. Save **7-OMSNewEmps.docx**.

Check Your Work

Inserting Comments in the Reviewing Pane

Reviewing Pane

Quick Steps

Insert a Comment in the Reviewing Pane
1. Click Review tab.
2. Click Reviewing Pane button.
3. Click New Comment button.
4. Type comment.

Comments can also be inserted with the Reviewing pane displayed on the screen. The Reviewing pane displays both inserted comments and changes recorded with the Track Changes feature. (Track Changes is covered later in this chapter.)

To display the Reviewing pane, click the Reviewing Pane button in the Tracking group on the Review tab. The Reviewing pane usually displays at the left side of the screen, as shown in Figure 7.2. Click the New Comment button in the Comments group and a comment icon and balloon displays in the right margin; the reviewer's name followed by "Commented" displays in the Reviewing pane. Type the comment and the text displays in the comment balloon and in the Reviewing pane. (The Reviewing pane might display along the bottom of the screen, rather than at the left side. To specify where the pane is to display, click the Reviewing Pane button arrow in the Tracking group on the Review tab and then click *Reviewing Pane Vertical* or *Reviewing Pane Horizontal*.)

Hint If your computer has a sound card and microphone, you can record voice comments.

A summary displays toward the top of the Reviewing pane and provides counts of the number of comments inserted and the types of changes that have been made to the document. After typing a comment in the Reviewing pane, close the pane by clicking the Reviewing Pane button in the Tracking group or by clicking the Close button in the upper right corner of the pane.

Figure 7.2 Vertical Reviewing Pane

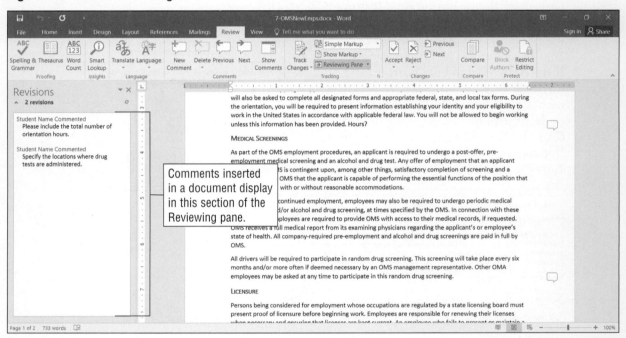

Project 1b Inserting a Comment in the Reviewing Pane

Part 2 of 4

1. With **7-OMSNewEmps.docx** open, show the comments in the Reviewing pane by completing the following steps:
   a. If necessary, click the Review tab.
   b. Click the Reviewing Pane button in the Tracking group.
   c. Click the Show Markup button in the Tracking group, point to *Balloons* at the drop-down list, and then click *Show All Revisions Inline* at the side menu.

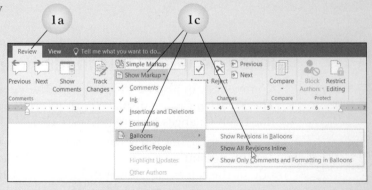

2. Insert a comment by completing the following steps:
   a. Move the insertion point to the end of the paragraph of text in the INTRODUCTORY PERIOD section.
   b. Press the spacebar once, type Maximum?, and then select *Maximum?*.
   c. Click the New Comment button in the Comments group on the Review tab.
   d. With the insertion point positioned in the Reviewing pane, type Please include in this section the maximum length of the probationary period.
3. Click the Reviewing Pane button in the Tracking group to turn off the display of the Reviewing pane.
4. Save **7-OMSNewEmps.docx**.

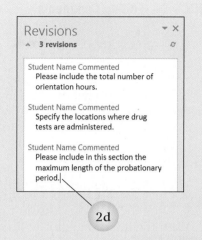

2d

Check Your Work

Navigating between Comments

 Previous

 Next

When working in a long document with many comments, use the Previous and Next buttons in the Comments group on the Review tab to move easily from comment to comment. Click the Next button to move the insertion point to the next comment or click the Previous button to move the insertion point to the previous comment.

Tutorial

Managing Comments

Edit a Comment
1. Click Review tab.
2. Click Reviewing Pane button.
3. Click in comment in pane.
4. Make changes.
OR
1. Click Review tab.
2. Turn on display of comment balloons.
3. Click in comment balloon.
4. Make changes.

Editing Comments

Edit a comment in the Reviewing pane or in a comment balloon. To edit a comment in the Reviewing pane, click the Reviewing Pane button to turn on the pane and then click in the comment to be edited. Make changes to the comment and then close the Reviewing pane. To edit a comment in a comment balloon, turn on the display of comment balloons, click in the comment balloon, and then make changes.

Showing Comments

The Comments group on the Review tab contains a Show Comments button. Click this button and comments display at the right side of the document. The Show Comments button is available only when the *Display for Review* option in the Tracking group is set to *Simple Markup*.

1. With **7-OMSNewEmps.docx** open, navigate from one comment to another by completing the following steps:
   a. Press Ctrl + Home to move the insertion point to the beginning of the document.
   b. If necessary, click the Review tab.
   c. Click the Next button in the Comments group. (This moves the insertion point to the first comment, opens the Reviewing pane, and inserts the insertion point in the pane.)
   d. Click the Next button to display the second comment.
   e. Click the Next button to display the third comment.
   f. Click the Previous button to display the second comment.
2. With the insertion point positioned in the Reviewing pane, edit the second comment to read as follows: *Specify the locations within OMS where drug tests are administered as well as any off-site locations.*
3. Click the Reviewing Pane button to close the pane.
4. Edit a comment in a comment balloon by completing the following steps:
   a. Click the Show Markup button in the Tracking group, point to *Balloons*, and then click *Show Only Comments and Formatting in Balloons* at the side menu.
   b. Click the Show Comments button in the Comments group to display the balloons at the right side of the document.
   c. Display the paragraph of text in the INTRODUCTORY PERIOD section and then click in the comment balloon that displays at the right.
   d. Edit the comment to read as follows: *Please include in this section the maximum probationary period, if any.*

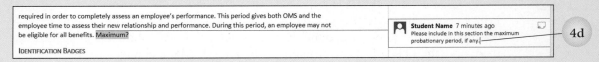

   e. Click in the document and then click the Show Comments button to turn off the display of comment balloons.
   f. Click the Show Markup button, point to *Balloons*, and then click *Show All Revisions Inline*.
5. Save **7-OMSNewEmps.docx**.

Check Your Work

Replying to Comments

During the review of a document, a reply can be made to a comment. To reply to a comment, open the comment balloon, hover the mouse pointer over the comment text, and then click the Reply button to the right of the reviewer's name. Type the reply in the window that opens below the comment. Other methods of replying to a comment are to click in a comment and then click the New Comment button in the Comments group and to right-click in a comment and then click *Reply to Comment* at the shortcut menu.

Printing Comments

Quick Steps

Print a Document with the Comments
1. Click File tab.
2. Click *Print* option.
3. Click first gallery in *Settings* category.
4. If necessary, click *Print Markup* to insert check mark.
5. Click Print button.

Print Only the Comments
1. Click File tab.
2. Click *Print* option.
3. Click first gallery in *Settings* category.
4. Click *List of Markup*.
5. Click Print button.

To print a document with the comments, display the Print backstage area and then click the first gallery in the *Settings* category (the gallery that contains the text *Print All Pages*). At the drop-down list, insert a check mark before the *Print Markup* option to print the document with the comments. To print the document without the comments, click *Print Markup* to remove the check mark.

To print only the comments and not the document, click *List of Markup* at the drop-down list. This prints the contents of the Reviewing pane, which may include comments, tracked changes, and changes to headers, footers, text boxes, footnotes, and endnotes.

Deleting Comments

Delete a comment by clicking the Next button in the Comments group on the Review tab until the specific comment is selected and then clicking the Delete button in the Comments group. To delete all the comments in a document, click the Delete button arrow and then click *Delete All Comments in Document* at the drop-down list. A comment can also be dimmed in a document without being deleted. To do this, right-click the comment and then click *Mark Comment Done* at the shortcut menu.

Delete

Quick Steps

Delete a Comment
1. Click Review tab.
2. Click Next button until comment is selected.
3. Click Delete button.

Change the User Name and Initials
1. Click File tab.
2. Click *Options*.
3. Type name in *User name* text box.
4. Type initials in *Initials* text box.
5. Click OK.

Distinguishing Comments from Different Users

More than one user can insert comments in the same document. Word uses different colors to distinguish comments inserted by different users, generally displaying the first user's comments in red and the second user's comments in blue. (These colors may vary.)

The user name and initials can be changed at the Word Options dialog box with *General* selected, as shown in Figure 7.3. To change the user name, select the name that displays in the *User name* text box and then type the new name. Complete similar steps to change the user initials in the *Initials* text box. A check mark may need to be inserted in the *Always use these values regardless of sign in to Office* check box.

Figure 7.3 Word Options Dialog Box with *General* Selected

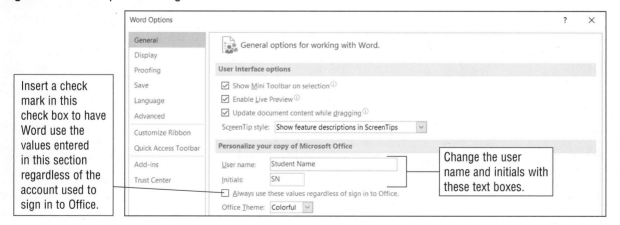

Insert a check mark in this check box to have Word use the values entered in this section regardless of the account used to sign in to Office.

Change the user name and initials with these text boxes.

1. With **7-OMSNewEmps.docx** open, change the user information by completing the following steps:
   a. Click the File tab.
   b. Click *Options*.
   c. At the Word Options dialog box, make sure *General* is selected in the left panel.
   d. Make a note of the current name and initials in the *Personalize your copy of Microsoft Office* section.
   e. Select the name displayed in the *User name* text box and then type Taylor Stanton.
   f. Select the initials displayed in the *Initials* text box and then type TS.
   g. Click the *Always use these values regardless of sign in to Office* check box to insert a check mark.
   h. Click OK to close the Word Options dialog box.

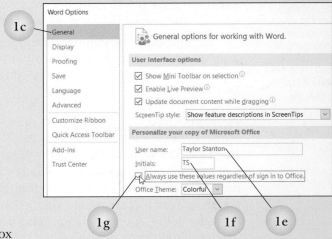

2. Insert a comment by completing the following steps:
   a. Move the insertion point to the end of the first paragraph of text in the section PERFORMANCE REVIEW.
   b. Click the New Comment button in the Comments group on the Review tab.
   c. Type Provide additional information on performance evaluation documentation. in the Reviewing pane.
   d. Click the Reviewing Pane button to close the pane.
3. Respond to a comment by completing the following steps:
   a. Press Ctrl + Home to move the insertion point to the beginning of the document.
   b. Click the Show Markup button, point to *Balloons*, and then click *Show Only Comments and Formatting in Balloons* at the drop-down list.
   c. Click the Next button in the Comments group. (This opens the comment balloon for the first comment.)
   d. Click the Reply button right of the reviewer's name in the comment balloon.

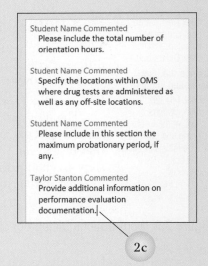

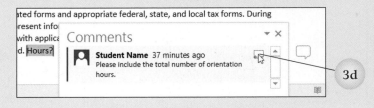

e. Type Check with Barb on the total number of orientation hours.

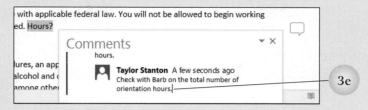

f. Click in the document to close the comment balloon.
4. Print only the information in the Reviewing pane by completing the following steps:
   a. Click the File tab and then click the *Print* option.
   b. At the Print backstage area, click the first gallery in the *Settings* category and then click *List of Markup* in the *Document Info* section of the drop-down list.

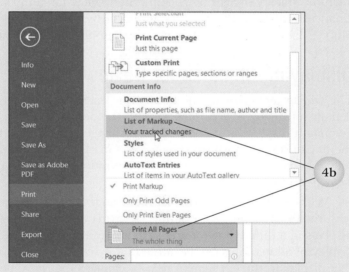

   c. Click the Print button.
5. Delete a comment by completing the following steps:
   a. Press Ctrl + Home.
   b. If necessary, click the Review tab.
   c. Click the Next button in the Comments group.
   d. Click the Next button again.
   e. Click the Next button again.
   f. Click the Delete button in the Comments group.
6. Print only the information in the Reviewing pane by completing Step 4.
7. Change the user information back to the default settings by completing the following steps:
   a. Click the File tab and then click *Options*.
   b. At the Word Options dialog box with *General* selected, select *Taylor Stanton* in the *User name* text box and then type the original name.
   c. Select the initials *TS* in the *Initials* text box and then type the original initials.
   d. Click the *Always use these values regardless of sign in to Office* check box to remove the check mark.
   e. Click OK to close the dialog box.
8. Save and then close **7-OMSNewEmps.docx**.

Check Your Work

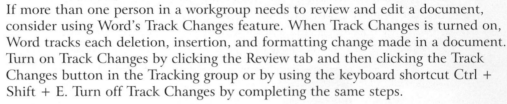

Preview Finished Project

Project 2 Track Changes in a Building Construction Agreement   4 Parts

You will open a building construction agreement, turn on Track Changes, and then make changes to the document. You will also customize Track Changes and accept and reject changes.

Preview Finished Project

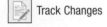

Tutorial

Tracking Changes
in a Document

Track Changes

Tracking Changes in a Document

If more than one person in a workgroup needs to review and edit a document, consider using Word's Track Changes feature. When Track Changes is turned on, Word tracks each deletion, insertion, and formatting change made in a document. Turn on Track Changes by clicking the Review tab and then clicking the Track Changes button in the Tracking group or by using the keyboard shortcut Ctrl + Shift + E. Turn off Track Changes by completing the same steps.

Tutorial

Displaying
Changes for
Review and
Showing Markup

Quick Steps

Turn on Track Changes
1. Click Review tab.
2. Click Track Changes button.
OR
Press Ctrl + Shift + E.

 Hint Each of the four options at the *Display for Review* option drop-down list displays a document at various stages in the editing process.

Displaying Changes for Review

The *Display for Review* option box in the Tracking group on the Review tab has a default setting of *Simple Markup*. With this setting applied, each change made to the document displays in it and a vertical change line displays in the left margin next to the line of text in which the change was made. To see the changes along with the original text, click the *Display for Review* option box arrow and then click the *All Markup* option.

With *All Markup* selected, all the changes display in the document along with the original text. For example, if text is deleted, it stays in the document but displays in a different color and with strikethrough characters through it. The display of all markups can be turned on by clicking one of the vertical change lines that display in the left margin next to changes that have been made or by clicking a comment balloon.

If changes have been made to a document with Track Changes turned on, the appearance of the final document with the changes applied can be previewed by clicking the *Display for Review* option box arrow and then clicking *No Markup* at the drop-down list. This displays the document with the changes made but does not actually make the changes to the document. To view the original document without any changes marked, click the *Display for Review* option box arrow and then click *Original* at the drop-down list.

Showing Markups

Show Markup

With the display of all markups turned on, specify what tracking information displays in the body of the document with options at the Balloons side menu. To show all the changes in balloons in the right margin, click the Show Markup button, point to *Balloons*, and then click *Show Revisions in Balloons* at the side menu. Click *Show All Revisions Inline* to display all the changes in the document with vertical change lines in the left margin next to the affected lines of text. Click the *Show Only Comments and Formatting in Balloons* option at the side menu and insertions and deletions display in the text while comments and formatting changes display in balloons in the right margin.

1. Open **Agreement.docx** and then save it with the name **7-Agreement**.

2. Turn on Track Changes by clicking the Review tab and then clicking the Track Changes button in the Tracking group.

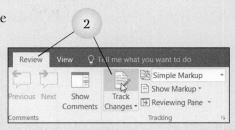

3. Type the word BUILDING between the words *THIS* and *AGREEMENT* in the first paragraph of the document.

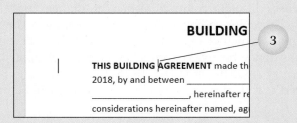

4. Show all markups by clicking the *Display for Review* option box arrow in the Tracking group and then clicking *All Markup* at the drop-down list. (Notice that the text *BUILDING* is underlined and displays in red in the document [the color may vary].)

5. Select and then delete *thirty (30)* in the second paragraph. (The deleted text displays in the document with strikethrough characters through it.)

6. Type sixty (60).

7. Move a paragraph of text by completing the following steps:

   a. Select the paragraph that begins *Supervision of Work* (including the paragraph mark that ends the paragraph).

   b. Press Ctrl + X to cut the text. (The text stays in the document and displays in red with strikethrough characters through it.)

   c. Position the insertion point immediately before the word *Start* (in the paragraph that begins *Start of Construction and Completion:*).

   d. Press Ctrl + V to paste the cut text in the new location. The inserted text displays in green and has a double underline below it. Notice that the text in the original location changes to green and has double-strikethrough characters through it.)

8. Turn off Track Changes by clicking the Track Changes button in the Tracking group.

9. Display revisions in balloons by clicking the Show Markup button, pointing to *Balloons*, and then clicking *Show Revisions in Balloons* at the side menu.

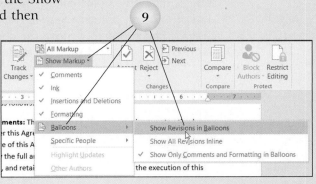

10. After looking at the revisions in balloons, click the Show Markup button, point to *Balloons,* and then click *Show All Revisions Inline* at the side menu.

11. Save **7-Agreement.docx**.

Check Your Work

Displaying Information about Tracked Changes

Display information about a specific tracked change by hovering the mouse pointer over it. After approximately one second, a box displays above the change that contains the author's name, the date and time the change was made, and the type of change (for example, whether it was a deletion or insertion). Information on tracked changes can also be displayed in the Reviewing pane, where each change is listed separately.

Changing User Information

Word uses different colors to record the changes made by different people (up to eight). This color coding allows anyone looking at the document to identify which users made which changes. How to change the user name and initials at the Word Options dialog box was covered earlier in the chapter (see the section *Distinguishing Comments from Different Users*). In Project 2b, the user name and initials will be changed and then additional tracked changes will be made.

Locking Track Changes

Quick Steps

Lock Track Changes
1. Click Review tab.
2. Click Track Changes button arrow.
3. Click *Lock Tracking*.
4. Type password.
5. Press Tab.
6. Type password.
7. Click OK.

To ensure that all the changes made to a document will be tracked, lock the Track Changes feature so it cannot be turned off. To do this, click the Track Changes button arrow and then click *Lock Tracking* at the drop-down list. At the Lock Tracking dialog box, type a password, press the Tab key, type the password again, and then click OK. Unlock Track Changes by clicking the Track Changes button arrow and then clicking *Lock Tracking*. At the Unlock Tracking dialog box, type the password and then click OK.

Tutorial

Customizing Track
Changes Options

Customizing Track Changes Options

Customize how tracked changes display in a document with options at the Show Markup button drop-down list. To show only one particular type of tracked change, remove the check marks before all the options except the specific one. For example, to view only formatting changes and not other types of changes, such as insertions and deletions, remove the check mark before each option except *Formatting*. Another method of customizing which tracked changes display is to use options at the Track Changes Options dialog box, shown in Figure 7.4. Display this dialog box by clicking the Tracking group dialog box launcher.

If the changes made by multiple reviewers have been tracked in a document, the changes made by a particular reviewer can be displayed. To do this, click the Show Markup button, point to *Specific People* at the drop-down list, and then click the *All Reviewers* check box to remove the check mark. Click the Show Markup button, point to *Reviewers*, and then click the check box of the specific reviewer.

Figure 7.4 Track Changes Options Dialog Box

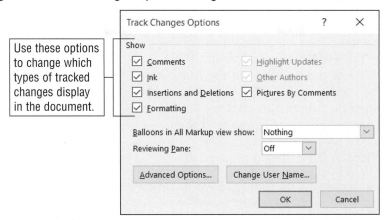

Use these options to change which types of tracked changes display in the document.

Project 2b Changing User Information and Tracking Changes

1. With **7-Agreement.docx** open, change the user information by completing the following steps:
   a. Click the File tab and then click *Options*.
   b. At the Word Options dialog box with *General* selected, select the current name in the *User name* text box and then type Julia Moore.
   c. Select the initials in the *Initials* text box and then type JM.
   d. Click the *Always use these values regardless of sign in to Office* check box to insert a check mark.
   e. Click OK to close the dialog box.
2. Make additional changes to the contract and track the changes by completing the following steps:
   a. Click the Track Changes button on the Review tab to turn on tracking.
   b. Select the title *BUILDING CONSTRUCTION AGREEMENT* and then change the font size to 14 points.
   c. Delete the text *at his option* (located in the second sentence in the second paragraph).
   d. Delete the text *and Completion* (located near the beginning of the fourth paragraph).

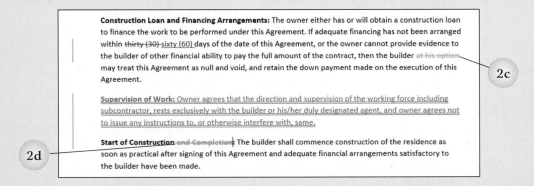

   e. Delete *thirty (30)* in the paragraph that begins *Builder's Right to Terminate the Contract:* (located on the second page).
   f. Type sixty (60).
   g. Select the text *IN WITNESS WHEREOF* (located near the bottom of the document) and then apply bold formatting.

3. Click the Review tab and then click the Track Changes button to turn off Track Changes.
4. Click the Reviewing Pane button to turn on the display of the Reviewing pane and then use the vertical scroll bar at the right side of the Reviewing pane to review the changes.
5. View the changes in balloons by clicking the Show Markup button, pointing to *Balloons*, and then clicking *Show Revisions in Balloons*.
6. Click the Reviewing Pane button to turn off the display of the pane.
7. Scroll through the document and view the changes in the balloons.
8. Click the Show Markup button, point to *Balloons*, and then click *Show All Revisions Inline* at the side menu.
9. Change the user information back to the original information by completing the following steps:
   a. Click the File tab and then click *Options*.
   b. At the Word Options dialog box, select *Julia Moore* in the *User name* text box and then type the original name.
   c. Select the initials *JM* in the *Initials* text box and then type the original initials.
   d. Click the *Always use these values regardless of sign in to Office* check box to remove the check mark.
   e. Click OK to close the dialog box.
10. Display only those changes made by Julia Moore by completing the following steps:
    a. Click the Show Markup button in the Tracking group and then point to *Specific People* at the drop-down list.
    b. Click *All Reviewers* at the side menu.

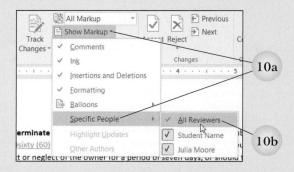

    c. Click the Show Markup button, point to *Specific People*, and then click *Julia Moore*.
    d. Scroll through the document and notice that only changes made by Julia Moore display.
    e. Return the display to all the reviewers by clicking the Show Markup button, pointing to *Specific People*, and then clicking *All Reviewers*.
11. Print the document with the markups by completing the following steps:
    a. Click the File tab and then click the *Print* option.
    b. At the Print backstage area, click the first gallery in the *Settings* category and then make sure a check mark displays before the *Print Markup* option. (If the *Print Markup* option is not preceded by a check mark, click the option.)
    c. Click the Print button.
12. Save **7-Agreement.docx**.

Check Your Work

Customizing Advanced Track Changes Options

How tracked changes display in a document is determined by default settings. For example, with all the markups showing, inserted text displays in red with an underline below it and deleted text displays in red with strikethrough characters through it. Moved text displays in the original location in green with double-strikethrough characters through it and in the new location in green with double-underlining below it.

Customize these options, along with others, at the Advanced Track Changes Options dialog box, shown in Figure 7.5. Use options at this dialog box to customize the display of markup text, moved text, table cell highlighting, formatting, and balloons. Display the dialog box by clicking the Tracking group dialog box launcher. At the Track Changes Options dialog box, click the Advanced Options button.

Figure 7.5 Advanced Track Changes Options Dialog Box

Change how the markups display with options in this section.

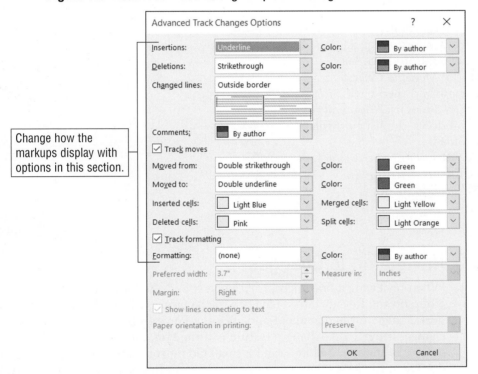

1. With **7-Agreement.docx** open, customize the Track Changes options by completing the following steps:
   a. If necessary, click the Review tab.
   b. Click the Tracking group dialog box launcher.
   c. Click the Advanced Options button at the Track Changes Options dialog box.
   d. At the Advanced Track Changes Options dialog box, click the *Insertions* option box arrow and then click *Double underline* at the drop-down list.
   e. Click the *Insertions Color* option box arrow and then click *Green* at the drop-down list. (You will need to scroll down the list to display this color.)
   f. Click the *Moved from Color* option box arrow and then click *Dark Blue* at the drop-down list.
   g. Click the *Moved to Color* option box arrow and then click *Violet* at the drop-down list. (You will need to scroll down the list to display this color.)
   h. Click OK to close the dialog box.
   i. Click OK to close the Track Changes Options dialog box.
2. Save **7-Agreement.docx**.

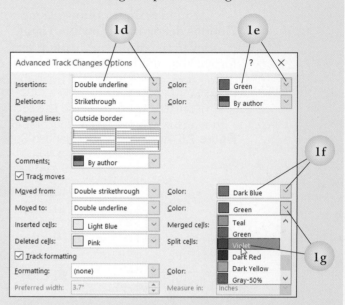

Check Your Work

 Next

 Previous

Navigating to Changes

When reviewing a document, use the Next and the Previous buttons in the Changes group on the Review tab to navigate to changes. Click the Next button to review the next change in the document and click the Previous button to review the previous change. If the Track Changes feature is turned on, move text and then turn on the display of revision balloons, and a small Go button (a blue right-pointing arrow) will display in the lower right corner of any balloon that identifies moved text. Click the Go button in the balloon identifying the original text to move the insertion point to the balloon identifying the moved text.

Accepting or Rejecting Changes

 Accept

 Reject

Tracked changes can be removed from a document only by accepting or rejecting them. Click the Accept button in the Changes group on the Review tab to accept a change and move to the next change or click the Reject button to reject a change and move to the next change. Click the Accept button arrow and a drop-down list displays with options to accept the change and move to the next change, accept the change, accept all the changes showing, and accept all the changes and stop tracking. Similar options are available at the Reject button drop-down list.

1. With **7-Agreement.docx** open, display all the tracked changes *except* formatting changes by completing the following steps:
   a. Click the Show Markup button in the Tracking group and then click *Formatting* at the drop-down list. (This removes the check mark before the option.)
   b. Scroll through the document and notice that the vertical change lines in the left margin next to the two formatting changes have been removed.
   c. Click the Show Markup button and then click *Formatting* at the drop-down list. (This inserts a check mark before the option.)
2. Navigate to review tracked changes by completing the following steps:
   a. Press Ctrl + Home to move the insertion point to the beginning of the document.
   b. Click the Next button in the Changes group to select the first change.
   c. Click the Next button again to select the second change.
   d. Click the Previous button to select the first change.
3. Navigate between the original and new locations of the moved text by completing the following steps:
   a. Press Ctrl + Home to move the insertion point to the beginning of the document.
   b. Click the Show Markup button, point to *Balloons*, and then click *Show Revisions in Balloons*.
   c. Click the Go button (a blue right-pointing arrow) in the lower right corner of the Moved balloon. (This selects the text in the Moved up balloon.)
   d. Click the Go button in the lower right corner of the Moved up balloon. (This selects the text in the Moved balloon.)
   e. Click the Show Markup button, point to *Balloons*, and then click *Show All Revisions Inline*.
4. Press Ctrl + Home to move the insertion point to the beginning of the document.
5. Display and then accept only formatting changes by completing the following steps:
   a. Click the Tracking group dialog box launcher.
   b. At the Track Changes Options dialog box, click the *Comments* check box to remove the check mark.
   c. Click the *Ink* check box to remove the check mark.
   d. Click the *Insertions and Deletions* check box to remove the check mark.
   e. Click OK to close the Track Changes Options dialog box.

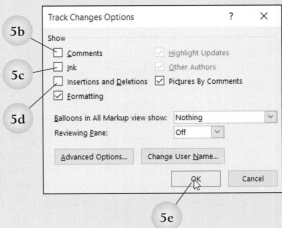

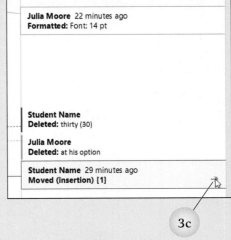

f. Click the Accept button arrow and then click *Accept All Changes Shown* at the drop-down list. (This accepts only the formatting changes in the document because those are the only changes showing.)

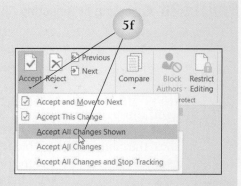

6. Redisplay all the changes by completing the following steps:
   a. Click the Tracking group dialog box launcher.
   b. Click the *Comments* check box to insert a check mark.
   c. Click the *Ink* check box to insert a check mark.
   d. Click the *Insertions and Deletions* check box to insert a check mark.
   e. Click OK to close the Track Changes Options dialog box.
7. Press Ctrl + Home to move the insertion point to the beginning of the document.
8. Reject the change that inserts the word *BUILDING* by clicking the Next button in the Changes group and then clicking the Reject button. (This rejects the change and moves to the next revision in the document.)
9. Click the Accept button to accept the change that deletes *thirty (30)*.
10. Click the Accept button to accept the change that inserts *sixty (60)*.
11. Click the Reject button to reject the change that deletes the words *at his option*.
12. Accept all the remaining changes by clicking the Accept button arrow and then clicking *Accept All Changes* at the drop-down list.

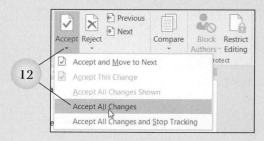

13. Return the track changes options to the default settings by completing the following steps:
   a. If necessary, click the Review tab.
   b. Click the Tracking group dialog box launcher.
   c. At the Track Changes Options dialog box, click the Advanced Options button.
   d. At the Advanced Track Changes Options dialog box, click the *Insertions* option box arrow and then click *Underline* at the drop-down list.
   e. Click the *Insertions Color* option box arrow and then click *By author* at the drop-down list. (You will need to scroll up the list to display this option.)
   f. Click the *Moved from Color* option box arrow and then click *Green* at the drop-down list. (You may need to scroll down the list to display this color.)
   g. Click the *Moved to Color* option box arrow and then click *Green* at the drop-down list.
   h. Click OK to close the dialog box.
   i. Click OK to close the Track Changes Options dialog box.

14. Check to make sure all the tracked changes are accepted or rejected by completing the following steps:
    a. Click the Reviewing Pane button in the Tracking group.
    b. Check the summary information at the top of the Reviewing pane and make sure that each option is followed by a 0. (You may need to click the up arrow right of *0 revisions* to display all the options.)
    c. Close the Reviewing pane.
15. Save, print, and then close **7-Agreement.docx**.

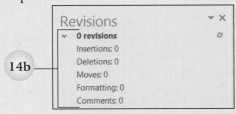

14b

Revisions

0 revisions
Insertions: 0
Deletions: 0
Moves: 0
Formatting: 0
Comments: 0

Check Your Work

Project 3 **Compare Lease Agreement Documents**   **2 Parts**

You will compare the contents of a lease agreement and an edited version of the lease agreement. You will then customize compare options and then compare the documents again.

Preview Finished Project

Tutorial

Comparing
Documents

 Compare

Comparing Documents

Word contains a Compare feature that will compare two documents and display the differences between them as tracked changes in a third document. To use this feature, click the Review tab, click the Compare button in the Compare group, and then click *Compare* at the drop-down list. This displays the Compare Documents dialog box, shown in Figure 7.6. At this dialog box, click the Browse for Original button. At the Open dialog box, navigate to the folder that contains the original document, and then double-click the document. Click the Browse for Revised button in the Compare Documents dialog box, navigate to the folder containing the revised document, and then double-click the document.

Quick Steps
Compare Documents
1. Click Review tab.
2. Click Compare button.
3. Click *Compare*.
4. Click Browse for Original button.
5. Double-click document.
6. Click Browse for Revised button.
7. Double-click document.
8. Click OK.

💡 **Hint** Word does not change the documents being compared.

Figure 7.6 Compare Documents Dialog Box

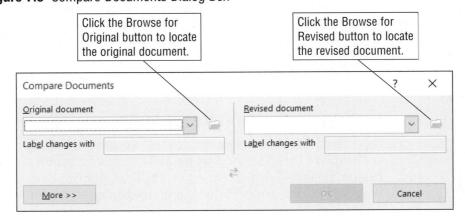

Click the Browse for Original button to locate the original document.

Click the Browse for Revised button to locate the revised document.

Compare Documents

Original document

Label changes with

Revised document

Label changes with

More >>   OK   Cancel

Viewing Compared Documents

Click OK at the Compare Documents dialog box and the compared document displays with the changes tracked. Other windows may also display, depending on the option selected at the Show Source Documents side menu. Display this side menu by clicking the Compare button and then pointing to *Show Source Documents*. Only the compared document may display or the compared document plus the Reviewing pane, original document, and/or revised document may display.

Project 3a **Comparing Documents**   Part 1 of 2

1. Close any open documents.
2. Click the Review tab.
3. Click the Compare button and then click *Compare* at the drop-down list.
4. At the Compare Documents dialog box, click the Browse for Original button.

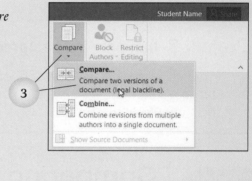

5. At the Open dialog box, navigate to the WL2C7 folder on your storage medium and then double-click *ComAgrmnt.docx*.
6. At the Compare Documents dialog box, click the Browse for Revised button.
7. At the Open dialog box, double-click *EditedComAgrmnt.docx*.
8. Click OK.
9. If the original and revised documents display along with the compared document, click the Compare button, point to *Show Source Documents* at the drop-down list, and then click *Hide Source Documents* at the side menu.

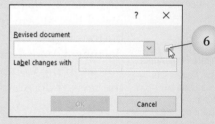

10. With the compared document active, print the document with markups.
11. Click the File tab and then click the *Close* option. At the message asking if you want to save changes, click the Don't Save button.

Check Your Work

Customizing Compare Options

By default, Word compares the original document with the revised document and displays the differences as tracked changes in a third document. Change this default along with others by expanding the Compare Documents dialog box. Click the More button and additional options display, as shown in Figure 7.7.

Figure 7.7 Expanded Compare Documents Dialog Box

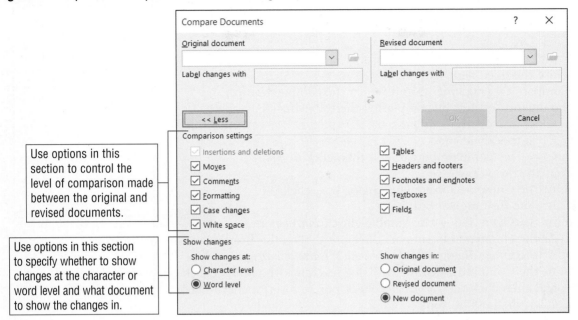

Use options in this section to control the level of comparison made between the original and revised documents.

Use options in this section to specify whether to show changes at the character or word level and what document to show the changes in.

Control the level of comparison that Word makes between the original and revised documents with options in the *Comparison settings* section of the dialog box. The *Show changes at* option in the *Show changes* section of the dialog box has a default setting of *Word level*. With this setting applied, Word shows changes to whole words rather than individual characters within the word. For example, if the letters *ed* are deleted from the end of a word, Word will display the entire word as a change rather than just the *ed*. To show changes by character, click the *Character level* option.

By default, Word displays differences between compared documents in a new document. With options in the *Show changes in* section, this default can be changed to *Original document* or *Revised document*. If changes are made to options in the expanded Compare Documents dialog box, the selected options will be the defaults the next time the dialog box is opened.

Project 3b Customizing Compare Options and Comparing Documents   Part 2 of 2

1. Close any open documents.
2. Click the Review tab.
3. Click the Compare button and then click *Compare* at the drop-down list.
4. At the Compare Documents dialog box, click the Browse for Original button.
5. At the Open dialog box, navigate to the WL2C7 folder on your storage medium and then double-click **ComAgrmnt.docx**.
6. At the Compare Documents dialog box, click the Browse for Revised button.
7. At the Open dialog box, double-click **EditedComAgrmnt.docx**.
8. At the Compare Documents dialog box, click the More button. (Skip this step if the dialog box displays expanded and a Less button displays above the *Comparison settings* section.)

9. Click the *Moves* check box and then click the *Formatting* check box to remove the check marks.
10. Click OK.
11. Print the document with markups.
12. Close the document without saving it.
13. Compare two documents and return the compare options to the default settings by completing the following steps:
    a. Close any open documents.
    b. Click the Review tab.
    c. Click the Compare button and then click *Compare* at the drop-down list.
    d. At the Compare Documents dialog box, click the Browse for Original button.
    e. At the Open dialog box, double-click ***ComAgrmnt.docx***.
    f. At the Compare Documents dialog box, click the Browse for Revised button.
    g. At the Open dialog box, double-click ***EditedComAgrmnt.docx***.
    h. At the Compare Documents dialog box, click the *Moves* check box to insert a check mark and then click the *Formatting* check box to insert a check mark.
    i. Click the Less button.
    j. Click OK.
14. At the new document, accept all the changes.
15. Save the document and name it **7-ComAgrmnt**.
16. Print and then close the document.

Check Your Work

Project 4 Combine Lease Agreement Documents   2 Parts

You will open a lease agreement document and then combine edited versions of the agreement with the original document.

Preview Finished Project

Tutorial

Combining Documents

Combining Documents

If several people have made changes to a document, their changed versions can be combined with the original document. Each person's changed document can be combined with the original until all the changes have been incorporated into the original document. To do this, open the Combine Documents dialog box, shown in Figure 7.8, by clicking the Compare button on the Review tab and then clicking *Combine* at the drop-down list. The Combine Documents dialog box contains many of the same options as the Compare Documents dialog box.

To combine documents at the Combine Documents dialog box, click the Browse for Original button, navigate to the specific folder, and then double-click the original document. Click the Browse for Revised button, navigate to the specific folder, and then double-click one of the documents containing revisions. Click the *Original document* option box arrow or the *Revised document* option box arrow and a drop-down list displays with the most recently selected documents.

Quick Steps
Combine Documents
1. Click Review tab.
2. Click Compare button.
3. Click *Combine*.
4. Click Browse for Original button.
5. Double-click document.
6. Click Browse for Revised button.
7. Double-click document.
8. Click OK.

Figure 7.8 Combine Documents Dialog Box

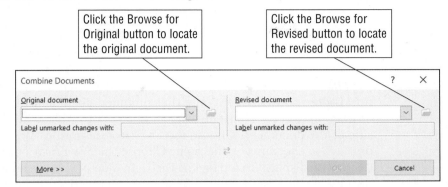

Combining and Merging Documents

Control how changes are combined with options at the expanded Combine Documents dialog box. This dialog box contains many of the same options as the expanded Compare Documents dialog box. By default, Word merges the changes in the revised document into the original document. Change this default setting with options in the *Show changes in* section. Use options in this section to show changes in the original document, the revised document, or a new document.

Project 4a Combining Documents

Part 1 of 2

1. Close all the open documents.
2. Click the Review tab.
3. Click the Compare button in the Compare group and then click *Combine* at the drop-down list.

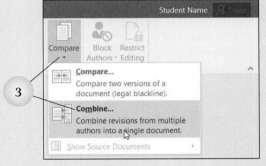

4. At the Combine Documents dialog box, click the More button to expand the dialog box.
5. Click the *Original document* option in the *Show changes in* section.

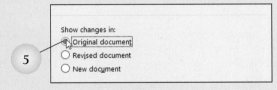

6. Click the Browse for Original button.
7. At the Open dialog box, navigate to the WL2C7 folder on your storage medium and then double-click **OriginalLease.docx**.
8. At the Combine Documents dialog box, click the Browse for Revised button.
9. At the Open dialog box, double-click **LeaseReviewer1.docx**.
10. Click OK.
11. Save the document and name it **7-CombinedLease**.

Check Your Work

Showing Source Documents

Use options in the Show Source Documents side menu to specify which source documents to display. Display this side menu by clicking the Compare button and then pointing to *Show Source Documents*. Four options display at the side menu: *Hide Source Documents*, *Show Original*, *Show Revised*, and *Show Both*. With the *Hide Source Documents* option selected, the original and revised documents do not display on the screen; only the combined document displays. With the *Show Original* option selected, the original document displays in a side panel at the right side of the document. Choose the *Show Revised* option and the revised document displays in the panel at the right. Choose the *Show Both* option and the original document displays in a panel at the right side of the screen and the revised document displays in a panel below the original document panel. Synchronous scrolling is selected by default, so scrolling in the combined document causes simultaneous scrolling in the other document.

Project 4b Combining and Showing Documents

Part 2 of 2

1. With **7-CombinedLease.docx** open, click the Compare button, point to *Show Source Documents*, and then click *Hide Source Documents* at the side menu if necessary. (This displays the original document with the combined document changes shown as tracked changes.)

2. Click the Compare button, point to *Show Source Documents*, and then click *Show Original* at the side menu. (This displays the original document at the right, the original document with tracked changes in the middle, and the Reviewing pane at the left side of the screen.)

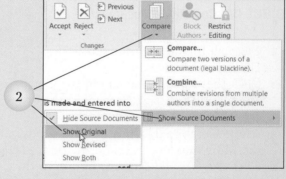

3. Click the Compare button, point to *Show Source Documents*, and then click *Show Revised*.

4. Click the Compare button, point to *Show Source Documents*, and then click *Show Both*. Scroll in the combined document and notice that the original document and revised document also scroll simultaneously.

5. Click the Compare button, point to *Show Source Documents*, and then click *Hide Source Documents*.

6. Close the Reviewing pane.

7. Click the Compare button and then click *Combine* at the drop-down list.

8. At the Combine Documents dialog box, click the Browse for Original button.

9. At the Open dialog box, double-click **7-CombinedLease.docx**.

10. At the Combine Documents dialog box, click the Browse for Revised button.

11. At the Open dialog box, double-click ***LeaseReviewer2.docx***.

12. At the Combine Documents dialog box, click OK.

13. Save **7-CombinedLease.docx**.

14. Print the document with markups.

15. Accept all the changes to the document.

16. Keep the heading *Damage to Premises* together with the next paragraph.

17. Save, print, and then close **7-CombinedLease.docx**.

Check Your Work

You will copy and embed Excel data into a Word document and then update the embedded data. You will also copy and link an Excel chart into a Word document and then update the data in the chart.

Preview Finished Project

Embedding and Linking Objects

One of the reasons the Microsoft Office suite is used extensively in business is that it allows data from one program to be seamlessly integrated into another program. For example, a chart depicting sales projections created in Excel can easily be added to a corporate report prepared in Word.

Integration is the process of adding content from other sources to a file. Integrating content is different from simply copying and pasting it. While it makes sense to copy and paste objects from one application to another when the content is not likely to change, if the content is dynamic, the copy and paste method becomes problematic and inefficient.

To illustrate this point, assume that one of the outcomes of presenting sales projections to the company's board of directors is revision of the projections; this means that the chart originally created in Excel has to be updated to reflect the new projections. If the first version of the chart was copied and pasted into Word, it would need to be deleted and then the revised Excel chart would need to be copied and pasted into the Word document again. Both Excel and Word would need to be opened and edited to reflect the changes in sales projections. In this case, copying and pasting the chart would not be efficient.

To eliminate the inefficiency of the copy and paste method, objects can be integrated between programs. An object can be text in a document, data in a table, a chart, a picture, or any combination of data to be shared between programs. The program that was used to create the object is called the *source* and the program the object is linked or embedded to is called the *destination*.

Embedding and linking are two methods for integrating data. Embedding an object means that the object is stored independently in both the source and the destination programs. When an embedded object is edited in the destination program, the source program opens to provide buttons and options for editing the object; however, the changes will not be reflected in the version of the object stored in the source program. If the object is changed in the source program, the changes will not be reflected in the version of the object stored in the destination program.

Linking inserts a code in the destination file that connects the destination to the name and location of the source object. The object is not stored within the destination file. When an object is linked, changes made to the content in the source program are automatically reflected in the destination program.

The decision to integrate data by embedding or linking will depend on whether the data is dynamic or static. If the data is dynamic, then linking the object is the most efficient method of integration.

Embedding an Object

An object that is embedded is stored in both the source and the destination programs. The content of the object can be edited in *either* the source or the destination; however, a change made in one will not be reflected in the other. The difference between copying and pasting and copying and embedding is that an embedded object can be edited with the buttons and options of the source program.

Since an embedded object is edited within the source program, that program must reside on the computer when the file is opened for editing. When preparing a Word document that will be edited on another computer, determine whether the other computer has both Word and the source program before embedding any objects.

To embed an object, open both programs and both files. In the source program, click the object and then click the Copy button in the Clipboard group on the Home tab. Click the button on the taskbar that represents the destination program file and then position the insertion point at the location the object is to be embedded. Click the Paste button arrow in the Clipboard group and then click *Paste Special* at the drop-down list. At the Paste Special dialog box, click the source of the object in the *As* list box and then click OK.

Edit an embedded object by double-clicking it. This displays the object with the source program buttons and options. Make any changes and then click outside the object to close the source program buttons and options.

Quick Steps

Embed an Object
1. Open source and destination programs and files.
2. Click object in source program.
3. Click Copy button.
4. Click taskbar button for destination program file.
5. Position insertion point in specific location.
6. Click Paste button arrow.
7. Click *Paste Special*.
8. Click source file format in *As* list box.
9. Click OK.

Project 5a Embedding Excel Data in a Document

Part 1 of 3

1. Open **DIRevs.docx** and then save it with the name **7-DIRevs**.
2. Open Excel and then open **DISales.xlsx** in the WL2C7 folder on your storage medium.
3. Select the range A2:F9.
4. Click the Copy button in the Clipboard group on the Home tab.
5. Click the Word button on the taskbar.
6. Press Ctrl + End to move the insertion point to the end of the document.
7. Click the Paste button arrow and then click *Paste Special* at the drop-down list.
8. At the Paste Special dialog box, click *Microsoft Excel Worksheet Object* in the *As* list box and then click OK.
9. Save **7-DIRevs.docx**.
10. Click the Excel button on the taskbar, close the workbook, and then close Excel.
11. With **7-DIRevs.docx** open, double-click in any cell in the Excel data. (This displays the Excel buttons and options for editing the data.)
12. Click in cell E3 (contains the amount *$89,231*), type 95000, and then press the Enter key.
13. Click in cell F9 and then double-click the AutoSum button in the Editing group on the Home tab. (This inserts the total *$1,258,643* in the cell.)
14. Click outside the Excel data to remove the Excel buttons and options.
15. Save, print, and then close **7-DIRevs.docx**.

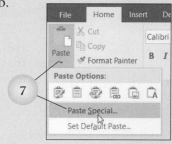

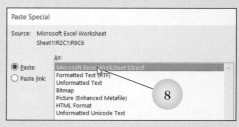

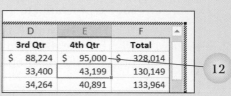

Check Your Work

Linking an Object

If the content of the object to be integrated between programs is likely to change, link the object from the source program to the destination program. Linking the object establishes a direct connection between the source and destination programs. The object is stored only in the source program and the destination program contains a code that indicates the name and location of the source of the object. Whenever the document containing the link is opened, a message displays indicating that the document contains links and asking if the link should be updated.

To link an object, open both programs and program files. In the source program file, click the object and then click the Copy button in the Clipboard group on the Home tab. Click the button on the taskbar that represents the destination program file and then position the insertion point where the object is to be inserted. Click the Paste button arrow in the Clipboard group on the Home tab and then click *Paste Special* at the drop-down list. At the Paste Special dialog box, click the source program for the object in the *As* list box, click the *Paste link* option at the left side of the *As* list box, and then click OK.

Quick Steps

Link an Object
1. Open source and destination programs and files.
2. Click object in source program.
3. Click Copy button.
4. Click taskbar button for destination program file.
5. Position insertion point.
6. Click Paste button arrow.
7. Click *Paste Special.*
8. Click source program for object in *As* list box.
9. Click *Paste link* option.
10. Click OK.

Project 5b Linking an Excel Chart to a Document   Part 2 of 3

1. Open **NSSCosts.docx** and then save it with the name **7-NSSCosts**.
2. Open Excel and then open **NSSDept%.xlsx** located in the WL2C7 folder on your storage medium.
3. Save the workbook and name it **7-NSSDept%**.
4. Copy and link the chart to the Word document by completing the following steps:
   a. Click the chart to select it.
   b. Click the Copy button in the Clipboard group on the Home tab.
   c. Click the Word button on the taskbar.
   d. Press Ctrl + End to move the insertion point to the end of the document.
   e. Click the Paste button arrow and then click *Paste Special* at the drop-down list.
   f. At the Paste Special dialog box, click the *Paste link* option.
   g. Click *Microsoft Excel Chart Object* in the *As* list box.

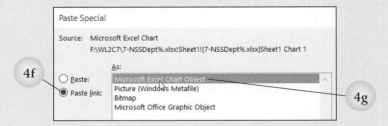

   h. Click OK.
5. Click the Excel button on the taskbar, close **7-NSSDept%.xlsx**, and then close Excel.
6. With **7-NSSCosts.docx** open on the screen, save, print, and then close the document.

Check Your Work

Editing a Linked Object

Edit a linked object in the source program in which it was created. Open the file containing the object, make the changes as required, and then save and close the file. If the source and destination programs are open at the same time, the changed content is reflected immediately in both.

Project 5c **Editing a Linked Excel Chart** **Part 3 of 3**

1. Open Excel and then open **7-NSSDept%.xlsx**.
2. Make the following changes to the data:
   a. In cell B4, change *18%* to *12%*.
   b. In cell B6, change *10%* to *13%*.
   c. In cell B8, change *5%* to *8%*.
3. Click the Save button on the Quick Access Toolbar to save the edited workbook.
4. Close **7-NSSDept%.xlsx** and then close Excel.
5. In Word, open **7-NSSCosts.docx**.
6. At the message stating that the document contains links, click the Yes button. (Notice the changes made to the chart data.)
7. Save, print, and then close **7-NSSCosts.docx**.

Check Your Work

Project 6 **Linking and Pasting Data into a Company Document** **2 Parts**

You will open a company document and then use the Insert File dialog box to paste a file into the company document as a linked object. You will also use the Paste Special dialog box to copy and paste the company name with formatting and copy and paste the company name and image as an object in a header.

Linking Data at the Insert File Dialog Box

In addition to linking an object using the Paste Special dialog box, data can be linked to a document at the Insert File dialog box. Display this dialog box by clicking the Insert tab, clicking the Object button arrow, and then clicking the *Text from File* option. At the dialog box, specify the file to be linked to the open document, click the Insert button arrow, and then click *Insert as Link* at the drop-down list. The data in the identified file is inserted into the open document as a linked object. If changes are made to the data in the original file, the data in the linked object will need to be updated. Update a link by clicking the object and then pressing the F9 function key or right-clicking the object and then clicking *Update Field* at the shortcut menu.

1. Open **ATSManagement.docx**, save it with the name **7-ATSManagement**, and then close the document.
2. Open **ATSDocument.docx** and then save it with the name **7-ATSDocument**.
3. Position the insertion point at the beginning of the heading *EMPLOYER COMMUNICATION*.
4. Link the table in *7-ATSManagement.docx* as an object to the open document by completing the following steps:
   a. Click the Insert tab.
   b. Click the Object button arrow and then click *Text from File* at the drop-down list.
   c. At the Insert File dialog box, click *7-ATSManagement.docx* in the Content pane.
   d. Click the Insert button arrow and then click *Insert as Link* at the drop-down list.

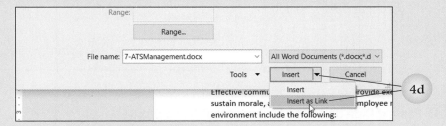

5. Save and then close **7-ATSDocument.docx**.
6. Open **7-ATSManagement.docx** and then make the following edits:
   a. Change the name *Genevieve Parkhurst* to *Noah Stein*.
   b. Change the extension *123* to *102*.

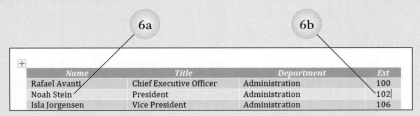

7. Save and then close **7-ATSManagement.docx**.
8. Open **7-ATSDocument.docx**.
9. Update the data in the table object by completing the following steps:
   a. Click in the table to select the table object.
   b. Press the F9 function key.
10. Save **7-ATSDocument.docx**.

Check Your Work

Using Paste Special

Use options at the Paste Special dialog box shown in Figure 7.9 to specify the formatting for pasted text and objects. Display the dialog box by clicking the Paste button arrow in the Clipboard group on the Home tab and then clicking *Paste Special* at the drop-down list. The options in the *As* list box vary depending on the cut or copied text or object and the source application. Text can be pasted with or without formatting and selected text can be pasted as an object. For example, in Project 6b, text will be copied in one document and then pasted into another document without the formatting. Also in the project, text and an image will be selected in one document and then pasted into another document as a Word object.

Figure 7.9 Paste Special Dialog Box

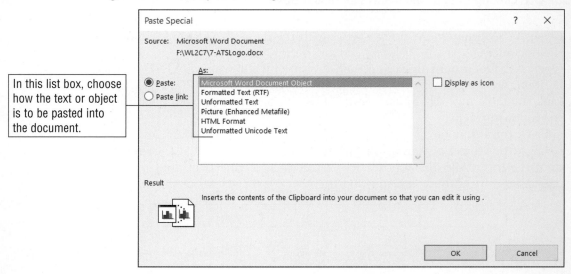

In this list box, choose how the text or object is to be pasted into the document.

Project 6b Pasting Data Using the Paste Special Dialog Box

1. With **7-ATSDocument.docx** open, press Ctrl + End to move the insertion point to the end of the document.
2. Open **ATSLogo.docx** and then save it with the name **7-ATSLogo.docx**.
3. Copy and paste the company name by completing the following steps:
   a. Select the company name *Advantage Transport Services*. (Select only the company name and not the image near the name.)
   b. Click the Copy button in the Clipboard group.
   c. Click the Word button on the taskbar and then click the *7-ATSDocument.docx* thumbnail.
   d. With the insertion point positioned at the end of the document, click the Paste button arrow and then click *Paste Special* at the drop-down list.
   e. At the Paste Special dialog box, click the *Unformatted Text* option in the *As* list box.
   f. Click OK.

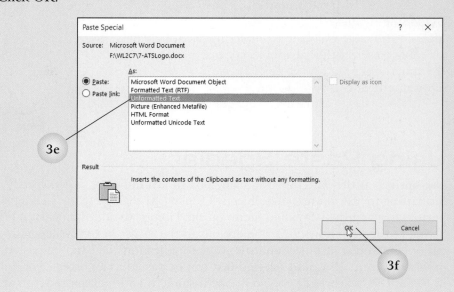

4. Copy the company name and image and then paste it as an object in the Header pane by completing the following steps:
   a. Click the Word button on the taskbar and then click the *7-ATSLogo.docx* thumbnail.
   b. Press Ctrl + A to select the entire document (the company name plus the road image).
   c. Click the Copy button.
   d. Click the Word button on the taskbar and then click the *7-ATSDocument.docx* thumbnail.
   e. Click the Insert tab.
   f. Click the Header button and then click *Edit Header* at the drop-down list.
   g. With the insertion point positioned in the Header pane, click the Home tab, click the Paste button arrow and then click *Paste Special* at the drop-down list.
   h. At the Paste Special dialog box, click the *Microsoft Word Document Object* option in the *As* list box.
   i. Click OK.

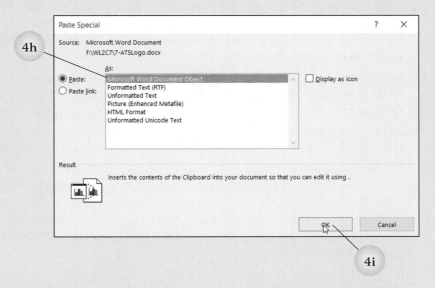

5. Increase the height of the pasted object by completing the following steps:
   a. Click the object to select it.
   b. Position the mouse pointer on the bottom middle sizing handle, click and hold down the mouse button, drag down approximately one-quarter inch, and then release the mouse button.
6. Close the Header pane by double-clicking in the document.
7. Save, print, and then close **7-ATSDocument.docx**.
8. Close **7-ATSLogo.docx**.

Check Your Work

Chapter Summary

- Insert a comment in a document by clicking the New Comment button in the Comments group on the Review tab; a comment balloon displays at the right margin. Depending on what previous settings have been applied, the Reviewing pane may display at the left side, rather than a comment balloon.

- Turn the display of the Reviewing pane on and off with the Reviewing Pane button in the Tracking group on the Review tab.

- Comments can be inserted in a document in the Reviewing pane. The summary that displays toward the top of the Reviewing pane provides counts of the numbers of comments inserted and changes made to the document.

- Navigate to review comments using the Previous and Next buttons in the Comments group on the Review tab.

- Edit a comment in the Reviewing pane by displaying the pane, clicking in the comment, and then making the change. Edit a comment in a comment balloon by turning on the display of comment balloons, clicking in the comment balloon, and then making the change.

- Click the Show Comments button in the Comments group on the Review tab to display comments. The Show Comments button is available only when the *Display for Review* option in the Tracking group is set to *Simple Markup*.

- Reply to a comment by clicking the Reply button to the right of the reviewer's name in the comment balloon and then typing the reply in the window that opens.

- Print a document with or without the comments or print only the comments and not the document.

- Delete a comment by clicking the Next button in the Comments group on the Review tab until the comment is selected and then clicking the Delete button in the Comments group.

- When changes are made to a document by another person with different user information, the changes display in a different color. Change the user name and initials at the Word Options dialog box with *General* selected.

- Use the Track Changes feature when more than one person is reviewing a document and making changes to it. Turn on Track Changes by clicking the Track Changes button in the Tracking group on the Review tab.

- Control how changes display in a document with the *Display for Review* option in the Tracking group on the Review tab. Control how markups display in a document with options at the Show Markup button drop-down list.

- Lock Track Changes so that all changes made to a document will be tracked. Lock Track Changes by clicking the Track Changes button arrow and then clicking *Lock Tracking*. Specify a password at the Lock Tracking dialog box that displays.

- Use options at the Show Markup button drop-down list or the Track Changes Options dialog box to customize the markup display. Click the Show Markup button in the Tracking group on the Review tab to display the drop-down list and click the Tracking group dialog box launcher to display the Track Changes Options dialog box.

- Display information about tracked changes—such as the author's name, date and time the change was made, and type of change—by hovering the mouse pointer over a change. After approximately one second, a box displays with the information. Information about tracked changes can also be displayed in the Reviewing pane.

- Change the Track Changes default settings with options at the Advanced Track Changes Options dialog box. Display this dialog box by clicking the Tracking group dialog box launcher. At the Track Changes Options dialog box, click the Advanced Options button.

- When reviewing a document, move to the next change by clicking the Next button in the Changes group on the Review tab and move to the previous change by clicking the Previous button.

- Use the Accept and Reject buttons in the Changes group on the Review tab to accept and reject changes made in a document.

- Use the Compare button in the Compare group on the Review tab to compare two documents and display the differences between them as tracked changes in a third document.

- Control how changes are combined with options at the expanded Compare Documents dialog box. Click the More button to display additional options.

- If several people have made changes to a document, their changed versions can be combined with the original document. Combine documents with options at the Combine Documents dialog box.

- Customize options for combining documents at the expanded Combine Documents dialog box. Click the More button to display additional options.

- Specify which source documents to display by clicking the Compare button in the Compare group on the Review tab, pointing to *Show Source Documents*, and then clicking an option at the side menu.

- An object created in one program in the Microsoft Office suite can be copied, linked, or embedded into another program in the suite. The program containing the original object is called the *source program* and the program in which it is inserted is called the *destination program*.

- An embedded object is stored in both the source and the destination programs. A linked object is stored only in the source program. Link an object if the content in the destination program should reflect changes made to the object stored in the source program.

- Data in one document can be linked to the open document at the Insert File dialog box by clicking the Insert button arrow in the dialog box and then clicking the *Insert as Link* option. Display the Insert File dialog box by clicking the Insert tab, clicking the Object button arrow, and then clicking the *Text from File* option.

- Use options at the Paste Special dialog box to specify the formatting for pasted text and objects. Display the Paste Special dialog box by clicking the Paste button arrow on the Home tab and then clicking *Paste Special* at the drop-down list.

Commands Review

FEATURE	RIBBON TAB, GROUP	BUTTON, OPTION	KEYBOARD SHORTCUT
accept change	Review, Changes		
Advanced Track Changes Options dialog box	Review, Tracking	, Advanced Options	
balloons	Review, Tracking	, Balloons	
Combine Documents dialog box	Review, Compare	, Combine	
Compare Documents dialog box	Review, Compare	, Compare	
delete comment	Review, Comments		
display for review	Review, Tracking		
Insert File dialog box	Insert, Text	, Text from File	
new comment	Review, Comments		
next comment	Review, Comments		
next revision	Review, Changes		
Paste Special dialog box	Home, Clipboard	, Paste Special	
previous comment	Review, Comments		
previous revision	Review, Changes		
reject change	Review, Changes		
Reviewing pane	Review, Tracking		
show markups	Review, Tracking		
show source documents	Review, Compare	, Show Source Documents	
Track Changes	Review, Tracking		Ctrl + Shift + E
Track Changes Options dialog box	Review, Tracking		

Workbook

Chapter study tools and assessment activities are available in the *Workbook* ebook. These resources are designed to help you further develop and demonstrate mastery of the skills learned in this chapter.

Microsoft®
Word

Protecting and Preparing Documents

CHAPTER

8

Performance Objectives

Upon successful completion of Chapter 8, you will be able to:

1 Restrict formatting and editing in a document and allow exceptions to restrictions

2 Protect a document with a password

3 Open a document in different views

4 Modify document properties

5 Mark a document as final

6 Encrypt a document with a password

7 Inspect a document for confidentiality, accessibility, and compatibility issues

8 Manage versions of a document

Precheck

Check your current skills to help focus your study.

In Chapter 7, you learned to perform workgroup activities such as inserting comments into a document, tracking changes made by other users, comparing documents, and combining documents from multiple users. In this chapter, you will learn how to protect the integrity of shared documents, limit the formatting and editing changes that users can make, and prepare documents for distribution.

SNAP

If you are a SNAP user, launch the Precheck and Tutorials from your Assignments page.

Data Files

Before beginning chapter work, copy the WL2C8 folder to your storage medium and then make WL2C8 the active folder.

Project 1 Restrict Formatting and Editing in a Company Report

3 Parts

You will open a company report document, restrict formatting and editing in the document, and insert a password.

Preview Finished Project

Protecting Documents

Within an organization, copies of a document may be distributed among members of a group. In some situations, the document may need to be protected and the changes that can be made to it need to be limited. If a document contains sensitive, restricted, or private information, consider protecting it by saving it as a read-only document or securing it with a password.

Use options in the Restrict Editing task pane to limit what formatting and editing users can perform on a document. Limiting formatting and editing is especially useful in a workgroup environment, in which a number of people review and edit the same document.

For example, suppose a company's annual report is being prepared and it contains information from a variety of departments, such as Finance, Human Resources, and Sales and Marketing. Access to the report can be restricted so only certain employees are allowed to edit specific parts of the document. For instance, the part of the report pertaining to finance can be restricted to allow only someone in the Finance Department to make edits. Similarly, the part of the report on employees can be restricted so only someone in Human Resources can make edits. By limiting others' options for editing, the integrity of the document can be protected.

Restrict Editing

To protect a document, display the Restrict Editing task pane, shown in Figure 8.1, by clicking the Review tab and then clicking the Restrict Editing button in the Protect group. Use options in the *Formatting restrictions* section to

Figure 8.1 Restrict Editing Task Pane

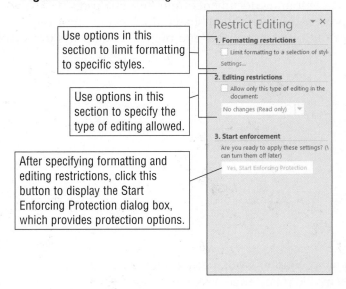

Use options in this section to limit formatting to specific styles.

Use options in this section to specify the type of editing allowed.

After specifying formatting and editing restrictions, click this button to display the Start Enforcing Protection dialog box, which provides protection options.

limit formatting to specific styles and use options in the *Editing restrictions* section to specify the type of editing allowed in the document.

The Protect group on the Review tab contains a Block Authors button when a document is saved to a Microsoft SharePoint site that supports workspaces. If the button is active, select the portion of the document to block from editing and then click the Block Authors button. To unblock authors, click in the locked section of the document and then click the Block Authors button.

Restricting Formatting

Quick Steps

Display the Formatting Restrictions Dialog Box
1. Click Review tab.
2. Click Restrict Editing button.
3. Click Settings hyperlink.

Use options in the *Formatting restrictions* section of the Restrict Editing task pane to lock specific styles used in a document, thus allowing the use of only those styles and prohibiting users from making other formatting changes. Click the Settings hyperlink in the *Formatting restrictions* section and the Formatting Restrictions dialog box displays, as shown in Figure 8.2.

Insert a check mark in the *Limit formatting to a selection of styles* check box and the styles become available in the *Checked styles are currently allowed* list box. In this list box, insert check marks in the check boxes preceding the styles that are allowed and remove check marks from the check boxes preceding the styles that are not allowed. Limit formatting to a minimum number of styles by clicking the Recommended Minimum button. This allows formatting with styles that Word uses for certain features, such as bulleted and numbered lists. Click the None button to remove all the check marks and prevent all the styles from being used in the document. Click the All button to insert check marks in all the check boxes and allow all the styles to be used in the document.

Use options in the *Formatting* section of the dialog box to allow or not allow AutoFormat to make changes in a document. Also use options in this section of the dialog box to allow or not allow users to switch themes or style sets.

Figure 8.2 Formatting Restrictions Dialog Box

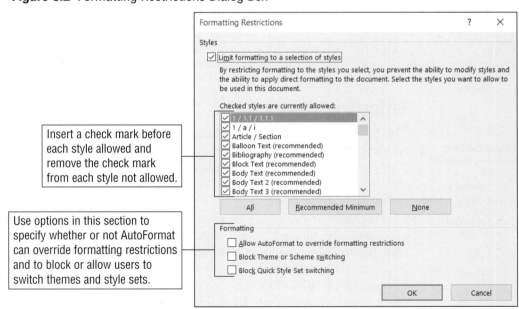

Insert a check mark before each style allowed and remove the check mark from each style not allowed.

Use options in this section to specify whether or not AutoFormat can override formatting restrictions and to block or allow users to switch themes and style sets.

1. Open **TECRpt.docx** and then save it with the name **8-TECRpt**.
2. Restrict formatting to the Heading 1 and Heading 2 styles by completing the following steps:
   a. Click the Review tab.
   b. Click the Restrict Editing button in the Protect group.

c. At the Restrict Editing task pane, click the *Limit formatting to a selection of styles* check box to insert a check mark. (Skip this step if the check box already contains a check mark.)
d. Click the Settings hyperlink.
e. At the Formatting Restrictions dialog box, click the None button.
f. Scroll down the *Checked styles are currently allowed* list box and then click to insert check marks in the *Heading 1* and *Heading 2* check boxes.
g. Click OK.
h. At the message stating that the document may contain direct formatting or styles that are not allowed and asking about removing them, click Yes.
3. Save **8-TECRpt.docx**.

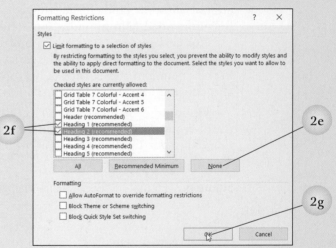

Enforcing Restrictions

The first step in protecting a document is to specify formatting and editing restrictions along with any exceptions to those restrictions. The second step is to start enforcing the restrictions. Click the Yes, Start Enforcing Protection button at the Restrict Editing task pane to display the Start Enforcing Protection dialog box, as shown in Figure 8.3.

At the Start Enforcing Protection dialog box, the *Password* option is automatically selected. To add a password, type it in the *Enter new password (optional)* text box. Click in the *Reenter password to confirm* text box and then type the same password again. Choose the *User authentication* option to use encryption to prevent any unauthorized changes. If Word does not recognize the password when a password-protected document is being opened, check to make sure Caps Lock is turned off and then try typing the password again.

Figure 8.3 Start Enforcing Protection Dialog Box

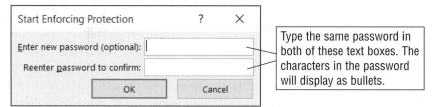

Type the same password in both of these text boxes. The characters in the password will display as bullets.

Project 1b Protecting a Document

Part 2 of 3

1. With **8-TECRpt.docx** open, click the Yes, Start Enforcing Protection button (at the bottom of the task pane).
2. At the Start Enforcing Protection dialog box, type formatting in the *Enter new password (optional)* text box. (Bullets will display in the text box, rather than the letters you type.)
3. Press the Tab key (which moves the insertion point to the *Reenter password to confirm* text box) and then type formatting. (Again, bullets will display in the text box, rather than the letters you type.)
4. Click OK to close the dialog box.

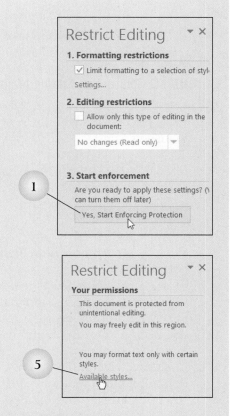

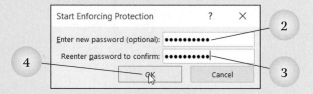

5. Read the information in the task pane stating that the document is protected and that text may be formatted only with certain styles. Click the <u>Available styles</u> hyperlink. (This displays the Styles task pane with four styles in the list box: *Clear All, Normal, Heading 1,* and *Heading 2.*)
6. Apply the Heading 1 style to the title *TANDEM ENERGY CORPORATION* and apply the Heading 2 style to the following headings: *Overview, Research and Development, Manufacturing,* and *Sales and Marketing.*
7. Close the Styles task pane.
8. Apply the Lines (Simple) style set.
9. At the message stating that some of the styles could not be updated, click OK.
10. Save the document.
11. Remove the password protection from the document by completing the following steps:
    a. Click the Stop Protection button at the bottom of the Restrict Editing task pane.
    b. At the Unprotect Document dialog box, type formatting in the *Password* text box.
    c. Click OK.
12. Save **8-TECRpt.docx**.

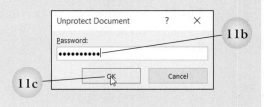

Check Your Work

Restricting Editing

Use the *Editing restrictions* option in the Restrict Editing task pane to limit the types of changes users can make to a document. Insert a check mark in the *Allow only this type of editing in the document* check box and the drop-down list below the option becomes active. Click the option box arrow and the following options become available: *Tracked changes*, *Comments*, *Filling in forms*, and *No changes (Read only)*.

To restrict users from making changes to a document, choose the *No changes (Read only)* option. Choose the *Tracked changes* option to allow users to make tracked changes in a document and choose the *Comments* option to allow users to insert comments in a document. These two options are useful in a workgroup environment, in which a document is routed to various individuals for review. Choose the *Filling in forms* option and users will be able to fill in the fields in a form but not make any other changes.

Project 1c Restricting Editing of and Protecting a Document

Part 3 of 3

1. With **8-TECRpt.docx** open, restrict editing to inserting comments by completing the following steps:
   a. Make sure the Restrict Editing task pane displays.
   b. Click the *Allow only this type of editing in the document* check box to insert a check mark.
   c. Click the option box arrow below *Allow only this type of editing in the document* and then click *Comments* at the drop-down list.
2. Click the Yes, Start Enforcing Protection button at the bottom of the task pane.
3. At the Start Enforcing Protection dialog box, click OK. (Adding a password is optional.)
4. Read the information in the task pane stating that the document is protected and that editing is restricted to inserting comments.
5. Click each ribbon tab and notice the buttons and options that are dimmed and unavailable.
6. Insert a comment by completing the following steps:
   a. Move the insertion point immediately to the right of the period that ends the last sentence in the second paragraph of the *Overview* section.
   b. Click the Review tab (if necessary), click the Show Markup button in the Tracking group, point to *Balloons*, and then click the *Show All Revisions Inline* option.
   c. Click the Reviewing Pane button to turn on the display of the Reviewing pane.
   d. Click the New Comment button in the Comments group on the Review tab.
   e. Type the following text in the Reviewing pane: Include additional information on the impact of this purchase.

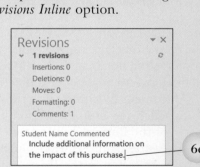

f. Close the Reviewing pane.

g. Click the Stop Protection button at the bottom of the Restrict Editing task pane.

h. Close the Restrict Editing task pane.

7. Save the document and then print only page 1.

8. Print only the comment. (To do this, display the Print backstage area, click the first gallery in the *Settings* category, click the *List of Markup* option, and then click the Print button.)

9. Close **8-TECRpt.docx**.

Check Your Work

Project 2 **Protect a Contract Document and Identify**   **2 Parts**
a Training Document as Read-Only

You will open a contract document and then protect it with a password. You will also open documents in different views.

Preview Finished Project

Protecting a Document with a Password

Tutorial

Protecting a Document with a Password

Quick Steps

Protect a Document with a Password
1. Press F12.
2. Click Tools button.
3. Click *General Options*.
4. Type password in *Password to modify* text box.
5. Press Enter.
6. Type same password again.
7. Press Enter.

Hint A strong password contains a mix of uppercase and lowercase letters as well as numbers and symbols.

In addition to protecting a document with a password using options at the Start Enforcing Protection dialog box, a document can be protected with a password using options at the General Options dialog box, shown in Figure 8.4. Display this dialog box by pressing the F12 function key to display the Save As dialog box, clicking the Tools button at the bottom of the dialog box next to the Save button, and then clicking *General Options* at the drop-down list.

Use options at the General Options dialog box to assign a password to open the document, modify the document, or both. To insert a password to open the document, click in the *Password to open* text box and then type the password. A password can contain up to 15 characters, should be at least 8 characters, and is case sensitive. Consider combining uppercase letters, lowercase letters, numbers, and/or symbols to make a password secure. Use the *Password to modify* option to create a password that someone must enter before being allowed to make edits to the document.

At the General Options dialog box, insert a check mark in the *Read-only recommended* check box to save a document as read-only. If a read-only document is opened and then changes are made to it, it must be saved with a new name. Use this option if the contents of the original document should not be changed.

Figure 8.4 General Options Dialog Box

Type a password in this text box to protect the document.

Click this check box to identify the document as read-only.

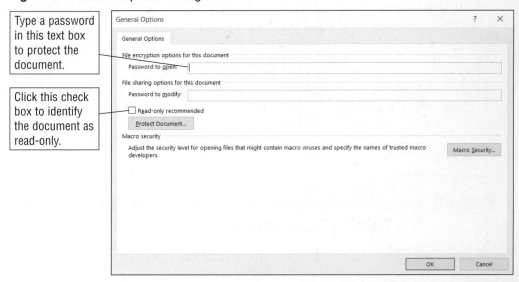

Project 2a Protecting a Document with a Password

Part 1 of 2

1. Open **TECContract.docx** and then save it with the name **8-TECContract**.
2. Save the document and protect it with a password by completing the following steps:
   a. Press the F12 function key to display the Save As dialog box.
   b. Click the Tools button at the bottom of the dialog box (next to the Save button) and then click *General Options* at the drop-down list.
   c. At the General Options dialog box, type your first name in the *Password to open* text box. (If your name is longer than 15 characters, abbreviate it. You will not see your name; Word inserts bullets in place of the letters.)
   d. After typing your name, press the Enter key.
   e. At the Confirm Password dialog box, type your name again in the *Reenter password to open* text box. (Be sure to type it exactly as you did in the *Password to open* text box, including the same uppercase and lowercase letters.) Press the Enter key.
   f. Click the Save button at the Save As dialog box.
3. Close **8-TECContract.docx**.
4. Open **8-TECContract.docx** and type your password when prompted in the *Enter password to open file* text box.
5. Close the document.

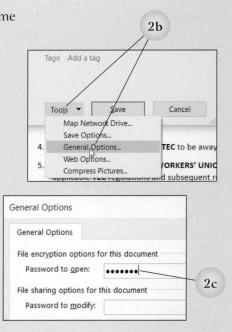

Opening a Document in Different Views

Quick Steps

Open a Document in Different Views
1. Display Open dialog box.
2. Click document name.
3. Click Open button arrow.
4. Click option at drop-down list.

Use the Open button at the Open dialog box to open a document in different views. At the Open dialog box, click the Open button arrow and a drop-down list of options displays. Click the *Open Read-Only* option and the document opens in Read Mode view and Read-Only mode. In Read-Only mode, changes can be made to the document but the document cannot be saved with the same name. Exit Read Mode view and display the document in Print Layout view by pressing the Esc key.

Click the *Open as Copy* option and a copy of the document opens with the text *Copy (1)* before the document name in the Title bar. Click the *Open in Protected View* option and the document opens with the text *(Protected View)* after the document name in the Title bar. A message bar displays above the document indicating that the file was opened in Protected view. To edit the document, click the Enable Editing button in the message bar. Open a document with the *Open and Repair* option and Word will open a new version of the document and attempt to resolve any issues.

Project 2b **Opening a Document in Different Views**   **Part 2 of 2**

1. Open **TECTraining.docx** and then save it with the name **8-TECTraining**.
2. Close **8-TECTraining.docx**.
3. Open a document as a read-only document by completing the following steps:
   a. Press Ctrl + F12 to display the Open dialog box and then navigate to the WL2C8 folder on your storage medium.
   b. Click the document name **8-TECTraining.docx**. (Click only one time.)
   c. Click the Open button arrow (in the bottom right corner of the dialog box) and then click *Open Read-Only* at the drop-down list.

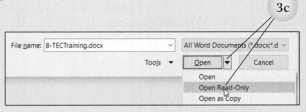

   d. The document opens in Read Mode view. Press the Esc key to exit Read Mode and display the document in Print Layout view. Notice that *[Read-Only]* displays after the name of the document in the Title bar.
   e. Close the document.
4. Open a document in Protected view by completing the following steps:
   a. Press Ctrl + F12 to display the Open dialog box.
   b. Click the document name *PremPro.docx*.
   c. Click the Open button arrow and then click *Open in Protected View* at the drop-down list.
   d. Press the Esc key to exit Read Mode view and display the document in Print Layout view. Notice the message bar that displays stating that the file was opened in Protected view.
   e. Click each tab and notice that most of the formatting options are dimmed.
   f. Click in the document and then click the Enable Editing button in the message bar. This removes *(Protected View)* after the document name in the Title bar and makes available the options on the tabs.

   g. Close the document.

You will open a real estate agreement and then prepare it for distribution by inserting document properties, marking it as final, and encrypting it with a password.

Preview Finished Project

Tutorial

Managing
Document
Properties

Managing Document Properties

Every document that is created has properties associated with it, such as the type of document, the location in which it has been saved, and when it was created, modified, and accessed. Document properties can be viewed and modified at the Info backstage area. To display information about the open document, click the File tab. Document property information displays at the right side of the Info backstage area, as shown in Figure 8.5.

The document property information that displays at the Info backstage area includes the file size, number of pages and words, total editing time, and any tags or comments that have been added. Add or update a document property by hovering the mouse pointer over the information that displays right of the property (a rectangular text box with a light-blue border displays), clicking in the text box, and then typing information. In the *Related Dates* section, dates display for when the document was created and when it was last modified and printed. The *Related People* section includes the name of the author of the document and provides options for adding additional author names. Display additional document properties by clicking the <u>Show All Properties</u> hyperlink.

Figure 8.5 Info Backstage Area

Click this button and then click the *Advanced Properties* option to display the Properties dialog box.

Click this button to display a drop-down list of options for protecting a document.

Click this button to display options for inspecting and checking the compatibility and accessibility of a document.

Click this button to recover and delete draft versions of a document.

Document property information is displayed in this area.

8-REAgrmnt.docx - Word

Student Name

Info

8-REAgrmnt

F: » WL2C8

Protect Document
Control what types of changes people can make to this document.

Inspect Document
Before publishing this file, be aware that it contains:
- Document properties and author's name

Manage Document
Check in, check out, and recover unsaved changes.
- There are no unsaved changes.

Properties ▾
Size	13.3KB
Pages	2
Words	589
Total Editing Time	1 Minute
Title	Add a title
Tags	Add a tag
Comments	Add comments

Related Dates
Last Modified	Today, 12:42 PM
Created	Today, 12:42 PM
Last Printed	

Related People
Author	Student Name
	Add an author
Last Modified By	Student Name

Related Documents
Open File Location

In addition to adding or updating document property information at the Info backstage area, specific information about a document can be viewed, added, edited, and customized with options at the Properties dialog box, shown in Figure 8.6. (The specific name of the dialog box reflects the currently open document.) Open the dialog box by displaying the Info backstage area, clicking the Properties button, and then clicking *Advanced Properties* at the drop-down list.

The Properties dialog box with the General tab selected displays information about the document type, size, and location. Click the Summary tab to view fields such as *Title*, *Subject*, *Author*, *Company*, *Category*, *Keywords*, and *Comments*. Some fields may contain data and others may be blank. Insert, edit, or delete text in the fields. With the Statistics tab selected, information displays such as the number of pages, paragraphs, lines, words, and characters. With the Contents tab selected, the dialog box displays the document title. Click the Custom tab to add custom properties to the document. For example, a property can be added that displays the date the document was completed, information on the department in which the document was created, and much more.

Another method for displaying document properties is to display the Open dialog box, click the document in the content pane, click the Organize button, and then click *Properties* at the drop-down list. Or right-click the file name in the content pane and then click *Properties* at the shortcut menu. The Properties dialog box that displays contains the tabs General, Security, Details, and Previous Versions. Some of the information in this Properties dialog box is the same as the information in the Properties dialog box that is accessed through the Info backstage area while some of the information varies between the two Properties dialog boxes. Generally, consider using the Properties dialog box accessed through the Info backstage area to add, edit, and create custom properties and use the Properties dialog box accessed through the Open dialog box to view document properties.

Figure 8.6 Properties Dialog Box with General Tab Selected

The Properties dialog box displays information about the document. Click each tab to display additional document information.

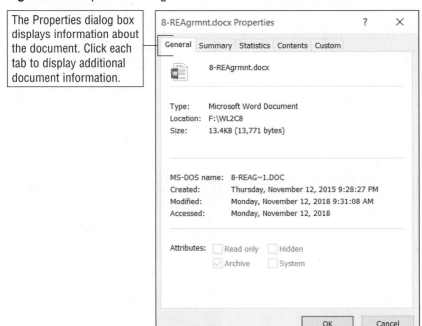

1. Open **REAgrmnt.docx** and then save it with the name **8-REAgrmnt**.
2. Make the following changes to the document:
   a. Insert page numbers that print at the top of each page at the right margin.
   b. Insert the footer *8-REAgrmnt.docx* centered on each page. (Do not set the footer text in italics. The footer text in this step was set in italics for emphasis only.)
3. Insert document properties by completing the following steps:
   a. Click the File tab. (Make sure the Info backstage area displays.)
   b. Hover the mouse pointer over the text *Add a title* that displays right of the *Title* document property, click in the text box that displays, and then type Real Estate Sale Agreement.
   c. Display the 8-REAgrmnt.docx Properties dialog box by clicking the Properties button and then clicking *Advanced Properties* at the drop-down list.
   d. At the 8-REAgrmnt.docx Properties dialog box with the Summary tab selected, press the Tab key to make the *Subject* text box active and then type Real Estate Sale Agreement.
   e. Click in the *Category* text box and then type Agreement.
   f. Press the Tab key and then type the following words, separated by commas, in the *Keywords* text box: real estate, agreement, contract, purchasing.
   g. Press the Tab key and then type the following text in the *Comments* text box: This is a real estate sale agreement between two parties.
4. Click OK to close the dialog box.
5. Press the Back button to return to the document.
6. Save **8-REAgrmnt.docx** and then print only the document properties by completing the following steps:
   a. Click the File tab and then click the *Print* option.
   b. At the Print backstage area, click the first gallery in the *Settings* category and then click *Document Info* at the drop-down list.
   c. Click the Print button.
7. Save **8-REAgrmnt.docx**.

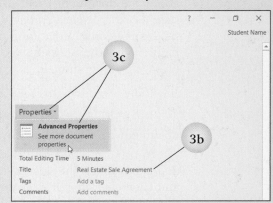

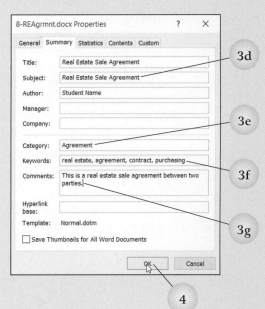

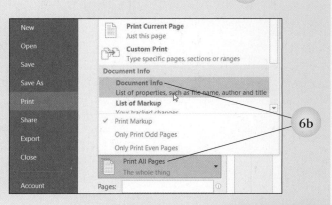

Check Your Work

Restricting Documents

The middle panel of the Info backstage area contains buttons for protecting a document, checking for issues in a document such as personal data and accessibility, and managing versions of a document. Click the Protect Document button in the middle panel and a drop-down list displays with the following options: *Mark as Final, Encrypt with Password, Restrict Editing*, and *Add a Digital Signature*.

🔒 Protect
Document

Marking a Document as Final

Click the *Mark as Final* option to save the document as a read-only document. Click this option and a message displays stating that the document will be marked and then saved. At this message, click OK. This displays another message stating that the document is the final version of the document. The message further states that when a document is marked as final, the status property is set to *Final*; typing, editing commands, and proofing marks are turned off; and the document can be identified by the Mark as Final icon, which displays on the Status bar. At this message, click OK. After a document is marked as final, the message *This document has been marked as final to discourage editing* displays to the right of the Protect Document button at the Info backstage area.

Project 3b Marking a Document as Final   Part 2 of 3

1. With **8-REAgrmnt.docx** open, mark the document as final by completing the following steps:
   a. Click the File tab.
   b. Click the Protect Document button at the Info backstage area and then click *Mark as Final* at the drop-down list.
   c. At the message stating that the document will be marked and saved, click OK.
   d. At the next message that displays, click OK. Notice the message that displays right of the Protect Document button.
   e. Click the Back button to return to the document.
2. In the document window, notice the message bar that displays at the top of the screen and then close the document.
3. Open **8-REAgrmnt.docx** and then click the Edit Anyway button on the yellow message bar.

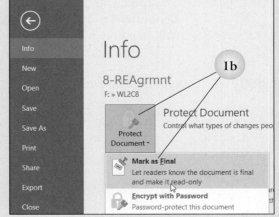

4. Save **8-REAgrmnt.docx**.

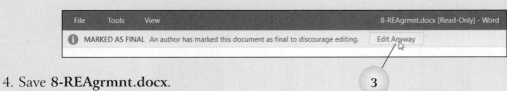

Encrypting a Document

Word provides a number of methods for protecting a document with a password. As previously discussed in this chapter, a document can be protected with a password using options at the Start Enforcing Protection dialog box and the General Options dialog box.

In addition to these two methods, a document can be protected with a password by clicking the Protect Document button at the Info backstage area and then clicking the *Encrypt with Password* option at the drop-down list. At the Encrypt Document dialog box that displays, type a password in the text box (the text will display as bullets) and then press the Enter key or click OK. At the Confirm Password dialog box, type the password again (the text will display as bullets) and then press the Enter key or click OK. When a password is applied to a document, the message *A password is required to open this document* displays right of the Protect Document button.

Quick Steps

Encrypt a Document
1. Click File tab.
2. Click Protect Document button.
3. Click *Encrypt with Password*.
4. Type password and then press Enter.
5. Type password again and then press Enter.

Restricting Editing

Click the Protect Document button at the Info backstage area and then click the *Restrict Editing* option at the drop-down list and the document displays with the Restrict Editing task pane open. This is the same task pane discussed previously in this chapter.

Adding a Digital Signature

Use the *Add a Digital Signature* option at the Protect Document button drop-down list to insert an invisible digital signature in a document. A digital signature is an electronic stamp that verifies the authenticity of the document. Before a digital signature can be added, it must be obtained. A digital signature can be obtained from a commercial certification authority.

Project 3c Encrypting a Document with a Password   Part 3 of 3

1. With **8-REAgrmnt.docx** open, encrypt the document with a password by completing the following steps:
   a. Click the File tab, click the Protect Document button at the Info backstage area, and then click *Encrypt with Password* at the drop-down list.
   b. At the Encrypt Document dialog box, type your initials in uppercase letters in the *Password* text box. (The text will display as bullets.)

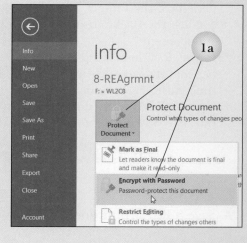

    c. Press the Enter key.

    d. At the Confirm Password dialog box, type your initials again in uppercase letters in the *Reenter password* text box (the text will display as bullets) and then press the Enter key.

2. Click the Back button to return to the document.

3. Save and then close the document.

4. Open **8-REAgrmnt.docx**.

5. At the Password dialog box, type your initials in uppercase letters in the *Enter password to open file* text box and then press the Enter key.

6. Save, print, and then close **8-REAgrmnt.docx**.

Check Your Work

Project 4   **Prepare and Inspect a Lease Agreement**   **1 Part**

You will open a lease agreement document, make tracked changes, hide text, and then inspect the document.

Preview Finished Project

Inspecting Documents

Use options from the Check for Issues button drop-down list at the Info backstage area to inspect a document for personal and hidden data along with compatibility and accessibility issues. Click the Check for Issues button at the Info backstage area and a drop-down list displays with the following options: *Inspect Document*, *Check Accessibility*, and *Check Compatibility*.

Using the Document Inspector

Use Word's Document Inspector feature to inspect a document for personal data, hidden data, and metadata (data that describes other data, such as document properties). In certain situations, some personal or hidden data may need to be removed before a document is shared with others. To check a document for personal and hidden data, click the File tab, click the Check for Issues button at the Info backstage area, and then click the *Inspect Document* option at the drop-down list. This displays the Document Inspector dialog box, shown in Figure 8.7.

 Check for Issues

By default, the Document Inspector checks all the items listed in the dialog box. To control what items are inspected in the document, remove the check marks preceding items that are not to be checked. For example, if the headers and footers in a document do not need to be checked, click the *Headers, Footers, and Watermarks* check box to remove the check mark. To scan the document to check for the selected items, click the Inspect button at the bottom of the dialog box.

When the inspection is complete, the results display in the Document Inspector dialog box. A check mark before an option indicates that the Document Inspector did not find the specific items. If an exclamation point displays before an option, it means that the items were found and a list of the items displays. To remove the found items, click the Remove All button right of the option. Click the Reinspect button to ensure that the specific items were removed and then click the Close button.

Figure 8.7 Document Inspector Dialog Box

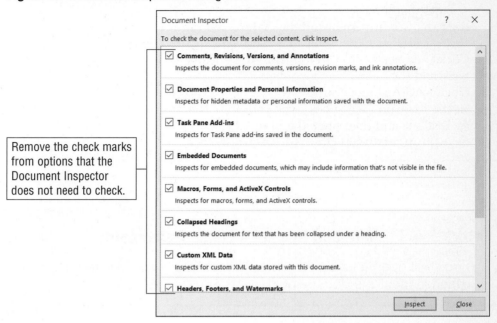

Remove the check marks from options that the Document Inspector does not need to check.

Project 4 Inspecting a Document

Part 1 of 1

1. Open **Lease.docx** and then save it with the name **8-Lease.docx**.
2. Make the following changes to the document:
   a. Turn on the Track Changes feature.
   b. Select the title *LEASE AGREEMENT* and then change the font size to 14 points.
   c. Delete the word *first* in the second numbered paragraph (the *RENT* paragraph) and then type fifteenth.
   d. Move the insertion point to the beginning of the text *IN WITNESS WHEREOF* (located on page 2) and then press the Tab key.
   e. Turn off Track Changes.
3. Hide text by completing the following steps:
   a. Move the insertion point to the end of the first paragraph of text in the document (one space after the period at the end of the sentence).
   b. Type The entire legal description of the property is required for this agreement to be valid.
   c. Select the text you just typed.
   d. Click the Home tab.
   e. Click the Font group dialog box launcher.
   f. At the Font dialog box, click the *Hidden* option in the *Effects* section.
   g. Click OK to close the dialog box.
4. Click the Save button on the Quick Access Toolbar.

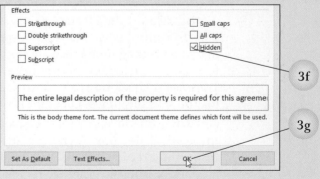

5. Inspect the document by completing the following steps:
   a. Click the File tab.
   b. Click the Check for Issues button at the Info backstage area and then click *Inspect Document* at the drop-down list.
   c. At the Document Inspector dialog box, specify not to check the document for extensible markup language (XML) data by clicking the *Custom XML Data* check box to remove the check mark.
   d. Click the Inspect button.

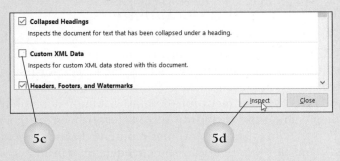

e. Read the inspection results and then remove all the hidden text by clicking the Remove All button at the right side of the *Hidden Text* section. (Make sure that a message displays below *Hidden Text* stating that the text was successfully removed.)

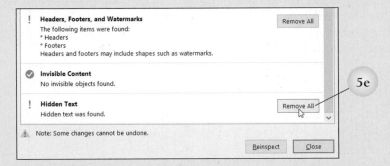

f. Click the Reinspect button.
   g. To keep the header and footer text in the document, click the *Headers, Footers, and Watermarks* check box to remove the check mark.
   h. Click the Inspect button.
   i. Read the inspection results and then remove all the revisions by clicking the Remove All button at the right side of the *Comments, Revisions, Versions, and Annotations* section.
   j. Click the Reinspect button.
   k. To leave the remaining items in the document, click the Close button.
6. Click the Back button to return to the document.
7. Save, print, and then close **8-Lease.docx**.

Check Your Work

You will open a document containing information on produce, check for accessibility issues, and check the compatibility of elements with previous versions of Word. You will also manage unsaved versions of the document.

Preview Finished Project

Checking the Accessibility of a Document

Word provides the Accessibility Checker feature to check a document for content that a person with disabilities (such as a visual impairment) might find difficult to read. Check the accessibility of a document by clicking the Check for Issues button at the Info backstage area and then clicking *Check Accessibility*. The Accessibility Checker examines the document for the most common accessibility problems in Word documents and sorts them into three categories: errors (content that is unreadable to a person who is blind); warnings (content that some readers will find difficult to read); and tips (content that some readers may or may not find difficult to read). The Accessibility Checker examines the document, closes the Info backstage area, and then displays the Accessibility Checker task pane.

In the Accessibility Checker task pane, passages of text that are unreadable are grouped in the *Errors* section, passages that are difficult to read are grouped in the *Warnings* section, and passages that may or may not be difficult to read are grouped in the *Tips* section. Select an issue in one of the sections, and an explanation of why it is an issue and how it can be corrected displays at the bottom of the task pane.

Quick Steps
Check Accessibility
1. Click File tab.
2. Click Check for Issues button.
3. Click *Check Accessibility*.

Project 5a **Checking the Accessibility of a Document**

Part 1 of 3

1. Open **PremPro.docx** and then save it with the name **8-PremPro**.
2. Complete an accessibility check by completing the following steps:
   a. Click the File tab.
   b. At the Info backstage area, click the Check for Issues button and then click *Check Accessibility* at the drop-down list.
   c. Notice the Accessibility Checker task pane at the right side of the screen, which contains an *Errors* section and a *Warnings* section. Click *Picture 4* in the *Errors* section and then read the information at the bottom of the task pane describing why the error should be fixed and how to fix it.

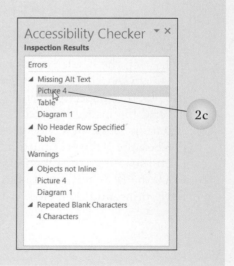

2c

3. Add alternate text (a text-based representation of the image) to the image by completing the following steps:

a. Right-click the selected image in the document and then click *Format Picture* at the shortcut menu.

b. At the Format Picture task pane, click the Layout & Properties icon and then click *Alt Text* to expand the options.

c. Click in the *Title* text box, type Cornucopia, and then press the Tab key. (This selects the default text in the *Description* text box.)

d. Type Cornucopia of fruits and vegetables representing Premium Produce.

e. Click the Close button to close the Format Picture task pane.

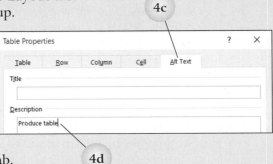

4. Click the first *Table* entry in the *Errors* section and then read the information at the bottom of the task pane about creating alternate text for a table. Add alternate text and repeat the header row by completing the following steps:

a. With the table selected, click the Table Tools Layout tab.

b. Click the Properties button in the Table group.

c. At the Table Properties dialog box, click the Alt Text tab.

d. Click in the *Description* text box and then type Produce table.

e. Click OK to close the dialog box.

f. Click anywhere in the first row in the table.

g. Click the Repeat Header Rows button in the Data group on the Table Tools Layout tab.

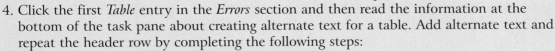

5. Click the *Diagram 1* entry in the *Errors* section and then add alternate text by completing the following steps:

a. Right-click the selected SmartArt graphic and then click *Format Object* at the shortcut menu.

b. At the Format Shape task pane, click the Layout & Properties icon and then, if necessary, click *Alt Text* to expand the options.

c. Click in the *Title* text box, type Graphic, and then press the Tab key.

d. In the Description text box, type SmartArt graphic with three shapes containing text on no pesticides, no herbicides, and organically grown produce.

e. Click the Close button to close the Format Shape task pane.

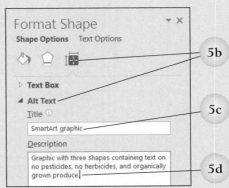

6. Click *Picture 4* in the *Warnings* section and then read the information about objects that are not inline with text. Do not make the change suggested because it will move the image to a different location on the page.

7. Click *Diagram 1* in the *Warnings* section and notice that the same information displays about objects that are not inline with text.

8. Close the Accessibility Checker task pane by clicking the Close button in the upper right corner of the task pane.

9. Save **8-PremPro.docx**.

Checking the Compatibility of a Document

Quick Steps
Check Compatibility
1. Click File tab.
2. Click Check for Issues button.
3. Click *Check Compatibility*.
4. Click OK.

Use one of the Check for Issues button drop-down options, *Check Compatibility*, to check a document and identify elements that are not supported or will function differently in previous versions of Word from Word 97 through Word 2010. To run the Compatibility Checker, open a document, click the Check for Issues button at the Info backstage area, and then click *Check Compatibility* at the drop-down list. This displays the Microsoft Word Compatibility Checker dialog box, which includes a summary of the elements in the document that are not compatible with previous versions of Word. This box also indicates what will happen when the document is saved and then opened in a previous version.

Project 5b Checking the Compatibility of Elements in a Document

Part 2 of 3

1. With **8-PremPro.docx** open, check the compatibility of elements in the document by completing the following steps:
   a. Click the File tab, click the Check for Issues button at the Info backstage area, and then click *Check Compatibility* at the drop-down list.
   b. At the Microsoft Word Compatibility Checker dialog box, read the information that displays in the *Summary* text box.
   c. Click the Select versions to show button and then click *Word 97-2003* at the drop-down list. (This removes the check mark from the option.) Notice that the information about SmartArt graphics being converted to static objects disappears from the *Summary* text box. This is because Word 2007, 2010, and 2013 all support SmartArt graphics.

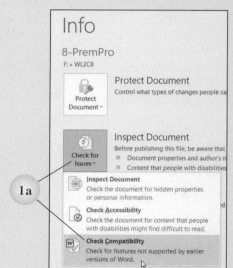

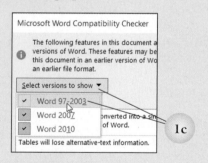

   d. Click OK to close the dialog box.
2. Save the document in Word 2003 format by completing the following steps:
   a. Press the F12 function key to display the Save As dialog box with WL2C8 the active folder.
   b. At the Save As dialog box, click the *Save as type* option box and then click *Word 97-2003 Document (*.doc)* at the drop-down list.
   c. Select the text in the *File name* text box and then type 8-PremPro-2003format.
   d. Click the Save button.
   e. Click the Continue button at the Microsoft Word Compatibility Checker dialog box.
3. Close **8-PremPro-2003format.doc**.

Manage
Document

Quick Steps

**Display the
UnsavedFiles Folder**
1. Click File tab.
2. Click Manage
   Document button.
3. Click *Recover
   Unsaved Documents.*
OR
1. Click File tab.
2. Click *Open* option.
3. Click Recover
   Unsaved Documents
   button.

**Delete an Autosave
Backup File**
1. Click File tab.
2. Right-click autosave
   backup file.
3. Click *Delete This
   Version* at shortcut
   menu.

**Delete All Unsaved
Files**
1. Click File tab.
2. Click Manage
   Document button.
3. Click *Delete All
   Unsaved Documents.*
4. Click Yes.

**Change the
AutoRecover Time**
1. Click File tab.
2. Click *Options.*
3. Click *Save.*
4. Type minutes in
   *Save AutoRecover
   information every*
   measurement box.
5. Click OK.

Managing Document Versions

When a document is being worked in, Word automatically saves it every 10 minutes. This automatic backup feature can be very helpful if the document is closed accidentally without saving it or the power to the computer is disrupted. As backups of the open document are automatically saved, they are listed right of the Manage Document button at the Info backstage area, as shown in Figure 8.8. Each autosave document displays with *Today*, followed by the time and *(autosave)*. When the document is saved and then closed, the autosave backup documents are deleted.

To open an autosave backup document, click the File tab and then click the autosave backup document. (Backup documents display right of the Manage Document button.) The document opens as a read-only document and a message bar displays with a Compare button and Restore button. Click the Compare button and the autosave document is compared to the original document. Review the comparison to decide which changes to accept and reject. Click the Restore button and a message displays stating that the selected version will overwrite the saved version. At this message, click OK.

When a document is saved, the autosave backup documents are deleted. However, if a document is closed without being saved (after 10 minutes) or the power is disrupted, Word keeps the autosave backup files in the UnsavedFiles folder on the hard drive. Access this folder by clicking the Manage Document button at the Info backstage area and then clicking *Recover Unsaved Documents*. At the Open dialog box, double-click the backup file to be opened. The UnsavedFiles folder can also be displayed at the Open dialog box by clicking the File tab, clicking the *Open* option, and then clicking the Recover Unsaved Documents button below the *Recent* option list. Files in the UnsavedFiles folder are kept for four days after a document is created. After that, they are automatically deleted.

Delete an autosave backup file by displaying the Info backstage area, right-clicking the autosave file (to the right of the Manage Document button), and then clicking *Delete This Version* at the shortcut menu. At the confirmation message that displays, click the Yes button. To delete all unsaved files from the UnsavedFiles folder, display a blank document, click the File tab, click the Manage Document button, and then click the *Delete All Unsaved Documents* option at the drop-down list. At the confirmation message that displays, click the Yes button.

As mentioned previously, Word automatically saves a backup of an unsaved document every 10 minutes. To change this default setting, click the File tab and then click *Options*. At the Word Options dialog box, click *Save* in the left panel. Notice that the *Save AutoRecover information every* measurement box is set at 10 minutes. To change this number, click the measurement box up arrow to increase the number of minutes between autosaves or click the down arrow to decrease the number of minutes.

Figure 8.9 Autosave Documents at Info Backstage Area

Info

8-PremPro
F: » WL2C8

Protect Document
Control what types of changes people can make to this document.

Inspect Document
Before publishing this file, be aware that it contains:
- Document properties and author's name
- Content that people with disabilities find difficult to read

Manage Document
Check in, check out, and recover unsaved changes.
Today, 12:25 PM (autosave)

> Word automatically creates backups of a document; these backups are deleted when the document is saved. To open a backup document, click an autosave version.

Project 5c Opening and Deleting an Autosave Document

1. At a blank screen, decrease the autosave time to 1 minute by completing the following steps:
   a. Click the File tab and then click *Options*.
   b. At the Word Options dialog box, click *Save* in the left panel.
   c. Click the *Save AutoRecover information every* measurement box down arrow until *1* displays.

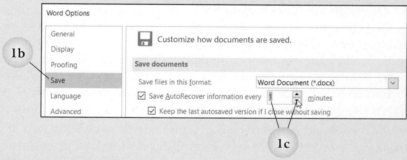

   d. Click OK to close the dialog box.
2. Open **8-PremPro.docx**.
3. Press Ctrl + End to move the insertion point to the end of the document and then type your first and last names.

4. Leave the document open for more than one minute without making any changes. After at least one minute has passed, click the File tab and then check to see if an autosave document displays right of the Manage Document button. (If not, click the Back button to return to the document and wait a few more minutes.)

5. When an autosave document displays at the Info backstage area, click the Back button to return to the document.

6. Select the SmartArt graphic and then delete it.

7. Click the File tab and then click the autosave document that displays right of the Manage Document button. If more than one autosave document displays, click the one at the top of the list (the most recent autosave document). This opens the autosave document as read-only.

8. Restore the document to the autosave version by clicking the Restore button in the message bar.

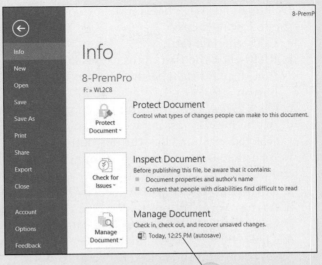

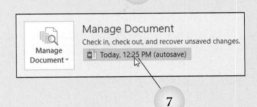

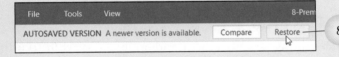

9. At the message that displays stating that the last saved version is about to be overwritten with the selected version, click OK. (This saves the document with the SmartArt.)

10. Press the Esc key to display the document in Normal view.

11. Check to see what versions of previous documents Word has saved by completing the following steps:
    a. Click the File tab.
    b. Click the Manage Document button and then click *Recover Unsaved Documents* at the drop-down list.
    c. At the Open dialog box, check the documents that display in the content pane.
    d. Click the Cancel button to close the Open dialog box.

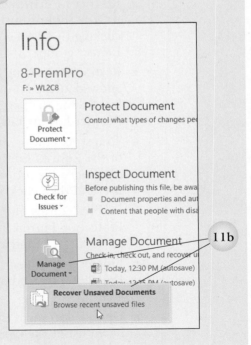

12. Delete an autosave backup file by completing the following steps:
    a. Click the File tab.
    b. Right-click the first autosave backup file name that displays right of the Manage Document button.
    c. Click *Delete This Version* at the shortcut menu.
    d. At the message asking whether to delete the selected version, click the Yes button.
13. Return the autosave time to 10 minutes by completing the following steps:
    a. At the Info backstage area, click *Options*.
    b. At the Word Options dialog box, click *Save* in the left panel.
    c. Click the *Save AutoRecover information every* measurement box up arrow until *10* displays.
    d. Click OK to close the dialog box.
14. Save, print, and then close **8-PremPro.docx**.
15. Delete all the unsaved backup files by completing the following steps:
    a. Press Ctrl + N to display a blank document.
    b. Click the File tab.
    c. Click the Manage Document button and then click *Delete All Unsaved Documents*.
    d. At the message that displays, click Yes.
16. Click the Back button to return to the blank document.

Check Your Work

Chapter Summary

- Restrict formatting and editing in a document and apply a password to protect it with options in the Restrict Editing task pane. Display this task pane by clicking the Review tab and then clicking the Restrict Editing button in the Protect group.

- Restrict formatting in a document by specifying what styles are and are not allowed at the Formatting Restrictions dialog box. Display this dialog box by clicking the Settings hyperlink in the *Formatting restrictions* section in the Restrict Editing task pane.

- To restrict editing in a document, use options in the *Editing restrictions* section of the Restrict Editing task pane. Insert a check mark in the *Allow only this type of editing in the document* check box, click the option box arrow at the drop-down list, and then click a specific option.

- Enforce editing and formatting restrictions by clicking the Yes, Start Enforcing Protection button in the Restrict Editing task pane and then enter a password at the Start Enforcing Protection dialog box.

- Protect a document with a password using options at the Start Enforcing Protection dialog box, the General Options dialog box, or the Info backstage area.

- Open a document in different views with options at the Open button drop-down list at the Open dialog box.

- Review and modify document properties at the Info backstage area.

- Display the Properties dialog box by clicking the Properties button at the Info backstage area and then clicking *Advanced Properties* at the drop-down list.

- When a document is marked as final, it is saved as a read-only document. Mark a document as final by clicking the Protect Document button at the Info backstage area and then clicking *Mark as Final* at the drop-down list. Typing, editing commands, and proofing marks are turned off when a document is marked as final.

- Another method for displaying the Restrict Editing task pane is to click the Protect Document button at the Info backstage area and then click *Restrict Editing* at the drop-down list.

- Insert a digital signature (an electronic stamp that verifies the authenticity of a document) in a document using the *Add a Digital Signature* option at the Protect Document button drop-down list. A digital signature can be obtained from a commercial certification authority.

- Inspect a document for personal data, hidden data, and metadata with options at the Document Inspector dialog box. Display this dialog box by clicking the Check for Issues button at the Info backstage area and then clicking *Inspect Document* at the drop-down list.

- The Accessibility Checker checks a document for content that a person with disabilities might find difficult to read. Run the Accessibility Checker by clicking the Check for Issues button at the Info backstage area and then clicking *Check Accessibility* at the drop-down list.

- Run the Compatibility Checker to check a document and identify elements that are not supported or that will function differently in previous versions of Word. To determine the compatibility of the features in a document, click the Check for Issues button at the Info backstage area and then click *Check Compatibility* at the drop-down list.

- By default, Word automatically saves a backup of an unsaved document every 10 minutes. A list of autosave backup documents displays right of the Manage Document button at the Info backstage area. Click the document name to open the autosave backup document.

- When a document is saved, Word automatically deletes the autosave backup documents. However, if a document is closed without saving it or the power to the computer is disrupted, Word keeps backup files in the UnsavedFiles folder on the hard drive. Display this folder by clicking the Manage Document button at the Info backstage area and then clicking *Recover Unsaved Documents* at the drop-down list.

- Delete an autosave backup file by displaying the Info backstage area, right-clicking the autosave backup file, and then clicking *Delete This Version* at the shortcut menu.

- Delete all the unsaved backup files by displaying a blank document, clicking the File tab, clicking the Manage Document button, and then clicking *Delete All Unsaved Documents*. At the confirmation message that displays, click the Yes button.

- Change the 10-minute autosave default setting by changing the *Save AutoRecover information every* measurement at the Word Options dialog box with *Save* selected in the left panel.

Commands Review

FEATURE	RIBBON TAB, GROUP/OPTION	BUTTON, OPTION
Accessibility Checker	File, *Info*	, Check Accessibility
Compatibility Checker	File, *Info*	, Check Compatibility
Document Inspector dialog box	File, *Info*	, Inspect Document
Encrypt Document dialog box	File, *Info*	, Encrypt with Password
Formatting Restrictions dialog box	Review, Protect	, Settings
General Options dialog box	File, *Save As, Browse*	Tools, General Options
Properties dialog box	File, *Info*	Properties ▾, Advanced Properties
Restrict Editing task pane	Review, Protect	
UnsavedFiles folder	File, *Info*	, Recover Unsaved Documents

Index

A

Absolute position option, 15
Accept button, 238
accessibility checker feature, 274–275
Add Gallery to Quick Access Toolbar, 100–102
Add Text button, 198
Advanced Track Changes Options dialog box, 237
Alignment option, 15
Allow overlap option, 15
alphanumeric sort, punctuation and symbols in, 158
American Psychological Association (APA) style, 176, 186–187
antonyms, 57
Artistic Effects button, 18
AutoCaption button, 205
AutoCorrect dialog box, 80
  with AutoFormatting options, 86
AutoCorrect Exceptions dialog box, 80–81
AutoCorrect feature, 80–88
  abbreviations and, 81
  adding words to, 81–82
  capitalization in index, 215–216, 218
  customizing AutoFormatting, 86–88
  deleting AutoCorrect text, 81, 87
  inserting symbols, 81, 84–85
  specifying exceptions for, 80–81
  using AutoCorrect Options button, 83–84
AutoCorrect Options button, 67, 80, 83–84
AutoExpansion feature, 66–67
AutoFormatting, customizing, 86–88
AutoMark button, 215

B

autosave backup document, 277–280
AutoText gallery, saving to content to, 92, 94–95

bibliography
  creating, 176–187
  formatting, 186–187
  inserting, 185
  managing sources, 182–184
  modifying and updating, 185–186
Bibliography button, 185
Block Authors button, 259
Book layout option, 15
Bookmark button, 144
Bookmark dialog box, 144–145
bookmarks
  deleting, 145
  displaying, 144–145
  inserting and navigating with, 144–146
  for insertion point at specific location, 145
  naming, 144
  for selected text, 145
Break Link button, 26, 27
Building Block Organizer dialog box, 104
building blocks
  defined, 88
  deleting, 104–107
  editing building block properties, 96–97
  inserting, 88–91
    as buttons on Quick Access Toolbar, 100–102
    custom, 97–102
    modifying custom, 100–102
  saving
    content as, 91–95
    content to Quick Part gallery, 93

in different template, 102–104
  sorting, 89
  table of contents, 90–91
Building Blocks.dotx template, 92, 93, 102–103
Building Blocks Organizer dialog box, 88–89
bullets
  AutoFormatting options, 86
  defining and inserting custom, 9–10
Bullets button, 4, 9

C

Caption dialog box, 202, 205
captions
  creating, 202, 206–207
  customizing, 205–207
changes, tracking, 232–244
Chart button, 66
Chart Elements button, 68–69, 71–73
Chart Filters button, 69
charts, 66–75
  changing
    color in, 68
    design of, 70–71
  creating
    column chart, 68
    pie chart, 73–74
  entering data in Excel worksheet to create, 66–67
  formatting
    with chart buttons, 68–70
    with Chart Tools Format tab buttons, 71–73
    with task pane options, 73–74
  linking chart to document, 249–250
Chart Styles button, 68–69
Chart Tools Design tab, 70
Chart Tools Format tab, 71–72
Check for Issues button, 271